I0633857

High-Yield
GARDENING

*How to get more from your garden space
and more from your gardening season*

MARJORIE B. HUNT and BRENDA BORTZ

Rodale Press, Emmaus, Pennsylvania

Copyright © 1986 by Rodale Press, Inc.

All rights reserved. No part of this publication may be reproduced or transmitted in any form or by any means, electronic or mechanical, including photocopy, recording, or any information storage and retrieval system, without the written permission of the publisher.

Printed in the United States of America on recycled paper containing a high percentage of de-inked fiber.

Book design by Mary Wise Smith
Illustrations by Frank Fretz

Library of Congress Cataloging in Publication Data
Hunt, Marjorie.
    High-yield gardening.

    Bibliography: p.
    Includes index.
    1. Vegetable gardening.   2. Organic gardening.
3. Fruit-culture.   4. Herb gardening.   I. Bortz,
Brenda.   II. Title.
SB324.3.H863   1986   635   85–24565
ISBN 0-87857-599-5   hardcover

2   4   6   8   10   9   7   5   3   1   hardcover

Contents

Acknowledgments

This book has been enriched by the collective wisdom of a group of talented and dedicated gardeners. For very generously sharing their expertise and experiences in the garden we want to thank John Bates, Diane Bilderback, Alan Brisley-Bown, Tom Butterworth, Lynn Coody, John Dromgoole, Jackie Eichhorn, Sherry Foreman, Pernell Gerver, Joey Massie, Walter Masson, Hugh Matthews, John Meeker, Shepherd Ogden, Bob Percival, Sandra Perrin, Mark Rames, William Rosenberg, Chris Seitz, Ramon Sohn, Netta Thompson, and Michael Wheeler.

The staff of the Rodale Research Center was an invaluable source of information and encouragement. In particular we want to acknowledge the contributions of Charles (Skip) Kauffman, Eileen Weinsteiger, Sarah Wolfgang, Anne Schauer, and Dave Matz.

We also want to thank Anne Thomas of the Rodale Product Testing Department for her prompt answers to all our queries.

And a very special thanks is due to Stevie Daniels for her assistance in this project.

Introduction

Close your eyes for a minute and imagine what your dream garden would look like. Don't let reality intrude—forget about frustrating limitations like poor soil, cramped space, and uncooperative weather. Let your mind wander and put together the garden you've always longed for. For many people it would probably look something like this: a lush area spilling over with brightly colored flowers, mounds of fragrant herbs, and vigorous, healthy vegetables just like the ones on the pages of seed catalogs. All the plants would be grouped in beds intersected by neatly mulched walkways. The whole garden would be an artful harmony of colors and so attractive that it could serve as the centerpiece of the landscape. The soil would be so soft and fluffy and free of rocks that it would take no effort to slide in a shovel. Excess water from heavy rainfalls would drain away quickly, but the humus-rich soil would guard moisture for roots in dry spells. This dream garden would of course need little maintenance and require little if any time spent hunched over pulling weeds.

The garden would also be bountiful and produce enough for the family to eat fresh and to preserve. The vegetables would ripen in steady batches—no frustrating feast or famine cycles. The boundaries of the standard growing season would be stretched to yield fresh vegetables long before the first signs of spring as well as a garden harvest to celebrate Thanksgiving and the winter holidays.

Don't dismiss this garden as mere fantasy—there is a way to make this dream come to life in your own backyard. A very special set of techniques, known as high-yield or intensive gardening, can overcome the limitations and harsh realities that interfere with the pleasure of having a garden. Let's visit one person who has put high-yield gardening to work to bring him closer to the garden of his dreams.

For Hugh Matthews, the move to high-yield gardening was a process that quite literally began from the ground up. His home in New Hampshire was built on a beautiful, wooded spot. The scenery was marvelous, but the soil was too rocky and poor to support much of a garden. So he bought topsoil, several truckloads of it, added amendments, and shaped the freshly conditioned "imported" soil into mounds. These mounds happened to sit on slight slope, and they stayed in place until the rains came. As Matthews says, "When I saw mud running down the hill, it looked like dollars to me."

His investment in soil is what prompted him to refine his bed-building techniques, so that now he has 1,100 square feet in beds enclosed by beams or rocks. "I just got hooked on making raised beds when I found out I didn't need a rotary tiller to prepare the garden anymore."

Now his 16-bed garden is a regular vegetable factory, producing fresh food for the table from May to October. Careful scheduling guarantees a regular progression of crops moving from seedling flats to garden beds to the kitchen.

Raised beds have made gardening easier and more enjoyable for Matthews. He has a 4 by 8-foot bed that is his favorite. When he goes out to work that bed, he knows he can turn and amend the soil, smooth it out, and plant it all in half an hour. The raised sides are convenient seats that take the back and knee strain out of planting and weeding. Beds like this one let him get an early start in the season since they dry out and warm up so fast in the spring. "People sometimes think I'm crazy because I've planted so early. Most people around here won't start gardening until around May 25. They think they are getting a jump on the season because they're putting their broccoli out then, but by May 25 I'll be eating broccoli from the garden." He also uses portable row covers and other protective devices to extend the season on the other end. He figures he makes his last zucchini harvest in October, long after zucchinis have vanished from most gardens.

Aside from these very practical considerations of yield and efficiency, Matthews likes the way his garden looks. His beds are filled to capacity with healthy, lush vegetables, punctuated here and there by mounds of bright marigolds and nasturtiums. Curtains of greenery appear where squash vines are trained up a trellis. The tidy beds are linked by neatly mulched paths. Overall, the garden gives the impression of a glorious quilt, with the beds and paths forming the design and nature's palette of greens, yellows, oranges, and reds creating the color scheme. "With this system of gardening, you end up with a much better looking garden. When you garden in beds it makes you more aware of what's going on, you tend the plants more, and you tend to want to keep the whole garden more attractive." Friends of his who say they have 100 different reasons why they can't garden and then come to visit and tour the garden go away thinking, "Gee, I could do that."

And that is precisely the message of this book. You, too, can have a more beautiful, more productive garden that's easier to tend. You don't have to face a situation as tough as gardening on an incline with poor soil, as Matthews did, to be interested in the benefits to be gained from high-yield gardening. Anyone anywhere with even the smallest bit of land can enjoy the same rewards Hugh Matthews has discovered in his garden.

What exactly are the techniques that go into high-yield gardening? In basic terms, this method pushes back the limits of space and time. You learn how to make every square foot of available space productive and how to gain the fullest use of the gardening season, no matter how long or short it might be.

Growing beds are the foundation of the system. They provide the most space and labor-efficient layout for the gardener and the most beneficial growing environment for the plants. In these beds, a rich medium must be maintained through conscientious soil care. This fertile soil is necessary to sustain a population of closely spaced plants in the growing areas.

THE ROOTS OF INTENSIVE GARDENING

What, you might ask, is the difference between oriental bed, French intensive, biodynamic, and biodynamic/French intensive gardening? These terms are interrelated and understandably often confused. The common denominator is that they are all forms of intensive gardening. What sets them apart is their unique blend of characteristics.

Oriental bed gardening has been practiced for centuries in the Far East. In this system, crops are grown closely spaced and often trellised in roughly 4-foot-wide mounds. The mounded beds are not deeply dug, the soil being loosened only 10 to 12 inches deep. Their gently sloping sides are usually not bordered by frames.

Beds with side supports are not a new invention. Drawings of medieval monastery gardens show herbs growing in beds enclosed by stones. Bed gardening really reached its peak in the nineteenth century with the market gardeners around Paris, who developed the system that is now known as French intensive gardening. These gardeners were searchng for an efficient and profitable system that would allow them to grow crops for the sizable and lucrative Parisian market year-round. The system that evolved was labor, manure, and space intensive. The basic principles are spelled out in a fascinating book first published in 1913, *Intensive Culture of Vegetables—French System.* It was written by a French gardener, known as Aquatias, who set down on paper techniques that had been evolving since the sixteenth century.

As practiced by those gardeners, French intensive relied on raised beds and bed covers of a uniform size. To be profitable, plants had to be kept growing at a productive rate, which called for massive quantities of manure and water. The gardeners gave the plants the growing conditions they needed even when the weather conspired against that, relying on cold frames, hot beds, cloches, and manure heat. Intercropping was also essential, for it allowed several different crops to be grown on the same piece of ground. Close spacing was used for a minimum of wasted, unproductive space.

Those French gardeners mastered the techniques so well that they could produce three to six crops a year. However, the advent of the railroad and the demise of horse-drawn vehicles spelled the end of their incredibly productive and efficient system. Fresh produce could be shipped into the city by rail, and the sources for the vast amounts of manure required slowly began to dwindle. Home gardeners on this continent are indebted to these prodigious and persevering market gardeners for the groundwork they laid in season-extending and small-space–enhancing techniques.

In the 1920s, Rudolf Steiner, a horticulturist and philosopher, began to spread the word about an approach to gardening he created called biodynamics. He believed that mental, spiritual, planetary, and cosmic forces affect the soil's productivity. His approach emphasized that gardeners must work with nature always keeping in mind that the earth is a living organism with a complex set of inter-relationships. The specific techniques he espoused include raised bed planting, organic fertilizers, companion planting, special herbal sprays to strengthen plants, and special preparations to activate the decomposition of materials in compost piles.

The late Alan Chadwick integrated Steiner's system with that of the French market gardeners to arrive at what he called the biodynamic/French intensive method. At the University of California at Santa Cruz, he put his theories to practice in a lush garden. He was the first to make the claim that it is possible to produce four times more vegetables per acre following his methods than by using mechanical and chemical methods. Chadwick popularized the idea of raised bed growing in the United States. He also advocated dense spacing, double digging, companion planting, and interplanting, and he arrived at a very specific recipe for composting that used very little or no manure.

John Jeavons, along with the group Ecology Action of the Midpeninsula, based in Palo Alto, California, wrote *How To Grow More Vegetables Than You Ever Thought Possible in Less Space Than You Can Imagine.* This widely read book puts forth the methods of biodynamic/French intensive gardening and has spread the work begun by Chadwick to a broad audience. Jeavons continues refining the biodynamic/ French intensive techniques in his gardens in the Willits Valley in California.

Interplantings, successions, and companion plantings are all employed to make sure that the space in beds is used as efficiently and as fully as possible, all season long. These strategies for arranging plants in the layout also ensure that crops are surrounded by neighbors that will help, not hinder, their growth.

Getting the most from the gardening season focuses not only on both ends—when the cooler weather and shorter daylengths usually conspire against plant growth—but even on the middle, when some plants need to be coaxed to grow beyond the built-in limits of their light and temperature tolerances. With careful attention to variety selection and wise use of season-extending structures, it's possible to keep something growing or at least harvestable in the garden all year-round.

Many people know this collection of techniques by the name of intensive gardening. We prefer to call it high-yield gardening, since that really emphasizes the greatest benefit—an amazingly abundant harvest from small, concentrated spaces. By its very name, "intensive" gardening sounds like it takes a lot of time, effort, and energy to do—and may be somewhat intimidating. But you'll find that once you've made the investment in time that goes into preparing the beds and fortifying the soil, there are time-savers built right into the system.

Growing areas contained in beds account for the efficiency of high-yield gardening. You can harvest more from 100 square feet in a bed than you could from 100 square feet in a conventional row garden. All 100 square feet in a bed are productive growing areas, while a standard garden has to sacrifice growing areas to accommodate foot paths. The figure commonly cited is that a garden tended intensively will give four times the yield of one grown using conventional methods—meaning rows and chemicals. Every garden is different; some gardeners feel they get more than four times the yield. This sort of claim is difficult to quantify, but setting numbers aside,

everything about the design and maintenance of beds increases the garden's potential to produce in copious quantities.

This enhanced productivity means you can direct your efforts onto a smaller area without any sacrifice in the amount of food you harvest. And a smaller garden means less area to prepare, plant, water, fertilize, and weed, which represents savings in labor and time. Hugh Matthews found that gardening intensively in beds has made it much easier to keep the garden neat and clean.

Most gardeners who practice intensive methods find that they spend the most time on soil preparation—double digging the beds, working in soil amendments, and making compost. But every year as the soil improves, they find they need to spend less time tending the soil.

Once the beds have been worked in the spring, gardeners report that they spend much less time weeding and watering than they had to in regular row gardens. The closely spaced plants grow together to form a leafy canopy that shades out weeds and acts as a living mulch to conserve soil moisture.

Perhaps the most encouraging words that intensive gardening isn't as intimidating as it sounds come from Alan Brisley-Bown of Washington, who tends beds that encompass 6,000 square feet of space. "In terms of time, you can spend just a little bit every day, and it's almost so joyful that it doesn't feel like work."

In the course of preparing this book, we spoke with dozens of gardeners across the United States who have intensive gardens. We asked them to explain the advantages they've discovered in gardening this way. As one person put it, "There are really nothing but benefits." It became very clear that backyard growers are turning to high-yield gardening because it is a productive, attractive way to raise healthy crops, especially in the face of space and other environmental limitations.

The benefits of high-yield gardening aren't limited exclusively to small-space gardeners. Even gardeners with lots of space at their disposal sing the praises of growing in beds. In some cases, a large yard is handicapped by soil that's rocky, sandy, clayey, packed hard, or otherwise inhospitable to raising plants.

Other gardeners who used to tend larger plots have scaled down to bed gardens because their families have gotten smaller and they don't see the need for the wasted space and labor of an expansive row garden. One gardener in his 70s switched to beds because he wanted to get more with less effort. People in these situations find they can avoid overplanting and grow just the right mix of vegetables so the harvests aren't overwhelming.

Consolidating a vegetable garden in beds leaves plenty of room for the other things you might want in your yard—an expanse of lawn, some fruit trees, flowers, and a swimming pool, for example.

Jackie Eichhorn, of Indiana, echoing the sentiments of many other gardeners, says that her bed garden is prettier than a standard row garden. "This sort of gardening challenges you to place things together that are pleasing aesthetically as well as good growing partners. I think that it makes you a little more conscious of how individual plants are progressing. If you have a long row of something, you don't worry as much if part of it doesn't look good. But when you have only a few plants, you take better care of them."

Beds make a gardener's planning and work easier, which ultimately means the plants receive the best sort of attention and growing conditions. In Michigan, Mark Rames likes the fact that it is easy to tailor each bed to the specific needs of the crops that are growing in it. It's easier for him to companion plant and much simpler to keep track of rotations.

New Hampshire gardener John Bates was drawn to high-yield gardening because of his belief that "the earth is a living thing, and my job and duty is to see that the soil is not only well but improved to the limit of my ability." As he stands in his garden he is amazed by "the volume this

friend of mine will give me if I treat it well." In his philosophy of gardening, high-yield isn't defined necessarily "in terms of quantity or quality only, but in the effect all of this has on your life and what you do."

As you can see, intensive gardening fills many different needs and confers a wide range of benefits. It's often said that gardening isn't a science but rather an art, and this particular form of gardening lends itself to a variety of very creative and practical expressions. The aim of *High-Yield Gardening* is to help you understand the basics so you can apply them to your own particular situation and modify them as suits your gardening style and your garden setting.

Over the years a great deal has been written about intensive gardening and many recommendations have been made. What sets this book apart is that we've tried to hold everything up against a "reality test." We wanted to make sure that the techniques and methods we discussed were really applicable to what gardeners do in their gardens. We asked ourselves these questions: Is it absolutely essential to double dig, or are there equally effective, less labor-intensive alternatives? Is there more than one way to raise a bed? Are cover crops really manageable in a small bed garden? Do bush varieties of vining crops really save space and produce as well as their lankier counterparts?

We've tried to shed light on those questions, among others, drawing upon work done at the Rodale Research Center in Maxatawny, Pennsylvania, and at other research centers across the country. We've also spoken with experienced gardeners from coast to coast who have been practicing intensive gardening. They very generously shared with us their insights and suggestions of what works and what doesn't work, and we share these with you in the pages of this book. (These gardeners, many of them finalists in the Organic Gardener of the Year contest sponsored by *Rodale's Organic Gardening*, are featured in a series of boxes called With the Master Gardeners.)

High-Yield Gardening is organized and the information is presented so that you can find what you're looking for quickly and easily. It's divided into three basic parts. Part 1, Getting More from Your Garden Space, tells you how to make every square foot of the garden productive. It covers soil preparation, building beds, and designing a garden in beds, then offers suggestions on the most productive and space-saving vegetables, fruits, and herbs to grow. Basic techniques for planting and caring for a high-yield garden are discussed, as well as special techniques you can use to boost yields.

Getting More from Your Gardening Season is the theme of part 2. The goal of this section is to help you overcome the limitations of your climate and grow as close to year-round as possible. Here you'll learn which techniques and crops to use to gain earlier starts and later finishes in the garden. There are discussions of homemade and commercial season extenders, from the simplest to the most elaborate, plus directions on how to use them and what crops to grow in them. One very useful chapter talks about specific regional problems and the ingenious ways in which gardeners have solved them.

The High-Yield Plant Guide is the third part of the book and no doubt the section you'll turn to frequently for reference as you plan and plant your garden. Ninety-nine vegetables, fruits, and herbs are featured, and for each one you'll find concise growing instructions specifically tailored to high-yield gardening. Intensive spacings, growing requirements, season-extending options, interplanting and succession planting suggestions, yield-improving techniques, and noteworthy varieties are all covered.

To round out the book, there is a Directory of Resources and a Recommended Reading list. Think of these as tools, as useful as your favorite spading fork and trowel. They can lead you directly to sources of supplies and information that can make gardening easier and more satisfying. In the directory you'll find an extensive listing of sources for seeds and plants. Many offer varieties that are suited to special regions, good for small spaces, cold or hot weather tolerant, or especially productive. This source listing is numbered. As you read the first three parts of the book, you'll notice that many varieties are followed by a number in parentheses. These numbers refer to the individual companies listed in the directory. Some varieties are widely available, and for those we've supplied no specific sources since you can find them in many catalogs and in seed racks in garden centers. But for the varieties that are not as well known or are only available from a limited number of sources, we've listed one or more sources to help you locate them.

The directory also includes mail-order sources for tools and other garden aids that are useful for high-yield gardening, such as special soil forks for double digging, season-extending structures, plant protectors, trellises, and special mulching materials.

Once you've spent some time in a garden you begin to understand that "yield" is measured in terms far greater than the bushels of tomatoes harvested. There is a deep reserve of pleasure from which to draw, day after day, as you behold a garden that is pleasing to look at and a joy, not a drudgery, to tend. The garden rewards your efforts many times over, in many ways.

We hope this book inspires you to break ground for a garden if you've never done so before. If you've been gardening, but in a conventional row plot, this book should encourage you to make the switch to high-yield gardening. And if you're an intensive veteran of many seasons, you're sure to find in the pages that lie ahead some ways to fine tune the techniques you've been using and perhaps even discover a few new ones to try.

The promise of a highly productive, attractive, easily maintained garden in a small amount of space isn't an empty one—you can have such a garden, no matter what limitations of space and climate you might face. And every year, your garden will only get better and better.

HOW HIGH-YIELD GARDENING CAN SOLVE THESE COMMON GARDENING PROBLEMS

According to a National Gardening Survey, the following are the most vexing problems that plague backyard growers. The techniques used in high-yield gardening can solve or even prevent these common dilemmas.

Not Enough Water
The high humus content, uncompacted soil, and the self-shading created by closely spaced plants act to conserve soil moisture deep down. Beds allow you to concentrate a limited water supply directly where it's needed; you won't waste water on pathways. It's easy to lay out an efficient drip irrigation system among beds. Plants growing in raised beds develop deep, probing root systems and are more resistant to drought.

Insects
Mixing plantings within a single bed (instead of growing row upon row of the same crop) confuses insects, making it harder for them to locate their host plants. It's much easier to monitor each plant's development in the confined areas of a bed, so insect problems can be caught early, when they're easier to treat. Entire beds can be outfitted with a cheese-cloth or other covering to keep egg-laying worms away.

Weeds
Closely spaced plants that form a "living" mulch in conjunction with standard mulches laid on the soil control weeds and cut down on the time spent weeding.

Hot Temperatures
Closely spaced plants shade the soil and each other, offering some relief from the heat. Interplanting taller and shorter crops shades the lower level planting. Lath or other shading structures are easy to set up to cover a whole bed.

Too Much Water
Raised beds drain very quickly and alleviate soggy soil conditions.

Animal Pests
Birds and rabbits can be kept at bay by covering beds with curved frames draped with plastic netting. You can get in and out easily, but the wild creatures can only gaze instead of graze.

Problems with Plant Growth and Soil Conditions
Raised beds overcome problem soils. You can create ideal growing mediums inside the beds by blending soil, sand, manure, peat moss, and other amendments. You can also tailor the soil to meet plants' specific nutrient needs. Because beds are never walked on, plants have a soft, deep area for excellent root development, which encourages strong, healthy plant growth.

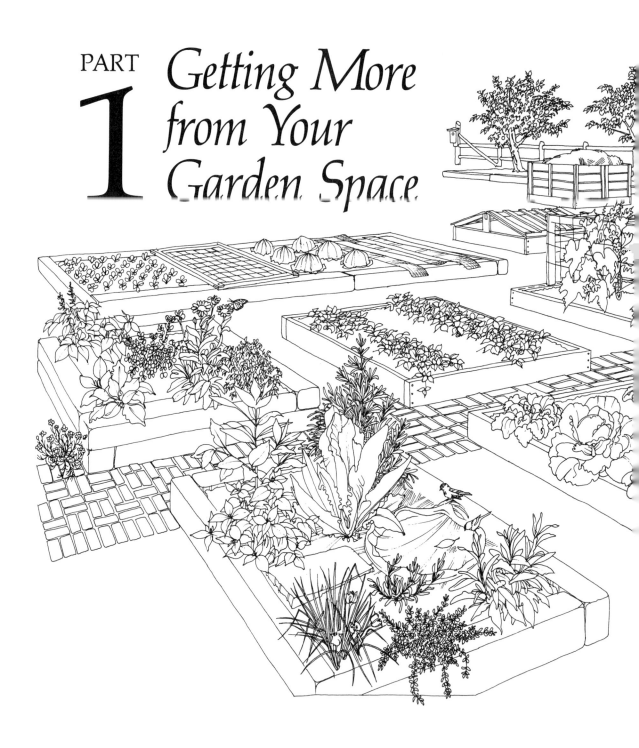

PART

1

Getting More from Your Garden Space

1

Preparing Soil for High-Yield Gardening

Spectacular yields depend first and foremost on soil so superbly conditioned it can handily meet the heavy demands of close planting, carefully timed successions, and a growing season stretched to its absolute limit at both ends. The master gardeners you'll meet in these pages have very different personalities and gardening styles, but they share one supremely important characteristic: All of them know their soil intimately and spend most of their gardening time conditioning it. Without exception, they consider those hours well spent, for they've made the beautiful discovery that if you feed your soil right, it will return the favor—tenfold. The constant soil care that is the price of such abundance centers on building and maintaining soil structure and fertility. And it all begins with getting to know your growing medium. The chart Discovering Your Soil Type Firsthand on page 4 can help you become acquainted.

Soil Testing—Necessary or Not?

Chances are you'll want to complement your visual and tactile examination of your soil with tests revealing its biochemical condition. But first, a caveat: Don't be too slavish about taking and evaluating soil tests. Experienced gardeners report testing their soil once early on, then retesting only if they are struggling with soil that is either very acid (pH below 5.0) or very alkaline (pH above 7.5), or if they notice a slump in yield that calls the availability of nutrients into question.

This relaxed attitude isn't as risky as it sounds, for although strongly acid soils reduce the availability of phosphorus, calcium, potassium, magnesium, and molybdenum, and very alkaline soils make boron, copper, zinc, manganese, and iron inaccessible, it's also true that most plants thrive in a pH range anywhere between 6.0 and 7.5. Difficulties—usually nutrient shortages—tend to arise only when soil is extremely acid or alkaline. Adding large volumes of organic material will buffer the impact of pH on yield. Because the organic content of a soil is directly correlated with the availability of its nutrients, superbly conditioned soils can be quite acidic or alkaline and still remain highly productive.

It's also true that pH and other soil measurements fluctuate madly—depending on when you take them. As Dr. Ehrenfried Pfeiffer noted long ago in his classic work *Bio-Dynamic Farming and Gardening* (Anthroposophic Press, 1943), in any location, the same soil sample will have its lowest pH in fall and its highest in winter. In soils on the acid side, the lowest reading will be in June, the highest in March. Neutral soils peak in pH in February and August and are at their lowest in May and October. Pfeiffer also documented double low and high points for nitrogen and humus content and noted that phosphoric acid is low in solubility in summer and high in fall and winter. Obviously, then, it's pointless to make and compare soil tests unless you're prepared to do this chore at the same time each year. In research begun in 1980 in Ohio, the levels of nine different soil nutrients were charted in six test plots over a 38-month period. The results made it plain that soil tests should be timed relative to both season and fertilizer application. The study also showed that fall is the best time to take soil samples if you're planning to fertilize in the spring.

Obviously, soil testing has its limitations. But that said, it must be added that periodic tests can help safeguard optimal yields by identifying small problems before they get big enough to make serious inroads on your garden's productivity. And they're definitely in order if you suspect the presence of toxic minerals such as lead. (By keeping your soil pH at 6.5 or above, you usually can assure that garden plants will pick up only trace amounts of any heavy metals in the soil.)

Then, too, acid rain seems to be lowering soil pH levels dramatically in New England and the Middle Atlantic states, while acid dust particles are beginning to change the soil picture in Great Plains states like Kansas. Experts now say that in as little as 20 years, the soil in America's heartland may become so acidic that neutral-soil crops like corn, wheat, and soybeans will no longer grow there. Monitoring pH regularly in such locations can't hurt—some New England gardeners are already discovering they need to lime their soil as often as every year or two.

Soil testing also can be used to make crop rotation schemes optimally effective. For example, gardeners who want to adjust the soil in various beds to suit the crops going in them the following spring can benefit by testing samples from those beds in fall. Conversely, regular soil testing can be a touchstone for bringing varying pHs in different parts of the garden in line so they don't interfere with a master rotation plan.

Soil Test Specifics

If you live in a rural area where soil has not been imported or excavated by building contractors, you can use a soil survey report to determine your garden soil's characteristics. Published by the Soil Conservation Service in Pennsylvania and many other states as well, these reports are done by county. Sometimes it is possible to scan the aerial photos they include to locate your plot and discover your soil type, texture, drainage, and many other facts about your particular growing medium. You can find and use this survey at your county's Cooperative Extension Service office or possibly at the nearest sizable public library.

You should also give your local extension agent a call if you wish to have soil from your plot tested. Usually that office can provide a special envelope and instructions on how to collect a sample and submit it to the state or province's agricultural experiment station for analysis. Some garden supply centers also distribute this packet as a service to their customers. A more expensive option is to submit soil samples to one of the growing number of private testing services. Make sure in advance, however, that if the fee includes an interpretation of the results and a remedial program, the service is able and willing to outline a nonchemical course of action.

Actually, it's fairly simple to test soil yourself. If pH is what you're after, you can use pHydrion paper obtained from a scientific supply house.

DISCOVERING YOUR SOIL TYPE FIRSTHAND

If It Looks . . .	And Feels . . .	And Is . . .
hard baked, crusty, and perhaps even deeply cracked when allowed to dry out	harsh and rock hard when dry	hard to work
scarce in pore spaces holding air and water	sticky, greasy, or rubbery when wet	very slow to absorb water and to dry out
devoid of individual particles		slow to warm up in spring
		likely to form large, congealed lumps if worked when wet
loose and friable	grainy and gritty	easy to work
quite porous	crumbly and won't hold its shape when squeezed	quick to warm up in spring
full of large, irregularly shaped mineral particles		fast drying
more or less devoid of larger pieces or granules		low in nutrients because soluble plant foods are lost through leaching
very dark brown	like moist peat moss when squeezed	easy to work
full of organic matter in varying stages of decay		slow to warm up and dry out in wet springs
granular and porous		slow to decompose
		low in minerals
full of crumbs of various sizes	spongy, compacting readily into a ball when squeezed, but falling apart readily when prodded	easy to work
quite porous		very productive
	or floury and talcum-powdery when dry and only moderately plastic when moist	well drained yet able to retain moisture as it is needed
		well aerated
		retentive of nutrients

(This comes in various ranges—chances are your soil falls between 4.5 and 8.5.) Once you've collected the soil sample, add mineral-free (distilled) water to make a slurry, then dip in the pHydrion paper and compare its color to those on the chart provided, which will let you come up with a pH calculated to one-tenth of a point.

If you'd like to test for pH plus key nutrients,

It's . . .	And It Needs . . .
CLAY If other kinds of particles are present in quantity, such soil can be classified as a stony clay, gravelly clay, sandy clay, or silty clay.	substantial additions of organic materials to break up the compaction and open channels for aeration and drainage. Some good choices: compost, manure, leaf mold, rice hulls, peat moss, coarse sand, sawdust, and wood chips. lime to improve its texture and free locked-up soil nutrients for the use of plants. leguminous green manure crops. spading or tilling in fall to expose massive solid clods to the weathering action of freezes and thaws.
SANDY Depending on the size and texture of the particles, such soil may be classified as gravelly, coarse, medium, fine, or loamy sand.	continual augmenting with large amounts of organic matter to hold water and nutrients within the range of plant roots. manure worked in deeply in autumn or winter. plentiful applications of peat moss, compost, leaf mold, or sawdust in topsoil layer. green manures to build structure.
MUCK or PEAT Peat is not fully decomposed. Muck is the same soil in a more advanced state of decay. It tends to be waterlogged and lacking in lime but rich in nutrients such as nitrogen.	layers of gravel or drainage tiles to improve drainage. lime added as needed.
LOAM A mixture of sand, silt, and clay, this close-to-ideal soil combines the best qualities of light and heavy growing media. Depending on the kind and size of the particles that predominate, a sample may be categorized as a coarse, sandy, medium sand, fine sand, silty, stony silt, or clay loam.	regular infusions of organic matter to maintain its already excellent fertility and structure.

look for a home test kit. Thanks to a breakthrough in filters, the Rapitest kit can give instant readings for pH, nitrogen, phosphorus, and potassium, together with instructions on how to adjust pH and correct nutrient deficiencies. (See the Garden Products section of the Directory of Resources for information on where to purchase this kit.) Soil test meters are an even more pain-

Soil Testing Options: Your local extension agent can supply a special envelope and instructions on collecting soil samples, as shown on the left. To do it yourself, there are home test kits available that give readings for pH and major nutrients.

less way to do home testing, but beware: the less expensive models often are not accurate.

Adjusting Alkaline Soil If your soil pH is alkaline, you can lower it to the neutral 6.0 to 7.0 range by adding sawdust, wood chips, leaf mold, peat moss, cottonseed meal, or pine needles. If you garden in an area with low rainfall, that high pH is probably linked to accumulated salts. These can be flushed below the root zone of sensitive plants such as beans, carrots, onions, and peppers by watering regularly with nonsaline water. Working in elemental sulfur or compost, mulch, or leaf mold also can help.

Adjusting Acid Soil An acid pH can be raised by working in bone meal; pulverized eggshells, clamshells, or oystershells; wood ashes (which also help discourage insects); or a form of fine-ground agricultural lime. Be sure to avoid hydrated lime—especially in springtime applications—because it's caustic and may burn seeds or transplants. Better choices are dolomitic lime or calcitic lime. If your soil test reveals a magne-

sium deficiency, use the dolomitic form. If calcium is low, choose the calcitic type. All else being equal, buy whichever one is cheaper.

Other imbalances shown in soil tests can be corrected by adding ample amounts of organic matter in the form of cover crops; compost; directly applied kitchen, yard, industrial, or seashore wastes; or rock powders.

Cover Crops

As soil conditioners, cover crops (also called green manures) are hard to beat. Costing just pennies per bed, these hardy workers will grow on in the garden over otherwise barren winter months. Their spring legacy is a wealth of moist and crumbly humus that improves the soil's structure and tilth, raising its organic content by an almost ideal 4 percent. There's also a heritage of stepped-up microbiological activity guaranteed to release minerals previously locked away from your plants and often the bonus of extra nitrogen.

Protecting the surface layer of the soil where the beneficial activity of bacteria, fungi, and

Collecting a Soil Sample: To prepare one sample, use a trowel to dig four or five 6-inch-deep holes in various areas of the garden or bed you are testing. Remove an even "slice" of soil from the side of each hole. Then, without touching the soil with your hands, mix the slabs of soil together gently.

earthworms takes place, cover crops also keep the growing medium from blowing or washing away, baking dry, or compacting under heavy rains. Green manures also help soil absorb more water. Quicker to break down in spring than thick mulches, they also have the advantage of manure, for instead of letting nutrients leach away when it rains, these "catch crops" keep soil nitrates and other plant foods locked up in their tissues until decay releases them for a succeeding crop. Some of the deeper-rooted green manures also aerate and enrich the subsoil, pumping up phosphorus, potassium, and vital trace minerals trapped there below the reach of most vegetable roots.

Planting several cover crops in succession— buckwheat followed by buckwheat followed by annual rye, for instance—can rid your garden of perennial weeds by shading them out. Indeed, certain cover crops (notably rye and wheat) contain natural toxins that will suppress weed growth or even pests in subsequent crops. Dr. Alan Putnam of Michigan State University uses fall-planted wheat and rye to successfully control annual weeds around fruit trees. (The crops are mowed in spring and the clippings left in place.) Putnam also has found residues of wheat and rye reduce weeds in subsequent plantings of vegetables such as legumes, cucumbers, and corn, while maintaining or even increasing their yields. Wheat, rye, and oat residues also help control wireworms in subsequently seeded carrots.

Astonishingly, green manure crops are ideal conditioners for troubled soils completely different in nature. In heavy clay, the humus they add

(continued on page 10)

With the Master Gardeners

SOIL CONDITIONING SECRETS

Russ and Madeline Wold have created their Eden in Pleasant Hill, California, a balmy place where the first frost doesn't arrive until mid-December, and the last one strikes just two months later. At first blush their growing conditions seem just right—warm enough to keep citrus trees alive by tossing a blanket over them on the coldest nights, yet cool enough to meet the chilling requirements for the apricots, peaches, apples, and walnuts they grow.

But these gardeners live with drought from June through October, and with summer temperatures usually in the nineties. And soil . . . well, when the Wolds started cultivating their one-third acre 24 years ago, the soil was so hard when dry that "you could bounce a pick off it" and so quicksandlike when wet that Russ remembers once losing his shoes just trying to walk across it. He also recalls using some of that unforgettable soil to fashion adobe bricks for one of his daughter's school projects: "You could throw the bricks as hard as you wanted against a wall and they'd bounce; they wouldn't break."

Madeline Wold counseled hauling the clay away and trucking in good topsoil, but her husband got stubborn. His degree in soil science from the University of Wisconsin helped him see that apparently hopeless clay as a challenge. Russ started to compost the family's kitchen wastes and the prunings and leaves from the yard, together with large volumes of grass clippings and horse manure. Using Sir Albert Howard's classic Indore Method—a layer of dry material, then a layer of succulent material, capped by a layer of soil, with the sequence repeated to a depth of 3 or 4 feet—Russ turned his heaps after six months. After a year, he dug the crumbly end product into the top 6 inches of his clay or used it as a mulch or to enrich the planting holes.

When Russ began to accumulate more trimmings from his maturing trees than he could cut up for composting by hand, he got a hammermill shredder. Soon all the available space in the yard was filled with compost piles, with material to

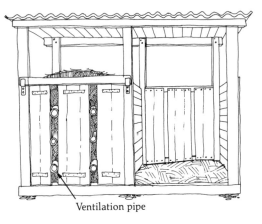

Ventilation pipe

Russ Wold's Compost Bins: Using his "sliding air tube method" and these specially designed compost bins, Wold produces 5 or 6 tons of compost a year with minimal effort.

spare. Figuring he could get finished compost faster if the heaps got more air, Russ came up with a strategy for making compost in six to eight weeks without turning it. The "sliding air tube method" as he dubbed it, features 5-foot lengths of 1½-inch black polyethylene water pipe, with ½-inch air holes drilled all the way through every 3 inches. Russ layers these ventilation pipes in with his compost, fitting 20 in each of his 4 by 5-foot covered bins. (The sides of the bins are constructed with gaps between the slats wide enough to let the pipes stick out by 6 inches on both sides.)

Thanks to this airy innovation, Russ Wold turns out five or six tons of compost a year, in half the space required by the traditional method and with far less work.

The action gets under way when he has accumulated enough material for at least one layer. Russ puts down 6 inches of high-carbon material (dried leaves and dead plants, shredded prunings, spoiled hay or straw, sawdust, or wood shavings), and about 4 inches of high-nitrogen material (kitchen garbage, manure, grass clippings), ending with about 2 inches of subsoil from the garden. (At this point, says Russ, most of the soil in his beds has been cycled through his compost bins three times.)

In the second foot-high layer and those that follow Russ places perforated pipes in the high-carbon tier, positioning them about a foot apart vertically and 2 feet apart horizontally so they can aerate the pile thoroughly.

After each heap-building session, Russ moistens the stack of materials and puts plastic or an old rug over the pile to keep it from drying out. The superb air circulation coupled with the right moisture level makes his "sliding air tube" compost heat up quickly and stay hot. "Cooking" for 30 to 50 days after the last layer is completed, the compost then cools to lukewarm (about 100°F) and is ready for Russ to use as a seed-starting medium for all the plants he starts in his greenhouse and as a replacement for the 12 inches of subsoil removed (and composted) in the fall when he prepares his 20-inch-deep tomato trench, which is rotated around the garden.

No wonder Russ Wold's soil produces tomato plants bearing up to 235 fruits. No wonder he and his wife were awarded first place in the 1983 Organic Gardener of the Year contest.

To the north of the Wolds, at the southern end of Oregon's Willamette Valley, live Lynn Coody and Jon Davis, the young gardeners who captured second place in the 1984 Organic Gardener of the Year competition. Like the Wolds, Coody and Davis do their growing on one-third of an acre. But for them the gardening life has become almost a full-time occupation. Once a neglected lawn rooted in heavy clay, their backyard now boasts 28 30-foot-long raised beds where these mini-farmers grow food for themselves and for 25 families participating in the subscription produce-buying plan they developed.

Like Russ Wold, Coody and Davis compost year-round. In 1985 they intended to make and apply 45 tons of compost. Eventually, though, the couple hopes to phase out composting and to condition their soil entirely through the use of green manure crops, which are already "a real important part of what we do." Even now, Coody reports, "at the very least" each bed gets cover-cropped in the fall and again in the spring.

Green manures are this hardworking couple's answer to the peculiarly different climate of the Maritime Northwest, which forces them to contend with "rain, rain, rain all winter" and super-dry summers with very cool nights. "That contrast makes soil preparation very difficult," says Lynn, "for going from very wet to very dry soils makes cement. Unless you have incorporated quite a bit of humus, you have a very short time in which to prepare your beds."

Together with mulching and composting—"we do it all, we have to!"—cover crops are vital to this garden's productivity. "They keep the soil moist in the summer and they help to pump water out in the springtime. We cut the tops off, leaving the roots, which act like little water pumps to get the sogginess out of the soil." Beds are treated with six or seven different green manures intermittently. These are planted year-round. Summer favorites are buckwheat—"a rich source of nectar for our bees"—and flax, "which germinates well on rough, poor ground." Winter choices are often crimson clover, hairy vetch, and Austrian field peas.

Jon Davis has developed his own effective techniques for managing these crops in beds. Scything the tops down, he then turns both tops and roots under by hand to a depth of 6 inches as he double digs. The idea is to bury the cover crops deeply so in decomposing they won't steal soil nitrogen needed by the crops planted on top. The deep-buried cover crops rot slowly through the growing season, releasing nutrients to plant roots as the roots reach the cover crops' level. Digging cover crops under that deeply also lets Coody and Davis plant the same day, which is why they do it. "We have a big production here, and we have to do things whenever we can."

Coody and Davis soil-condition new areas with cover crops for at least three years before they even try to grow food there. When they are putting in a green manure as a fallowing technique, they don't double dig beds before planting the next cover crop. Instead, the previous cover crop is tilled under. Next the bed is raked up, for the cover crop fluffs it up quite a bit. Then the new cover crop is planted on top.

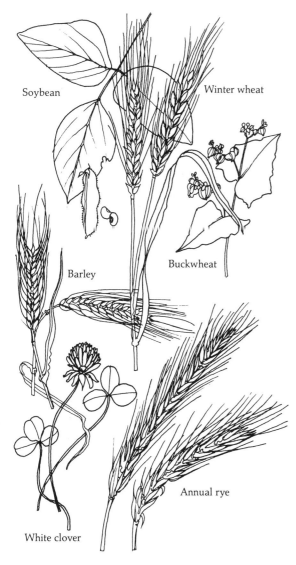

Soybean

Winter wheat

Buckwheat

Barley

White clover

Annual rye

Cover Crops: Also called green manures, these crops can improve even the most troublesome soils. Grains like rye and wheat improve soil texture and legumes like soybeans boost nitrogen levels.

and the microorganisms they stimulate work to loosen rock-hard compaction and create a crumbly,

well-aerated, and well-drained soil structure. Particularly recommended are legumes. In sandy soils, the bulky, deep-penetrating roots of cereal crops act to bring up needed nutrients that have leached into the subsoil. As they decompose, the matted roots give the soil enough body to hold onto both nutrients and water that otherwise would quickly drain below the reach of vegetables.

Cover crops also can be used to correct specific problems revealed by soil tests. As a rule of thumb, legumes are chosen to raise nitrogen levels and grains to improve soil texture and tilth. Interestingly, however, new research suggests that the rhizobia (soil dwelling bacteria) associated with the roots of legume crops may well remove as much fixed nitrogen from soils as they add. But it's also just been discovered that even though annual legumes are relatively low in root mass, they are way ahead of other crops (including grains) in the ability to promote beneficial soil biological activities. It may be that this characteristic accounts more than any other for legumes' positive impact on soil nutrition. Whatever the mechanism, if your garden has reasonably good, well-drained soil but is low in nitrogen, alfalfa or white clover will be effective. On the other hand, if your soil is somewhat poor in quality—or if you're in the first or second year of gardening in raised beds—better choices to remedy nitrogen deficiency are the less demanding soybeans, peas, or hairy vetch. Buckwheat can be used to treat a low phosphorus reading, and wheat, rye, barley, or oats are antidotes for poor potassium. Zinc-deficient soil benefits from an alfalfa cover crop, while molybdenum levels are raised by vetch.

As if all this isn't enough, cover crops actually have the potential to become the only source of nutrients your garden needs. Dick Raymond, author of *Garden Way's Joy of Gardening* (Garden Way, 1982), has completed more than ten years of research on an "Eternal Yield" plot, on which he grows only sequences of green manure crops followed by corn. His results indicate that if a gardener follows a two-year rotation, planting peas/snap beans/ annual rye the first year, followed by sweet corn (or another heavy feeder)/annual rye the second year, and returning all residues to the soil, no other fertilizers of any kind are necessary. Raymond is convinced the vast amounts of organic matter such a scheme adds to the soil act to set free unlimited amounts of phosphorus, potassium, and other nutrients usually locked away in insoluble compounds.

Along these lines, longtime gardener and author Gene Logsdon goes so far as to recommend that growers in the North create two gardens—one for vegetables, one for green manures. By rotating the plots yearly, says Logsdon, gardeners would virtually eliminate the need for fertilizers other than mulches and would prevent insect and disease buildups. In the South two gardens aren't necessary, for certain legumes can be grown over the winter, just as rye, winter wheat, and oats are grown in the North.

The disadvantages of growing cover crops are few but formidable. For those who perform all garden chores by hand, dealing with mature green manures can be incredibly labor intensive. In fact, turning under a long-term cover crop manually has to rank right up there with double digging as one of the most physically demanding tasks in all of gardening. Too, covercropping during the growing season in northern gardens or any time at all in year-round gardening locales uses up space that could be producing generous amounts of food. Understandably, intensive gardeners in such areas with small or moderately sized growing spaces are loath to let any of their land go fallow, especially since they can rely on compost or other "off-site" nutrient sources. Another drawback is that if a gardener with raised beds wants to turn under cover crops the easy way—with a tiller, disk, or plow—beds with contained sides must be ruled out. Also, beds being covercropped must be completely broken down and reshaped and probably subjected to

the weight of machinery, which could contribute to soil compaction.

Managing Green Manure Crops in Beds

To plant all or part of a bed in a cover crop, turn the soil with a tiller or spade, or just rough up open spaces with a hoe. Raking the surface smooth, sprinkle the seed on as evenly as you can, then rake or hoe lightly to cover the seed a little. You can turn under the green manure crop anytime between greening and flowering. However, if you'll have the help of a power mower and a tiller, it's definitely to your soil's advantage to delay digging under the cover crop as long as your planting schedule for a given bed permits.

A delay of at least 7 to 10 days for legume crops and 14 days or more for cereal covers is usually recommended between turning under and planting. That's because in the first days of decomposition those heavy masses of green manure give off ethylene gas, which inhibits seed germination. Too, the microorganisms that multiply to break down the humus-to-be tend to commandeer available soil nitrogen for their own use. The temporary deficiency will hinder seeds or transplants put in before the extra soil organisms die off and free the nitrogen supply for the plants.

Tips for Working by Hand If you are going to be turning under your cover crops entirely by hand, choose and time them carefully. Even totally committed intensive gardeners who enjoy working up a good sweat avoid rye as a winter cover crop unless they can get into the garden to turn it under very early in spring. Otherwise, this abundant grower gets so tall and so formidably rooted that it's backbreaking to turn under and must be chopped and worked over and over to prevent rerooting. Moreover, in the absence of pulverizing mower and tiller action, a well-developed stand of rye may take a month or more to break down sufficiently to permit planting.

(continued on page 15)

COVER CROP PLANTING GUIDE

Keep in mind that the characteristics of each green manure crop will vary according to climate and growing conditions. Before resorting to the seed sources listed, you may want to check out local garden centers and farm supply stores for varieties that will grow best in your area. Contact your Cooperative Extension Service for local planting dates.

Crop	N Fixed per Year, Average (lbs./acre)	Soil Preference	Soil Fertility Needs	Tolerates Low pH
LEGUMES				
Alfalfa	158–250	Well drained, loamy, neutral pH	High	No
Beans, garden	40	Loam	Medium	No
Clover:				
Alsike	119	Heavy loam	High	Yes
Crimson	94	Widely adaptable, good in sandy loam	Medium	No
Red*	103–151	Loam	High	No
Sweet White	93–168	Heavy loam	High	No
Sweet Yellow	93–168	Widely adaptable	Medium	No
White Dutch	103–133	Heavy loam	High	No
White Ladino	179	Sandy loam	Medium	No
Fava Beans	71	Widely adaptable	Low	Yes
Peas, field	32–48	Heavy loam	Low	No
Soybeans	58–105	Loam	Medium	No
Vetch, hairy	80	Widely adaptable, good in sandy soil	Low	Yes
GRAINS‡				
Barley	0	Loamy, neutral to alkaline pH	Medium	No
Bromegrass	0	Widely adaptable	Medium	Yes
Buckwheat	0	Widely adaptable	Low	Yes
Millet	0	Loam	Low	Yes
Oats	0	Widely adaptable	Medium	Yes
Rye, winter	0	Widely adaptable	Medium	No
Sudangrass	0	Widely adaptable	Medium	Yes
Wheat, spring	0	Loam	Medium	No
Wheat, winter	0	Loam	Medium	No
MIXTURES	Varies	Varies	Varies	Varies

No insulation needed.

‡ *For information on the best varieties for your area and local grain harvest dates, contact your Cooperative Extension Service.*

Drought Tolerance	Seeding Rate (oz. per 100 sq. ft.)	Depth to Cover Seed (in.)	When to Sow	When to Turn Under	Seed Sources
High	1/2	1/2	Spring Fall	Fall Spring	24, 41
Medium	4	1½	Spring	Fall	Widely available
High	1/4	1/2	Spring Fall	Fall Spring	†
Medium	1/2–2/3	1/2	Spring Fall	Fall Spring	†
Low	1/3	1/2	Spring Fall	Fall Spring	34, 41
Medium	1/2	1/2	Spring Fall	Fall Spring	34
High	1	1/2	Spring Fall	Fall Spring	34
Medium	1/4	1/2	Spring Summer	Fall	34
Medium	1/3	1/2	Spring Fall	Fall Spring	†
Medium	8-in. centers	1/8–1/4	Spring Fall	Fall Spring	25, 26, 64
Medium	4	1½	Spring	Fall	†
Medium	2–3	1½	Spring	Fall	34, 41
High	2½	3/4	Spring Fall	Fall or Spring Spring	41
High	4	3/4	Fall Spring	Spring Fall	†
Medium	2	1/2	Spring Summer Fall	Fall Fall or Spring Spring	†
Medium	2½	3/4	Spring Summer	Summer Fall	34, 41
High	2	1/2	Spring	Fall	34
Low	4	1	Spring Fall	Summer Spring	34
High	4	3/4	Fall	Spring	34, 41
Low	2	3/4	Spring Summer	Summer Fall	25, 41
High	4	3/4	Spring	Fall	34
High	4	3/4	Fall	Spring	34
Varies	Varies	Varies	Varies	Varies	28, 64

†Not included in the numbered listing of seed source in the back of the book are two suppliers of these noted cover crops. Serving Canadian customers only is Bishop's Farm Seeds, PO Box 338, Belleville, Ontario, Canada, K8N 5A5. Agway is a northeastern chain; contact Agway at the following address for the name of a store nearest you or for ordering information: Agway Inc., Corporate Library, Box 4933, Syracuse, NY, 13221.

Turning Under Cover Crops: Cut back heavy topgrowth in very early spring with a sickle, scythe, or mower, as shown top left. Before turning it under, spread a layer of compost or manure over the stubble to speed decomposition (bottom left). Make several passes with a rotary mower to chop the green matter into degradable pieces (top right). This keeps long, lush tops from getting caught in your tiller. (Tops can also be bagged and put on a compost pile or rototilled into another bed scheduled to be planted later.) Tillers are the best choice to dig under the crop, and rear-tine tillers are better than front-mounted types. Go over the bed once lengthwise and once crosswise. If the topgrowth isn't excessive, at this stage keep working in the cover crop until you have created a manageable seedbed, then plant the same day. If the tops are lush and heavy, after two passes with the tiller let the clods and pieces of sod dry out for a day or two. At this point a watering or rainfall will help speed decay. When the bed has dried out somewhat, go over it a couple more times, wait until it's dry again, then till the soil a final time and plant.

No-Till Cover Crops: To make hand-turning easier, bend over the topgrowth and cover with a thick layer of wet newspaper or black plastic anchored with a mulch of shredded leaves (shown on top). This will encourage decomposition, making the cover crop easier to manage with hand tools. To keep the bed in use while you're waiting for the topgrowth to break down, cut out strips of mulch and plant rows of peas or other legumes.

On the other hand, rye fall-sown with clover is much more manageable in spring. And the hollow, tender stem of buckwheat makes this short-term summer cover relatively easy to chop through by hand. Gardeners without machines also should consider planting fall cover crops that will sooner or later succumb to winter kill in their area. If you seed such crops in available spaces from mid-July to September or October (depending on how early your first frost comes), by early the following spring you'll have a well-decomposed source of humus and nitrogen that can be turned over easily by hand. True, this halfway measure won't give you the volume of organic matter and/or nitrogen you would reap from a full season's growth, but it costs so little and saves so much labor that is just may be the only mode of covercropping worth your while.

If you're hand gardening but still want to grow hardy cover crops over the winter, there's an emergency technique you can use to cope with those that get away from you. Instead of fighting to subdue all that luxuriant growth, simply bend it over and cover it with a thick layer of wet newspaper or biodegradable black plastic held down by a thick mulch of shredded leaves. While you're waiting for the cover crop to decompose sufficiently to be turned under by hand, you can keep the bed in use by cutting out narrow strips from the mulch and putting in rows of peas, fava beans, or other legumes. When the

RHIZOBIA TO USE FOR INOCULATION

Legume Group	Rhizobium Species	Use For
Alfalfa	R. meliloti	Alfalfa
		Sweet clover
		Fenugreek
Clover	R. trifolii	Clovers
Pea	R. leguminosarum	Pea, Vetch, Sweetpea, Lentil
Bean	R. phaseoli	Beans
Lupine	R. lupini	Lupines
		Serradella
Soybean	R. japonicum	Soybean
Cowpea		Cowpea, Lespedeza, Crotalaria, Kudzu, Peanut, Lima bean

Source: Martin Alexander, Introduction to Soil Microbiology, *2nd ed. (New York: Wiley Press, 1977), 307.*

crop is harvested, it will be relatively easy to turn under the partially decomposed cover crop. Or you can leave the cover crop, mulch, and pea roots in place and plant nitrogen-loving vine crops such as squashes or cucumbers, which will recline in comfort atop the cushiony bed for the rest of the growing season.

More Time and Space-Saving Techniques with Cover Crops

Whenever possible, plant cover crops you can eat. Peas, fava beans, soybeans, crowder peas, snap beans, and limas all stimulate soil life as they grow. At harvest time you can leave the roots in place and either toss the tops on the compost heap or chop them into small pieces and bury in the same bed with a little manure or compost. Put legumes in rows or block plantings here and there as part or all of a bed opens up. Or succession plant an entire bed in peas, followed by beans or soybeans for an entire growing season, then grow heavy feeders there with little or no fertilizer the following year. In year-round gar-

dening climates like the Gulf Coast, it can be a good idea to put in a crop of the heat-resistant LADY CREAM crowder peas in summer and follow up with winter and early-season crops like brassicas, spinach, lettuce, collards, and radishes. (Whatever legumes you grow, for best results inoculate the seed with the appropriate strain of rhizobia bacteria. If you can't purchase this at a farm or garden supply store, try Agricultural Laboratories, listed under Garden Products in the Directory of Resources at the back of the book.)

Consider getting double use from a bed with a cover crop by mowing it and overseeding large-seeded vegetables such as legumes or putting in transplants. In studies done at the Rodale Research Center in Maxatawny, Pennsylvania, that focused on planting vegetables in established legume sod, the legumes that survived a Pennsylvania winter with least damage and tolerated two or three mowings to control weed growth were WHITE DUTCH clover, which formed a lush, thick sod and suffered no winter kill, and MEDIUM RED CLOVER, which gave a fair to good stand but experienced minor winter damage.

Try sowing cover crops while vegetables are still growing. You can broadcast winter rye among your crops in early fall and can sometimes plant cowpeas and soybeans under taller vegetables as a living mulch. Such newcomers won't compete with well-developed plants but will provide a bonus of humus and heightened soil microbe activity. You can start overseeding most cover crops among vegetables from late July for a thick stand by frost. According to northeastern Pennsylvania Extension Agent Tom Jurchak, this technique works best with beans, brassicas, peppers, potatoes, sweet corn, and tomatoes and probably should not be used with low growers such as cucumbers and melons. Cover crops like alfalfa, buckwheat, or soybeans make superb interplantings with corn (especially in hot, windy, arid places), and favas do well interplanted with lettuce and other spring crops.

Schedule a cover crop wherever and whenever you have a month or more of garden time available. Nonlegumes in particular produce substantial topgrowth in amazingly little time. Buckwheat, for example, is a good, quick cover in warm weather months, growing knee-high in 45 days. In cooler regions, it's possible to put in a cover crop like oats as soon as the ground can be worked and turn under as much as 22 inches of topgrowth by the time it's safe to set out tomatoes. Other quickie crops that can benefit your soil in just a few weeks of growing time are turnips and fodder radishes, which loosen heavy clay soils, and mustard and rape, cole crops that can survive longer into fall than buckwheat. If a narrow strip opens anywhere in the garden, pop in a row of short-season edible soybeans. Should a root or other crop finish early, sneak in an extra green manure crop of buckwheat or oats, then plant winter wheat at the beginning of October or later.

Compost

It's no accident that the gardeners with the best yields tend to be fervent large-scale composters, whose idea of a good time is cruising to stables or sawmills in the pickup . . . or scavenging the woods for leaves or the beach for seaweed . . . or rescuing endless bags of grass clippings or leaf mulch from neighborhood curbsides. However it's concocted, compost is the great equalizer. Capable of normalizing every problem soil, it can bring life to sand dunes or rock-hard red clay, to patches of slick, shiny black wax gumbo, or to hard-scrabble, high-limestone earth with barely a trace of topsoil.

By heating organic wastes to 160°F, the composting process deactivates weed seeds and reduces levels of plant pathogens and toxic substances, producing sweet-smelling crumbly humus. Because compost releases its nitrogen slowly, it creates lower concentrations of nitrates in nitrate-storing leafy vegetables like lettuce than chemical fertilizers with an equivalent amount of N-P-K—an important plus since high nitrate levels in food have been linked to some kinds of cancer.

Compost is a strong alternative to cover crops, for it, too, can contribute a high volume of top-quality organic matter to the soil, and it doesn't tie up garden space to do it. According to a study done at the Hungarian Academy of Sciences, if adequate nitrogen and phosphorus are present, organic soil content is the characteristic that most influences soil respiration and decomposition of cellulose, biological activities firmly linked to nutrient availability and high yield. (Because of the vital connection between organic matter and soil life, compost will be even more effective if it is supplemented with mulch, for as the mulch breaks down, the soil organisms that multiply to degrade it will reinforce the uptake of nitrogen from the compost.)

Unlike chemical fertilizers, compost attracts earthworms, which feed mostly on organic tidbits and return them further enriched to the soil in the form of castings. While mineral fertilizers used alone tend to lower soil fertility and pH, the manure typically found in compost acts to maintain or even improve the physiochemical balance

RAISING CROPS FOR THE COMPOST PILE

Ecology Action of the Midpeninsula, a California-based environmental organization devoted to biodynamic/French intensive gardening, maintains that ideally each garden should produce its own organic enrichment for self-sustenance. In other words, you should grow crops specifically for composting. Just to give you an idea how much composting material is needed by a raised bed garden, let's examine the group's figures. In regions with a four-month growing season, Ecology Action claims between one-fifth and one-half of the garden area should be given over to the growing of plants specifically for the compost pile, while in areas with a six-month season, between one-eighth and one-third of the garden area should be used in this manner.

For gardeners with a limited amount of space, turning over productive area to feed the compost pile probably will not be a very appealing idea. After all, you can always compost what's left behind from edible crops that have been harvested and eaten. But for gardeners with the space who are serious about conditioning their soils, this might be an interesting alternative. Let's see how two Oregon gardeners have adopted this system.

Lynn Coody and Jon Davis are very earnest composters. As Coody says, "We have a winter composting system and a summer composting system. We put inches and inches of compost everywhere. Jon says everything that doesn't move we put compost on." That includes all the fruit trees, berry bushes, and vegetables they grow on one-third of an acre.

This generous use of compost necessitates, of course, an abundant, convenient source of compostable materials. In addition to collecting organic matter, they have begun to grow their own. Coody explains, "We have pasture grasses that we grow and orchard grasses between our fruit trees that we cut specifically for composting and mulch for the trees." These grasses are cut before they go to seed, three to four times in their wet Oregon spring season.

Many of the green manures they grow are raised for composting and for cover crop use at the same time. They cut annual rye and hairy vetch and compost the tops. Coody cautions, "You have to be careful not to cut hairy vetch down too close." Sometimes they let these covers regrow and turn them under or cut off the tops again, compost them, and then turn in the roots.

---

of the soil and by heightening bacterial activity increases the value and effectiveness of small amounts of mineral powders used in the compost or separately.

Not surprisingly, gardeners trying to wrest heavy yields from small spaces find compost almost indispensable. This is especially true of those struggling to fit three crops into a 90-day growing season or battling intense heat, which burns up organic matter at a phenomenal rate. Compost also makes an especially important contribution to high yields when it is used lavishly in growing frames brought into action to extend the season at both ends. The low soil temperatures and crowded conditions in these structures mandate a growing medium that is at once highly fertile, light, well aerated, and well drained. It is, in a word, compost.

Alternatives to Standard Compost Piles

Because there are many ways of composting, experienced gardeners often have an assortment of heaps ripening at different rates. There's no need to go by the book, either. Traditional compost starters such as manure can be eliminated in the presence of such free and easy nitrogen sources

COMPOSTING MATERIALS

Material	Source	Comments
Bone meal†	Garden centers	Very high P* source
Coffee grounds	Restaurants, offices	Good N* source
Corncobs and stalks	Farms, canneries, garden refuse	Best when ground or used as a soil texturizer or mulch; high in C*
Cottonseed†	Garden centers, gins	High in N and P
Cowpeas (green stalks)	Farms, gardens	N and K* source
Eggshells	Egg farms, restaurants	Supplies calcium and N
Fish scraps and shellfish wastes	Canneries, fisheries, fish markets, restaurants	High in N and trace minerals, but odoriferous
Fruit wastes	Canneries, restaurants, market dumps, restaurants	Banana peels are rich in K
Grass clippings	Lawn mowing, lawn services, neighbors' bags set at curbside	Use only clippings from herbicide-free lawns; very high in N; decompose rapidly and help create necessary heat to break down other materials in pile; odoriferous unless blended well with C-rich materials
Hair (animal and human)	Barber and beauty shops, pet groomers	Good N source, but slow to break down; avoid human hair that's been dyed
Hay	Farms	Bulky, high in C; alfalfa highest in N
Hoof and horn meal†	Slaughterhouses, garden centers	High in N; slow to break down
Hops (spent)	Breweries	Wet and hard to manage; rich in N; odoriferous
Leather wastes	Tanneries, manufacturers	Good N source, but slow to break down
Leaves	Woods, dumpings in parks or at curbsides	When decomposed to the form of leaf mold, make an excellent soil texturizer; contain growth inhibitors if not first composted; shred before adding to pile
Manure	Farms, stables, poultry houses, circuses, feed lots	Listed from high to low N: pigeon, chicken, duck, horse, rabbit, pig, cow, sheep, goat
Peanut shells	Farms, gardens, peanut butter processors	Good soil texturizer with moderate humus potential; slow to break down; high in C and K
Pine needles	Woods, evergreen plantings	Highly acid N source; use on acid-loving crops or with neutralizer
Sawdust, shavings, wood chips	Lumberyards, tree surgeons, sawmills, carpentry shops, furniture makers, utility crews for chips	High in N, P, and C; exceedingly slow to break down; never add fresh sawdust directly to soil
Seaweed	Beaches	High in N and K, but odoriferous
Soy meal, soy pulp, and other oil-pressing wastes	Garden stores for meal; oil processors of tung nuts, castor beans, sunflowers, rapeseed, linseed, and so on for other materials	High in N, but often hard to find

(continued)

*N = nitrogen, P = phosphorus, K = potassium, C = carbon
† Unless they're bought in bulk, these materials can be expensive. Most gardeners prefer to add them directly to the garden soil rather than fortify the compost pile with them.

COMPOSTING MATERIALS— *Continued*

Material	Source	Comments
Spice waste	Spice makers	Mustard seeds are high in N
Stable bedding, sweepings	Stables, farms	Better nutrient balance than manure alone
Sugarcane and sugar beet waste	Refineries	N source, but hard to work with
Vegetable waste	Canneries, restaurants (especially vegetarian ones), sorted garbage, food stores, farm markets	Pea pods are especially high in N
Weeds	Gardens, fields, road sides, pond dredgings	Cut before seeds set, or use in hot compost pile; purslane is very high in N
Wheat straw, oat straw	Farms	High in C; slow to break down
Wood ash	Fireplaces, wood stoves, wood furnaces, bonfires	K and P but no N; strongly alkaline; don't use ashes from fires started with charcoal
Wool wastes	Mills	High in N but low humus potential; slow to break down
Worm culture soil†	Wholesale worm farms, fishing worm dealers	Rich in N from castings

as grass clippings or corncobs and husks. Some innovative people fire their heaps with unconventional choices such as human urine (which is odorless and safe to use) mixed with sawdust, or wheat bran or alfalfa purchased in bulk at feed stores. Others in climates at least moderately warm and wet have discovered layering, turning, and watering are all unnecessary. Shoveling any and all garden and other organic wastes into pits, they cover the completed collection with a few inches of soil, and dig up finished compost within a year. (Small kitchen scraps will break down in as little as six weeks if the hole is filled in early summer.)

If you lack the space for composting on a grand or even small scale, why not leave the root systems of all your nonroot crops in the ground to break down there? Weighing up to half as much as the aboveground, harvested part of the plant, such material can contribute significant amounts of organic matter to your soil, functioning

as a kind of on-site compost. You also can hand dig or till under plant tops at the end of the season. Another possibility is hand-digging or tilling under produce wastes from a supermarket or farmers' market a few weeks or more before planting. If put through a grinder, this nitrogen-rich material will spread like grass clippings. Although directly applied wastes lack some of the advantages of compost, new findings from the Department of Plant and Soil Science at the University of Vermont suggest they may have just as great an impact on fertility factors such as soil nitrogen availability and organic content and structure.

Compost in a Hurry

In the rush of the season, compost making is sometimes neglected. If, toward the end of the summer, you've used all the spring-made compost on seedlings and in compost tea, it is good to know how to make a replacement batch by the

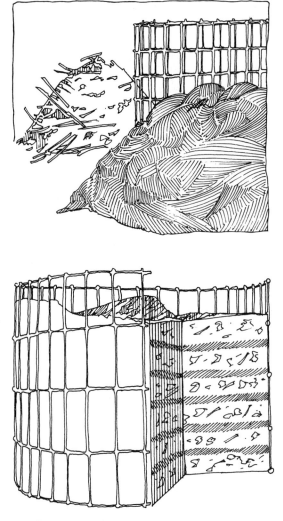

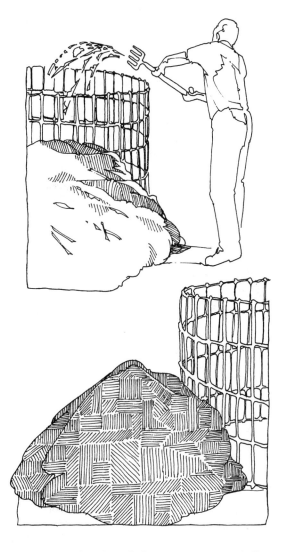

Quick Compost

Step 1: Use a bin, pen, or wire container that admits air. The capacity should be at least 1 cubic yard, and the height 4 feet or more. Assemble organic materials. Divide them into two categories: green and wet (high in nitrogen); and dry and coarse (high in carbon). Chop everything into pieces of less than 6 inches.

Step 2: Fork layers of dry and wet materials into the bin, alternating 4 inches of dry material with a sprinkling of wet matter. Add water between layers until the material glistens but is not sodden. Stop layering when the pile reaches 3 feet high.

Step 3: Three days later, fork out the contents. Fluff and aerate it as you toss it back into the bin, placing the outside of the old pile on the inside of the new pile. Add water until the material glistens. Skip a day and turn the pile, then skip another day and repeat, making sure each particle has spent some time in the interior of the pile. (If you're in a hurry toss once a day to speed the process even more.)

Step 4: When the pile cools to 110°F, move it out of the bin and let it age for a week or two before using in the garden.

With the Master Gardeners

TILLER-TURNED COMPOST

A tiller can take the back-straining labor out of turning the compost pile. And as one fan of the tiller method has found, a batch of compost made this way is ready in an easy month and a half.

Mark Rames, a finalist in the 1985 Organic Gardener of the Year contest, needs a large and steady supply of compost to overcome the clay in his Michigan garden. He uses compost in his orchard, side-dresses 24 beds of vegetables with it, and even plants hills of cantaloupes in deep pockets of compost. He's devised a system that allows him to make as much compost as he needs throughout the season, letting his rotary tiller bear the brunt of the pile-turning.

Rames starts with a truckful of manure (preferably free of sawdust and straw). He spreads this out in a layer 6 inches thick, 4 to 5 feet wide and as long as it will stretch. The next layer is green material gathered from kitchen wastes and visits to local fruit and vegetable stands, augmented by garden wastes and grass clippings.

Revving up the rotary tiller, he makes a pass across the pile, mixing the manure with the green matter. He then adds a 3 to 4-inch layer of straw to one half of the pile, from end to end. At this point he used to shovel and rake the uncovered half of the pile onto the straw-covered half, but now thanks to a blade attachment meant to pile snow he can do this work with the tiller.

The pile gets a plastic cover and is allowed to sit for one to two weeks. At the end of the rest, the plastic comes off and Rames makes another pass with the tiller to flatten the pile. He adds another layer of green matter, tills it in, and with the blade attachment mounds the pile again. This pile heats up quickly and Rames knows it's ready when it cools down.

Besides saving his back and a good bit of time that would otherwise be spent turning by hand, Rames admits that it's "really nice to be able to use compost so freely," knowing that there's an abundant supply on hand.

fast method. Many good intensive gardeners use only this method to provide themselves with abundant compost throughout the year.

The product of fast-style compost making is more alkaline and lower in nitrogen than slowly made compost, but the high temperatures reached in the almost totally aerobic, quickly made pile will destroy all weed seeds. Each gardener will develop variations on the method to suit facilities and materials, but the basic steps are shown in the illustration on the preceding page.

Other Soil Amendments

If planting green manure crops and/or composting are not part of your gardening plans, you can get by with high-nitrogen substitutes such as grass clippings or manure. Manure, for example, is superior to mineral fertilizers over the long term because it intensifies the mineralization of carbon, which increases the stability of organic matter. According to Dr. Emmett Schulte, a professor of soil science at the University of Wisconsin at Madison, applying 230 to 460 pounds of such high nitrogen material to each 100 square feet of soil once a year can provide all the nitrogen, phosphorus, and potassium needed in most gardening situations. United States Department of Agriculture soil scientist Dr. Sharon Hornick says you'll see noticeable improvement in most soils by applying just 230 pounds of organic matter per 100 square feet and that in the clay and loam

NUTRIENT PROFILES OF COMMON ORGANIC AMENDMENTS

Organic Material	Nitrogen	Phosphorus	Potassium	Rate of Release
Activated sludge	5.0	3.0	0	Medium
Alfalfa hay	2.5	0.5	2.1	—
Animal tankage	8.0	20.0	0	Medium
Apple leaves	1.0	0.2	0.4	—
Basic slag	0	0.8	0	Rapid
Bloodmeal	15.0	1.3	0.7	—
Bone meal (steamed)	4.0	21.0	0.2	Slow
Brewers' grains (wet)	0.9	0.5	0.1	—
Castor pomace	5.5	1.5	1.3	Slow
Cattle manure (dried)	2.0	1.8	2.2	Medium
Cattle manure (fresh)	0.3	0.2	0.4	Medium
Cocoa shell dust	1.0	1.5	2.7	Slow
Coffee grounds (dried)	2.0	0.4	0.7	—
Colloidal phosphate	0	18–24	0	Slow
Cornstalks	0.8	0.4	0.9	—
Cottonseed	3.2	1.3	1.2	—
Cottonseed meal	7.0	2.5	1.5	Slow–medium
Dried blood	12–15	3.0	0	Medium–rapid
Fish emulsion	5.0	2.0	2.0	Medium–rapid
Fish meal	10.0	4.0	0	Slow
Fish scrap	7.8	13.0	3.8	Slow
Granite dust	0	0	5.0	Slow
Greensand	0	1.5	5.0	Very slow
Guano	12.0	8.0	3.0	Medium
Hoof meal and horn dust	12.5	1.8	0	Slow
Horse manure (composted)	0.7	0.3	0.6	Medium
Horse manure (fresh)	0.4	0.2	0.4	Medium
Leaf mold (composted	0.6	0.2	0.4	Medium
Mushroom compost	0.4–0.7	57–62	0.5–1.5	Slow
Oak leaves	0.8	0.4	0.2	Rapid
Peach leaves	0.9	0.2	0.6	—
Phosphate rock	0	30–32	0	Very slow
Pig manure (fresh)	0.6	0.4	0.1	Medium
Pine needles	0.5	0.1	0	—
Poultry manure (fresh)	2.0	1.9	1.9	Medium–rapid
Rabbit manure (fresh)	2.4	0.6	0.1	Medium
Roses (flower)	0.3	0.1	0.4	—
Sawdust	4.0	2.0	4.0	Very slow
Seaweed	1.7	0.8	5.0	Slow–medium
Sheep manure (fresh)	0.6	0.3	0.2	Medium
Soybean meal	6.7	1.6	2.3	Slow–medium
Tankage	6.0	8.0	0	—
Tobacco stems	2.0	0	7.0	Slow
Wood ashes	0	1.5	7.0	Rapid

soils of the Northeast and Midwest, even 115 pounds will yield results.

Extension Horticulturist Dr. William S. Peavy of El Paso, Texas, advises gardeners to halve the first year's application in subsequent years to allow for the fact that organic materials have a "half-life" rate of release. That is, they surrender half their nutrients the first year, half of the remaining half the second year, and so on. According to Peavy, if all crop residues are returned to the soil from the second year on, then just one-quarter of the original amount will be needed yearly.

Fresh manure, of course, can burn plants, as can other relatively quick-releasing fertilizers, so use them carefully. Even spent mushroom soil should be at least a year old before going in the garden. Fresh manure is preferably applied in the fall, but in a pinch you might want to work it in thoroughly, then risk being guided by farmers' wisdom, which holds it is safe to plant when your soil has stopped giving off the pungent odor of dung and started to exude the more pleasant aroma of good, earthy compost. This is likely to take three or four weeks.

To improve your soil's ability to speedily decompose and make use of organic material in whatever form you add it, you may want to consider spraying on supplemental soil bacteria every other year or so. Some gardeners find this practice especially helpful in conditioning clay soils.

If your soil is rich enough in organic content to supply or release from the soil sufficient amounts of the major nutrients (nitrogen, phosphorus, and potassium), the chances are excellent that the micronutrients are also around in soluble form in the very small amounts required. The most usual exception to this rule is iron, which often remains unavailable in highly alkaline soils. If your soil has a very high pH, more of its iron reserves can be brought into solution by the chelating action of humus, so step up your efforts to boost the organic content of your growing medium.

Make Growing Beds for Bigger Yields

Besides the issue of getting the soil into good shape for growing, there's also the question of what shape the garden will take. For gardeners seeking high yields, there's a very basic answer— growing beds. As you'll see in this section, beds can take many forms, from flat to raised, each with interesting variations.

Beds versus Rows

Rows running from north to south can be compatible with intensive gardening if you're growing large plants that cast lots of shade or if you're trellising plants inside the garden rather than along the northern or eastern borders. Too, some high-yield gardeners with large growing areas prefer straight, single, widely spaced columns of slow-germinating crops such as carrots and beets simply because they can remove weeds in record time just by pulling a 5-inch-wide hoe between the rows. The advantage becomes even greater if the garden area is being mulched with uncomposted manure, which has weed seeds in it.

As a rule, though, a planting scheme based on long skinny rows separated by wide expanses of cleanly cultivated soil makes sense only on farms, where vast acres of cropland are cultivated by machine. Most gardeners work primarily with hand tools, plus their arms and legs, and to use time and energy most efficiently, it's supremely desirable to bring as many plants as possible within reach of an outstretched hand or hoe. The answer, of course, is to position plants in groups — an arrangement that proves of great value not just to the gardener but to the plants, for the microenvironment created this way has powerful implications for plant health and productivity.

Plants clustered in growing areas shaped as squares, rectangles, circles, or whatever are being grown in beds. By definition, beds eliminate at least some of the extra spacing that distinguishes plants in adjoining rows from plants within a row. Often seeds or transplants are placed so as to form a grid of squares. Even more effective as a space-saving device is equidistant spacing, in which plants are treated as circles and planted in hexagonal or diagonal offset patterns. (These patterns are discussed in more detail in chapter 4.)

As you might guess, the smaller the distance between plants, the greater the advantages of beds in terms of space efficiency. In a conventional garden in which plants are placed 2 inches apart in rows spaced 12 inches apart, two 5-foot by 20-foot areas will yield only 12 rows. When the same space is equidistantly planted with 2 inches between plants on all sides, it will accommodate 50 rows—over four times more plants! With larger plants positioned 18 inches apart in

rows 36 inches apart, there will be 4 rows; equidistant spacing, which calls for the same 18-inch spacing from center to center with only 15 inches between rows, makes possible 8 rows—that's twice as many plants.

When the space needed for paths is factored in, it's possible to see even more clearly how beds permit gardeners to fit in many extra plants per square foot of growing space. For example, in a typical row garden of 10 by 20 feet with 2-foot-wide paths for a rotary tiller, you migh have two 20-foot-long rows of carrots spaced 2 inches apart, for a total of 400 carrots from a productive area roughly 3½ by 20 feet. In a bed garden measuring the same 10 by 20 feet and featuring two 4-foot-wide beds—one on each side of a 2-foot-wide center path—you could plant a total of 432

Space-Efficient Beds: Given the same amount of garden area, beds make better use of the space than a conventional row garden. Valuable space isn't wasted on paths between rows of plants, and the prime condition of the soil allows for close spacing.

carrots 2 inches apart in a portion of the bed measuring just 2½ by 4 feet. Similarly a total of 200 bush bean plants planted 4 inches apart within two 20-foot rows compares unfavorably with the 216 green bean plants that can be fitted into a 4 by 5-foot section of a wide row using the same spacing between plants. You can get a quite vivid sense of the benefits of beds by converting row-feet into square feet of bed. For example, it's possible to fit 66 row feet of alternating leafy greens and root crops into an 18-square foot bed (a 3 by 6-foot bed with 22 rows 3 inches apart) and 60 row feet into a 27-square-foot area (a 3 by 9-foot bed with 20 rows 5 inches apart).

If your soil is highly fertile and well-conditioned, such close planting is likely to reduce the productivity of individual plants slightly but will increase yields on a square-foot basis dramatically. In one comparative study done by the Asgrow Seed Company, equidistantly planted soybeans outperformed those in rows by 24 percent.

The heightened productivity of a stand of closely spaced plants may be traced to a more supportive environment that helps plants come closer to realizing their fullest growth potential. For starters, positioning plants so their leaves touch reduces stress by slowing the rate at which the air temperature changes within the garden and by working in several ways to let plants make the fullest use of water falling on the garden from above. For one thing, the relatively dense network of roots in a bed and the relative infrequency of paths assures that precious moisture is retained in the growing area instead of running off to puddle pointlessly in nonproductive places. (The same benefit applies to fertilizers applied during the growing season.) Also, the shade supplied by the living canopy of mulch that blankets closely planted beds slows the evaporation of water from the surface of the beds.

These conditions enhance productivity by approximating more nearly than row culture can the circumstances enjoyed by plants growing in the wild. By not subjecting the soil that supports plant life to human weight, a garden designed in beds and permanent paths mimics a natural eco-system in another critically important way. One of the most subtle but powerful factors limiting plant growth is soil compaction, which crushes particles together and forces oxygen and water-holding spaces out of the growing medium. The result all too often is an almost impenetrable layer of hardpan that prevents relatively delicate plant roots from reaching deep into the earth and making use of the abundant trace minerals and moisture stored there. If unimpeded, the roots of even small plants such as beets will travel downward as much as 10 feet, but in airless, rock hard soils, plant roots are forced to spread sideways instead of continuing their vertical progress as decreed by gravity. As a result, if you plant closely in compacted soil, the horizontally moving root systems of neighboring plants will compete with each other for a relatively limited supply of oxygen, water, and nutrients, and yield will be reduced accordingly.

Soil under cultivation is always quicker to compact than that left undisturbed, and topsoil tends to compact faster than subsoil. That being the case, it is enormously important for a garden to be fashioned so that growing areas are never walked on—an ideal possible only when you forsake large plots crisscrossed by paths that are relocated each year for narrow beds separated by permanent walkways. Double digging, a technique of bed preparation designed for use with growing beds anywhere from 2½ to 5 feet wide, also fights soil compaction.

In addition to upgrading the milieu in which your plants grow, beds also help yields by making harvested areas more noticeable and therefore encouraging prompt, easy succession planting. This is especially true for gardeners putting in block plantings of single crops. Unlike rows, beds also lend themselves to broadcast sowing of salad crops, kale, turnip greens, and so on for early spring greens.

The closer planting and better yields associated with beds also make it possible and desirable to spot-harvest part of most crops when the vegetables are young and tender, staggering the yield in a helpful way. Because plants overlap somewhat, some mature faster than others, prolonging the harvest from a single planting longer than would be possible with row plants, which tend to mature within a few days of each other.

Dividing the garden into distinctly separate sections also lets you do custom soil conditioning, manipulating the pH or other characteristics to meet the special needs of the crop to come. For instance, potatoes can be given the slightly acid soil they favor, while in the bed next door extra lime can be applied for an anticipated planting of peas or beans, or an added measure of manure provided for heavy feeders such as lettuce, cauliflower, tomatoes, beets, eggplants, or corn.

As this implies, gardening in beds rather than narrow strips makes it far easier to plan and carry out crop rotation schemes, which impact on yields by preventing the buildup of certain soil diseases and confusing insects looking for a free lunch. With beds, the covercropping so significant to rotation plans also becomes surprisingly manageable in a garden context. As

individual beds open up, grains or legumes can be sown here and there in time slots as short as four weeks.

Wide-Rows and Other Flat Beds

Once you've made the decision to convert from rows to beds you'll need to decide whether to choose a form of flat bed gardening or "go all the way" to raised beds. Continuing to garden on the level offers certain obvious advantages. For one thing, flat beds are easy to prepare and maintain with rotary tillers and tractors. For this reason alone they're often favored by those working large areas. No time is spent shaping raised surfaces and, of course, there's really no need to go to the trouble and expense of building sides to contain the beds.

When to Consider Flat Beds If these considerations don't make up your mind one way or the other, factor in your basic soil type, the rainfall in your area, and other relevant climatic characteristics such as frost dates and windiness. As you'll see, raised beds are a marvelous advantage in many gardening situations. Even so, flat bed gardening is by no means incompatible with heavy yields and under some circumstances is

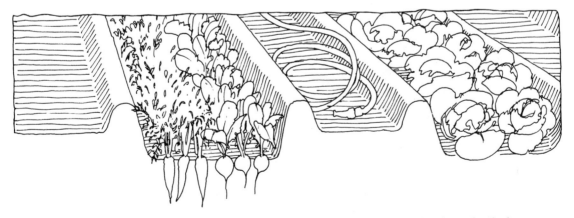

Basin Beds: Gardeners in dry areas might want to try these variations on raised beds. The sunken beds are surrounded by 12-inch retaining walls that hold in water.

preferable. For example, the exposed sides of uncontained raised beds cause them to dry out faster on hot windy days—especially when seedlings have not yet developed to the point of shading the bed. It follows that if you garden in sandy, fast-draining soil in a scorching, gusty, arid climate, you might find it best to keep a low profile with heavily mulched flat beds.

Indeed, keeping raised beds from eroding under such circumstances may be difficult even if your soil is incredibly rich in organic matter. Why bother to raise a bed when it will be leveled by the end of the season? That's the prognosis in very hot, sandy places with low humidity and little rainfall. Cooked by intense sunlight, organic matter disappears with appalling rapidity. As

one dazed grower in cactus country puts it, "When you water, your soil disappears into the soil." The antidote is repeated applications of organic matter and a carefully managed watering program. Some gardeners in the Southwest are trying basin beds, also called waffle beds or pans. These beds are sunk 3 to 6 inches below ground level and are surrounded by retaining walls at least 12 inches high.

Flat Bed Options If flat-bed culture is your choice, there are several ways to go about it. Some people forfeit the advantage permanent paths offer for reducing soil compaction, preferring to grow crops such as peas, beans, and limas in block plantings as large as 25 square feet.

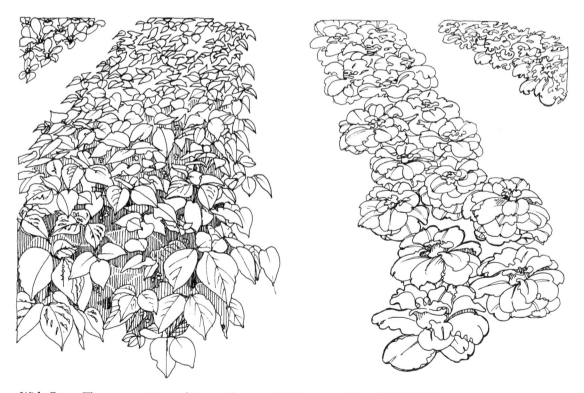

Wide-Rows: These are an intermediate step between single rows and broad beds. Wide-rows can range from 10 to 36 inches across. Crops are densely spaced so that leaves of adjacent plants just touch each other.

Wide-row gardening authority Dick Raymond alternates such larger patches with a 3 by 3-foot or 4 by 4-foot flat bed and long broad rows ranging anywhere from 10 to 12 to 36 inches in width. Despite the fact that he is often photo-graphed standing or harvesting from a stool smack in the middle of his broad beds, Raymond reports phenomenal yields from his block plantings. Among his secrets are super-rich soil, sowing seeds at rates 20 percent higher than average, and rigorous, regular harvesting (he uses a cut-and-come-again strategy for leafy greens and eats some of each crop when it's quite young and tender).

Another strategy for intensive growing in flat beds comes from Mel Bartholomew, who developed the square foot gardening method. Claiming that wide-rows and beds lead people to overplant and to be overwhelmed with too much food all at once, Bartholomew advocates dividing garden space into 1 by 1-foot squares. These are grouped into larger 4 by 4-foot units surrounded by permanent paths. Each square foot is closely planted with one crop at a time, and vining crops are trellised. Rodale Research Center staffers

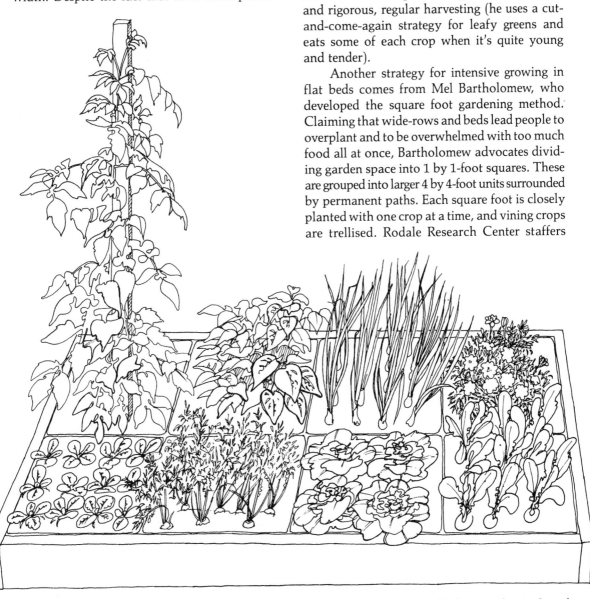

Square Foot Gardening: This highly organized system is based on 1-foot-square units. Each square foot is planted with one crop, and four or more of these units are grouped together and surrounded by permanent paths.

experimented with this approach over one summer and reported, "It proved very productive, especially for salad crops. Using pre-started plants, five succession plantings were harvested during the growing season." Meticulous and small scale in its orientation, square foot gardening seems most realistic for small-space gardeners. Bartholomew maintains that it produces the same amount of food as a conventional row garden with one-fifth the space and work, offering the benefit of a logical, automatically controlled harvest together with "all the advantages of crop rotation, soil improvement, and companion planting."

Gardeners intent on the ultimate in yields and willing to put forth more effort might try using the square foot gardening layout and planting techniques in tandem with 4 to 4½-foot-wide raised beds with flat tops or contained sides. With double digging thrown in, the results could be outstanding!

A variation of the square-foot approach calls for combining different plants within each square foot of the garden, thus obtaining the benefits of interplanting herbs and vegetables and working toward maximum efficiency in the use of space. Choose the plants to fit together in space and time, and arrange them like the pieces of a jigsaw puzzle to complement each other's height, growing time, shading requirements, and so forth. In such a system, the idea is to fill each small square with a major plant, then to fill in with a smaller transplant and seeds of low-growing plants, which are broadcast into any open areas. (For more information on choosing complementary plants to share growing space, see chapter 5.)

The Benefits of Raised Beds

By raising the height of your planting beds by 4 to 8 inches or more above that of the surrounding soil, you can enjoy all the blessings of flat bed plantings and add a raft of new ones. Some of the added elevation of raised beds comes naturally as the soil becomes increasingly loosened and aerated via double digging and the activity of plant roots, soil organisms, and worms. This progressive fluffing of the soil is augmented by the regular addition of organic matter so that the height of the beds increases by 3 to 6 inches each year. Some experienced gardeners boast flat-topped beds 16 to 18 inches high, their sides decorated with mosses and liverworts that discourage erosion. Like wide-rows, raised beds allow for equidistant and other planting schemes that enable you to squeeze more plants into your growing space. If you choose the rounded style, which has a gently curved top that allows you to plant down the sides of the bed, you'll have somewhat more planting surface than in a wide-row of the same surface dimensions and anywhere from 10 to 20 percent more planting space than is provided in a flat-topped raised bed.

For a number of reasons, the yield from close-planted raised beds is likely to be greater than that from similarly planted flat beds. The raised, fluffed growing surface lets more solar energy, air, water, and other growth-stimulating elements enter and intermingle in the growing medium. As the ancient Greeks discovered by observing the aftermath of landslides, plant life prospers in piles of disturbed soil. The mounds you construct will have the further advantage of being conditioned by organic matter. Well drained, this heaped soil warms up earlier in spring and holds heat longer at day's end and in the fall—obvious advantages if you garden in a northern or high-altitude location with a short, cool growing season. The extra warmth also helps if you experience cool, cloudy summers and want to grow heat-lovers such as tomatoes, melons, and summer squash.

The improved soil aeration and texture characteristic of raised beds contribute to their better drainage, so that surface soil dries faster as water seeps to the soil in the root zone, where it does the most good. This exceptional drainage means raised beds are probably of greatest value to those gardening in poor-draining, heavy clay soils in places with high precipitation. In climates where winters are very wet but mild, or springs cold and flood-prone, raised bed gardeners are able to plant and harvest in mist and drizzle while their neighbors are looking out the window at seas of boot-sucking mud.

That kind of superb drainage coupled with greater warmth gives a two to six-week jump on the gardening season. In Portland, Oregon, for example, it's quite possible to start hardy vegetables in early February and to feast on fresh peas, lettuce, broccoli, and Chinese vegetables in mid-May . . . to the sound of your neighbor rototilling!

Happily, given their added warmth, raised beds that are closely planted also are capable of functioning like a water-conserving mulch, should that be necessary. In cucumber and eggplant trials done at the University of Delaware's Georgetown Extension Center, raised beds gave roughly the same improvement in yield as areas treated with black plastic mulch. It's true, however, that raised beds tend to dry out faster than level plots high in organic content in intensely hot, dry weather

and/or when the beds contain sandy loam.

On the other hand, the height of a raised bed is a definite advantage in plots where the subsoil begins 11 or 12 inches down. Raised beds allow for more root development and help lessen the limiting effect of soil compaction on yield. Coupled with close planting, that countering of compaction means less space is needed to get the same yield as before: One commercial herb grower now harvests more from less than 2,500 square feet of raised beds than she did from more than 32,500 square feet on the level.

Together, the cutback in space needed and reduction in the area given over to paths make possible enormous savings in the amount of fertilizer, compost, water, and fuel needed to grow a fixed amount of food. John Jeavons's meticulous records for Ecology Action of the Midpeninsula's double-dug raised bed garden show he uses anywhere from $\frac{1}{4}$ to $\frac{1}{62}$ of the fertilizer required in conventional plots, only $\frac{1}{2}$ to $\frac{1}{16}$ of the water, and only $\frac{1}{100}$ as much fossil fuel energy.

The Comfort of a Raised Bed: Uncomfortable straining and stooping are no part of gardening in raised beds. Planting, weeding, and harvesting can all be done from a convenient perch on the side of the bed.

Jeavons's extraordinarily low material input relative to outcome may be partly attributed to the extra labor he invests, for his beds are not only raised but double dug between each crop. But no matter how you dig your raised beds, their height in combination with well-conditioned soil and close planting will allow economies that justify using these techniques—even if you have unlimited growing space.

Raised beds also are an improvement over flatland gardening in regard to convenience, for they make the hand cultivation linked to this style of gardening physically easier. Many gardeners enjoy sitting on double-tiered railroad ties, beams, or other materials retaining the growing soil when they plant, weed, or harvest. Even beds without contained sides are high enough and narrow enough to make the bending and reaching of gardening seem almost like fun, and to bring your face and eyes pleasantly close to your young plants when you hunker down in an adjacent path. This close proximity of gardener and garden seems to create a particularly strong bond between raised bed gardeners and their plants, which are seen and cared for on a more individual basis. The elevation of the planting surface also lets gardeners with limited flexibility perform many of their chores from a footstool set in the path.

Sizing Beds and Paths

Before you lay out and dig up your beds, think ahead. If you are opting for permanently located beds and paths and fully intend never to set foot (or lean arm!) in your growing space, you'll want to make your beds narrow enough so you and anyone else planting and harvesting them can comfortably reach to the middle from either side. That means each strip will be anywhere from 3 to 6 feet wide (narrower when you have access from only one side, wider when you have access from both). Should you plan to use a tiller on the beds after your permanent paths have been established, choose a bed width that also will accommodate your machine, allowing for two passes with considerable overlap in the middle of the bed. (A large tiller covers an area almost 3 feet across.)

Thinking of putting up commercial cloches or homemade polyethylene tunnels or a cold frame to extend the gardening season at both ends? Then size some or all of your beds accordingly: cold frames are often 4 feet wide, and 2½ or 3 feet is a convenient width for a homemade cloche setup.

Whatever width you choose, try if possible to employ it throughout your garden, since a standard width is desirable for interchanging bed frames, trellises, cold frames, and other "accessories." Because the advantages of close spacing increase with the width of a growing area, you'll probably want to make your beds as wide as you comfortably can, remembering that the width of any sides you may construct for the beds must be subtracted from actual growing space and calculations for seeding, fertilizers, and so on. The width favored by most raised-bed practitioners is 4 feet, although 3 and 5-foot beds also have their boosters.

A sensible idea is to start with the width best for you, then arrive at a length that will give you a multiple of 100. That way each bed will cover 100 square feet—the most convenient area for reckoning the amount of soil amendments, seeds, or transplants needed since such information is usually given on that basis. Beds of a uniform size also make it much easier to plan and carry out crop rotations.

There may, however, be compelling reasons to waive the 100-square-foot rule by making beds longer or shorter. For instance, framing materials are easy to find if you're working with standard lumberyard dimensions of 4 and 8 feet, and gardeners with small, attractively designed garden areas like the handsome, easily worked 84 by 36-inch-wide planting rectangle that can be created with two 8-foot and two 4-foot-long 6-inch-square beams. Some gardeners with larger

A SURVEY OF RAISED BEDS

ROUNDED

Description: Curved mound with gradually sloping sides.

Advantages: Because of its rounded contour and gently curved sides, which can be planted all the way down, this style of bed offers somewhat more planting space than indicated by its width at ground level and significantly more than beds with straight, angled sides. For example, a 5-foot-wide bed with a rounded top has over 20 percent more planting space than a 5-foot-wide bed with straight sides angled at 45 degrees. It is also relatively easy to shape.

Disadvantages: Plants closest to the edges of the bed may sidle or droop over into the walkway, necessitating wider paths. (To prevent this, plant small or narrow, stiffly erect plants at sides of the bed.) Also, lack of any drainage trough means that water may run out of the bed and into surrounding paths, taking planting soil along with it.

When recommended: Most feasible for good, well-conditioned soil rich in organic matter and soil that is porous and able to hold moisture well.

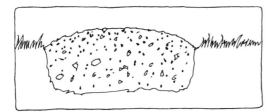

FLAT-TOP

Description: Level bed surface with straight sides angled 45 degrees from horizontal, forming an angled drainage ditch on each side of the bed where it merges with the path.

Advantages: Flat top and trenches work against water and soil loss from the growing area.

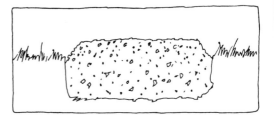

Disadvantages: Slanted sides reduce space available for planting and may require extra effort to construct and maintain.

When recommended: Good option for soils low in organic matter, for extremely heavy clay soils, and for beginning intensive gardeners.

WALLED-IN FLAT-TOP

Description: Level surface surrounded by ridges of soil around the perimeter of the bed. Straight sides slanted at 45-degree angle to horizontal.

Advantages: Ridges hold water and soil on top of bed within planted area.

Disadvantages: Has the least growing space of any type of raised bed. (To optimize what's there, position larger plants near the sides of the bed so one vertical-half of their upper growth extends out over unplanted sides of the bed.)

When recommended: Helpful where water is limited and erosion is a problem, or where capacity of the soil to hold water needs considerable improvement.

(continued)

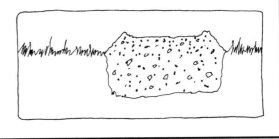

A SURVEY OF RAISED BEDS—*Continued*

CONTAINED

Description: Soil is held in place by wood, stone, or other material forming sides 6 to 24 inches high.

Advantages: Attractive, neat appearance. Sides keep soil and water in beds and effectively separate growing area from invasive grasses and weeds. Sides slow drying out of the soil and if made of thick materials may help bed retain heat longer and offer some protection against light frost. Frame can be used as starting point for season extending or shade structures or trellises or as a support for netting.

Disadvantages: Containing beds requires additional time and effort and usually the added expense of purchasing railroad ties, rot-resistant wood, or other construction materials. Sides can interfere with rototilling or double digging and can prove difficult to disassemble and relocate. Insects and slugs may be attracted to the dark moist area between the soil and sides.

When recommended: A splendid choice for those who value an aesthetically appealing garden. Can be of practical help if the growing medium is not rich enough in organic matter to resist erosion from wind and water and to hold its shape. Sides help counter the sinking of perennial beds, which are not mounded up and renewed through repeated double digging or tilling. They also can keep invasive perennial vegetables and herbs from taking over the garden.

plots prefer 30-foot beds, which they feel permit a more efficient use of space and labor. Remember, though, that the longer your beds, the more gardening time you'll spend walking around them. Jumping over a raised bed is never a good idea because of the compaction (not to mention the general destruction) that would occur if you miscalculated and sank a shoe into all that fluffy, superbly aerated, closely planted soil. Consequently, since "walk, don't jump!" is the rule, remember the corollary, which is that surprisingly often you will find yourself walking as much as the entire length of your bed plus its width to perform a gardening chore in the soil directly across from you (this is the case when you are gardening in the middle of a bed). If your bed is 20 by 5, your farthest journey will be 25 feet. If it is 30 by 5, 35 feet. Over a long, active gardening season multiplied by many beds, those extra feet could turn into miles! For that reason, you probably will not want the length of your beds to exceed 50 feet.

The permanent paths in your intensive garden should be at least 12 to 18 inches wide and a minimum of 24 inches wide if you need to accommodate a tiller or shredder. Although 1-foot paths may tempt you if you have just a small growing area and want to squeeze in an extra bed, be forewarned that many gardeners have found such narrow walkways to be disastrous and have ended by doing them over. The problem comes well into the season when plants "in aisle seats"— especially those planted down the sides of rounded beds—begin to compete with you for the air space above the paths. If your plants are growing as profusely as you hope they will, you will find it tricky just to turn around and out of the question to kneel down to take care of them without being molested.

On the other hand, paths 24 inches wide will allow you to maneuver a wheelbarrow and to kneel and weed without gouging the bed behind you with your feet. Paths this generous or more so become even more desirable if you plan to till and reshape your beds regularly or if you have grass or rye or clover in your paths and want to mow them. Some gardeners put 3-foot paths in areas where they plan to bring out and use shredders and other gardening equipment. It's also sensible to have a broad path that cuts across

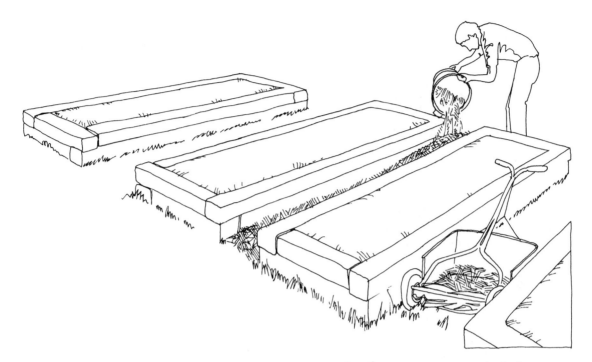

Space-Conserving Paths: This realistic approach saves space but also allows easy access to garden beds. Between a series of parallel beds 2-foot-wide grass-strip paths alternate with narrower, cultivated walkways. Clippings from the grass paths can be used to mulch the narrower ones.

the center of a long garden for convenient access by machine. One realistic yet space-conserving approach for those with a series of parallel beds is to have grass-strip paths 2 or 2½ feet wide alternating with narrower, cultivated walkways. That way you can bring a wheelbarrow or other piece of equipment next to each bed from one side of it and can keep those major paths groomed with a lawn mower. One drawback of sod strips as paths is that the grass will tend to invade your beds, so they work best in conjunction with contained growing spaces. In any case, if you are maintaining strips of lawn between your growing beds, make sure they are wide enough to match your mower's cutting width.

There are lots of other pathway treatments to use if you don't want to add to your lawn

mowing chores. See the box Novel Ways to Cover Paths on page 49 for more ideas.

The Pros and Cons of Double Digging

One way to elevate your beds is to double dig them. This labor-intensive approach adds volumes of air and inches of height to a growing medium, a triumph achieved by removing the topsoil to a depth of about 11 or 12 inches, loosening the next 12 inches of subsoil with a spading fork, then returning the topsoil and laying on and sifting in manure, pH modifiers, trace minerals, and other nutrients as needed. Double digging is a powerful antidote to soil compaction, which closes the pore spaces between soil particles, slowing the movement of air, water, and nutrients to plants and limiting their growth. According to the latest research, in soils susceptible to compaction, doubling the compaction pressure decreases the soil's ability to transmit water by a factor of 10. It follows that double digging can be enormously helpful to gardeners intent on getting top yields from heavy clay soils that are normally quite dry.

The method was perfected and proved under just such conditions in coastal California, where John Jeavons's Ecology Action group used it to transform four acres of hard-baked alkaline clay with a 35 percent rock content, little nitrogen, and just a trace of phosphorus and potassium into a green oasis yielding an average of four times as much food per square foot as gardens conventionally prepared.

The benefits of double digging are obviously considerable. The drawback, of course, is the formidable amount of time and physical energy it demands, for both these commodities may have to be rationed by gardeners with full-time jobs or a substantial number of growing beds to prepare for planting. The time and stamina required to convert a sodded 4 by 20-foot strip into a planted, double-dug bed are hard to estimate, depending on the soil type and on the double digger's abilities, conditioning, and physical strength. Chances are the task will take between 5 and 15 hours the first time around and anywhere from 4 to 6 hours on subsequent go-throughs. By way of contrast, hand spading the same sized bed to a depth of 12 inches will take 1 hour, and rototilling it thoroughly to a depth of 8 inches will use up all of 3 to 5 minutes.

Making the Decision to Double Dig

Do *you* need to double dig for top yields? Consider it seriously if you're gardening in heavy clay in an area with low rainfall. Such parched soils are prone to compaction, and the more impenetrable the hardpan the more necessary it may be to loosen the subsoil regularly. Indeed, if great productivity is your goal, it may be essential to double dig not just yearly, but every time you put in a crop. (Jeavons's phenomenal yields were the result of double digging every time he planted.) According to Stephen Gliessman, who directs the Agroecology Program in Santa Cruz, California, heavy clay soils planted with shallow-rooted crops where rainfall is high are also likely to compact fast and require yearly double digging.

There is some evidence, though, that all that work may be both unnecessary and futile in New England, the Pacific Northwest, or parts of the Gulf states, where the problem is waterlogged soil. For six years, Dr. Franklin P. Eggert, professor of horticulture at the University of Maine at Orono, ran side-by-side trials comparing double digging and rototilling in the wet sandy loam and clay soils of coastal Maine. Eggert's experiences convinced him that double digging is effective in arid areas primarily because it breaks up the hardpan and lets roots search more deeply for water. On the other hand, says this plant scientist, Maine has a fairly heavy rainfall, and the challenge in spring "isn't getting the water in, it's getting the water out," for the water table may rise to within 12 inches of the surface. Under such circumstances, he reports, gardeners trying to reach a depth of 2 feet will be shoveling mud and "poking holes in water." Perhaps more to the point, Eggert found that no statistically significant increases in yields of carrots, tomatoes, and dry beans were obtained by double digging. He's convinced that the higher yields associated with the method are actually coming from close planting.

It's probable that the discrepancy between Eggert's findings in Maine and Jeavons's results in coastal California is related not just to differences in rainfall but to the effects of a harsh versus a very mild climate. New England winters cause soils there to freeze to a depth well below 2 feet, and Eggert theorizes that the formation of ice in the soil has an effect similar to double digging. He believes that using frost to prepare growing beds is the ultimate in energy efficiency, "and at least in Maine a very dependable substitute for the time and effort of double digging."

Jeavons feels Eggert's results are indicative of superior soil and agrees that "if you have a really good soil—as he evidently does—or a sandy loam or any good rich garden loam, you may *not* have to double dig." Like most of us, you probably live with soil somewhere in between Jeavons's and Eggert's. If so, there is a simple test that can tell you immediately whether you can skip double digging and still enjoy magnificent harvests. Just push a pointed metal rod straight down into one of your growing beds after a light rain. If you can insert the rod at least 24 inches, double digging isn't for you—unless you want the exercise!

If the rod test tells you double digging may be important to achieve high yields in your first season of intensive gardening, you may find yourself walking in the footsteps of various master gardeners who double dug their beds when starting out but went on to condition their soil and loft their beds so skillfully that they were able to discontinue double digging with no noticeable loss of productivity. Should your soil be a clay type both susceptible to compaction and responsive to double digging, it might be more prudent to double dig the first two years, then in alternate years. When this system is under way, in a given year double dig just half your beds, and spade or till the other half to a depth of 12 inches, working in fertilizer and compost.

Step-by-Step Guide to a Double-Dug Bed

Whether you raise your beds by double digging or any of the other options described in this chapter, you may want to do the job in fall instead of just before spring planting. Tests with raised bed plantings done at the University of Delaware's Georgetown Extension Center revealed that when beds were prepared in December, there was less sandblasting of the mounds by heavy winds when crops were planted the next spring. Beds turned and shaped before the onset of freezing temperatures also appeared to have fewer weed problems.

Step 1 Mark the dimensions. Do this by driving in a stick or stake at each corner of the bed and running a string all the way around it.

Step 2 Water the bed-to-be thoroughly.

Step 3 Remove the sod. If you are preparing your bed a couple weeks or more before you plan to plant it, you can simplify this job by covering the sod with a heavy mulch or black plastic for at least two weeks. If this delay isn't possible, wait a day or two after watering, then use a straightedge spade to cut through the sod to a depth of about 4 inches, using as your guide the string outlining the bed. Angle the spade so you can reach and cut under the sod inside one end of the bed to about 1 inch.

From this start, work the blade further under the sod, until the spade is a full length under the sod. Then lift the handle to break off the roots. Do this all the way across the bed, rolling the sod back as you go to clearly expose the place where you wish to drive in the spade tip next.

Continue working across the bed in sections the width of the spade, taking up the sod and a 1-inch depth of root mat. Whenever you get a couple feet of sod rolled, cut it off and put it aside. Be sure to leave a few inches to roll over so you can continue to scrape the rest of the bed. (It's sometimes possible to kneel behind a lifted flap of sod, grasp it with your gloved hands, and peel it back toward you at a sharp angle. If this technique works, you can rip off most of a cross-strip at one time by pulling steadily—it's worth a try and can shorten sod-removal time considerably.) The sod you take off can be saved to be layered in the bed during the double digging process, or it can be stacked, like-side to like-side, to form a compost pile that will decompose into fine potting soil within a year. Or you can always use it to patch up areas in your lawn.

Step 4 Turn over a shovelful of soil and make sure it is ready for digging. Soil moistened just right is critical to success in double digging. If you dig when the soil is so wet that it sticks to the spade, the soil you cut through will glue itself back together again just as tightly when you withdraw your shovel. On the other hand, digging soil when it is so dry it won't hold its shape after being squeezed will break down its structure. Just as importantly, soil at the right moisture level digs four times easier. If your soil seems quite wet, wait a while before digging (protect it with plastic in the event of rain). If the bed is too dry and compact to dig, wet it thoroughly again— preferably for 2 hours with an oscillating sprinkler—and wait a day, then loosen the top 12 inches with a fork.

Step 5 Dig a trench one spade deep and two spades wide across one end of the bed. The top-soil you remove will be used to fill the trench at the other end of the bed (or the trench nearest you in an adjacent bed if you happen to be digging beds side by side), so put it in a wheelbarrow or pile it at the head of the bed next door.

Step 6 With a spading fork, step into the newly dug trench and begin to break up the solid layer of subsoil now exposed. Work the fork back and forth, side to side, until you have broken up the subsoil to a depth 20 to 24 inches below ground level all the way across the bed. If

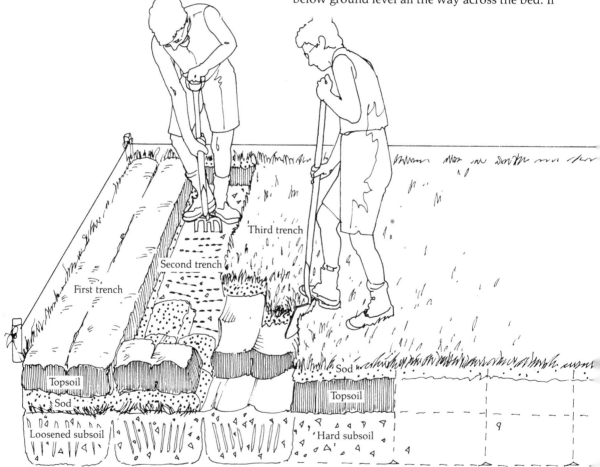

Third trench

Second trench

First trench

Topsoil

Sod

Loosened subsoil

Sod

Topsoil

Hard subsoil

Double-Digging: To start, mark bed dimensions and water the area thoroughly. Remove the sod from one end and dig a trench one spade deep and two spades wide. Move this sod and topsoil to the far end of the bed, where they'll be used to fill the final trench. Loosen the subsoil in the first trench with a spading fork. Remove the sod

the soil is extremely compacted, you may have to lift it and break it with the fork, but be as gentle as you can, remembering that you don't want to disturb the natural layering of the soil any more than necessary. To avoid stepping on parts of the subsoil you have already forked, leave the 10-inch sections at each end of the trench until last, bending over and working on them while you're standing at ground level.

Step 7 Refill the trench. If you have sod you want to add to the bed, do it now, placing a single layer on top of the aerated subsoil, grass side down. Use the spade to chop it into smaller pieces, so the roots of vegetables can pass through this layer easily even before the sod is rotted away. Either after this is done or immediately after subsoiling, replace the topsoil removed earlier with an equivalent amount dug from the next two-spade-wide strip. Don't try to fill the trench in a hurry by taking large slices with your

spade: that much soil will be awkward to handle and you may interfere with the soil layers more than you need to. Your goal should be to cover the two-spade width of bed with four to six vertical cuts of the spade, moving each multilayered slice of topsoil all the way over to the previously dug trench, sliding it off the spade right side up, then coming back for another one. This way, in four to six passes across, you will fill the trench just forked while digging a new trench, to be forked in its turn.

Step 8 Fork the subsoil in the second trench. Then proceed to fill it with topsoil from the third.

Step 9 Continue down the length of the bed. Fill the final trench with the topsoil taken from the first trench or with topsoil left over from a previously prepared bed.

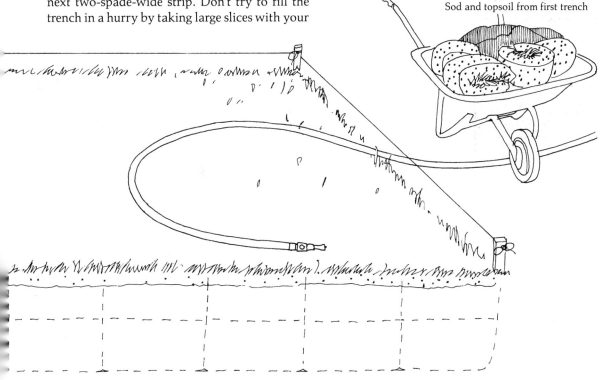

Sod and topsoil from first trench

from the second trench, place it on the subsoil of the first, and then move the topsoil over. Loosen the subsoil in the second trench, then fill it with the sod and topsoil from the third trench. Continue in this fashion until you've worked the entire bed.

Step 10 Use the back of the spading fork to break up the raised slices of soil that now form the bedtop.

Step 11 Let the roughly shaped bed rest for several days. Water it lightly each day to help any remaining chunks of soil break down further.

Step 12 Add soil amendments. Sprinkle them over the bed one layer at a time at the standard rate of application. Work the various nutrient sources into the top 3 or 4 inches of the soil with a spading fork or the corner of a spade.

Step 13 Allow the prepared bed to settle for two or three days.

Step 14 Shape as desired.

(NOTE: The tasks in steps 10 and 12 also can be performed with a tiller.)

Other Ways of Preparing Beds

The most obvious alternative to double digging is the ever popular single digging, which consists of turning the soil as deeply as you can with the tool of your choice. The garden implement most often linked with bed preparation in intensive gardening is the U-bar, a carefully crafted fork with five or six long tines and long, parallel handles that allow the gardener to work with a straight spine and to exert maximum leverage. Used by French intensive gardeners for decades, often in two-man versions that allowed a pair of market gardeners working side by side to till a large bed in a flash, U-bars penetrate the soil to 11 inches or more, lifting and aerating winter-compacted chunks without interfering with natural stratification. Even the smaller, lighter American versions are wonderful labor and time-savers, allowing one person to loosen almost three times more soil on each thrust than a run-of-the-mill spading fork.

John Jeavons recommends using the U-bar alone to prepare beds that have already experienced one formal double digging, working down the length of a bed from one or both sides, depending on the length of the tines and the

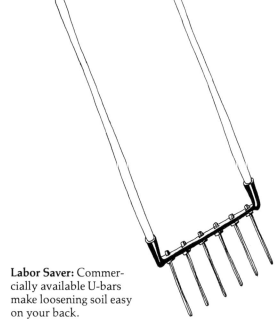

Labor Saver: Commercially available U-bars make loosening soil easy on your back.

width of the bed. The version Jeavons favors is almost 30 inches wide and has 18-inch tines, so it can reach three-quarters of the depth attained in traditional double digging. He has found digging with a U-bar cuts down the time needed to dig a 100-square-foot bed to 20 minutes or less.

Assuming soil that is relatively friable, there is no reason why the U-bar can't be used in place of a less efficiently designed spade or fork by gardeners who prefer to single dig their beds by hand. Lightweight, relatively short-tined versions of this tool are available from sources listed under Garden Products in the Directory of Resources.

Using a Tiller Many gardeners single dig with a tiller to a depth of anywhere from 7 to 11 or 12 inches, mixing in layers of manure, compost, or wintered-over leaf mulch as they go. (The best choice for this purpose is a rear-tine tiller, which makes it possible to till a bed while standing on the adjacent path. You can thereby avoid imposing your weight on the just-loosened soil and recompacting it almost immediately.) Gardeners who pull back with the tiller, piling up the soil and thus working it to a depth of about a foot, are getting closer to the deep cultivation characteristic of double digging. Indeed, a kind of quasi-double digging can be done with a tiller on which the standard tines can be replaced with a shovellike attachment called a hiller. This method, called hilling and tilling, consists of tilling the growing bed to a depth of 11 inches, then switching to the hiller, which can slice through the soil down to a depth of 24 inches, pulverizing it further. The hiller then makes it possible to direct the cultivated soil to create an almost perfectly shaped growing bed. (Hilling should be repeated at least twice during the season to keep fresh soil turned against the growing plants and to add support while feeding shallow roots.)

Using a Plow Some intensive gardeners with a lot of ground to cover used a double-disk plow pulled by a tractor. Marking off beds 5 feet wide, they plow twin furrows the length of the garden, then turn the tractor and plow up a double furrow on the other side of the strip, throwing dirt against the first furrows and forming a bed 5 feet wide at the bottom and 3 feet wide at the top. Nutrients such as composted leaves, cow manure, and wood ashes are then shoveled out of the back of a slow-moving pickup truck straddling each bed, and the amendments are worked in with a rear-tine tiller.

Barney Volak of the Rodale Research Center recommends a tractor-pulled Rotavator with a packer wheel behind it to make, level, and firm attractive beds. Another option is a rotary tiller with a bed-shaper mounted on the rear. This approach will give you beds tilled to 6 inches or more, then raised to a maximum of 4 inches.

Working by Hand If you're single digging by hand, or if the machinery you're using doesn't raise and contour the beds for you, you can turn the soil, then dig out the paths between beds to a level of 6 to 12 inches and add that topsoil to your bed tops. Depending on the width of your paths relative to that of the beds, this easy variation and the "free" soil it provides can add up to 6 instant inches to the height of your growing areas. (If you wish, you can dig a layer of crumbled leaves, sawdust, compost, rotted manure, or grass clippings into each bed before adding the layer of topsoil from the pathways.)

Working from the Ground Up For many gardeners, the most sensible alternative to double digging is not to work downward but to build up from ground level. Those afflicted with thin topsoil or a backyard a contractor has graded and filled in with stony subsoil often choose to have topsoil for their raised beds trucked in. Or they create their own soil by sheet composting various organic materials they purchase or scavenge, then burying the materials under a couple inches of topsoil. After the bed is filled, it can be wet down, then covered with black plastic to retain heat and speed decomposition of the sheet compost.

Building up is an especially convenient alternative for raised beds fashioned from barn beams or railroad ties and also can be used in conjunction with growing boxes, which can be filled with lightweight growing media and set on porches, patios, or driveways for the summer, then carried indoors for winter production under growlights.

Beds can be built up from ground level without removing the sod first (see Converting Gradually to Raised Beds in the next chapter). The soil cover will kill and decompose the sod in as little as six weeks, or you can kill the grass by watering it well, then covering it with black plastic or thick layers of mulch or newspapers for at least two weeks before you begin to lay on additional organic matter. Crops without taproots or deep root systems can be grown in such beds right away and deeper rooted crops a year later. For high yields, however, this approach is best used on light and sandy soils and the bed pre-

With the Master Gardeners

INTUITIVE ALTERNATIVES TO DOUBLE DIGGING

A soft-spoken man, Michael Wheeler of Kentucky coaxes his bumper crops from 3,000 square feet of close-planted raised beds, which look like "a real jungle by July or August." In the first of the five years Wheeler has been gardening, he worked the soil conventionally and wasn't interested in the organic approach. But in year two of his backyard odyssey, he discovered mulch and began his joyous evolution into no-work gardening.

"I don't till or plow or anything like that anymore," he reports. Instead he spends most of his gardening time gathering and spreading mulch . . . and harvesting all the food he raises. "We feed ourselves very well from our garden." Wheeler never did double dig. Originally a poor-draining orange clay, his soil is littered with rocks so huge he can barely turn them over, let alone lift them, the legacy of bulldozing done by a contractor grading the soil. "I hit rocks periodically," Wheeler offers, "and I just didn't want to tackle double digging because I thought it would be so frustrating."

Actually, this gentle gardener's style of bed preparation is as far from double digging as you can get, for once he has created a bed by tilling to 7 or 8 inches and throwing additional soil on it from neighboring pathways, he never turns the soil there again. "I pretty much just add layers of mulch and compost to the surface and let the worms do the digging." The closest he gets to tilling "is when I level off the top of the beds to plant. I rake a little bit of the mulch off to the side, just so I have a flat surface to plant on."

Wheeler's approach to soil cultivation is a conscious imitation of the way nature creates and cultivates the soil. Much as natural processes do, he is constantly littering the soil with organic material;

in his case, about 2 to 4 inches a year of mostly fall-gathered sawdust, horse manure, and leaves. In his plot, as in nature, these wastes eventually turn to humus through the action of earthworms and other insects and microorganisms.

An Organic Gardener of the Year finalist in 1984, Wheeler applies mulch anytime around the year, "whenever it looks like it is getting pretty thin or weeds are coming up." When he plants in spring he puts a mulch "right on top of the seeds, and as they grow I will add mulch around the plant." Except when he plants, Wheeler's topsoil remains undisturbed: "Anytime I interfere with what naturally happens in nature I really have to think a long time about it. How would *I* feel if my house was turned upside down every year?"

When this respectful gardener cuts through his soil for any reason, he can see the various levels and all the aeration and drainage channels created by his enthusiastic crew of earthworms. "Sometimes I just dig down there to look at it." All that humus makes Wheeler's garden immune to erosion, even though his beds run across a slight slope. The proof of that pudding came one recent spring when his soil absorbed 12 inches of rain in three days: "It just drank it all up." The thick layer of water-holding material also comes in handy during Kentucky's summer dry spells, which can last as long as six weeks.

Wheeler's style of gardening makes covercropping seem both irrelevant and irreverent, and sure enough, he's found that a fall cover crop of rye takes entirely too much time and effort to turn under and keep under. "I gave it a try but it's not worth it because I had to keep cutting the tops off with a stirrup hoe over and over."

pared the fall before spring planting. If you're "building up" and want plant roots to have an easy time penetrating the original soil below the bed, remember to aerate the ground with an iron bar or long-tined fork before constructing the above-ground bed.

No-Till Mounds Gardeners who want to build up uncontained beds sometimes add materials layer by layer, never mixing or cultivating them in any way. The German version of this no-till method—called *hugelkultur* (mound culture) —involves digging out a trench 6 inches deep

Far north of Michael Wheeler's Kentucky home, another gardener who "grows rocks" practices a very different kind of soil care. An ex-aerospace engineer "burned out from urban living and trying to measure everything precisely," John Bates freely admits he and his wife returned to her family's abandoned homestead in New Hampshire to regenerate themselves as well as the land.

The farm that is their challenge lies at 1,200 feet on the "morning side" of a rocky hill. Stressed by high winds and limited sun, their garden experiences lows of light and sharp dips of temperature throughout the growing season: "After a tremendously hot day it can go down into the forties." There are extremes of wet and dry, too. "We can go from dead drought to a monsoon and have to fight erosion problems as well as actual physical damage to the plants."

Like Michael Wheeler, John Bates reveres nature and its ways, spending much of his time in the garden "doing nothing—just walking around trying to feel it." Happy to have left behind what he calls "the agony of ultraprecision," Bates is a highly intuitive steward of the land who tries hard to "understand what the soil wants to do."

But Bates diverges dramatically from Wheeler —and from the proponents of double digging— by not being particularly concerned with imitating or maintaining the soil stratification practiced by nature. He does a good deal of hand spading and is forever moving his soil around. "You talk about crop rotation," he laughs. "Well, we rotate the soil."

Bates regularly raids the garden beds for soil for the greenhouse, where it gets enriched with compost, sand, and vermiculite. "Then," he adds, "as soil from the greenhouse is used, I like to take it out and let it weather and sort of purify and get mixed with new soils." The same active approach to soil improvement characterizes Bates's attitude toward his growing beds, which are prepared by the addition of more soil and cover crops. "We have very thin soil," he says, "so we scrape up soil wherever it is, and try to put it where we can use it and try to improve it."

In one experiment he calls "walking mulch," Bates is preparing a garden bed over a time frame of several years. In fall he piled hay a foot thick on a "painfully rocky, mossy 100-square-foot piece of ground with maybe an inch of topsoil." Peeling back the hay the next spring he found the old growth had been killed out. Spading the area by hand, he tested for pH, which was 4.2, then "added a good pailful of woodashes and seeded it heavily with winter rye. When it reaches 4 or 5 inches tall, I will probably spade that over and plant red clover."

One of Bates's strategies is a "soil bank" that "has developed just from soil recovery to an actual development program." The agenda here calls for "digging up soil wherever it is and putting it in a place and planting something in it. Then when that crop gets to the size where it has some body, I spade it back in and plant something else. The soil just seems to love this treatment."

More specifically, the soil bank is land Bates keeps constantly mulched with cover crop hay, later tilled under, or covercropped with buckwheat, winter rye soybeans, sweet clover, or hairy vetch. "When I need soil for any purpose, I go and take some from the soil bank."

Some of the soil he enriches finds its way to his "plant hospital"—a raised framed bed 4 by 16 feet, used as a starting bed and a place to put ailing plants for closer observation and "for ultra-treatment."

Deeply philosophical, this regional winner in the 1983 Organic Gardener of the Year contest prepares his garden beds by working to make the soil productive "not just in my terms, but in its own terms." But then for him, there's no difference: "I am that soil. And that's no metaphor."

and 5 or 6 feet wide in either fall or spring, then laying down a layer of sticks and twigs, which is topped by layers of compostable materials and spiked with manure, seaweed, comfrey, or other compost starters.

Ideally positioned to run north-south, the mounds are constructed to a height of 18 to 30 inches, with sides that slope no more than 40 degrees. These truly hot beds are covered with a 2½-inch layer of topsoil. After the top of each is flattened for 15 inches across, a furrow is made in the center of the flat top (which slopes prefera-

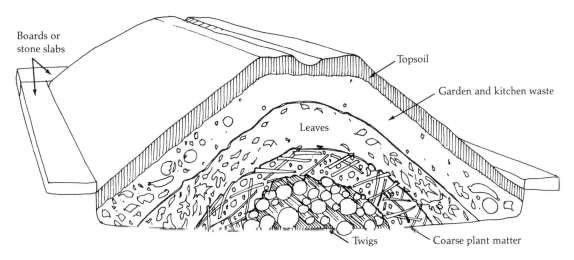

Boards or
stone slabs

Topsoil

Garden and kitchen waste

Leaves

Twigs   Coarse plant matter

Hugelkultur: This German method of mound culture allows gardeners to build up uncontained beds by layering compostable materials. Each mound is 5 to 6 feet wide at its base, 15 inches wide on top, and 18 to 24 inches tall. The mounds last from four to seven years and flatten gradually as the materials decompose.

bly from north to south) so the mound can be watered by a trickle from a hose. Crops are contour-planted closely around the mound, with sun-lovers at the top and moisture-lovers at the bottom (stakes can be driven in for tomatoes and such). Early and late vegetables can be alternated with each other in the same contour circle for efficiency.

Each mound lasts from four to seven years, flattening gradually. The recommended rotation sequence features heavy feeders (tomatoes, cucumbers, leaf, and head vegetables) in the first year, followed by root crops, then legumes, with potatoes planted in the fourth year or later, when the heap is almost flattened. Finally it can be planted with perennials.

Deep Compost Beds Another approach to bed preparation involves building compost heaps under the ground, instead of above it. Garden writer Norm Lee moves aside the soil in his 3-foot-wide beds to a depth of 2 feet with a backhoe, then puts down 6 inches of brush and prunings, followed by a sprinkling of topsoil and manure. The next layer is 6 inches of aged hay and dry or green weeds, succeeded by a sprinkle of manure, then

by 6 inches of topsoil, 3 or more inches of old or fresh manure, and 3 inches of any organic material on hand. By this time, the bed has reached ground level. Lee finishes his mound-building by putting on 6 inches of wet spoiled hay, 3 inches of finished compost, and 3 more of topsoil. After this initial labor, he maintains these deep compost beds just be adding manures and compost annually.

Plants That Do the Digging One of the more effortless alternatives to double digging is simply to plant deep-rooted legumes and other cover crops whenever and wherever you can. These plants provide the ample organic matter needed to maintain a stable, porous soil structure and in effect will do your double digging for you, breaking up hardpan as they go. Smart gardeners plant cover crops in time slots as short as one month, turning them under by hand or with a tiller. (For tips on handling cover crops effectively in beds, see the earlier section on Managing Green Manure Crops in Beds.)

Even a few inches of green manure turned under will help fight the tendency of heavy soils to recompact in the wake of being watered. Actually, in chronically wet, heavy soils cover crops may prove more effective than the most enthusiastic double digging, for tests done at Ohio State University show that if subsoil is broken up by a blade when the ground is at all wet, the soggy clay will recompact as tightly as ever when the blade is removed. Nevertheless, for green manure crops to substitute effectively for the labor of double digging, they must grow long enough to send roots into the subsoil. Alfalfa and sweet clover, for example, won't put down roots deeply enough to relieve the problem if the soil is wet and poorly drained.

Adding Nutrients When You Make Your Beds

Whether you're tilling, double digging, or just plying a spading fork, if you're using traditional growing beds, you'll probably want to work additional nutrients into the soil as you prepare them. There are many ways of doing this.

If you have a cover crop or a blanket of leaves on your garden, most experts recommend turning this material under at least 10 to 14 days before planting so the nutrient source has time to decompose. (See Cover Crops and the box on Soil Conditioning Secrets for ways of getting around this delay.) You may want to coordinate green manuring or mulching with rotations so that only late-planted crops go in beds fertilized this way. Depending on your climate and how late you'll be planting beds treated in this fashion, you can work the nitrogen-containing material in several weeks or more before preparing your beds or do so just before you double dig or otherwise ready your beds.

In the event that you are adding manure, compost, or other nitrogen sources at the time you make or refurbish your beds, it's best to till or double dig first, then mix the material into the top few inches of topsoil. This style of application will slow the rate at which the nutrients leach deep into the bed. It's an especially good

idea if you have sandy fast-draining soil, for if you diffuse the fertilizer throughout the full 10 or 11-inch layer of topsoil, the nitrogen, which is water-soluble, will quickly be carried below and beyond the root-range of your crops, and yields will slump dramatically.

The amount of nitrogen-rich fertilizer you'll want to add at bed preparation time will depend primarily on the original quality of your soil and how well you've been feeding it previously. Assuming you haven't been covercropping or laying on lots of organic matter in the fall, Dr. Franklin Eggert suggests applying four bushels of composted poultry manure or six bushels of combined hay and stable manure to every 100-square-foot bed each spring.

John Jeavons's soil-building program for beds with very poor soil calls for 3 inches of compost or aged manure to be worked into the top 12 inches of each bed during the inaugural double digging. If the bed has good soil, Jeavons advocates only a 1-inch layer of compost or manure. Should a soil test show other nutrients are needed, Jeavons adds suitable amounts of organic nitrogen, phosphorus, potassium, calcium, trace mineral fertilizers, and pH modifiers to the top layer of soil after the bed has been double dug. (Ecology Action gardeners use leaf or pine needle compost to make soil less alkaline and limestone to make it less acid.)

For raised beds that have been double dug previously, Jeavons suggests adding a 1-inch layer of compost and a ½-inch layer of aged manure at the time you sprinkle on any other needed fertilizers and pH modifiers—that is, *after* the bed has been dug and shaped. He feels this procedure helps counter the tendency toward more rapid leaching as the soil becomes increasingly loose. According to Jeavons, amendments spread or sprinkled on the bed after shaping should be "sifted in" gently by inserting a spading fork into the top 2 or 3 inches of soil, then jiggling it a little as you lift it upward.

If thin topsoil is your garden's lot, you may need to add more to your beds after they're dug.

A nutrient-rich alternative that works well with clay soils is based on a mixture of equal parts of garden soil, compost, and rotted sawdust (or sphagnum moss). To three parts of this blended mixture add one part of dune or fine river sand. This custom-made topsoil for use in topping off beds is high in organic matter and very moisture retentive. It can be enriched further by additions of rotted manure, wood ashes, and rock phosphate.

Not all successful intensive gardeners add fertilizers to their beds as a whole when preparing them for planting. Some rely on a heavy leaf mulch or cover crop undertaken the previous fall, then apply a combination of nutrients to individual plants when they are put in the garden.

Finishing Touches

Whether you're raising your beds with muscle or machine-power, you can custom-contour their tops to suit your situation. But before you smooth and shape those newly dug or tilled beds, use a sprinkler or wait for a good rain to wet them down well and reveal rocks or other near-surface debris, which should then be removed. Once that job has been taken care of, while your beds are still slightly moist, take a rake and shape them

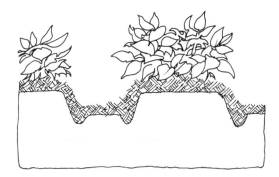

Mulched Bed with Trenches: If you're planning to mulch your raised beds but live where strong winds blow, you might want to extend the angled sides of your beds below path level. The resulting V-shaped trenches will help trap the mulch on the beds.

in any of the basic ways reviewed earlier in the box A Survey of Raised Beds. If you like, fine-tune the fundamental shapes even further. If you garden in the North or anywhere sunshine and warmth are in short supply, consider sloping your bed tops toward the south so the sun's rays strike them closer to the perpendicular in spring and fall. An angle of 20 to 40 or 45 degrees—the farther north, the more desirable a steep slope—will let such beds receive and store more heat and should benefit all your crops, especially the heat-lovers.

Needless to say, relentlessly bright and hot gardening sites call for a different style of bed shaping, because uncontained raised beds (especially those constructed of sandy loam) are vulnerable to increased evaporation. So if you're among the 40 percent of American gardeners whose biggest problem is inadequate water, you may want to improve the water-trapping abilities of the flat-top or walled-in flat-top bed by making the surface slightly concave or even using the basin beds described earlier in the chapter. These water-saving techniques spare potential plants, too, since any seeds dislodged by watering will stay in the beds instead of being washed into the paths. More suggestions for water-saving modifications appear in chapter 4 under Watering Devices and Systems.

Building Sides for Beds

If you choose to contain your beds, put their sides in place before you add the final applications of topsoil, manure, and compost that will loft them to their ultimate height. If wood is your style, but your construction skills are limited, consider holding in your soil with single or double courses of old barn beams (in a pinch, the 8 by 8's are wide enough to also serve as a path between two beds), logs, or old telephone poles or railroad ties. Make sure, however, that any creosote applied to such wood has soaked in or worn off. This cheap preservative wards off molds and pests for two years, but it is toxic to plants and for a full year after application will burn any that come in contact with it. Some gardeners using beams or similar self-supporting materials leave openings at diagonally opposed corners so they can get inside the bed with a rotary tiller or a shredder.

If you don't mind doing some construction work on your frames, you can improvise bed sides using scrap wood from crates and pallets. For long-lasting, stronger movable frames, many knowledgeable bed gardeners prefer to invest in rough-cut economy grade redwood heartwood, which should last for 20 years. Also acceptable are rough-cut select tight-knot cedar, which is another naturally rot-resistant wood, and pressure-treated pine (which has a lifespan of about 15 years). If you choose other lumber, make sure it is treated with a nontoxic wood preservative that can protect lumber in direct contact with soil. The best choice for this purpose is probably Cuprinol 10 or another product containing copper naphthenate, which will safeguard bedding frames for up to 4 years and is believed to be harmless to people and plants.

Most long-time gardeners work with lumber 1 or 2 inches thick and 6, 8, or 10 inches wide. You may want to base your decision about the width of the boards (which will determine the height of the growing bed) on how deeply you cultivate your soil. Obviously, beds constructed entirely above ground level will need to be well raised to provide adequate root room; 10 inches of growing medium and sides to match would provide the growing conditions most conducive to high yields under such circumstances. On the other hand, if you're planning to double dig and thereby assure 24 inches of noncompacted soil below ground level, you can make do nicely with beds that top out at 5 or 6 inches with sides 6 inches high. When deciding the width of the lumber, also consider whether you will be setting the frame on top of bricks around the bed or flush on the ground, or sinking it several inches into the soil.

In putting together your frames, you can miter the corners for an attractive look or use standard butt joints if you're working with a handsaw. It's a good idea to put cross braces at 6 or 8-foot intervals to keep the sides aligned. For ultra stability you can sink 4-inch-square corner posts a foot longer than your lumber is wide into holes 12 inches deep and fill them with concrete. The mitered short and long sides of the bed are then joined and attached to the outside of the posts with 16-penny nails or 3½ or 4-inch Ardox spiral nails. On the other hand, excellent portable posts and stakes can be fashioned from 2 by 4s (4 by 4s for the corners) cut 30 inches long, with their ends sharpened. These should be driven 16 to 18 inches into the soil, at each corner and at 30-inch intervals *outside* the sides of the bed so the force of the raised soil holds the boards in place. For greatest support, nail the stakes to the frame. Their tops can be sawed off when the beds are done.

In the South and other places where moisture and termites make short work of wood, many gardeners contain their beds with cement blocks or bricks. Another bug and water-impervious option is corrugated fiberglass. This long-lasting, relatively cheap material can be cut with a saw into panels 8 or 10 inches high that are overlapped by 2 inches and pushed into the soil. The frame is then staked in place with ½-inch galvanized electrical conduit cut into 12-inch lengths. The stakes should be driven in on the outside of the fiberglass and positioned so one is at each overlap and one at the center of each panel.

If you live in the Southwest you can surround your raised beds with adobe walls 4 to 6 inches thick and about 8 inches above ground level. Once the mud has dried, fill the bed with soil and organic matter and plant it. In Guatemala, where adobe beds are traditionally used in flower growing, they last about three years.

New England gardeners or others growing great crops of rocks or stone can build sides for

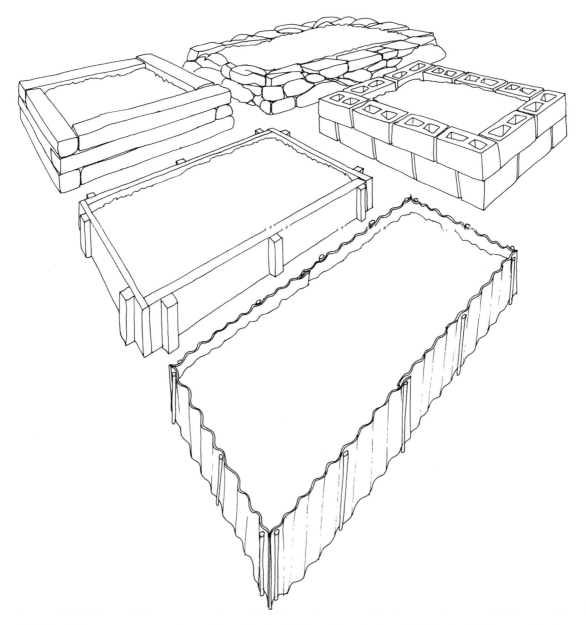

Bed Sides: There are many ways to contain garden beds. Choose the technique that is best suited to your climate and makes use of materials already on hand or easy to find. On the left, from front to back, beds are framed with fiberglass, lumber, and railroad ties. On the right, beds are built from cinder blocks and layered rocks.

their beds as they dig them! The idea is to stack relatively flat rocks in overlapping courses to fashion mortarless drywalls up to 2 feet high.

Once you've added the finishing touches to your beds, let them settle for a few days before planting. The respite will allow air to leave the top layer of soil and assure that the seeds you plant will come in solid contact with the soil. If you don't want to postpone planting for that long, you can walk across your beds on a 12-inch-wide board—a maneuver that will firm the soil without compacting it.

NOVEL WAYS TO COVER PATHS

Paths are the only large untended space in a garden of raised beds. Weeds and grasses that seek open spaces will spread easily from paths to productive areas in beds. The point is to keep them from finding a staging area for their assault. Mulch is too dignified a word for the material that inhibits weeds in paths. What you need there is a weed-stifling cover of almost any kind. It need not be chemically balanced, permeable to rain or air, or even organic. Here are some ideas for path treatments.

• Rocks, concrete, gravel, flagstones, tiles, builder's sand, or slate paving.
• Black plastic strips of heavy thickness, preferably covered with an attractive organic material such as bark or wood chips.
• Roofing or tar paper, heavy cardboard from boxes or fabric bolt holders, corrugated tin strips, or shingles.
• Bark shreds, sawdust, buckwheat hulls, bran, shredded cornstalks or corncobs, cocoa bean hulls, chopped leaves, wood chips, or other high-carbon organic material. Cornstalk mulch tends to become soggy and some of the lighter materials may have to be weighted with stones to keep them from blowing into the beds. Grass clippings are another option. After these path covers have been broken down by trampling feet you can shovel them onto the beds for the winter, then turn under the next spring.
• Sowings of alfalfa and rye, rye alone, WHITE DUTCH clover, Irish moss, veronica, thyme, perennial chamomile, vetch, or grass, or extra thick sowings of field beans. The moss, veronica, thyme, and chamomile don't need mowing, but the others must be cut frequently. The mowings can be used for bed mulch or added to compost.
• Books of wheat straw, oat straw, or hay, or loose spoiled hay or leaves piled to at least a 4-inch thickness. Of these, hay will be most likely to contain seeds, which, when germinated and growing, should be pulled from the path and added to the mulch layer. When material has been trampled into fine particles in the paths, it can be placed on the beds as mulch, and the paths replenished.
• Carpet strips or carpet scraps, linoleum or vinyl strips or tiles, treated plywood or other flat building material, including paneling.
• If waterlogged paths are not a problem where you live, collect so-called "end rolls" of unused newspaper 14½ or 19 inches wide from your local newspaper's print shop. Usually free for the asking, these waste spools contain anywhere from 10 feet to several hundred feet of clean white paper that can be unrolled for use as path covers or mulch.
• If you have lowered your paths to raise your beds and/or have a high water table or frequent heavy rains, you may choose to fight the mud by letting weeds come up there. Some gardeners have found that pests are more attracted to wet weeds than to their vegetables. The wild plants also can provide a home for beneficial insects and make added fodder for a compost heap.

2 *Designing a Garden in Beds*

When you're gearing up for high-yield gardening, a very logical progression of thought takes you in increments from the soil to growing beds to the garden itself. This is the point where you begin to put the smaller pieces together and fit them into a grand plan. Before you take shovel in hand, you should give some thought to how the beds will be arranged and integrated into the landscape. Investing time in planning will earn you dividends of healthy, productive crops. How you locate beds and rotate and situate plants will affect yields. And using special garden design options will help you overcome any topographical limitations of size and shape and slope that may present themselves.

Converting Gradually to Raised Beds

If you're transforming grass into garden, there are a number of ways you can convert gradually to raised beds. If you like, get started in fall by outlining your bed-to-be with string around stakes, then laying down several inches of fresh manure and covering this with 6 to 8 inches of old hay. The next spring, push aside the mulch and insert transplants or large seeds into the rotted sod. If you don't get around to burying the sod until spring, there's still time. Just lay black plastic over the wetted-down manure and hay and let it compost for eight weeks. Then remove the plastic and set in heat-loving late-planted crops such as tomatoes and peppers. Add more mulch as the vegetables grow and again in fall if you like. The next spring, till or double dig the converted area. Voila—a new raised bed!

Another approach you can undertake just before planting is to aerate a patch of lawn intended for a bed by driving in an iron rod or spading fork. Then frame the area with railroad ties or barn beams. Cover the sod inside with trucked-in topsoil or perhaps with subsoil mixed with purchased loam, and work in some compost. Then plant—preferably with shallow-rooted crops the first time around.

Easier yet is digging up narrow strips of sod in a lawn or in a field with perennial grass. If you like, kill the sod first by burying it for a week or more under black plastic or 6 inches of grass clippings, alfalfa, or hay (one bale will cover a 5 by 20-foot bed-to-be). If you prefer, you can simply remove plugs of turf, pop in transplants or large seeds, then mulch the sod all around them to the borders of your eventual bed. By converting in this way, you can enjoy the advantages of grass pathways around the new beds or even around individual plants. The mat of sod will act like mulch, keeping the soil moist and cool in the hottest and driest of summers. Moreover, until you have time to plant the new area closely, the dense grass cover will go on capturing solar energy for you there, producing high nitrogen green matter you can mow and share directly with the plants as mulch or add to a compost heap.

Tests at the Rodale Research Center in Maxatawny, Pennsylvania, on planting in sod prove this low-work method has a lot going for it as a transition to raised bed gardening. In some trial plots, tomatoes were grown in 4-inch-square openings in 20-inch-wide growing strips in which the sod was simply covered with a biodegradable black plastic called Ecolite. Plants given this treatment outyielded those grown with Ecolite in tilled soil by almost 14 percent. The mulched, no-till tomatoes also outperformed those grown without plastic in tilled soil by almost 18 percent. According to Project Director Steve Ganser, the sodded, mulched growing strips required no weeding all season. Best of all, says Ganser, when ground is left essentially undisturbed, "the soil structure isn't broken down or compacted, soil organisms aren't disturbed, and roots aren't ripped apart from tilling."

Tests confirmed that the soil in the mulched, sod-planted plots was richer and more friable than soil in the cultivated plots where tilling had exposed the organic matter and increased the rate at which it disappeared. Ganser noted, "In the sod-planted plots, the roots really penetrated through the soil." After you harvest sod-grown

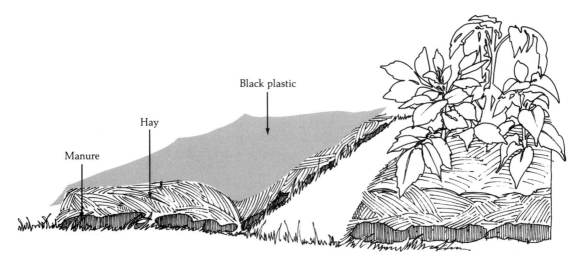

Black plastic

Hay

Manure

Converting Grass into Garden: An easy no-dig way to make the transformation to a raised bed is to layer fresh manure and hay over the designated bed area. Cover with black plastic and let it sit for eight weeks. Lift off the plastic and set in transplants.

crops in fall, it's an easy matter to till the strips thoroughly and lay on more organic matter to raise the beds higher. The following spring you'll have made a relatively painless conversion to one or more raised beds surrounded by grass paths. At that point, you can till again or double dig. (For ease in tilling and double digging later, the transitional growing strips should probably be at least 3 feet wide.)

Expanding your garden space by planting directly in grass is as close as you can get to a no-work, problem-free changeover to intensive gardening. Bear in mind, though, that these Rodale Research Center tests were done using traditional, generous spacing. If you're in a hurry to condition soil more intensely so you can close-plant for greatest yields, you may want to put forth more effort so you can go one step further toward raised beds that first season.

To do this, kill the sod over an area wide enough and long enough to give you a growing bed together with a pathway on each side. Next, chop up all the dead sod thoroughly with a spade or tiller and turn it under, working the soil vigorously. Then move down each of the pathways, heaping 6 to 8 inches of their blend of chopped sod and topsoil onto the bed between them. Add composted manure and other amendments to the top 3 or 4 inches of the new raised bed. After such rough-hewn, transitional beds have been wetted down by a good watering or rainfall, you can plant crops that don't require highly cultivated soil (for example, peas, pole beans, soybeans, and lettuce). Legumes especially will stimulate soil microorganisms that will help break down chunks of organic matter and improve the soil's texture. Later in the season or the following spring, you can till or double dig the new bed to prepare it for more demanding crops.

Changing from Rows to Beds If your garden is already in place under cultivation, and you're merely switching from rows to raised beds, your lot is an easier one. Starting at one side of the garden, each gardening season you can mark off and double dig or till one or two beds, raising them with soil dug out from the path on either side. If you're in the mood, you can even convert a section of the garden in midseason, just before you put in a succession crop.

Some gardeners prefer to start making the transition in fall, when there's no need to struggle against spring-rain–soaked soil or to rush to meet a planting schedule. In autumn, the pace can be more leisurely and the digging spaced out over five to ten weekends in northern gardens—which is how much time you may have, depending on climatic variations, between the first killing frost and the hard freezing of the soil. The time is right to shred or just turn under garden residues and to raise the beds-to-be further by dumping on pulverized leaves garnered through last mowings—or first rakings—of the lawn. You can also layer on sand, lime, compost, or whatever else your situation calls for. Winter freezes and thaws will work to break down hunks of organic matter and improve the soil texture of the new beds while you relax indoors. And as soon as the ice leaves the soil in spring, you'll be able, not just ready and willing, to plant.

Placing Beds for Best Results

There are a few general considerations to keep in mind when siting your beds and laying out your garden as a whole. If at all possible, arrange matters so the longest dimension of the garden area and of the individual beds runs from north to south. Such a layout minimizes problems linked to plants' shading each other and is particularly desirable in intensive gardening because plants in beds tend to be crowded much closer on all sides than those in rows.

If your beds must run east to west, make sure you put the taller or more shade-tolerant crops along their northern sides, for plant scien-

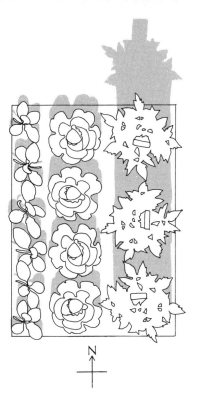

N

Orienting Beds: If you have a choice, orient your beds like the one on the left, so the longest sides run from north to south. This minimizes shading problems. If the beds must run east to west, put the shortest crops on the southern side and the tallest ones on the northern side. Their shadows will fall outside the garden area.

tists have discovered the shading factor creates significant microclimatic differences in various parts of wide-rows planted in an east-west direction. Plants on the brighter and therefore warmer southern side mature earlier than those on the shaded, cooler northern edge. So, if you use equidistant spacing and want crops in a bed to ripen rapidly and at the same rate, make sure the patch runs north-south. Beds oriented east-west will present you with a more staggered harvest that may be lower in total weight.

Ideally, your garden should be situated so all of your plants receive at least six, and preferably eight, hours of full sun every day. If that's not possible, try to site your beds so they catch the morning sun. Should shade problems affect all or part of the garden, try to orient it north-south so you can use vertical growing structures within the beds as well as along the sides of the plot. This exposes a maximum of leaf surface to whatever sun gets through.

It's best to site a garden well away from trees, not just because of the shade they cast, but because of the possible effect of their root systems and leaves on garden productivity. Black walnut trees release a potent substance called juglone from their roots and leaves. (Plants That Work against High Yields in chapter 5 discusses this phenomenon.) The tannin found in pine tree needles and oak leaves also inhibits numerous garden crops—strawberries are one of the few plants not affected.

If at all possible, avoid situating your vegetable patch over your septic system. That way you will avoid any chance of your produce encountering pathogens sometimes found in sewage. You should be particularly careful in this respect if your soil drains poorly. If drainage is good and there's nowhere else for the garden, you can plant fruiting vegetables like tomatoes, peas, beans, or peppers over a septic field. To be on the safe side, however, forgo root and leafy crops, which can become contaminated with bacteria. Although fruit trees should not be planted in such areas because their roots can damage drainage pipes, shallow-rooted bushes such as blueberries and raspberries should be safe bets.

Using Space Well

In planning your intensive garden-to-be on paper or in your head, try to "tie in" every suitable site on your property. And don't overlook small or odd-shaped parcels of land, which can boost productivity surprisingly.

In many yards, the long narrow strips of land along the foundation of a house and garage all by themselves add up to a good-sized garden. Spaces as narrow as 1½ feet make excellent beds for crops to be grown up vertical supports and also are prime locations for perennials, which do not effectively fill larger beds for several years and can more readily be controlled in areas away from the garden proper. Many gardeners take special delight in such border gardens, for they

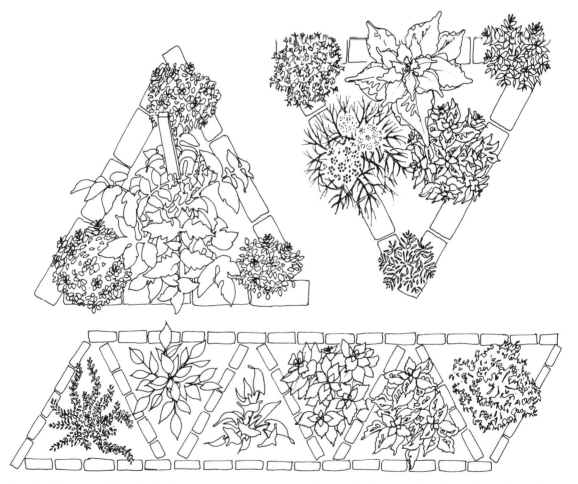

Garden Geometry: Triangular beds can be a nice variation on the standard rectangular shape. A triangle with 3-foot sides can hold a staked tomato plant and dwarf basil plants (shown top left), or an array of six compact annual herbs (top right). Interlocking triangles can also form an interesting garden mosaic. The bed shown here is filled with an assortment of annual and perennial herbs.

can be planted, weeded, and harvested from a lawn or sidewalk. Besides, grass clippings or shredded leaves can be blown directly onto the plants or raked in readily from adjacent lawn areas. Such edge gardens also make succession plantings seem easier because of their accessibility.

Remember, too, that no law says your growing space has to be square or rectangular. Why not try other geometric shapes? Rhomboids, hexagons, star shapes—take your pick! Such surprising forms can make delightful minigardens here and there or join forces for a beautifully eclectic effect. For instance, on their own or interfacing, triangles with 3-foot sides are attractive basic units for herb plantings. The dimensions can easily be laid out with stakes and string, and each triangle planted with one large plant in the center or a smaller one at each corner. Up to six smaller annual herbs will fit into one triangle. Used individually or interlocked to form a bed, triangles can give you attractively shaped masses of foliage and usable amounts of herbs. If you're up to a more intricate design, three-sided figures also can be effectively grouped around rectangles.

Also pleasing in a garden setting are rounded forms. One sure-fire attention getter is the round tomato bed originated by Robert E. Sanders. Described in *Flower and Garden* magazine (April/May 1981), Sanders's "circle of cages" method makes possible incredible yields—upwards of 1,000 tomatoes from a circle 8 feet in diameter—while creating an attractive design motif. The round accommodates 5 caged plants planted 2 feet apart and an assortment of low-growing crops that fill in toward the outer edge of the circle.

The high-yield secret of the tomato circle is a 12-inch-wide, 24-inch-deep minicircle in its center, which is primed with fish emulsion fertilizer in water, then filled with a rich layering of manure or compost, followed by bone meal and grass clippings, and topped by manure to bring the compost to ground level. Sanders then recommends moving out 6 inches and constructing a 6-inch-wide, 9-inch-deep watering trough. The bottom of this concentric circle should hold ½

inch of bone meal covered with ½ inch of dried manure. Other nutrients can be added through the growing season as the circle of cages is watered. To complete the basic arrangement, five tomato plants are planted around the 2½-foot space remaining between the outside of the trough and the outer perimeter of the 8-foot circle. (Sanders arranges the plants equidistantly with the help of a garbage can lid and recommends planting the tomatoes very deeply in richly prepared holes 12 inches wide and 24 inches deep.) For added beauty, the circle of cages can be ringed by 15-inch-high garden fencing and surrounded by colorful flowers, which will help assure good pollination of the tomatoes.

Several different climbing crops can be grown in one circle of cages. Or an entire garden can be planned around such circles, simply by choosing climbing varieties of all fruiting crops and filling in around them with root and leaf vegetables.

If you prefer, an entire garden can take the form of a large circle bisected by one or more wide paths and narrow walkways that divide the halves or quarters of the round into wedges. For more growing space and beauty, the circular garden can be ringed by a wide path, which itself can be surrounded with a circular bed enclosed by a curving fence that doubles as a trellis. Practical as well as charming to contemplate, a circle garden of this kind designed to have a 100-foot diameter can be watered without effort—simply by putting a revolving sprinkler on a tripod at its very center. Run just once a week for 12 to 14 hours, such a watering device will give the entire garden the equivalent of 1 inch of rain.

If your gardening space is more limited, consider a circle garden just 20 feet in diameter, which will accommodate rotations beautifully. The round can be divided into eight pie-shaped beds by narrow, sunken pathways. Or room can be left in the center for a "hub." This smaller circle can be surrounded by fencing to make a circular trellis. (Leave the circle partly open for access to create a compost hole or heap at its center.)

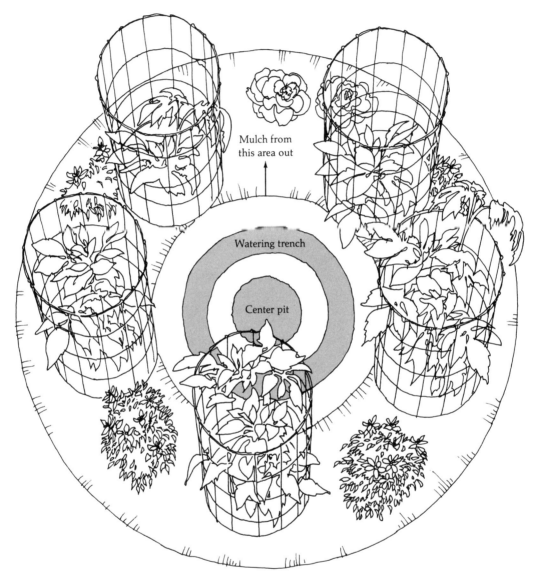

Tomato Circle: A pit filled with compost, bone meal, grass clippings, and manure serves as the fertile center for this 8-foot circle. Ringing the pit is a watering trench. Five caged tomato plants occupy the outer area, interspersed with basil and lettuce plants.

Designing a Modular System

As you plan your garden, hold firmly to the thought that you may at some point want to cover your raised beds with various growing structures. A likely addition would be a movable wooden cold frame or perhaps a permanent cold frame constructed of brick, masonry, or cinder block—perhaps even a soil-bermed structure. To make this development possible, make sure any beds that could be affected are of an appropriate

Gardening "Islands": For a change, plan a garden by creating "islands" of circles, semicircles, or ovals outlined in decorative fencing and bisected by paths. One 25-foot roll of 15-inch fencing can define a circular bed 8 feet in diameter with about 50 square feet of growing space or an oval with the same coverage. A more elongated oval can be created by joining two rolls and creating 150 square feet of space. Cover the walkways with grass clippings and straw or wood chips. The rounded beds can be divided into wedges or planted in concentric circles with staked or caged vine crops at their centers. This kind of massing cools both plants and soil and can be a good design choice for hot, dry climates.

width and oriented so the cold frame's angled top will be maximally exposed to the winter sun. That is, the front of the structure should face due south or no more than 20 degrees to the east or west. Be particularly careful to position a potential cold frame site away from trees or any objects that could shade it immediately or eventually.

As you grow in skill and ambition, it's also likely that you'll find yourself wanting to add compost bins, nursery areas, shading devices, and/or trellises to your raised bed garden. If you are planning to establish permanent beds, it's important to prepare for this eventuality from

the very beginning by creating beds that are uniform at least in width. If your property has odd dimensions, shading problems, or any other characteristics that make same-sized beds impossible, try at least to have four beds or four sections of a single long bed appropriately and uniformly sized so you can satisfactorily rotate

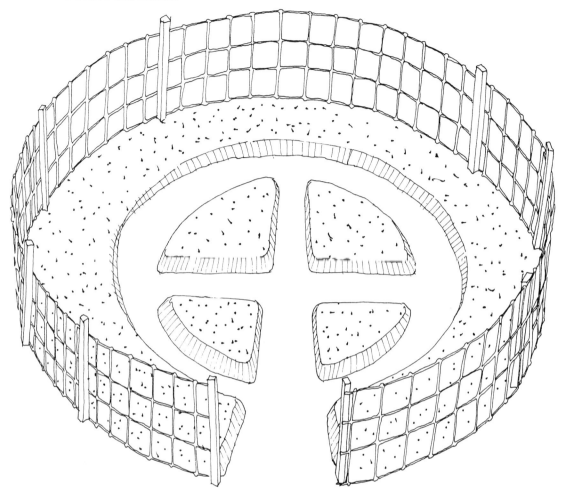

Gardening in the Round: For a neatly contained garden area, try this layout. The center bed is divided by paths and all four sections are easily accessible from all sides. Along the perimeter bed, grow vining crops to take advantage of the wire fencing that acts as a built-in trellis. Watering is easy when you set a revolving sprinkler in the center.

cold frame, shading, nursery, and trellising appa-ratuses yearly without having to break down and reconstruct your beds and paths.

Actually, there are certain advantages in moving directly to a completely integrated sys-tem in which all beds and gardening appliances are standardized for complete interchangeabil-ity. Though some gardeners find this kind of component-oriented approach too regimented for their taste, others take enormous pleasure in the greater efficiency and attractiveness it brings

to the garden. The harmony of dimension and materials that characterizes modular systems is pleasing to the eye and also motivates the proud owner to keep up that nice appearance by weeding and succession planting promptly. Setting up the garden in interchangeable units also makes crop rotations wonderfully easy.

One Homemade System

You can, of course, construct a modular system entirely on your own. One enterprising gardener framed the perimeter of his garden with lengths of 4 by 4 lumber. He then built 16 4-foot-square beds, each sharing at least one side with the outside frame. Leaving a 2-foot-wide path down the middle of the two rows of beds, he also allowed 18 inches between the beds on each side and covered all the paths with builder's sand. One bed became the basis for a cold frame constructed of 2 by 12s covered with a storm window glazed on both sides with polyethylene. Seven trellises made of ½-inch metal pipe from the junkyard were added to some of the beds to increase the small garden's productivity. Completing this homemade modular system are two cloches sized to the standardized beds. These are framed in 2 by 2s and have polyethylene stretched over them. Strips of leather nailed to the wood at the top of opposite sides provide a handle so the plastic glazing gets less wear. (Although this unit is heavy enough to stay in place even in a strong wind, such add-on accessories can, of course, be attached with hooks.)

Ready-Made Plans

If improvising a modular garden system is beyond your scope, you can always follow step-by-step plans and build the 4-in-1 setup developed by the Rodale Design Group. The Rodale system is organized around square modules, but the raised bed frame it includes can be adapted to make 4-foot-wide beds of any length. The accessories—a 4-foot-high trellis, a 22½-inch-high compost bin, a Poisson-pod style cold frame, and a slotted shading device—are all sized to fit a 4 by 4-foot section of raised bed.

Two sides of the raised beds are made from 2 by 10s, but the other two are constructed of two 1 by 10s with spacers in between. The spacers form slots that the accessories lock into, an advantageous feature that makes the various appli-

Modular Garden System: All the interchangeable components of this system—trellis, compost bin, cold frame, and shading device—are sized to fit 4 by 4-foot raised beds with wooden frames. Complete plans for this build-it-yourself project are available (see the Directory of Resources).

ances easier to set up and much more stable. The cold frame, for example, can't get bumped out of line so cold air sneaks in, and the trellis is anchored much more firmly than one simply shoved into the ground. To obtain complete plans for the Rodale Design Group's modular raised-bed system, see the address given in the Garden Products Section of the Directory of Resources.

Some Special Design Options

Gardening on a slope? Be sure to run the length of your beds across it and to maintain a sod strip between them to prevent your garden soil from washing downhill. If the angle of the slope is greater than 10 degrees, don't take the safety risk of gardening with machines. Instead, work your beds by hand.

In gardens that vertical, you also should consider contour planting along the natural lay of the land to control erosion and distribute water evenly across the slope. You can find contour lines quite easily by mounting an ordinary carpenter's level in the center of a 2 by 4. Beginning at about the center of the slope at one side of it, lay the 2 by 4 horizontally and move one end up or down until the bubble on the level is centered. Mark that spot with a stake and continue across the slope, placing markers as you go to define the contour guide line.

Then plant your vegetables parallel to this line, leaving channels between the rows to collect and hold water. To carry away drainage or rainwater with the potential to erode your angled garden, you can make a diversion terrace, which is nothing more than a ridge with a shallow channel on the upper side. Grade the terrace slightly so water entering it flows off into a grassy area away from the garden.

If you're gardening on a fairly steep slope, you may have to build retaining walls to assure your plants of an adequate supply of moisture and to combat soil loss. You need to put forth this added effort if:

• The growing surface of a given bed is more than 18 inches above the adjacent lawn (there's clear danger of erosion if the slope is more than 1 to 2 feet high).

• The slope has a fall of at least 1 foot for every 100 horizontal feet.

• Water is carrying off soil from a garden now on the slope.

• Water is flowing from a neighbor's property into a garden now on the slope .

• The embankment is freshly cut (steeper slopes just machine dug require thicker retaining walls to hold back the weight of the dirt).

The easiest way to retain terraced beds is to build mortarless drywalls of flat rocks. If you are constructing very low terraces, rocks can simply

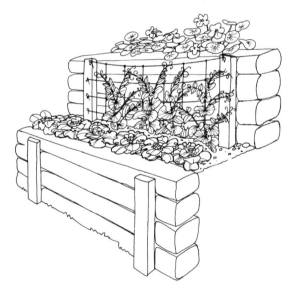

Growing on a Slope: If you're not averse to digging post holes, you can construct attractive beds with retaining walls. Sink sturdy posts and on the uphill side set double courses of railroad ties, barn beams, or telephone poles in place to hold back the soil. Trellised crops can be grown on fencing ties or tacked to the support posts.

be stood on edge in the soil to make beds 2 to 4 feet wide, depending on the angle of the original slope. Each bed should slant slightly downhill. For higher terraces on steeper slopes, you can stack flat rocks to make wide walls. Irregularly shaped stones are better for this purpose than

Terraced Beds: Irregularly shaped, flat stones make stable retaining walls on minor slopes. Stood on edge in the soil, stones can be fit together snugly without mortar to form beds 2 to 4 feet wide.

bricks or blocks, which are certain to be moved out of line when the soil heaves. If flattish rocks aren't plentiful where you live, consider using boulders, cut stone, or broken concrete, which often can be scavenged from the local dump or carted off when neighborhood sidewalks are torn up and redone. In either case, this novel building

material will cost you nothing but the price of a pair of rugged work gloves to protect your hands. Gardeners who use this ploy receive many compliments: usually admiring neighbors refuse to believe those handsome retaining walls aren't fashioned from rock until they check for themselves.

Step-by-Step Guide to Building a Stone Retaining Wall

Step 1 Calculate the height and width of the wall. Remember that the width of its base should be at least two-thirds of its height.

Step 2 Prepare the foundation. If your wall is to be less than 3 feet high, you need only to level a strip equal to the wall's bottom dimensions. For taller walls, dig a trench 1 to 2 feet deep, tamping down firmly any loose dirt.

Step 3 Put down the foundation layer. Embed the largest stones you have securely in the soil, surrounding them with smaller rocks and gravel for drainage. Lean the rock face slightly toward the embankment to use the force of gravity in your favor and prevent heaving during winter freezes. By angling the stones so the buried end is lower than the bottom of the exposed face, you also will keep the soil from washing out.

Step 4 Build the first aboveground layer. Use the next biggest rocks so you don't have to lift them too high. Stuff soil around and on top of the stones.

Step 5 Keep building upward. Using a mixture of large and small stones on each layer, begin to apply the basic construction principle that calls for one stone to be placed over two stones and two stones to be positioned over one. In other words, position the stones so that the one going on top always covers the space between at least two stones beneath it. This technique will guarantee that there will be no vertical fissures where the wall can separate.

Step 6 Check as you go for lack of stability and unevenness. When you notice rocks that seem shaky, reposition them or chip off knobs or

Building a Stone Retaining Wall

Prepare the foundation with large stones embedded firmly in the soil, surrounded by smaller rocks and gravel.

Build upward, adding layers of stones. Mix large and small stones and anchor them with soil. Position the stones so that the one going on top always covers the space between at least two stones beneath it.

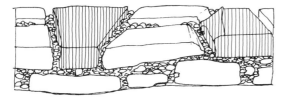

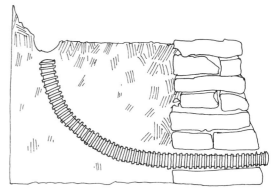

To improve drainage, consider laying a pipe through the wall as you build. This will collect water from a drainage ditch at the back of the growing bed.

"Tie" stones, or elongated stones that run from front to back, add to the wall's stability.

The biggest, flattest rocks make the best ends. For a finishing touch, add a layer of flat stones on the top.

points to make them fit more solidly. You also should go across the layers with a level and adjust stones accordingly. Make the construction job easier by using the flattest sides to form the tops and bottoms of each layer. The next flattest sides should form the outside face of the wall.

Step 7 Include "tie" stones every 6 to 8 feet. By putting down elongated stones that run from the front of the wall to the back, in effect you can bind one face of the wall to the other and add to its transverse strength.

Step 8 Give special attention to ends and corners. Save your biggest, flattest rocks with square ends for these important places. An end area should contain as many long rocks as possible and should feature tie rocks on alternating layers. When you make a corner, use plenty of tie stones, and cover as many joints as possible with each one, since the corner must be tied into both lengths of wall. Ideally, try to have tie rocks running from the corner into each wall on each layer.

Step 9 Consider laying a terra-cotta or metal pipe through the wall as you build. Its uphill end could collect water from a drainage ditch constructed parallel to the wall on the opposite side of your 2 to 4-foot-wide growing bed.

Step 10 Finish the wall with a layer of flat stones on top.

Raised Beds for Special Gardeners

Intensive gardening in raised beds is ideally suited to the physically handicapped or others for whom the bending, twisting, and lifting motions of garden tasks are difficult if not impossible. Board-contained growing areas that are 2½ feet wide or less and built up from ground level to a height of 24 inches or so should be completely accessible to a person in a wheelchair reaching to the left or right—provided of course, there are paths on both sides. Trellises mounted on the ends of the beds can add a vertical growing panel 2 to 3 feet high to further enlarge the harvest within arm's reach. Beds built to waist height would be perfect

Wheelchair Garden: A raised bed that allows a seated gardener to roll partway under the unit brings the growing area within reach.

for gardeners unable to crouch and bend over.

Gardens for wheelchair growers should be located on a level site, and the aisles should be 2½ feet wide or more and relatively smooth, hard, and stable. Although close-cut sod might be adequate in relatively dry, well-drained areas, concrete, brick, or embedded flagstone is usually preferable.

To spare a wheelchair gardener the need to twist to the side, a raised bed also can be created in a grow box constructed with a slatted or drilled bottom for drainage. One such successful setup, created for an adult, consists of a box 15 inches deep, 5 feet wide, and 12 feet long, with a trellis attached. When there's access from only one side, a 3 or 4-foot or even narrower width growing area would be appropriate. You'd probably want to alter the width, too, for a child's garden.

Such units are raised by screwing on wooden legs and setting them inside a frame with legs attached. Or they can be suspended on construction horses or concrete blocks. Either way, the seated gardener can roll part way under the bed itself. This option allows for full-face contact with the planted area and makes it possible to reach all, or nearly all, the way across the growing area with both hands at the same time. The movable beds created can be enjoyed as part of a family garden or placed on a deck or patio or even in a sunny corner of a porch.

Accommodating Perennials

"Any perennial is well suited to intensive gardening," says Dick Meiners of Pinetree Garden Seeds. And it's hard to disagree with him. Multiplying their own number and yield as the years go by, perennials also make fewer demands on the soil than nutrient-hungry annuals, which must fuel and finish their entire life cycle over one short growing season. Tending to be relatively disease and pest-free once established, perennials help make up for the delay until harvest by being surprisingly high in yield. Jerusalem artichokes, for instance, are five times more productive than potatoes. What's more, perennial yields are being steadily improved. New varieties now on the market—many of them hybrids—are now outproducing older strains by up to 30 percent (BROCK IMPERIAL asparagus comes to mind, among others that are discussed in the next chapter). Breeders also are making these plants more feasible for yield-oriented gardeners by shrinking their dimensions. The new, dwarf SUNCHOKE (64) Jerusalem artichoke is a full one-third smaller than older types but has tubers the same size.

Many perennials also earn a place in the garden by virtue of their very high nutritional value. Asparagus ranks a surprising sixth in major vitamin and mineral content among the 39 most widely eaten vegetables and fruits. And the globe artichoke is right behind it in seventh place.

On the negative side, a large number of perennials in the garden can wreak havoc with crop rotation plans, and they also preclude renewing the soil regularly through covercropping. Interestingly, however, it's possible, and may even be desirable, to move some of these "permanent" plantings every third or fourth year. (See the box Perennial Pains and Pleasures.) Perennial herbs even take well to being divided and transferred to a new bed every spring. Long-lasting plants handled this way can participate at least partially in the benefits of rotation and green manuring.

Perennial vegetables and herbs also tend to be space-invaders. This tendency can be checked by isolating them in foundation plantings along the side of a house or garage. Such sites are often partially shaded and characterized by soil less well conditioned than that in the garden proper. Actually, such liabilities can be helpful in slowing the growth and spread of very exuberant perennials that you may not wish to produce in great quantity. Some experienced gardeners deliberately plant vigorous growers like the Jerusalem artichoke in a less than optimal soil and situation. This strategy reserves more productive spaces

for plants needing more encouragement to yield well. Border beds also tend to be narrower than those in garden areas, and since perennials often take many years to spread throughout a generously sized bed, it makes for an efficient use of space to assign them to smaller quarters.

In fitting these long-lived plants into your garden layout, you might also site them under trees. Boxed-in rhubarb makes an attractive ground cover under an ornamental specimen while strawberries will grow quite successfully in a 2 to 3-foot radius around a dwarf fruit tree, where they will create a living mulch and permit double use of each application of fertilizer. You can also surround trees with 4-foot-square plantings of low-growing perennial herbs such as thyme, ginger mint, basil, Greek oregano, or tarragon. (See Two-Story Sharing in chapter 5 for some more ideas on fitting crops around trees.) Or set aside such sites (or perhaps a bed or portion of a bed) for biennial herbs, replanting half of the area each year, while the other half features the same herbs in their second year of growth.

Bush and bramble fruits create a different challenge in garden design. In most instances you'll need to plant at least two varieties for cross-pollination, and you may well want to include early, mid-season, and late varieties for an extended, staggered harvest. These considerations and the fact that it's practical to cover the fruits with netting to thwart bird gourmands mean that block plantings are often a good arrangement. Bramble fruits that need trellising can do well in border beds just 1 to 2 feet wide. To make brambles space efficient, plant them in the center of 3-foot-wide beds, and train the canes up wires running the length of each side of the bed. During the first summer after setting out the brambles you can plant vegetables such as beans, peas, or cabbage in the bed to keep it in production.

To avoid disease problems, experienced fruit grower Gene Logsdon transplants young canes of his fall-bearing raspberries in the spring of

With the Master Gardeners

PERENNIAL PAINS AND PLEASURES

Mark Rames has energy to burn. Or at least energy to work up to 60 hours a week as a switching equipment technician for a telephone company and still co-create a lush oasis right next door to Michigan soybean fields.

Converting from chemicals just five years ago, Mark and his wife, Carol, have transformed "real nasty yellow clay" littered with trash, nails, broken glass, coal cinders, and other unmentionables into a 1½-acre vegetable kingdom featuring 24 beds framed in rough oak and surrounding rows of corn, tomatoes, potatoes, melons, and cucumbers. Framed by flowering shrubs, a hedgerow of rugosa roses, and young blue spruce trees in combination with a privet hedge, the couple's property includes an old brick farm house shaded by walnut trees and sugar maples.

To complete the inviting picture, they've put in an herb patch, a clutch of berry bushes, a vineyard with a dozen varieties of grapes, and an orchard boasting nearly 40 different varieties of apples, cherries, peaches, pears, nectarines, plums, and apricots. All that beauty and productivity brought Mark and Carol third-place honors in the 1984 Organic Gardener of the Year Contest.

With all these plants to tend, you wouldn't think there would be any time left to pamper perennials, but Mark has brought his thoughtful, vigorous care to this aspect of gardening. Like many seasoned gardeners, he's been exasperated by some of the more rambunctious perennials. "Once you get things like Jerusalem artichokes going you can never get rid of them. One little shred of root in the ground and it will come back up again. And comfrey is a real nice herb, but I want it to stay where I put it." Mark finds even garlic can pose a challenge. "It's got such a gripping root that if it gets into a vegetable planting you can't pull it up. It just breaks off at the top before it will come out of the ground and you have to dig it out."

To control such incorrigibles, Mark has devised a 6 by 10-foot containment bed divided in three compartments. Step one consisted of digging a 12-inch-deep trench along the perimeter of the bed

Containment Beds: Mark Rames devised this setup to keep rambunctious plants under control. Cement blocks set in a 12-inch-deep trench and topped with a wooden frame keep plants like Jerusalem artichokes from taking over the garden.

and setting a single layer of cement blocks inside. Constructing a wooden frame box to fit the dimensions of the bed, he then set the frame on the cement blocks. Next he lined the inside of the box with rubber sheeting he had on hand, "so the root couldn't get between the board and the cement block." According to Mark, "A tractor inner tube slit to make a long strip would work in the same way."

Fitting the box with boards across the center before filling it with the excavated soil, Mark created a large compartment for comfrey and two smaller ones for garlic and Jerusalem artichokes. The containment bed has held up well for five years, and "no one's escaped yet. They're all still captive."

Unlike Rames, Jackie Eichhorn of Indiana isn't bothered by the invasive tendencies of perennials. In fact, self-renewing herbs, vegetables, and flow-

(continued)

PERENNIAL PAINS AND PLEASURES—*Continued*

ers take pride of place in the intricately designed and interplanted garden landscape she has created. Jackie and her husband, Doug, fashioned a garden including 135 perennials next to an old brick warehouse they renovated into a home and shops.

Jackie has permanent plantings of asparagus, rhubarb, Egyptian onions, Jerusalem artichokes, pokeweed, and dandelion, and she even put in a special row of daylilies to supply blossoms for cooking purposes. "I love finding perennial vegetables," she confides, "and I'd like to have even more. They're such a time-saver, and they produce very well, too."

Far from confining her vegetable perennials to permanent beds, Jackie has discovered that they do better if she moves them every three or four years "just to freshen the soil." Although she keeps one permanent planting of Egyptian onions going to

get sets to grow elsewhere as scallions, she digs up and relocates the mother bed of this vegetable quite matter-of-factly. "It just seems that after a few years you run into a few problems—some kind of worm will get into it or something. When we lived across the street, I had an Egyptian onion bed that I left in place for four years and the fourth year, even though I was fertilizing and doing everything that I had done before, it didn't perform quite so well. I figured it was simpler to replant it somewhere else."

In Jackie's experience, even Jerusalem artichokes have proved cooperative. "You know, people say once you have it, you'll always have it, but that just isn't true." Like her other perennials, the tubers of this troublemaker are deliberately rotated around the garden. "If you miss some," she adds, "they'll eventually come to the surface, and then you just dig them out."

---

every fourth year and harvests them the same fall. For a painless transition he recommends letting the old border or bed planting produce for another year and planting the young canes just 1 or 2 feet apart in the new location for heavy early production.

Putting Together Rotations That Can Boost Yields

Seasoned growers intent on getting big harvests without resorting to chemicals pay a lot of attention to crop rotation. They make sure full-season plants such as tomatoes, pole beans, cabbages, and melons are sited in different garden spaces over a period of at least three or four years. It's also possible and helpful to use the principles of year-to-year rotations in planting successions of short-term crops during a growing season. One master gardener educated in ecology makes a point of telling rookies, "If you don't do anything else special in the garden, rotate your crops!"

The reasons for such enthusiasm aren't hard to find. For starters, it's known that plants release toxins that over a period of time can build up in the soil to a level capable of severely stunting or even killing the very species that produced them. Called autoallelopathy, this phenomenon is known to affect cauliflower if it is grown in the same location repeatedly and also creates problems if growers try to replant old orchards where apples, peaches, cherries, plums, and apricots grew.

On the other hand, it's also been discovered that certain chemicals plants leave behind can have a positive, growth-enhancing impact on successor plants of another family. Sometimes, as in a two-crop rotation of soybeans and corn, each crop produces better when it follows the other. Where legumes are concerned, the greater yields that result in subsequent plantings of crops like corn also have been linked to changes in soil texture and increased nitrogen. Tests done at Kansas State University suggest that cover crops such as soybeans and wheat also raise the productiv-

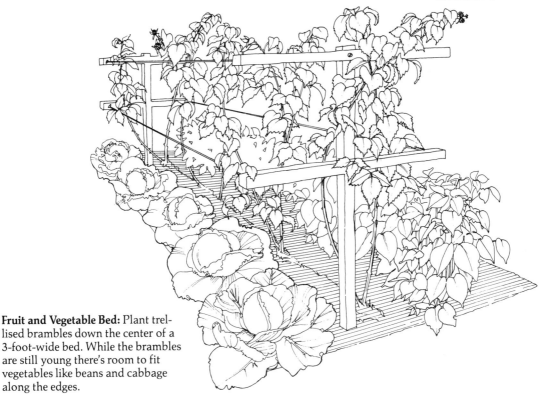

Fruit and Vegetable Bed: Plant trellised brambles down the center of a 3-foot-wide bed. While the brambles are still young there's room to fit vegetables like beans and cabbage along the edges.

ity of crops that follow them in dry climates because they use relatively little water and therefore leave more soil moisture behind.

Rotations also contribute to better yields by interrupting disease cycles linked to specific plants and thwarting the build-up of fungi and other harmful soil organisms and insects. Root crops, brassicas, and solanaceous crops such as tomatoes, eggplants, peppers, and potatoes are especially vulnerable to insects and disease and as a result benefit substantially from crop rotation.

Basic Rotations

The general principles of rotation are fairly easy to grasp. Many experienced gardeners get by handsomely simply by remembering to never plant a crop in the same place two years in a row and to alternate crops harvested for their aboveground parts with those grown for their roots. (Along these lines, it can help to bear in mind that leaf crops need primarily nitrogen; roots,

potassium; and fruiting crops, phosphorus.)

If you're ready to refine your rotation scheme further, you can start factoring in soil-building crops. One approach is to concentrate on working up three-year rotations featuring heavy feeders, light feeders, and soil builders as listed in the chart Plants Grouped According to Nutrient Needs on page 69. Any sequence featuring a vegetable from each column is acceptable as long as you remember never to follow a light feeder immediately with a heavy feeder—unless you lay on an extra application of compost or manure. An easy-to-remember four-year rotation pattern consists of legumes/brassicas/root crops/leafy greens. You also can start out with well-manured soil and do the following sequence: fruiting plants/leafy greens/root crops/cover crops.

For an added challenge, in planning rotations go beyond the major nutrient needs of your crops to consider their pH requirements. For example, legumes should thrive right after lime has been applied, while brassicas do best a season or two later. Potatoes can be grown profit-

GROUPS OF PLANTS SUSCEPTIBLE TO THE SAME DISEASES

Cantaloupes	Broccoli	Eggplants	Beets	Beans
Cucumbers	Brussels sprouts	Okra	Carrots	Peas
Pumpkins	Cabbage	Peppers	Garlic	
Squashes	Cauliflower	Potatoes	Onions	
Watermelons	Collards	Tomatoes	Parsnips	
	Mustard		Shallots	
	Radishes			
	Rutabagas			
	Turnips			

ably at the end of the liming cycle since they prefer slightly acidic soil. (See Rotations Balancing pH and Soil Needs on page 70 for more ideas.)

Whatever method you choose, make a mental note *not* to plant any member of the solanaceous family in a given spot more often than every fourth year. Remember, too, that if you're succession planting one or more of the brassicas in a bed over a growing season, it's good practice to work against the build-up of soil toxins by introducing another plant family to that bed the following year. (To help your planning, each vegetable featured in the High-Yield Plant Guide lists its family affiliation.)

Ways to Make Rotations Easier

There are several steps you can take to make crop rotations easier to plan and carry out. It helps, of course, to devote each section of your garden or perhaps each bed to block plantings or interplantings of plants in the same family or at least of the same type (root, leaf, or fruiting). If you're working with a small number of beds but still want to follow a comprehensive rotation scheme, divide your beds into blocks; 4 by 4-foot or 5 by 5-foot squares can work well. The more squares you make, the more rotations you can undertake and the longer you'll be able to wait before you have to replant the same vegetable—or better

yet, a member of the same vegetable family—in a given square.

For planning purposes, if you have more than a few beds and/or if they're subdivided into blocks, you'll want to put your garden layout on paper, numbering each bed and giving any subdivisions within it a letter as well. You may want to keep separate charts for your fall and spring plantings. Actually, it can be easy and pleasant to keep track of rotations by taking photographs of your garden each year.

Gardeners with really poor soil or those who want to rely almost entirely on cover crops for soil building sometimes plant two gardens and rotate *them* from year to year. If you do block plantings you can get the same effect by dividing a good-sized square or rectangle in half, then rotating the sides each growing season.

Rotating crops becomes more difficult if part of your garden is in shade for some of the day. To counter the problem without limiting your rotation options too greatly, consider trellising or caging plants in the affected areas. Certainly, you'll want enough vertical growing setups to allow for a three-year rotation of disease-prone crops such as tomatoes. Planning adequate crop rotations in such circumstances may be difficult, since many of the popular vining plants are in the cucurbit family.

PLANTS GROUPED ACCORDING TO NUTRIENT NEEDS

Heavy Feeders	Light Feeders	Soil Builders
Asparagus	Carrots	Alfalfa
Beets	Garlic	Beans
Broccoli*	Leeks	broad
Brussels sprouts*	Mustard greens	lima
Cabbage*	Onions	snap
Cantaloupes*	Parsnips	Clover
Cauliflower	Peppers	Peas
Celery	Potatoes	Peanuts
Collards	Rutabagas	Soybeans
Corn	Shallots	
Cucumbers*	Sweet potatoes	
Eggplants*	Swiss chard	
Endive	Turnips	
Kale		
Kohlrabi		
Lettuce		
Okra		
Parsley		
Pumpkins*		
Radishes		
Rhubarb		
Spinach		
Squash		
summer*		
winter*		
Strawberries		
Sunflowers		
Tomatoes		
Watermelons*		

Fertilize twice

Rotation also gets problematic if you are growing various crops in very different quantities. If this is the case, you may not be able to devote a whole bed or even a good-sized portion of a bed to a regular rotation sequence. If that's so, keep a journal recording what was planted where. If you want to stay with units of identical size, try adding annual flowers or herbs to beds or blocks where you want to grow less of a given vegetable. You'll be a little less efficient in your use of space, but you'll enjoy more diverse harvests and learn valuable lessons in companion planting.

When interplanting, plan your rotation around the main crop. Should you add new beds to your garden, arrange the rotation so heavy feeders go in the older beds, which will probably be richer in humus, and put soil-building crops in the newly cultivated places. One final tip: certain root crops such as carrots and beets and various cucurbits may not do well planted directly after a legume. On the other hand, you'll probably enjoy especially good yields from leafy vegetables if you slot them in after legumes.

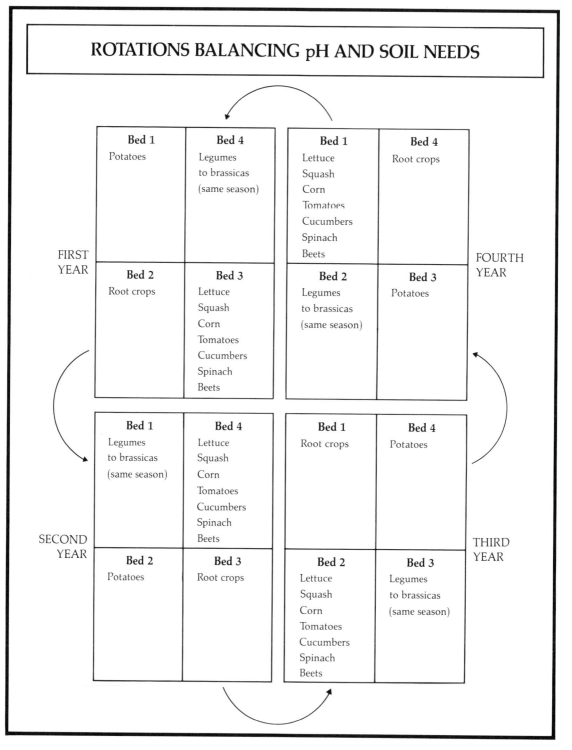

ROTATIONS BALANCING pH AND SOIL NEEDS

FIRST YEAR

Bed 1
Potatoes

Bed 4
Legumes
to brassicas
(same season)

Bed 2
Root crops

Bed 3
Lettuce
Squash
Corn
Tomatoes
Cucumbers
Spinach
Beets

FOURTH YEAR

Bed 1
Lettuce
Squash
Corn
Tomatoes
Cucumbers
Spinach
Beets

Bed 4
Root crops

Bed 2
Legumes
to brassicas
(same season)

Bed 3
Potatoes

SECOND YEAR

Bed 1
Legumes
to brassicas
(same season)

Bed 4
Lettuce
Squash
Corn
Tomatoes
Cucumbers
Spinach
Beets

Bed 2
Potatoes

Bed 3
Root crops

THIRD YEAR

Bed 1
Root crops

Bed 4
Potatoes

Bed 2
Lettuce
Squash
Corn
Tomatoes
Cucumbers
Spinach
Beets

Bed 3
Legumes
to brassicas
(same season)

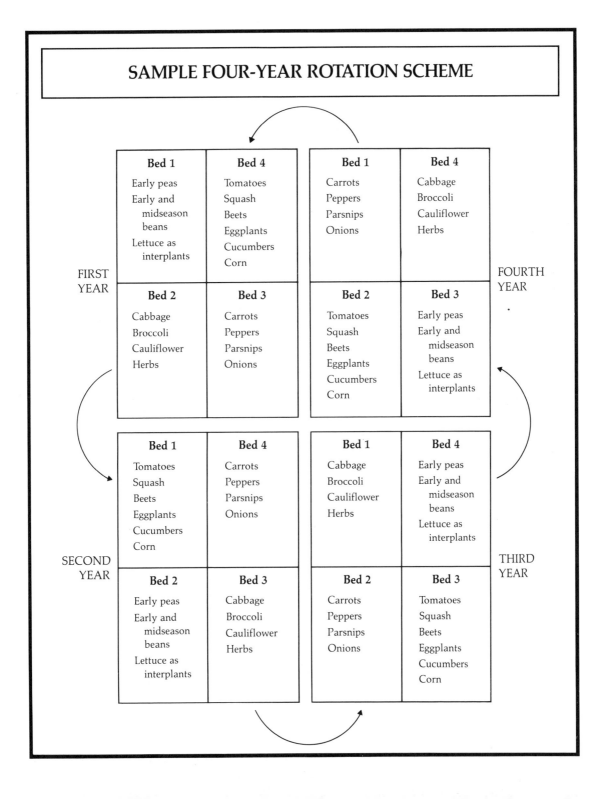

SAMPLE FOUR-YEAR ROTATION SCHEME

FIRST YEAR

Bed 1
Early peas
Early and
   midseason
   beans
Lettuce as
   interplants

Bed 4
Tomatoes
Squash
Beets
Eggplants
Cucumbers
Corn

Bed 2
Cabbage
Broccoli
Cauliflower
Herbs

Bed 3
Carrots
Peppers
Parsnips
Onions

FOURTH YEAR

Bed 1
Carrots
Peppers
Parsnips
Onions

Bed 4
Cabbage
Broccoli
Cauliflower
Herbs

Bed 2
Tomatoes
Squash
Beets
Eggplants
Cucumbers
Corn

Bed 3
Early peas
Early and
   midseason
   beans
Lettuce as
   interplants

SECOND YEAR

Bed 1
Tomatoes
Squash
Beets
Eggplants
Cucumbers
Corn

Bed 4
Carrots
Peppers
Parsnips
Onions

Bed 2
Early peas
Early and
   midseason
   beans
Lettuce as
   interplants

Bed 3
Cabbage
Broccoli
Cauliflower
Herbs

THIRD YEAR

Bed 1
Cabbage
Broccoli
Cauliflower
Herbs

Bed 4
Early peas
Early and
   midseason
   beans
Lettuce as
   interplants

Bed 2
Carrots
Peppers
Parsnips
Onions

Bed 3
Tomatoes
Squash
Beets
Eggplants
Cucumbers
Corn

3

What to Grow for Highest Yields

To get the absolute most from your intensive garden, you'll need to complement your careful preparation of soil and beds with close attention to varietal selection. Next to savoring the year's first snap peas right in the patch, hunting through seed racks and catalogs has to provide some of the purest pleasure in gardening. The imagination soars—tethered to Earth only by niggling afterthoughts of growing conditions and space (no longer) available!

As a gardener intent on maximum returns, you'll find that there are many ingenious ways to heighten overall productivity through plant selection. We'll explore some major ones here.

Highest Yielding Crops and Varieties

The most obvious way to get more from your garden is to feature crops and varieties offering the greatest yield relative to the garden space and garden time they require. Clearly the poorest returns are most likely to come from vegetables and fruits that must spend an extended growing season in the patch. Crops such as large bulbing onions, peanuts, sweet potatoes, parsnips, salsify, and larger pumpkins must stay put for as long as 120 to 150 days. Other poor bets for intensive production are crops relatively low yielding and so tall and/or wide they can't be planted closely—a category that includes full-sized sweet corn varieties and globe artichokes. Asparagus, rhubarb, and other perennial vegetables and fruits that yield little or nothing for their first two or three years in the garden also may be hard to justify in terms of quantity of output.

Conversely, high yields relative to space and time are linked to fast-growing crops such as radishes, mustard greens, turnips, scallions, spinach, loosehead lettuce, bush snap beans, summer squash, kohlrabi, Swiss chard, okra, cucumbers, beets, early peas, and kale, which take only 22 to 55 days from seed to harvest. For long-maturing crops, you can boost the return relative to the amount of time they take in the garden by starting them as well-developed transplants. For instance, giant sweet onions take five months from seed but just three and a half months if you start from onion seedlings.

Crops more high yielding by nature include those ideal for close planting because they are relatively low growing and most of their growth is on a vertical plane. Particularly impressive yields are possible with relatively fast-maturing elongated root vegetables such as the 6 to 8-inch-long beet CYLINDRA (8, 17, 22) and mild white Japanese radishes like the MINOWASE daikon (25), which can grow 24 inches long. Then there are the spectacular producers like tomatoes, cucumbers, and summer squash, which form startling numbers of sizable fruits for yields of up to several hundred pounds per plant.

Several elaborate studies have been done to determine exactly which crops are the most worthwhile for backyard growers. A two-year project at Brigham Young University in Utah found that beets, cabbage, carrots, onions, potatoes, and summer squash are the most efficient vegetables in relation to labor and land used. In a survey of three dozen top home garden experts by the National Garden Bureau, the criteria of value factored in were total yield per square foot, average value per pound harvested, and seed-to-harvest time. The ten top scorers under these rules are tomatoes grown on supports, green bunching onions, leaf lettuce, turnips harvested for both roots and greens, summer squash, edible-podded peas, onion bulbs, pole beans, beets grown for roots and tops, and bush beans.

Hybrid Vigor

When specific varieties rather than crops are considered, perhaps the surest route to better yields is to grow hybrids, which exhibit a striking vigor that translates into faster growth and more flavorful, abundant, better-keeping yields. Two or three-pound hybrid tomatoes are commonplace, as are large numbers of fruits per plant—one thrilled gardener harvested 280 1½-pound BETTER BOY tomatoes from a single vine! Dramatically improved yields and characteristics are found in

Encouraging More Greens: Fast-growing greens such as cress, mustard, Swiss chard, looseleaf lettuce, and spinach can be made to yield more prolifically by cutting them back to 2 inches or less several times during the growing season.

SOME HIGH-YIELD, LOW-SPACE
VERSIONS OF POPULAR VEGETABLES

The garden crops featured here rank among the top 20 both for popularity among gardeners and for their value (derived by factoring in total yield per square foot, average value per pound harvested, and seed-to-harvest time). Varieties were chosen for their relatively compact habit and abundant yield per square foot of gardening space and are listed alphabetically.

Tomatoes (Bush types with full-sized fruits*)
    Better Bush VFN (3)
    Celebrity (9, 26, 34, 50)
    Pik-Red (26)
    Super Bush (25, 22)

Sweet Bell Peppers
    Golden Bell (26, 48)
    Gypsy (6, 9, 26, 50)
    Lady Bell (26)
    Park's Whopper (48)

Snap Beans (Bush types*)
    Astro (48)
    Blue Lake (28)
    Bush Kentucky Wonder (25, 26)
    Earli-Serve (25)
    Early Contender (25)
    Jumbo (25, 48, 50)
    Provider (26, 28)
    Roma II (26)
    Top Crop (25)

Cucumbers (Bush types*)
    Bush Champion (9)
    Cucumber Burpless Bush (48)
    Hybrid Pot Luck (25)
    Hybrid Surecrop (25)
    Patio Pik Hybrid (28)
    Spacemaster (9)

Looseleaf Lettuce
    Black-Seeded Simpson (25, 26)
    Crispy Sweet (48)
    Green Ice (9)
    Prizehead (25)
    Royal Oak Leaf (9)
    Salad Bowl (26)

Summer Squash (Bush types)
    Dark Green (28)
    Dixie (48)
    Gold Crest (50)
    Gold Rush (9)
    Green Magic (48)
    Hybrid Daytona (25)
    Park's Creamy Hybrid (48)
    Sunburst Hybrid (9)
    Table Gold (65)
    Tara (26)

Carrots
    Danvers Half-Long (25)
    Gold Pak (25)
    Improved Imperator 58 (25)
    Oxheart (25)
    Pioneer (26)
    Red-Cored Chantenay (28)
    Scarlet Nantes (25)

Edible-Podded Peas
  Bush sugar-snaps:
    Early Snap (26)
    Sugar Ann (26, 34)
    Sugar Bon (9, 48)
    Sugar Mel (25, 48)
  Bush snow peas:
    Dwarf White Sugar (25)
    Snowbird (9)
    Snowflake (34)

Beets
    Cylindra (8, 17, 22)
    Early Wonder Staysgreen (34)
    Forono (50)
    Green Top Bunching (48)
    Ruby Queen (25)

Broccoli
    Green Comet (25, 26)
    Green Dwarf #36 (48)
    Hybrid Citation (25)
    Packman (50)

*You'll gain greater yields relative to horizontal growing space by growing the larger, indeterminate, vining types on stakes or trellises. See the section later on Vertical Growing—The Ultimate in Space Saving.

a wide array of vegetable hybrids. MELODY hybrid spinach offers substantially more greens earlier in the season, and the new BROCK IMPERIAL asparagus hybrid puts forth a profusion of spears both thick and tender, producing up to 30 percent more than the old, standard strains. HYBRID CITATION broccoli turns out an 8-inch-wide head on a plant little more than twice that high. Another hybrid, the new CRYSTAL potato, yielded an astonishing 27,300 pounds per acre in Idaho trials (all available from 25). JADE CROSS, a hybrid Brussels sprout, has been rated one of the top dozen vegetable introductions by a panel of experts.

Disease Resistance

Critical to the dependable high yields of such hybrids is their improved disease resistance. In tomatoes this is announced by a string of capital letters after the variety's name, each standing for a disease to which the plant is resistant. V is for verticillium wilt, F stands for fusarium wilt 1 or 2, N means nematodes, T signifies tobacco mosaic, and A represents alternaria, or crown wilt. The All-America winner CELEBRITY (9, 26, 34) sports VFFNT in its catalog credits, while Park's QUICK PICK VFFNTA (48) offers six-way disease resistance together with very early, very heavy yields.

Choosing vigorous, strongly disease-resistant hybrids obviously becomes almost essential if you garden organically in a humid, hot area where plant diseases and pests thrive or anywhere else climatic extremes stress plants and make them more vulnerable to bacteria, viruses, and bugs. It also makes good sense to favor hybrids of crops that tend to be disease-prone or in other ways benefit enormously from hybridization. This group would include corn, melons, peppers, and tomatoes.

Compact Size

Another important characteristic to factor in when selecting varieties for highest yield is compactness. Today's gardeners respond enthusiastically to densely constructed varieties such as LITTLE GEM romaine (64), which is 6 inches high and just 4

inches around and yields heavily even when planted just 6½ inches apart. The popular clamor for such "spacesaver" varieties has caused seed company breeders to concentrate on this line of development. As a result, one compact variety is rapidly succeeded by a yet smaller one guaranteed to produce an even tastier, earlier, and more abundant harvest. As varietal specialist George B. Park, Jr., says, "We're talking about a moving target," so it's important to scan the latest catalogs to discover the strongest options in pint-sized plants.

If your gardening space is very limited, such space-efficient varieties will make it possible for you to grow a much greater variety of foods. This gives you a greater amount of different vegetables you can use to make up more of your meals at any given time. This can be a great boon, preventing the waste of garden space implied when you wind up giving away bushels of squash and tomatoes.

It's equally true, however, that even though small varieties can be planted closer, their yield per square foot may be disappointing. This is always the case with so-called "miniatures" or "minivegetables," in which not just the plant but the size of the individual vegetable is minuscule. Dick Meiners of Pinetree Garden Seeds, which specializes in space-efficient varieties, reports most of these midgets "are gimmicks which we eschew." Often, even larger compact types with standard-sized fruits cannot justify the space saved. For example, several relatively high-yielding American eggplants are 6 to 8 inches shorter than the Japanese hybrid ICHIBAN (9), but ICHIBAN's yield per plant in some trials has been over three times greater.

When comparing yields of smaller and larger varieties, you also have to factor in time to maturity. A surprising number of spacesavers take considerably longer to start yielding than their larger relatives. For example, the petite bush melon HONEYDEW OLIVER'S PEARL CLUSTER (50) takes only 4 square feet of garden space but requires an outrageous 110 days to produce edible fruit! Compare that to the vining but larger-fruited, heavy-cropping VENUS HYBRID HONEYDEW that matures in only 88 days (9). Or to the heavy and long-bearing SWEET 'N' EARLY hybrid cantaloupe (9), which delivers in just 75 days. Then there's GREEN DWARF #36 hybrid broccoli (48), only 8 inches tall, with a 5½-inch head that permits close planting. This compact variety takes 90 days to maturity from setting out, versus extra early larger-headed hybrids like CLEOPATRA and GREEN COMET, which are ready in 55 days. Is the space saved by planting the more compact melon and broccoli worth that extra 35 days of garden time? Probably not.

On the other hand, the availability of dwarfed varieties may help you justify growing certain crops. For example, lima beans aren't very competitive on a yield per square foot basis—except in the South, where they produce in hot weather. But it's hard to resist the compact BRIDGETON (48), which happens to be the most productive, disease resistant, and just about earliest of limas at 65 days. New compact versions also can help change your mind about crops that used to seem too tall and wide for your garden scheme: the LONG ISLAND IMPROVED Brussels sprout is just 20 inches high, and DWARF LONG GREEN POD okra (9, 25) tops out at 24 to 30 inches. Even sweet corn begins to look feasible when you can choose early varieties often less than a yard high that can be crowded into 8 to 12-inch spacings and yield four or more ears per plant. Examples of these include GOLDEN MIDGET, HONEY CREAM (35), and MASON'S MIDGET (3).

Bush-type compact varieties can also tempt you to find just a little space for long-season crops like the PORTO RICO sweet potato (9), which is quite compact and very heavy yielding.

Compact forms seem most essential to yield-oriented gardeners who have little space but a big yen to grow long-season vining crops like squashes and melons. When full sized these sprawlers take three or four times the horizontal room of spacesaver types. Certainly, it's hard to resist the logic of triple-benefit winter squash and melons that combine compact size with early, heavy yields. Some of the current best bets in bush or short-vined acorn-type winter squashes are GOLD NUGGET, BUSH ACORN TABLE KING, BUSH TABLE QUEEN, and JERSEY GOLDEN ACORN. Best compact butternut-types include BUTTERBUSH (9) and the somewhat larger EARLY BUTTERNUT hybrid (25, 26, 48). Top buttercups or turban-shaped winter squash are KINDRED (20, 59) and SWEET MAMA hybrid (9, 48).

Gardeners looking for compact cantaloupes should consider three hybrids—BUSH STAR (22, 26, 65), BUSHWHOPPER (48), and GIANT HYBRID (25), which brings forth jumbo fruits of up to 18 pounds from relatively compact vines in just 80 days. Watermelon winners for postage-stamp-sized plots include BABY FUN hybrid (28,50), BUSH JUBILEE (26), SWEET BABY HYBRID (26), and WATERMELON BUSH BABY (48).

Early-Maturing Varieties for Fast-Moving Successions

No matter where you live and garden, if total productivity is one of your top priorities, *always* give preference to compact or vertically grown varieties that are early bearing. As southern seedsman George B. Park, Jr., puts it, "The more crops you can fit into a growing season, the longer the eating season you'll have."

If you're getting by on a skimpy ration of 90 to 120 frost-free days per year, look for varieties you can sow early because they are tolerant of low soil and air temperatures. And plant them in black plastic mulch, which can shorten the time to maturity by an additional 4 to 7 days.

You can get the same effect, of course, by starting early bearers indoors and setting out the transplants as early as possible. (For more pointers on these techniques and on how to extend the season with smart crop selections, see chapter 6.)

Even if they're not the top-yielding varieties of their kind, "quickies" like the 50-day LITTLE FINGER (9, 50) carrot and the 30-day TOKYO CROSS HYBRID (50) turnip justify themselves by freeing garden space 20 or 30 days earlier than a somewhat more productive variety. Best of all, of course, are varieties outstanding for both earliness and abundant yield of full-sized vegetables or fruits per square foot. Here's just a sampling of such treasures:

Beets: EARLY WONDER—50 days (34, 59); RED ACE hybrid—50 days (34); FORONO—54 days (50).

Bush Beans: BOUNTIFUL—46 days (9, 14, 50); TOP CROP—49 days (50); PROVIDER—50 days (26).

Broccoli: SPARTAN EARLY—60 days (50).

Cabbage: BABY EARLY hybrid—50 days (50); STONEHEAD—55 days (50); All-America winner EMERALD CROSS HYBRID—63 days (9).

Cauliflower: SNOW KING hybrid—50 days (9, 22, 35); SNOWBALL T-3—51 days (34, 59); ALERT—52 days (34, 59); SNOW CROWN hybrid—53 days (26, 50).

Chinese Cabbage: EARLY HYBRID G—50–60 days (26); TWO SEASONS HYBRID—62 days (9).

Corn: EARLY KING hybrid—63 days (35, 56); BLITZ hybrid—64 days (26); GOLD RUSH hybrid—66 days (17, 47).

Cucumbers (pickling): PEPPI hybrid—48 days (48,59); PIONEER female hybrid—48–55 days (10, 46, 48); SPARTAN DAWN hybrid—49 days (8, 17, 25).

Cucumbers (slicing): EXTRA EARLY EXPRESS—45 days (17); FORCE BEAUTY HYBRID—45 days (49); STOKES EARLY HYBRID—55 days (59).

Peppers (sweet): PARK'S EARLY THICKSET hybrid—48 days (48); EARLY PROLIFIC—62 days (50).

Pumpkins: semi-bush SPIRIT HYBRID—99 days (9, 50).

Spinach: INDIAN SUMMER hybrid—39 days (34).

Tomatoes: climbing EARLY GIRL hybrid—54–62 days (8, 9); climbing BALL EXTRA EARLY—55 days (6); short-vined BURGESS HYBRID NO. 1—55 days (8, 47); SUPER BUSH hybrid—63 days (50).

Watermelons: SUGAR BALL—65 days (39, 49); STOKES SUGAR hybrid—70 days (59, 62); SUGAR DOLL HYBRID—72 days (28, 48); BABY FUN hybrid—82 days (50).

(For additional early varieties of various crops, see chapters 6 and 9.)

You can also increase your garden's effective productivity by staggering the harvest over time. By dividing space devoted to major crops such as cabbage, carrots, peppers, and tomatoes among early, mid-season, and late-maturing varieties, you work against the temptation to overplant relative to your rate of consumption. This avoids the painful necessity of giving away most of what you grow or, heaven forbid, letting part of your too-abundant harvest rot in the garden. This kind of anticipatory strategy is especially important in intensive gardening, since your yields may be three or four times greater than before.

Wide-row gardening expert Dick Raymond staggers his sweet corn yields in Vermont by growing early and mid-season varieties with 7 to 10 days difference in their times to maturity. His lineup includes SPANCROSS at 62 days (47, 49, 62), SUGAR 'N' GOLD at 67 days (3, 27, 49), BUTTER 'N' SUGAR at 73 days, and PLATINUM LADY at 80 days (50). The Burpee catalog advocates a combination planting that provides fresh tomatoes from early summer to late winter: EARLY PICK HYBRID VF (for an early crop at 62 days), VF HYBRID (for a major crop at 80 days), SUPERSTEAK HYBRID VFN (for a late crop at 80 days), and LONG KEEPER (for

Staggered Plantings: Enhance your garden's productivity by staggering the harvest over time. Some crops, such as corn and cabbage, come in early, mid, and late-season varieties. Planted at the same time, these crops mature in stages, preventing a wasteful glut.

tomatoes that will stay fresh in winter storage for up to three months). All of these are available from 9.

If you prefer, you can stagger a harvest by choosing distinctively different varieties that satisfy various tastes and purposes. Consider, for example, planting either the midget MORDEN DWARF cabbage (20) or the hybrid MARKET VICTOR (26)—both ideal for close spacing—for a harvest of small heads at 60 to 65 days from transplanting. Then savor RED ACRE in colorful slaw at 76 days and end the season with PENN STATE BALLHEAD (20, 41, 59) for storage and krautmaking at 105 days.

You can still space out yields even if you're growing just one variety. The trick is to choose hybrids that are long-bearing. For example, you might try BONANZA hybrid broccoli (9), bred to keep producing 3 to 5-inch-wide side shoots, and the hybrid tomato BETTER BUSH (48), which combines the compact habit of single-cropping, determinate tomatoes with the long-bearing trait of the indeterminate, long-vined types.

Vertical Growing—The Ultimate in Space Saving

Compact, bush varieties of vine crops such as green and lima beans, cucumbers, melons, peas, pumpkins, squashes, sweet potatoes, and tomatoes have been making a strong showing in catalogs and seed racks in recent years. But although these short-vined varieties bear earlier than their sprawling or crawling counterparts, they are not nearly as productive. By nature, the short-viners are determinate plants, which grow and set fruit for a limited time. They simply can't compete in yield per plant with long-vined indeterminate versions of the same crop, for when harvested regularly, these lanky types flower and fruit as long as the weather allows.

The heavier, more prolonged yield coming from vining plants, which often produce from early summer all the way to frost, means you need fewer plants of each type and can thereby save some garden space. But the really enormous contribution such vining crops can make to intensive gardens comes when they are grown vertically.

Even at their most compact, vines allowed to sprawl use up far more space aboveground than below. In the case of indeterminate types, square foot gardening expert Mel Bartholomew claims that only 10 percent of the horizontal space covered by a sprawling tomato plant and just 5 percent of that consumed by a rampaging winter squash is needed to anchor and nourish those plants. For that reason, such vine crops don't really capitalize on the advantages of raised beds. Instead, it's far better to grow vining varieties that measure 3 feet or longer up supports in the narrow "waste spaces" along the foundation of your house or garage or garden fence, or to erect trellises at the north end of the garden.

In that sort of arrangement each plant needs as little as ½ to 1 square foot of horizontal garden space, and you can harvest incredible yields from as much as 10 to 12 feet of vine literally growing on air. The space you save by training plants upward is astonishing: if you construct an 8-foot-high trellis next to a growing bed just 20 inches wide and 16 feet long, you are creating the equivalent of 150 square feet of growing space at a "cost" of just 27 square feet of surface garden soil! (See chapter 5 for more information on how to provide support for upwardly mobile crops.)

Numerous United States Department of Agriculture (USDA) extension service studies in which cucumbers were grown vertically show a consistent *doubling* of yields when a variety is grown vertically rather than horizontally. The key factor contributing to this phenomenal productivity seems to be the increased photosynthesis that takes place when more of a plant's leaf surface is exposed to the sun. Scientists say food crops grown traditionally use only about $\frac{1}{12}$ of the sun's energy available to them and that just a small increase in that capability could increase yields significantly. Vertical growing is a rela-

(continued on page 82)

HIGH-YIELDING VARIETIES FOR VERTICAL GROWING

Variety	Comments	Sources
BEANS		
Green		
Dade	Bred for fall planting in hot, humid climates. Rust resistant.	28
Kentucky Wonder	Good, climbing, heavy producer of very tasty 7 to 9-in. pods.	9
Romano	Tender, stringless, wide, flat Italian bean yielding up to 20 lbs. per plant.	9, 50
Stringless Blue Lake FM 1	Fiberless high-quality bean that bears early (60 days).	28, 48
Lima		
Burpee's Best	Quality of Fordhook Bush but higher yields on vines of 10–12 ft.	9, 62
Carolina (also called Sieva)	Early bearing (78 days).	9, 28
King of the Garden	Enormous crops of giant beans on 8-ft. vines	9, 25, 28
Prizetaker	Giant beans of top quality and flavor	9, 41
CUCUMBERS		
Burpless		
Green King 29	Best performer for early, total productivity in one University of Tennessee study. Resistant to many diseases.	64
Green Knight	Heat-resistant, widely adapted hybrid with fruits 16–18 in. long.	9, 26
Sweet Success	All-America selection. Female hybrid that is self-pollinating. Fruits up to 12 in. long.	9, 26
Slicing		
Early Pride Hybrid	Long-bearing gynoecious type producing up to 50 lbs. per plant.	9
Saladin Hybrid	Very disease-resistant All-America winner. Good for salads or pickles.	9, 48
Victory	Disease-resistant gynoecious giving top yields in North.	9, 10, 20
Pickling		
Liberty	Hybrid All-America winner.	9
National Pickling	Super yields in 55 days.	41, 46
Spartan Dawn	Yields up to 50 percent more than standard varieties.	8, 17, 25
MELONS		
Cantaloupe		
Honey Gold No. 9	Small, edible-skinned Japanese melons that don't slip off the vine.	34
Jenny Lind	Very prolific sweet melon that does well as far north as Maine.	50
Mainstream	Up to 10 3-lb. melons per plant.	10, 70
Sakata's Sweet	See Honey Gold No. 9.	34
Saticoy	A highly disease-resistant hybrid with 4-lb. fruits with deep orange flesh.	14, 26, 48
Honeydew		
Early Dew	Hybrid bred for earliest maturity of 5-lb. honeydews. Fruit "slips" so use slings.	34
Watermelon		
Baby Fun	Hybrid producing 15-lb. fruits in just 82 days. Melons don't slip off the vine.	50

Variety	Comments	Sources
Watermelon (continued)		
Sugar Baby	Round, 7-in. fruits that don't need slings.	8, 17
Yellow Baby	An All-America hybrid yielding 10-lb. yellow fleshed melons with relatively few seeds.	14, 20, 39
PEAS		
Shelling		
Green Arrow	Very high yielding, very hardy variety ideal for coastal regions and the North.	14, 20, 39
Maestro	Early and high yielding, with 8–10 peas per pod.	9
Victory Freezer	All-America midseason type that's very resistant to disease.	17, 25, 64
Alderman	Largest pods and longest vines. Produces high-quality peas.	26, 46
Wando	Most productive hot weather–tolerant pea.	9, 48
EDIBLE-PODDED		
Snow pea		
Mammoth Melting Sugar	Huge meaty-but-tender pods. Plant early for best results.	8, 14
Snap pea		
Oregon Sugar Pod II	Very large crop on 28-in. vines.	9
Sugar Daddy	Stringless version of Sugar Snap.	22, 48, 59
Sugar Mel	A top yielder among snap peas. Although dwarf, does best trellised.	25, 48
PUMPKINS		
Small Sugar	Fruits 7 in. across and 5–8 lbs. appear in 95–100 days.	48, 50
Sprite	The only All-America pumpkin. A semibush type yielding 12-in. pumpkins.	48, 50
SQUASH		
Summer		
Elite	An extra-early, abundant yielding hybrid.	26
Winter		
Golden Delicious	Giant yields of oblong, golden fleshed fruits on spreading vines.	25, 26
Vegetable Spaghetti	A 10-ft. vine yielding up to 18 fruits.	9, 17, 25
Waltham Butternut	Deep orange fleshed All-America winner with a small seed cavity.	9, 10
SWEET POTATO		
Allgold	Golden yellow, very early, highly nutritious midwestern favorite. Good for storing.	20, 22
Centennial	Early, with fine-textured, bright copper flesh.	22, 25, 39, 48
Jewell	Early, top yielder that holds flavor well.	25, 47
TOMATO		
Better Boy VFN	Heavy yielder of big fruits. Produces almost 1 bushel per plant	9, 25
Climbing Trip-L-Crop	Yields about 2–3 bushels from each 8-ft. vine.	48
Early Girl	The earliest indeterminate tomato hybrid.	9, 62
Fantastic	Very early, high-yielding producer of medium-sized tomatoes.	10, 46, 48
Park's Whopper VFNT	Huge yields of 4-in.-diameter tomatoes over a long season starting 70 days from setting out.	48

tively simple and convenient way to do just that by making plants more sun efficient.

The increased light reaching plants that are stalked or trellised makes it possible for them to mature more of the fruits they set. While bush melons often produce only 2 or 3 fruits, vining types turn out as many as 15. Although such fruits may be somewhat smaller, the weight of the total harvest per plant will be much higher. Stepping up photosynthesis at the bottom of vining plants is especially important to yields if you happen to be growing the highly productive gynoecious (female) cucumbers. The added light that reaches the leaves reduces the tendency of female flowers to abort at lower nodes, thus greatly boosting the number of fruits that are set per plant.

Besides the almost automatic assurance of higher yields, there are many other advantages in growing crops vertically. A major one is that the greater circulation of air under foliage reduces the chance of disease—a particularly valuable benefit to gardeners in humid regions such as the Southeast. Because they never touch the ground, fruits also escape the attentions of many insects and are less prone to rot and mold. Plus, they're often better shaped and of higher quality, in addition to being delightfully clean and close at hand for harvesting. And because plants are up in the air and out of the way, you're less likely to injure them as you weed and harvest.

For all these reasons, when you're seeking high yields you should grow as many crops as possible vertically. Even varieties without tendrils can readily be tied to supports as they grow. Upright growing is an especially important option for those with gardens short on sunshine and horizontal space. You can raise a surprising number of crops in this fashion—including the twining green Malabar spinach (23, 45). Although some vertical gardeners use only varieties bearing fruits of 5 pounds or less, others claim excellent results with much heavier melons and pumpkins. These gardeners choose types that

Vertical Vines: Train vining plants upward to save space and expose more of their photosynthesizing leaves to the sun. Cucumbers, melons, squashes, and pumpkins can all be grown this way.

stay on the vine well and support the growing fruits with slings made of old panty hose, cheesecloth, nylon netting, or rags.

If you do venture into vertical growing, consider removing the lateral stems on certain crops. When you prune plants this way they can be set much closer together. In addition, the very experienced Mel Bartholomew, author of *Square Foot*

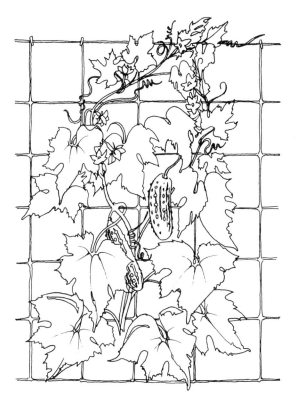

Trellising for Even More Cucumbers: Gynoecious (female) cucumbers are super-productive because nearly all of their flowers set fruit. Trellising these plants even further enhances their productivity.

Gardening (Rodale Press, 1981), insists that taking off tomato suckers promotes earlier and larger tomatoes on the central stem. And cucumber studies reveal that removing lateral branches from the bottom 18 inches of a plant delays and reduces early yields somewhat but results in greater total production over the growing season.

Super-Nutritious Crops for a Higher Nutrient Yield

Another approach to boosting your plot's productivity is to include those crops and varieties richest in nutritional value. A few years back, two California scientists ranked 39 of America's most widely eaten vegetables and fruits according to their popularity. The crops were then ranked again for their overall content of major vitamins and minerals.

Significantly, many of the most nutrition-packed vegetables were among those least consumed. In fact, only two of the top ten nutritional standouts—carrots and sweet potatoes—also ranked in the top ten for popularity. You can remedy this state of affairs for your own household by giving top planting priority to crops that give the greatest return in food value and health benefits.

Heading that list is broccoli, which was head and leaves above all other major fruits and vegetables in total food value. Particularly rich in vitamins A and C, in the major B vitamin riboflavin, and in iron, broccoli also offers almost as much calcium as whole milk.

The second most nutritionally valuable crop is spinach, which ranked first in iron content, second in calcium and riboflavin, and third in potassium and vitamin A. Third place belongs to Brussels sprouts, which scored third in vitamin C, fourth for iron and riboflavin, and also made the top ten for potassium, niacin, thiamine, and calcium. Fourth in overall nutrition is the lima bean, while fifth place goes to peas. The remaining top ten vegetables are asparagus, globe artichokes, cauliflower, sweet potatoes, and carrots.

Although not evaluated in the California study, collards deserve mention as an outstanding source of calcium, vitamin A, and vitamin C. Kale is noteworthy as an excellent source of vitamin C, a very good source of calcium and vitamin A, and a good source of riboflavin and iron.

You can increase the nutritional value of all these superstars even further by seeking out varieties extra-high in vitamins or minerals. For instance, the popular DWARF SCOTCH is the most high-powered kale. And lima bean varieties such

Putting Shade to Good Use: Use the dappled shade created by tall vines to shelter heat-sensitive greens like lettuce or to cool a patio, porch, or house wall.

as BURPEE'S BEST or CANGREEN BUSH (28, 35, 39) move this vegetable into the top ten for vitamin C. The early-bearing pea ALASKA also lifts peas into the ten best for ascorbic acid.

The popular cauliflower EARLY SNOWBALL is higher in vitamin A than most other cauliflowers (much of it in the tender leaves around the head), and the already superb vitamin A content of the sweet potato is at its peak in the stem-rot resistant variety ALLGOLD (20, 22, 26), which also happens to be a high yielder. Considerable efforts have been made to boost the vitamin A value of

carrots. The two most recent breakthroughs are the bolt and crack-resistant ORLANDO GOLD (22, 25, 59), which contains 50 percent more carotene (the element that is converted into vitamin A) than the very popular IMPERATOR 58 (25), and the newer hybrid A PLUS (35, 39), which has 76 percent more carotene than the IMPERATOR and has been judged superior in taste to eight commercial hybrids.

Tomato lovers should consider supernutritious types such as CARO-RICH (8), a sweet-flavored, low-acid, orange-fleshed tomato that boasts ten times the vitamin A content of ordinary tomatoes. Then there's DOUBLERICH (8, 20), which contains twice the vitamin C of other tomatoes. And don't overlook the high-C, high-yielding SWEET 100 (48) hybrid, offering a hundred or more 1-inch fruits on each of its many long branches (48).

Top nutrient value among lettuce, a crop often enjoyed with tomatoes, is found in loose-leaf varieties such as Burpee's PARIS WHITE COS, which offer much more vitamin A than iceberg strains. Then there's corn salad, a tender and delicious salad green that has one-third more iron than spinach.

Several nutrient-rich squashes can be used to raise the value of these sprawling crops, which can be disappointing when you judge them on a yield-per-square-foot basis. You can harvest the compact, prolific KUTA (48) as either a summer or winter squash. It offers up to double the calcium and phosphorus of other squashes. EAT-ALL (20) features a bonus of mineral-rich edible seeds that are 35 percent protein. An analogous NAKED SEEDED PUMPKIN (1, 51) is very productive and very early. The 1982 All-America selection JERSEY GOLDEN ACORN (9, 48) is a bush-type winter squash with three times as much vitamin A as standard green acorns.

Another vine crop with a nutrient yield that can be improved through careful variety selection is the watermelon. Look for types with deep red flesh such as the BUSH CHARLESTON GRAY (25)—they're highest in vitamin A. Spud fanciers might try the outstanding new baking potato, BUTTE (25), which was developed at the University of Idaho. It offers 58 percent more vitamin C and 20 percent more protein than the standard RUSSET BURBANK (48).

To harvest top quality vegetable protein from your backyard patch, consider fast-maturing new dwarf varieties of the edible soybean, which can be eaten green like fresh limas, or dried. EDIBLE EARLY HAKUCHO matures in only 65 days, setting pods heavily on plants just a foot high (48). Containing 39 to 40 percent protein, the slightly taller FISKEBY V is even earlier, thriving in cool, bright areas with short growing seasons (48).

Varieties Adapted to Difficult Growing Conditions

You can frequently improve yields by stocking the garden with varieties highly adapted to the growing conditions in your particular area. This strategy can be critically important if you are struggling against dry, scorching, wind-whipped summers or cool, overcast, soggy ones. Other challenges that can clobber even the most widely adapted hybrids are the endlessly varied microclimates found in the Rockies and other mountainous regions, maddeningly short growing seasons, or year-round growing environments threatened by frosts and freezes when cold fronts move southward in the middle of the winter gardening season.

Matching varieties to such a crazy quilt of diverse conditions is not getting easier. The increasing concentration of plant breeding and production in fewer and fewer geographical areas is decreasing the diversity in plant materials being sold wholesale throughout the nation. Economic pressures have forced many seed houses that once catered to regional differences to become mere clearinghouses for varieties developed for national or even world markets. More and more, regionally adapted "heirloom" varieties that fail to sell at least 500 packets a year are being crowded out of seed catalogs by newly patented varieties that can do fairly well just about anywhere. According to Kent Whealy, who heads the Seed Savers Exchange, "The garden seeds currently being dropped from the catalogs are the best home garden varieties we will ever see."

As an intensive gardener looking for top yields, you should seek out plant materials developed for your area, or at least field-tested there, by seedsmen specializing in regional selections. Companies like Johnny's Selected Seeds (New England), Stokes Seeds (Canada and northern United States), Harris Moran (northern states), Hastings (South), and Gurney Seed and Nursery (Midwest and Plains states) do their own breeding and field trials, evaluating and selecting new varieties on the basis of how well they do along a certain latitudinal or regional line.

In addition to emphasizing these locally adapted varieties and telling regional gardeners in detail how to grow them, the catalogs of these regionally oriented seed houses also are more likely to spell out how to adapt varieties sold nationwide to their special area.

Help in tracking down heirloom varieties for your area also is available from a host of small seed suppliers who painstakingly collect these rarities. An extended list of such "traditional" vegetable seed companies has been published in the Graham Center Seed and Nursery Directory, available from The Rural Advancement Fund, P.O. Box 1029, Pittsboro, NC 27312 for $2. Or you can obtain seeds from other gardeners via the Seed Savers Exchange, 203 Rural Avenue, Decorah, IA 52101.

In chapter 9, where the six major types of growing conditions in North America are discussed, you'll find a generous sampling of varieties well suited to the rigors of each area. Use these suggested varieties to regionalize your garden—and make better yields more likely.

Top-Yielding Fruits for Small Spaces

Should fruits other than melons be included in your intensive garden plan? Maybe so, maybe not. Gardeners committed to organic culture who hanker to grow perennial fruits must come to grips early on with the problem of pest and disease control. The importance of choosing disease-resistant fruits and varieties—and making sure plant material is disease-free when purchased—can hardly be overstated. If you're realistic, you'll bypass even the most tempting spacesaving varieties in favor of a smaller number of larger ones bred to resist or tolerate fungus and insect diseases. (Recover space lost by this primary precaution by choosing self-pollinating varieties; then you won't need to plant two varieties of each fruit to assure good yields.)

As an intensive organic gardener, you also should be especially careful to match fruits to their growing conditions. South Carolinians are well advised to choose blueberries rather than peaches because of persistent insect and disease pests there. And what benefit is to be gained if an intensive gardener in the southeastern United States or northwestern California plants even the most high-yielding of miniature apricots? The fact is, apricots simply do not do well in those places.

Similarly, southern gardeners should stay with apples and cherries bred to require few hours of winter chilling. And northerners who don't live where winters are tempered by large bodies of water had better forgo peaches, for even varieties bred farther North will often fail under such conditions.

Tree Fruits

All that said, it's also true that breeding breakthroughs are producing a spate of compact, heavy-yielding fruits that may be worth the gamble. This is particularly true of tree fruits, for the new genetically dwarfed apples, peaches, apricots, nectarines, plums, cherries, and figs usually reach just 4 to 8 feet above the ground, can be planted 6 feet or less apart (that's nine or more in a 12 by 12-foot plot!) and yield up to a bushel of full-sized fruits yearly when mature.

Genetic dwarfs—often called miniatures or extra-dwarfs in catalogs—are always self-fertile and start yielding a few pounds of fruit the year after setting out. Like vegetables, these petite trees benefit from being interplanted with each other, apple next to cherry, apricot next to peach, and so on. A varied environment invites insect-eating predators and fights the spread of viruses

Fruit in the High-Yield Garden: Select dwarf fruit trees that save space and come into bearing sooner than full-size ones. A bed full of strawberries will yield heavily and quickly in a relatively small space. Brambles are less space efficient than strawberries but can share space with vegetables in beds.

that sometimes occurs when fruits of the same species make root contact.

Like the breeding of spacesaving vegetables, the development of small fruit varieties is an active field of research. Early genetic dwarfs like the BONANZA peach have long been surpassed by new strains offering fruits of vastly improved taste and texture. Less hardy than grafted dwarf fruits, the genetic types do best in the South and West and are likely to survive in the North only up to hardiness zone 5, although some can be grown successfully as far north as zone 4 if they are planted in movable tubs and given winter protection in a garage.

Some genetic dwarfs are spur types developed from a mutant branch of a standard tree. They are characterized by short, fruit-bearing spurs rather than long and leafy branches. Although often not as small as other genetic dwarfs, spur types are smaller and slower growing than standard trees and produce larger crops earlier in their lives. Stark Brothers offers a line of "Stark-spur" apples from 8 to 10 feet tall at maturity for zones 4 through 7. Some nurseries, like Bountiful Ridge, feature spur apple varieties for zones 4 to 6 grafted on the very dwarf M27 interstem. These trees bear in their second year, can be kept under 6 feet, produce two bushels of apples yearly, and can be planted 5 feet apart in rows spaced 10 feet apart.

Though not a spur type, the scab, blight, mildew, and apple blotch-resistant PRIMA (73) apple (for zones 5 to 8) also is available in this miniature form. Another multi-disease-resistant apple—the hardy, highly productive LIBERTY—is offered as a larger semidwarf by Kelly Brothers, where it has been the best-selling variety since its introduction in 1980. Bountiful Ridge has the early-ripening, fireblight, blight, mildew, and apple blotch-resistant semidwarf pear MOONGLOW (for zones 5 to 7).

Such semidwarfs make sense for gardeners who put disease protection first. And the so-called "5-in-1" semidwarfs can function as real space-savers, for they provide several kinds of apples or pears ripening at different times on one self-pollinating tree just 10 to 15 feet high (9, 25, 74).

If you choose one of the larger dwarfs, it's still possible to save space by planting three trees in one hole and pruning them as one. This can be done with apples and pears or with any deciduous fruit trees having an open form. Avoid using genetic dwarf peaches and nectarines since they tend to have dense growth. You can also compensate for larger fruit trees by making them the

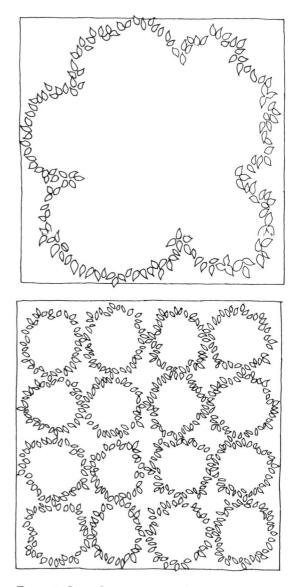

Dramatic Space Savings: You can fit 16 dwarf fruit trees in the same space it takes to grow one standard-size tree.

basis of a bilevel arrangement featuring early planted, fast-maturing vegetables on ground level.

Whatever the size of the fruit trees you choose,

you'll want to shorten the delay until bearing by planting in fall, for trees planted then often begin producing a year before those set out in spring. According to William Kurle of the North American Fruit Explorers, apple growers who want early yields should cut back trees severely at planting time so they form low heads, for such trees begin bearing before others.

If your gardening space is quite limited, you might do well to consider berry vines or bushes before fruit trees. These require less space, yield more fruit earlier, and are usually far less troubled by insects and diseases than are tree fruits. More easily trained and confined than the smallest dwarf trees, berries don't cast shadows or interfere with head space like trees, and a wide row of them can be made to harmonize readily with your vegetable beds and landscape.

Strawberries

The obvious first choice among nontree fruits is the strawberry, for no fruit is easier to grow and yields more heavily or more quickly in less space. John Jeavons reports yields of up to 30 to 40 gallons per 100 square feet when one-year-old plants are set on 12-inch centers and grown under intensive culture. Delightfully thorn and pest-free, strawberries need no trellis or other support as do many other small fruits, and they are ideally suited to raised bed culture. This is especially true when they're grown in the eastern United States where winters are not too severe on heavier, slow-to-drain soils. Look for disease-resistant high-yielding varieties suited to your area. The top everbearer for zones 6 through 8 is OZARK BEAUTY, which resists leaf spot and leaf scorch and yielded over 12,000 quarts per acre in tests at Iowa State

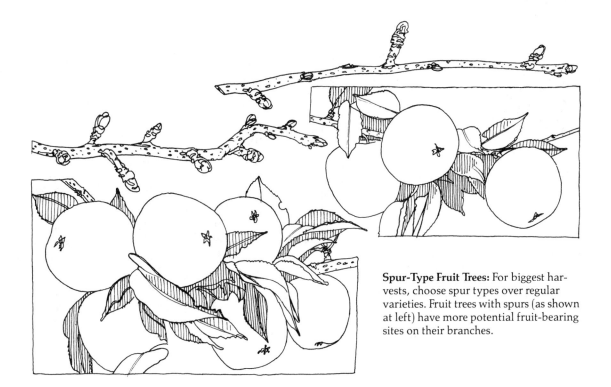

Spur-Type Fruit Trees: For biggest harvests, choose spur types over regular varieties. Fruit trees with spurs (as shown at left) have more potential fruit-bearing sites on their branches.

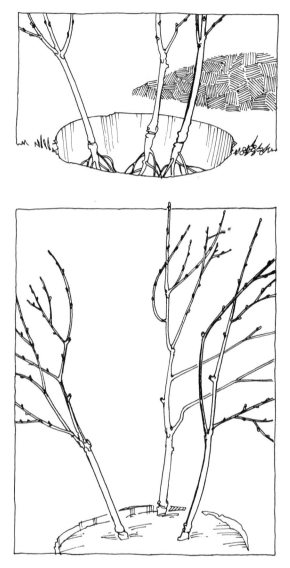

Three-in-One Planting: This space-saving scheme treats three dwarf trees as if they were one. For best results, use trees with similar rootstocks and topgrowth. Dig a hole large enough to allow the trees to be set 1 foot apart. Slant the trees toward the outside of the hole. To prune, treat all three trees as one and remove branches as needed to keep the center open.

University. Or consider the very productive and everbearing runnerless bush strawberry BORDU-RELLA (both available from 25).

Blueberries

A productive bush fruit for small spaces is the blueberry. Mature bushes yield up to 15 quarts of fruit from a 4-foot circle. Moreover, breeders are steadily shrinking the size and extending the growing range of blueberry bushes, making them ever more feasible for gardeners with little space. Just 20 to 24 inches tall, the NORTHBLUE (20) lowbush-highbush cross yields 3 to 5 pounds, and survives cold down to −30°F. NORTHSKY (20) is even hardier and only 18 inches high. Also hardy in the North, the self-fertile TOPHAT grows 2 feet tall (25).

Some of the best-yielding, heat-tolerant rabbiteye blueberries suited to the South (north of Florida) and central California are TIFBLUE and the disease-tolerant PREMIERE. There are also new tetraploid blueberry hybrids that yield greatly improved fruits clear to the south of Florida. Varieties include CLIMAX, SOUTHLAND, and WOODARD (all available from 28 and 78).

Brambles

Bramble fruits, most notably raspberries, are less space thrifty relative to yield and are often plagued by viral and bacterial diseases that can't be controlled. You can count on them to produce only about 5 pints per plant at best. If you grow brambles, choose unusually disease-resistant hybrids like the ROYALTY raspberry (9, 48) and heavier-yielding large-fruited strains such as the thornless blackberry BLACK SATIN THORNFREE (25). For tips on how to make brambles space efficient and to fit them into beds, see Accommodating Perennials in chapter 2.

FLOWERS FOR THE HIGH-YIELD GARDEN

The buds, blossoms, or leaves of plants valued for their beauty can nourish the body as well as the soul.

Some edible flowers can also contribute to garden yields by repelling pests or diseases or by attracting bees for better pollination of fruit-setting plants. Such multipurpose flowers make superb borders or interplantings for the high-yield garden. Here is a brief sampling of some useful and versatile edible flowers that can add both eye appeal and food value to your garden beds.

Borage Boasting bright blue (and sometimes pink) star-shaped flowers, borage is often planted to lure bees to enhance fruit-set on tomatoes, winter squash, strawberries, and other plants needing pollination in mid and late summer. You can candy the edible flowers of borage for decorating cakes and cookies or use fresh flowers to garnish summer drinks.

Edible Flowers: Besides perking up garden beds, the flowers and sometimes the leaves of (left to right) nasturtiums, borage, and marigolds can be used in the kitchen.

Borage leaves have the flavor of cucumbers and are a pleasant addition to salads and soups and add a unique taste to iced tea and fruit drinks such as cider, punch, and lemonade. This novel green also can be enjoyed cooked like spinach. You can peel the stalk of the plant and cut it into cucumberlike chunks to add crunch to salads. Borage prefers moist, fairly rich soil and is a good companion to tomatoes, squash, and strawberries. Some gardeners find that it deters tomato worms and improves the growth and flavor of tomatoes and squash. Borage is also believed to strengthen the resistance of plants around it to insects and disease.

Marigold The radiant red and orange flowers of this popular ornamental can contribute splashes of color and pungent flavor to rice, soups, and stews while the plants left behind protect the vegetable harvest. French marigolds (*Tagetes patula*) and African marigolds (*T. erecta*) have been proved potent natural nematode fighters and are also believed to ward off Mexican bean beetles and other insects. One of the stars of companion planting, marigolds are recommended for use throughout the garden but are especially helpful near beans, corn, cucumbers, eggplants, potatoes, pumpkins, squashes, and tomatoes.

Nasturtium The low, compact dwarf varieties of the easy-to-please, cheerful nasturtium can be put to a host of uses. Thriving in average well-drained soil or even in dry problem areas, nasturtiums are available in a rainbow of colors. The flowers make a spectacular garnish for salads and also can be minced and added to butter or other spreads. Tangy like watercress, the rounded leaves add a peppery flavor to soups and salads and make a fine substitute for lettuce in sandwiches. You can even pickle the tender young seed pods in vinegar like capers. Another hardworking companion plant, nasturtiums are thought to benefit radishes, cabbage, cucurbits, and fruit trees. The flowers attract aphids so the insects can be handpicked efficiently, and they repel whiteflies, squash bugs, and striped cucumber beetles. Gardeners often find that nasturtiums improve neighboring crops' growth and flavor.

Herbs in the High-Yield Garden

Most of the more popular cooking herbs are modest-sized plants, and those that are abundant producers with a variety of culinary uses can earn their way in an intensive garden that values diversity of production. Try companion-planting annual herbs with vegetables to help repel pests and growing tender or hardy perennials capable of wintering over in your climate in their own raised bed.

According to commercial growers, herbs grown only for their leaves are highly compatible with each other, so they can share space in a bed with no ill effects. Beware, however, of spacing perennials too closely, for more invasive types like French tarragon and mint can stunt slow-growing neighbors like thyme. Planting herbs, both annuals and perennials, in raised beds guarantees the superb drainage they crave. In fact, the key to wintering over perennial herbs successfully in the North hinges on raised beds and superior drainage, along with protection from heavy spring rains and a soil with a neutral pH.

Bedded Herbs: Raised beds provide the excellent drainage herbs need for good growth. To make tending herbs easier, give perennials their own bed (shown on left) apart from the annuals (right) that will be replanted every season.

Garden varieties specialist George B. Park, Jr., predicts that within the next five or ten years home growers will be able to choose from among many new herb varieties showing greater compactness and even earlier yields. In the meantime, high-yield gardeners can concentrate on herb species and varieties professional growers have found to be most versatile in their culinary uses and most productive per square foot. Some of these are featured in the box The Twelve Most Versatile and Productive Herbs on the next page.

Controlling Herbs in Close Quarters: In intensive gardening it can be a good idea to control the size and spread of faster-growing herbs like mint and tarragon. Confine them in sunken chimney tiles or large coffee cans with holes cut in the bottom. Dig a hole to bury the tile or can, set the herb plant inside, and fill with soil.

THE TWELVE MOST VERSATILE AND PRODUCTIVE HERBS

With the help of herb nurseries all over the country we've put together a list of the most versatile and productive herbs you can grow. Despite the geographic distance separating the participants in our informal survey, there was a surprising unanimity of response when we asked them to choose the 10 herbs they would most recommend to intensive gardeners in their part of the country. In fact, the same 10 herbs appeared on half or more of the lists submitted. Here, then, are the top 12 scorers, grouped in the order of their popularity with our cross section of growers.

FIRST GROUP

Basil

This tremendously productive annual imparts a unique flavor to sauces, stuffings, soups, salads, and meat dishes. Good bets are the compact 18-inch-high BUSH BASIL and the larger-leaved LETTUCE LEAF, which is great for drying. Other recommended varieties are FESTIVAL SWEETS, DARK OPAL, and LEMON, which is strongly favored by The Liberty Herb Farm in Maine, because "it makes wonderful herb vinegar and is excellent with fish and salad." BASIL SPICY GLOBE (48) is a spacesaver.

Oregano

The most frequently mentioned variety of this tomato-mate and meat stew and salad-enhancing herb is the tender evergreen GREEK form, which grows to 18 inches or more. According to Carol Hildebrand of Casa Yerba in Oregon, GREEK is best for long-cooked dishes, while the 16-inch-high ITALIAN oregano excels in quickly pepared soups and salad dressings.

Thyme

Thyme is superb mixed with soft cheeses and as a seasoning in stuffing, salad dressings, gravies and sauces, and egg and meat dishes. Marilyn Hempstead of Fox Hill Farm in Michigan reports that both ENGLISH and LEMON thyme "offer a big return for the space." The ABC Herb Nursery in Missouri recommends the "really high-yielding" ST. LOUIS thyme.

SECOND GROUP

Chives

This grassy, bunching, 12 to 18-inch-high perennial member of the onion family is endlessly useful as a flavoring agent in sauces, soups, and salads of all kinds. Many herb growers also recommend garlic chives, which combine the flavor of mild garlic and chives.

French sorrel

An extremely hardy perennial, French sorrel grows 2 to 3 feet high. Its tart green leaves are high in vitamin C and make a tangy addition to salads or are tasty cooked together with other greens like spinach or cabbage. This herb also is the star of a famous French soup.

Unusually prolific and adaptable, this 2 to 2¼-foot-high self-renewing perennial is tasty as a solo tea or added to tea and other beverages. It also contributes a pleasant subtlety to vegetable and fruit salads. Lemon balm attracts bees for better pollination of other garden plants.

Though not as sweet as the curly form, flat-leaved parsley is recommended by Kent Taylor of Taylor's Herb Gardens in California and by Anna Smith of Country Herbs in Massachusetts, who cited its "tremendous yield" and suitability for most cooking purposes.

A perennial herb that blends well with eggs, soups, gravies, stuffings, fish, and meats, sage comes in several varieties, some quite ornamental. The yard-high HOLT'S MAMMOTH is favored by one southern herb farm because it is fast growing and doesn't die back. But a better choice in intensive gardens might be DWARF SAGE—a 12-inch-high form that is less likely to be winter-killed in northern areas.

The French form of this anise-flavored, 2½-foot-tall perennial is the most superior. According to Fairman Jayne of The Sandy Mush Herb Nursery in North Carolina, French tarragon loses no flavor "even when grown under very intensive conditions." Much more flavorful fresh than dried, this herb makes a delightful vinegar and is superb in tartar and other white sauces, and with fish, cheese, eggs, and cauliflower.

THIRD GROUP

Hardy and self-seeding, this fernlike annual attracts honeybees when allowed to mature to 2 or 3 feet. Dill needs just 8-inch spacing on all sides. If harvested young, it can be interplanted with cabbage, carrots, cucumbers, lettuce, and onions. Dillweed is a tasty addition to cheese or tofu dips, soups, salads, and creamed entrées. It's also a staple in making vinegars and pickles.

Upright forms of this elegant tender perennial are often recommended, but North Carolina grower Fairman Jayne says the most productive variety for small spaces is the foot-long creeping HUNTINGTON CARPET rosemary. North of Virginia, rosemary must be protected over the winter or taken indoors. This very decorative herb makes an unforgettable accompaniment to meat and poultry and is also memorable in soups, stuffings, gravies, sauces, and salad dressings.

The compact, 1½-foot-high annual SUMMER variety of this spicy plant was preferred by all but one of the growers who included it on their lists. Once called "poor man's pepper," savory's small, zingy leaves can be used to perk up soups, salads, sauces, or sandwiches.

4 *Planting and Caring for the High-Yield Garden*

Comparing high-yield intensive gardening to ordinary gardening is like comparing tournament chess to casual Sunday afternoon checkers. The real difference comes in the degree of complexity. Intensive gardeners are always thinking two or three moves ahead of themselves. Bed rotation can require planning up to several years in advance, but even during one season, the sequence from sowing to harvesting of a single crop, and the subsequent use of that crop's space by a second planting, will demand able timing and fast decision making. (For assistance in these areas, see chapter 5.)

Timing will be more finely tuned and decisions wiser if all the peripheral aspects of gardening are set in order early. You may be gardening in rectangles, but the last thing you need is to have to stop and return to square one to reexamine the basics.

Size and Site

It all begins, of course, with the selection of a site and a size for your garden. Start small, and you will learn the skills of intensive gardening quickly. Experience, knowledge, and confidence, like vegetables, grow most productively in small spaces where success can be cultivated intensively.

If your first raised beds are to be on newly broken land, choose a spot with full sunlight, a southern exposure, and good air drainage. A gentle south-facing slope is ideal. Check the site for signs of early and late frost. If you find you have chosen a frost pocket, consider erecting a barrier to prevent cold air from settling in your garden. It can be in the form of a slatted fence, a hedge, or even a row of hay bales on the north, or windward, side of the plot. If the land is flat, make sure no rain puddles on it. Puddles mean poor drainage, possibly due to a rock or clay subsoil.

Look for large weeds or thick stands of grass, which indicate good soil. Starting with rich, well-balanced soil will save you some of the time it takes to build soil to your plants' requirements. Within the prospective plot, look for microclimates. Mark out the sunniest, highest, most protected area for the bed that will hold your first plantings.

Especially if you are just beginning to garden intensively, it's wise to locate the beds as close to your home as is practical. You'll no doubt be spending a lot of time out there (as much out of pleasure as by necessity), and you'll appreciate being able to reach the beds quickly and effortlessly. The gardener is, after all, the most essential ingredient of the intensive garden.

When you hear that the raised bed garden is labor intensive, don't think that means you'll be spending hours at hard labor after the initial digging. What it does mean is that you'll have to be available for frequent inspections, timely troubleshooting, and general surveillance. Raised bed gardening is a little like bread baking in its demands. The total labor is slight, but the job requires commitment if the results are to be spectacular. A daily visit of less than half an hour may serve to keep weeds and visiting pests in check, to prevent drought damage, and, most important, to bring in a harvest of perfect ripeness.

Basic Needs: Water and Fertilizer

In the early stages, before a vegetable leaf canopy has been established, a garden of intensive beds may require more water than a row garden of the same size. You'll save yourself a lot of effort by locating intensive beds near a water source. The watering device can be as simple as a bucket that is carried from a nearby tap or as complex as a subsoil, automatically timed drip irrigation system. A host of hoses, sprinklers, and simple drip systems lie between the two extremes. Have your watering system well thought out before you set up your beds. Alternative systems are discussed later under Watering.

In the intensive garden with its dense spacing, you'll be asking a lot of the soil. If you've gardened at all, you know that soil rewards you in direct proportion to how you treat it. It isn't a mine from which to remove riches; it's a living substance that must receive in order to give. With the loss of 50 percent or more of its original organic matter, soil becomes more and more dense and its potential for growing good yields is correspondingly decreased.

The material you return to your soil should be organic fertilizer, like homemade compost. However many paths you lay in your garden, one of the most traveled of them all should be the path from the compost pile to the beds. Keep it short and wide. You'll be carting plant residues and weeds from the garden to the compost pile, but in the opposite direction will flow the stuff of life for your gardening beds. Early in the spring will come the heaviest loads, but throughout the season the need for compost continues.

Obtaining Compost Materials Whatever green material comes from the garden in the form of tough outer leaves, young weeds that haven't developed seeds yet, disease-free plants past bearing, stalks, and, of course, the bean ends, lima pods, corncobs, and parings that make up a gardener's garbage are the beginnings of a compost pile. Some gardeners even grow their own material specifically for composting (see chapter 1). In addition, however, outside sources of composting materials will generally be required by most raised bed gardeners.

You'll have to learn when these materials will become available, where to find them, and how to bring them to your compost "kitchen." If compost is to be available when the beds are dug, either it must have been stockpiled the previous season, or it must be made by the quick method discussed in chapter 1 under Compost. For ideas on where to find free or inexpensive compost materials, see the chart on page 19. To collect many of these materials in practical quantity, you will need to own, borrow, or rent a truck. In planning your garden layout, be sure to provide truck access to the compost area. Budget the time for material delivery and for compost making.

Once you start making arrangements for outside materials, your own time will not be the only schedule you will have to consider. Pick-up arrangements must be worked out with farmers, manufacturers, and stable owners. Straw, for example, may cost you less when bought at the time of wheat or oat harvest, but you must be alert to harvest times. Road crews can sometimes be persuaded to dump leaves or wood chips they have gathered in their work, but the dumping will seldom be done if it costs much crew time.

The compost-making and mulch storage areas of your garden complex should be efficiently arranged and well organized. For rapid compost making, you will have to sort materials into categories. This calls for room for several piles and, if possible, at least two bins. Have these available before the season begins. Also make sure a water source reaches the compost pile. Slow composting can continue through the winter if you arrange a storage area for dry material like ground-up leaves or aged sawdust that you can use to cover layers of household garbage. Purchased amendments like soybean meal or greensand, whether used in compost or directly as fertilizers, should also be given safe, dry storage.

Equipment Needs

Some bed gardeners use rotary tillers and plows more commonly associated with conventional row gardens. There are some other tools and devices of special use to the intensive gardener. Among hand tools, the most useful will be shovels, forks, spades, hoes (especially narrow, shallow-bladed, and triangular ones), back-saving sub-soil loosening forks, rakes, trowels, and bulb planters or dibbles. In working out the precise spacing of plants and seeds, measuring rods or spacing devices are helpful. (These are discussed in more detail later under How to Space Plants and Seeds.)

The intensive gardener strives to keep harvests going as long as possible by stretching the season in both directions. The second part of this book is devoted to simple and complex frames, bed covers, tunnels, and individual protective devices that can keep plants producing from earliest spring into, and sometimes through, winter. The larger and most effective of these are permanently installed over a raised bed, either in the garden or near the house. The smaller devices, designed to protect individual plants or groups of plants, are handy for seasonal use and adapt well to raised beds, particularly those contained in wooden frames. They will, however, require convenient, nearby storage when not in use. Any garden plan should include a storage area for season-extending devices and tools—a shed, basement, or an accessible closet or corner of a garage, for example. Rigid devices can be hung on hooks or set on racks, while several types of tunnels and cloches can be disassembled for flat storage. Efficient garden planning involves matching protective devices to the storage facilities available for them.

Seedling Space

The first seedlings to go into the beds in spring will have been started inside under growing lights in a basement, or an enclosed and heated porch, on a window sill, or in a greenhouse if you're fortunate enough to have one. Insulated cold frames are also excellent places to start seedlings. As the season progresses, new flats of plants growing toward transplant size can spend a longer portion of their lives outdoors, as part of the hardening-off process. Many gardeners find it convenient to keep flats of plants awaiting transplanting close to the garden, where seedlings can be given attention at the same time garden plants are being cared for. Tiers of shelves on one side of a garden shed or garage, plant benches, or an old picnic table set next to the garden will make for efficient timing of transplanting, because they assure that the next move in the gardening chess game is never far from

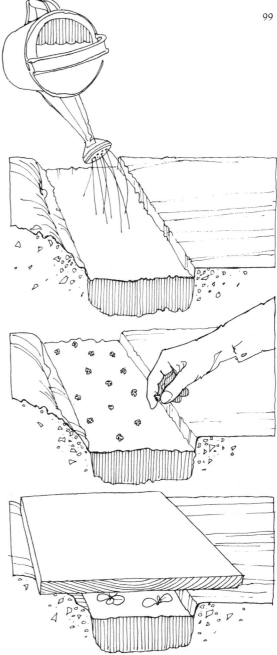

Make Room for Seedlings: Shelves built onto the outside of a shed or garage make a handy waiting area for seedlings ready to be moved to the garden.

mind. Remember that seedling plants need special care and should be given shade, ample water, and protection from garden insects.

As an alternative to shelves or a table of seedling flats, many gardeners devote one of a series of small raised beds to use as a seedling nursery. Soil in this bed is prepared with special attention, raked or sifted to great fineness, and lightened with peat moss or vermiculite. Either the bed is situated where it receives shade in the afternoon, or it is fitted with a cloth or lath cover.

If you wish to keep a seedling bed for use throughout the season, consider converting one bed to an insulated cold frame. If an electrical outlet is nearby, you can also install a heating cable and do all your seed starting in the covered bed, even when snow covers the rest of the ground.

Summer Seed Germinating: To get seeds to sprout in the heat of summer, dig a 6-inch trench. Fill it to 1 inch from the top with seed-starting medium. Wet the trench thoroughly, then sow seeds. Cover the trench with a board that rests on the edges and doesn't press down on the planted row. Check daily until seedlings appear, and water when the soil is dry. Once seedlings are up, remove the board and shade the plants with a screen or fabric "roof."

A seedling nursery of 2 by 4 feet, plus a smaller germinating area, will be sufficient for most gardens. The space may be located at one end of a larger bed. Having the nursery close to the other beds will allow you to locate candidates for transfer to more permanent plantings quickly whenever a space becomes open through harvest.

Nursery beds are most useful in replenishing salad plantings that mature quickly and require frequent replacement throughout the season. A skillful intensive gardener always has a full salad bed and a nursery bed full of younger replacement greens ready to move into it when they are needed. Try not to delay moving larger vegetables into their permanent beds. According to research done at the Virginia Truck and Ornamental Research Station in Virginia Beach, Virginia, plants that have been held back in starting media or have been overhardened often fail to begin growth quickly after they are moved.

Determining Your Seed and Plant Needs

Gardening is ultimately a personal matter. To tell a person what and how much to grow without first knowing all about the person's food preferences, family size, appetite, nutritional requirements, available time, gardening space, storage and processing facilities, budget, degree of ambition, and general temperament is at least as much of an affront as to give advice on what to read or how to dress without first becoming acquainted with a person.

On the other hand, to a gardener unaccustomed to intensive practice, and perhaps skeptical of claims to high yields made by intensive proponents, decisions about how much seed to order can be intimidating. What's more, seeds must often be ordered long before the season begins and without the instruction of experience. In gardening, as in other activities, we must learn from the experience of other people before we

accumulate our own. Here, then, is the system one gardener used to determine how much food his family needed and how many plants and how much space it would take to provide that food.

A Family Food Inventory

The starting point in this system is to establish a family food inventory. This helps you decide how much of each vegetable to raise based on what you actually need. There's only one way to be sure of what your family eats, and that's to keep a two-week food diary. Guesswork can inflate or underestimate your family's food consumption.

Follow the example set by the gardener who devised this system and post a piece of paper on front of the refrigerator. Mark it off into 14 boxes, each labeled with a date. Each day record every vegetable the family eats (if you grow fruit, keep track of the amount of fruit consumed). List the vegetables by name and estimate as closely as possible how much is eaten for a given meal.

At the end of the two weeks, you're ready to move on to the next phase, organizing the information from the inventory. List all the vegetables in a vertical column from A to Z. Call that column "Vegetables We Eat." Label the next column "What to Grow" and the third "What to Buy."

In the first column, write in the total amount of each vegetable your family ate for the two weeks. Then estimate, based on the eating habits of your family, how much of each you would consume in a year. (Ask yourself questions like these: Do you eat a salad every day, cauliflower once a week, carrots three times a week, cabbage once a month?) Based on your season length and garden space available, figure out how much of that yearly amount you can realistically grow yourself. That is noted in the "What to Grow" column. The balance that won't come from your garden should fill the third column.

Once you've reached this point, you'll need to translate those figures into numbers that relate directly to the garden and seed order forms—how much space each crop will take and how

SAMPLE FAMILY FOOD INVENTORY

Vegetable	Amount We Eat		What to Grow	What to Buy
	TWO WEEKS	YEAR		
Asparagus	24 spears	624 spears	—	All
Beans (snap)	3 lb.	72 lb.	288 plants	—
Beets	2	52	52 plants	—
Broccoli	1 lb.	26 lb.	36 plants	—
Cauliflower	1 head	12 heads	8 plants	4 heads
Corn	20 ears	120 ears (3 months)	—	120 ears
Lettuce	2 heads	112 heads	84 plants	28 heads
Melons	2	12 (3 months)	6 plants	—
Onions	6	156	78 plants	78 onions
Peppers	2	70	3 plants	34 peppers
Tomatoes	4	104 (fresh use, 3 months)	3 plants	—

many plants you'll need to produce the desired amounts. To do those calculations you'll need to know: the total amount of each vegetable you're seeking to raise; how much an individual plant yields (see the chart, What One Plant Will Yield); and the spacings you'll be using in the garden.

To give you an example of how this is done, here's the reasoning the gardener who developed this system used for a year-round supply of snap beans. He figured that his family used 6 pounds of beans a month. Thirty-six plants will produce that amount. Spaced 4 inches apart they'll occupy a 2 by 2-foot area. Three plantings a season will yield a total of 18 pounds of snap beans. To increase the total quantity to 72 pounds (6 pounds a month for a year), of which 54 pounds would be frozen, the bean plot would need to be enlarged to 4 by 4 feet. Each of the three plantings would include 144 plants. This gardener might also have planted one triple-sized bed designated for freezing and kept smaller plantings for fresh eating.

If space is tight you might want to divide your inventory into two categories: staple crops like potatoes, onions, peas, and beans, and seasonal favorites like corn and cantaloupes. Whenever you're cramped for space opt for a staple over a seasonal crop, which could be purchased fresh at a farmers' market or roadside stand.

Other Ways of Assessing Food Needs

This model, with its finely tuned relationship between production and use is not, however, a suitable model for all families. The first thing to consider in making your own projection of need is what vegetables you really like to eat. Even a casual inventory, less thorough than the one described above, will give you a notion of what vegetables are actually making their way to your table, either directly or from storage.

Also consider which vegetables you can store most easily. Potatoes, onions, carrots, and rutabagas require no special processing before storing. Kale, Brussels sprouts, and parsnips can be ground stored or picked under mulch in the garden, but tomatoes, corn, spinach, peas, beans, broccoli, and many others will require additional labor

WHAT ONE PLANT WILL YIELD

Knowing how many pounds of peas that one plant, or seed, will produce or how many cucumbers to expect from one vine is invaluable when you're planning your garden. For vegetables that yield once per plant, like carrots and onions, the figuring is easy. But what about all those that yield steadily over weeks? Here is a list of vegetables and the yield you can expect from one plant of each.

One Plant	Produces		How Often
	QUANTITY	WEIGHT (LB.)	
Asparagus	1 spear	$1/12$	per week for 4 weeks
Beans (lima)	—	$1/25$	per week
Beans (snap)	—	$1/10$	per week for 2 weeks
Broccoli	—	$2/3$	main head plus $1/3$ lb. per season
Brussels sprouts	100 sprouts	3	per season
Cantaloupes	2 cantaloupes	2	per season
Cucumbers	2 cucumbers	1	per week
Eggplants	1 eggplant	$1/2$	per week
Peas	—	$1/16$	per week for 4 weeks
Peppers	1 pepper	$1/4$	per week
Potatoes	—	$2\frac{3}{4}$	per season
Squash (summer)	3 squash	1	per week
Squash (winter)	1 squash	1	per season
Sweet potatoes	—	1	per season
Tomatoes	3 tomatoes	1	per week

and equipment before you can depend on a year-round supply.

Some families will happily feast on fresh-picked asparagus twice a day for the whole month of May, moving on to a pea-dominated diet in June, while others, perhaps spoiled by supermarket variety, tire of one taste quickly. For those who binge on single vegetables at their peak, a two-week inventory will be of little use, if it is made in the heart of a specific ripening season. The gardener who developed it made his inventory in November, a time of year when more produce is usually coming to the table from the market, storage, and cold frames than from the main beds.

If you start small—many experts recommend planting no more than 750 square feet for the first intensive garden—you may wish to specialize with a raised bed or two of salad and soup crops like lettuce, carrots, spinach, onions, and turnips. A salad bed will develop a sense of discipline and hone your skills of continuous harvest production. In the second season, you can double the space and add five or six crops intended for storage or staple eating—beans, peas, potatoes, squash, limas, and onions, for example. Remember that among the principal practices of intensive gardening are keeping the season going for as long as possible and supplying the table at a steady rate. Intensive gardeners, therefore, need less storage food because they will be producing more fresh food. Fresh is always best.

If you do decide to grow crops for storage and preserving, once again it pays to calculate your needs. The very best guide, of course, is experience. One normal year of management by estimate will tell you in certain terms just what is left over and what you ran out of. All the evidence you need will be there in empty shelves or in the still-full freezer. The following season you can adjust your plantings to meet your newly discovered needs.

If your goal is not to match your vegetable production to your consumption, but rather to grow the maximum amount that will fit into a bed you have room for and are certain you can take care of, the following formula may be helpful:

$$\frac{L \times W}{D^2} = P$$

This will tell you the number of plants in a rectangular raised bed (P) when L equals the length of the bed (in inches), W is the width of the raised bed (in inches), and D equals the distance between plants (in inches).

Let's say your raised bed is 20 feet long and 4 feet wide and you'll be growing a mix of salad greens that can be spaced 6 inches apart. Following the formula you multiply 240 inches by 48 inches and divide by 36 inches. The answer tells you that you'll need 320 plants to fill that bed.

Of Time and the Garden

How much time does an intensive garden require? That depends on the size of the beds and their

---

GUIDE TO ORDERING SEED AMOUNTS

Do you have any idea how many seeds you get in a packet? And do you know how that number relates to the garden space you intend to plant? Most gardeners aren't clear on that relationship, and this uncertainty can make filling out seed order forms an exercise in creative guesswork. Seed catalogs offer varying degrees of assistance. The most helpful tell you how many ounces of seed a packet contains, how many plants a packet produces, and how many feet of row that fills. Other catalogs offer slightly less complete information, and some provide no help at all.

When you're in a quandary over how much seed you need to order, refer to the following listing of vegetables for some guidance. It should help you avoid ordering three times as much turnip seed as you really need or having to scramble and reorder snap beans for a midseason succession planting.

Vegetable	How Many Feet of Row Will One Packet Plant?
Asparagus	One packet produces 60 roots; need 15–20 roots to plant 25-ft. row.
Beans	
Fava	2-oz. packet contains 35–40 seeds, enough to plant a 20-ft. row.
Lima (bush)	2-oz. packet contains 115–130 of small-seeded variety, 45–50 of large-seeded variety; large-seeded packet will sow 15-ft. row, small-seeded packet will sow longer row.
Lima (pole)	One packet will plant 10 poles or 10-ft. row.
Snap (bush)	2-oz. packet contains 130–150 seeds, enough to sow 25-ft. row.
Snap (pole)	2-oz. packet contains 100 seeds, enough to sow 16 poles or 25-ft. row.
Soybean	2-oz. packet contains 200–400 seeds; depending on variety, enough to plant 33 to 66-ft. row.
Beets	½-oz. packet contains 600 seeds, enough to sow 50-ft. row.
Broccoli	1½-g. packet contains 375 seeds, enough to sow 30-ft. row; 1-oz. packet produces 2,500–3,500 plants.
Brussels sprouts	1-g. packet contains 250 seeds, enough to plant 25-ft. row; 1-oz. packet produces 2,500–3,000 plants.
Cabbage	see Brussels sprouts

(continued)

GUIDE TO ORDERING SEED AMOUNTS— *Continued*

Vegetable	How Many Feet of Row Will One Packet Plant?
Cantaloupes	4-g. packet contains 140 seeds, enough to transplant 30-ft. row or 12 hills.
Carrots	2-g. packet contains 960 seeds, enough to sow 20-ft. row; 1-oz. packet contains 6,000–9,000 seeds, enough to sow 250–300-ft. row.
Cauliflower	0.75-g. packet contains 225 seeds, enough to transplant 20-ft. row.
Celery	0.5-g. packet contains 900 seeds.
Chinese cabbage	1-g. packet contains 500 seeds, enough to plant 30-ft. row.
Corn	2-oz. packet contains 200 seeds, enough to plant 50–100-ft. row.
Cress, garden	¼-oz. packet contains 250–300 seeds, enough to plant 25-ft. row.
Cucumbers	2.5-g. packet contains 83 seeds, enough to plant 12-ft. row.
Eggplants	0.25-g. packet contains 50 seeds, enough to transplant 100-ft. row.
Garlic	1 lb. of sets plants 20-ft. row.
Kale	2-g. packet contains 500 seeds, enough to sow 45–50 ft. row.
Kohlrabi	2-g. packet contains 400 seeds, enough to sow 40–60-ft. row.
Leeks	2-g. packet contains 750 seeds, enough to transplant 100-ft. row.
Lettuce	
Loosehead	1-g. packet contains 670 seeds, enough to sow 30-ft. row.
Looseleaf	see Loosehead lettuce
Romaine	see Loosehead lettuce
Mustard	1-g. packet contains 500 seeds, enough to plant 30-ft. row.
Onions	
Plants	75 plants will cover 18-ft. row.
Seeds	5-g. packet contains 1,700 seeds, enough to sow 50-ft. row.
Sets	1 lb. will plant 50-ft. row.
Parsley	1.2-g. packet contains 600 seeds, enough to plant 20-ft. row.
Parsnips	4-g. packet contains 1,400 seeds, enough to sow 50-ft. row.
Peas	
Edible-podded	4-oz. packet contains 500 seeds, enough to sow 25-ft. row.
Garden	see Edible-podded peas
Snap	see Edible-podded peas
Peppers	
Hot	0.5-g. packet contains 50 seeds, enough to transplant 30-ft. row.
Sweet	see Hot peppers
Pumpkins	Packet containing 30 seeds will sow 10–15-ft. row.
Radishes	5-g. packet contains 350 seeds, enough to sow 25–30-ft. row.
Rhubarb	8 roots are enough to plant 25-ft. row.
Rutabagas	2-g. packet contains 570 seeds, enough to plant 50-ft. row.
Salsify	¼-oz. packet will sow 25-ft. row.
Spinach	5-g. packet contains enough seed to plant 20-ft. row.
Squash	
Summer	4-g. packet contains 35 seeds, enough to plant 10–15-ft. row.
Winter	Packet containing 30 seeds will plant 10–15-ft. row.
Sunflowers	Packet containing 50–75 seeds will plant 25-ft. row.
Swiss chard	5-g. packet will plant 30-ft. row.
Tomatoes	0.5-g. packet contains 150 seeds; 8 to 10 plants needed to transplant 25-ft. row.
Turnips	2.5-g. packet contains 938 seeds, enough to plant 20-ft. row.
Watermelons	2.5-g. packet contains 50 seeds, enough to transplant 15-ft. row.

number, on the crops to be grown, on season length and other factors of locality, and on the standards, strength, agility, ingenuity, and fastidiousness of the gardener.

The fact is that good gardeners become so engrossed in their work that they seldom keep a clock on themselves, making gardening time estimates hard to come by. There's also the matter of

EASY FIGURING FOR SEEDLING NEEDS

Michigan gardener Mark Rames was looking for a quick and accurate way to figure out how many seedlings he should start or buy for each season's garden. Since all his beds are a standard 9 feet long, he devised a simple chart. He wrote down the common spacings used within the garden rows, and then figured out how many plants it takes to fill a row at each spacing in one of his beds. When his garden plan indicates, for example, two rows of cauliflower in a bed, he looks at the 24-inch spacing on the chart and sees that he needs four plants per row, or eight total for the bed.

If you plant single crop beds and have a standard size for all your beds, you might want to refine this system a bit. List all the plants you grow and the spacing used for each. In a third column translate each spacing into the number of plants it takes to fill a standard-sized bed. (Use the equation on page 103.) In a glance you can see how many seedlings you should start or buy to fill a bed.

whether compost making, path mowing, seed starting, preserving, and the quiet evening tours of satisfaction all gardeners allow themselves should be included in the count.

If your time is as limited as your space, or more so, you've already selected the best possible method of saving time when you decided to opt for raised bed gardening. Automatically, you've eliminated the time that goes into watering, making compost for, cultivating, and weeding all the wasted room that used to lie between the rows. Just the sheer act of walking up and down rows to get from one part of a row garden to another takes more time than you might think. With raised beds, you can stand, or sit, in one place and reach many crops just by extending your arm.

The most time-consuming part of intensive gardening is the first step—digging the beds. Double digging and thorough subsoil loosening, texturizing, and fertilizing can take as much as 12 hours for a 100-square-foot bed. Once established, however, the bed will require a fraction of that time to maintain and renew.

In a nine-month growing season, only about half an hour a day is required to tend a 500-square-foot area. With a shorter growing season, the time will be slightly more per day. Three hours a week is the time estimate given by one garden writer who raises all the vegetables her family eats year-round, yet calls her garden small. A weekend gardener estimates that he spends six hours every other weekend on the average, but points out that hours are long in spring and dwindle to almost nothing by midsummer.

Managing Time

It's not the total amount of time that concerns many people when they set out to garden; it's the distribution of time. Gardening is an activity with prime times. If midsummer heat slows down some vegetable growth, it certainly slows down people, too. No one wants to be forced out into the blazing August sun for heavy labor. And no gardener really needs to be, especially when the garden is small and intensive. In summer, early mornings, late afternoons, and evenings are the prime times for the weeding, watering, transplanting (evening only), and harvesting that need to be done.

If you work outside the home, budget your time carefully so that as much of your after-hours time as possible can be spent in the garden. Daylight-saving time will help you. You may

GARDEN TIME-SAVERS

Here are a few suggestions for shortcuts and ways to plan a more time-economical garden.

• Instead of double digging your beds, use a tiller, a plow, or any of the alternatives presented in chapter 1.

• Mulch all paths and mulch the areas between widely spaced crops after the plants are well established and the ground is warm. This will cut down your watering and weeding time.

• Make your beds small, less than 10 feet long, Steps will be saved.

• Use dependable varieties of a few basic vegetables only. Eliminate those that are inexpensive and readily available at stores.

• Don't grow any crop that does poorly in your climate or requires much attention to grow well. Crops to examine critically for possible elimination are: celery, peas, cauliflower, artichokes, melons, watermelons, peanuts, eggplants, and cucumbers.

• Set aside a small section of a bed to experiment on new vegetables and new varieties before you introduce them into your main beds. This way, you'll feel free to learn what you need to know about growing a new crop without committing yourself to a lot of time in exchange for questionable reward. You can also use the section as a "gambler's bed" for experimenting with very early or late planting times.

• Group your vegetables by a sensible scheme to save walking and labor. Examples of groupings include vegetables requiring frequent pickings, such as beans, leaf lettuce, and peas; vegetables that remain in the bed all season and mature close to the same time, such as tomatoes, peppers, Brussels sprouts, cantaloupes, and eggplants; vegetables for storage, such as onions, potatoes, garlic, and carrots; vegetables requiring frequent watering, such as cucumbers and lettuce; vegetables, like salad crops, that grow quickly and require replacement; vegetables, such as onions, that need frequent weeding; and vegetables, like potatoes and onions, that do well under heavy mulch.

• Install an automatic watering system.

• Choose compact vegetable varieties and ones that bear heavily. Examples include pole beans that will bear longer than bush beans, short-cored cabbages that have more edible inner leaves than other cabbages, and snap peas that require less time than garden peas to prepare. Use vegetables like kale, tomatoes, broccoli, carrots, and cabbage that can be depended upon to produce harvests for a month or more. Growing determinate tomatoes will spare you the time it takes to prune and stake.

• Don't try to process food for storage. Instead, choose crops that store well fresh in or out of the garden and try to extend your season as long as possible.

• Buy your seedlings from a dependable source instead of growing them. Seedling production is time consuming. If you plan ahead, you may find a small greenhouse that will raise seedlings for you to your schedule specifications.

• Hire occasional help in the garden. Summer help is usually easy to find, especially if you look among the young and the retired.

• Agree with a gardening friend to specialize in certain crops and trade vegetables. One person may, for example, have more room for corn than the other has, while the second person may possess a special talent for lettuce growing.

• Cultivate early, before the weeds become established. Early hoeing or raking up of weeds will often prevent future emergence.

• Don't be too finicky about small weeds once your plants are large and strong enough to withstand the competition.

• Concentrate on having something growing for as many months as possible, instead of trying to produce large quantities.

---

have to work out understandings with those you live with, sharing responsibilities of child care, or food preparation at other times, to keep your evenings free. Almost certainly, you will have to change your pattern of television viewing in early evening. Perhaps you will find the dishes can be left in the sink and washed after dark.

You'll make matters easier for yourself if you plan ahead. Winter months can be used, for example, to freeze healthy versions of prepackaged meals for easy summer preparation.

The weekend gardener will soon distinguish major chores requiring weekends from those chores that can be squeezed into the mornings and evenings of a five-day work schedule. Some vegetables, for example, demand almost daily picking at the height of their season. These include peas, beans, asparagus, and zucchini. Others will wait for the weekend with no loss in quality.

One problem shared by almost all weekend gardeners is the tendency to run back and forth as frantically as a frightened rabbit once the weekend finally comes, hopping from job to job in an uneconomical fashion. And what a catastrophe a weekend of rain presents, however much it is needed! Good organization can cure job hopping. Make lists of tasks and set them in order of priority. Smaller beds will have the benevolent effect of placing limits on the job hopper. It's easy to say, "This weekend I'll weed and tend two beds," when the beds are small and the chances of finishing the job are good.

Cooperative gardening is another way of going about gardening on a limited time budget. If your friends are also gardeners, they will appreciate the time-sharing schemes you propose. "Help me put my peas in this weekend," you may say, "and I'll turn your compost for you the next time you make it." Time sharing works particularly well in community gardens.

Within households, time sharing is even more important. If the whole family appreciates the bounty of the garden, they may also be willing to make gardening a family activity. When sharing tasks with a number of people, however, make certain understandings are firm. Some gardening groups and busy couples use something like a blackboard on a tool shed wall to let others know that, for example, the beans have already been picked for the day.

Arranging Crops in Beds

You've prepared the beds, the soil is soft and fluffy and awaits planting—now the moment of truth arrives. How are you going to arrange the plants within the borders of your beds?

There are two basic patterns from which to choose, blocks or rows, plus the option of vertical growing. This section explains the pros and cons of all these arrangements and gives pointers on how to use them successfully.

Block Planting

The square foot garden devised by Mel Bartholomew is one intensive gardening scheme that makes use of the block system of planting. Plants of one vegetable are concentrated in a single area, in this case a square-foot block. Block planting may also be done in monocropped rectangles, whole beds, or bands that run the length or the width of beds. Triangular or wedge-shaped plantings within a circular bed are also considered block plantings. The basic principle involved is that if a certain vegetable will do well at a given spacing within a row, it will also do well in rows spaced at that same distance within blocks.

Monocropped blocks have several advantages. They are easy to take care of, the vegetables in them can be harvested and replaced all at once, they simplify planning, and they make soil nutrient, crop protection, and water needs uniform for a given area. However, monocrop planting in any form also has a major disadvantage: once a disease or pest has found a favored crop, destruction can be rapid and devastating. Monocrop planting also misses out on the mutual advantages mixed crops impart to one another in the way of shading, pest protection, beneficial chemical interaction, and soil nutrient sharing.

The warning about disease and pest damage in monocropped blocks need not disturb you if you are planning to use small blocks of compact vegetables like lettuce within a larger, mixed vegetable bed. These small squares need not be set

Block Planting: Grouping plants of a single crop closely in a bed or in portions of a bed is the essence of this arrangement. Monocropping is simple to plan and makes nutrient and water needs uniform for a given area.

next to each other but can be spotted throughout the bed, checkerboard style, to give them many of the benefits of mixed or narrow-row planting, while preserving the major advantage of the block—rapid harvest and replacement.

Row Planting

The major alternative to the monocrop block is the narrow row pattern. In this system, a bed resembles a miniature row garden but with much smaller distances between rows. Several crops are grown together in one bed, arranged to provide for individual space needs but also placed to maximize mutual benefits. The narrow row method allows for a more diversified plant mix than is possible with the block method. Rather than being devoted to a single crop, a bed section may contain, for example, alternate rows of bush beans and head lettuce. Bush beans shade the lettuce, and the lettuce makes use of the understory space next to bean plants, space that would go to waste in a monocrop system. Increased production is possible when you exploit growing space to the maximum.

Just as alternate narrow rows of shorter and taller vegetables make good use of the space above ground, so alternate rows of leaf and root crops assure that underground space is shared efficiently. Planting short, crosswise rows in a raised bed, each of a different vegetable, will get you used to some of the challenges of interplanting, companion planting, and space sharing (all of which are discussed in chapter 5). It will also teach you enough about spacing needs so that you can eventually move on to more complex and sophisticated planting patterns in which vegetables are mixed within rows, or rows are abandoned entirely in favor of a mosaic of larger and smaller plants, each spaced according to its needs.

Matching Crops to Planting Patterns

Before you decide on either the row or the block system, consider the special needs and the mature size of the vegetables you plan to grow. Many gardeners use mixed systems, tailoring beds to the crops they hold. Corn, for example, benefits from block planting for best pollination. Although smaller vegetables can be grown with corn in a raised bed and will benefit from the shade the corn throws, a single long row of corn in a bed

Row Planting: Unlike monocropped blocks, a row-planted bed contains a more diversified mixture of crops. Rows in beds are placed more closely together than rows in conventional nonbed gardens. Here, tomatoes are flanked by lettuce and beans.

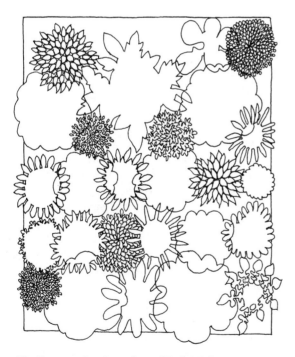

The Beauty of an Interplanted Bed: With experience comes the ability to create a colorful, closely spaced mosaic of plants, where each crop has the room it needs. In this bed, herbs and flowers are interspersed among vegetables for an eye-pleasing effect.

will not do as well as two or more rows blocked together.

Crops like storage carrots or potatoes, which are harvested and stored all at one time, make natural block plantings. If your potatoes were row-planted, interspersed with fall broccoli, for example, it would be almost impossible not to uproot the broccoli in digging the potatoes. Most perennials are also naturals for block plantings, and so are those ground-stored crops that need an especially heavy mulch to take them through winter. Sprawling plants like squashes, watermelons, cantaloupes, and sweet potatoes tend to overwhelm their smaller neighbors, and for that reason, they are often given beds, or blocks within beds, all to themselves. Alternatively, you can train sprawling crops upward, choose compact varieties, or plant them at the ends or sides of your raised beds and let them sprawl in the paths. When using vertical supporting devices, always consider the effect on other vegetables of the shade thrown by trained plants. If you have beds with one end close to a building, use that end for vertical growing. A trellis or supporting poles can be propped against the structure. (For more tips on vertical growing techniques, see chapter 5.)

The Fourth Dimension

When you plan the placement of crops within your beds, remember the fourth dimension in the chess game of intensive gardening—time. Large plants like peppers, eggplants, tomatoes, melons, squashes, sweet potatoes, and corn will need to occupy a comparatively large space as mature plants, but they also require a long time to reach maturity. Borrow their growing room temporarily for your fast-maturing crops like spring onions, radishes, spring turnips, short carrots, young beets, Chinese cabbages, lettuce, and spinach. The loan will be paid back at high interest. (Chapter 5 goes into more detail on planning succession plantings.)

Spacing

Eugene P. Odum, professor of zoology at the University of Georgia, reports that plant scientists have consistently found maximum broad leaf crop production is achieved when the total leaf surface equals four to five times the surface area of the garden. Obviously, no gardener is going to spend precious time measuring leaf surfaces to determine the optimum spacing for plantings, but the principle illustrated by this research is basic to intensive gardening: Crops grow better if tightly spaced.

The reasons behind the principle are many, complex, and not all understood. We do know that plants close together benefit one another, and, through shading, modify soil temperatures and conserve water. When plant nutrition and care are of high quality, tight spacing can lead to healthier, and often faster, plant growth.

Set your plants and seeds close together, but not too close. An overcrowded bed is not a pleasant or well-organized one. Overcrowded plants become tangled, block each other's sun, and steal one another's food and water, making for spindly, poorly bearing crops.

The best guide to planting distance is experience. If you have been in the habit of setting eggplant seedlings 24 inches apart in your old garden rows (which were 24 to 36 inches apart), use 24-inch spacings in all directions when you move to intensive beds, but watch to see if the eggplants actually use the space they are given. If the leaves of eggplant plants next to each other do not meet, next season you can feel free to decrease the distance, or, perhaps better, to plant something else between every two plants. Always observe full-grown vegetables carefully to learn their ideal mature size. Measuring and keeping records is very much in order, but "getting the feel" is just as crucial.

It is the fertile, friable soil of a raised bed that allows for close spacing. Roots, finding little resistance in the loose soil under them, move downward, instead of reaching out laterally to rob the nutrients sought by their neighboring plants. If you space closely you *must* attend to the tilth, fertility, and moisture level of your beds. You must also harvest vegetables promptly, or as soon as they begin to compete with their neighboring plants. This will mean, for example, that you may sometimes have to pick head lettuces slightly immature if they have begun to crowd the broccoli interplanted with them. Alternatively, if you are determined to harvest full-sized head lettuce, set it out early, before you transplant your broccoli seedlings. This means you'll have to learn the days to maturity of both vegetables to do your planning. In determining the best spacings, there are several other factors to consider:

Climate In wet, humid, and hot, or misty, cool climates diseases spread quickly from plant to plant. In such climates, wider spacing is advised. In localities with little sun, spacing too closely may interfere with soil warming and ripening. In unusually dry climates where water is scarce, wider spacing may be required for individual plants to be sustained in their moisture requirements. Ground shading between tightly spaced plants will, it is true, slow down the evaporation of available water, but in times of drought, plants will be healthier if given more room for their roots to spread. Wider spacing is recommended for winter planting, especially in moist climates.

Soil Fertility Heavy feeding crops need slightly wider spacing than light feeders. (See the chart on page 69 for a listing of light and heavy feeders.) Unless you are certain your soil is highly fertile, do not use minimal spacing for these crops. You may wish to group heavy feeders in a specially enriched bed or give periodic feedings to these plants throughout their growth.

Shade Tight spacing will interfere with the light requirements of smaller plants unless the beds are planned to avoid the problem. If the bed itself is shaded by trees or structures, space the whole bed more widely. Always place the taller, more vigorous plants where their shade won't inhibit the smaller ones. If your beds run east and west, plant staked tomatoes or pole beans in a single row on the north side of the beds. Most plants can benefit from afternoon shade in the summer, but not in the fall. Spot lone, tall plants at the edge of the garden, where their shadows will be narrow and will rotate 180 degrees during the day. Dwarf corn will cause fewer shading problems than tall corn.

If shade limits your beds, look for shade-loving vegetables and varieties. As a rule, leafy greens, some root crops, and a few other vegetables will tolerate partial shade (two hours of direct sun daily with shade or indirect light for the rest of the daylight hours). This group includes beets, broccoli, cabbage, carrots, leaf lettuce, bunching onions, peas, spinach, Swiss chard, and turnips.

Time of Year The first goal of your planting plan should be to establish a soil-shading canopy as rapidly as possible. This will save time in watering and weeding. To shade the ground quickly, use fast-maturing, small vegetables for your first plantings and space them closely.

As you add the seedlings of larger plants like tomatoes and peppers, make sure the small vegetables planted near them will crowd out any early weeds, but also calculate on having the smaller vegetables gone by the time the large ones need more room and are big enough to provide their own shade. Early in the season, if the smaller vegetables are removed for harvest, or die, have ready replacements of a similar mature size. On the other hand, if your early-season vegetables are ones you want to reach full size—beets, for example—give them more space than you would if they were principally there to inhibit weeds and produce fast growth.

Later in the season, space more widely to lessen plants' competition for nutrients. The shading out of weeds will, by this time, no longer be a problem. If spaces remain, apply a layer of mulch. (At this point there's no danger that the soil will remain too cool beneath it.) Wider spacing in midsummer prevents insect infestation and promotes air circulation.

In autumn, close spacing again becomes desirable, this time for the mutual protection of plants whose growth has been slowed by cool temperatures. The exception to this rule is in moist climates and shady locations. Some gardeners find that tomatoes bear longer into fall if tightly spaced and given sun.

Harvest Method If you're planning to use the cut-and-come-again method of harvesting, cutting only the mature outer leaves of your leaf crops, then your spacing can be tighter than if you plan to harvest the whole vegetable.

Carrots grown for storage can be harvested by the shovel load if sown tightly. If larger, single carrots are needed, space more widely. For medium-sized carrots to eat early in the season, for example, five to seven plants per square foot are best, while for late-season storage carrots, 1½-inch spacing, or 20 plants per square foot, is possible. If broccoli is to be used for side shoots as well as for heads, it will remain in the ground longer and will need more nutrients and hence more space.

Differences among Vegetables The seed that germinates first in a planting will produce a slightly larger vegetable that needs proportionately more room than its neighboring siblings. Because of such small individual differences, it is wise not to become too rigid or mathematical in planning spacings between plants. Be ready to retransplant a few inches when one particular plant outstrips its space allotment. When an individual plant looks stunted, try removing the competing plants nearest to it.

Spacing plants to allow for maximum yield may not be your cup of tea. Yield is not always the first consideration of the gardener, after all, for gardening is more than a competitive sport. The highest yield of onions per square foot, for example, produces onions only an inch and a half in diameter. If you can't use golf-ball–size onions, be more generous with your spacing.

Methods of Planting Exact and intricate spacing is much more difficult when you direct seed than when you transplant. (This is especially true when you're working with tiny seeds like carrots and onions.) Broadcasting and single-seed methods of sowing are not for beginners. Exact spacing, even if it is achieved by a master sower, may come to naught if a seed fails to germinate, and precious time must go into starting over again before a canopy—and a harvest—can be achieved. Save your fancier spacings for your transplanted crops until you've had a few seasons of experience.

Sow quick-to-harvest, small-seeded vegetables like carrots and lettuce as thinly as you reasonably can, and expect to do some thinning and even some transplanting to achieve better spacing and placement. In good soil and with shading devices, it is not hard to move small plants after they have grown in the wrong place for a short time.

Varietal Difference Especially large or especially small varieties of vegetables require wider or closer spacings. Space requirements for unusual varieties are best learned by experience. Start with the within-row spacings given on the seed packets.

Spacings to Use in Beds

Careful experimentation and record keeping have given us charts of suggested distances between common vegetables. By using these distances, it is claimed, production can be tripled over the average yields in row gardens. If the vegetable you wish to grow does not appear on the chart Intensive Spacings for Vegetables, use the recommended distance *between plants*, not between rows, given on the seed packet or in the catalog from which you ordered seed. After a year's experience, reduce this distance by up to three-quarters unless crowding has occurred.

As you use the chart, please bear in mind that your direct knowledge of a vegetable's possiblities and limitations, along with your knowledge of a climate and growing situation, are worth more than any generalized listing of spacings. Indeed, a chart is just a starting place. Consult this vegetable spacing chart to confirm or modify spacings in your garden. You may also find it useful to look at the charts of intensive spacings for herbs and fruits on page 114.

In monocropped beds, bed cross-sections, or blocks within beds, the twin techniques of square center and equidistant plantings are most economical of space. This is also true when you are interplanting different vegetables that require the same amount of room. Square center spacing works like a grid system, with the center of each plant set at an equal distance from its neighbors. Equidistant spacing is slightly more condensed. In this spacing pattern the distance between the centers of mature plants is calculated and the bed is visualized as a constellation of touching growing circles. The plant centers are staggered and not perpendicular to each other, so the rows can be even closer together than in square center

INTENSIVE SPACINGS FOR VEGETABLES

Listed below are popular garden vegetables with recommendations for intensive spacings. Keep in mind that your climate, the condition of the soil, and your skill as a gardener all have an effect on how well close spacings work. Experience and careful observation of how well your plants do at various spacings will always be the best guidelines for your garden. Use the following spacings as starting points.

Vegetable	Spacing (in inches)
Asparagus	12–18
Beans (lima)	4–9
Beans (snap)	4–6
Beets	2–6
Broccoli	15–18
Brussels sprouts	15–18
Cabbage	15–18
Carrots	2–3
Cauliflower	15–18
Celery	6–9
Chinese cabbage	10–12
Collards	12–15
Corn	18
Cucumbers	18–36
Eggplants	18–24
Endive	15–18
Garlic	2–6
Kale	15–18
Kohlrabi	6–9
Leeks	2–6
Lettuce (head)	10–12
Lettuce (leaf)	6–9
Melons	24–36
Mustard	6–9
New Zealand spinach	10–12
Okra	12–18
Onions (bulb)	4–6
Onions (bunching)	2–3
Parsley	4–6
Parsnips	4–6
Peanuts	12–18
Peas	2–6
Peppers	12–15
Potatoes	10–12
Pumpkins	24–36
Radishes	2–3
Rhubarb	24–36
Rutabagas	6–9
Salsify	2–6
Spinach	4–6
Squash (summer)	24–36
Squash (winter)	24–36
Sunflowers	18–24
Sweet potatoes	10–12
Swiss chard	6–9
Tomatoes	18–24
Turnips	4–6

INTENSIVE SPACINGS FOR HERBS

The following are recommended close spacings for some commonly grown annual herbs.

Herb	Spacing (in inches)
Basil	12–18
Dill	10–12
Sage	18–24
Summer savory	12

the advantages of equidistant over square center spacing diminishes.

In planting adjacent rows with different vegetables in them, you will need to be able to calculate how far apart to set the rows. There is a formula for this: add the respective recommended spacings for the two vegetables and divide the sum by two to arrive at the average. For example, if you want a row of head lettuce (12 inches) next to a row of bush beans (4 inches) add 12 and 4 to get 16 and divide by 2. Eight inches will be the proper spacing between rows. If you are alternating bush bean and head lettuce plants within one row, space them 8 inches apart. If you find after a year's experience that neither crop is hampered by shading or competition, set lettuce and beans 6 inches apart the next time you interplant in an equidistant spacing pattern and watch to see how they do.

spacing. Equidistant spacing is most often recommended for small vegetables. As the recommended spacing between plants increases,

INTENSIVE SPACINGS FOR FRUITS

A fruit tree is not the same as a cabbage; with an annual vegetable, if you don't get the spacing quite right you can always try again. But with a tree you get only one chance. Home growers with a limited amount of space may wonder how close they can plant without hindering the trees' growth and yield. A survey of nurseries across the country led to the following listing of distances. Remember that the particular rootstock of a tree can determine its optimum spacing (this is especially true with apples). When in doubt on how close to safely space your trees, consult the nursery that supplied them. This chart features dwarfs and semidwarfs since they're the most space-saving types. Remember that genetic dwarfs of most fruits can be planted 6 feet apart or less.

Fruit	Spacing (in feet)		
	Dwarf	Semidwarf	Standard
Apple	8–12*	12–18	—
Apricot	8–12	10–12	—
Blueberry	—	—	6–8
Cherry (sour)	10–15	10–15	—
Cherry (sweet)	12	18	—
Grapes	—	—	7–10†
Peaches and Nectarines	8–10	10–16	—
Pears	8–15	12–14	—
Plums	8–12	12–14	—
Strawberries	—	—	1–1½

One nurseryman reported that he has a four-year-old planting of apples spaced 5 feet apart; this dense planting has created an "apple hedge" with no appreciable stress to the trees or drop in yield. Also see page 119 for research that shows 5-foot spacings can increase apple yields.
†*Depends on variety and soil condition.*

Square Center Spacing: This economical spacing pattern works like a grid. The center of each plant is set at an equal distance from its neighbors.

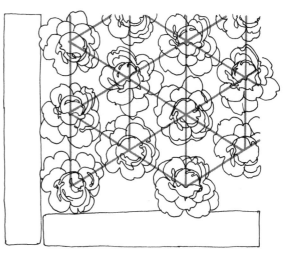

Equidistant Spacing: This pattern is even more space efficient than square center spacing. The plant centers are staggered, not perpendicular to each other, so the rows can be set even closer together.

How to Space Plants and Seeds

As we have already observed, equidistant spacing is far easier to achieve when setting out transplants than when planting seeds. Peter Chan, a proponent of the oriental bed gardening method, uses a bulb planter to plant his seedlings. He makes a clean cut in the soil, places dried chicken manure (compost would also work) in the hole, and sets the seedling into it, forming the soil around the roots. He uses the length of the bulb planter to measure the distance between plants. (Some planters very conveniently have inch increments marked on their cylindrical bases.)

Measuring sticks of the length of each of the common between-plant spacings are useful. Using a yardstick marked at intervals with a bright waterproof marker is a slightly less convenient alternative suitable for small beds. To get the row straight, run a string from one end of the bed to the other and move the yardstick along the string as you plant. Boxed beds are easy to "wire" with string. As you get better at transplanting, you'll find you can "sight" a row as expertly as an old-fashioned farmer used to plow a straight furrow.

One spacing device that is particularly easy to store is a collapsible wooden gate usually used to protect young children from falls down stairs. With its adjustable diagonal grid, it makes equidistant placement easy. Center each seedling in the middle of a diamond-shaped opening after the gate is laid over the bed surface. A length of wooden trellis can be used in a similar manner.

For a frequently used spacing, you might consider making a triangle out of scrap wood, with each side equaling the desired spacing. To use, set the triangle in place and plant at each point. Flip it over and continue planting at the points.

A similar design offers more versatility because it allows you to mark many different distances. Cut a triangle out of waxed cardboard or other waterproof, slightly stiff material. The sides should all measure 36 inches. With a ruler, draw lines parallel to one of the sides at 6-inch increments, from 36 to 6. These lines will create a series of smaller and smaller equilateral triangles.

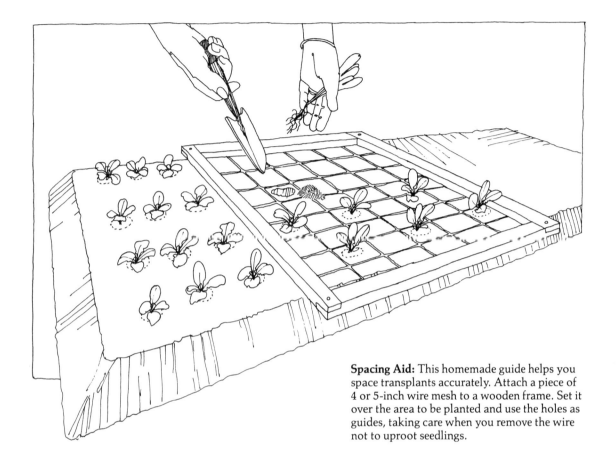

Spacing Aid: This homemade guide helps you space transplants accurately. Attach a piece of 4 or 5-inch wire mesh to a wooden frame. Set it over the area to be planted and use the holes as guides, taking care when you remove the wire not to uproot seedlings.

Mark each line with its length. When you want to plant at 24 inches, you simply mark the soil at both ends of the 24-inch line and at the facing point of the triangle. To make this device even more useful, write the names of crops at their corresponding spacings.

For quick marking of equidistant seed spacings, take a board and glue or nail in place pieces of dowel ½ inch long and ½ or ¾ inch in diameter at the appropriate spacings. Don't forget to stagger the rows. You might want to make several of these with the spacings you use most often, say 6 inches for salad greens or 2 inches for peas. A coat of wood preservative will guarantee many seasons' worth of use.

An inexpensive and easy-to-make spacing marker is as handy as yesterday's newspaper. Take three sheets, staple them together, and fold into accordian pleats. Punch holes at the desired spacing. This task is easy when you use a piece of pipe and a hammer and work on a soft surface that allows the pipe to punch through the layers of paper. Unfold and hold this marking guide in place with rocks as you plant.

Sowing Seeds Individually In the prime of the season, both plants and gardeners prefer the out-of-doors, and the enthusiasm of even the most ardent indoor seed starter will predictably wane. At this point it is wise to learn the art of

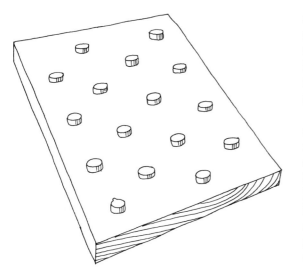

Easy Marker: To mark seed spacings quickly, attach pieces of dowel to a board at the appropriate distances. A handle on the other side makes it simple to press this device into a prepared seed bed. Make several of these boards with the spacings you use most often.

individual seed sowing, difficult though it may be. There are also certain crops that do best when direct sown. (These are the Temperamental Transplants mentioned on page 183).

Precise individual placement of seeds has many advantages. Both space and seed are conserved, thinning is eliminated, emerging plants begin life without competition, and when you weed, there is never the danger of pulling up a valued plant instead of an intruder. You know exactly where your plants will be the moment your seeds hit the ground, and you can assume that everything else is out of place. If you plant by the square center method, you can even cultivate with safety before your plants emerge by raking down the intersecting rows.

A French proverb says, "He who sows thickly harvests thinly." The psychological urge is to plant more than enough to harvest enough, but in intensive gardening the urge must be curbed

and the proverb remembered. The conditon of soil in raised beds is superior, making germination conditions ideal and seed loss less likely. Single-seed sowing of most vegetables is a far less tedious and time-consuming job than the task of thinning, which it eliminates.

To sow seeds individually, you must literally place each seed exactly where you want a mature plant to stand. Obviously, this will be easier with large seeds like peas, beans, corn, and beets than with the more vexing carrot, celery, or lettuce seeds. To help with placement, use a portable measuring device similar to those we have mentioned as useful for transplanting—a yardstick or wooden rod, a triangle or hexagon, or a wire or wooden screen of the proper mesh. By using 2-inch chicken wire, you can set seeds through every other opening in a row and achieve 4-inch spacing. For wider spacing, use a larger mesh wire, or skip more openings.

Another precision method of sowing is to cut an 18 to 24-inch-wide strip of plywood to the width or half the width of the bed and drill holes through the wood at the spacing your seeds require. A handle will make it easier to lower and raise this planting guide. Drop seeds through the holes, lift off the strip, and add a covering of soil.

Alternatives to Individual Sowing Carrots, it has been found, will yield as well in narrowly spaced rows as in regular equidistant spacings, even when the spacings within the rows are not entirely uniform. If carrots are sown or thinned to about an inch apart in furrows spaced 4 inches from each other, they yield as well as when they are spaced 2 inches apart in all directions. In fact, there is some evidence that carrots are self-spacing. Fewer germinate in thick sowings. Thick sowings of small-seeded vegetables like carrots also have the advantage of establishing a canopy quickly to make weeding less necessary.

Another method of sowing small vegetable seeds, as well as larger ones, is to broadcast or scatter the seed over a designated area. John Jeavons and the late Alan Chadwick, principal proponents of the biodynamic/French intensive method, consider broadcast sowing within mono-cropped areas of beds the most economical and productive of sowing methods. Broadcasting, however, requires a learned manual skill and sacrifices order to quantity.

Beginners almost always broadcast too thickly. The trick is to swing the arm in a wide arc or a series of scalloped motions over the full width of the bed or row, letting a few seeds slide between your fingers while your arm is in motion. The wider the arc, the more even the distribution. Avoid dropping seed in clumps or leaving bare spots. A master broadcast sower can achieve a remarkable evenness of distribution. With larger seeds, let a seed or two fall between your fingers as your arm moves. Smaller seeds will flow between fingers in a thin stream. Another method for small seeds is to put them in a jar with holes in the top just a little larger than the seeds. Shake the jar vigorously over the bed. After sowing by either method, cover with soil and tamp with a hoe. Broadcast only on windless days. It may be

a good idea to perfect your skill by practicing with sand on a sheet or blanket spread on a driveway.

Broadcasting is most satisfactory for mono-cropped areas or entire beds and for fast-growing, small plants like turnip greens, radishes, dwarf peas, beets, and leaf lettuce. Among larger vegetables, beans adapt best to broadcasting, but they should be thinned to 4 to 5-inch equidistant spacings. Other crops frequently broadcast in small beds are kale, endive, chicory, rocket, and the smaller oriental greens. The chief advantage of the method is that it allows relatively large monocropped areas to be planted quickly. The chief disadvantage is a serious one: weeding of broadcast-sown beds is extremely difficult, and preemergent weeding is impossible. Weeds will outpace the seedlings and may steal soil nutrients from carrots and beets when they are broadcast sown. Frequent hand weeding must be done in the first three weeks after sowing to prevent crop stunting. After that period is over, the carrots or beets will hold their own against

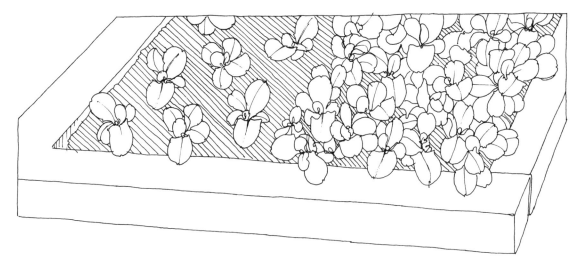

Broadcast Bed: Broadcasting contributes to higher yields by making it possible to fill a growing area with a sun-catching layer of plant leaves in record time. In this bed, the lettuce seedlings on the right have yet to be thinned. The seedlings on the left will have to be thinned one more time as they expand.

Close Spacing for Fruit Trees: Close spacing and careful placement have advantages beyond the garden beds. Fruit trees also benefit from being placed so that their limbs barely touch but do not overlap. In research done at Auburn University in 1974, it was discovered that six-year-old apple trees on dwarfing rootstocks at 5-foot spacings outyielded similar trees spaced at 10-foot intervals by 247 bushels per acre. Trees spaced 5 feet apart formed solid fruit walls where their limbs touched without training, while 10-foot spacings required the tying of limbs.

weeds and provide shade to discourage weed growth. Another disadvantage to broadcast sowing is the likelihood that some thinning must be done after germination to ensure that the developing plants are barely touching their neighbors.

Taking Care of the High-Yield Garden

You may be able to set each seed and every transplant exactly where you want it to grow, but you can't expect the plants to produce until you've provided the right conditions for them. The cultural requirements of the intensive garden are those of any well-managed growing area—water, fertilizer, and weeding—but the use of densely planted beds will demand certain refinements of general practices.

Watering

John Jeavons claims that the biodynamic/French intensive garden uses one-eighth of the water that commercial agriculture requires. Most of the water savings is realized through reduced evaporation due to a leafy canopy that acts as a living mulch. Another obvious savings the gardener will appreciate is of watering time. With fewer square feet and no need to water unproductive areas between beds, neither water nor time is wasted. Per square foot of *productive* space, however, raised beds may require *more* water and watering time than row gardens. Tightly spaced plants are thirsty plants, growing rapidly and therefore transpiring heavily. Loose soil soaks up water in large quantity.

Many factors affect the water requirement of gardens: available groundwater, rooting characteristics and water requirements of the plants being grown, degree of exposure to sunlight, temperature and humidity, time of year, and soil composition. Of these, the last, soil composition, is the most important for conventional gardeners, but it's the one that least affects raised bed gardeners, who already know their carefully prepared humus-filled soil will protect them from drought or flood. Compost holds six times its weight in water. Double digging creates a loose soil deep down to retain moisture and makes groundwater readily available. In deeply loosened soil water can easily travel upward, drawn by capillary action into root zones. The plant roots can also travel down and penetrate to, or toward the groundwater.

Incidentally, the contrast of the soil in your raised beds and the soil of surrounding untended areas may be useful. Look to your paths and nearby fallow fields for an early warning system for threatening drought. Plants there will begin to wilt before the garden crops do.

In general, watering too frequently and too heavily is as hard on plants as too little watering. Excessive watering washes nutrients from the soil, displaces needed soil air, and may uproot seedlings, while frequent watering encourages shallow roots and creates an artificial water dependency. Too much water at the wrong time may also cause leafy growth at the expense of flowers and fruit. See the chart Critical Times for Watering for some guidelines. Here are some other factors to keep in mind as you plan a watering system and a watering schedule for your raised beds.

• Some vegetables, and vegetables at certain stages of development, require more water with each irrigation, but fewer irrigations.

• Watering at certain stages of plant growth reduces the quality of some edible crops.

• In regions with early falls, heavy watering late in summer interferes with hardening-off and reduces frost resistance.

• Giving plants enough water to allow them to transpire freely keeps them cool in the heat of summer. Leaves are cooled by evaporation.

• The higher the air temperature and the lower the humidity, the greater the need for water. Dry winds dehydrate plants.

• Plants that have been exposed to low temperatures become dehydrated more slowly in time of drought than plants whose total growth has occurred under high temperature conditions. Lack of water inhibits the growth of cucumbers the most, for example, when they have been transplanted late in the season.

Defensive planting prevents drought damage. Choose drought-resistant varieties and concentrate on such vegetables as asparagus (the most drought resistant of all), if water shortages plague your area and irrigation water is scarce. Use windbreaks. Mulch or covercrop to protect all vacant spaces. Increase the distances between plants in midsummer. Save rainwater and air conditioner drips for the garden and investigate the use of filtered household graywater. Make basins around larger plants to retain irrigation and rainwater. Water at night when evaporation is lowest.

• The general rule of thumb is that mature plants need 1 to 2 inches of rain per week in summer. You should provide whatever portion of this moisture is lacking. One inch of rain equals 65 gallons per 100 square feet of garden space. Do not, however, interpret the rule too rigidly. Observations of plants both in and near the garden can tell you as much as your rain gauge does. In irrigating, consider individual plant needs as much as you heed the rule of thumb.

• Learn where your groundwater level stands. See how deep you have to dig before you come to moisture. To maintain the capillary process that makes groundwater available to your plants, some slight moisture should be present in the soil all the way from the ground surface to the groundwater table. Experiment to find how much water

CRITICAL TIMES FOR WATERING

Plant	Critical Time Period	Amount of Water
Beans (dried, lima, snap)	Pollination and pod development; pod enlargement; delay may cause pod drop	Dried: ¾ gal. per foot of row a week Lima: 1 gal. per foot of row a week Snap: 1 gal. per foot of row a week
Beets	Throughout growing season; avoid erratic watering	¾–1 gal. per foot of row a week
Broccoli	Early in season to prevent buttoning	1 gal. per plant a week
Cabbage	Head development; too much water later will cause splitting heads	1½ gal. per plant a week or 12 in. per season, less after development
Cantaloupes	Flowering and fruit development	1½ gal. per plant a week or 18 in. per season
Carrots	Throughout growing period	¾ gal. per foot of row a week or 18 in. per season
Cauliflower	Early in season to prevent buttoning	1 gal. per plant a week
Cucumbers	Flowering and fruit development	1½ gal. per plant a week or 25 in. per season
Eggplants	Flowering through harvest	1½ gal. per plant a week or 18 in. per season
Fruit trees	Flowering and near harvest when fruit growth is most rapid	—
Herbs	Do best with less water; wait until they begin to wilt	1½ gal. per plant a week
Lettuce	For loosehead and iceberg types, during head development; for leaf lettuce, throughout growing season	For both types of lettuce: ¾ gal. per foot of row a week or 9 in. per season
Onions	Bulb enlargement; stop when tops fall or ripening may be delayed	1 gal. per foot of row a week or 15 in. per season
Peas	Flowering and pod development	1 gal. per foot of row a week or 18 in. per season
Peppers	Flowering through harvest	1 pt. per plant a week when young, increasing to 1½ gal. per plant a week or 18 in. per season
Radishes	Throughout growing period	¾ gal. per foot of row a week
Squashes (summer and winter)	Bud development and flowering	1–1½ gal. per plant a week or 18 in. per season
Strawberries	Flowering and during runner development	—
Swiss chard	Throughout growing season	1 gal. per foot of row a week or 9 in. per season
Tomatoes	Flowering through harvest, an even supply is important; older, late-maturing varieties require less water	2½ gal. per plant a week or 24 in. per season; more for unmulched, staked plants
Turnips	Beginning of root development	¾ gal. per foot of row a week

Note: Adapted from a chart by Libby J. Goldstein of the Philadelphia County Extension Service.

you must add to achieve this. Keep apprised, through Agricultural Extension reports and the weather news, of any remarkable drops in your local groundwater level. Use a rain gauge or a calibrated can to determine your per-week rainfall.

• Heavy watering after transplating stimulates root growth, reduces transplant shock, and helps plants to become established and benefit from soil nutrition quickly.

• Seeds require water to germinate. Unless rain is expected, always water after seeding.

Light or Heavy: The Gardener's Dilemma

When experts disagree, the amateur suffers. There are two firm schools of thought about the best way to water. One insists on light, frequent waterings; the other calls for deep, weekly soakings whenever the rainfall comes to less than an inch a week. Each school presents sound arguments.

Master gardener John Jeavons is a light, frequent waterer, irrigating all his beds once a day, and old, compacted beds and seedlings twice a day, so that the top several inches of soil, the plants' root zones, are damp at all times. Frequent, light watering speeds early plant growth by releasing soil nutrients. It assures proper aeration by never saturating the soil beyond its field capacity, and the showerlike delivery never compacts the soil. Light watering, just enough to achieve a shiny look on the soil surface, is, he argues, particulary appropriate to the raised bed garden, where soil drains quickly and dries out rapidly because of the many air pockets. Ecology Action computes the need of a 114-square-foot bed at 10 to 30 gallons a day, or 1.7 inches per week, compared to 1.5 inches for a row garden of the same area.

Proponents of the heavy-and-infrequent method insist that such daily watering encourages shallow roots. Infrequent, heavy watering, they say, makes full use of groundwater to supplement rainfall. Plant roots, forced deeper into soil, penetrate to nutrient-rich strata, anchor plants more firmly, and often produce better topgrowth.

They admit, however, that deep heavy waterings have a tendency to compact the soil and make it less workable the day after irrigation. This technique also wastes some water in the soil outside the root zones, thus encouraging weeds.

The best systems for accomplishing light frequent watering are sprinkler cans with a rose, or perforated cap, that points upward to simulate rain; buried or surface drip irrigation systems that deliver water directly to the root zone in small quantities and can be used for short periods of time each day, sometimes automatically; spray wands that deliver water manually to the base of plants from a hose attachment; trickle wick installations for individual plants; soaker hoses with a small, constant delivery; and sprinkler systems adjusted to bed size.

For heavy watering the best systems are trench, furrow, and flood irrigation; sprinklers designed to soak a whole bed; drip irrigation systems used over long periods of time; soaker hoses with relatively high delivery rates; and hand dipping from buckets to flood plant areas.

Seasonal Patterns of Watering Those of us who live in regions where rainfall alone will not meet the needs for healthy plant growth would do well to look to Nature for a model delivery system. In fruitful, temperate regions, spring and fall rains are light and frequent; summer rains infrequent and heavy. To simulate natural growing conditions, tailor your watering method to the age of your crop. Water transplants heavily to prevent shock, but then depend on light rains to carry them through their early growth period. If such rains don't materialize, water lightly, taking care not to saturate the bed but to deliver as much of the water as possible to the root zone. Once you have started a daily light watering in a dry spring, you must continue it. Hardly anything is worse for plants than infrequent light watering.

As the young plants begin to develop a leafy canopy, start weaning them to less frequent watering. Wait for a heavy rain, then gradually lengthen the period between waterings. Your plants will adapt to this, for they are now strong, less challenged by weed competition and well adjusted to the soil. After the transition period, water thoroughly and deeply to encourage deep root penetration, but only do this at the first sign of plant stress or after a full, hot week without rain. A general sign of stress is, of course, wilting; on corn plants leaves curl and on tomatoes the lower leaves appear blanched.

The second phase of your watering system may require a change in method. For example, you may switch from a gentle drip system to a soaker hose, or from a sprinkler to the individual flooding of basins around large plants.

As fall approaches, go back to the light-and-frequent method to let your hardier plants harden-off. As new seedlings join the beds in the middle of the season, make sure that they are given individual light waterings when rain is scarce, even when the rest of the garden is being soaked infrequently. Summer-planted seedlings are more vulnerable to drought than spring planted ones. The groundwater level will be lower, the seedlings will be less resistant for having been started under warmer conditons, and the potential damage from dry winds and bright sun will be greater.

Having tailored your watering system to your climate and the different parts of your season, you must also tailor it to individual crops and growth periods for these crops. This may require grouping plants of like water needs together in one bed, or it may mean doing more individual watering at the critical period for a given crop. (Take another look at the earlier chart Critical Times for Watering for a reminder of when these periods occur.)

If experts divide on the quantity of water to give at one time, they also disagree about the hour of the day when it's best to water. In dry climates, watering late in the day or at night will waste the least amount of moisture to evaporation, but in wetter climates early morning watering is

Water Needs: Group plants with the same water needs together in one bed. The shallow-rooted leaf and head crops shown at top do better with constant, light waterings of their root zones. Deep-rooted crops like beans, squashes, melons, and peppers grow best with deep but infrequent watering.

advised for crops and localities susceptible to mold, mildew, and fungal infections. Never sprinkle plants directly in hot sun. Leaves and fruits may be damaged by the combination of heat and water.

Watering Devices and Systems

Ways of delivering water to beds and plants are many and diverse, ranging from the very simple to the complex. What follows is a rundown of seven watering options, describing their advantages and drawbacks.

Watering Cans These are good for watering individual plants when transplanting or when you need to keep the foliage dry. They are also useful for delivering liquid fertilizers. Pick a solid, rustproof watering can that fits under the outside tap and won't splash during use. The rose, or perforated plate over the spout, should be oval, and the perforations many and small enough to produce a fine spray. Long spouts that send water upward in an arc simulate gentle rain, while downward-pointing ones give more accurate water placement.

Hoses and Nozzles With adequate water pressure, to get the most water to one spot you need the shortest hose that will reach. Choose ⅝ to ¾-inch diameter hoses. These will spread an inch of water over a 5,000-square-foot area in about four and one half hours.

The most durable hoses are rubber, but these are expensive, sometimes costing more than a dollar per foot. Hoses with rubber interiors and reinforced vinyl exteriors are almost as durable and cost about half as much. Be sure that your hoses have durable brass couplings.

Nozzles should also be brass. They should allow for accurate and easy control of water flow. The twist-grip types with separate spray nozzles for hard and soft spray are easier to use than variable-spray, pistol-grip ones.

Fine sprays are useful for misting small plants, for cooling plants in heat waves and for the first few waterings of seedbeds. Hand-held hoses, however, are inefficient and time consuming and should never be relied on for general bed watering where better distribution of water is required than they can provide. It takes at least an hour with a hand-held hose to put enough water on a 10 by 10-foot bed to soak the root zone. Most gardeners can think of better ways to spend an hour.

Sprinklers When left in one place, a sprinkler will wet soil to a foot or more in an hour. The most basic sprinkler has a weighted spray head that makes it stationary. It uses the force of the water to make it spin. Sometimes it has rotary arms that throw water in a circular pattern. Such a sprinkler is suitable only for a circular bed. Impulse sprinklers also cover a circular area, and often produce too rough a flow for young plants.

Most raised bed gardeners require a rectangular pattern with even, not overlapping, coverage. Pick an oscillating or stationary sprinkler that can be adjusted to cover the exact area of your beds. Make sure that it does not deposit a surplus of water at the point where it changes directions or at the center of the rectangle. Test the sprinkler by letting it run for one hour and measuring the water at several points on the bed with tin can collectors.

Sprinklers have helped some crops survive heat waves. In tests at the University of Hawaii, sprinkling increased yields of watercress by 5 to 6 percent and lowered the underleaf temperature by almost 5°F.

The chief disadvantage of sprinkler systems is the possible buildup of salts on leaves and in root zones when water from wells or from public drinking supplies is used. By its indiscriminate watering of bare spaces, and through evaporation as it throws water into the air, sprinkling wastes water.

Never sprinkle in a wind over five miles per hour or the water distribution will be thrown off. Fixed, buried sprinkling systems are often used on lawns, but they are generally uneconomical for the bed garden and may interfere with cultivation. Some gardeners report success using a fine-misting butterfly sprinkler mounted on bed-spanning elevated tripods. This setup is a miniature version of field-watering irrigators.

Soaker and Dew Hoses The traditional soaker hose is relatively inexpensive, needs no assembly, and can be laid down between small plants and narrow rows without difficulty. Some soaker hoses are flexible enough to be woven in and out between vegetables in an interplanted, equidistantly spaced bed. Soakers are particularly useful for the occasional slow, thorough soaking of single rows of vegetables.

Soakers fall into several categories. Some, known as dew hoses, ooze water over their entire

Soaker Hose: In a densely planted bed, use a flexible hose that can be woven in and out between plants.

length through porous sides. Others spurt water through small perforations. Some are made of canvas, others of plastics of various kinds and various degrees of flexibility, and still others of rubber.

A Rodale Product Testing Department survey conducted in 1985 concluded that in selecting a soaker hose, the three main factors to take into account are ease of placement, durability, and flow rate. Polyester and canvas soakers are easiest to maneuver between plants. Some rigid vinyl models and rubber soakers are hard to lay flat and cannot be bent easily. Polyester, polyethylene, rubber, and vinyl soakers are resistant to fungal attack and seldom develop leaks at couplings or seams. This means such hoses can be left in the beds for long periods of time without danger. Canvas hoses, in contrast, are susceptible to mold and mildew and, to be protected from rotting, should be drained and dried daily. Vinyl hoses with perforations or slits in them, although durable, may become clogged and require periodic flushing.

Polyethylene and rubber models release the smallest quantity of water at one time. This feature is useful for early, light, root zone watering but not for heavy soaking. Fully swollen canvas and polyester soaker hoses emit the largest amount of water, while vinyl hoses fall between the two categories in their flow. Some vinyl hoses, however, must be run at low pressure only or they will erode the soil. Two-tube vinyl sprinklers, on the other hand, release a fine stream but will tolerate a high flow rate. They also tend to be more flexible than other vinyl soakers, and some models may be adjusted to various lengths by moving an end clip.

A soaker hose will give most of the advantages of an installed drip irrigation system at a fraction of the cost. Soakers save water, they slowly concentrate moisture in the root zones while keeping leaves dry, and their flow is controlled easily to meet the demands of the soil and the plants. One advantage they do not share with more sophisticated drip systems is the ability to tailor delivery to individual crops, since flow emerges evenly the length of the soaker.

The price of a soaker hose is determined more by the material from which it is made than by its length. On the average, soaker hoses cost between 5 and 20 dollars and come in lengths of 25, 30, and 50 feet.

Traditional Individual Drip Systems Pitcher irrigation is a low-cost method of delivering water to individual plants or groups of small plants in dry soil. It is the traditional method of Indians in the Southwest. Water is placed, often by hose, in large, 3-gallon baked, but unglazed, earthenware jugs or pitchers that are porous enough to allow slow seepage into the root zone. Unglazed pots are available in Mexico and in some garden centers in the Southwest. If a heavy clay wash has been applied to the outside of the vessel, you must sand it off.

In the pitcher irrigation method, pits are dug at intervals near large, drought-prone vegetables or within rings of smaller crops. A pitcher is sunk into each pit with its mouth at soil level. Pitchers are covered to prevent evaporation, and refilled every four or five days, or when they are half empty. Bags of compost or aged manure can be

Pitcher Irrigation: Developed in the arid Southwest, this method delivers a slow, steady supply of water to individual plants or groups of plants. An unglazed pot or jug is buried among plants in the garden, filled with water, and covered to prevent evaporation.

Homemade Watering Devices: These waterers work well set next to large individual plants. Punch a few holes in the screw-type lid of a large wine jug. Invert the jug and bury it upside down to the depth of the shoulder (shown on top). Transform plastic jugs by slitting them on the side, near the bottom, and inserting a length of vinyl tubing or a wick, which will conduct water to the root zone. Place the tubing on the soil surface at the base of the plant and bury the wick in the root zone.

suspended in the pitchers to provide nutrients.

The method works best with vigorous-rooted vegetables such as melons and squash and least well with root crops and shallow-rooted vegetables. Pitcher irrigation uses between one-sixth and one-eighth the amount of water required by conventional flood or sprinkle irrigation. The earthenware filters out salts that are prevalent in arid regions. Pitchers should be flushed periodically to remove the alkaline deposit.

Drip Irrigation Systems Drip irrigation, developed in Israel, delivers water a drop at a time to plant root zones, where it can penetrate immediately and deeply, leaving empty spaces dry. Slowly applied water will penetrate to the depth of a foot in 15 minutes.

Drip or trickle systems cause no salt buildup or water stress. Water flows through a thin plastic pipe into flexible plastic tubing of very small diameter and then to an adjustable emitter placed at each garden plant. These emitters can be opened wide to allow for a fast drip of water or closed down for a very slow flow. Drip irrigation, therefore, adapts to both the light and the heavy method of watering.

Drip systems may be designed with compatible components that allow them to be customized to bed size and even to individual crop use. Water in one customized system, for example, flows the length of the bed through a main manifold pipe and then branches off into as many as 25 row pipes. A gate valve controls every 5 pipes. Crops that require much water, like cucumbers or celery, may be irrigated at the same time other vegetables in the same bed, or the same row, receive no water at all. A short section of microtubing, also called spaghetti or transfer tubing, runs to the root zone of every large plant.

For unusually tightly grown vegetables like carrots, emitters are not used. Instead, holes are punched in a ½-inch pipe at intervals of every 3 inches or so, and water oozes out.

If you install pipes under the bed surface, you can plant seeds and transplant seedlings near the emittors. On the other hand, cultivating in a tube-laced soil may be difficult. Some systems need to be unearthed and removed at the end of the season to keep them from freezing.

With surface installations, plastic component tubes will be subject to faster deterioration than is found in subsurface systems, but clogging, which leads to uneven watering, will be less of a problem.

The rigid main pipe may be connected to a hose. Several hoses may be used at once for different beds if a Y-connection is fitted to the faucet. Flow-reducing washers control the volume of water that moves through the hoses. Shut-off valves allow manual control at the beds, and antisyphon valves, required by many health codes, prevent water from returning to the house system. The latter are especially important when you're using the drip system for liquid fertilizer feeding. Filters are used to prevent clogging.

Assembling a drip system seldom takes more than a few hours, but much careful advanced planning is necessary before you choose a series of components. The more carefully you plan the beds, the more useful the system will be.

Most home water systems deliver more than enough water (300 to 600 gallons per hour) to supply the average drip system. Vegetable gardens usually use from ½ to 1 gallon per hour for closely spaced plants, and 1 gallon per hour for large plants.

Many suppliers now stock equipment and may be helpful in designing systems to your specifications. Agricultural Extension Offices, particularly in western states, can provide information. Prepackaged kits are generally less expensive than materials for customizing, but they are also less adaptable. A typical kit costs 25 to 200 dollars, and customized components can run much higher. No drip system is perfect. Hoses and pipes rot or deteriorate and need to be replaced, and a clogged emitter can cause problems from spotty watering to major erosion. The close spacing of intensive

Drip Irrigation: Drip systems can be customized to fit your bed size. The adjustable emitters placed at individual plants allow you to change the water flow from heavy to light, as plants require.

gardens makes the use of many of the inexpensive drip irrigation kits impractical. Some kits, for example, are calculated for root crops placed 30 to 35 inches apart. In areas of adequate rainfall, the customized system, on the other hand, must still be considered something of a luxury. (See the Garden Products section of the Directory of Resources for the names of some companies that sell drip irrigation kits.)

Even more of a luxury are the automatic timing devices that use a drip system to water on a schedule. One such device allows you to dial the number of gallons you want in each bed right at the faucet. But unless you also have a device like the osmotic pressure gauge to let you know how much water your soil requires at a given time, automatic watering may quickly become overwatering.

So far, scientific research on drip irrigation in commercial agriculture has shown mixed results. Yields have been increased dramatically over results from sprinkle or flood irrigation on water-loving crops like melons and on those vegetables like potatoes that thrive on a steady supply of water. In dry periods, drip irrigation increases almost all vegetable yields. Shallow-rooted vegetables like lettuce, however, have been found to produce as well with sprinkle watering as with a drip system. In one experiment, cabbage production was decreased when irrigation was used.

Fruit trees have been shown to yield more produce when watered by this method. In a study done at the University of Georgia by J. L. Chesness and G. A. Couvillon, drip-irrigated peach trees showed an increase in total fruit volume and size and had a significantly larger total yield per tree than nonirrigated peach trees.

Flood, Furrow, and Basin Irrigation Flooding is one of the oldest irrigation methods, but in general, it adapts poorly to the raised bed garden. It works well in arid areas where intensive beds are sunken instead of raised, and it is good to keep in mind for extreme drought emergency. In the flood method, water is poured onto the bed until the soil surface is completely covered. On flat-topped beds a shallow dam must be built to confine the water and prevent runoff. The bed is submerged for several hours. Flooding leaches salt, but it compacts soil and wastes water, and sometimes it uproots young plants, cuts off soil air, and depletes soil nutrients.

Furrow and basin irrigation work well for deep-rooted crops on level land or in flat-topped beds. In this method, water is flooded into straight trenches in the middle of beds, serpentine shallow ditches between rows or plants, or basins around large plants. The water is allowed to seep in. The trenches and ditches can be filled with mulch at the beginning of the season to keep down weeds and flooded with water during hot

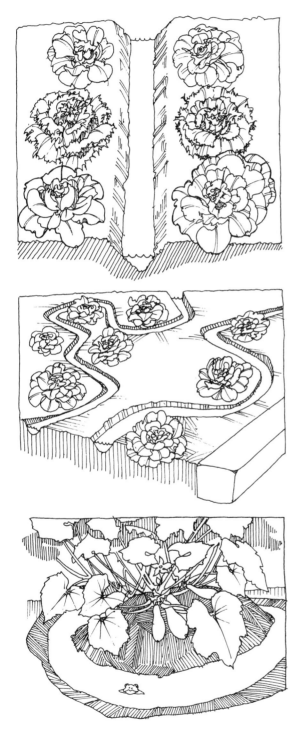

Irrigation Variations: At top is a bed with a straight trench dug through the middle. In the center, shallow ditches wind between closely spaced groupings of plants. At bottom, a hill of squash is surrounded by a moat. Fill these trenches with mulch at the start of the season to suppress weeds and flood with water during hot spells.

spells. The decomposed mulch can be raked into the bed at the end of the growing season. The dangers in furrow and basin irrigation are salt buildup and fruit rot. The method is, however, useful in arid areas and on clay soil.

Fertilizing

Plants in high concentrations not only require more water than widely spaced plants; they also need better nutrition. The long seasons made possible by intensive gardening practices exact a toll on soil nutrients. Fast-growing young plants have the heartiest appetites of all, and in the high-yield garden, young seedlings are being relayed into the soil rapidly at all points of the growing season.

In spring, when the largest number of young plants are in the beds, you will already have spread a lavish feast for them by preparing the beds with compost and other soil amendments. Nothing else you have done, or can do, for them is more essential. Compost feeds the soil to allow soil organisms to feed the plants. Although it measures low in nutrients on a chemical scale, it is, indeed, a gift that goes on giving, assuring a slow release of soil nutrients throughout the season.

As you add new transplants to the beds, or prepare new rows for sowing, put a handful of compost in each planting hole or seedling furrow. Young plants and long-season or heavy-feeding vegetables like spinach, squashes, tomatoes, eggplants, and peppers also benefit from a fast-acting pick-me-up or snack. This will speed them along the way or spur more growth at a demanding phase like the period of fruit development.

When we speak of a quick pick-me-up, we are not talking about the junk food of chemical fertilizers, which interferes with natural plant processes, establishes dependency, leads to unbalanced growth, and often invites insect attack. Summer fertilizers should always be organic, slow acting when compared to chemicals, and easy for plants to digest. To see the release rates of organic materials and their nutrient content, refer to the chart on page 23.

Liquid fertilizers are favored for use in intensive beds during the season. Because the liquids move through soil and are absorbed into plants rapidly, results are easy to see. Most liquid fertilizers are balanced enough that in dilute solutions they will not burn seedlings. Because they keep plants growing at maximum rates, they make any intensive bed extremely productive.

One excellent liquid fertilizer is fish emulsion, which is made from soluble fish canning wastes. Fish emulsion is not an entirely balanced fertilizer. It is low in calcium and high in nitrogen when compared, for example, to compost. If your bed soil is low in calcium, the extensive use of fish emulsion may lead to blossom-end rot in tomatoes and peppers. Never use solutions stronger than 1 tablespoon to a gallon of water. Fish emulsion delays aging in some plants, making them productive longer, but it can also delay flowering by a week, so it should not be used late in the season. Do not use fish emulsion on salad crops near harvest time; it imparts a fishy taste. Use it sparingly, if at all, on young root crops. The high nitrogen content may cause forking. Also be aware that dogs seem particularly attracted to it; the family pet might cause some damage trampling and rolling around in a freshly fertilized patch.

The nitrogen content of liquid seaweed is lower than that of fish emulsion, but seaweed liquid also contains phosphorus and potassium along with some trace minerals. Unlike fish emulsion, it can be used safely on beans and other legumes. There are also seaweed/fish emulsion blends available. These have a balanced nutrient content, offering roughly equivalent amounts of nitrogen, phosphorus, and potassium.

To deliver liquid supplements, use dipping cups, watering cans, or any of the simple setups discussed earlier under Watering Devices and Systems—inverted jugs fitted with tubing, for example. If adapting drip irrigation systems to manure or compost tea feedings, be sure to employ filters, or strain the solution thoroughly before introducing it into the system.

Another means of delivering liquid fertilizer is through foliar sprays. Leaves absorb nutrients quickly and are more selective than roots, taking up only what the plant needs to complete its nutritional balance. Foliar spray works well in conjunction with a slow-release fertilizer like compost, because the spray provides a boost at any stage of development and can be used on all crops safely. In a tightly spaced garden foliar spraying may be the easiest way to deliver nutri-

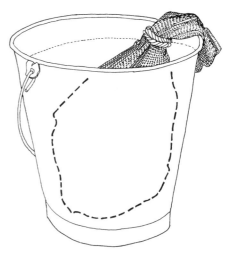

Brewing Garden Teas: Compost or manure teas are the least expensive liquid fertilizers. Scoop compost or manure into a burlap bag and suspend in a bucket of water. Steep for a week or two, moving the bag around once every couple days. Use full strength or dilute to the color of weak tea. Chopped alfalfa, wood ashes, seaweed, bloodmeal, or bone meal may be added to the "tea" bag. Chopped fresh comfrey is used for a potassium-rich tea that will benefit cucumbers, beans, and tomatoes.

ents to young seedlings and to mature plants with suspected nutrient deficiencies. The use of fish emulsion foliar spray will correct nitrogen and phosphorus deficiencies and has been known to increase tomato yields by 16 percent. Seaweed foliar spray is highest in trace elements, and comfrey tea is best for meeting potassium needs. Spray plants every three to four weeks with a solution only half as strong as you would apply to soil. Once you have started a foliar spray feeding program, you must continue it regularly. Use watering cans with finely pierced roses, or use pressurized hand sprayers.

If you build soil tilth and increase the humus content of your garden beds before and after each season, you should soon find no need for liquid supplements. Build in humus by spading in compost, dressing your beds with manure or compost in fall or using a cover crop and spading it under before you plant as described in more detail in chapter 1. Onions and the brassicas may do better in soil that has been sprinkled with wood ashes, and potatoes benefit from additions of aged leaf mold, but compost is most important of all to any crop.

Mulching

Mulch has often been called, next to compost, the best friend of the organic gardener. The shift to raised beds will bring to your life a change somewhat like the one a new job or a move causes. Friends will be kept, but friendships will alter in subtle ways. No longer will you have to cover great, weed-prone stretches between rows, but if you have already formed the habit of buying or cutting hay or straw and saving autumn leaves, do not abandon it. Mulching is still useful in the raised bed garden; it just has to be done a little differently.

Mulches, organic and synthetic, are used to conserve water; raise or lower soil temperature by absorbing or shielding the sun's radiation; reduce leaching and nutrient loss; increase the density and spread of roots; mitigate the harmful effects of soil fungi and nematodes; improve soil

structure by encouraging earthworms; prevent compaction by heavy rains; and keep sprawling plants and low-hanging fruit from becoming dirty. Organic mulches also add matter to the soil as they decay.

There's a host of different mulching materials available, and each has its own characteristics that make it suited to performing specific functions in the high-yield garden.

Soil Warming Plastics have the distinction of raising the soil temperature. Among the many forms, clear plastic is better at this than green or black opaque plastics, but the clear form does encourage weed growth. Gardeners use plastics to advance planting dates or to give heat-loving crops a little extra care in cool or short-season areas (more about the use of plastic mulch in chapter 6).

A few cautions about the use of plastics, however, are in order. When certain plastics are in place all season long they cut off air and moisture, which can lead to unbalanced and fungus-prone soil and even to toxic conditions. Plastic mulching of tender plants when soil is wet can also result in damping-off disease.

Not all plastic mulches interfere with the passage of air and moisture. Some mulching sheets are slit for ventilation and newer plastics are often woven, or spun, to make them air and water permeable. Astroturflike materials and non-woven mats, increasingly used commercially, are also slightly permeable. Recent University of Wisconsin studies have shown, however, that all plastics of this type fail to produce the benefits of increased soil temperature. Temperatures under woven and spun plastics are very close to the temperatures of bare soil. The Wisconsin study showed that the heavy, green, Astroturflike material and one of the nonwoven mats produced slightly higher ground temperatures. Heavy-duty impermeable plastic mulches remain the most effective for warming the soil and promoting early growth in heat-loving vegetables, according to the study.

Controlling Weeds Although black polyethylene and woven plastic give the best weed control, a shredded bark mulch is almost as effective. Straw and hay often contribute to the problem of weeding because they contain seeds. Both are usually too cumbersome to use between narrowly spaced rows and should be confined to the unplanted spaces around large vegetables like melons and potatoes.

Moderating Soil Temperature For reducing soil temperatures and creating a moderate soil miniclimate, straw is the best material. Between small vegetables in raised beds, grass clippings are an effective straw substitute. Aluminum foil is another good temperature-reducing mulch for it reflects back the sunlight. A combined mulch of clear plastic over black plastic over leaves cools soil the most. Leaves should not be used alone in summer. They contain phenols, which may inhibit plant growth when leached into the soil. (For more on how to use these cooling mulches, see Mulches in chapter 6.)

Retaining Moisture For holding in moisture, shredded bark mulches work best, followed by straw and grass. Bark and straw, however, are high-carbon materials and may deplete soil nitrogen unless used with a nitrogen source such as soy meal or bloodmeal. Oat straw has a better nitrogen-carbon ratio than wheat straw so you don't need to worry about supplying more nitrogen to the soil.

Promoting Higher Yields No single mulch will stimulate growth and produce higher yields in all vegetables. Bark, in the Wisconsin experiment, produced the highest yields in snap beans and cucumbers. Lettuce yields appeared to be unaffected by mulch.

In another experiment, this one conducted at the University of New Mexico Agricultural Experiment Station, alfalfa hay produced the largest yields in apples. In Ohio, grapevines did best when mulched in a layer of straw, while straw-mulched strawberries showed a 10 percent increase

in yield over unmulched, cultivated plants. Blueberries do best mulched with peat moss or sawdust; in Ohio, these mulches increased yields up to an impressive 152 percent. Salt hay has been found to be good for peanuts, watermelons, strawberries, and radishes. In an Auburn University test, pole beans under oat straw outyielded all others, and tomatoes under peanut hulls dramatically increased in yield over unmulched tomatoes. Seaweed has increased yields in beets, kale, corn, and broccoli.

Improving the Soil All organic mulches help build soil by contributing nutrients and humus. Oat straw, bran, leguminous hays, seaweed, and grass clippings do the most to increase soil fertility. Don't place seaweed, fresh alfalfa, grass clippings, or bran directly next to plants because as these high-nitrogen, wet, green materials are attacked by bacteria, they heat up. When this occurs the nitrogen is volatized in the form of ammonia, which can "burn" tender seedlings. In wet climates, never use absorbent mulches like paper. They will become soggy and then, as they dry, will harden into a crust that cuts off air from soil and encourages conditions that favor diseases.

Best All-Around Mulch Probably the most useful all-around mulch for raised bed gardens is grass clippings. They fit between small vegetables, are easily obtained from your own or your neighbors' property, add nitrogen to the soil, and improve its texture, and they moderate soil temperatures if they are piled to a depth of 4 inches. Campuses, golf courses, and other wide grassy areas will often provide a source of grass clippings for gardeners. Be certain the grass has not been treated with herbicides. If you use mowings from road crews, be wary of lead from automobile exhaust and of thistle and other pernicious weed seed that may be in the mowings.

By midsummer, the living mulch of healthy, growing leaves will protect the soil around most small vegetables in a raised bed. Larger vegetables like potatoes, peanuts, storage onions, corn, tomatoes, peppers, eggplants, and melons should be mulched, especially in time of drought, if not surrounded by a living mulch of small vegetables. Lay the mulch after a soaking rain when the ground is wet but not soggy. With raised beds, you need not worry about compacting the soil as you perform the task. If no rains come, water thoroughly before you mulch. You may leave your soaker hose or drip irrigation system in place under the protecting mulch layer.

Weeding

Weeds are generally regarded by gardeners as persistent troublemakers, and rightly so. Weeds steal water and soil nutrients needed by edible plants, thereby reducing garden yields. They harbor insects and diseases. Weeds also compete for sun, and since they usually grow more quickly and vigorously than most vegetables, they often win the competition. A row of vegetable seedlings can be easily smothered by weeds.

By starting with a garden of raised beds and tightly, evenly spaced plantings, you have already given yourself a major advantage in the battle against weeds. When you double dig and bring in relatively weed-free compost to add to the soil, you have an opportunity to remove, or bury deeply, the roots and stems of perennial plagues like crabgrass, quack grass, and bindweed and to reduce the number of annual weed seeds near the surface of your soil. As your seedlings grow, the living mulch of vegetable leaves will stifle, or shade out, many of the weeds that do grow in your beds. You may also be using grass clippings or another weed-inhibiting mulch between narrow rows or in spaces around larger vegetables. As the soil of the raised beds washes down over the years exposing new layers, weed seed in the entire bed will be reduced gradually.

Do not deceive yourself into thinking, however, that in a raised bed you'll never see a weed. Remember that you have created an ideal environment in your soil, and weeds, like edible plants, seek out and thrive in such environments. Some

hand weeding will be part of your life as a raised bed gardener.

The careful spacing of intensive beds makes the most important weeding you do into an easy task. This weeding begins long before you ever see a full-sized weed, or a direct-seeded vegetable. Do it within three days after seeding or transplanting, preferably after a rain or a watering, or when you first notice tiny flecks of green between your plantings. Since you know exactly where seeds or plants have been placed, you can assume that anything else that's green should be removed. Use a hand cultivator, a rake, or a hoe to barely scrape the soil surface to less than an inch deep, uprooting the tiny weeds. If you continue this practice every few days until your plantings are established and beginning to cast a shadow, it may be the only weeding you have to do, apart from hand pulling of occasional weeds very close to plants.

While plants are in the period of rapid growth but have not yet formed a shading canopy and when soil is still too cool to mulch or you haven't had time to mulch it yet, it is a good idea to set up a schedule for cultivating and hand weeding. With small raised beds, it will be easy to designate a bed or two a week to weed thoroughly.

Oregon growers with a very large garden report that they weed 2 of their 28 beds each day. Weeding each bed at least once every two weeks assures weeds don't have time to go to seed. These Oregon market gardeners move a small stick (painted with the words "Weed Me Next") from bed to bed so that each person working in the garden can keep track of which bed is next on the agenda.

As you become more experienced, you'll learn which vegetables require the most weeding to sustain high yields, and you can concentrate your weeding energies on those crops. Onions and carrots, for example, require much weeding early in their growth, before you mulch them.

The height of the beds will allow you to sit or kneel in the paths while reaching into the center of the beds. The time you spend weeding will not be unpleasant, and it will give you occasion to check the progress of your garden and to look for insect damage.

Cultivating for an Almost Weed-Free Garden

When you cultivate during the season of rapid growth, what you are actually doing is forcing the germination of subsurface weed seeds and then destroying the weed seedlings that germinate. Contrary to general belief, most weed seeds don't blow in from fields and waste areas; they come from the soil, where they have remained viable for many years. An experiment in Vermont using sterilized soil over weed-infested land and cultivating to various depths proved that seeds of pigweed, lamb's-quarters, and ragweed are inhibited from germination if they are buried deeper than 1 to 2 inches. When you cultivate to a depth of more than 2 inches, you kill off many thousands of weeds that have already germinated, but you also bring up a whole new layer of soil full of thousands of weed seeds that will then begin to germinate. In one experiment, one field was found to contain more than a billion weed seeds an acre.

If you keep cultivating to a 2-inch depth, or less, you can eventually force the germination of, and kill, a large percentage of the annual weeds in your beds. A large row garden requires the periodic use of a rotary tiller, which stirs weed seeds buried deep below the surface. Weeds in the row garden, therefore, will always remain in large number. With raised beds, if you cultivate shallowly and avoid using a rotary•tiller, each year your beds will have fewer weeds. One estimate, made at Louisiana State University, is that weed seed declines 50 to 75 percent each year under repeated, shallow cultivation.

Once the leaf canopy of vegetables is formed, or mulch has been laid, it is still a good idea to cultivate shallowly occasionally. Always culti-vate when you replace vegetables. Gardeners who stop hoeing when their plants stop growing may be adding to their weed problems in future years.

Weeding at the Right Time

With some gardeners, the quest for a weed-free garden becomes an obsession, and too much precious gardening time goes into producing manicured spaces—time that would better be spent on making compost, working out faster successions, or planning more beds. A compulsive weeder is no more pleasant to live with than a compulsive house cleaner. In reining back an obsession, use new research to direct weeding energies.

A 1984 study at Canada's Harrow, Ontario, Research Station suggests that the time at which we weed matters more than how often we weed. With transplanted early EMERALD ACRE cabbages and direct-seeded PETO TRIPLEMECH pickling cucumbers, for example, a single weeding is sometimes enough to prevent yield loss. Cabbage yields were not reduced when cabbage plots were kept weed-free for the first three weeks after transplanting or when one thorough weeding was done at any point between three and five weeks after transplanting. Yields under both these circumstances were the same as in plots kept weed-free all season.

In plantings of pickling cucumbers, plots that were kept free of weeds for the first four weeks after direct seeding and those beds that were thoroughly weeded three weeks after seeding equaled weed-free controls in terms of yield.

An earlier Harrow experiment with SPRINGSET tomato transplants showed that the critical period for keeping tomatoes weed-free is five weeks after transplanting. A thorough weeding at four to five weeks after transplanting prevented yield reductions.

Other Natural Weed Controls

Birds and insects eat a vast number of weed seeds and seedlings. Birds are almost always found in a raised bed garden. Insects are generally less welcome, with a few notable exceptions, but nearby weeds may appease them into staying out of the garden. We should remember that weeds, too, are part of the balance of nature. A few weeds near (but outside) the beds will encourage not only insects but also insect predators that you will welcome to your garden. For example, you can encourage parasites of caterpillars into orchards by allowing wildflowers to grow there.

There is at least one more way to control weeds, should you find that too much of your time is going into pulling and cultivating. Certain vegetable varieties hold their own against weeds better than do others. GREEN MOUNTAIN (27) and NORCHIP (79) potatoes are the best competitors with broad-leaved weeds, yellow nutsedge, pigweed, and lamb's-quarters. HUDSON potatoes compete well with yellow nutsedge, while KATAHDIN (62) and SEBAGO (47) compete poorly. Cornell University researchers attribute the ability to compete to early emergence, rapid growth, and the capacity to form a dense canopy.

EBONY (10, 14) acorn squash, a vine crop, competes best with pigweed and lamb's-quarters if planted early. The squash BUSH TABLE QUEEN and BUSH EBONY (63), a semibush, compete with yellow nutsedge, even when planted late, but only at the expense of some of their yield.

Winterizing the Garden

In intensive gardening, the season never really ends if planning and practice are at their best. However, there will be a sorting out that compares with the putting to bed of the ordinary garden. Different treatments will be necessary for separate beds and bed sections.

Perennial Beds Strawberries, asparagus, Jerusalem artichokes, bramble crops, blueberries, horseradish, and large perennial herb plantings should be cleared of weeds and dead or diseased vegetation, and then mulched very heavily after the first frost. If possible, use a mulch that meets the nutritional requirements of the crop. To encourage healthy renewal, add a layer of compost or rotted manure. If cutting back the stalks of Jerusalem artichokes, be certain to leave enough stalk to mark the plants, in case you wish to continue your harvest through winter.

Storage Beds See Ground Storage in chapter 6 for pointers on how to prepare for in-ground storage and the names of crops that can be carried over this way.

Beds for Winter Growing By the end of summer, you should have designated one bed or more for winter growing of lettuce, spinach, kale, oriental greens, and other hardy vegetables. Try to use beds that have not been given over to heavy feeders during the main season. Legume beds are ideal. Winter beds are fitted with growing devices that cover them. Consult chapters 7 and 8 for further information on winter growing inside protective structures. Chapter 6 suggests reliable varieties and planting dates.

Beds for Early Spring Use If possible, select a bed that has not been used for heavy feeders during the past season. The bed from which you have just removed your late lima beans is ideal. After the first hard freeze, add a 3-inch layer of hay, leaves, pine needles, straw, grass, or other porous material. This will prevent erosion as well as alternate freezing and thawing of the soil. Remove the mulch as early in spring as you are ready to think about planting, and you will find that you've spared yourself much hard preparatory work. See Techniques for an Early Start in chapter 6 for some useful information on early-season gardening.

Beds for Mid to Late Spring Planting These are the beds that will have the time to be given the full winter recovery treatment and rest cure. Plan so that at least some of your beds are empty before the fall is over, and you will have time to plant a cover crop. For a complete discussion of cover crops and their care, consult chapter 1.

5 *Special Techniques for Even Higher Yields*

The perfect positioning of five white daisies within a riotous August bouquet is a small gesture — a fine point, perhaps, but also a sign of thoughtful caring that gives a finish and a patina to human enterprise. So, too, in gardening, small gestures distinguish the true expert from the competent practitioner and the bumper crop from the adequate harvest.

A well-tended narrow row of a single vegetable will bear generously for the average raised bed gardener. The master high-yield gardener is looking for more. Adding an extra flourish, a grace note, the expert carefully matches two vegetables and makes the garden space do double duty for the highest possible yield.

Sometimes a proper balance must be struck between two gardening goals. Here again, it is the skillful gardener who moves with sureness, knowing when to prune to produce one large, perfect apple instead of three small ones, or when to nip off buds to ripen a reluctant melon before frost. Sound, sure judgment and the patience for extra care come with experience. In the long run, learning the fine points will always bring reward.

Interplanting

When we discussed raised bed spacing options in chapter 4, you were introduced to space-sharing plans that allow two vegetable plants to grow in close proximity to make optimum use of a given area. Options included making use of otherwise wasted space around large vegetables, closely spacing two different crops within one row, and setting separate vegetables in adjacent rows, strips, or blocks. Another word for this kind of space sharing is interplanting. The name is derived from an agricultural practice known as intercropping.

In intercropping, two or more crops are grown at the same time in one field. Each planting yields less than it would if given the entire field to itself, but, if compatible crops are chosen, the total yield of the field is greater than it would have been with a monocrop culture. For example, in a 1974 New York State study involving kidney beans and corn, it was shown that a 30 percent greater common yield due to intercropping is quite common.

Intercropping of tomatoes and beans has increased tomato yields in locations from Michigan to Costa Rica by up to 40 percent. When a four-vegetable intercropping of tomatoes, snap beans, peas, and cabbage was used in a Michigan State University experiment, tomato and snap bean yields were reduced, but cabbage and pea yields increased, producing a total crop of higher market value.

Granted, all this evidence that interplanting brings higher yields was gleaned from agricultural research. But even on the reduced scale of the backyard garden, the benefits of interplanting will be similar. You'll harvest more per square foot of garden area, making better use of the available space.

Another benefit you'll notice is a more aesthetic one — your garden will look lusher and like a mosaic, with different shades of green dotted with the bright yellows, deep reds, burnished oranges, and delicate lilacs that make up the garden's palette. Purple basil planted among eggplants, a fringe of scallions around a head of cabbage — these pairings do more than make good use of space; they delight the gardener's eye. Keep in mind this other dimension to plant pairings as you read the following suggestions for interplantings.

Jigsaw Fit Aboveground

The art of garden interplanting begins with finding out which crops are compatible. Plants get along together in a number of different ways. To begin with, they can complement one another in

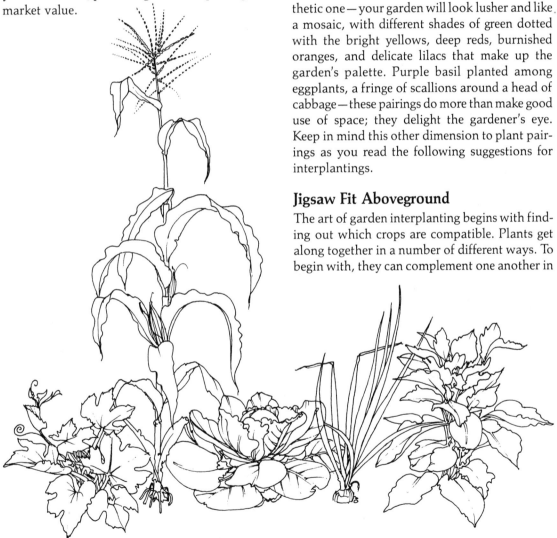

Good Neighbor Policy: Plants with complementary topgrowth can share close quarters in a garden bed. Compatible growers include, from left, squash, corn, cabbage, onion, and eggplant.

ABOVEGROUND GROWTH PATTERNS

These vegetable combinations may be interplanted successfully because of their complementary physical growth patterns.

Beans—celery	Corn—Chinese cabbage	Melons—radishes
Beans—corn	Corn—lettuce	Onions—cabbage
Beans—corn—squash, melons, cucumbers	Corn—potatoes	Onions—carrots
Beans—radishes	Corn—squash, melons, cucumbers	Onions—eggplants
Beans—tomatoes (staked)	Cucumbers—okra	Onions—peppers
Cabbage—chives	Kohlrabi—beets	Onions—spinach
Cabbage—peppers	Leeks—carrots	Peas on trellis—cole crops, turnips,
Cabbage—squash, melons, cucumbers	Leeks—parsley	lettuce, carrots, kohlrabi,
Cabbage—tomatoes	Lettuce—carrots—onions	spinach, radishes
Cole crops—carrots	Lettuce—onions	Sweet potatoes—pumpkins
Corn—cabbage	Lettuce—radishes	

the shape of their topgrowth so that they will tuck in next to each other in a row as neatly as two stones in a well-made wall. When plants fit tightly together, no space remains to invite weeds. Some plants make extremely efficient couples. Corn and mung beans, for example, when planted together intercept 90 percent of available sunlight after only 50 days of growth. For a guide to matchmaking in your own garden, see the pairings listed in the chart Aboveground Growth Patterns.

Two-Story Sharing

You will notice that whenever radishes appear on the chart Aboveground Growth Patterns they are always listed along with a larger vegetable. Of course, this can be accounted for by the fact that few vegetables are smaller than radishes, but it also illustrates another interplanting strategy. Think of your intensive plantings as having not only width, but also height. Use the understory space pocket created by plants that spread out a little over the ground (like beans), or left by those plants that soar straight up (like corn), for smaller vegetables like radishes, lettuce, and spinach. Keep

in mind, however, that understory vegetables must be tolerant of shade. For possible combinations of light-loving with shade-loving vegetables see the chart Light and Shade-Tolerant Plants on page 140. Early in the season, shade-loving crops will be mostly salad vegetables, but by midsummer when the sun shines longer and warmer, members of the cabbage family can be included.

Take care to give your shade-tolerant understory plants some light and sufficient water and nutrients. If an understory crop is being forced to grow abnormally tall and spindly or its normal color has dulled, it is probably not getting enough light because of overcrowding. The cucumber is one vegetable often given more shade than it should have. Slightly cool conditions benefit its growth, but it needs full sunshine.

Corn and sunflowers, which produce food with unusual efficiency if given high levels of light, are ideal upper story plants. However, for reasons to be discussed later under Plants That Work against High Yields, sunflowers should not be planted too close to other vegetables.

Sometimes the upper story is way, way up there. European market gardeners, especially on the island of Majorca, and tropical farmers in Indonesia and Nepal traditionally plant vegetables around their ornamental and fruit trees to make full use of both space and shade. Garlic or radishes are set under fruit trees and soybeans are sometimes used under walnut trees. Here in North America, one gardener in North Carolina grows parsnips and squash under her dwarf fruit trees.

Jigsaw Fit Underground

Don't limit your thinking to topgrowth when you plan interplantings. Plants relate to each other underground as well.

The association of two plants with compatible root systems makes full use of underground space. Deep roots feed below shallow roots, tapping different levels of nutrients and water, thereby avoiding direct competition.

Although the root system of each individual vegetable differs slightly from that of all other plants, there are two main categories of roots, taproots and fibrous roots.

Taproots are the primary roots on seedlings. In some vegetables these first roots become en-

Two-Story Interplanting: Tall crops, like staked tomatoes and corn, leave plenty of space for ground-hugging plants like leafy greens, radishes, and celery. Make sure understory plants can tolerate shade.

LIGHT AND SHADE-TOLERANT PLANTS

These pairings combine plants with differing light needs that grow well together. The left half of the pairing prefers full sun, while the right half tolerates shade.

Beans (bush)—celery
Beans (bush or pole)—lettuce
Beans (bush or pole)—spinach
Cole crops—celery
Cole crops—lettuce

Cole crops—spinach
Corn—lettuce
Cucumbers (trellised)—celery
Cucumbers (trellised)—lettuce
Eggplants—celery

Okra—cucumbers
Onions—carrots—lettuce
Peas (trellised)—lettuce
Peas (trellised)—spinach
Tomatoes (staked)—lettuce

Fruit and Vegetable Combination: Try filling the empty space under dwarf fruit trees with root crops and vining plants like squash.

larged after transplanting and sometimes furnish the most edible part of the plant, as in carrots, parsnips, radishes, and turnips. Generally there are also smaller secondary roots on taprooted vegetables.

In some taprooted seedlings like the brassicas, eggplants, peppers, and tomatoes, the taproot breaks up after transplanting and the secondary roots branch out dramatically to become the sustaining root system of the plant.

Still other vegetables like the legumes and the cucurbits have taproots that remain small, reaching about the same depth as their secondary roots, to give them a root system resembling that of a fibrous-rooted vegetable.

True fibrous-rooted vegetables have roots that branch out early in the development of the plant. Their primary roots stop growing and small roots grow out of the stem or from nodes and travel laterally and shallowly. Members of the onion family and of the grass family, like corn, have fibrous systems.

When you use members of different plant families with different root patterns—taproot, modified taproot, and fibrous—in your inter-

CHARACTERISTIC ROOTING DEPTH

Shallow Rooting (18 to 36 inches)	**Medium Rooting** (36 to 48 inches)	**Deep Rooting** (more than 48 inches)
Broccoli	Beans (snap)	Artichokes
Brussels sprouts	Beets	Asparagus
Cabbage	Carrots	Beans (lima)
Cauliflower	Cucumbers	Parsnips
Celery	Eggplants	Pumpkins
Chinese cabbage	Mustard	Squash (winter)
Corn	Peas	Sweet potaotes
Endive	Peppers	Tomatoes
Garlic	Rutabagas	
Leeks	Squash (summer)	
Lettuce	Swiss chard	
Onions	Turnips	
Parsley		
Potatoes		
Radishes		
Spinach		

planting schemes, you make certain that the root systems of individual plants set close to one another will not crowd or compete but will share underground space. For example, you can plant vegetables like radishes with small taproots next to plants with extensive branched systems like tomatoes or peppers. Shallow-rooted plants like cucumbers and onions can be planted with deeper-rooted plants like beans or Swiss chard.

Nutrient Sharing

When too many plants compete for the same nutrients and water, stunting and poor growth occur. Even in highly fertile raised beds, soil nutrients must be rationed out equitably. Nitrogen is the element most essential to plant growth. Growing interplantings composed entirely of heavy-feeding crops—those that require much nitrogen

—will not only result in poor yields, but it will also drain the supply of soil nitrogen quickly. In general, heavy-feeding crops are those with broad leaf areas.

Most interplanting schemes designed to share light and aboveground and underground space also make for good distribution of soil nutrients. For example, beans, peas, and soybeans, whose aboveground shapes allow light to reach smaller heavy feeders like radishes or parsley, actually help to build nitrogen into the soil. Carrots, garlic, potatoes, parsnips, turnips, and most other root or tuber crops are light feeders and will not interfere with the nutrient demand of the crops they are most likely to share root space with, such as broccoli, eggplants, or spinach.

Carrots, leeks, potatoes, and turnips all require large amounts of potassium and should not be

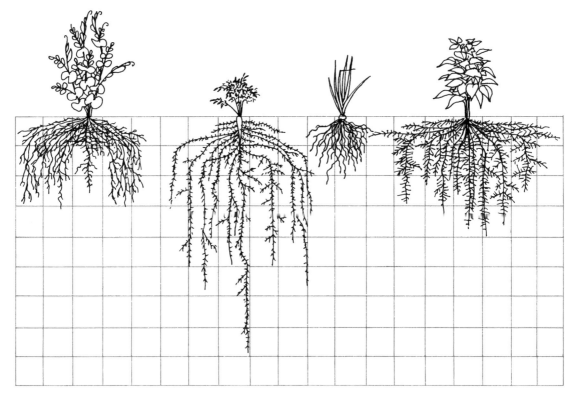

Root Systems: When planning close spacings, it helps to consider compatible root systems. Representing the basic kinds of roots (with variations) are, from left, a pea vine with a small taproot, carrot with a full-fledged taproot, fibrous-rooted onion, and pepper with a modified taproot.

planted together repeatedly in the same bed unless wood ashes are added to the soil. In general, very sprawling plants with large leaves like potatoes, squashes, and sweet potatoes interplant poorly and should be given wider spacing if they are grouped.

Some Favorite Combinations

Each high-yield gardener develops sets of favorite vegetable combinations that achieve economy of space without interference. Once you have found interplanting schemes that work for

you, rotate the whole combination to a different bed the next season.

In planning combinations, use the same common sense you would in arranging your living room furniture. Start with big, space-occupying, long-lasting items (couches and chairs in the living room, tomatoes or squash in the garden), and then work in smaller, more adaptable items that are more easily replaced (lamps and end tables in the living room, lettuce and radishes in the garden).

Interplanting schemes of all sorts have additional advantages. Through their diversity, they

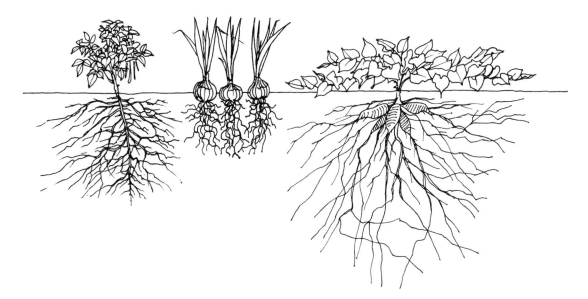

Underground Companions: Make sure plants in beds get along underground. Try to alternate medium-rooting (represented here by bush beans), shallow-rooting (onions), and deep-rooting (sweet potatoes) crops so there is minimal competition for water and nutrients at the same soil level.

SPACE-EFFICIENT ROOT PATTERNS

The pairings below match crops with complementary root growth patterns. Planted next to each other, roots won't compete and will make the best use of the available space underground.

Beans—carrots	Melons—radishes
Beans—celery	Onions—cabbage
Beans—corn	Onions—carrots
Beans—cucumbers	Onions—eggplants
Beans—onions	Onions—peppers
Beans—radishes	Onions—radishes
Beans—squashes	Onions—spinach
Corn—lettuce	Parsnips—lettuce
Corn—potatoes	Peas—radishes
Kohlrabi—beets	Peas—turnips
Leeks—carrots	Salsify—lettuce
Lettuce—carrots—onions	Swiss chard—cucumbers
Lettuce—radishes	

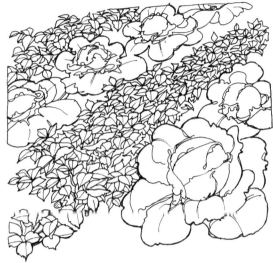

Sharing Soil Nutrients: In the garden, a trio like this won't compete for nutrients. The pea will build nitrogen into the soil, a bonus for the broccoli. The light-feeding carrot won't interfere with the broccoli's nutrient demands.

Cabbages among the Strawberries: Some gardeners transplant cabbage seedlings into strawberry patches when the berry harvest is over. This stretches the productivity of the garden bed.

create complex ecosystems that imitate the rich mosaic of nature and therefore encourage spiders, toads, and other valuable insect predators and discourage the spread of crop-specific pests and diseases.

One of the best known interplanting combinations is shell beans and corn, the staple of Central American diets and a duo to which North American Indians added pumpkin or squash. The leaves of corn and bean plants are at different heights so the crops don't compete for light. The subsurface roots are of different types, fibrous (corn) and modified taproot (beans), but, even more important, the beans help the heavy-feeding corn by harboring the bacteria that will put nitrogen into the soil. The deeper roots of the beans draw nutrients from levels below the soil occu-

pied by the shallow corn roots.

A traditional combination that was used in the extra-dense plantings of French market gardeners' glass-covered winter beds is carrots, lettuce, and radishes. Spinach and celery share space well. Peas, cabbage, and winter lettuce group well in short rows. Cucumbers and corn, although often used, are less successful unless a Bantam variety of corn is one of the partners. Taller corn interferes with the cucumbers' need for light.

Among master gardeners, onion sets, broccoli, herbs, and marigolds is one favorite grouping, and onions, tomatoes, and basil a second. Swiss chard, beets, and carrots are grown together through winter in an Oregon garden, while in Mississippi parsley, celery, Brussels sprouts, and

Traditional Combination: Beans and corn are a classic pair. The difference in heights and root systems means there is no competition above or below ground. The beans boost the soil's nitrogen level, which aids the heavy-feeding corn.

spinach share space. A North Carolinian favors spinach among the strawberries, okra with the Swiss chard, and cucumbers next to the grapevines. Squash and blueberries share a bed in Iowa. Beets live among corn, and leeks among brassicas, in a Washington garden, while in Kansas it is lettuce, radishes, and tomatoes that make up the salad bed.

Successions

It's possible to add a new dimension to interplanting—the dimension of time. If interplanting is the sharing of space, then succession planting is the sharing of space *in time*. Of all the strate-

gies for increasing the yield of a given space, succession planting is the most crucial and the most productive when it comes to the small intensive garden. Idle spaces produce no crops. Spaces that are used in sequence by as many crops as possible, it stands to reason, are most productive.

Most row gardeners practice some form of haphazard succession. Usually when one crop, or one vegetable plant, is harvested they look around for something to put in its place or fill the gap. Intensive gardeners have to do better than that. They should know ahead of time exactly what the replacement crop will be and, whenever possible, they should have on hand transplant-size seedlings of the replacement crop at the exact moment of the turnover. Timing is the key to successful intensive gardening.

To get your timing on the mark, you will have to learn, or keep on record, the days to maturity of each of the vegetables (and, if possible, individual varieties of the vegetables) you plan to use. Using a combination of early, middle, and late varieties planted simultaneously will provide a continuous harvest of one vegetable. For example, early cabbage matures in 55 days, while late cabbage may take as many as 105 days. By planting both and also using a midseason cabbage with an 80-day maturity, you can supply your table with crisp green cabbage the better part of three months. This is the simplest kind of succession planning.

Simple succession is related to the agricultural practice of double cropping. Farmers plant winter wheat in September, harvest it in June, and immediately use the same field for a crop of soybeans to be harvested the following fall. The gardener will not, of course, be working with whole fields but at most with beds and more usually with narrow rows or individual vegetable spaces.

A slightly more complex form of succession planting is the use of one vegetable variety with

(continued on page 148)

With the Master Gardeners

BACKYARD INNOVATIONS IN INTERPLANTING

There's a lot to be learned about gardening from books, magazines, seed catalogs, and the backs of seed packets. But often the very best way to learn is from other gardeners. Here are interplantings master gardeners across the country have tried, some to great success, others with less than desired results.

In Texas, John Dromgoole puts sunflowers, pumpkins, and cucumbers in the corn patch and, like a good Italian chef, "garlic with everything." "The most important thing," he says, "is never letting a space go vacant." Seedling onions and lettuce are best for the kind of space fillers that lead to constant harvest, but he's found that herbs that have medium to low light requirements are the plants to look for if you're filling in under the shade of taller plants.

Organic Gardener of the Year contest winner Lynn Coody of Oregon divides her market garden into six basic rotated areas based on vegetable family affiliations, but she also interplants for beauty as well as for benefit. Lettuce is interplanted with artichokes, cauliflower with broccoli and lettuce, and flowers and herbs are mixed with many crops. "It takes me three weeks to make the garden plan in January," she confesses.

One area in which Coody has been experimenting recently is multilayered planting—finding things that like to grow in the shade, like lettuce, spinach, and some of the mustards and planting them underneath plants that are taller. Using a multi-story system helps cover the ground and extends the season of the shade-loving crops. Coody has succeeded in keeping lettuce from bolting "even into the middle of summer" by planting it under sunflowers and corn. She's also grown lettuce underneath cabbages. Lettuce grows wider while the cabbage grows taller, and by the time the cabbage starts expanding its girth, the lettuce is ready to cut.

Mark Rames of Michigan, another Organic Gardener of the Year finalist, has learned almost as much from combinations that didn't work as from ones that did. "It didn't work real well for us to interplant root crops," he reports. "If you wanted to get a carrot or an onion out, you had to disturb the vegetable next to it." Now he puts all his onions in one bed and his carrots in another.

Some interplanting schemes, on the other hand, have worked well for him—parsley with celery, Brussels sprouts with spinach, and Swiss chard with cauliflower. The larger, taller vegetables, he finds, can go down to the center of the bed, and the spinach or chard can fill out the rest of the ground and cover it. He plants lettuce between pepper plants to protect it from the sun and often mixes in some radishes. Peas, celery, and spinach, he's found, are an especially good combination.

In Kansas, Chris Seitz is always looking at her garden with a critical eye. "Yesterday I was saying I could be growing beets in all that space between the tomatoes." She already has lettuce and radishes there and "it's working out fine. As the weather gets hotter, the tomatoes shade the lettuce and the lettuce gradually dies out." One combination that didn't work for Seitz was dill and potatoes. The potatoes grew past the dill and shaded it out completely.

Vermont market gardener and proprietor of The Cook's Garden, Shepherd Ogden, has another place for dill. It goes with his cabbage. He's not sure it keeps the bugs away, but it "grows up to a nice size for me to sell, and then I cut it and the cabbage expands."

"You have to plant things somewhere, and I figure if you can confuse any insect with a variety of smells, that's worth doing." That's the way New Hampshire Organic Gardener of the Year Hugh Matthews makes his case for interplanting. One of his successful interplanting recipes is this: Plant a row of broccoli near one side of a raised bed. Interplant with onion sets. Using staggered placement, add a row of cauliflower and then a row of cabbage. As the weather warms up, add a couple of herbs and put some marigolds on either end of the rows. Another of Matthews's favorite bed combinations is a row of peppers next to a row of mixed carrots and onions. His broccoli, carrots, cauliflower, and early cabbages are planted together in a zigzag pattern.

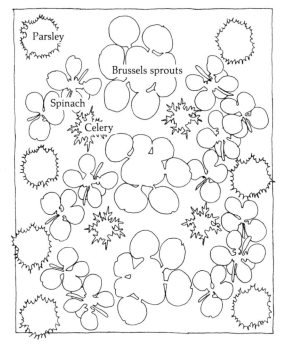

Innovative Interplantings
Brussels sprouts, parsley, spinach, and celery share space in this bed.

Peppers, basil, and tomatoes make good neighbors.

Radishes, lettuce, and peppers are companions in this dense planting.

Peas, lettuce, and cabbage are space-conscious bed mates.

staggered plantings. If, for example, you do small sowings of radish seeds every two weeks from April until late June, you will be assured of a few fresh radishes at almost every meal for almost three months. The staggered plantings help you avoid the dismal feast or famine cycle of harvesting. These radishes could theoretically be grown in the same space each time or in different spaces.

How to Succeed with Successions

So far, we've been talking about single vegetables, and we have temporarily set aside our discussion of shared space and mixed plantings. Now let's return to the mixed crop bed. We've said earlier that when it comes to making the best use of space, it is common sense to start planning around the space-demanding crops you wish to grow. In planning the use of space in time, the crops that stay in the beds the longest are the ones you have to think of first. See the chart Long-Season Crops for a handy listing.

Warmth-loving, long-season crops are usually in the soil from May until August or even longer in many parts of this country. Cold-loving crops may occupy space from March until June, from August into October, or for shorter periods of time.

List all the long-growers you plan to use, including all crops that occupy space for 70 days or more from planting until harvest. Divide these into heat-loving and cold-loving. Now, using the times to maturity listed on the seed packets, or in notes you have taken from your own experience

LONG-SEASON CROPS

Crop	Average Days to Maturity	Season of Growth
Beans (pole)	108	Midseason
Broccoli	110 (60 after transplanting)	Early or late
Brussels sprouts	130 (85 after transplanting)	Whole season
Cabbage	140 (90 after transplanting)	Early or late
Cauliflower	110 (60 after transplanting)	Early or late
Corn	70–90	Midseason
Eggplants	120 (70 after transplanting)	Midseason
Garlic	90	Mid to whole season
Leeks	150	Whole season
Melons	90	Midseason
Onions (storage)	100	Whole season
Parsley	80	Whole season
Parsnips	120	Whole season
Peanuts	120–140	Whole season
Peas	70	Early or late
Peppers	125 (75 after transplanting)	Midseason
Potatoes (sweet)	140–150	Whole season
Potatoes (white)	80–140	Mid to whole season
Pumpkins	110–120	Whole season
Salsify	120	Whole season
Squash (winter)	80–100	Mid to whole season
Tomatoes	126 (70 after transplanting)	Midseason
Watermelons	75–90	Midseason

SUCCESSIONS AT A GLANCE

This sample chart should give you an idea of how to plot a time line of successions. In this sample garden bed, beets, carrots, and early cabbage vacate areas for peppers and tomatoes. Early staggered plantings of radishes give way to staggered bush beans. At the end of the beans, the fall crop of cabbage and carrots goes in. Graph paper makes it easy to plot times to maturity, especially when you make one square equal to one week.

	March	April	May	June	July	August	September
Beets 60 days							
Carrots 70 days							
Broccoli 60 days*							
Cabbage 55 days*							
Radishes 25 days							
Beans (snap) 50 days							
Peppers 75 days*†							
Tomatoes 70 days*†							

*Days from transplanting
†Although these long-season crops take 70 to 75 days to mature their first crop, they continue to produce until frost.

with them, or in the High-Yield Plant Guide at the back of this book, designate a period during which space will be reserved in your beds for each of these crops. If you have an option, pick the earliest possible starting date for each vegetable and select a variety that, through quick growing habit or heat or cold tolerance, will permit the date you have chosen.

On a piece of graph paper, prepare a chart similar to Successions at a Glance on the preceding page. Put your own calculated days to maturity under the vegetable name and mark off a time bar across the appropriate month columns. In effect, you will be hanging a "this time reserved" sign on various parts of your garden plan.

Now comes the chess game. First, calculate the longest possible total growing season your climate will allow, taking limited risk on frost damage. Then, using heat-loving and cool-loving long-growers, try to mesh growing times as much as possible. The growing periods indicated by your time bars should either meet exactly or overlap slightly. Keep in mind that certain crops, like some of the brassicas and oriental greens, do better in fall than in spring. Make sure that follow-up crops are given long enough to mature before heavy frosts come.

Now, consult the chart Short-Season Crops for a list of vegetables with short growing times. Crop by crop try to fit as many short-season growing periods as possible on either side of your time lines for long growers. The short and long growing lines can overlap slightly.

When you begin to examine the relative rates of maturity of various crops you'll discover many possibilities; for example, three relays of radishes could precede a broccoli planting, and five or more staggered radish sowings could mature in the time left over after the broccoli harvest. Head lettuce can come out of the garden around the time peppers go into the beds, allowing the two crops to share one space during a season. A crop of okra can fit neatly between an early and a late planting of cabbage. These are just a few of an endless number of combinations.

In addition to using quick-maturing varieties, you can speed up successions in your beds by transplanting as many of your vegetables as possible. When you put plants in the garden at transplant stage instead of sowing seeds, you can

SHORT-SEASON CROPS

Crop	Days to Maturity	Season
Arugula	45	Early
Beets	50–60	Early or late
Carrots	70	Early or late
Garden cress	10–20	Early or late
Kohlrabi	45–55	Early or late
Lettuce, loosehead	55–70	Early or late
Lettuce, leaf (heat-resistant types)	45–60	Any
Onions, green (from sets)	30–40	Any
Radishes	20–25	Any
Spinach	45–50	Early or late
Spinach, New Zealand	55	Midseason
Swiss chard	55–60	Any
Turnips	40–75	Early or late

subtract the time they would take from sowing to reach that stage, and thus achieve faster turnover. To have plants at exactly the right stage for transplanting when the time comes to replace crops, learn the number of days from sowing to transplanting for each of your vegetables and start the seeds at the correct time. (This information is given for individual vegetables in the High-Yield Plant Guide.)

Some midsummer replacement sowings may take less time than usual to germinate and mature since the soil is already warm. But some late summer successions like peas and lettuce will be stubborn germinators precisely *because* the soil is warm. Their overall development may be a bit slower than spring-started counterparts. Another factor to keep in mind with midsummer replacements is the shortening daylength. Seed packet days-to-maturity figures are usually based on spring planting. Some gardeners add two weeks to the estimated maturity date for crops growing into the fall.

Relay Planting

Overlapping growing periods allow for a special kind of succession planting called relay planting.

By the time you harvest your spring cabbage, the leaf lettuce will be ready to thin.

Soon after tomato plants are set out, the lettuce will be finishing. By the time the expanding tomato plants need the room, they'll be able to take over the space that has already produced two crops.

Three-Way Garden Relay: Set out early cabbage plants in mid-March. In early April sow leaf lettuce between the cabbages. (Indoors, start tomato seedlings for mid-May transplanting.)

Ordinary succession planting is following one crop with another, while relay planting is putting in a second crop before the first crop is harvested. To achieve a perfectly timed relay interplanting, plant new seedlings between, or immediately alongside of, established initial plantings. By the time the relay crop needs more space, the initial planting will have been harvested.

Favorite Relays and Successions

Where you live determines how many successions you can squeeze into a season. Southern

SUCCESSIONS FOR SOUTHERN GARDENS

These successions were developed by Professor William Poillion of the Southeast Horticultural Experimental Station in Hammond, Louisiana, for gardeners' use in his geographical area. The planting dates and harvest periods should be modified for use in localities with shorter seasons.

Vegetable*	Date Planted	Harvest Period
COMBINATION ONE		
Tomatoes†	Apr. 5	June 9–July 6
Cantaloupes†	Apr. 20	June 19–July 6
Broccoli	July 26	Oct. 7–21
Turnips	Oct. 27	Feb. 13–Mar. 29
COMBINATION TWO		
Sweet corn	Apr. 11	June 20
Cucumbers	June 21	Aug. 1–15
Beans (bush)	Aug. 16	Sept. 26–Oct. 10
Cabbage	Oct. 11	Jan. 1–Feb. 1
COMBINATION THREE		
Peppers (hot)†	Mar. 29	May 30–Oct. 26
Cucumbers†	Apr. 10	May 31–June 26
Cantaloupes†	July 3	Sept. 10–Oct. 21
COMBINATION FOUR		
Broccoli	Mar. 14	Apr. 28–June 2
Sweet corn	June 21	Aug. 22
Cucumbers	Aug. 29	Oct. 16–31
COMBINATION FIVE		
Sweet corn	Apr. 10	June 21–26
Tomatoes†	July 6	Nov. 8
Cantaloupes†	July 11	Sept. 27–Oct. 25
COMBINATION SIX		
Red beans	Apr. 12	June 27
Broccoli	July 10	Sept. 22–Oct. 20
Cabbage	Oct. 21	Jan. 28
COMBINATION SEVEN		
Sweet corn†	Apr. 11	June 20
Southern peas†	June 3	Aug. 25–Sept. 15
Cabbage	Sept. 16	Dec. 1–Jan. 1
COMBINATION EIGHT		
Sweet corn	Apr. 11	June 20–26
Pumpkins	July 1	Sept. 28
COMBINATION NINE		
Yellow squash	Apr. 12	May 22–June 29
Beans (bush)	July 21	Sept. 17
Carrots	Sept. 15	Feb. 12

All vegetables in each combination were not necessarily grown in the same rows but were grown in the time period as shown.
†Interplanted
Source: Louisiana Agriculture vol. 24, no. 2 (Winter 1980–81):19.

SUCCESSIONS FOR NORTHERN GARDENS

Two-Way Relays

Early peas	followed by	Carrots
		Corn
		Cucumbers
		Swiss chard
Early peas	followed by	Leeks
		Melons
		Onions
		Potatoes
		Squash
		Tomatoes
Lettuce or spinach	followed by	Beans (pole)
		Carrots
		Eggplants
		Peanuts
		Peppers
		Potatoes
		Tomatoes
Bunching onions	followed by	Beans (pole)
		Eggplants
		Peppers
		Potatoes
		Swiss chard
		Tomatoes
Chinese cabbage	followed by	Beans (pole)
		Carrots
		Eggplants
		Peppers
		Squash
		Tomatoes
		Turnips

Three-Way Relays

Early peas—Broccoli—Squash (summer)
Early peas—Tomatoes—Cress
Broccoli—Beans (bush)—Lettuce
Chinese cabbage—Beans (bush)—Kohlrabi
Spinach—Cucumbers—Radishes
Lettuce—Onions—Beans (bush)

Four-Way Relays

Early peas—Broccoli—Beans (bush)—Beets
Early peas—Spinach—Melons—Turnips
Chinese cabbage—Beans (bush)—Lettuce—Onions
Spinach—Radishes—Beans (bush)—Chinese cabbage
Early peas—Onions—Swiss chard—Broccoli

Source: Anna Carr, Good Neighbors: Companion Planting for Gardeners. *(Emmaus, Pa.: Rodale Press, 1985).*

gardeners have the luxury of a longer time to fill. But industrious northerners who use season-extending devices can fit three and maybe even four relays into a season. For some ideas on regional planting, see the charts Successions for Southern and Northern Gardens.

Jack Ruttle, an editor with *Rodale's Organic Gardening,* shares his favorite succession, a complex one: He direct-sows spinach as early as the ground can be worked (from March 25 to April 1

in his garden), seeding a small raised bed at 4-inch intervals. When the spinach is up, he plants parsnips on the south side of the bed, 10 to 12 inches apart, pulling a few spinach plants to make room. On June 15, he transplants Brussels sprouts to the north side of the bed, replacing the spinach there. If room permits, he adds broccoli before July 1. As the rest of the spinach is removed from the center rows of the bed, it is replaced by parsley and by successive sowings of heat-resistant

Simple Relays: Transplant broccoli among established lettuce in midspring. Set melons, cucumbers, or pumpkins alongside a planting of peas in June. The peas will be gone by the time the vining crop needs the trellis.

lettuce. On August 1, Ruttle transplants Chinese cabbages and Egyptian onions into the bed to replace the lettuce.

Some gardeners have good results planting an early corn variety, then following it with indoor-started peppers, bush beans, or carrots. The cornstalks can also be stripped after harvest and used for a climbing-bean trellis.

An Alternative Strategy

Successions are good for the gardener, but they're not always good for the garden soil. Some gardeners who worry about the fertility of their soil adopt a different strategy of successions. They grow crops together in densely planted beds, choosing the members of the group by the time of their intended harvest.

In a bed designed for simultaneous harvest, not all vegetables are planted at the same time. Some shorter-growing crops are added gradually after the ones with the longest number of days to harvest are already in place. For example, in one raised bed three crops with similar growing periods of around 60 days—kohlrabi, beets, and cauliflower—are sown together. One week later, broccoli is started inside at the same time that onion sets are added to the original trio. The broccoli seedlings go into the bed and snap beans are added by direct sowing a month after the initial planting of kohlrabi, beets, and cauliflower.

Simultaneously harvested beds have two main advantages. Digging one crop for harvest will not damage a still-developing crop, and the bed can be refertilized in preparation for a spring-to-fall turnover of crops. If your beds are of questionable fertility, either use this method or allow more than the recommended spacing between initial plantings.

Successions' Impact on Yields

The research on extra yields achieved from succession planting is sparse and provides only mixed conclusions. Total yields will be up when the most possible use is made of space throughout the season, but will individual vegetables produce better when used in successions?

In an experiment conducted at the Research Station of the Research Branch of Agriculture Canada in St. Jean, Quebec, and reported in 1976, crop sequences affected yields significantly. Carrots, onions, celery, and lettuce were grown in various sequences for purposes of the study. It was found that carrot yields were significantly greater when carrots followed celery or lettuce than when they followed earlier carrots or onions. Onion yields were greatest after celery or lettuce, less after onions, and least after carrots. Celery yields were greatest after celery or lettuce, less after onions, and least after carrots. Lettuce yields were greater after lettuce or celery than after onions or carrots. The experimenters hypothesized that the depletion of potassium in the soil by the carrots and onions detrimentally affected subsequent crops.

Once more, as in our study of interplanting, we see that an important part of time and space sharing involves nutrient sharing. In choosing one crop to follow another, keep in mind everything you have learned about crop rotation. Successions should be a sort of rotation in fast time. As you would do in bed rotations involving whole-season sequences, follow heavy feeders with light feeders, light feeders with soil-building legumes, and legumes with heavy feeders whenever possible. Try not to plant the same crop, or crops of similar nutrient demands, two times in a row in the same space, particularly when dealing with heavy feeders, potassium-draining root crops, or crops susceptible to diseases or pests you have experienced in your garden. See chapter 2 for more information on vegetable rotations and for a chart listing heavy and light feeders and soil-building crops.

Combining Successions with Interplanting

When there are too many lists to check and criteria to examine before you can make a simple decision about what to plant, the timid, impatient, or inexperienced gardener feels undermined. Suppose, for example, that you find that a fall planting of Brussels sprouts intermixed with spinach fits into the seasonal calendar beautifully after a spring planting of broccoli interplanted with leaf lettuce. The roots of the Brussels sprouts and spinach mesh just as well as the lettuce and broccoli roots did, and the topgrowth patterns complement each other and give the spinach the shade it needs. Then all of a sudden a problem emerges. If Brussels sprouts replace the broccoli, two vegetables from the same family with the same nutrient demands and disease susceptibilities are being asked to share the same ground in sequence—something that the charts tell you should be avoided. But should it be avoided, when everything else works out so well? Not necessarily.

One consideration may outweigh and overrule another when it comes to plant placement and use in sequence. There's one more list you need—a sensible order of priorities from most important to least important:

• Try to share space between long-growing and short-term vegetables.
• Mesh aboveground growing patterns for maximum use of light, choosing sun-lovers over shade-lovers.
• Follow heavy feeders with light feeders or legumes whenever possible, especially late in the season or when soil is not optimally fertile.
• Mesh rooting patterns within the underground space you use.

• Allow for any suspected, but not necessarily documented, growth-enhancing benefits one plant may give to another. (These are discussed in the following section.)

Companion Planting

Companion planting is a form of interplanting in which the space-sharing plants are selected on the basis of their ability to enhance one another's growth. Companion planting is an age-old practice that is thought to confer a number of benefits on the paired plants. Among these are pest, weed, and disease control and growth and flavor enhancement. Some classic companions are tomatoes and basil, nasturtiums and squash, and beans and marigolds.

Probably more has been written and less actually proven about companion planting than about any other aspect of organic gardening. Until recently, the literature has been in large part anecdotal, although sanctioned by long tradition and passionate belief. Recently, however, a growing body of controlled scientific experiments has tested hypotheses and offered scientific explanations for certain plant interactions. This research has generally concentrated on protection against insect attack and growth enhancement. So far, some of the experimental evidence has been contradictory and much of it inconclusive, but some progress is being made toward identifying companions that are mutually beneficial. We now know that marigolds deter soil-dwelling nematodes and that tansy can repel insects like aphids, squash bugs, and Colorado potato beetles. Until researchers can come up with more findings to substantiate traditional companion plant pairings, the best place to turn for information is your own garden. Gardener and author Anna Carr, in *Good Neighbors: Companion Planting for Gardeners* (Rodale Press, 1985), suggests that home growers run controlled experiments on plant pairings to see if the benefits are really there.

Carr points out that every garden is unique because of different conditions of weather, soil, surrounding vegetation, and cropping history. For this reason, and for the obvious additional reason that factors like flavor will always remain matters of personal judgment, gardeners are urged to carefully keep track of those paired plantings of vegetables, herbs, and flowers that have flourished or failed.

Observe carefully and keep accurate records. Repeat all combinations that have worked for you. Exercise imagination, especially in the combination of edible and inedible aromatic plants with those vegetables you wish to protect from insects. Aromatics include marigolds, borage, onions, garlic, leeks, shallots, tomatoes, rosemary, basil, oregano, sage, wormwood, rue, hyssop, lavender, thyme, cabbage and other brassicas, dill, chamomile, mints, nasturtiums, chrysanthemums, tansy, monarda, and many fragrant weeds.

Plants That Work against High Yields

Just as there are good companions in the garden, there are also bad ones that exert a harmful influence on their neighbors. Some of the deficiencies and patterns of poor growth once thought to have been caused by overcompetition, "worn out soil," and poor nutrient balance have been found to come instead from root secretions that certain plants leave in the soil and pass on to the roots of their neighbors. This process is known as allelopathy.

Notice which plants (excluding those that cast a deep shade) require the least weeding in your beds. The chances are that the lack of weeds is caused by growth-inhibiting chemicals. You can sometimes take advantage of one plant's self-weeding ability by planting a weed-prone plant next to it, but there is always a risk involved. Test in small quantity to make sure the weed inhibitor won't turn on the crop you have chosen for its companion.

Black walnut trees are famous for clearing out the ground around themselves, but they do not harm all crops. They've been shown to stunt, wilt, or even kill alfalfa, apples, blackberries, blueberries, peas, peppers, potatoes, and tomatoes.

TRADITIONAL COMPANIONS

Crop	Traditional Friends (enhance growth)	Traditional Enemies (hinder growth)	Research Findings
Asparagus	Tomatoes repel asparagus beetles; parsley and basil help growth.	Onion family	No data is available to confirm the traditions.
Beans	Potatoes repel Mexican bean beetles; corn improves growth; rosemary repels insects; catnip repels flea beetles; celery helps growth.	Fennel, gladiolus, onion family	Marigolds and potatoes were shown by certain studies to reduce bean beetles.
Beets	Onion family repels insects.	Beans (pole)	No evidence is available to confirm the traditions.
Cabbage family (broccoli, Brussels sprouts, cabbage, cauliflower, collards, kale, kohlrabi)	Celery repels cabbage worms; onion family deters maggots; rosemary, sage, and thyme repel insects.	Beans (pole), strawberries tomatoes	In some studies, supposed enemies tomatoes were shown to keep whiteflies and diamond-back moths away from cabbages.
Carrots	Peas add nutrients; onion family repels carrot flies; rosemary and sage repel insects.	Dill	No conclusive results are available on the traditional pairings.
Celery	Cabbage repels insects.	Carrots, parsnips	No evidence confirms the status of friends or enemies.
Corn	Beans and peas add nutrients; potatoes repel insects; soybeans deter chinch bugs.	Tomatoes	In various studies, bean inter-plants reduced numbers of fall army worms. Alfalfa cover crops, grown yearly, have reduced wireworm populations.
Cucumbers	Radishes deter cucumber beetles; beans add nutrients.	Potatoes, sage	Corn or broccoli companions have reduced striped cucumber beetle populations. Radishes have been proved to deter the same beetles.
Eggplants	Green beans deter Colorado potato beetles; potatoes can be used as trap plant.	None	No data is available to confirm the traditional friends.
Lettuce	Carrots, radishes	None	No evidence is available on the status of traditional companions.
Melons	Corn; nasturtiums and radishes repel cucumber beetles.	None	Research hasn't been able to confirm the benefits of pairing melons with nasturtiums.
Onion family (bulb onions, garlic, leeks, scallions, shallots)	Beets, carrots	Beans, peas	No evidence confirms the status of friends or enemies.
Peas	Carrots, turnips	Gladiolus, onion family	No evidence confirms the traditions. But in one study, tomato/pea intercropping brought higher pea yields. Cole crop companions deter pea root rot.

(continued)

TRADITIONAL COMPANIONS — *Continued*

Crop	Traditional Friends (enhance growth)	Traditional Enemies (hinder growth)	Research Findings
Peppers	Carrots	Fennel, kohlrabi	No research is available to confirm the traditions.
Potatoes	Beans and corn repel insects; use eggplant as trap plant.	Apples, pumpkins, raspberries, tomatoes	None of the traditional friends have been confirmed. But toxic jimsonweed and deadly night-shade lure egg-laying potato beetles and poison the larvae.
Pumpkins	Corn	Potatoes	No evidence confirms the roles of traditional friends and enemies.
Radishes	Cucumbers repel insects; lettuce.	Hyssop	No research is available on the status of traditional companions.
Spinach	Strawberries	Potatoes	No research confirms the roles of friends and enemies.
Squash	Corn	Potatoes	No data is available to confirm the traditions.
Swiss chard	Onion family	Beans (pole)	No research is available on traditional companions.
Tomatoes	Asparagus and basil repel insects; parsley helps growth.	Corn, dill, kohlrabi, potatoes	No research confirms the roles of friends and enemies.
Turnips	Peas help growth.	Potatoes	No research is available on the status of traditional companions.

Plants that tolerate the presence of black walnut include beans, corn, grapes, onions, and raspberries. Sunflowers have been found to suppress from 50 to 75 percent of the weeds that might otherwise grow near them. For this reason, it is not wise to plant valued crops close to sunflowers without first testing the association by a small planting.

The seeds of some weeds like Bishop's weed can prevent other seeds from germinating. Indeed, almost every plant family has a few pariahs that assure their own comparative solitude through means of chemical warfare. Scientists, however, differ in the weight they give to allelopathy as a force in agriculture.

Expand the Garden with Containers

After reading about the deterrent qualities of aromatics like mint, an inexperienced gardener may decide that peppermint is exactly the thing to plant between cabbages, just on the chance that the old tradition of cabbage butterflies being held at bay by a minty-fresh odor should pay off. Anyone who has ever grown peppermint, on the other hand, will smile with a shake of the head at such an idea, knowing that of all plants, mints are the most likely to get out of hand and invade the whole garden.

Wouldn't it be great if you could bring in the peppermint when cabbage butterflies appear and then quickly take it away again? Of if you could keep all occasionally helpful but space-consuming plants on retainer, so to speak, letting them ride like the cavalry to rout the "bad guys"?

The dream of a portable garden entices even more when you consider other possibilities like being able to remove a star vegetable from danger of early frost, insect invasion, or bird attack. Sun-lovers could be toted around from sun patch to sun patch in a shady garden and ideal microclimates could be sought out hour by hour. And think of the space it would add to the regular garden plot. You'd have more growing area without having to dig more garden beds. More growing space means more to harvest and enjoy. All these dreams become realities when containers are used as adjuncts to a raised bed garden. Some enterprising container growers even use children's wagons or special deep carts to make their plants not only portable but mobile.

Of course, there are also a few drawbacks to gardening in containers. The system is less natural than raised bed gardening, relying less on normal rooting systems and soil nutrient use patterns. If you've ever raised house plants you know that when you garden in pots many things can go wrong. Containers can be expensive. Moving large pots and tubs around is heavy and time-consuming work. The soil in the pots must be changed every two years, and all containers require heavier and more frequent watering and fertilizing than do beds.

To some extent the container garden is the logical extension of the intensive plot. Instead of planting by the square foot, you plant by the cubic foot in a barrel, bucket, tub, or large clay or plastic pot. Plants in containers need deep, light soil—at least 24 inches deep, or up to 5 gallons worth for one squash plant. Smaller herbs can be grown in 4 to 8-inch pots. All containers must have adequate drainage, for they will be watered daily. Whenever possible, use compact, bush-type varieties and start with transplants, not seeds. Vining varieties can be used as long as you practice the vertical growing techniques of staking, pruning, and tying. Allow wider spacing within large containers than in raised beds, and make sure individual containers are deep enough for the vegetables they contain.

Pots and tubs may be set in paths in a raised bed garden. If space is lacking they can be grouped in tiers on risers set near the beds. Low walls, patios, and terraces are also ideal spots for container gardening.

Here are some keys to successful container growing. Never use plain garden soil. In garden beds it works fine, but in containers it tends to become waterlogged, a condition that can suffocate plant roots. Always lighten soil with peat moss, perlite, vermiculite, or sand.

Plants confined to pots need more frequent watering. Check them *daily*. Concerning fertilizing, a good rule of thumb is to feed once a week. Good container fertilizers include manure tea and seaweed or fish emulsion. Foliar feeding works particularly well.

Some Creative Containers

Portable framed beds without bottoms are an easy kind of container culture. For these you assemble a frame on a lawn, patio, or concrete driveway, fill it with enriched soil, plant it like a raised bed, and, when the season is over, disassemble for storage. (Be forewarned that the grass under a framed bed will die out, and draining water will ooze out onto patios and driveways.) In the soil they use and the manner in which they are planted, these frames bear more resemblance to raised beds than to portable pots and, of course, once they are filled they are no longer portable at all. The soil of a portable bed will never be as deep as the soil of a double dug garden bed, so large vegetables may do poorly in such frames. Stick to the more shallow-rooted vegetables.

Pillow or bag gardening is an innovative form of container gardening. Fill large, heavyweight plastic bags with the same light soil or soilless medium you use for house plants or seedling starting. Lay the bags flat and make slits through the uppermost surface so that seedlings may be set into them. On the underside, punch holes for drainage. Tomatoes and potatoes require 18-inch-deep bags that are often set into large cans to make them more portable. Trying to pick up a large soil-filled pillow that has not been given structure by a can is a wrestling match you're not likely to enjoy. Also, be aware that when you water some soil is going to leak out.

Commercial grow-bags are also sold, sometimes preplanted. The ones used in commercial greenhouses hold 2½ cubic feet of planting medium and are much praised by some growers for the healthy crops they make possible. No weeding is ever required. One New England grower reported in the *Christian Science Monitor* that he grew two tomato plants in each bag and that before having to replace the soil at the end of two years he could produce 80 to 100 pounds of tomatoes from each planting. Grow-bags can be used with a drip irrigation system, but for small-scale use they are usually watered by hand daily.

Fruit Trees as Container Plants

Dwarf fruit trees make spectacular container plantings that can be carted into the garden area for landscape accent and to encourage pollinat-

Expanding the Garden: Container growing adds versatility to the raised bed garden. Plants that need special care (full-day sun, pest control) can be moved around and given the ideal microclimate. Containers add to the growing space without the need to dig more garden beds.

ing insects. Citrus trees are popular container plantings since they can be moved indoors over winter in marginal climates and made to yield when they otherwise might not.

All container-grown trees, including even winter-hardy species like dwarf apples, cherries, pears, and plums, must be given some additional protection during cold weather, because their roots are more easily chilled than are those of trees grown in ground. Temperatures of 10 to 15°F may endanger roots of potted trees.

During an experiment at the Rodale Research Center in Maxatawny, Pennsylvania, one group of potted fruit trees was placed in an unheated shed, while a second group was kept in the garden in a 2-foot trench lined with hardware cloth and filled with soil and sawdust. Both groups of trees survived the winter equally well. Shed storage has the advantage of allowing you to evade late frost damage in spring by artificially delaying blossom time. Fruit trees bloom later when kept in shelter and darkness.

Dwarf trees, like other plants grown in containers, require periodic repotting to change their soil. Many of them also need both root and limb pruning to limit their size. Techniques for pruning dwarf trees will be discussed in the following section. Potted trees require more frequent watering and feeding than soil-grown trees. Container-grown citrus should be watched carefully for micronutrient deficiencies and, if necessary, should be given extra supplements of a liquid fertilizer rich in manganese and zinc, such as fish emulsion or a fish/seaweed blend emulsion.

Vertical Growing Techniques

To get the greatest return per square foot from indeterminate plants that set fruit throughout the growing season, you must train these sprawlers and crawlers up dependable vertical supports. You can guide climbing plants relatively low in weight (twining greens, peas, and beans) up the trunks of small fruit trees or up brush or branches stuck upright in the beds. The handiest solution, of course, is a fence already in place: if it's metal, though, and your summers are intensely hot, remember that the hot wire can burn tender shoots.

Perhaps the next easiest approach to vertical growing is to drive pointed wooden stakes 1 to 2 feet into the ground and train or tie individual plants to them. To give extra stability to a row of staked plants you may want to erect metal poles at 8-foot intervals, connecting them with wire a few feet off the ground. The stakes to which the plants are tied can then be lashed to the wire.

A variant would be to build "tepees" by lashing together three dried sunflower stalks or dried cornstalks with their bases driven several inches into the ground. Such improvised setups have a tendency to collapse under peak loads, and for increased stability for heavier crops you may want to use 5 or 8-foot bamboo poles sold at most garden centers or 8-foot-long 1 by 2-inch furring strips available at building supply stores.

Vertical growing panels for the sides and ends of beds can be made by nailing together laths or by stapling or tying nylon netting or the more expensive plastic-coated wire, chicken wire, or concrete reinforcing wire to wooden uprights made of scrap lumber or saplings driven 1 to 2 feet into the soil. Such arrangements work best for weighty plants like cucumbers when the uprights are no more than 4 to 6 feet apart and when horizontal crosspieces are nailed or screwed across the top and bottom of the uprights. The bottom of the netting or wire can be as much as 6 inches above soil level (3 or 4 inches if you're growing peas and want to secure the delicate shoots early against the wind).

If nylon netting is used, it should be stretched tight when anchored to counter the sagging that occurs when heavy vegetables or fruits develop. (In *Rodale's Organic Gardening* tests, Burpee's Garden Trellis Netting outperformed Ross Gronet and Fanon Vegetable Trellis, proving least likely to stretch or break.) Choose mesh size

Fruit in Containers: Dwarf fruit trees thrive in containers and can be located strategically among a garden of raised beds to receive ample sunlight and provide attractive accents.

according to the crop grown. Squashes, melons, and cucumbers do best on 5 or 6½-inch squares, while peas and beans prefer 1½-inch mesh, which keeps them from intertwining, clumping, and growing away from the trellis. In situations where harvesting from one side is desirable, choose trellising material with spacing ample enough to let you reach a hand through and bring back the vegetable or fruit. If your uprights top out at only 4 or 5 feet, you can always extend their height temporarily—to accommodate 8-foot peas, for example—by tying on boards or sticks to

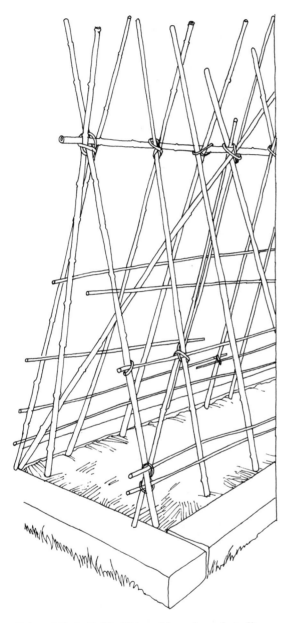

Oriental-Style Trellis: This stable and sturdy trellis can be created by positioning a series of bamboo tepees down a 3½-foot-wide bed and connecting them with horizontal crossbars at top and along the sides.

which you've attached another 3 or 4-foot-high section of netting.

An easy A-frame trellis can be made by bending a length of fencing wire. This strategy is especially appealing for a bed with contained sides since the frame can be held in place by wedging each end inside a side of the bed. Or the frame can be butted against oak stakes—often available free at mills or wood shops. With a little more effort you can make a portable A-frame by nailing 2-inch mesh poultry wire to two wooden frames 5 feet high by 6 feet long, then hinging or very loosely tying the frames together at the top. This self-supporting structure can be laid flat for storage.

Lumber used for such vertical growing units should be treated with a nontoxic wood preservative. A good choice would be a product such as Woodguard, which lasts up to eight years and contains copper-8-quinolinate—a compound the government allows to be used on wood in direct contact with agricultural products. Other nontoxic possibilities are Zar Clear Wood Preservative (lasts at least three years), and Olympic Wood Preservative (lasts less than three years). If substantial parts of the trellis are to be in contact with the ground, be sure to use a copper-naphthenate–based product such as Cuprinol 10, which is tough enough to protect the trellis yet has been proved completely harmless to seeds and plants and lasts up to four years.

For even more durable portable, stockable, lightweight frames, use ¾-inch PVC water pipe and fittings to make a structure as large as 9 feet long and 5 feet high. Then lash 4-inch fencing wire to it. Capable of being used in pairs as an A-frame or separated and laid down horizontally, such setups can be covered and used to shade lettuce or even as the top of a quickly improvised cold frame on cold nights in spring or fall.

A-frame setups, trellises leaned against fences, and tepees and other pyramidlike growth frames cover more garden surface than strictly vertical

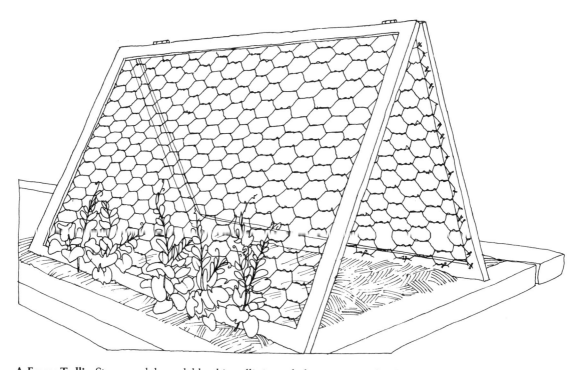

A-Frame Trellis: Strong and dependable, this trellis is made from two wooden frames, 5 by 6 feet, covered with poultry wire and hinged at the top.

growing panels. But these options allow you to double-crop by planting fast-growing, somewhat shade-tolerant plants under the unit. One possibility is a pyramid trellis that features a frame made of 1 by 2s covered by string or wire. A setup like this measuring 92 inches by 94 inches at its base would permit you to plant four rows of pole beans (at 4-inch intervals) around the outside of the frame, for a total of 32 row feet of growing space, and four more rows around the inside of the frame, for 27 additional row feet. In the 2 by 2-foot-square growing area in the center of the pyramid, you can put fast-maturing crops that are harvested before bean vines cover the trellis overhead.

Another good bet for peas or pole beans is to create what looks like a horizontal ladder a couple feet above the ground by lashing tree or shrub prunings to twine running the length of both sides of a growing bed. Some growers swear by cages made of concrete reinforcing wire for tomatoes, cucumbers, and other viners, claiming that the electromagnetic field created contributes to mammoth yields. Whatever the reason, experiments have shown tomatoes in 24-inch-diameter cages perform very well, achieving better foliage cover and more protection against sunscald than those staked or allowed to sprawl.

A more permanent structure is favored by a committed vertical grower, seedsman Dick Meiners of Pinetree Garden Seeds in Maine. Meiners advocates growing tomatoes up 6-foot strings attached to overhead bars. Removing suckers, he positions the plants at 12-inch intervals for a yield of

20 to 40 pounds per plant. The bars may be suspended from the eaves of a porch or house roof facing south or west or from the crosspiece of a wooden or metal-pipe–frame trellis.

Another long-term approach involves sinking treated wooden posts into the beds, then attaching heavy wire across their tops and bottoms. Strings can be tied vertically at 4-inch intervals for peas and beans or at 1 to 2-foot intervals for tomato plants. Panels of 6-inch wire mesh can be tacked on where or when you're growing squash or melons, and nylon netting tied or tacked on for other crops. The deeply imbedded permanent posts allow you to grow any crop without resorting to guy wires and make it possible to arch wire mesh overhead between parallel beds to create a shaded bower or walkway.

The possibilities for improvised trellises are endless. For example, plastic holders from six-packs of beer or soft drinks can be lashed together with wire ties, then hung from an overhead wire. You could also recycle wire clothes hangers, attaching them with U-staples to 2 by 2-inch

Shaded Walkway: For respite from the summer sun, join two parallel trellises with an arched wire "canopy." Growing vines will blanket the wire and give you a cool spot to beat the heat.

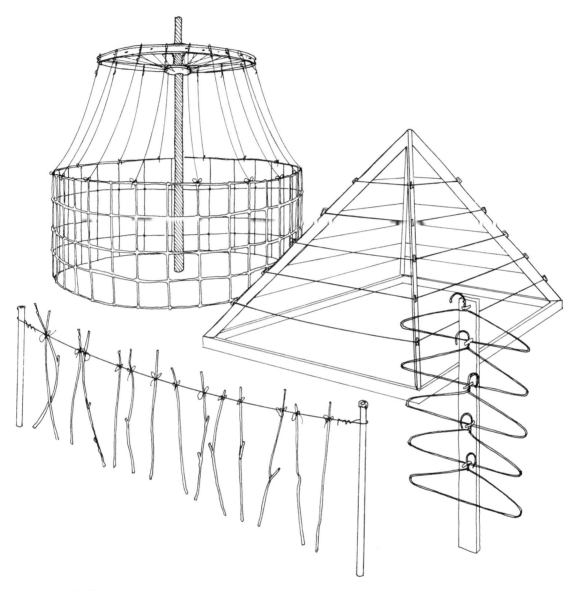

Improvised Trellises: From top left, moving clockwise: A suspended bicycle wheel rim is linked to a circle of wire fence. A pyramid, built from 1 by 2 pieces of wood, is covered by string or wire. Wire hangers, attached to a post or furring strip, do a fine job of holding up vertical growers. What looks like a ladder set on its side is really a length of string run between posts with prunings lashed on to serve as the vertical "rungs."

posts or furring strips driven a foot into the ground. These hanger trellises can be placed side by side for a "fence row" or joined with plastic ties or twine to form square cages. If you'd like to improve on the space efficiency of tepee trellises and fences, you can fashion a discarded 24-inch bicycle wheel rim, a piece of wood or pipe, fishing tackle, and a 36-inch circle of wire fence into a bean support. Attaching the center of the rim to the top of a piece of scrap wood or pipe with a bolt or long nail, drive the wood or pipe into the soil. Then tie fishing line, string, or even ribbon to each spoke where it joins the rim. Fasten the other end of these pieces to the circle of fence you have placed on the ground around the rim. This adaptable trellis can be as tall or short as the piece of wood or pipe at its center.

If imagination and energy fail, you always can order an array of prefabricated vertical growing setups. Gurney offers the "tomato web"—a 5-foot-tall, 18-inch-diameter net tube that can be nailed on top of a garden stake. Burpee's "bean tower" consists of 70 feet of string attached to hoops at the top and bottom of a 6-foot pole and can accommodate at least 12 pole bean plants or around 36 snap pea vines. Strawberry growers can pack up to 50 plants in as little as 4 square feet with the help of Hasting's movable, rot-resistant "strawberry tower."

Siting and Training Vertical Growers

You may want to reserve the northernmost 2 feet of each garden bed for vertical growing setups on an east-west axis. However, trellises also can be positioned to run north-south along the eastern border of the plot or even a few feet to the west so shade-tolerant crops like lettuce to the east are placed in shadow during hot afternoons. (Pole beans and limas tolerate shade best of all the vining crops.) If part of the garden abuts the house or garage, use that end for your high risers. Unless your vertical structures are secured by guy wires and pegs or sturdy posts set quite deep, make sure setups in exposed areas are erected parallel to the prevailing winds—east-west, for example, if winds usually blow from the West. Best of all is a sheltered location buffering high-speed gusts that could flatten a heavily laden plant support.

Put up your trellis before you plant, for if you wait until the vines develop you could damage plant roots. Seeds or transplants should be positioned 6 inches from the structure and on its windward side, so that when the prevailing wind blows, tendrils and fruits will move toward the trellis instead of away from it. Guide or tie young plants to the support when they're about 6 inches tall—earlier for delicate peas in danger of being blown down by wind. In the case of tomatoes growing up strings, wrap the twine around the tip of the plant every week or so to keep it upright. More pliable vining plants can be gently wrapped around string and in and out of netting or wire mesh as they grow. Nontwining types can be secured with plastic ties, string, strips of cloth, or pieces of nylon stocking. Melons and squash can be supported from the time they're half grown by slings made from mesh onion bags or a length of nylon stocking knotted at the bottom with an opening created for the fruit's stem. You can also make slings from squares cut from old sheets or cast-off clothes: just cut a hole in each corner and run string around the edges, tying the pouch and its contents to the support.

More Techniques for High-Quality Yields

In the chess game of intensive gardening, each player will develop a set of "trade secrets" for coaxing the highest possible yields from individual vegetables. One gardener, for example, may put great trust in pea or bean inoculants, even for established beds, while another with different experience may call them a waste of time and money. Just as each gardener by trial and error, or by controlled experiment, selects groupings of plants that work well together, either in terms of space, time, or nutrient sharing or for the more ineffable benefits of companionship, so every gardener gathers a different "bag of tricks" when it comes to individual crops. Some master potato growers, for example, claim that by allowing their seed potatoes to develop sprouts up to 12 inches long before they are planted, potato yields can be increased dramatically. Not only, they

With the Master Gardeners

TRELLISING TRICKS OF THE TRADE

Ron and Sherry Foreman of North Carolina have turned sand into a garden that was a regional winner in both the 1983 and 1984 Organic Gardener of the Year Contests. Sherry reports building up their low-lying garden and boosting yields via a vertical growing technique she developed to meet the challenge of their seaside location. "With our sandy soil, we have to fertilize almost constantly. Yet because we also have a problem with poor drainage, we can't really use liquid fertilizer very effectively."

To solve that set of problems, the Foremans devised an ingenious way to compost in wire rings set right on top of their raised beds. Filling a ring about 3 feet in diameter—"you can make it any height you want"—with 4-inch layers of leaves alternated with sprinkles of manure, they plant tomatoes and other vine crops around the outside of the wire circle. "In between the tomatoes we usually plant shorter crops like carrots. Last year, though, we put in green beans, and as they grew we wrapped them around the tomato plants and the wire. So they actually tied up the tomato plants for us."

Helped by rain or regular watering, the couple's hot climate breaks down those 4-foot-high stacks of compost nicely, and the rich runoff provides liquid manure for the surrounding vegetables all summer. "We get 8-foot tomato plants," Sherry says happily. At season's end, the rings are lifted and the compost spread over the raised bed to raise it even more.

Out in Kansas, Chris Seitz has evolved her own version of the compost ring. Digging an 18-inch-deep, 3½-foot-diameter hole, Seitz fills it with compost. Then she plants melons, squashes, pumpkins, and gourds alternately around the inside and outside of cages 5 feet high and 3 feet in diameter, which she centers over the larger, compost-filled area.

Walter Masson's towering achievement is his 8-foot-high tepees, which each year hide hundreds of cucumbers under a wealth of morning glories. In his garden in Massachusetts, Masson makes his "old-fashioned tepees" out of three 1½ by 1-inch pieces of scrap wood that he lashes together at the top and pushes into the soil to a depth of 5 inches. "Then I wrap poultry wire all around for the vines to climb on, tying it on with twistems." Costing just 4 square feet of horizontal garden space, each tepee supports a half dozen prolific female cucumber vines. This seasoned Yankee gardener lets the cukes establish themselves, "then I plant morning glories by June and let them grow right over the vines to give it some beauty."

say, does the trick permit earlier growth for an earlier start, but it also leads to more tubers since the many nodes on the long shoot all develop underground.

Properly, gardening is an idiosyncratic and a pragmatic business. Do whatever works for you, your plants, and your soil, as long as it doesn't harm the environment.

Among time-tested ways to increase the quantity or the quality of fruit and vegetable yields are pruning, training, and harvesting practices. We'll take a close look at some of these effective techniques in this section.

Root and Tip Pruning of Seedlings

Root pruning encourages the rapid development of the fibrous roots that supply many vegetable plants with water and nourishment. There is some evidence that seedlings of tomatoes and lettuce and other leafy crops produce more rapidly when their primary taproots are removed artificially before transplanting, forcing early emergence of an alternative root system.

With tomato seedlings, cut back the long taproot and clip off lower leaves, leaving the top two large leaves and the top rosette of smaller leaves. Set the seedling deeply into the ground, digging a trench for the stem and laying it in so the top leaves protrude aboveground. The nodes on the stem, now underground, will sprout new roots, giving the plant access to nutrients in a wide area of soil. With a larger than normal supply of nutrients, topgrowth becomes rapid and the plant starts blossoming and bearing fruit earlier, and often more heavily, than it normally would.

With salad greens and leeks, trim back the taproot (or, in the case of leeks, the tips of the cluster of fibrous roots) and shorten the leaf tips or topgrowth. This trimming restores a proper top-to-root balance and stimulates the plant into a vigorous renewal made possible by a stockier root system. The trimming of leeks and salad greens is a technique long practiced by French market gardeners.

Root pruning is also done when older plants or seedlings with unusually extensive root systems are transplanted into already occupied beds as relays. In order not to disturb the established root systems of plants in the bed, trim the roots

Easy Transplanting: Using a bulb planter to prepare holes for seedlings is a good idea, for it will do the least amount of damage to the seedlings' new neighbors in a closely planted bed.

of the new additions into compact balls with no straggling roots. You must also cut back the topgrowth so the top-to-root balance will not be upset. A rule of thumb is to cut back the tops by one-third to one-half. Always prune in direct proportion to the amount of root growth that's been cut away.

Pinching

The pinching back of indeterminate tomato plants is a sort of gentle pruning done after the plants are in the ground to encourage stockiness at the expense of height. It also limits the number of branching stems to concentrate the plant's energy into producing and ripening fruit. When the height of a tomato plant or the number of its branches is reduced, the fruit yield per plant will be cut, but the total yield of the garden area, in many cases, will be increased. The garden can accommodate more plants per square foot when the size of each plant is restricted. This leads to higher total yields per bed.

If you plan to stake indeterminate tomato plants, pinch off all but one side shoot or sucker, using your thumb and forefinger. The remaining main stem and the sucker you preserved will become the two main shoots, which will be tied to the stake. After the initial pinching, allow no additional side shoots to grow more than 6 inches before you cut them off with a sharp knife. To limit the height of the plant (this applies to plants in cages as well as to those on stakes), pinch all topgrowth back when it has reached the desired height. Fruits will be more uniform but no larger than on unpruned tomato plants.

Cucurbits are also pinched back, especially late in the season. When you remove blossoms, immature fruits, and unfruitful branches from melon, cucumber, squash, and pumpkin vines, the plants concentrate their energies on ripening the fruit that remains. Pinch off all immature fruits that appear within 50 days of the first expected fall frost. At least 45 days are needed from pollination to harvest, and in cool climates more will be required. Because the remaining fruit matures faster, following this practice may help you to rescue a few fruits from an anticipated early fall frost instead of losing an entire immature crop.

Pruning Dwarf Fruit Trees

Conventional wisdom held that fruit trees should be pruned heavily before planting to help offset the trauma the roots would undergo when set into the ground. This pruning was intended to get the trees off to a solid start. This practice is out of favor with many horticultural experts these days.

Larry J. Kuhns, extension specialist in Ornamental Horticulture at Pennsylvania State University, for example, believes that pruning nursery-grown trees before planting should be done only to reduce the shoot-to-root ratio when growing conditions are poor or when the seed-

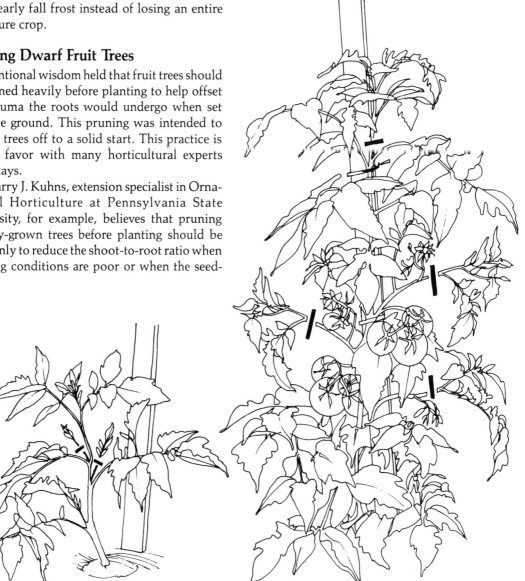

Tomato Pruning: To keep rambunctious indeterminate tomato plants under control in tightly spaced beds, begin pruning soon after transplanting. Clip off all but one sucker to create two main shoots. Prune side shoots when they grow longer than 6 inches and pinch back topgrowth to keep it at a manageable height.

ling trees are damaged, unhealthy, improperly dug, or advanced past bud opening stage.

Carl Whitcomb, a nursery researcher at Oklahoma State University, found that in 6 to 8-foot, year-old dwarf Elberta peaches and Kieffer pear trees, pruning did not affect the start of growth after planting, but 30 percent pruning of topgrowth did result in long sprouts that had to be pruned in subsequent years to improve the shape of the trees. He recommends pruning only to remove weak forks and broken limbs, to encourage low branching and strong structures on apple, pear, and cherry trees that will support heavy yields of fruit, and to open up the centers of trees so sun can get through to ripen the fruit.

Robert Carlson of Michigan State University, one expert who disagrees with the trend toward less pruning, recommends topping one-year-old dwarf trees at 18 to 20 inches from the ground to head the fruiting limbs low for heavier, healthier yields. William Kurle, head of the North American Fruit Explorers, also advocates cutting back at planting to promote earlier bearing.

In general, trees should be pruned while they are still dormant in late winter. Thin apple blossoms at flowering to prevent biennial bearing, and remove all blossoms from one-year-old dwarf trees. Three to four weeks after petal fall, thin immature fruits to their proper spacing so they don't crowd or bruise one another as they mature. Although this reduces the number of fruits, it improves their size and quality and may, by reducing fruit fall, increase the total harvest.

From mid-July to late August or early September, perform gradual light summer pruning on all closely planted dwarf fruit trees, especially those that are trained in espalier and those that are in containers. Summer pruning forces early fruiting the next year and encourages dwarfing by altering the carbohydrate balance to work a physiological change on trees. When you cut back new shoots, a new relationship is set up between the living material of the tree and the amount of nourishment it has in storage. By removing the summer's nonfruiting wood, you

Cucurbit Pruning: As shown on this watermelon, pinch back cucurbits late in the season to hasten ripening. Remove any blossoms and immature fruits (shown by the arrows) so the plant can channel its energy into the fruit that remains.

A NEW TREE SHAPE FOR MORE AND EARLIER APPLES

The key to boosting apple yields is sunlight, pure and simple. The more sunlight that reaches the leaves, the more energy the tree can produce to generate an apple crop. An apple grower in Washington State, Carl Perleberg, has devised a new trellising system that allows trees to capture 15 percent more sunlight than conventionally pruned central leader trees.

In Perleberg's system, trees are trained to double leaders with a 30-degree angle between the limbs. He feels this is the optimum angle for capturing sunlight. The branches are maintained at the correct angle by a central trellis post fitted with two wood crosspieces and a top support wire. He begins installing the crosspieces once the trees have been growing for three years.

Perleberg uses a 4 by 18-foot spacing for high-density plantings. The trees are kept at a maximum height of 13 feet. Viewed from the side, the trees in this trellising system resemble the letter M.

M-Shaped Trellising System: The first wooden crosspiece, 4 feet long, is bolted to the tree at a height of 3½ feet. As the tree grows, the second crosspiece is installed at a height of 80 inches. The final level is a support wire at 10 feet. The maximum height for the tree is 13 feet.

encourage the development of more fruit-bearing sites for the next crop.

Mike Yawarosky, a grower of dwarf fruit trees in eastern Pennsylvania, removes about 40 percent of the leaf area of his trees each year in late summer and finds that fruit is forced earlier, dwarfing is encouraged, pests are physically removed, and, most important, the yield is higher. One of his dwarf GOLDEN DELICIOUS apple trees is only 6 feet high but bears as many as 75 apples a season.

For suggestions about various forms to which dwarf trees can be pruned, consult *Backyard Fruits and Berries* (Rodale Press, 1984). Pruning to an open center or vase shape is better for dwarf peach and nectarine trees, while pruning

to a pyramid shape by using the central leader technique works best with apples, apricots, cherries, pears, and plums.

No dwarf tree should be allowed to grow to a height taller than can be reached for picking, and container trees should be pruned enough to keep them from becoming top-heavy. When repotting container trees, trim an inch or two from the coarse, fibrous lateral roots and the thick, downward-pointing taproots. Don't trim the bunches of fine, fibrous roots. Encourage an open growth habit in dwarf trees by spreading the branches so they come out from the trunk at 60-degree angles. This encourages early flowering and a beneficial growth cycle that means a healthier and more productive tree.

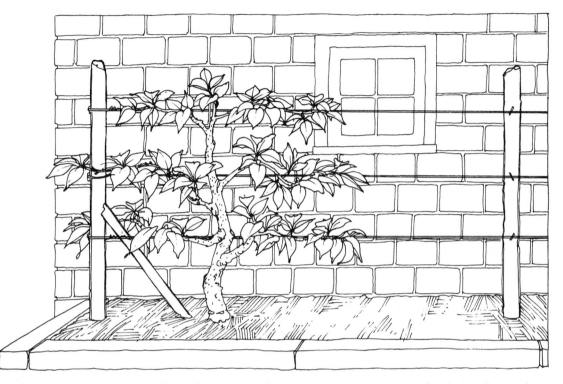

Espaliered Fruit Tree: For sweeter, larger, better quality fruit try training a tree in an espalier form. When sited against a masonry wall (that acts as a solar collector), the tree will be protected from sudden drops in temperature.

Espalier

Espalier is a time-honored European method of directing the growth of plants, most frequently of fruit trees, so that their stems, or trunks, and their branches grow flat along a wall, fence, or trellis. In common with intensive gardening, espalier seeks the most economical use of space for the highest possible yields.

In espalier, training dictates the growth pattern, elaborate or simple, and pruning maintains the desired shape. Growth is always restricted in some manner, so all espaliered trees are relatively small. But because of their economical use of space that might otherwise go to waste—space

near foundations or walls—espaliered trees increase the total yield of the garden.

Espaliered trees come into production much sooner than standard trees of the same species and variety, often requiring half as many years before the first harvestable fruit is produced. A standard apple tree, for example, needs 35 to 40 leaves to produce a high-quality apple. An espaliered tree, although kept smaller than any dwarf variety, can produce a good apple with only 25 leaves.

The fruit of espaliered trees is generally thought to be sweeter, larger, and of better qual-

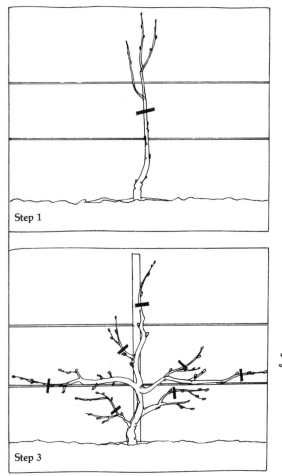

Step 1

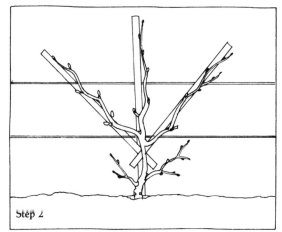

Step 2

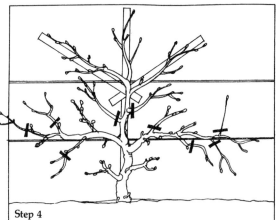

Step 4

Step 3

Espalier Training

Step 1 Start by cutting back the young tree to 15 inches from the ground. **Step 2** Train the top shoot vertically and coax two opposing branches into 45-degree angles from the center stem. Provide a stabilizing support in addition to the wires. **Step 3** Lower the two bottom branches and tie them to the horizontal wires. (Best done while plant is dormant.) Cut back these branches by one-third. Prune away any growth below the second wire. Look for three buds near the second wire that can serve as the second tier of branches and an extension of the center stem. **Step 4** Repeat the pruning and training you used for the first tier of branches. **Step 5** When the tree has achieved the size and shape you want, spot prune to remove lateral branches that emerge from the horizontal ones.

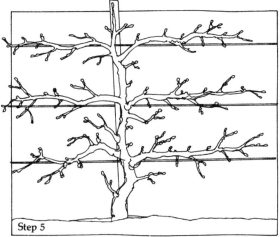

Step 5

ity than the fruit of standard trees. Sunshine is vital to even ripening, sweetness, and good color in fruits like apples. When a tree is trained to a masonry wall, the wall functions as a solar collector to release energy both day and night, energy the tree uses in growth and ripening. Heat-retaining walls protect trees from sudden drops in temperature. In northern climates, they may make the growing of some tender fruit trees possible. Espaliered peach trees, for example, will grow in areas where the temperature descends to −10°F when given the protection of a plastic tarp attached to a supporting wall. The combination of a tarp and a wall will also create a solar-greenhouse effect, bringing trees into blossom and harvest earlier than normal.

Already trained six to seven-year-old espaliered trees are available from nurseries at a cost from 75 dollars upward. To train your own tree, start with a whip, a tree that has had one season's growth since the time of its grafting. Choose a dwarf or semidwarf variety. Select a spot with fertile, loose soil along a wall or fence, making sure that the location receives at least six hours of full sunshine a day. Erect a trellis of 10 to 14-gauge rustproof wire. This should be set at least 1 foot out from the wall or fence. Planting too close to a wall, or failing to use an additional freestanding support, may result in sunburned bark, especially in warm climates.

Pruning of espaliered trees is done twice a year, once heavily in late winter and once lightly in summer. Winter pruning determines the tree's shape, while summer pruning controls the growth of new foliage and encourages the production of fruit. Leaving only 6 inches of new wood when pruning in winter will make for the sturdiest and most compact growth. As with the pruning of nonespaliered dwarf and container trees, the summer pruning should be done gradually. It concentrates the tree's energy into the production of fruit, making high yields possible.

Apple and pear trees make the best espalier, but all fruit trees and vining fruits are amenable to some form of trellising.

Pruning Grapevines

Grapevine pruning is done during winter dormancy. Late winter pruning will delay budding as much as ten days and may save a vine from damage by late frost, but it does cause bleeding, a harmless but potentially disease-attracting loss of sap.

A. J. Winkler of the University of California at Davis proved by experiments conducted more than 50 years ago that the heavy pruning of grapevines stunts them and causes a 31 percent loss of growth during a season. Lighter pruning coupled with cluster thinning produces crops up to 50 percent larger than those produced with traditional heavy pruning.

If you leave between 50 and 75 buds per vine and pinch off one-third of the tiny clusters of immature grapes in spring, you save the vines the burden of an overlarge crop and still provide for the healthy growth of vines for future bearing. The pruned and thinned vine leafs out several weeks before a heavily pruned vine does and starts with a larger reserve of food to help it grow faster. Faster growth provides more nourishment for the grapes. The clusters grow larger, so the yield is heavier. Grapes are also sweeter, more uniform, and of better quality.

For heavy harvests, it is also important that sun reaches as many grape leaves as possible. This can be achieved by training a leaf canopy to spread over the top of a broad trellis.

Pruning Brambles and Blueberries

Bramble vines will bear more heavily if you remove all canes that have produced fruit and thin the remaining canes to four or five per foot. After thinning, head back all remaining canes to a height of 24 to 30 inches and remove all suckers. If a trellis is used, the canes will be higher. Pinch new shoots of black or purple raspberries when they are 18 to 24 inches high to encourage branching, which in turn encourages heavier yields the following season. Bush blackberries should be pinched back in summer to 30 to 36 inches and then pruned in winter to 8 to 12 inches.

Double-Duty Canopy: In this garden, the end-of-the-bed canopy trellis supports grapevines and casts a welcome shadow over shade-loving crops and seedlings.

Careful annual pruning will increase the yield and improve the quality of your blueberry harvest. Blueberries produce fruit on the wood of the previous season's growth. The pruning program begins at the end of the third season of growth with the purpose of keeping the bushes open enough to allow sun to reach all branches. Cut off branches an inch or thicker, keeping those small shoots that rise from roots or from near the base of the bush. Remove all low-spreading limbs that clutter the inside of the bush and all shoots from the previous season that are less than 3 inches long. Look down from the top of the bush and make sure the sun can reach all parts. Erect-growing varieties require more inside pruning, while those of spreading habit require the removal of lower, drooping branches.

Harvesting Techniques for Higher Yields

Your last chance to increase the yield of your vegetable plants may also be one of your best chances. Some crops respond spectacularly to prompt and thorough harvesting by continuing to bear heavily. Asparagus, beans, peas, squash, and cucumbers produce more flowers or flower stalks and continue to bear longer if they are picked early and regularly.

If you grow cucumbers for pickling, for example, be sure to pick the cucumbers when they are small. If you allow them to grow large, not only will your pickles be less crisp, but the vines may bear only 5 to 12 cucumbers apiece, instead of the 35 to 50 they would bear if picked earlier.

Even if your bush bean harvest gets ahead of you and you have no use for the beans, you'll find it is better to throw the unwanted pickings into the compost or give them away than to stop harvesting for a few days. Leaving the pods on the plant will send a signal to discontinue setting beans. Pole beans will also produce only as long as they are picked regularly and promptly. If you go a few weeks without picking them, the flowering and the yields may drop by half or more.

When you pick vegetables before their seeds are mature, many plants will continue producing in an attempt to reproduce themselves. Broccoli, left unharvested, seldom produces side shoots.

Contrary to general belief, onion bulb growth continues even after onion leaves have shriveled and fallen over. Yields increase when you refrain from knocking over all the onions in a bed after only the first few in a planting have fallen on their own. In most regions there will be time to let the onions fall over naturally before frost.

In harvesting leafy crops like lettuce, Swiss chard, collards, turnip greens, mustard, spinach, and endive by the cut-and-come-again method, you'll find that more growth will come after cutting if you clean out all growth over an inch high. Leave at least six leaves so the plants can renew their growth. New, tender leaves will appear quickly to replace all the growth that has been removed. Some gardeners have found, after having groundhogs nibble plants to the ground, that many greens can come back from roots alone. Kale is an exception. The center bud must be intact if kale is to replace itself.

In experiments conducted at the Rodale Research Center in 1981 and 1982, spring and fall plantings of six leafy greens—heading Chinese cabbage, celery cabbage, nonheading Chinese cabbage, mustard, lettuce, and spinach—all grown in a heated Quonset hut greenhouse were measured for comparison of two harvest methods. The first method was the harvest of the whole plant at one time and the second was the harvest of outer leaves three or four times, followed by the final harvest of the plant.

Leafy greens that had outer leaves harvested over time showed a 30 to 40 percent reduction in total yield when compared with plants harvested once only. However, when the outer-leaf method was used, harvest began earlier.

The decision about which method to use would most sensibly be based on your daily need for greens. Although outer-leaf harvest may produce less in total, it may be more important to you to keep a small, steady supply coming to the table than to increase total yield.

PART

2 Getting More from Your Gardening Season

6 Extending the Season with Crops

So far, in discussing intensive gardening techniques, we've been concentrating on how to get the highest yields from the given area that is your garden. With skillful manipulation you can increase the size of harvests without adding to the gardening space. Now, the question is, can you manipulate time so that your garden remains productive for as long as possible throughout the year? That's what this part of the book is all about.

A gardener's season has its limits. Cold areas won't let heat-loving vegetables grow to harvestable maturity unprotected out-of-doors. Cold-loving vegetables, on the other hand, just won't grow in the blazing sun of a southern summer. Your goal is to extend these seasonal limitations by keeping the garden productive during times when the weather is least hospitable to growing crops. The ideal is to have something growing or at least harvestable in the garden year-round.

In this chapter you'll learn which special techniques and hardy crops will give you an extra-early start for early harvests. You'll also see how to coax plants beyond their natural limitations by keeping cool-loving crops going in warm weather and by accelerating hot-weather crops in cool, short-season areas. As a grand finale, you'll find out which crops make great late finishes and can be held over, in harvestable form, from fall through late winter.

Some General Techniques to Help with Season Extending

No matter whether you're trying to gain an earlier start or a later finish, timing, or choosing the right moment to put plants in the garden, is everything. Many gardeners rely on indoor-started plants to help them gain time and/or keep the garden on a productive schedule. In this section we'll weigh the pros and cons of transplanting against direct seeding for the time-conscious intensive gardener. And we'll also discover some seed-starting tricks that can be used to ensure good, timely germination. After all, if seeds take their time to sprout or even fail to sprout, your season-extending efforts are going to be hampered.

The Old Dispute: Direct Seeding versus Transplanting

As long as hoes and seeding flats are in existence, gardeners will be debating the merits of starting crops indoors. Those in favor of using transplants say they gain more control over the timing of successions and interplantings, and they're able to plan the spacings and layout more precisely. Gardeners eager for an early harvest point out that plants started from transplants are ready two to three weeks before direct-seeded crops. Gardeners less enamored of starting seeds indoors cite the six weeks or so of coddling that must be done before seedlings are ready to occupy the garden. They're not convinced this extra time, not to mention the space and cost that seed-starting paraphernalia require, are worth it.

In general, intensive gardeners concerned with getting maximum use out of garden space

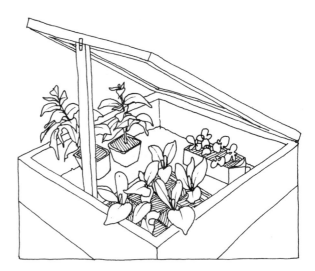

On the first day, have the 1 to 2-hour outing correspond with the warmest part of the day. Set the seedlings so they receive dappled, not direct, sunlight. Bring them in at night. Increase exposure by an hour or so each day until a week has passed, and also increase the intensity of light. At the end of the week risk a couple of nights out for your seedlings. During this time you should be cutting back on watering.

Hardening-Off: No matter whether seedlings are the first spring plants, midseason replacements, or fall recruits, they all must be acclimated to outdoor conditions. Hardening-off prepares coddled indoor plants for what lies ahead—stronger light, stronger winds, deeper cold, and greater temperature fluctuation. One week before transplanting begin withholding food and water. Set plants outdoors in a sheltered area like a porch or cold frame.

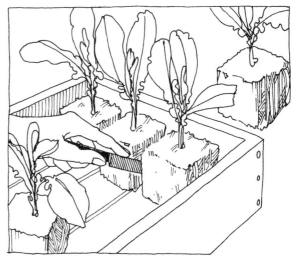

If the plants are growing in a flat, now is the time to cut the soil into blocks to give the roots a chance to heal before transplanting. Slice cleanly around the seedlings so that each has an ample-size rootball.

DIRECT SEEDING VERSUS TRANSPLANTING

DIRECT SEEDING

Risks
- Killing frosts may destroy plants if they germinate too early and are caught by surprise.
- Early growth may be stunted by spring drought. The mechanics of watering are more cumbersome in early spring, when hoses are in storage and outside faucets are turned off.
- Seeds may rot if the ground is too wet and too cold.
- Seedlings are exposed to insects and pests at a tender age.
- Seeds or seedlings may wash out in spring rains.

Benefits
- Germination starts the very moment the soil is warm enough, eliminating guesswork and the need for artificial heat.
- Plants never experience transplant shock and root damage. Hardening-off occurs naturally, making plants more resistant to later stresses.
- Roots almost always develop as fast as, or faster than, the tops. This means they're able to seek out and supply the nutrients the developing plant needs.

TRANSPLANTING

Risks
- Brittle or succulent stems may break in handling.
- The shock of transplanting sets back growth. Sometimes it takes a long time for a plant to repair its tissue and reestablish its feeding system. While this is going on, little further development or growth occurs. Some sensitive plants, when threatened by setback, prematurely bolt or form small heads too early. Early starts can be cancelled out easily by transplant shock.
- Indoor plants require more watching and more of your time than their direct-seeded garden counterparts.
- Lamps, heating elements, and containers can add to gardening expense. They also take up space when in use and in storage.

Benefits
- Transplants are ready for harvest two to three weeks earlier than direct-seeded crops.
- You control the timing. Harvested plants can be replaced with new ones at any point in the season.
- Root systems, though smaller, are more compact and efficient when they have been restricted to pots.
- Nourishment, moisture, light, and warmth can be given where and when needed.
- You have the opportunity to inspect roots at any point and cull poor plants, so only healthy seedlings go into the beds.
- Hard-to-start seeds can receive special attention.
- All growing space in the beds can be filled with healthy maturing plants.
- Tender seedlings aren't exposed to garden pests and diseases.
- The early start allows northerners to grow crops they couldn't mature otherwise—tomatoes, eggplants, melons.

TEMPERAMENTAL TRANSPLANTS

A gardener's rule of thumb is that transplants shorten the time to harvest. But for some plants, the rough handling during transplanting can actually delay their maturity or even threaten their very survival. If you don't handle these temperamental transplants just right, you can defeat the whole purpose of using them in the first place.

Some plants, like tomatoes and lettuce, seem to thrive on successive repottings. But the touchy vegetables—root crops, cucurbits, and legumes, plus a few others—resent any disturbance to their roots. You must take some precautions while handling these seedlings to make sure the transfer to the garden is a success.

Never start any of the vegetables listed below in communal flats—always give them their own containers. Plant three or four seeds to a container, and once they've sprouted thin the extras by cutting rather than lifting. Some gardeners find that Styrofoam cups or plastic containers work better than peat pots for these crops.

Before transplanting, water the plants well so the soil sticks together to form a protective ball around the roots. Tear away the sides of Styrofoam cups, or carefully ease plants out of plastic containers. Set the seedlings into prepared holes as gently as possible. Throughout this process, try not to handle or manipulate the roots. With just the right touch, these plants should get off to a good start in the garden.

Beans*	Peanuts*
Beets	Peas*
Carrots	Pumpkins
Corn*	Spinach
Cucumbers	Squashes (summer and winter)
Okra*	Swiss chard
Parsnips	Turnips

*These plants are very temperamental and are a bit trickier to transplant than the others. Handle them with extra care.

and accelerating harvests prefer to give as many vegetables as possible indoor starts. With every vegetable, however, benefits must be weighed against risks.

According to Nancy Bubel, whose *The Seed-Starter's Handbook* (Rodale Press, 1978) is required reading for all indoor seeders, the vegetables that benefit most from successive repottings before going into garden beds are tomatoes, peppers, lettuce (especially heading types), members of the cabbage family, onions, eggplants, celeriac, endive, and escarole. These vegetables have root systems and stems that are relatively flexible and can be handled without undue damage. They repair themselves quickly. Lettuce goes outside so early that a good root system will give it a crucial edge on rapid growth once it is transplanted.

Some favorite garden crops, such as corn and cucurbits, don't take kindly to having their roots disturbed. See Temperamental Transplants for tips on handling these. To schedule seed-starting and setting-out activities, see the Guide to Timing Transplanting on the next page.

Tricks for Starting Seeds

When time is of the essence and you have a schedule established for moving crops in and out of the garden, seeds that take their time, or worse yet, fail to germinate, can spoil the whole show. Slow germination can completely wipe out any time advantage you were seeking by starting transplants indoors. Out in the garden you can lose precious time if you seed, wait, then have to

GUIDE TO TIMING TRANSPLANTING

Transplants help you gain a head start on the gardening season, but only if you time the seed-starting and setting-out dates well. After all, there's not much to be gained by setting out tender cucumber seedlings while temperatures are still low and there's a chance of lingering frost. And starting any transplant, tender or hardy, too far ahead of setting out means you'll probably end up with a leggy plant with cramped roots that's ill-equipped to stand up to the rigors of the outdoor garden. Use this chart to guide your indoor seed-starting and outdoor transplanting activities.

Vegetable	Weeks to Transplant Size (from time of sowing)	Spring Setting-Out Dates (in relation to frost-free date)	
		Weeks Before	Weeks After
Asparagus	12–14	—	4
Beans (lima)	3–4	—	1–2
Beans (snap)	3–4	—	1–2
Beets	4	4	—
Broccoli	6–8	4	2–3
Brussels sprouts	6–8	4	2–3
Cabbage	6–8	5	2–3
Carrots	5–6	4	—
Chinese cabbage	4	4–6	—
Collards	6–8	4	2
Corn	4	—	2–3
Cucumbers	2–3	1	—
Eggplants	8–10	—	2–3
Endive	4–5	4	2
Garlic	4–6	2–4	1
Kale	6–8	5	2
Kohlrabi	6–8	5	2
Leeks	4–6	5	2
Lettuce	4–6	2	3
Melons	2–4	—	4
Mustard	4–6	5	2
Okra	6–8	—	3–4
Onions (bulbing)	4–6	6	2
Onions (bunching)	4–6	4–5	2
Parsley	4–6	4–6	4–6
Parsnips	4–6	4	3–4
Peanuts	4–6	Plant on	frost-free date
Peas	4	4	2–3
Peppers	6–8	—	2–3
Spinach	4–6	3–6	—
Squash (summer)	4	—	4
Squash (winter)	4	—	3–4
Sweet potatoes	6–8	—	2–3
Swiss chard	4	3–4	—
Tomatoes	6–10	—	4
Turnips	3–4	4	—

reseed all over again. In the interest of saving you time and effort, here are some tips to ensure that notoriously difficult seeds will sprout.

Problem: New Zealand spinach, asparagus, parsley, beets, and, to a lesser extent, spinach and okra are tough seeds. Their seed coats are too resistant for water to penetrate easily or contain germination inhibitors.

Solution: Soak seeds overnight in warm water, whether planting indoors or out. Before soaking, scar the outside of the seed coat with a file or blunt instrument, or shake seeds in a bag of stones. For small seeds like parsley, rub them between two sheets of sandpaper. For spinach, instead of water you may use a dilute solution of vinegar as long as you rinse it off before planting. For okra, some gardeners use a very dilute chlorine bleach solution. Dry seeds after soaking by setting them in a single layer on paper towels or newspapers in a warm, but not hot, place. Put them near, but not on, a radiator or wood stove, or roll and pat them gently in a double or triple layer of paper towels. This will prevent clumping. Be extra gentle if some of them have sprouted.

Problem: Seeds of parsley, carrots, parsnips, celery, and peppers are exceedingly slow to germinate if soil is under 78°F. All of these may take as long as three weeks.

Solution: Presoak overnight, then freeze for a week. (Be sure to allow time for this in your scheduling.) Dry the seeds on paper towels, or mix them with dry material like sand or cornmeal before planting, so they won't clump. If that sounds like too much work, pour boiling water over the planted flat. Handle parsnip seed extremely carefully when soaking or drying because it's quite fragile. Outdoors, some gardeners cover parsley and parsnip sowings with a board to encourage faster germination.

Problem: Some seeds require very warm soil (70 to 80°F) if they are to germinate in a reasonable amount of time. These warmth lovers include squash, okra, eggplants, cantaloupes, peppers, lima beans, black-eyed peas, and corn.

Solution: For indoor starts, set flats on water heaters, furnaces, inside a sink cabinet, or wherever you would sprout seeds for eating. Use thermostat-controlled heating pads or plate

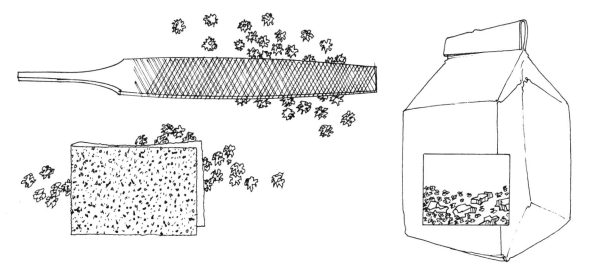

Seed Treatments: Seeds like beets and parsley can be stubborn germinators. To speed the process, scar seeds with a file, shake them in a bag with stones, or rub them between two sheets of sandpaper.

warmers, or better yet, use a heating cable installed in a flat according to the manufacturer's instructions. Cable-wired heating tiles are also available. Soak lima beans briefly in warm water to encourage sprouting. Too long a soak will waterlog them. Plant limas shallowly, eye down. Outdoors, delay planting heat-loving seeds until the soil is thoroughly warm. A soil thermometer is the most reliable gauge of when the soil has warmed sufficiently. Planting too early, while the soil is still cool, doesn't gain any time, for these seeds will simply lie dormant or even rot.

Problem: Seeds of spinach and lettuce sown in the heat of midsummer often fail to sprout

Solution: Hot weather shuts down these seeds. Always store seed packets in a cool place. Give them an extra cold treatment one to two weeks before planting by chilling in the freezer.

Problem: Cucurbit seeds rot easily after planting, especially naked seed pumpkin varieties.

Solution: Presprout cucurbits on wet paper towels before planting indoors or out. Handle them with care.

Techniques for an Early Start

Southern and some coastal gardeners will experience hardly any break in the gardening season. For them, crops already in the ground since autumn will harbinger spring by setting forth hopeful growth the way crocuses and snowdrops do for the rest of us. In the snowbound North, however, the sooner we get going in the spring, the longer and more productive our season will be.

One of the most important forms of insurance for early starts is advanced planning. All too often there comes an absentmindedness with the smell of a wood fire. Fortunately, seed companies jolt us from our long winter's nap with glossy reminders that spring is coming. When catalogs start arriving with January mail, we count the leftover seed packets or the envelopes of seed we've gathered and dried ourselves, and

we order supplements. We get out graph paper and gardening notebooks and begin our delightful planning daydreams while snowflakes still fall.

In January, however, it will be too late, or too early, to prepare the seedbeds. For early starts, soil preparation should be done in the fall. Raised beds in good, friable condition, full of compost and mulched, will make spring tasks easier. They also allow you to plant sooner. While neighbors with conventional plots must wait to till the soil before planting, you can get right down to business as soon as the soil becomes workable. And the light, well-draining soil in raised beds will usually be workable before the soil in a compacted, conventional plot is.

According to Timothy Fisher and Kathleen Kolb, Vermont gardeners and two of the authors of *Intensive Gardening Round the Year* (Stephen Greene Press, 1981), a sprinkling of wood ashes will cause snow to melt over beds faster. Another method is to cover beds in fall, either with portable cold frames or other protective devices or with a mulch of hay or leaves. For fast-frozen soil under mulch, spread a sheet of clear plastic and let the sun thaw and warm the soil for you.

Soon after snow is removed, take the soil's temperature with a soil thermometer. Few seeds will survive long in wet, cold ground, even if you can get a spade through it to break up the frozen clods. Lettuce and spinach seed, among the hardiest, will germinate at no lower than 35°F.

Hardy seedlings, set out as early as possible, will give you a jump on the season. For instance, if extra-early lettuce is your goal, you can subtract 10 to 15 days from the 42 days to maturity of the popular BLACK-SEEDED SIMPSON if you start seeds indoors four to five weeks before it's warm enough to transplant. See the earlier Guide to Timing Transplanting for help in scheduling seed-starting and setting-out activities.

One way to achieve super-early harvests is to overwinter certain rugged plants right in the garden. If you live in a moist, protected, well-drained location in hardiness zone 4, or live in hardiness zones 5 or 6 or in a northwestern coastal region where winters are even milder, you can encourage your garden to keep going during winter months that ordinarily would be lost to food production. By fall planting hardy varieties that have a fighting chance to grow on intermittently despite the cold, you'll enjoy an extra harvest in early spring long before most people have put away their snow shovels.

Hot prospects for this kind of cold growing include kale, collards, lettuce, spinach, sweet onions, and sprouting broccoli. You can also overwinter seeds to get off to a fast start in spring. Try seeding peas, lettuce, New Zealand spinach, spinach, and other cool-weather crops right before the ground freezes in the fall. These fall-planted seeds will emerge earlier and develop faster than their spring-seeded counterparts.

In the following pages, individual crops that can take the cold and are suited for early starts are discussed. Under each vegetable you'll find specific techniques and varieties that will bring you an early harvest. Each of these vegetables either commences growing at the onset of spring or can be set outside extra early from an indoor start. Most of them withstand frost when young. Some, through the choice of suitable varieties and by employing special gardening practices, can be made to produce for a very long season. Some can even be planted at the other end of the season for late harvests, which will be discussed in more detail under Late Finishes. Also, some of the crops discussed later under Oriental Vegetables are good for early starts.

Beans

To extend the normal bean-growing season use cool-loving favas for an early start. Although these shelled beans take three months to mature, they can be planted as early as peas, or seven weeks before the last spring frost. Their harvest will be under way about the time limas, which they resemble in flavor, are being planted. Two reliable favas are IPRO and WINDSOR (both available from 29).

To make the crop an even earlier one, start favas indoors in individual pots in February, and have them ready to go outside as soon as the ground can be worked. Give the young plants protection at times of heavy frost.

A continuous bean harvest starts with favas, progresses first to early, then to later, snap beans, and moves on to the new early limas like the bush variety GENEVA (34), which tolerates cool soil and can be planted two weeks earlier than other limas in northern gardens. Next come the later-planted traditional bush limas, a grand panoply of shell beans, green soybeans, pole snap beans, pole limas, and finally dried beans for winter eating.

A few snap beans have been bred to germinate in cool soil, and these you can plant as much as a week before the last spring frost. These include ROYAL BURGUNDY and LIMELIGHT (64), a flat Italian type. All other beans must wait until spring frosts are over.

Beets

Sow beet seeds indoors for a quick start out in the garden. These hardy plants can be set out as early as one month before frosts end. Give nighttime protection for a week after transplanting if temperatures drop below freezing. Young beet seedlings are quite hardy. Hot weather makes beets woody, so early starts give you better quality harvests. For spring crops, use quick-maturing varieties that will be ready for harvest before heavy moisture followed by summer drought causes banded roots.

Three quick-maturing varieties for spring use are RED ACE, 50 days to maturity, EARLY WONDER, 55 days, and LITTLE BALL (9), 56 days. LITTLE BALL is compact and ideal for both growing frames and tightly spaced, interplanted beds. It can be direct-seeded in a cold frame in late February or early March. BOLTARDY (57, 67) is another good beet for earliest spring planting since it's extremely cold and bolt resistant.

Broccoli

For an early start in spring, sow broccoli seeds indoors. You can transplant out as early as one month before the last expected frost. Broccoli will not be harmed by a light frost. An early start will help you to beat the flea beetles and the cabbage butterflies and will also allow time for a gradual harvest of the side shoots after the main head is cut. If heat threatens, provide sun-shading devices to keep the plants from bolting.

Among the hardiest and fastest-growing varieties for spring are GREEN COMET, PACKMAN (50), EMPEROR (34), GREEN GOLIATH (59), DE CICCO, and BRAVO.

Any broccoli plants you've wintered over will very likely sprout again in early spring. Your first taste of fresh broccoli will be from these plants. Extra-hardy CALABRESE, when mulched heavily, will go through winter and sprout again in early spring.

Another winter-worker is the OVERWINTER-ING (45, 64) heading broccoli, ideal for late sum-mer or early fall planting in the Pacific North-west for spring harvest. CHRISTMAS PURPLE SPROUTING (45) broccoli comes through even earlier, providing a welcome late January harvest in the Pacific Northwest. EARLY PURPLE SPROUTING and LATE WHITE SPROUTING (both available from 64 and 67) sown in May or June will survive winters in zone 5 and further north with protection. Broccoli raabs—actually sprouting turnips—such as FALL BROCCOLI RAAB (17) and RAAB 7 TOP (64) also overwinter cheerfully, sending up 12-inch asparaguslike shoots in early spring.

Cabbage

For the earliest start on the cabbage season, plant fast-maturing cabbages as soon as the ground can be worked, using transplants started indoors and giving them protection under cloches or frames. An advantage to using quick-maturing varieties is that they will beat the heat.

PRIMAX (29, 34), a good variety, has been indoor started in New Hampshire to produce by early June. GOLDEN ACRE, at 62 days, is often called the earliest of all, but like any early varieties, it may show yellow leaves and poorly formed heads. PRINCESS (63), which matures in 66 days, is better looking. SALARITE (63), 57 days, is a semisavoy with crinkled leaves tender enough

EXTENDING THE ASPARAGUS SEASON

For gardeners, tender shoots of asparagus are as much a sign of spring as a plump robin hunting worms in the yard. Once a bed is established, asparagus is one of the first garden-fresh vegetables ready for harvest in the spring.

Unfortunately, once it's begun, asparagus season is over all too quickly. There is a way you can stretch out the season by delaying the harvest of a few plants in the bed. Researchers in New Zealand found that by letting the first spear that emerges develop completely, you can delay the start of harvesting from seven to ten days. You'll get the same total yield from the bed, but you'll be able to savor fresh asparagus for a bit longer.

for slaw. EARLY JERSEY WAKEFIELD, at 62 days, is a very popular early cabbage.

Carrots

For a speedy spring harvest, choose quickly maturing carrot varieties that will develop before the temperature climbs over 75°F. Raised beds are ideal for carrots because the soil warms quickly and root growth, finding less resistance in loose soil, is rapid. LINDORO (48) matures a week before Nantes types. Small-rooted carrots like LITTLE FINGER (9, 50), BABY FINGER (38, 42), KUNDULUS (48), and PLANET (57, 59) can also be harvested early and are ideal for cold frames. HIPACK (26) can be planted densely in frames or beds without the roots becoming distorted. GONSENHEIMER TREIB (67) can be forced under cloches or planted outside earlier than other varieties. Plant GOKUWASE 3-SUN (67) very early under plastic mulch for an extra-early harvest.

For early starts, sprout seeds indoors, using heating cables to warm the soil to 78°F. Sow seed every two or three weeks for staggered transplantings, and transplant when outdoor temperatures reach the mid-60s. (See the box on Temperamental Transplants for pointers on how to handle carrot seedlings.) During periods of nighttime frost, give protection after setting out. Carrots are moderately frost hardy.

Endive

Endive makes a good lettuce substitute for impatient gardeners. Its coarse texture and slight bitterness may disturb finicky eaters, but it is hardier and less perishable in storage than lettuce, and it can grow well into spring—a month longer than the early lettuces. Best of all, as a biennial it produces seed only in its second spring and therefore is bolt-proof.

Curly endive, the most hardy, can be planted in late winter for early spring harvesting. GREEN CURLED and SALAD KING are two popular curly endive varieties. Another type, usually marketed as escarole, is lighter green, with smooth, broad

Extended Broccoli Harvest: An early-planted crop of broccoli gives you an extended harvest. After cutting the main head, the plant will continue to produce tender side shoots. Broccoli raab, shown on right, overwinters well for extra-early harvests in spring.

leaves. It is usually planted late spring to midsummer. Varieties include FULL HEART BATAVIAN (36) and BROAD LEAVED BATAVIAN (9).

To hasten harvests, start seeds indoors. For longer harvests, stagger plantings every two weeks. You can start picking immature leaves within 30 days of transplanting.

Kohlrabi

Fast-growing varieties of kohlrabi, started indoors and set out five weeks before last frosts in spring, will help round out your early harvesting season. Kohlrabi, like cabbages, will stand light frost but not hard freeze, so you should be ready to protect your seedlings. Kohlrabi will be ready to harvest 12 weeks after setting out, when the enlarged stem has reached 2 to 3 inches in diameter. For a long harvest, plant several varieties and have seedlings ready to transplant every two weeks until mid-June.

Best for spring are the fast-growing varieties that mature while days are cool, including GRAND DUKE, 45 days, KARLA (34), 42 days, and EARLY WHITE VIENNA, 50 days.

Lettuce

A commercial market grower in the short-season region of Vermont keeps lettuce producing outdoors from June through November by carefully manipulating environments and choosing the right varieties. Home gardeners with growing frames may succeed in producing it even longer, especially if they live farther south or have insulated growing frames. Even with a standard cold frame it's possible to produce lettuce in April in the North, advancing the season by up to two months.

Early spring lettuce is usually started indoors from mid-February on so that it will be ready to go into the beds as early as possible. Continue starting plants indoors every two weeks until May, using quick-to-mature varieties. From flats, transplant two-week-old seedlings to pots and, two weeks later, move them outdoors.

THE HARDY VEGETABLE LINE-UP

Listed below you'll find hardy vegetables ranked by degrees of cold-tolerance—from least hardy to most hardy.

Least Hardy	Cauliflower
	Kohlrabi
	Rutabagas
	Onions
	Lettuce
	Carrots
	Celeriac
	Broccoli
	Cabbage
	Mustard
	Turnips
	Beets
	Radishes
	Celtuce
	Swiss chard
	Chinese cabbage (heading type)
	Endive
	Collards
	Parsley
	Garlic
	Brussels sprouts
	Leeks
	Spinach
	Salsify
	Parsnips
	Jerusalem artichokes
	Corn salad
Most Hardy	Kale

Early leaf lettuce and loosehead and fast-growing head lettuces resist light frost and can be set out soon after the soil can be worked, although the protection of cloches, cold frames, or tunnels is advised when nights are below freezing. If the young plants do freeze, there will be some browning along the leaf edges. A little of this "burning" won't interfere with the plants' development as the weather improves. The Vermont commercial grower sets out his first-planted lettuces under tunnels in mid-April and finds that tunnels speed the growth. Pick leaf and loosehead types by the cut-and-come-again method for longest harvests.

Early lettuces include the heading types TANIA (14, 26), 65 days, GRAND RAPIDS, 45 days, ITHICA, 60 days, and PRIZEHEAD, 48 days. There are also fast-growing head types like VANGUARD, 90 days, which has been interbred with wild lettuce, and SALINAS (21), 75 days, a crinkled-leaf variety. There are many early leaf types, including BLACK-SEEDED SIMPSON, 42 days, and RED SAILS, 50 days. Looseheads include the small TOM THUMB (15), 49 days, and GREEN ICE (9), 45 days.

Depending on how cold your winters are, you might want to try overwintering a young crop of lettuce plants. The plants that survive will respond quickly to the onset of spring weather by putting on new growth and will give you your first lettuce harvest well in advance of even the earliest spring-planted crops. Sow these lettuces in late summer so they'll have time to produce six to eight leaves and reach 4 to 6 inches across before the soil freezes. If you have a cold frame, sow them in there. Otherwise, be ready to cover the plants as cold weather settles in so they'll last through the winter. Tougher lettuce strains will intermittently grow in temperatures as low as 12°F, but you'll really notice a flurry of growth as the days lengthen and begin to warm. Abundant Life Seed Foundation in Fort Townsend, Washington, reports successfully overwintering the romaines WINTER DENSITY, WINTER MARVEL, and ALL YEAR ROUND (all available from 1, 15 and 55) despite winter weather in the teens. Other gardeners have had good results with VALDOR (15) and LITTLE GEM (64).

Onions

By proper planning and making use of seeds, sets, and transplants, it is possible to produce fresh onions for use eight months of the year, with storage onions to fill in the other four. Now how's that for extending the season? Here we'll talk about spring and summer onions; for fall harvests see Late Finishes.

Grow bunching onions for spring use from seeds started indoors, or in a cold frame, in midwinter. These will be ready to go outside as seedlings in March, or two months before the last spring frost. You can start harvesting immature plants in April. As an alternative, or supplement, you may start sets as soon as the ground can be worked and harvest them immature as soon as their stems are as big around as a pencil. Some of

---

FOUR SEASONS OF LETTUCE

With some planning and enlightened variety selection, you can be enjoying home-grown salads nearly year-round. Here's a summary of the planting techniques that will give you lettuce in each season.

Spring	Summer	Fall	Winter
Plants that have wintered over. Transplants set out early with protection. Direct-sown seed.	Heat-resistant varieties started indoors, set out, and given shading.	Frost-resistant, quick-maturing varieties that are direct-sown, with mature plants protected from frost.	Winter-hardy varieties started in September, raised in growing frames.

the best varieties for spring green onions are EVERGREEN BUNCHING, ISHIKURA LONG (34), BELTSVILLE BUNCHING, EVERGREEN HARDY WHITE, SOUTHPORT BUNCHING (26), and KUJO GREEN MULTISTALK (34). WHITE PORTUGAL and SILVER SKIN sets also make good green onions. When using sets, hill them to produce long white stems.

The next onions you eat in spring will be the bunching onions you have started the previous fall. SWEET WINTER (48), EXPRESS YELLOW (64), and WALLA WALLA SWEET (34) will be ready to harvest by May or June. Seed them directly in August, or ten weeks before the first fall frost, and by October they should be 6 to 8 inches high. During the winter they stop growing in most areas, but they resume in early spring. SWEET WINTER seedlings can endure spells as low as −20°F and WALLA WALLA SWEET withstands temperatures down to −10°F. Because these onions have been bred to bulb in response to daylengths of 11 hours, they will have reached almost full bulb size by late May.

For the next in the sequence of onion harvests, start Sweet Spanish and Bermuda varieties from seed indoors in January. Transplant out in March, after very careful hardening-off. When the length of the days goes over 12 hours, they will be almost at full bulb size, and they can be harvested from early summer to midsummer. Among the summer onions are YELLOW BERMUDA, CRYSTAL WHITE WAX (the earliest), and RINGMASTER. All are poor for storage. The Spanish, or Valencia, type includes the UTAH strain of YELLOW SWEET SPANISH, (2, 8, 47) an unusually large summer onion.

Late summer onion harvest consists of the later types of Spanish onions, which include the YELLOW SWEET SPANISH PECKAM (34) strain, and the later Bermudas, along with common storage onions.

Peas

The earlier you plant peas, the longer you harvest them. Although they'll take chills of 19°F, warm weather slows and toughens them. Plant as soon as the ground can be worked. Peas transplant poorly and germinate in relatively cool ground, so indoor starts are seldom useful. In extremely cold areas or places with brief springs, transplanting may be necessary. See the box Temperamental Transplants for pointers on how to handle peas with care. Soak the seed when starting indoors or if planting into dry soil.

The 1985 catalog from Johnny's Selected Seeds in Maine offers these tricks for an early start in spring, the prime pea-planting time. Use

---

FOUR SEASONS OF ONIONS

It's possible to have a home-grown supply of onions all through the year. Here's a summary of the onions you can be eating in each season.

Spring	Summer	Fall	Winter
Bunching onions that have wintered over. Bunching onions from transplants or immature sets.	Bulbing onions from sets and spring transplants.	Bunching onions direct-sown in spring. Bulbing onions from sets and spring transplants.	Storage onions harvested in fall. Bunching onions in growing frames or mulched in the garden.

well-prepared, well-drained raised beds or rows; select a sunny, warm place in the garden; melt the snow and warm the ground with a sheet of clear plastic before planting; and add potassium-rich supplements or wood ashes to sweeten the soil. Frequent cultivation will also keep the soil warm and prevent waterlogging during germination and the first, early growth.

Always use an early maturing variety for the first planting. Among these are the heavy-bearing garden pea dwarfs KNIGHT and SPARKLE, and the larger, sweeter climbers FREEZONIAN, THOMAS LAXTON, and MAESTRO.

Keep the pea season going with a second planting of a later-bearing variety that is heat resistant. These include LINCOLN, ALDERMAN, and WANDO (17, 34, 35).

Snow peas are at least as hardy as the earlier garden peas and can be harvested sooner, because they are eaten immature. Reliable varieties include MAMMOTH MELTING SUGAR and SNOW-FLAKE (8, 14).

The snap peas, which are eaten mature, develop over a slightly longer period. They will be ready to pick just before the later varieties of garden peas, making the spring harvest continuous. Quick-to-mature vining types are SUGAR SNAP (9, 48) 62 days, and SWEET SNAP (9, 47), 64 days. Dwarf sugar snaps include SUGAR DADDY (22, 48, 59), 68 days, SUGAR RAE (34, 48), 66 days, SUGAR ANN (26, 34), 55 days, SUGAR MEL (25, 48), 70 days, EARLY SNAP (26), 62 days, and SUGAR BON (9, 48), 56 days.

Radishes

If you're weary of waiting for something to harvest fresh from the garden, try these robust little roots that bring rapid rewards. CHERRY BEAUTY (64), when planted as soon as the ground can be worked, may be pulled ripe in just 28 days. SAXA (17, 25) is still faster—18 days for that crisp red marble. For silver-dollar size, try CHAMPION, ready in 27 days. Less crisp, but carrot-sized, are WHITE ICICLE and LONG SCARLET.

Remember, though, one little heat wave in the 80s and you'll be biting wood and swallowing fire. Radishes remain in prime form for only a few days. Plant them early and harvest them fresh and small. They are usually direct-seeded in staggered small batches as close together as a week, spring and fall. They won't take freezes or store in the ground.

Spinach

Spinach germinates and grows best in cool ground and in air temperatures in the 60s, so if your soil thaws as early as the beginning of March, you'll probably find little advantage to starting it inside.

For the fullest and longest harvests in spring, plant spinach outdoors every two weeks until the last frost. Within a month of the last frost, start planting heat and bolt-resistant varieties. These include BLOOMSDALE LONGSTANDING, POPEYE'S CHOICE (69), and TYEE (50).

For the very earliest starts, backtrack two seasons. Plant spinach in fall, mulch, and expect renewed growth in the spring, up to three months before last frost. For fall plantings, you may want to start seeds inside without bottom heating. Once the small plants are about 2 to 4 inches high and have four leaves, give them a dose of liquid fertilizer to speed growth. After first fall frost, set the seedlings out in newly emptied and cultivated beds. Feed them again with bloodmeal or more liquid fertilizer. By the time the temperature sinks to the 30s, new leaves will have developed. Light mulching is beneficial, but it is not essential in areas with snow cover. Snow lets the light through to the spinach, while keeping out the cold and insulating against freeze and thaw. Don't use light-blocking mulches.

In early March, or when crocuses are up but not yet open, fertilize again. Fall-planted spinach will be the first greens in the garden, unless you have managed to winter over oriental greens or winter lettuces. Its growth will be more luxuriant and tender than the growth on any spinach you grow later in the season. For fall-planted spinach, use the hardiest varieties you can find. These will include the savoy types such as INDIAN SUMMER (34), MELODY, VIRGINIA SAVOY (17), WINTER BLOOMSDALE (29), GIANT WINTER (1), and AMERICA.

Swiss Chard

We're so used to thinking of Swiss chard as a summer substitute for spinach that we forget how hardy it is. It will easily survive 10°F and, in many areas, can be mulched for early spring renewal. Cut back the stalks in fall before applying a heavy layer of mulch. Since Swiss chard takes 60 days to mature from direct seeding, it should be planted a week or two before the last spring frost. To get a head start, consider using transplants.

Dependable varieties are FORDHOOK GIANT, LUCULLUS, and RHUBARB, a red-stalked plant.

Turnips

Among the earliest and quickest-maturing turnips are YORII SPRING (34), 38 days, TOKYO CROSS HYBRID (50), 35 days, and MILAN (9, 14), 40 days. Start them indoors and transplant by mid-April or a month before the last frost. Turnips are hardy to 20°F and grow best at 40 to 60°F. No protection is necessary after transplanting, unless frosts are very severe.

Cool-Weather Greens for Early and Late Harvests

Two main trends have enlarged the repertoire of the cool-weather gardener in recent years. An increased interest in edible wild plants has resulted in their introduction into the garden in tamed form, and, in North America, the internationalization of cuisines has spread interest in cold-weather vegetables long used in other parts of the world. In addition, a few new varieties have been developed to combine features of old favorites. All of these are hardy enough to be started early in cold frames or under other protection; some will winter over for extra-early harvests and may even remain harvestable late in the fall.

Arugula Also called rucola, roquette, or rocket, this plant is used for early spring greens that are coarser and more flavorful than leaf lettuce. Sow it as soon as the ground is workable, or set out transplants at frequent intervals from earliest spring until hot days come. Space plants closely so they benefit from self-shading. Arugula matures in 40 days. Pick and eat the leaves while they're young and tender. In the South, arugula can be wintered over like the hardier radicchio. ROSSA DE VERONA is a good Italian variety. Arugula makes a good cold frame crop (available from 29 and 67).

Celtuce This is a crop that comes in two installments. The leaf crop, ready for harvest in 45 days, forms in a rosette around the stem. The celerylike, but ribless, seedstalk matures a few weeks later. The early leaves, which resemble romaine lettuce, should be eaten before the plant matures to bolting stage, for afterward they become bitter and milky. The stem, however, remains edible after bolting and tastes best when it is an inch in diameter at the base. It has a slight cucumber taste and is usually peeled to remove the bitter outside sap tubes.

Southern gardeners set celtuce outside in February or early spring after an indoor start in winter. Northerners sow it as soon as the soil is workable or set it out a month before last frost after indoor starting (available from 68).

Corn Salad Sometimes known as lamb's lettuce, this is another plant that has come in from the wild to serve as a winter lettuce substitute in the South and as an early lettuce, or spinach, substitute where springs come quickly.

Start seeds indoors two to three weeks before last frost and set out seedlings one week after frost. Direct-seed as soon as the soil is workable. Spoon-shaped leaves grow up to a foot in 55 to 60 days but can be eaten after 45 days from seeding, or sometimes earlier. The plant forms loose rosettes that will resist frost. Corn salad can also be grown as a fall crop, sown in August and later mulched. Harvest until early winter, or leave plants undisturbed for extra-early spring greens. If grown in summer, it requires some shading. Sow thickly to compensate for poor germination. Corn salad has a nutty flavor and a delicate texture. RONDE MARAICHERE (15, 67) is a particularly early and productive variety.

Dandelions Yes, plant dandelions, but don't tell the neighbors. Young, tender dandelion greens are piquant additions to early salads. The thick-leaved dandelion has been improved to produce broad, flavorful leaves. When planted midsummer, cultivated dandelions will provide roots for winter forcing. Planted in early spring as soon as the ground thraws, they will give you very early, nutritious greens within a month. (What the neigh-

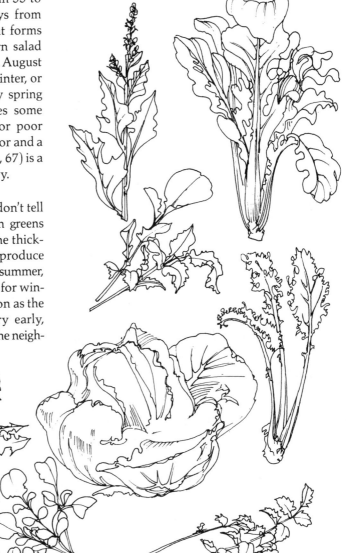

Greens for Cool Weather: All of the greens assembled here thrive under cool growing conditions. From lower left they include garden cress, corn salad, dandelion, upland cress, salad burnet, radicchio, sea kale, arugula, celtuce (top right), and Good King Henry.

bors will give you if they find out is better left unsaid.) (Available from 15, 17, 57, and 67.)

Garden Cress This form of cress matures in ten days and can be sown shortly before the spring frosts end. Harvest the leaves and flowers while they are still on the stalk. With frequent cutting, they will come back again (available from 16 and 52).

Good King Henry This self-sowing perennial potherb produces young leaves that can be eaten like spinach, as well as shoots and flower heads to prepare like asparagus. The shoots come up nice and early along with asparagus, and the leaves soon follow. Start it from seed indoors in early spring, from seedlings found in the wild, or use root divisions. Good King Henry is best mulched and given its own bed, where it should be thinned and divided frequently to keep it from growing rank (available from 55 and 67).

Mustard India and white mustards are the best for greens. Varieties include SOUTHERN GIANT CURLED, a pungent, 3-foot-tall plant best grown in fall, and GREEN WAVE, a bolt-resistant, hot-tasting variety that can be planted two months before last frost. FLORIDA BROAD LEAF, with its large leaves and tender ribs, is also bolt resistant. More mellow in taste is FORDHOOK FANCY.

Mustard is a hardy short-day crop that is good for cool seasons but bolts so easily in early spring that it is usually grown only in fall. If planted before mid-April, or three weeks before the last expected frost of spring, some varieties will mature to harvesting size without first bolting, provided the temperature doesn't sink rapidly during an early spring cold snap. In hot weather, mustard becomes too hot in flavor to be eaten raw without discomfort. Boiling, however, will mellow the taste.

Mustard Spinach This is a name given to the TENDERGREEN (9) variety of India mustard. Just to confuse things, there is also a mustard cabbage variety with the name TENDERGREEN (this is discussed in a later section on oriental vegetables). Mustard spinach resembles spinach in appearance but not in taste. If you take one bite of it raw, you'll know it's a mustard. It matures in 25 days, a shorter period than is common for other mustards. Even more important for home gardeners, it is hardy enough to be the first plant in the garden in spring. Plant mustard spinach two months before last frost in spring or wait until after August and overwinter it. If you pick the small outer leaves one at a time, you will find them crisp and surprisingly mild.

Radicchio Long a favorite Italian salad ingredient, red, green, or variegated radicchio can be planted for early spring enjoyment. It matures in 85 days and grows better when sown in mid-July for a fall crop. Radicchio will survive freezing under mulch for renewed growth when temperatures return to the 40s. Rosettes of leaves develop before the plant bolts in May. Sowing seed thickly as soon as the soil can be worked in spring will provide a less long-lasting crop. Plant it densely so that leaves will be kept mild flavored by self-shading. Radicchio can also be grown from indoor starts sown a month before last frost. VERONA RED (23), sometimes listed as ROSSA DI VERONA (64), is a favorite variety.

Salad Burnet A perennial sometimes grown as an annual, salad burnet remains green and edible through winter in all but the coldest parts of the United States and Canada. It needs full sunlight but will germinate outdoors within ten days if planted at the time of the last spring frost. It matures within two months and self-seeds from ruby-colored flowers late in the season. When the rubies have faded, cut back the plant and mulch it for renewed winter and early spring growth. Salad burnet produces small, tasty, cucumber-flavored leaves on branching stems.

Sea Kale This relatively unknown perennial is used for its leaves and shoots. Like asparagus, which it resembles, sea kale is usually transplanted to a permanent bed, where it reaches edible size in its second or third year and continues bearing for six years or more. It can be started from seed, but for a more quickly established bed, find some-one growing sea kale who is willing to share some roots with you. Dig 4 to 6-inch roots in fall, store them, and replant in spring for harvest the following spring. In early spring, blanch shoots as they appear by covering them with flower pots or mounding them with earth. During blanching, a small leaf develops at the top of the leafstalk. Harvest sea kale like asparagus until the full leaf appears, removing the soil or blanching device when frosts are over. The flowers, which come in summer, should be cut off. In winter, clean up the bed and mulch heavily. Sea kale, which has a less bitter taste than Belgian endive, can be forced indoors from crowns in winter. (For directions, see the box later in the chapter on Winter Gardening Indoors.) It is also grown in cold frames for an extra-early harvest of tender shoots (available from 67).

Upland Cress Also called winter cress, these fast-growing greens can be sown in mild climates from July to September, for winter and spring use. The quality of the leaf flavor is improved by a cold winter under mulch, but cresses can also be planted in early spring in cold areas. Cress germinates in four to five days and matures within two weeks. Harvest young leaves as needed for salads or steaming, but parboil the tougher outer leaves (available from 9, 55, and 57).

Carrying Cool Crops into Warm Weather

A very common complaint among gardeners is that just about the time the tomatoes are ripening, there's no decent lettuce to be had. If only the prime spring greens season could overlap with tomato time, then garden-fresh tossed salads with these two favorite ingredients would be possible. Getting the most out of the growing season means

being able to extend the time cool-weather crops like lettuce remain productive and even finding some suitable substitutes that can stand up to higher temperatures.

Sun Shading

One of the outstanding features of a closely spaced intensive bed is that the leaves of the plants almost meet to shade the soil beneath them, creating a microclimate both cooler and more moist than the surrounding open spaces. Cool, moist conditions are what early spring and late fall vegetables thrive in, so it should come as no surprise to learn that they can be maintained at bearing stage longer in intensive gardens than in conventional ones. Another characteristic of inten-sive beds is the high humus content of their soil. Organic matter serves as a buffer to moderate soil temperatures so the ground is likely to stay cooler than the air that is warming with the long days of summer.

When heat waves come unusually early, or otherwise intrude upon the growing time of cool crops, however, it is smart to have a few tricks up the sleeve of your gardening coveralls. Interplant-ing small plants like lettuce, radishes, early cab-bage, or spinach in the shade of taller, stocky plants like Swiss chard, bush beans, or peppers will give them a leafy awning to protect against wilting.

A deep straw or hay mulch applied in early June to nestle around the plants will hold mois-ture and coolness in the soil and keep early plants from bolting. It puts another layer between the heat source and the roots and traps cool air in the air pockets next to the vegetables. It will also offer some shade to low-growing vegetables.

Judicious use of water will also cool the soil. Lettuce, for example, benefits from constantly moist, but not wet, soil going 12 inches down. Mulch lettuce and other cool greens thickly in hot weather and irrigate when the soil under the mulch dries out.

Shading Devices: These structures can range from full-scale lathhouses to a row of bamboo sticks pushed into the soil (shown on top). A miniature lath or bamboo fence covered with burlap or muslin (center) will throw an afternoon shadow that may save your lettuce. Or drape bent-wire tunnels with light-permeable fabric such as cheesecloth or Reemay. (This can replace the original, frost-fighting plastic of early spring.)

Cool Crops to Coax into Summer

Remember that you're going against the natural inclination of cool-weather crops to ask them to produce well as the temperature rises. You'll have a better chance of success if you carefully select varieties that exhibit heat tolerance.

Beets Sow GREEN TOPS and GREEN TOP BUNCHING (48) directly after the soil has warmed to the high

60s and frosts are over. They will produce late summer and fall greens, replacing spinach in hot weather. The roots, however, are less satisfactory.

Cabbage For a good summer harvest, geographical location is the most critical factor. The best growing conditions are moist and neither too hot nor too cold, so only foggy maritime regions with temperatures under 80°F will produce fine-quality summer cabbage heads. Gardeners in other regions should try STONEHEAD, a fast-maturing variety that develops well in hot weather, and SAVOY KING, which is heat resistant (both available from 28).

Carrots KINKO (34), a heat-resistant carrot, if seeded directly in May, will produce early June crops to extend the carrot harvest into warm weather.

Lettuce and Spinach To keep harvesting these greens into or through the summer, start heat-resistant varieties indoors in late April for mid-May transplanting. Continue setting them out until mid-June, leaving two-week intervals between sowings. Transplant out when 2 inches high. For this group you can use the Bibbs KAGRAN SUMMER (34), and BURPEE BIBB; leaf types GREEN ICE (9), SLO-BOLT (14, 20), and OAK LEAF; and looseheads RED FIRE and GREEN WAVE (both available from 68). Hot-weather lettuces also include the heading types MINETTO (36) and MANTILLA (57) and the butterheads BUTTERKING (55), AUGUSTA (48), ALL YEAR ROUND (also drought resistant), and MERVEILLE DES QUATRE SAISONS (both available from 67). If these are chosen for lengthening maturing times, they will keep the harvest going into early fall. Also plant long-maturing but slow-to-bolt varieties like the crisphead BALLADE (68) and the romaines PARRIS ISLAND COS (14, 21) and LOBJOIT'S GREEN COS (17, 67). These do best in fall but may need shading as seedlings, if the weather is hot.

One spinach that's billed as being heat tolerant is ITALIAN SUMMER (57). A high-yielding plant, it is more bolt resistant than other spinach. The leaves are thick and semicrinkly.

In hot weather, pick lettuce (and spinach, if you're lucky enough to keep that growing) before it is fully mature. Leaf lettuce should be picked at between half and three-quarter size and head lettuce when the heads are formed, but not solid.

Radishes A few summer radishes extend the season into hot weather. These include the heat-tolerant SUMMER CROSS (9), WHITE AND LONG (60), and MINOWASE EARLY (34). BLACK SPANISH has black skin, stores well, and needs 60 days to mature.

Substitute Crops

In hot weather, gardeners have to be just as adaptable as they were during cool weather, and sometimes that will involve running in a substitute for an adversely affected favorite.

For greens to substitute for spinach in the heat of summer, try New Zealand spinach, which will neither bolt nor become bitter. Its leaves are succulent enough to resist drought, and its sprawling habit makes it self-mulching and partly self-shading. Start it inside in late winter after checking the earlier section Tricks for Starting Seeds, and transplant it after danger of frost has passed. Harvest, or pinch out, the growing tip, and the plant will branch for a more productive harvest of leaves. New Zealand spinach will self-sow and overwinter under mulch in all but very cold climates. It tastes very similar to spinach and can be used as a spinach substitute in any recipe.

The inner leaves of Swiss chard are edible straight through the summer, and, when the plants are cut back, they will send up tender new leaves within a month. Chard's deep roots make it drought resistant. These greens have a full-bodied flavor, more intense than spinach, and are best when used young.

Vegetable amaranth is sometimes listed as tampala or *hinn choy* in seed catalogs. Pick the growing tips young and tender, and a bed of 24

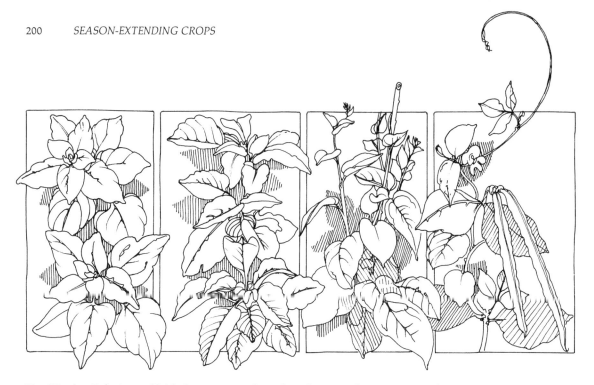

Hot Weather Substitutes: Unlike lettuce, spinach, and garden peas, these crops grow best in the heat. They include, from left, New Zealand spinach, vegetable amaranth, Malabar spinach, and crowder peas.

plants will produce up to 2½ pounds of greens a week. When cut, the plants respond by growing bushier. Amaranth transplants well, so start it inside, and transplant it out after frosts are over. Ideally, it can replace peas in the garden, if started three weeks before the end of the pea harvest. Vegetable amaranth has a rich green flavor all its own. Young leaves are fine for salads, but older ones are better when steamed (available from 52).

Malabar spinach, or basella, needs nighttime temperatures above 58°F, so it is usually started indoors and transplanted out in early summer after all chance of frost is over. It needs a trellis and much moisture and is usually eaten raw. It has a delicate flavor, milder than Swiss chard and turnip greens.

Orach plants thrive on heat. Start them inside one week before the last frost for transplanting out two weeks after frost danger is over. Pick leaves young like those of amaranth. The flavor is definite and strong.

Garden peas won't go into hot weather, but crowder peas—so called because they crowd each other in the shell—will, and that's why they have been southern favorites for generations. In terms of taste and use, crowder peas are a little closer to beans than to garden peas, but some varieties do have a flavor approaching garden peas. There are over 150 varieties of crowders, including ones of the black-eyed, field, proto, Southern, cream, and cowpea types. Plant them at the same time you plant limas and squash. The vines benefit from tying to trellises since they have no tendrils. They can wander on the ground if necessary.

Northerners should use only short-season varieties. Harvest 16 days after bloom if you plan to use the peas green and slightly immature. They may also be grown longer and dried on the vine. TEXAS CREAM #40 and CREAM 8 (both available from 28) are high-yielding varieties of the cream pea type. PINK EYE PURPLE HULL (28, 47) cowpeas have bushy vines and a flavor good for

Mexican dishes that's better, some people say, than the starchier brown peas many southerners prefer. BLACK EYE BEAN, also known as QUEEN ANNE (47), tastes the most like a garden pea. Its pods are 7 to 8 inches long and very full.

Extending the Season for Hot-Weather Crops

We know for certain that dependable hot-weather vegetables will come through the summer. After all, most of them have tropical ancestors. These crops—corn, melons, tomatoes, peppers, beans, squashes, cucumbers, pumpkins, and sweet potatoes—are also among the ones most familiar and dear to North American gardeners. What we need to learn about them now is how to extend their growing season in both directions so we can harvest them longer and grow them successfully in cooler climates. A slightly different strategy for warmer climates is to give these heat-lovers optimum conditions for rapid growth so they will occupy their beds for a shorter time and allow room for replacement or relay planting.

Beans

We've already discussed early beans, including the favas, but with careful selection and tending, many snap beans will produce for a long season. As much as six weeks' picking can come from a single sowing if you carefully select the variety and tend it well. All bush varieties were originally bred from vining beans to suit the commercial grower's convenience by stopping growth at a certain determined point instead of continuing on, like the indeterminate pole beans, to produce blossoms repeatedly until frost.

Any gardener with trellises or poles can use indeterminate pole beans of many varieties to achieve a continuous harvest. Most varieties start ripening one to two weeks after bush beans, and if selected carefully, will carry the harvest on when the bush beans stop bearing. Among climb-

ing bean varieties are WREN'S EGG POLE BEAN (55, 68), also called SPECKLED CRANBERRY, which will yield prolifically in a small area, providing its first harvest 65 days after sowing. It is usually used for shelled beans. ROMANO ITALIAN, 70 days, has stringless snap beans. BLUE LAKE, 64 days, is noted for its fine flavor, but KENTUCKY WONDER, 64 days, a heavy bearer, is probably the most popular. SELMA ZEBRA (48), a purple-striped variety, starts producing in 58 days, as early as a bush bean.

Bush beans include some varieties that are less determinate than others. For extra-long harvests without the need to provide supports, and in limited space, these are the ones to choose. To be sure you'll be picking all summer, select among both early and longer-to-bearing varieties. BLUE BUSH LAKE 141 (48), 55 days, for example, has an everbearing habit combined with the attributes of the other members of the Blue Lake series. MOUNTAINEER WHITE HALF-RUNNER (48) has vines 3 to 4 feet long and if given a little support from a low fence or cage will bear for six weeks or more. GREEN CROP, 51 days, and CONTENDER, 49 days, are a bit smaller but equally productive. CONTENDER, with its short period to bearing, makes a good late-season bean. Also consider BLACK VALENTINE (68), 70 days, good in cold weather, CHEROKEE WAX, 50 days, and JUMBO (48, 64), 54 days. A May planting of JUMBO has been known to bear until frost in Maine.

There are certain things you can do to keep any bush bean producing. Always keep the plants picked, even if you're so swamped with beans that they end up in the compost. Pick them slightly immature. Fully ripened beans signal the plant to stop flowering. Water encourages longer growth and is especially crucial a week before the heaviest bloom. When beans produce over a long period, their nutrient need goes up. If growth slows due to plant "hunger" or "thirst," or because of pest infestation or disease, flowering will also diminish.

It is sometimes worthwhile to continue caring for healthy plants when they stop producing.

The most common cause of interrupted bloom is a sudden change in weather. When weather returns to normal, you may get a second bloom and a second harvest. Late-planted beans will continue to grow up to the time average daily temperatures reach 55°F. They are unaffected by daylength. When planting for autumn production, add 15 days to the growing time to allow for cooler temperatures during the maturing period. This will mean that as far north as central New York State or southern Wisconsin, a 45-day bean can be planted safely before mid-July.

Cantaloupes

These melons can be grown as far north as the Canadian border if they're started from pre-sprouted seeds in individual pots six weeks before the ground is thoroughly warm. Choose the earliest maturing varieties, which include MAINEROCK (2, 20), 75 days, FAR NORTH (25), 70 days, GOLDEN HONEY (22), 73 days, GOLDEN CHAMPLAIN (25), 68 days, ALASKA (2, 28), 70 days, and GOLDEN CRISPY (33), 75 days.

Seeds should germinate in five to ten days. Grow seedlings at warm temperatures of 70 to 80°F and never below 55°F. Soil temperature should be in the 60s. Gradual hardening-off is crucial to successful transplanting. Give developing vines abundant sunshine and water, irrigating often until the melons form. Black plastic mulch over raised beds is helpful for fast starts in cold climates. Use large cloches, bed covers, or other protection in cold spells. As the end of the season approaches, cut off all immature fruits and concentrate the plant's energy on ripening the few larger melons on the vines.

Corn

All corn, even early corn, demands a soil temperature of 50°F to germinate. Southern gardeners, and some coastal ones, can work up a seedbed in early March for sowing in late March. Northerners who produce commercially use special raised beds with bottom heat and covers. They plant in January for June harvest. You don't have to go to

quite that extreme; indoor starts in bottom-heated flats or pots will also allow early production. If you can maintain an air temperature of 70°F inside and give bottom heat with heating cables or hot pads, and plenty of light, you should be able to start corn inside. Corn needs lots of warmth for germination and early growth.

Use peat pots or other individual containers for easy transplanting, and presoak or sprout the seed. See the earlier box Temperamental Transplants for pointers on how to handle corn seedlings. The young plants will be ready for setting out in about a month, so make sure conditions will be suitable for them in your beds then. That means temperatures are reaching the 70s and there is no danger of frost. When the corn reaches knee high, keep it from tipping over by mounding the earth around the base of the stalks. Water the crop generously when it tassels. Early corn will always be small in stature.

POLAR VEE (9, 59) matures in 53 days and ROYAL CREST in 60 under optimum conditions. EARLIVEE (34) and NORTHERN VEE (9, 59) are also fast maturing. An early planting will allow time for another relay crop to be harvested from the same garden bed. Choose your later corn varieties to produce over the longest possible period in sequence, or plant the same variety in relay. Toward midsummer, use rapidly maturing varieties again.

Cucumbers

Gynoecious hybrids will give you an early start because they produce only female flowers. Most monoecious (male and female flowered) cucumbers delay setting fruit until both the male and the slower female flowers are blooming. The female flowers on the gynoecious plants open early and are ready to be pollinated by the male flowers on accompanying pollinator plants (marked seeds for these male plants are included in seed packets). Gynoecious plants are early and heavy producers, but they do require more watering and feeding.

One drawback to gynoecious hybrids is that they also stop bearing early. To prolong the cucumber season, plant a mixture of gynoecious and monoecious varieties.

The usual planting advice is to sow cucumber seeds outside two weeks after the last frost in spring, if air temperature is in the 60s and the soil is thoroughly warm. In regions with very short seasons, of course, this is unrealistic. Instead, start them inside two weeks before last frost, using peat pots of ample size. Black or clear plastic mulch will warm the soil so transplants can be slipped out into the garden earlier. It's generally safe to transplant two weeks after last frost. Make sure the soil comes almost to the withered cotyledon or seed leaf and well over the original soil ball. In midsummer, a second cucumber planting is possible from indoor-started transplants as far north as Pennsylvania.

Keep the soil moist, but not wet, throughout the growing time but especially at flowering. Raised beds work well for cucumbers, but, in addition, they need the support of a trellis, low fence, or portable A-frame to continue producing well. Pruning the vines by pinching off the first five or six lateral shoots along the bottom 18 inches of stem produces more fruit longer but also delays the first fruit. Another way to prolong the season is by picking all cucumbers young. Excessive loads of fruit shorten the plant's life, and mature fruit left on the vine signals the plant to stop producing blossoms.

Gynoecious hybrids include COUNTY FAIR, VICTORY, and TRIUMPH. Some monoecious hybrids are BURPLESS HYBRID, BURPLESS TASTY GREEN, and SPARTAN VALOR. Open-pollinated varieties are POINSETT 76, STRAIGHT 8, and MARKETER. KYOTO THREE FEET (33, 60, 67) is said to produce best in cool weather until frost. TOKIWA JIHAI (67) bears well in summer and in the cooler conditions of spring and fall. This is a good variety to use for early starts.

Summer Squash

One of the ironies of growing squash is that if you set out transplants for an earlier harvest,

these plants are most vulnerable to pest attack and may end up giving you no harvest at all. Save some of the seedlings for replacement plantings. Set out in mid-July, they will escape some of the squash bug damage inflicted on earlier plantings. These later plantings will mature in early September in Pennsylvania and continue bearing until frost.

One South Carolina gardener plants summer squash outdoors two weeks before the last frost in spring, hilling it in soil and rabbit manure and covering it with a large, bottomless glass jug. Her harvest begins in April. Indoor starting in large peat pots, bottom-heated by cables or pads, will produce plants ready to set out when frosts are over.

Squash planted early, however, won't tolerate heat as well as later plantings, so the South Carolinian follows her first planting with another outdoor planting a month later, this time using the space between early cole crops and carrots that will soon leave the ground. She makes four plantings in all, the last in late August or early September. Even in South Carolina, the last-planted crop must be given protection, but it often does better than the insect-prone midseason ones.

Most squash takes around 50 days to mature, but VEGETABLE MARROW WHITE BUSH HYBRID (68) is a little faster at 43 days, and SCALLOP YELLOW BUSH (68) and AMBASSADOR follow at 49 days. Among zucchinis, BLACK MAGIC is a 44-day variety and GOLD RUSH takes 45 days.

Sweet Potatoes

These warmth-lovers get an early start when you grow your own slips from the previous year's rootstock. As far north as northern Indiana, start cutting the old tubers in half lengthwise in mid-March, dry them, and set them in flats full of moistened sand. Keep them at 80 to 90°F for six to eight weeks with the lights left on up to 24 hours a day. Slips will be ready for separation from the tubers in early May. Plant these in individual containers full of light soil, potting

Early Start for Squash: Start seeds indoors to have seedlings ready to set out two weeks before the last frost. Prepare fertile hills of soil and rotted manure. Be sure to provide frost protection, shown here in the form of a large, bottomless, glass jug.

mixture, or compost, and keep them inside at daytime temperatures of 75 to 80°F and nighttime ones no lower than 55°F.

When outdoor soil is warm and dry in late May, set the slips out. Water well in early August during tuber formation, but otherwise keep the soil fairly dry. The early start will permit northerners to harvest ripe sweet potatoes immediately after the first light frost. If the first frost is very light, remove all blackened or damaged leaves and the tubers will continue to mature. This must be done immediately, however, or the roots will take on a bitter taste.

By using black plastic as a mulch for raised beds, growers can double their yields of harvestable 3 to 9-inch sweet potatoes as far north as Massachusetts, where soil takes a long time to warm. Unmulched beds gave four times as many useless, undersize culls as mulched ones in a study done at the University of Massachusetts. Further south, mulch can be removed when the ground is thoroughly warm.

JEWELL and CENTENNIAL sweet potatoes mature early. VARDAMAN and VINELESS PORTO RICO (both available from 68), bush varieties, grow well in limited space. All sweet potatoes take

about 120 days to mature from transplanting. They also require curing at temperatures approaching 90°F with 90 pecent humidity for a week, if they are to store well, but they can be cooked and frozen or canned if curing isn't feasible.

Tomatoes

The tomato is the darling of the backyard gardener, and the first tomato fruit produced in a neighborhood in summer is an acclaimed symbol of gardening status. See the illustration on page 206 for a few tricks for producing early tomatoes.

Tomatoes, like beans, come in determinate and indeterminate form. Indeterminate types grow and produce until frost, often reaching heights of 6 feet or more, if staked or grown in cages. They branch when pruned back. Determinate varieties stop growing when fruit sets on the terminal bud. Their foliage is more compact, and fruits ripen over a shorter period. Determinates should not be pruned.

Arrange a continuous supply of tomatoes by picking a succession of varieties for their ripening dates. All plants may be set outdoors when the ground is warm, but they will develop and start to produce on different schedules. In

Sweet Potato Rooting

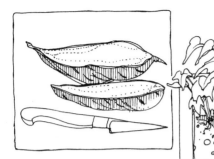

Step One Setting out pre-sprouted sweet potatoes in the spring gives these plants a head start. Begin by cutting a sweet potato in half lengthwise and allowing the halves to dry.

Step Two Set half a tuber, cut side down, in a flat filled with moistened sand. Keep the flat at 80 to 90°F for six to eight weeks. Shoots will begin to appear and develop leaves and roots.

Step Three The slips are ready to separate from the tuber when they're 4 to 8 inches tall and have four or five leaves.

Step Four Plant individual slips in containers full of a light-textured soil mix.

choosing varieties, also allow for special uses and for different tastes, nutritional values, shapes, sizes, and even colors. Paste-type tomatoes like ROMA, 76 days, and BELLSTAR (34), 70 days, are vital for making good tomato sauce and paste, while the large, juicy fruits of varieties like BEEFSTEAK, 80 days, and BURPEE'S BIG BOY HYBRID, 78 days, are better for slicing raw. Among the earliest tomatoes is SIBERIA (58), 65 days, which is frost resistant enough to be planted in early April in northern Indiana. It begins to bloom when only 4 inches tall and sets fruit at 38°F. SPRINGSET is another plant that sets fruits while nights are still cool. Other extra-early tomatoes include SUB-ARCTIC PLENTY (34, 51), 58 days, SUB-ARCTIC MAXI (58), 62 days, and EARLIBRIGHT (59), 63 days.

A few side shoots can be rooted from established tomato plants to carry on harvests when earlier plantings are past their prime. This can be done up to mid-July in Pennsylvania, for late fall harvesting. This technique is useful for replacing earlier transplants that have died or been slowed by disease.

When the season begins to wane, long after the last plants have gone into the ground in mid-July, there are several ways to prolong the harvest. On indeterminates, pick off all flowers and all fruits unlikely to ripen by frost. This will speed the ripening of the more mature fruit. Have frost protection ready for chilly nights. Often a good Indian summer ripening period lies on the far side of the first fall frost.

An excellent late storage tomato called LONG KEEPER (9) is planted four to six weeks after the main-season crop and does most of its ripening inside after being picked pink or greenish yellow· at frost time. Its care and storage will be discussed later under Late Finishes.

Watermelons

G. W. Elmstrom of the Leesburg Agricultural Research Center in Florida determined several years ago that direct-seeded watermelons develop deep taproots, while transplanted watermelons have shallow, but extensive, root systems. For many northerners, the only way to grow watermelons to maturity is to start them inside. You should be aware that the unnatural root development on transplants means that more irrigation will be required when pot-grown melons are set outside.

There are now plenty of watermelons for northern gardeners. NEW HAMPSHIRE MIDGET (9) matures in just 70 days and is good for intensive gardens of limited space, requiring only a 4-foot-square area. HONEY CREAM (45), a larger variety, matures 65 days after sprouting.

Mulching watermelons conserves water, controls weeds, and prevents rotting but should be started only after the ground is warm to the touch. If you put it down too soon, the watermelons' growth will be hampered.

Southern and northern gardeners can produce early crops by presprouting seeds and planting them in large pots. If you keep the soil around 68°F, germination should take five to ten days. To learn how to transplant successfully, see the earlier box on Temperamental Transplants.

In short-season areas, it's practical to limit the number of fruits on the vine to no more than three. This diverts plant energy from growing more fruit to enlarging and ripening what it already has.

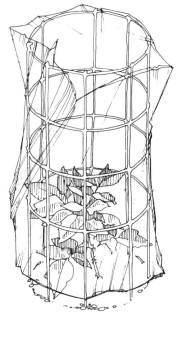

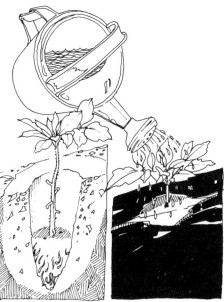

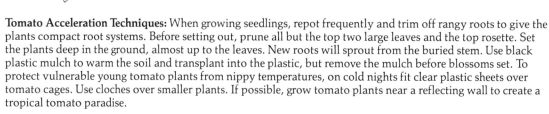

Tomato Acceleration Techniques: When growing seedlings, repot frequently and trim off rangy roots to give the plants compact root systems. Before setting out, prune all but the top two large leaves and the top rosette. Set the plants deep in the ground, almost up to the leaves. New roots will sprout from the buried stem. Use black plastic mulch to warm the soil and transplant into the plastic, but remove the mulch before blossoms set. To protect vulnerable young tomato plants from nippy temperatures, on cold nights fit clear plastic sheets over tomato cages. Use cloches over smaller plants. If possible, grow tomato plants near a reflecting wall to create a tropical tomato paradise.

With the Master Gardeners

SECRETS TO BETTER MELONS

No crop on earth brings out the competitive spirit of a northern gardener more than the melon. Whatever amount of trouble it takes, each northerner must challenge cold springs, short seasons, and early frost if only for the sake of one juicy bite of cantaloupe.

"I've had trouble growing cantaloupes," admits 1983 Organic Gardener of the Year finalist Hugh Matthews, who battles the late springs of New Hampshire. Over the years, he has developed a cantaloupe strategy. In early spring, he turns the soil and fills holes spaced 2 feet apart with compost and bone meal. Then he puts down a sheet of black plastic. As the soil warms up in May, he sets a soaker hose down the middle of the row under the plastic, and over the row he puts up a plastic tunnel. "Then," he reports, "I go back and put in a couple of cantaloupe seedlings every 2 feet. That way, I don't have to get underneath the plastic to really water it."

He starts his cantaloupe seedlings in his solar greenhouse and finds that with the added watering system, the well-warmed soil, and the tunnel protection, the melons have just the warm, moist environment they need for a fast, early start.

For Michigan gardener Mark Rames, an Organic Gardener of the Year in 1984, the secret for producing good melons is mulch. "I dig a nice little hole," he explains, "and fill it with compost. I plant the melons in there, and I mulch real heavily." Rames knows for certain that the mulch makes the difference. "I had two plots, one that I mulched and one that I didn't. The plants that were mulched grew so lushly that they just completely covered the soil," while the unmulched melon bed had "some sparse spaces where the ground was exposed and the weeds were spilling out there." He thinks the difference can be accounted for by the higher temperature and moisture level in the mulched soil. Whenever he plants vine crops, Rames spaces them close enough that good ground coverage is assured, but for holding in moisture, he says, mulch is the answer.

Accelerating Growth

So far in our discussion of ways to shorten the maturing time of heat-loving crops, we've concentrated on finding varieties adapted to shorter growth periods. Now, we will turn to another principle of intensive gardening: if you can't change the plant, change its environment. Actually, you already put this principle to work when you use growing lights and heating coils to speed up seedlings. But what can you do for plants once they're in the ground? Have you turned them over to powers beyond your control? Sometimes it seems so. But just recall that even the soil you put them in is to a certain extent artificial—richer, looser, more balanced than anything in untouched nature. What more can you do to improve their environment?

Row Covers

In searching for ways to extend the growing season into and through winter, horticulturists at the Rodale Research Center in Maxatawny, Pennsylvania in 1982 conducted experiments with several types of unheated plastic row covers. (These experiments will be discussed in more detail in chapter 7.) In spite of the fact that they learned that none of the row covers would grow tender crops through the winter, the researchers proved the effectiveness of row covers in accelerating the growth of both warm-season and cool-season vegetables. Row covers increased the soil temperature up to 20°F above that of uncovered soil. The temperature of the air surrounding the plants ranged between 10 and

30°F higher than the outside air. Because they were being given higher temperatures during early stages of growth, warm-season vegetables under covers produced harvests four to five weeks earlier than normal plantings, and cool-season vegetables were harvested four to six weeks earlier than their unprotected counterparts. We use the conclusions of this experiment not to steal thunder from the section of this book on the use of growing structures, but to give the most dramatic example we can find of how radical plant growth acceleration can be when environment is controlled.

Mulches

In chapter 4 the noteworthy characteristics of organic and inorganic mulches were discussed. Now it's time to talk about how to use these mulches throughout the year to accelerate or encourage good growth. Contrary to some popular belief, not all mulches can do everything.

In the ideal use, mulches are matched with individual crops, plant growth periods, tempera-

At that point, remove the warming mulch and cultivate. Water well and leave the soil bare for about a week.

Next, add a mulch of grass clippings, oat straw, or hay, which allows rain to soak in and keep the soil cool. Warming mulches left on after fruit sets tend to encourage blossom-end rot.

Changing Mulches with the Season: Vegetables like tomatoes with high temperature needs benefit from a warming mulch from transplanting until the first few fruits have set.

tures, and weather conditions. They are also frequently combined. Use cooling mulches (aluminum foil, paper, grass clippings, leaves over black plastic, spoiled hay or straw over plastic, or spoiled hay or straw alone) next to cool-weather crops in hot weather. Soil under leaves heaped on black plastic was 20 degrees cooler than bare soil in a Connecticut Agricultural Experiment Station study conducted from 1978 to 1981. Use warming mulches (black, green, or clear plastic, black paper, compost) next to warm-weather crops in cool weather.

In early spring, you can gain some time by covering whole unplanted beds with warming mulches. Clear plastic raises soil temperatures more than opaque colored plastic—by about 12°F in a late midspring afternoon, according to one study where bare ground was the control treatment.

After young plants are set out, or seeds planted, plastic mulches may be set around them, or slits may be made in the plastic already in place to permit planting. Air and soil temperatures near the plants will rise and this change in microclimate early in the season will speed their growth. This in turn will allow faster replacement of crops.

With the use of black plastic sheets, Connecticut researchers harvested peppers ten weeks after planting, which was two weeks before peppers were ready when grown on bare ground. Higher *total* yields, however, were produced by pepper plants grown in the ground-cooling mulch of clear plastic over black plastic over leaves, a mulch that lowered the soil temperature 15 degrees more than that of black plastic–mulched soil. Warming mulches left on after fruit set tend to encourage blossom-end rot, especially in tomatoes and peppers, according to this study.

Timing is critical to the success of a plastic mulch. Northern gardeners have found that if a dark, opaque, impermeable mulch is applied near heat-loving plants before the ground is thoroughly warm, it may delay ripening by cutting off radiation from the ground. Studies have found that the best yields result when mulching is delayed until the ground temperature reaches 78°F 3 to 4 inches below the surface. In Vermont, this may be as late as the third week in June.

What does mulch research have to offer the intensive gardener? It tells us that vegetables with common high temperature requirements for fast early growth, and with equally long seasons, can be grouped together in beds. Mulch with compost, or punctured plastic sheets, from time of transplanting until the rapid growth is complete and the first few fruits have set. Then remove the mulch and hand cultivate the ground shallowly. Water well and leave the ground bare for a week or so. Replace the first mulch with grass clippings, oat straw, or hay, which allow for the passage of rainwater and keep the ground cool.

If long-season crops are still in your mulched bed when the season starts waning and chilling, reverse the process and return to the use of compost or plastic strips. Since plants will already be in place in the garden, sheets will no longer be practical. Laying down strips between the plants is much easier than cutting holes and fitting sheets over maturing plants.

A warming plastic mulch used all season will give an earlier harvest, but an organic one may provide a larger yield. All-season use of plastic also cuts off air and water to the soil. To alleviate these problems, slit the plastic sheets across the surface of the beds or even remove them occasionally to cultivate and water. In wet climates, never use absorbent mulches like paper. They will become soggy and then, as they dry, will harden into a crust that cuts off air from soil and encourages conditions that favor diseases.

Stone mulches, which make your beds look like plant-growing ornamental terraces, are particularly useful during cool weather in early spring and fall. Late-planted fall crops of beets, lettuce, and broccoli can be kept productive weeks after growth has stopped in the same crops on bare ground. Hardy herbs, like parsley, sown in cold soil in fall to overwinter, produce healthier plants when sown among rocks. As you know if you've ever sat on a rock by the seashore or on a mountain top, rocks absorb heat on sunny days and release it slowly on cloudy days and at night. In nature, herbs like thyme, frequently grow well

Mulching with Stones: In early spring, set large flat stones over a prepared bed and along the sides (shown left). These stones, which are removed for planting, will prewarm the soil. Or consider setting smaller stones between plants in a bed to act as a permanent mulch. In hot weather, cover stones with grass clippings to keep the soil cool.

on rocky hillsides. Rocks are among the original solar collectors.

There are at least two ways you can use rock mulches in the intensive garden. In early spring, set large flat stones (or roof slates, or quarry or roofing tiles, if you have them) over the surface of prepared beds, laying them close together. Tilt additional stones against the exposed edges of raised beds. Before transplanting, remove the stones and rake the soil surface to aerate and dispel moisture. In beds of larger plants, smaller stones may be set between plantings to serve as a permanent mulch. Square quarry tiles will help you in regularizing planting intervals. Cover the rocks with grass clippings in hot weather to prevent overheating of the soil.

Late Finishes

On the whole, people have been better at learning how to extend the growing season by getting early starts in spring than at acquiring the techniques of late finishes. If the gardener's cry of greeting, "Got your peas in yet?" resounds with the calls of north-flying geese, then, all too often, south-flying geese overhear, "Garden all done with?"

Good intensive gardeners are deaf to that question, finding late-season gardening the most challenging and satisfying of all. "Surrender?" they ask. "Why, we have just begun!" But true autumn gardeners, like their crops, must be hardy and persevering. They must also know which crops will take the cold and how to coax less tolerant plants into staying around a little longer than they'd really like to.

There is much overlap, but not total, between early spring and late fall crops. Spring and fall are not, after all, mirror images of one another. Temperatures may sink more rapidly in fall than they rise in spring, or more gradually, depending on location and many other factors. Moisture, too, may come in different amounts, at different rates, or even in different forms. Most important, by the time fall arrives, the days have already considerably shortened. June 21, the daylength turning point, is hardly the center of the gardening season. Many plants respond to decreasing daylength by putting up seedstalks and becoming useless for eating. Gardeners have to be able to recognize the bad actors that have this particular habit.

Some plants like to start off cool and mature in heat, while others like the reverse pattern: first hot, then cool. The latter, of course, make the best fall crops. At the same time you are learning the techniques of fall gardening, you will find you are becoming a better spring gardener, since spring and fall, for all their differences, have more in common than the other two seasons. They represent the outer limits, the frontiers, of gardening in the North, and the very heart of the southern growing season.

Before we take a look at the best crops for late finishes, we'll learn about some techniques that keep the garden productive for longer into the fall and winter. For help in scheduling fall planting, see the chart How to Figure Fall Planting Dates on page 213.

Frost Protection

When frost threatens, spring or fall, intensive gardeners find themselves distinctly advantaged when compared to their conventionally gardening neighbors. In fall, with a long winter harvest ahead of them, they hear no funeral knell. In both seasons, they can rejoice that they have less territory to cover. They are also often equipped with protective devices such as growing tunnels and portable growing frames that can be pressed into immediate use as bed covers. In protecting frost-sensitive vegetables, however, anything goes, as long as it will work by holding heat in the immediate vicinity of plants—flower pots, inverted baskets or dishpans, large cardboard boxes, even literal bed covers like old blankets and quilts.

Many of these homemade or scavenged frost barriers will do more harm than good, however, if they are relied on for heavy frost, or if, unventilated, they are left over plants in bright sun. Soaking the beds in late evening prior to temperature drops also wards off light frost. Mulches are useful, too. The intensive gardener's learned aptitude for planning will also serve well at frost time, for protection involves preparation and the laying in of supplies.

Group your late-planted or long-to-mature crops according to their frost hardiness. Put tomatoes and peppers, or sweet potatoes, for example, in one bed, or in adjacent beds, for easy covering. Rodale Research Center trials of bed covers showed that temperatures rose higher in those covering larger areas up to bed, or two-row, size. This finding is as useful for frost prevention as it is for growth acceleration. A supply of tarps, blankets, heavy sheet plastic, painting throws, tent ground sheets, and large blocks of canvas is useful for covering whole trellises, pole bean tepees, and A-frame supports. You can also drape them over tomato cages and suspend them over stakes driven into the soil around growing beds. Especially when fitting plastic over plants, be sure to allow enough air room. When leaves come in contact with very hot or very cold plastic they may sunscald or freeze. Covered cages should be well vented. Often in the mid-North, a stray first, light frost is followed by a superb ripening period. Don't miss out on that time by being caught with your canvas down.

Ground Storage

Although technically this can't be viewed as a "growing" technique, storing rugged crops in place in the garden is one way to keep the garden productive during a time when active growth isn't possible. Storing cold-hardy vegetables in the ground gives you a place to hold the latest of the late-finishing crops until you're ready to use them. The discussions of individual crops that follow in this section mention which ones are suited to ground storage.

THE DIFFERENT DEGREES OF FROST

When the weather forecast warns of frost, all good gardeners think of their plants. What they may not realize is that there are actually different degrees of frost, and these together with conditions in the garden as well as the state of the plants determine how much effect the cold has.

A light or white frost occurs when moisture in the evening air condenses on cool plant surfaces and the air temperature drops to around 32°F. The white crystals on the plants' surfaces usually won't cause any harm. When the sun comes up, the frost melts and the dew evaporates.

A heavy or black frost is the one that causes the damage. This occurs when temperatures sink to the low 20s or teens, causing the plants to wilt and even collapse. Blackening of plant parts will show up from a few hours to a day later. Because of the internal injury it causes, this sort of cold is a killing frost.

However, the effects of frost in your garden aren't as clear cut as they might appear from these descriptions. Have you ever noticed that under the identical conditions some pepper plants are blackened by an early frost, while other peppers come through intact? Perhaps some years you've noticed that a sudden cold snap in October causes more injury than the same or lower temperatures in December? You can't always assume that just because the thermometer shows 26°F a killing frost is going to ravage your garden. As Dr. Charles Williams in the Plant Science Department at the University of New Hampshire explains, there are a number of variables at work that determine the impact frost has on plants.

The location of the garden and its particular microclimate can temper or alter air temperature and the conditions causing frost. If you're in a sheltered area and your neighbor's garden is in a frost pocket, his garden may suffer and yours may be unharmed on a night when frost has been predicted.

Plants themselves have different thresholds of frost tolerance. You know from your own experience that a cucumber plant succumbs to cold much faster than a head of cabbage. The difference in hardiness among annuals and between annuals and perennials has to do with the amount of internal "antifreeze" each contains. The cells and spaces between cells aren't filled with pure water; there are sugars and starches and other dissolved substances. Their presence means that most plants will not suffer from internal freezing at 32°F—it takes a lower temperature to cause damage. The more of this antifreeze a plant has, the lower temperatures it can tolerate without internal injury.

The age of a plant can also determine frost's effects. A young plant with tender new growth will be injured at a higher temperature than a more mature one. The plant's stage of maturity also counts. A fruit tree or perennial herb is more susceptible to damage as it's just beginning to grow in spring or harden off in fall. That explains why a tree may be damaged by a 32°F frost in early spring or late fall but will be unaffected by much lower temperatures in the winter.

The condition of the plant also decides how well it will withstand frost. A seedling that's been hardened-off by exposure to gradually cooler temperatures is more likely to tolerate lower temperatures than one that's been moved directly from the warmth of a windowsill to a garden bed. Here at least is one area where the gardener can contribute to a plant's frost survival.

Horticulturists have established temperatures at which various crops will suffer cold damage. Throughout the book, these temperature guidelines have been given. As you read them, keep in mind the other variables that affect an individual plant's cold tolerance in your garden.

The use of mulch for ground storage or winter protection in cold climates is really a different subject from the growing-season mulching we've discussed earlier. In winter, mulch is used for two reasons: to trap warmer air close to crops that are dormant, or no longer growing rapidly, to

HOW TO FIGURE FALL PLANTING DATES

		Days to Maturity*	+	Days to Germination†	+	Days to Transplanting	+	Short-Day Factor‡	=	Days to Count Back from First Frost Date
SURVIVE HEAVY FROST	Beets	55		5		direct-seed		14		74
	Cauliflower	50		5		21		14		90
	Endive	95		12		21		14		142
	Kohlrabi	65		7		direct-seed		14		86
	Lettuce (head)	65		3		14		14		96
	Lettuce (leaf)	45		3		14		14		76
	Peas	50		6		direct-seed		14		70
SURVIVE LIGHT FROST	Broccoli	55		5		21		14		95
	Brussels sprouts	80		5		21		14		120
	Cabbage	60		4		21		14		99
	Carrots	65		6		direct-seed		14		85
	Chard	50		5		direct-seed		14		69
	Collards	55		4		21		14		94
	Radishes	25		3		direct-seed		14		42
	Spinach	45		5		direct-seed		14		64

*These figures are for the fastest-maturing varieties we could find. Fast-maturing varieties are best for fall crops. But for the variety you have, get the correct number of days from your seed catalog.

†These figures for days to germination assume a soil temperature of 80°F.

‡The short-day factor is necessary because the time to maturity in seed catalogs always assumes the long days and warm temperatures of early summer. Crops always take longer in the late summer and fall.

keep them from freezing solid; and to keep the ground loose and spare it from experiencing both repeated deep freezings and rapid thaws.

As frosts approach, remove any mulches that have been in place during the growing season to give vegetables a chance to harden off and so the radiant heat retained in the soil will be released to them at night. Reapply mulch after the first hard frost, using deep, 1 to 2-foot layers of organic mulch with a loose texture. Choose ones like hay or straw that have many air pockets and are composed of resistant fibers that will not become waterlogged. Mulches made of coarse, semirotted sawdust, wood chips, and especially leaves—materials you would hesitate to use in the growing season—will not decompose into

soil appreciably during winter, so you don't have to worry about depleting soil nitrogen reserves. Be sure to remove them in spring.

Besides covering those crops you're storing for winter use, cover all perennial beds, such as asparagus beds, and beds containing vegetables that winter over for spring use, such as bunching onions.

Some gardeners prefer to let the ground become lightly frozen, down to a half inch, before applying winter mulch. This discourages field mice from moving in under the mulch and making use of your storage trove.

Indoor and outdoor frame, barrel, and root cellar storage also, of course, prolong the usefulness of your harvests, but they are outside the scope

Getting Ready for Winter: To keep hardy vegetables in harvestable shape as the weather cools, mulch with a 1 to 2-foot layer of hay or straw. The crops awaiting mulch in this garden include Brussels sprouts, cabbages, carrots, beets, Swiss chard, leeks, and bunching onions.

of this book. Intensive gardeners with bed-covering frames will find them especially useful for winter storage of mature vegetables. For a more in-depth look at storage, consult *Root Cellaring* by Mike and Nancy Bubel (Rodale Press, 1979).

Beets

Direct-sow fall storage beets 74 days before the first expected fall frost. LUTZ GREENLEAF can be planted in midsummer (late summer in the South)

for greens in late summer and early fall, and storage roots in fall and winter.

Fall storage beets can be left in the ground under a loose mulch and harvested until deep cold comes or, in milder areas, throughout the winter. LUTZ GREENLEAF and WINTER KEEPER (14) will not become woody when they are ground stored. You can also cover the beet bed with a cold frame and prolong the harvest a full month.

In early August, or 60 days before the first

expected frost, early beets that need 60 days or less to mature can be direct-sown to make a second crop. This second crop, however, should be dug promptly or mulched very heavily. The beets will be smaller than those of the spring crop. DETROIT DARK RED (17), 60 days, is unusually hardy and can be grown spring or fall. It requires less mulching than the other early beets.

Broccoli

Long-season and heat-resistant varieties like WALTHAM, GREEN VALIANT F1 (69), and GREEN MOUNTAIN (5) are often chosen for fall planting. These are grown from indoor starts and are timed to mature before first fall frosts arrive. With protection, they can be grown past frost, although their growth will be slow. If you use varieties known for sprouting, you can prolong the harvest of side shoots into December without protection. Sprouting varieties include EARLY SPARTAN, DE CICCO, and ITALIAN GREEN SPROUTING.

For growing into or through winter, use the extra-hardy CALABRESE. With a heavy mulch it will last the winter and sprout again in spring. For cold-frame growing, Chinese broccoli, which will be discussed later under Oriental Vegetables, will come through the winter.

A perennial sprouting broccoli, NINE STAR (64, 67), will yield several crops a year in mild, maritime areas and remain in the bed for three to five years. Start seeds in May or June, set out in June or July, and space plants 3 feet apart. By next March you'll be harvesting a central head and smaller side shoots. Feed the plants and don't let them go to seed for a continuous harvest.

Brussels Sprouts

With the possible exception of kale, Brussels sprouts are the most frost resistant of all cole crops. Fortunately, these little cabbage heads on a stalk also resist heat, for there is no such thing as a quick-maturing variety, and the crop must be started in spring a long 95 days before harvest.

For the longest harvests in the North, start Brussels sprouts indoors, or in a cold frame, three to four months before the first fall frost, depending on the maturing time of the variety. A choice of several varieties will keep a harvest going from August until late December.

Start to pick the sprouts when they are firm. Pick from the bottom of the stalk upward, and the higher sprouts will develop faster. To mature them more evenly for quantity picking, break off the top rosette when it develops. The later-harvested varieties, picked after frost, will have the best flavor. Where frost is not severe, you can harvest them straight through winter. In colder areas, bend the stalk to the ground and mulch it heavily. Some gardeners lift the plants before the ground freezes and hang them upside down in a cool basement or garage. If the sprouts should freeze on the plants, you can still use them. Just be sure to cook them immediately, for if they're allowed to thaw, the texture will become mushy.

EARLY DWARF DANISH (34, 55, 63), 95 days, PRINCE MARVEL HYBRID (48), 90 days, and JADE CROSS, 95 days, are early maturing, while FOCUS F1 (64) is extra hardy and will go through the winter unmulched in Ohio. A new variety, ORMAVON (64), produces a cabbage head in the place of a top rosette.

Cabbage

Fall cabbage does well where autumns are sunny, for like many cole crops, cabbage thrives on decreasing daylengths. Fall plantings grow more slowly than the earlier spring crops. Select varieties that develop well over a longer period for the fall, when dropping temperatures slow growth. In autumn, a supposed 90-day variety may actually take 120 days. For a long harvest period, choose fall varieties with various maturing times from short to long.

Start cabbages indoors about 10 to 14 weeks before the first expected fall frosts. Set them out when they're three weeks old. To encourage stocky root growth in fall, give wider-than-usual spac-

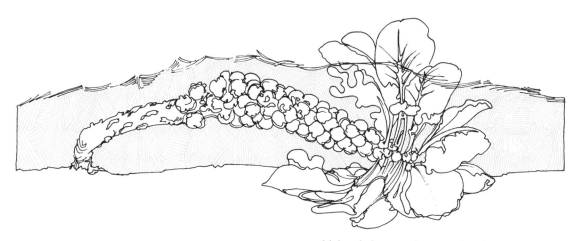

Winterized Brussels Sprouts: In areas where winters are very cold, bend plants to the ground and cover them with a layer of mulch. To harvest, brush off any snow, push aside mulch, pick the sprouts, and cover again.

ing so that the plants will receive plenty of sunshine. Give them protection from light frosts on. Cabbage will continue to grow at air temperatures below freezing.

Among late cabbages, JANUARY KING (63) and DRUMHEAD SAVOY are good for maritime areas, where they head by October and stay in the ground all winter. WISCONSIN 8 (47) makes a good late crop, while STONEHEAD (28) stores well. LATE FLAT DUTCH, DANISH BALLHEAD, EXCELL, and GREEN WINTER mature slowly, and MARKET PRIZE holds for a long time without splitting when grown from Canada to Florida. GLORY OF ENKHUIZEN (2), and the newer ERDENO and LATE DANISH (both available from 34) are noted for storing well. In general, European-bred cabbages hold better than fast-growing American varieties. To ground store, mulch cabbage plants heavily.

Carrots

For extending the carrot harvest into fall, plant longer-to-mature varieties 60 days before the first fall frost. This is usually done by direct-seeding in early August. Mulch when the ground freezes ¼ to ½ inch deep, and carrots will ground store through moderately cold winters. If carrot tissue is frozen solid and then thawed, however, the texture will become mushy.

ROYAL CHANTENAY and SCARLET KEEPER (34, 55) remain tender when ground stored all winter. TOUCHON (5, 17), a 70-day variety, is 7 inches long and good for ground storage. As an alternative or supplement to mulching, set a growing frame over the carrot bed for easy winter harvesting.

Celeriac

Its slow growth makes this one of the last crops to mature in the garden. That's a good thing, too, because celeriac's flavor is greatly enhanced by early frosts.

Celeriac matures in 110 to 120 days, but its early development is so slow that it is usually sown inside in February for setting out after frost, or when it reaches 6 inches in height. On a mature plant, the crown rises above the ground and benefits from mulching if overwintered in mild areas. Mulched, celeriac will remain in the ground into November in the North, or about a month after first frost. Among European varieties are PRESIDENT and ST. LAURENT (both available from 67). American varieties include GIANT SMOOTH PRAGUE and the larger ALABASTER. Celeriac has a mild parsley flavor but is most often

Fresh Carrots in Winter: In-ground storage works very well with carrots. After the ground freezes about ½ inch deep, add a thick, fluffy layer of mulch. In areas with harsh winters, you might wat to set a cold frame over the mulched carrot bed. To harvest, shovel aside the snow, lift the mulch, and dig as many carrots as you need.

used in place of celery. The knobby, semicrisp root can be eaten raw or cooked.

Collards

The collard plant, closely related to kale, is dependable year-round in the South, except where midsummer heat causes it to bolt. To lengthen its growing season in the North, plant collards in late July or August from indoor starts, and begin harvesting small leaves in two months. Continue the gradual harvest, giving protection on cold nights after it starts developing a head. A collard plant, when gradually harvested, will provide 115 pounds of greens in an average season.

After the head is cut, a second, smaller head will often appear for late fall, or early winter, harvesting. Mulching and shielding from sunscald are good practices during frosts. Collards, a southern favorite, are less hardy than kale. Temperatures as low as 12°F may kill the plants unless they are protected.

Collards give the advantage of a harvest that continues into hot weather without danger of bolting or toughness. GEORGIA and VATES are old dependable 60-day varieties. CHAMPION (34) is a newer one that stands heat well and is compact enough for a small growing frame or bed. It can withstand cold down to 10°F.

Endive

July is the best planting time for endives that will last into late fall. Most varieties take 95 days to mature. Endive is an excellent crop for winter growing frames because of its cold tolerance. When plants are set closely in frames or beds, the hearts will blanch by themselves. ROUGE DE VERONE (67) has very large, frost-resistant leaves. After you harvest the main head in fall, the plants will produce smaller secondary heads of crisp, red leaves for winter harvesting.

You can lift endive roots from the garden and force them indoors for a harvest of Belgian endive, or, more accurately, chicons. This indoor harvest gives you gourmet ingredients at a time of year when fresh, home-grown salads are a rarity. For more on this technique, see the box Winter Gardening Indoors on page 230.

Hamburg Parsley

Also known as Dutch or turnip-rooted parsley, this plant is suited to late finishes in the garden because it takes most of the season to mature and, once established, can withstand cold temperatures. It differs from other parsley because it is used for its root. The root looks like a parsnip's and is prepared similarly, but it tastes more like celeriac. The foliage can also be eaten. Like other parsley, Hamburg grows best between 50 and 70°F and slows considerably above 75°F or below 45°F. It will, however, survive freezing. A biennial, it bolts in warm weather in its second year.

In regions with moderate winters sow it in early spring, and in very cold ones sow in July to overwinter under mulch for a spring crop. This root needs a long season; March-sown Hamburg parsley is seldom harvested before late October (34).

Horseradish

The horseradish needs cold autumns and winters to intensify its flavor. It can be mulched and dug for winter use and is also forced indoors to produce tasty leaves for winter salads. (For more instructions on how to do this, see the box Winter Gardening Indoors.) In spring, the first leaves that appear in the garden are often used for potherbs, but the hot reputation of horseradish really rests on its use as a condiment.

Common varieties are NEW BOHEMIA and MALINER KREN (9). The horseradish, a member of the mustard family, is propagated from root cuttings or crowns and planted in the spring. In a short growing season planting works best if the whole root with crown attached can be taken from another garden in fall or very early spring.

Jerusalem Artichoke

Just now coming into its own in supermarket produce departments, the Jerusalem artichoke is a hardy perennial that substitutes for potatoes if boiled or steamed, and for Chinese water chestnuts if raw or stir-fried. It deserves a bed of its own, and it better be given one, or it may help itself to the whole garden. Jerusalem artichokes are sweetest in late winter and can be stored under mulch for winter digging. They extend the harvest season through winter, even in cold areas.

Like the potato, the Jerusalem artichoke is usually started from eyes of stored tubers, which can be purchased. These small tubers form on lateral roots and are the parts harvested. So why, then, is this unusual vegetable treated like a perennial? Because, try as you may, you'll never be able to dig every last tuber from a planted area, and year after year new, sunflowerlike shoots will greet you in the spring. Plant spring or fall.

Kale

Kale is so hardy that winter harvests are almost guaranteed. It survives 10°F unprotected and grows at 40°F. Kale's nutritious dark green leaves are great for beating the midwinter doldrums, and frost only sweetens their flavor. In severe climates, use the protection of a mulch or grow it under a frame or a tunnel.

Grow kale from transplants, setting small plants out two months before the first heavy frost of fall. Start clipping individual leaves after frost. In unprotected beds, kale will produce well into December in most areas. If the sun is strong after freezes, use burlap sun screens to protect the frozen leaves from sunscalding.

Unlike collards, its slightly less hardy southern counterpart, kale is unsuitable for growing into hot weather. In heat, its high fiber content will be appreciated only by livestock.

There are about 16 varieties in two main categories, Siberian and Scotch. Most people prefer the flavor of Scotch. The discriminating eat only the tender outer leaves of Siberian, breaking them off one by one at an immature stage. By this method, the tender inner rosette remains to be harvested as the season's grand finale. Real

EXTENDING THE FRESH HERB HARVEST

Some gardeners may not feel the the need to try to keep the herb harvest going, since leaves are so easy to harvest and dry (or in some cases, such as basil, even freeze) for culinary use. But for those people who prefer to use their herbs fresh, here are some ways you can keep a small harvest going.

Stop harvesting the leaves of perennials a month before the first expected frost. If you pick leaves too close to frost, the plants will develop new growth that will be tender and susceptible to cold damage, perhaps destroying the whole plant in the process. You may resume light cutting after freeze and continue until the leaves die back from the cold.

Try mulching semihardy herbs several inches deep around their bases, or provide them with winter frames, tunnels, or cloches. Or carefully move smaller herb plants to a cold frame, where they will hold until spring. During winter you can pick a few leaves as they are needed, but don't disturb their dormancy by heavy picking. Among the commonly used perennials you can treat this way are mints, Roman or German chamomile, parsley, catnip, winter savory, creeping thyme, coriander, sage, chives, French sorrel, and sweet cicely.

The slightly more tender perennials, including tarragon, lemon balm, oregano, and germander, should be given protection from winds by heavy mulching, frames with covers, or tepee windbreaks made of evergreen branches. Don't pick from these plants until spring.

For fresh harvests through winter, consider moving some plants indoors. In cold areas, dig tender herbs like bay, basil, lemon verbena, sweet marjoram, and rosemary before hard frost. Select small plants, pot them carefully, and move them inside a month before the furnace goes on or the wood stove is in use. They will become gradually acclimated to indoor surroundings. This moving strategy, however, is not always successful. You may have better luck by growing herbs in containers right from the start, setting them out over the summer, and then bringing them in as winter approaches.

A few biennial plants, while not able to survive northern winters, should be left in a permanent bed because of their ability to self-sow. These "volunteers" will come up early, giving you an effortless head start on the herb-growing season. Self-sown seed often produces growth before indoor-started replacement plants can be set outdoors safely. Among self-sowers are dill, sage, chervil, and more hardy herbs such as lovage, chamomile, and borage. In early spring, new self-sown seedlings can be used to replace plants grown too rank for use.

---

kale connoisseurs vote for a newly available type, Chinese kale, which is discussed later in the section on oriental greens. Unlike Siberian, Chinese kale can be eaten stalks and all. EVERGREEN GEM (17), a Siberian type, is hardiest but inclined to toughness. WINTERBOR (34), a new variety, and PENTLAND BRIG (64) are almost as hardy. (WINTERBOR is a good candidate to overwinter mulched for early spring greens.) BLUE SIBERIAN (17) and DWARF BLUE CURLED SCOTCH (also called BLOOMSDALE) are particularly dependable, and KONSERVA (34), a Scotch type, has enormous yields. NIEDRIGER GRUNER KRAUSER (67), a variety developed in Germany, has very thick compact growth, which helps it stay in good shape under snow cover. VERDURA (57), a Dutch variety, is very productive and noted for withstanding cold weather well.

For fall planting timed to mature just before the first heavy frost, use longer-maturing, cold-resistant varieties like EARLY WHITE VIENNA, 55 to 60 days, and PURPLE VIENNA, 65 to 70 days. European varieties are usually purple and include AZURE STAR (48) and BLUE DANISH (34). Kohlrabi stores well under a heavy mulch but seldom survives beyond late December in cold areas.

Sun Protection: Overwintered kale resists plummeting temperatures well, but its frozen leaves can be damaged by the sun. Protect your winter greens with an improvised burlap screen.

Leeks

Leeks are desirable as a certain crop for ground storage and winter eating. WINTA, ALASKA (18, 49, 59), ELECTRA (26), CATALINA (65, 67), and INVERNO (34) are among the most hardy, but all leeks can be kept in the garden if the ground around them is mulched heavily enough to keep it from freezing.

Leeks require a long season of 75 to 190 days to mature. Start them indoors in March, or two months before the last frost. Transplant to a cold frame, or to individual containers, as soon as the small plants can be handled easily. Take them outside to their beds in June. Before setting

out leeks, cut back the stems to 4 inches and trim off any rangy roots. Then plant the seedlings deep enough to almost cover the tops. You may set them into holes or trenches.

Leek harvest can begin in autumn, but it will continue longer and give you more flavor if you use your leek bed as a winter storage area and keep digging leeks through the winter.

Lettuce

For fall crops of lettuce, return to the quick-maturing types that are frost resistant (listed on page 191), but this time direct-seed. Refer back to the section Tricks for Starting Seeds to find ways to encourage lettuce to germinate in warm soil. Autumn lettuce is often sown thickly and then thinned to save only the sturdiest plants. This system usually works better than transplanting. Fall lettuce will take longer to mature than spring lettuce because of the short fall daylengths, but it will mature before heavy frost, as long as it's sown in August. Protect the plants in tunnels or cloches as frost approaches.

With protective devices you can lengthen the season on into late fall or winter by using European winter lettuces that have been bred for short daylengths and cold temperatures. They are usually sown inside in September and transplanted to a bed or frame for an April harvest. REINE DE MAI (16), sometimes called MAY QUEEN, and VAL D'ORGE (15) are two Belgian butterheads of this type. Another winter butterhead is NORTH POLE (45), which can be started two or three weeks before the first fall frost for a winter crop with an early spring harvest. ARCTIC KING (15) has large heads with crinkled, cold-resistant leaves, and WINTER DENSITY (1, 15, 55) is an English cross between a butterhead and a cos. IMPERIAL WINTER (52), another winter lettuce, and KLOCK and KWIEK (both available from 15) are three varieties commonly grown in Europe for late winter/early spring use.

All winter lettuces are tolerant of moderate frost, and because of their shorter-than-normal daylength requirement they will grow faster in winter than other cold-tolerant lettuce varieties. Even in a protective frame, however, they may stop growing and then resume in early spring. In the South, their growth is more continuous, and two plantings are possible in mild areas, making lettuce almost a year-round crop.

Onions

The onions you'll be harvesting in fall as the season winds down are the ones you'll store in the pantry for winter use. Storage onions are usually started from sets in March, or two months before the last frost. They begin forming bulbs when daylengths reach 16 hours. These include YELLOW GLOBE, YELLOW GLOBE DANVERS, DOWNING YELLOW GLOBE, and EBENEZER. Earlier maturing storage onions are ORBIT (34), EARLY YELLOW GLOBE, and COPRA (34). White storage onions such as SOUTHPORT WHITE GLOBE (10, 17) should be stored only if their necks are small. Red storage varieties include WETHERSFIELD (47) and SOUTHPORT RED GLOBE.

By sowing seeds of EVERGREEN LONG WHITE BUNCHING after frosts are over in the spring, you can obtain clumps of mild green onions in late autumn and on into winter and have some left to overwinter for early spring use. They can also be grown through the winter in cold frames. Occasionally, Japanese bunching onions will bulb in time for late winter eating. Bunching onion IWATSUKI (67) is so hardy that it will not even require mulching when left in the bed all winter. Even without fresh onions from the garden, you will still have storage onions for winter use and may never have to shop for store-bought onions again.

Parsnips

If you mulch to keep them from freezing solid, you can dig parsnips all winter. Some people say they are not worth eating until heavy frost has concentrated their sugar content. As a season extender, the parsnip is a star of late autumn and winter.

In the North and Midwest, plant parsnips from mid-April to early June to mature about 120 days later. The best planting time is when daffodils bloom. Parsnip seed is very perishable. It germinates slowly and, in damp soil, poorly. Indoor starting will guarantee better germination. See the box on Temperamental Transplants earlier in the chapter for some guidelines. If you're sowing outdoors, mark plantings, firm the ground, and allow three weeks before giving up all hope.

Don't rush the harvest. Wait for at least a month of hard frost before digging roots. Lay on mulch just before the ground would freeze solid without it. The parsnip harvest continues until March, when leaves begin to form and root sugar reverts to starch.

HARRIS MODEL is a good 120-day parsnip with a long tapering root. ALL AMERICAN is shorter and bigger around the shoulders and takes only 105 days. HOLLOW CROWN (17, 20), also 105 days, is known for its fine-grained flesh.

Peas

In most regions, peas bear sparsely in fall because of the lack of combined cool weather and long hours of sunshine. However, in some dry areas and in places where springs are short, a fall crop is the only possible one. A pea breeder at Cornell University, G. A. Marx, suggests planting disease-resistant varieties in late summer. Healthy vines are better able to tolerate the heat. Some gardeners produce their snap and snow peas in the fall. The presence of an edible pod, they figure, makes up for the lack of harvestable quantity. Edible-pod peas planted in July, or early August, will produce until hard frost in November.

If the soil is too warm for starting peas in late summer, try starting them indoors in peat pots for later transfer outside. Since they can be a little tricky to transplant, review the tips given earlier in the box Temperamental Transplants. Keep this fall crop cool with mulch, ample water, and a shading device. Be prepared with frost protection. Young pea shoots can withstand temperatures down to 17°F, but older plants are very susceptible to frost.

Radishes

The pungent radishes you enjoy in spring won't be of much help in the fall or winter garden since they don't stay in good shape when exposed to cold temperatures. For more robust roots to round out the season, try daikons, or Japanese radishes. They rival their cousins the turnips in usefulness, store well, and sometimes reach stupendous sizes. Even the leaves can be steamed. CHINA ROSE and CHINESE WHITE CELESTIAL need 55 days to mature. MIYASHIGE (34), a 60-day variety, planted in mid-summer to early August, is the best daikon for fall storage. Plant TOKINASHI or ALL SEASON, a 65-day daikon, two to three months before the first fall frost for a late autumn harvest. It is well adapted to summer growing. SAKURAJIMA MAMMOTH, 70 days to harvest, is the monster of them all, having reached 100 pounds on occasion. Grow it for fall use and serve it cooked.

Even the mighty daikons stand less frost than turnips. Mulch them well and they will last until deep cold comes, or at least as long as carrots do.

Rutabagas

Rutabagas are large yellow roots grown for storage that require a long, 90-day season that extends into the late fall. As far north as Canada, they are planted in late June, three months before frost. They stand more cold than their purple and white cousins, turnips. Frost improves their flavor. Mulch them in fall and they will thrive in weather as cold as you find in a Minnesota November and will remain in good shape late into winter. LAURENTIAN is a widely known variety.

Salsify

Also called oyster plant for its flavor, this is another biennial root crop that can stay in the garden over winter to prolong the harvest. It needs four months to mature but is otherwise similar to parsnips in growth pattern and also has perishable seed and a long germination period. Plant salsify in June to mature in October in mild areas, but in the North, plant it in midspring. In the far North it must be planted as soon as the ground can be worked to mature in late fall. The tops resemble daffodil foliage and should be cut in the fall. If mulched well, salsify will survive frost with improved flavor and will go into late November. Young shoots of overwintered salsify grown in milder areas are similar to asparagus. They, and the new green leaves that follow, may be eaten (available from 41 and 69).

Spinach

Spinach is hardy enough to keep growing as the temperatures drop, and the shortening daylengths in fall mean the plants won't be tempted to bolt.

As far south as Arkansas, September plantings yield a small crop of leaves in October, then go on from mulched stumps to produce a better crop in spring. Further north, if autumns are cool enough, a fall-harvested spinach crop is possible. Mulch the plants when a hard freeze threatens, or cover them with cloches or tunnels. Small, immature plants may also be dug and transferred to a cold frame, where they will continue to produce a modest crop of leaves.

Spinach is a good growing-frame crop. You can sow it directly in the frame or transplant there from indoor starts in late winter or fall. It will grow dependably, though less productively than the oriental greens do. For longest harvests in frames or beds, cut a few individual leaves at a time, rather than taking the whole plant at once.

Swiss Chard

In the fall, mulch Swiss chard plants at night and on very cold days, or protect them with covers. In many areas they will remain harvestable until Thanksgiving. Chard also does very well in a large growing frame, where it will give a small but steady harvest through the winter. To overwinter for early spring use, cut the chard plants back by removing the high outer leaves. Keep a few small center leaves intact for renewed growth when the weather warms.

Turnips

Fall turnips are traditionally planted on July 25 in the Northeast. To produce small roots in fall, use the same, or similar, quickly maturing varieties mentioned on page 194. For longer-growing and larger turnips, use a standard variety like PURPLE TOP WHITE GLOBE, which is ready for harvest in 55 days. Time your fall planting to mature just before the last frost.

Few turnip varieties will store well in the garden. Decreasing temperatures followed by warm weather cause a bolting reaction. Frost damage followed by a thaw or sitting in damp, cold soil causes sprouting. For these reasons, rutabagas make a better storage crop than turnips. DES VERTUS MARTEAU (67) is one turnip that resists sprouting and bolting in fall and is therefore good for short-term ground storing under mulch.

For greens that will grow into late fall, use slow-bolting varieties like SEVEN TOP or CHARLESTOWNE (46). Mulch when using for greens, and harvest as needed until severe cold comes.

Oriental Vegetables

These hardy specimens deserve a section all their own because they're exceptional season extenders. Although they stretch the season more on the fall end, some are good candidates for early starts in the spring. All of these vegetables have been bred to tolerate low light and cool conditions. They do well in the garden and are standouts in growing frames. Tips on how to raise them in these structures are covered in chapter 8. In this chapter we'll focus on growing them out in the garden.

Some gardeners who have tried raising oriental brassicas (most of these vegetables are members of the cabbage family) in the past have complained of their tendency to bolt. Breeders have been working to tame this habit, and more and more varieties are appearing on the market that are bolt resistant. Oriental vegetables also have a rather limited temperature range for optimum growth. But oriental brassicas in general make ideal cool-weather crops. They tolerate temperature fluctuations better than spinach or lettuce, and they are extraordinarily productive and nutritious. Too much heat, though, and they stress wilt and turn pungent or bitter.

In the spring, you can set out transplants up to a month before last frost. Their growth really won't take off until temperatures reach 60°F. As fall settles in, you can leave a second planting out in the garden. The centers of heading-type oriental brassicas will remain in good shape down to 15°F and will hold up better than nonheading types. Although oriental brassicas can last without mulching, you might want to add a covering of straw or Reemay for extra cold insurance. Harvest overwintered orientals a couple leaves at a time. Strip away the outer, frost-damaged wrapper leaves of heading plants. The inner leaves are of better quality, but even they are best suited to soups and stews since they tend to be a bit watery. Plants will remain harvestable to November in Pennsylvania, later in gardens farther south and not as long in gardens farther north.

Chinese Cabbage

Chinese cabbage offers our first excursion into the mysteries of the Orient, where several forms of it have been grown for centuries, sometimes through the winter. Although members of the cabbage family, Chinese cabbages are more delicately flavored than most coles. The biggest problem you may encounter with Chinese or oriental cabbages is in keeping them sorted out in your mind, for there are several categories and many confusing names.

Chinese cabbage is *Siew choy* in Cantonese parlance, *Wong bok* or *Pe-Tsai* in other parts of China, and *Haku-sai* in Japan. Some Japanese

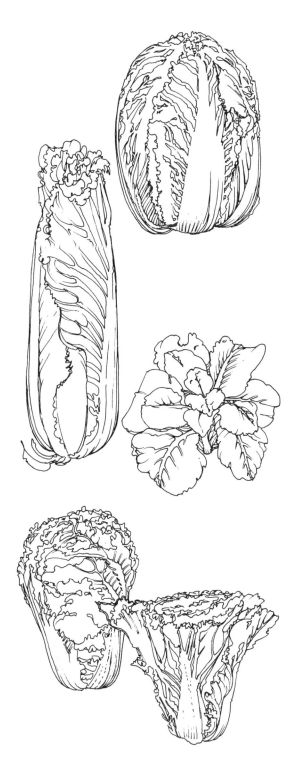

seed companies call it *Nagaoka*, and on the West Coast it is often known as *Napa* cabbage. There are two main forms, which differ from one another in habit and growing pattern.

Chinese heading cabbage produces a well-developed terminal bud that forms a head in which leaf tips close in an overlapping pattern at the top. Heads can be oval, flat topped, or cylindrical, and they weigh from 3 to 6 pounds. Chinese heading cabbage requires a comparatively long growing period.

Chinese nonheading cabbages include both looseleaf and semiheading varieties. The looseleaf type has an underdeveloped terminal bud and forms no leaf head. Leaves either spread out in a rosette or stand erect. This type is used for greens.

The semiheading type does have a terminal bud, but the head formed from it has a hollow center inside a rosette of large leaves. Nonheading varieties require less time to mature than heading ones and are therefore good for planting in arid, cool climates where growing time is limited.

Since 1978, the Rodale Research Center has been performing a service for growers and home gardeners by conducting experiments with varieties and growing patterns among oriental brassicas. For all Chinese cabbages, they recommend allowing 28 days between seeding indoors and spring transplanting to fields or beds, and 21 days from sowing to fall transplanting. Spring seedlings take longer due to lower light intensities. Of 26 varieties tested, the heading cabbages HAKUCHO (72), 72 days, CHON'S ALL-SEASON (13), 65 days, MARVEL (70), 72 days, and JUNE BRIDE (70), 73 days, held without bolting when transplanted on April 19. (The days to maturity indicate the time from transplanting to harvestable size.) Among nonheading cabbages, harvested

Oriental Cabbages: These related plants come in a variety of interesting shapes and sizes. Clockwise from top right are oval heading, looseleaf, semiheading, flat-topped heading, and cylindrical heading cabbages.

46 days from transplanting, SEOUL CABBAGE (72), OSAKA LARGE LATEST (52), VITAMIN GREEN (72), and SHIRONA (4) didn't bolt when transplanted in April. With fall transplantings on August 26, however, almost none of the heading or nonheading cabbages bolted.

This study indicates that the gardener should either plant all types of Chinese cabbage only in fall or should select nonbolting varieties for spring plantings. The most recently developed heading cabbages bred to be bolt resistant include TIP-TOP HYBRID (60, 67), HARUMAKI OHGATA (67), NAGAOKA SPRING (33), TROPICANA (33), SALADEER (33), TROPICAL PRIDE (60), SPRING A-1 (60), and EARLY TOP (60). All of these are suited to spring sowing, are heat resistant, and mature quickly, taking 60 to 65 days. Although fall conditions prevent bolting, growth was found to be slower in the short days of fall when temperatures sank below 60°F. This means that to mature before frost, the slower-maturing heading types should be sown early in fall, preferably in July for August transplanting in those areas where first frost comes in October.

The heaviest producers of the fall-sown Chinese heading cabbages tested were CHON'S BEST (13) and SUNKISS (4). Of the nonheading cabbages, MATSUSITIMA (34) and KASHIN (72) were the best yielders, while the faster-maturing MARUBO SANTO LOOSE (67) also did well. (However, some people who have tasted MATSUSITIMA report that it may not be worth growing!)

One of the first varieties to be introduced, and still the most common, is the cylindrical MICHIHILI. This cabbage not only has a tendency to produce nonuniform heads, but it is also less palatable than other varieties that are coming onto the market and into the garden. It is unfortunate that other Chinese cabbages have been rejected through association with MICHIHILI. Among the tastier new varieties are STATUE HYBRID (65) and MONUMENT (33, 34).

Chinese cabbages will be more tender and flavorful if they are grown quickly to maturity and if they are grown at temperatures between 60 and 75°F. Within this range, yield decreases with increasing temperature for Chinese heading cabbage while increasing for nonheading and for celery cabbage, a related crop that will be described later. A tendency to transplant shock in some varieties suggests that some Chinese cabbages mature faster when directly seeded. This is particularly true for heading cabbage varieties.

Chinese Celery Cabbage

This plant is probably the most dependably productive of the oriental brassicas. It is also known as white cabbage, as pak choi, or occasionally as bok choi. It has long, white or, more rarely, green leaf stems with bright, dark green leaves. In some varieties the leaf stems are quite broad. Leaves are oval and wide, with wavy or smooth margins. Much smaller than Chinese cabbage of either type, celery cabbages weigh less than a pound. They generally take 30 to 50 days to mature from seeding, depending on the season. Their tendency to bolt limits the growing of celery cabbages to fall. In the Rodale Research Center trials, however, a few varieties, including CHINA SHAKU-SHIMA (37), held without bolting when transplanted in mid-April.

In the Rodale Research Center's fall planting in late August, there was no significant bolting of celery cabbages. Among the highest-yielding varieties in the fall planting were CHINA SHAKUSHIMA and TAI-SAI SEPPAKU (30).

Like Chinese nonheading cabbage, celery cabbage increases in yield as temperatures increase toward 75°F. In areas as far north as Michigan, its planting can be held off until June so that the longer days and higher and more stable temperatures will prevent bolting. Rodale Research Center tests indicated that transplanted crops of celery cabbage may give higher yields than direct-seeded ones.

Chinese Mustard

This crop is sometimes called mustard cabbage because it has a strong mustard flavor when eaten raw and a less pronounced one when steamed or boiled. It is usually the least acceptable to the American palate of the oriental brassicas. Mustard cabbage, a form of India mustard, has broadly oval leaves that taper to the base. Leaf margins are curled, scalloped, or frilled, depending on the variety. Plants are more or less spreading. Leaves range from bright green to purple.

Mustard greens are the group of oriental brassicas most susceptible to bolting in cool temperatures. In Rodale Research Center spring trials, only two varieties, AKA CHIRIMEN (72) and KYO MIZUNA (1, 12, 72), grew without bolting when transplanted on April 30. In fall transplantings on September 10, in contrast, only NANFOON (52) bolted prematurely. HYBRID TENDERGREEN II proved to be the most productive and uniform of the fall-tested varieties, but in general, spring and warm weather growth was more rapid than growth during September and October. The variety GREEN IN SNOW (60) is exceptionally hardy and is a good choice for late harvests.

Flowering Chinese Cabbage

This brassica is grown both for leaves and for the flower stalk, which appears soon after the plant

has reached full size. Flowering Chinese cabbage has rounded, distinctly stalked leaves that nar-

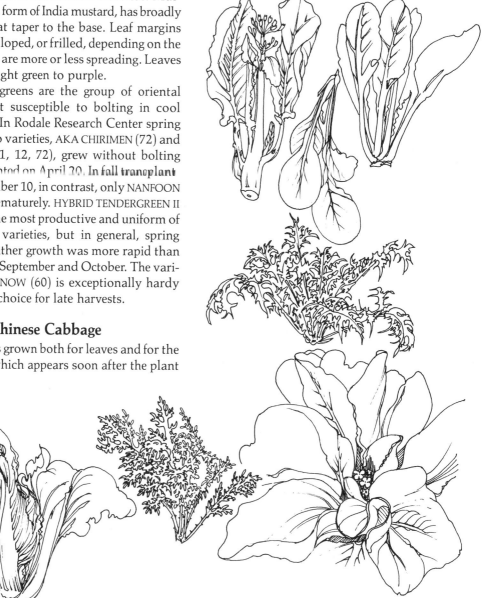

Oriental Vegetable Portrait: Assembled here are some of the interesting greens that can add an exotic touch to your garden. From lower left they are Chinese mustard, shungiku, flowering Chinese cabbage, Japanese mizuna, Japanese chard (top right), komatsuna, and Chinese broccoli.

row toward their base. While blooming, the plant grows fuller.

In Rodale Research Center spring trials, all varieties bolted 28 to 35 days after seeding, producing only spindly stalks. In fall, only three varieties were tested but all did well, and CHOY SUM-BAILY (41) was outstanding.

Chinese Broccoli

Also called Chinese kale, this plant closely resembles regular broccoli, except that it has longer stems and larger flowers. The stems and head are picked before the flowers open. The plant is hardier than broccoli, but it is low yielding when compared with other oriental brassicas. It grows well in a cold frame and matures in about 84 days from direct seeding.

Japanese Chard

Spring plantings yielded more than fall plantings in Rodale Research Center trials and spring-grown plants didn't bolt. Japanese chard's yield was superior to that of Swiss chard. In the garden, you'll be struck by its resemblance to the red-stalked varieties of Swiss chard.

Sow Japanese chard inside eight weeks before the last spring frost, and transplant it a month before last frost. It can be harvested a few leaves at a time or all at once. The harvest is longer with the first method. Japanese chard is an excellent cold frame crop (available from 72).

Japanese Komatsuna

Also called mustard spinach, the plant resembles regular mustard but grows faster and larger. Leaves are dark green, broad, and oval. Japanese komatsuna can be grown through the year in most areas, since it is tolerant of both hot and cold weather. It makes a good winter greens crop. Plants are 10 inches tall and slow to bolt. They do well in large cold frames (available from 23 and 52).

Japanese Mizuna

This is a large plant, over a foot high, that matures in 40 to 65 days, depending on the variety. Dark green leaves are narrow, numerous, deeply lobed, pointed, and sometimes hairy. Leafstalks are white. The leaves are picked young throughout the growing season. Although the plant is easy to grow and is very frost tolerant, the texture and hairiness of the leaves make it less desirable for greens than other oriental brassicas. Sow inside six weeks before the last frost and transplant out two weeks before last frost. Japanese mizuna is too large for most cold frames (available from 52).

Shungiku

Sometimes called chop suey green or edible chrysanthemum, this plant is grown for its shoots and fleshy leaves. If allowed to develop, it produces yellow flowers. The medium-leafed varieties are more productive than the broad-leafed ones.

Shungiku can be sown directly into a bed as soon as the ground can be worked in spring or sown indoors eight weeks before last frost and transplanted a month before last frost. It requires 50 to 84 days to mature and may bolt in warming weather. Begin picking the side leaves at ground level when they are 5 inches long, or harvest the whole plant at that time. If you wait and let the leaves grow longer, they will be stringy. If given a permanent bed, shungiku will self-sow and may be treated like a perennial in milder climates. Shading in spring may delay bolting.

The chrysanthemum flavor of shungiku is too strong for many American palates, so the crop is normally used in small quantities in salads with other ingredients or treated like a seasoning. It can be grown in a large cold frame and is usually direct-seeded into the frame (available from 29 and 67).

Life after Harvest

Extending the season takes on another meaning when you look for ways to get immature crops that couldn't ripen fully in the garden to ripen indoors. In this section we'll look at two ways to extend the season by expanding upon the time crops have to ripen.

Ripening Harvested Vegetables Indoors

Any tomato picked with a modest blush of red or yellow on its skin on the day before a killing frost will ripen indoors, if it is thoroughly sound, is full sized, and has begun the ripening process. Contrary to general belief, bright sunshine is not necessary for the process, but many a kitchen windowsill has been used to good advantage during the late fall months.

LONG KEEPER (9) has the advantage of ripening slowly and maintaining freshness over a long period. Keep picking until frost, and sort the fruit by ripeness—orange-green to pale yellow-pink. Set it in a cool place in categories arranged according to ripeness, and take care that none of the fruits touch. Keep the temperature around 60°F. By six weeks after picking, the skin of even the greener LONG KEEPERS will have reached a persimmon yellow. You'll still proclaim them unripe until you cut into one and see the deep ketchup-red flesh. The sight of that color may, however, raise your hopes too high. The flavor is only a pale imitation of a vine-ripened variety, but it's better than anything you'll find in a supermarket in winter. Many growers, if they regularly cull all fruit that looks the least bit soft or blemished, can hold LONG KEEPERS until spring. Once rot gets started on a ripening shelf, however, it's a sad and messy business.

An old-fashioned tomato variety called GARDEN PEACH was found by the Rodale Test Kitchens to have keeping qualities equal to LONG KEEPER, and its flavor was generally preferred. Seeds are available only through the Seed Savers Exchange. (See page 86 for the address of this group.)

Some winter squash continue to ripen indoors if picked close to ripeness and put in a warm place. Some people hang tomato vines they've pulled from the garden, fruit and all, upside down in a

Tomato Ripening: For Long Keeper and other tomatoes you hope to ripen indoors, set up a system like the one shown here. Segregate the tomatoes into groups according to their stage of ripeness, and keep checking to dispose of any that are spoiling.

warm shed or basement for continued vine-ripening. Peanuts, definitely a southern crop unless started inside, are traditionally cured by shed hanging, and although this is principally to harden and dry them, some ripening also continues.

Even frost-nipped vegetables can be used if the softened or damaged tissue is trimmed away before slicing or cooking. There are also many relish and condiment recipes that call for green tomatoes, so they don't have to go to waste.

Moving Plants Inside

Occasionally, a clever gardener may succeed in potting a mature vegetable from the garden and moving it to warmer quarters to continue ripening its crop. Mature plants with their developed and complex root systems, however, transplant poorly, so the success rate isn't very high.

A much better alternative is to plan ahead for this transfer and grow some crops from the start in containers. Crops that benefit from this season extension are cucumbers, eggplants, melons, peppers, and tomatoes.

Don't expect to move a plant that's spent the summer outdoors into the house overnight. Just as you hardened-off seedlings, so must you acclimate these mature plants to the special conditions indoors. In late August, start to bring them in at night, but put them back out during the day. As the days begin to cool, keep them inside for progressively longer periods until they've made the change to indoor growing.

Light will determine the measure of success you have with these plants. Natural light won't be sufficient unless you have a greenhouse. Plan on providing 16 hours of supplemental light.

You shouldn't have unrealistic expectations about these plants. With luck they'll ripen the fruits that were already set before the plants moved indoors. Don't expect to see any new cucumbers or tomatoes forming.

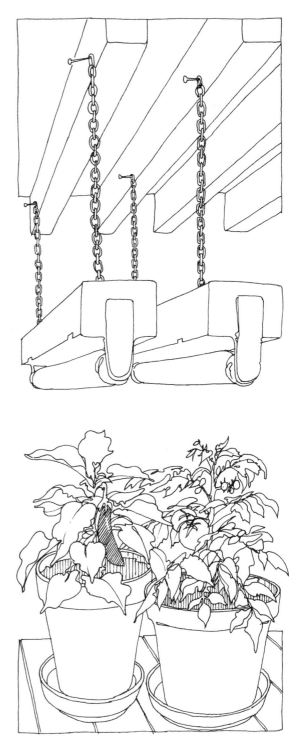

The Garden Moves Indoors: To ripen fruit that has already set in the garden, move plants like tomatoes and eggplants indoors. This transfer is made easier when plants are already growing in pots and are gradually acclimated to indoor conditions. Provide 16 hours of supplemental light.

WINTER GARDENING INDOORS

Keep the harvest going by moving your gardening activities indoors over the winter. There are a number of root crops that you can dig, relocate indoors, and force for midwinter greens. The basic equipment is an ample container such as a garbage can, plastic tub, or large pot, a batch of well-draining soil mix, and a watering can. You won't need to worry about supplemental lighting since nearly all these plants need darkness to sprout.

Asparagus In the fall before the ground freezes hard, dig some large roots, at least three years old. If you've been meaning to thin the bed, this is a good use for the excess roots. Replant them in a soil-filled container. Don't water and set it in a cool garage, shed, or unheated room for six weeks. This chill breaks their dormancy.

Next, move the container to a site where the temperature is 60 to 65°F. Water enough to keep the soil evenly moist, but don't overdo. The shoots will emerge regardless of whether they're kept in light or darkness. You won't harvest a bumper crop, but you will get just enough for a delightful preview of the coming asparagus season. Once the roots have been forced, toss them out, since they've used all their energy reserves.

Belgian Endive These creamy sprouts, also called chicons, are a gourmet's delight. It's hard to find them in grocery stores, but it's so simple to have a winter-long supply when you grow your own (available from 67).

To start, you must plant seeds of Witloof chicory in the outdoor garden in early spring or summer. By fall, the plants should have developed 10 to 12-inch-long roots. Before the ground freezes hard, dig the roots, trim the leaves to 1-inch stubs, and replant in a soil-filled container, leaving the top inch of the roots exposed. You can plant them shoulder to shoulder. Cover the roots with a 6 to 8-inch layer of damp sand or sawdust. Keep the soil evenly moist. Give the roots a cool (50 to 60°F) and dark rest for 3 to 5 weeks. Soon you should see the sprouts or chicons poking their way through the sand. Snap them off and leave the roots in place for a second harvest. Some gardeners have been able to harvest twice a week for two months from a garbage can full of forced chicory roots.

Horseradish   Adventuresome salad makers can dig horseradish roots in fall and treat as described for Belgian endive. The tender new leaves that appear will have a bite to them, so mix these greens with other milder ones to temper their flavor (available from 9).

Rhubarb   Although this perennial is an early producer in spring, you can enjoy a small but even earlier harvest by forcing roots. The roots should be exposed to a few frosts before being moved indoors, so wait to dig until just before the ground freezes hard. Two to three-year-old roots are best.

Bury them in containers filled with soil and store dry in a dark, cool place for one month. At that time, put a cover on the container, and expose it to 44°F for 10 days. Then move it to a place where the temperature is 50 to 60°F. Keep the soil evenly moist. In four to six weeks, ruby red stalks should be peeking through the soil.

Sea Kale   Although this perennial is relatively unknown to North American gardeners, it deserves more recognition for its mildly nutty-flavored stalks. Dig crowns when the tops die back in the fall, and treat as described for rhubarb. Use sea kale as you would asparagus (available from 67).

Shallots   A large clay pot full of shallots perched on a sunny window ledge should give you a small but steady source of snipped greens to use for flavorings and in salads. Plant the bulbs to half their depth in a rich, well-draining soil mix, give them full sun, and keep them at room temperature. Water to keep the soil evenly moist. In a couple weeks the greens should appear. When you clip the tops, don't injure the central shoot to ensure an ongoing harvest.

The bulbs will never grow as large as those on garden plants, but within several months they should reach the size of bunching onion bulbs. At that point you can harvest them (available from 22, 25, and 28).

CHAPTER

7 *Extending the Season with Simple Devices*

Give a high-yield gardener a peck of perfect peppers in August, and he or she will start asking for more peppers in October. Habitually discontent? Spoiled rotten? Perennially restless? Well, maybe, but then haven't both culture and agriculture always been pushed or tugged ahead by the restlessness of frustrated perfectionists?

It's easy to see where the frustration begins. Large, high-quality, continuous yields have come to the table from midspring through summer with nary a hitch and with much less work than you'd expected now that your beds are raised and your soil is in good tilth. You're finally getting into the swing of it, even working out successions long in advance and starting seedlings for transplanting at just the right time. Then, one late September or early October morning you look out the window and—wham!

"That's all folks," seems to be written all over the screen between you and your garden, for there sit the vegetables, fallen and blackened, their floppy, transparent leaves bringing you news of an unexpected frost. Alarmed and distressed in the morning, you're despondent by afternoon. By then, the temperature has risen into the high 70s and a glowing gardening day has dawned over the deserted scene of carnage that was once your raised bed garden. If you live in one of the more moderate weather zones, you know that if you could figure on only the *daytime* temperatures, good gardening weather would go on another full two months before winter began in earnest. Think of it—two full months that easily would have ripened those smitten green tomatoes. Why, in two months you could even grow two plantings of leaf lettuce!

What is really disturbing is that for the first time since spring you have lost control over things. And soon, if you're like most high-yield gardeners, you begin plotting ways to get the control back again. You may decide that the time has come to acquire some kind of permanent device that will be a good deal more dependable than the motley collection of overturned bushel baskets and bottomless plastic jugs you've been setting over your tender vegetables on cold nights. Indeed, what you want is something that will positively guarantee freedom from nighttime frost damage and give you an extended season.

Ambitious and hopeful gardeners (like amateur crooks who have hit on the idea of a cover-up) begin to think season-extending devices will take care of everything. Here are some of the minor miracles we expect from protective devices like cloches, tunnels, and growing frames.

- Warming the soil in spring.
- Starting early, hardy vegetables a month or so earlier than they can be started outside.
- Hardening-off seedlings for transplanting.
- Protecting early and late vegetables from cold winds and heavy rains.
- Giving an early and rapid start to warmth-loving vegetables like beans, peppers, and tomatoes.
- Ripening frost-threatened crops in the fall.
- Carrying crops started in or under the device into or through winter.
- Forcing vegetable production out of season.

Protective devices come in many shapes and sizes and offer a wide range of protection. However, few, if any, devices will perform all eight miracles for us. Before you select devices to use as covers or adjuncts for your raised beds, here are some questions you must ask yourself.

- How long is your normal winter?
- What is the time interval in your area between first light frost and the onset of daily daytime temperatures below 40°F? Many plants cease growth at 43°F.
- How much money are you prepared to spend to lengthen your season?
- How much time do you have to devote to the project, both for building the device and for tending it?
- Would it be worth the expense of a growing device or several devices to lengthen your season by three weeks? By a month on either end of the season? By six weeks, spring and fall?
- Would you realize the greatest savings by concentrating on getting late crops through early

frost, speeding early crops, or being able to grow something fresh to eat each day of the year?

To your ears these questions may have the ring of the interrogations family members are apt to direct at you when trying to talk you out of one of your more ambitious or costly projects. They are not intended that way. If you are to be satisfied with the devices you choose, however, it does make a difference what part of the country you live in and what you most want to accomplish in season extending. In the mid to deep South, for example, even small, inexpensive devices can make the difference between a 9-month and a 12-month growing season. In the Pacific Northwest, where hard rains and cloudy days do as much to discourage fall and spring gardening as do temperatures, many different kinds of devices have a place in or near the garden. In the Far North, it may be impossible to find a device airtight enough to protect from really deep freeze, but, on the other hand, there are some crops like melons and peppers that wouldn't get to the table at all without devices that lengthen the season from two months to almost three. No device will produce all vegetables year-round in an area further north than South Carolina.

Devices for Individual Plants

The most basic form of protection involves setting a device over a single plant. With varying degrees of innovation and elaboration, this is exactly what gardeners have been doing for centuries. The materials range from glass to plastic, and the shapes are diverse, but the goal is always the same—to offset less-than-perfect climatic conditions to encourage good plant growth.

The Bell Jar

One of the simplest plant protectors, the bell jar or glass cloche, is also one of the oldest, having been used in Europe since ancient times and especially prized among French market garden-

Bell Jars: These molded glass covers were favorites with French market gardeners. The model on the left has to be propped open at the bottom for venting. The bell jar on the right has a knob that can be removed to permit easy venting.

ers from the seventeenth through the nineteenth century. The molded glass cover, 1 to 1½ feet in diameter, is large enough to protect either a group of seedlings or a single vegetable as large as a bean plant. Originally it was tinted blue in the mistaken belief that blue pigment screened the rays of the sun.

The market garden area of France, surrounding Paris, has a moderate climate often lacking sun in winter, but seldom falling below freezing for more than a few days at a time. Although less variable and slightly cooler, the climate resembles that of the San Francisco Bay Area. In France, manure hotbeds were used to produce heat to force crops out of season. The purpose of the cloche was simply to make the fullest possible use of the sun's warmth and growth-accelerating potential while protecting individual plants from cold winds and rains.

When the short ultraviolet rays of the sun pass through an enclosing glass vessel, they warm

both the air around a plant and the soil under it. Soil, especially loose, dark soil, is an excellent solar collector and storage unit, storing energy in the form of heat. The soil releases the heat in long, infrared rays that pass back through glass at a slower rate than the short rays passed into the glass. In effect, heat is stored in the soil that sits under the glass. The principle involved is called the greenhouse effect, and we will observe it in action whenever glass is used in protective devices.

Not only are daytime temperatures inside glass cloches often many degrees higher than the

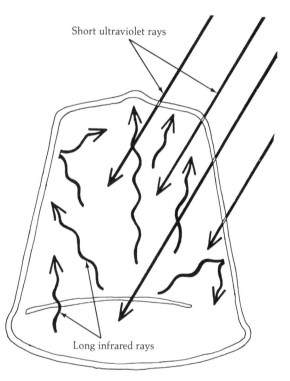

Short ultraviolet rays

Long infrared rays

Heat Storage: Sunlight passes through a glass cloche as short, ultraviolet rays to warm the enclosed soil and air. The soil releases the sun's energy stored as heat in the form of long, infrared rays. These pass through glass more slowly than short rays. This heat storage phenomenon is known as the greenhouse effect.

temperatures of the surrounding or ambient air, but at night stored heat is released from the soil under the glass slowly and trapped within the glass. The glass allows only minimal passage of heat, thus decreasing the day-to-night differential within the glass cloche. Moisture inside the cloches condenses against the glass as it cools at night, providing an additional barrier to heat loss.

Glass cloches offer adequate protection to keep some vegetables from frost damage in early spring and late fall. Perhaps even more usefully, glass cloches produce a warm, moist microclimate conducive to rapid growth of seedlings and heat-loving plants. The air and soil space within a cloche is too small to retain enough heat to sustain plant growth when there is little sunshine and daytime temperatures fall consistently to below 40°F with nighttime temperatures below freezing. Therefore, cloches alone will not see vegetables very far into winter in the northern part of this country. Failure to hold enough heat to sustain winter growth, however, is not the only problem with the bell jar, or even the biggest problem.

The original bell jars were unventilated. To let in air so as to reduce inside temperatures, bell jars either had to be lifted and removed individually, or propped at an angle to permit the passage of air at their bottoms. Later cloches were made with small wooden knobs that served as handles and could also be removed to allow air to enter from the top. In bright sunshine temperatures inside cloches can soar to 100°F even on days of moderate outside temperatures. High temperatures injure plants by dehydration, by encouraging disease, and by simple cooking of the foliage. Heat places extreme stress on cool-weather crops, especially newly transplanted ones.

The bright sun and the spring and fall fluctuations of temperature in most parts of this country make the use of bell jars impractical. Exceptions would be in mild, foggy coastal areas. Even there, some ventilating scheme must be devised to prevent disease.

Homemade Glass Cloches A cover very similar to the bell jar can be homemade simply and economically. Collect large, gallon-size glass jugs used for cider, vinegar, fruit juice, or wine. Wearing protective goggles and gloves, score the glass in a continuous line about an inch from the bottom with a tool made for glass cutting. The jug may be rotated firmly against a cutting tool that is held fixed in a vise, or a cutting tool may be securely attached to a 2-by-4 and rotated firmly around the jug.

After the glass has been scored, turn the jug upside down and tightly wrap densely woven string made of natural fibers around the scored line. Knot the string. Ease the string off over the jug bottom and tighten the knot. Trim the ends of the knot. Soak the string in alcohol for a few minutes and return it to the jug again, pressing it against the scored line.

With a wooden match, carefully set fire to the string at several places, making certain that the whole length heats up uniformly. The flame will not be bright. The glass will make a pinging noise as it responds to the heat by breaking along the score line. As you turn the jug right side up again, the bottom should drop off. If it does not, tap it gently against a wooden surface, holding the jug at an angle as you tap. This should release the bottom. Sandpaper any rough edges.

Bottomless glass jugs are durable, hold heat as well as any individual cover, and fit over all but the largest plants. They can be carried, or set in place, by the glass loop handle. Best of all, unlike the original glass cloche, the glass jug contains a built-in ventilator, the metal cap. To make ventilating and closing easier, punch a hole in the cap and attach it to the handle with a loop of wire or string so that it won't be misplaced when removed. Over the winter, store jugs in divided wine or beverage cartons.

The Tent and the Barn Cloche

Not long after French cloches made the channel crossing to what we consider foggy England, they were judged unsuitable for the climate. It was the English who insisted on a design that included built-in ventilation. The simplest form of the English cloche is an A-frame made of two pieces of glass leaning against each other and held in place by springs, wires, and clips that allow an adjustable gap at the peak for ventilation. The open ends are closed, but not sealed, with yet more glass. In their more elaborate forms, English cloches took on barn and lantern shapes. Like the French bell jars, they were movable. Placed end to end, they could be used to form long tunnels.

English gardeners, both commercial and amateur, continue to prize their glass cloches, finding they provide protection from chilling winds and battering rains as well as from light frosts at both ends of the season. In England, cloches allow the planting of beans and the transplanting of tomatoes, melons, and cucumbers six weeks before the last frost in late winter. They provide nearly perfect germination conditions for seedling starting because of the moist, even warmth they hold. English gardeners use cloches to get full use of their beds throughout a growing season by accelerating each crop in turn. They work out row successions so that the cloches can be moved from early crops to later ones with a minimum of motion. Cloches also reduce the need to water under conditions of the English climate, for they hold in condensation and prevent rapid evaporation, giving a steady, light supply of moisture to plant leaves. In England, some crops like winter lettuces are held from fall planting until spring by means of the cloche, stretching the growing season even further. In this country, you'll have to experiment to see which of these season-extending practices are possible in your particular climate.

Even ventilated tent or barn cloches should be checked frequently during sunny weather so that high temperatures inside them do not endanger plants. In cold weather it is important to make certain that plant leaves do not come into con-

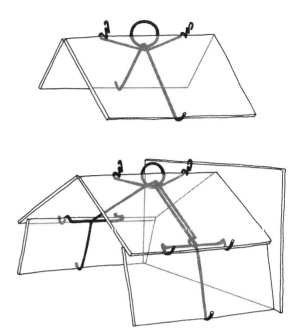

Tent and Barn Cloches: These English designs have built-in ventilation. The system of springs, wires, and clips lets you adjust a gap at the peak for ventilation. Both the tent (shown on top) and the barn cloche can be closed off on both ends with extra pieces of glass.

tact with the cold glass of cloches during nighttime dips of temperature.

Outside of England, one catalog supplier provides the component wire clips, and glass panes must be purchased separately. If you want to construct your own individual tent or barn cloche, order Rumsey clips for the appropriate model from Walter F. Nicke (see the Garden Products section of the Directory of Resources).

At the time you order the clips, ask for information about constructing the type of cloche you want. Buy glass panes precut from a glass dealer. Heavy glass intended for horticultural use is the most satisfactory. For a tent cloche that will be secured with Rumsey clips, you will need two identical pieces no larger than 24 inches long and 12 inches high. For barn cloches, you will need four panes. Possible dimensions would be two panes 12 inches high by 9 inches and two panes 12 inches high by 6 inches. A width greater than 24 inches makes the cloche unstable. The lower panes of the barn cloche should never be higher than they are wide. If you wish to make your own wire frames for barn cloches study the pictures of frames carefully and bend #8 or #9 galvanized wire to hold the glass panes.

With all glass cloches, breakage is always a problem, especially in areas subject to high winds or hail, or to romping children, vandals, or animals. Adequate off-season storage should be provided for cloches, and they must be washed from time to time to keep them functioning well. Glass, especially the heavier glass that is most effective in cloches, is expensive. When preassembled glass cloches are sold in other countries they cost as much as 30 dollars per section. In short, individual glass cloches are seldom economically feasible in this country except perhaps for use over prize botanical specimens or food crops of high commercial value.

Plastic Cloches

In the United States, glass cloches may be a rarity, but plastic covers, sometimes called cloches, are becoming more and more common. Although almost all garden suppliers carry some form of plastic plant cover, and plastic covers are much less expensive than glass ones, the plastic milk jug with the bottom cut off and the screw top removed for ventilation is still the individual cloche of choice for most gardeners.

Commercially made individual plastic cloches come in several shapes and sizes. Generally, they are intended for use over individual plants of moderate size or over groups of seedlings. Among the more popular of the commercial models now being sold are the following. (For the names of suppliers see the Garden Products Section of the Directory of Resources.)

The Wall O' Water consists of an upright ring of 18-inch, narrow plastic tubes to be filled with water, 25 pounds of it in all, for solar heat storage. The stored heat in the water is released to plants at night, speeding their growth. In cold weather when the device is set over seedling plants the top can be closed by tilting the tubes inward into a tepee shape. One garden supplier recommends setting the Wall O' Water out in closed position, and only opening the tops when the normal planting time for the protected seedlings has arrived.

The Whiting Mini-Hothouse looks like a round stovepipe hat. It is 10 inches across and made of rigid opaque plastic. The device is intended to be anchored by mounding soil over the horizontal base, or "hat brim." A dome-shaped cap fits on top of the base and can be removed in warm or sunny weather.

The Fabro Expanding Tomato Cover comes from Switzerland and consists of a roll of thin plastic film with small splits running across it. It is to be unrolled and cut into lengths to fit over small vegetables. Stakes are placed close to newly planted seedlings. A long tube or cone of the plastic is slid over the stake and secured to it with a twist tie. As the seedling grows, the film is pushed outward, opening the slits to let in more air. Many other slitted plastics will adapt to homemade and less expensive versions of this device. Slitted plastics, often of heavier grades than the one in the Fabro kit, are sold in rolls of 50 or 500 feet.

Sun Hats are tall, narrow cones 8½ inches high with a 7-inch base. The original commercial ones came from England. Two bottom tabs provide anchoring spots for pegs or stakes that are to be supplied by the gardener. Sun Hats, also sometimes sold as Grow-Cones, have green vertical stripes for shading alternating around the cone with stripes of clear Mylar plastic. The cost of Sun Hats and Grow-Cones is less than a dollar apiece and they are sold at retail outlets. They usually come in packages of ten, and they are reusable but will not last more than a few seasons. These devices are ventilated with a top opening.

A more durable design is the Solar Cone, designed by Leandre Poisson and sold through Solar Survival. This cone comes in various sizes and is fashioned from semirigid reinforced fiberglass acrylic sheets originally developed for solar collectors. The sides of the cone are held together with screws, and ventilation takes place through the top of the cone. The shape of the device and the weight of the material make the Solar Cone an extremely stable cloche that stays in place but is easy to move and to store. The largest size Solar Cone will protect large plants through killing frost in autumn, but very bushy or branchng plants will be cramped by the cone shape. The cone should always be removed when inside temperatures begin to approach 80°F. For very large plants, a cylinder slightly larger than the base of the cone can be used as a riser.

Homemade Plastic Cloches Even the least expensive individual plastic cloche has a price tag. That fact may account for the popularity of the bottomless plastic jug as a protector of single plants. There's no need for fancy cutting tools when you are working with the gallon jugs that come filled with bleach, juice, cooking oil, liquid detergent, and other products. A less-than-good

pair of utility scissors or a knife will help you remove the bottom. The jug will cover medium-

Commercial Plastic Cloches: Starting at the lower left, ready-made cloches you can buy include the Solar Cone, Whiting Mini-Hothouse, Fabro Expanding Tomato Cover, Wall O' Water, and Sun Hat.

EVALUATING PLASTIC CLOCHES

Of the several styles of individual plastic cloches tested in the gardens of the Rodale Research Center in 1984, none provided significant protection from frost damage at temperatures of 20°F or less. Two commercial models, the Wall O' Water and the Whiting's Mini-Hothouse, saved from frost a portion of the tomato seedlings used, but only at the expense of their later healthy growth. Tomatoes were used in the experiment because they were the vegetables most frequently pictured in advertising literature for cloches, but Rodale testers agreed that tomatoes are less successfully cloche-grown than cool-loving crops. Indeed, tomato seedlings used in the experiment were found to mature later when covered than when grown in the open air.

It was claimed for both of the two more successful commercial plastic cloches that they would permit outdoor plantings up to six weeks earlier than normal. The Rodale tests did not support that claim. The Fabro Expanding Tomato Cover was said to provide only three weeks' head start, but it also failed either to protect from frost or to produce earlier yields of tomatoes. Nighttime temperatures under all of the commercial products tested were close to the temperatures on exposed soils.

The Rodale Research Center recommends transplanting tomato seedlings under plastic cloches at most only three weeks before they would survive outdoors unprotected. In cold climates gardeners may find that a three-week head start is seldom worth the expense of commercial cloches.

Bottomless plastic jugs also failed the Research Center's tests. At 20°F tomato seedlings under plastic jugs were frost-killed. On the other hand, in an earlier experiment both bottomless jugs and commercial plastic covers protected broccoli seedlings to 19°F and also accelerated their early growth. (The seedlings were covered for the first three weeks of their growth after transplanting in mid-April.) Being able to produce broccoli two weeks earlier than normal might justify the expense of cloches to some gardeners or at least it might justify the time it takes to make homemade models such as the ones described in the text.

size plants and, like its glass counterpart, is automatically ventilated when you remove the lid. It may, however, need to be wedged between stakes to anchor it in windy weather.

We have already mentioned the idea of making your own plastic tents from lengths of the slitted plastic that comes in rolls. Another homemade possibility is to use discarded elastic-and-plastic shower caps on your smaller plants. Plastic storage containers, plastic ice cream containers, or clear plastic pails, tubs, buckets, or bowls, if adequately ventilated with punched holes or faithfully removed on sunny days, may hasten plants a few days in spring or protect them from light frost in fall.

Another idea is to make small individual frames for tender vegetables. A square frame can be made of scrap lumber, and chicken wire may be attached to it using a stapler. Cut the chicken wire square larger than the frame and bend it into a dome shape. The larger you cut the wire, the higher it will dome. Staple the wire to all four sides of the frame. You will have to gather the edges of the wire a bit to make it fit the frame. Fit a large clear plastic bag or sheet of plastic over the whole frame. Puncture the plastic at several spots and attach all thicknesses to the chicken wire with twist ties. The plastic will have to be replaced every year, but the frame will last a long time and will also afford protection, with plastic

Homemade Plastic Protectors: Look around the house for handy, inexpensive single-plant protectors. Shower caps (top left) and plastic ice cream tubs (right) given a few ventilation holes will do in a pinch. To make milk jugs handier to use, cut the bottom on three sides and fold it back to form a flap. Use a stone to anchor the flap. A string attaching the lid to the jug handle makes it easy to take on and off for venting.

removed, to small cole crops and lettuce where rabbits are a menace.

Cubic wooden frames can also be covered with plastic sheeting on all but the bottom side for a more conventional cover for individual vegetables. If unslitted plastic is used, these frames should be removed in sunny weather.

Heavy plastic cones similar to the Leandre Poisson Solar Cone can be made with lengths of fiberglass acrylic sheets. Make sure the material you purchase is thin enough and flexible enough to allow you to bend it or roll it into a cone shape. Unless you have special equipment, you will not be able to bend and secure fiberglass as heavy as that used in the Solar Cone. Cut a large circular shape from the sheet, make a single cut to the center of the circle, and roll the plastic into a cone shape, leaving an opening at the top. Drill holes through both thicknesses along the overlapped outside edge of the material and insert screws, small bolts, or sturdy two-pronged note-

book fasteners. Trim the bottom of the cone as needed so that it will sit flat on the ground.

What Individual Plastic Covers Will Do for Plants

Many gardeners, unfortunately, expect too much of plastic covers. Only heavy glass, opaque materials, and some forms of double-glazed plastic with an air space sandwiched between hard plastic layers are sufficient to sustain plants within individual cloches on a frosty night. Most plastic, unlike glass, permits the rapid exit of long, infrared rays. Polyethylene, the most common material for homemade plastic cloches, loses heat readily. Inside a polyethylene protector the air at night is often no warmer than the outside air.

Since it is lighter than glass, plastic blows away easily, tips over to injure plants, and often requires additional anchoring even when sunk into soil. Anchoring stakes for lightweight devices

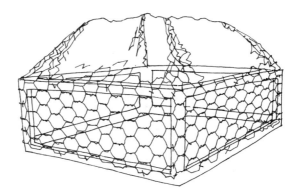

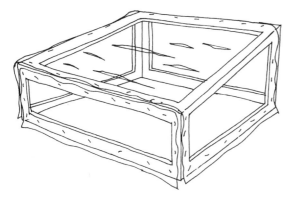

Home-Style Plant Protectors: Scrap lumber and leftover chicken wire can be put to good use to build the structure shown on top. A large plastic bag or sheet of plastic can be fitted over the frame. Without the plastic, the frame can keep away hungry wildlife. The structure on the bottom is the same basic design, minus the wire. Clear plastic is stapled to all five surfaces. Both these protectors can accommodate groupings of small plants. The top structure affords more "headroom."

pull out easily from the loose soil of raised beds. Many plastics also deteriorate quickly or yellow to become opaque when exposed to the ultraviolet rays of direct sunlight.

Plastic cloches, especially the heavier, better insulated ones, are useful for accelerating seedling growth in spring and fall, permitting some crops to produce earlier yields. However, not all crops bear earlier when their early growth is accelerated under plastic.

Plastic cloches are designed to be left in place day and night for several weeks from early spring to early summer. They serve as miniature greenhouses, making full use of the sun's heat. Warm daytime temperatures hasten the plants' uptake of moisture and nutrients, causing plants to grow faster and mature more rapidly.

Individual Paper Covers

Hot caps are another form of individual plant protector. They are nothing more than small domes made of waxed paper reinforced with manila tape. The most successful of these are made with slightly opaque paper and are anchored to the soil with a stake. Others are cone shaped and are anchored with soil. They are unventilated, but the material itself is somewhat porous. The opaque material offers better cold protection than light plastic does, but it cuts off some of the growth-stimulating sunlight. Later in the season, if left in place, hot caps can be ventilated by slitting or by cutting off the top of the cone. Waxed paper cones are inexpensive and may last as long as two seasons if they are the reinforced type. They hold soil moisture, reducing the need to water.

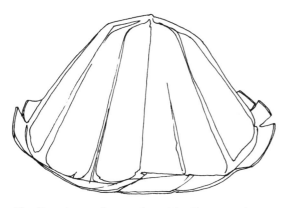

Hot Cap: A waxed paper dome like this is suited to covering individual seedlings and transplants. It can be ventilated by cutting slits or making a hole in the top. The flaps around the bottom can be covered with soil to anchor the cap.

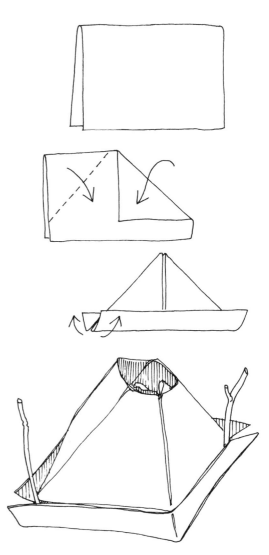

Generally they come in two sizes, 6 inches high and 9½ inches high, both 11 inches at the base. They are too small to be used for many mature plants and are better suited to protecting seedlings and transplants.

Not even the sturdiest paper cloche will protect from heavy frost. Paper hats, like other individual cloches, are most useful in places like the San Francisco Bay Area, the Pacific Northwest, and the maritime areas of the mid-Atlantic states where lack of sunlight, cold winds, and excessive rain pose greater limits to extending the growing season than do low temperatures. Because waxed paper is opaque and cuts off sunlight, it is most successfully used over crops with low light requirements, like oriental brassicas in their early stages or young cole crops.

Growing Tunnels: The Continuous Cloche

When the original glass bell jar was brought to England, you will recall, it evolved into the indi-

Fold-Your-Own Paper Hot Cap: Take the Sunday paper and enlist your family's aid to fold a supply of hot caps. Take a whole sheet of paper (four individual pages) and place the fold away from you. Fold the outer corners toward the center. Fold the bottom flaps up to form the brim. In the garden set the hot cap over a seedling and anchor with twigs. A hole cut in the top will provide ventilation.

vidual tent cloche, a two-sided tent with removable end pieces. The tent cloche, which remains

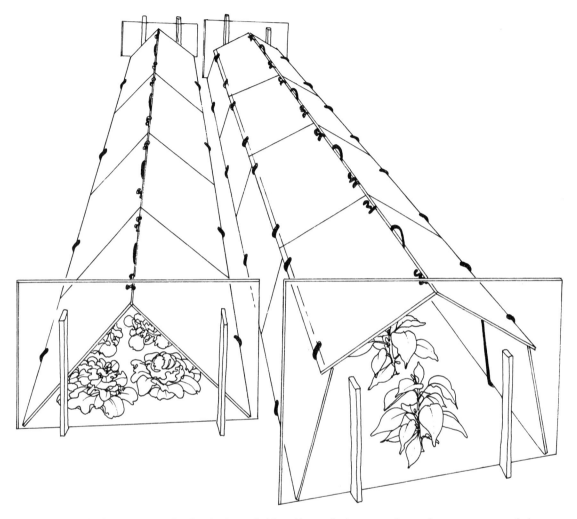

Glass Tunnel Cloches: A series of individual tent (left) and barn cloches set end to end can cover rows of plants in garden beds. To close off the ends, set panes of glass in place with support stakes.

in use today, is seldom used to cover individual plants. Rather, tents are set directly next to each other, open ends together, to make long row-covering tunnels. End pieces are placed only at either end of the row. The tent cloche tunnel was the original continuous cloche, or growing tunnel.

Tunnels of cloche segments are moved from row to row in English gardens as earlier, and then later, crops mature. The whole cloched part of the garden is carefully planned to allow for the shifting of tunnels.

Tent cloches are usually only large enough to fit over a row of lettuce and carry it to mature size. They adapt to the raised bed garden for use over smaller vegetables and seedlings only. If used over larger plants there is the danger that the cramped leaves within the continuous tent will come into contact with the glass, resulting in frost damage in cold weather and sunscald in hot weather. Spacing within raised beds should be wider than normal if tent cloches are to be used.

The objection to the leaf-cramping quality of the tent cloche was soon overcome with the development of the barn cloche. The barn cloche uses four panes of glass, two set perpendicular to the ground and two rising above them to form a tent or roof. Barn cloches come in various dimensions, some shallow-sided with low roof pitch and some steeply rising with a high pitch. A few models even come with risers that will allow them to be used to cover quite tall plants. The most common modern barn cloche used in England is 24 inches long, 22 inches wide, and about 19 inches high, or large enough to fit over two narrow rows of small vegetables in a raised bed garden. Barn cloches are moved by means of a top handle that also controls the spring-operated venting gap.

Utility or tomato cloches are composed of three panes of glass and are flat topped with slightly inward-sloping sides, offering greater height, but less width than a barn cloche. Although often used to protect individual large plants, utility cloches adapt to tunnel use. Barn and tent cloches can also be turned on their sides to make windscreens for taller vegetables.

Glass tunnels have all the advantages and disadvantages of individual glass cloches. They retain heat well and offer a real boost to early growth, but they are expensive, breakable, and hard to find. Temperatures inside tunnels, even with top ventilation gaps opened wide, often rise higher than those under individual glass cloches. Glass tunnels should not be used in sunny areas in warm weather or in cold sunny weather without frequent checking.

Plastic Row Tunnels

Plastic row tunnels are much more readily available in this country than the glass ones. Some models can be homemade without purchasing special clips and frames. They are lighter and less breakable than glass and therefore can be made in continuous lengths without combining individual segments. On the other hand, they are generally less durable than glass and most of them provide less warmth. Plastic tunnels can be rigid and molded, semirigid and bent to form, or composed of plastic sheeting stretched over a supporting and strengthening structure.

Corrugated fiberglass sheeting molded into an arc can be set over rows and the ends closed using small sheets of plastic. You can ventilate tunnels by removing the end pieces or by drilling holes in the top surface. Although it is only translucent, not transparent, fiberglass transmits light fairly well and holds heat well enough to lengthen either end of the season by a few weeks and to provide protection against light frost. Tunnels made of fiberglass will last about five years and are moderate in cost when compared with glass.

Molded acrylic is slightly more durable than fiberglass, remains anchored in the soil better, transmits light at least as well, and shares the other advantages of molded plastic.

Semirigid plastic materials include polypropylene, a double-layered woven plastic with a corrugated appearance. Unlike other plastic materials, it provides better thermal insulation than glass, but it transmits light less well because it is a milky white opaque. Barn-shaped cloches of this material can sometimes be found commercially. They will last about five years.

In general, rigid or semirigid plastic row covers are designed for use in conventional row gardens and are too long and often too wide for growing beds with narrow rows. If you do use one in your garden, anchor it in high winds and provide for ventilation.

Homemade Plastic Tunnels The way around the problem of awkward lengths in commercial tunnels is, of course, to make your own. In making a tunnel cloche of semirigid plastic you must find some means of keeping the plastic bent to the desired arching shape. One method, popularized by the late gardening expert James Underwood Crockett, is to make a wire framework to set over the bent plastic. Heavy #8 or #9 coiled galvanized wire may sometimes be purchased precut, but the usual procedure is to buy it in rolls and to cut it into lengths with a wire cutter or cutting torch. When purchased in rolls, the wire will already be arched by the rolling. Several arches, shaped like croquet wickets, are pushed into the soil 4 inches deep at intervals. These hold the bent plastic in place over a row of plants. Another approach is to string straightened wire through holes punched near the base of the curved plastic. These wires draw the plastic into a permanent arch.

Wire-reinforced plastics are also used to make tunnels. These materials can be bent into high and narrow or low and squat shapes as desired. They last about three years and require anchoring against high winds. Wire-reinforced plastics are sometimes sold in tunnel kits containing 3 by 100-foot or 6 by 100-foot rolls of material. To span 2 feet or more, this material requires additional support, but it can be bent to form narrow tunnels that hold their shape well and would be suitable for a raised bed garden. Bending some wire-reinforced plastics sold in kits is a time-consuming process. During trials at the Rodale Research Center in Maxatawny, Pennsylvania, one kit assembly required almost half an hour to bend correctly. The cost for this material is less than that of polypropylene.

Besides the time needed for assembly, another problem with wire-reinforced plastic tunnels is that watering and weeding under them is difficult, requiring the temporary removal of the tunnel.

Tunnel Kits

The materials for plastic tunnels are often sold in kits containing flexible plastic (usually thin sheet plastic) and the supporting device over which it

is to be secured. Tunnel kits are designed for the long rows of conventional gardens, but most of them may be adapted to short rows or bed lengths by cutting them into sections. You'll have to decide whether it would be easier to adapt a kit or to start from materials similar to the ones in the kit and custom-tailor the tunnel to your garden. As we examine the various kits available and tested by the Rodale Product Testing Department, a discussion of materials will be included to assist you in devising your own. The kits tested included the Spring Garden Row Cover, Great Vegetable Cover-Up, Tunnel Grow System, Key-Lite, Select Greenhouse Tunnel, and Warp's Row Cover and Mulch Kit. See the Garden Products section of the Directory of Resources for the addresses of suppliers of these kits.

Tunnel Dimensions In choosing a plastic tunnel kit, size is an important factor. Commercial tunnel cloche kits tested ranged in length from 13 to 25 feet; in width from 12 to 24 inches; and in height from 10 to 16 inches. The Tunnel Grow System was the widest and highest. In the raised bed garden where plastic will have to be cut before it can be used over short rows, length is not a limiting factor for tunnels that are to be fitted with sheet plastics. Tunnel kits containing heavy semirigid plastic, on the other hand, may have to be ruled out entirely unless they can be used the length of the bed. The plastic may be too heavy to cut without special tools.

Height and width measurements will determine which crops can be protected by the tunnels. A 10-inch-high tunnel, for example, will accommodate vegetables no larger than 6 inches tall and therefore will be most useful for starting seedlings. The most spacious kit tunnels tested (the Tunnel Grow System and Warp's Row Cover and Mulch Kit) allowed room for mature rows of spinach, lettuce, kale, beets, carrots, turnips, cauliflower, and some low-growing broccoli. Most kits are designed to cover a single row in a small row garden. This may limit their usefulness in raised beds if rows are narrow or if a staggered form of spacing is used.

Both rigid and semirigid plastic tunnels are difficult to move once they are installed, much more so than individual plant covers. Because of their light weight, they are most frequently anchored against wind by sinking their edges into the soil. In a tightly spaced raised bed garden, moving a tunnel may mean uprooting a neighboring plant or row of plants. The same problem occurs with the most popular form of row tunnel, made from plastic sheeting draped over a structural frame.

Grades of Plastic Sheet plastic, most commonly polyethylene, comes in various thicknesses and weights and is sometimes slitted at ¾-inch intervals with 5-inch-long openings to allow air circulation. (Some slitted plastics have smaller slits.) Sheet plastic is by far the most popular material for homemade tunnels. To construct tunnels from sheet plastic, the material may be stretched over a variety of frames including hoops of wire or bent wood, bent plastic tubing, and square wooden supporting frames.

Among the tunnel kits tested by the Product Testing Department, the Great Vegetable Cover-Up, Tunnel Grow System, and Warp's Row Cover and Mulch Kit contained sheet plastic, generally polyethylene 1 or 2 mils thick (1 mil equals 1/1000 of an inch), the same thickness used by commercial growers. (These sheets were to be used in single layers, and all but the Tunnel Grow System came with ventilation slits already cut.) Heavier sheets, although more durable and less easily damaged by wind, tend to sag between support hoops and also reduce the light that reaches plants. The Spring Garden Row Cover and Select Greenhouse Tunnel contained unslitted plastic sheets intended for use in double thickness. Double thicknesses of polyethylene function much as double glazing does, trapping air between layers for added insulation. The double-thickness covers were found to give 2 to 4 degrees greater protection against frost than the slitted sheets

that were tested, while also producing higher levels of heat and moisture on warm, sunny days. Double layers of unslitted plastic require that tunnels be opened occasionally on one side for venting to prevent injury to plants.

Tunnel Supports The tunnel kits tested generally contained supports in the form of hoops bent from #8 or #9 wire. These hoops were either prebent or required bending. One kit, the Spring Garden Row Cover, contained flexible wooden support hoops already preinserted into pockets stitched in double layers of polyethylene. The supports were usually spaced from 2 to 4 feet apart and were meant to be pushed into the soil at an angle and to a depth of 6 inches, so that the top of the frame extended 12 to 16 inches above the ground.

Setting Up the Tunnels Following the instructions with the kits, furrows were dug on each side of the row that was to be covered. A 6 to 8-inch trench was also dug at each end of the row, allowing for the outside ends of the covers to be buried for anchoring.

The need for furrows and trenches may make tunnel row covers impractical for raised bed gardens with tight spacing. A bed intended for tunnel cleching should be spaced more widely than normal and ample room should be left at each end of it for cover-end anchoring. In raised beds, it may be more practical to extend the covers beyond the supporting hoops and to anchor them with rocks or bricks or boards in the path area immediately beyond and below the beds. Unvented covers set at one end of a raised bed can be raised along one long side for venting if stones or boards are used to anchor that side.

Conclusions from the Study The self-venting polyethylene material reduced light transmission by 14.3 to 16.7 percent, while double-layered polyethylene reduced light by 18.9 to 22.5 percent. The one wire-reinforced polyethylene material tested (Key-Lite) reduced light the most, by 26.1 percent. Light transmission was reduced further in the course of the testing due to condensation

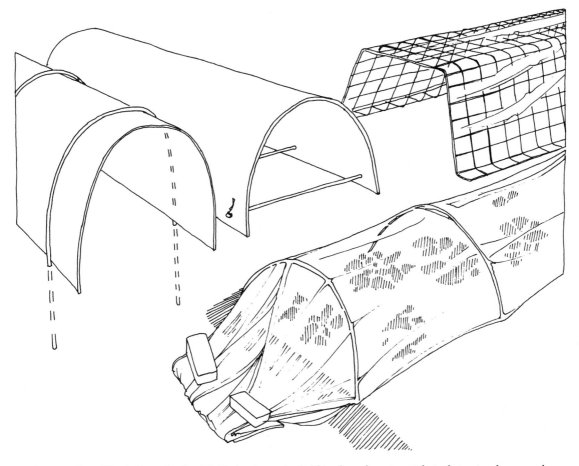

Make Your Own Plastic Tunnels: Semirigid plastic can be held in shape by wire wickets that act as braces or by wire pieces threaded through the bottom edges of the plastic (shown top left and center). Wire-reinforced plastic (top right) can be shaped into an arched tunnel form (you'll probably need an extra pair of hands for this). At bottom is a popular design—wire wickets that support a length of clear plastic sheeting. The sides are held down by soil. The long plastic ends are anchored by bricks or stones. Arrange the tunnel so that the excess at the ends can fall in the area beyond the bed to avoid wasting growing space.

deposit, dust, and marks of abrasion that accumulated on the material.

The self-ventilating, slitted tunnels required less labor after installation than the double-layer ones because venting was less frequent, but also because weeding, watering, and harvesting could be done through the slits in the material. (It should be pointed out that some slitted plastics available have slits too small to accommodate an arm.) All double-layered covers had to be raised frequently on sunny days to prevent heavy condensation, as well as to protect the plants from overheating. However, one of the slitted plastics also became fogged with condensation.

All covers tested were fairly easy to disassemble and store, especially the larger ones without preinserted hoops. The most time consuming to set up was the Key-Lite kit containing wire-

GROWING PLANTS IN PLASTIC TUNNELS

The air inside plastic tunnels by day can reach 85°F when the outside temperature is only 55°F, but nighttime temperatures inside the tunnels come much closer to ambient air temperatures. Overheating on sunny days can present a problem in plastic tunnels of all styles and materials. Cool-growing crops of moderate size like head lettuce and carrots seem to benefit most from the protection of plastic tunnels. High relative humidity and carbon dioxide levels are often reached within the tunnels by day, resulting in the rapid growth of young plants. An additional advantage of tunnel growing is the protection tunnels offer the soil. Protected soil holds tilth longer and requires less frequent watering.

In growing medium to late-maturing vegetables in row tunnels in the fall, it is necessary to start plants early enough so that they are approaching maturity before early winter nighttime temperatures slow their growth. The plants will grow very little after cold weather begins, and they will hold their own better if they are mature or nearly mature by then. Oriental brassicas are the most feasible crops for growing into early winter under plastic tunnels and row covers. It's also sometimes possible to harvest an early spring crop of oriental greens from an autumn planting, or start an extra-early spring crop.

Oriental brassicas, winter spinach, and frost-resistant lettuce planted on March 10 in eastern Pennsylvania and tunnel-covered were harvested after only five to eight weeks, giving a five-week advantage over normal, unprotected planting. Quick-maturing varieties of cool-season vegetables planted in the fall can be harvested in mid to late winter with minimum frost damage if tunnels are used to protect them and if outside temperatures remain above or only slightly below freezing at night. They should, however, be grown to maturity before a hard frost comes, for tunnels will not offer sufficient protection from below-freezing temperatures.

reinforced plastic. It required two people to set it in place.

The Rodale researchers concluded that since both slitted and double-layered materials promoted fast early growth in many plants, the choice among kits is most reasonably made on the basis of the size of tunnel desired. Larger tunnels will be needed for fall protection than for spring seedlings. Other important considerations are the amount of labor required to set up, service, and maintain each tunnel. By these criteria, the most satisfactory tunnels tested were large in size and used slitted materials. In terms of cost, however, double-layer tunnels are more durable, and hence more cost efficient, than slitted ones. In autumn, when plants must be protected from cold nights, double-layer covers are the better choice.

Tunnel kits are available at garden centers, at some hardware stores, and through catalog garden suppliers. Money can always be saved by purchasing the materials separately and doing your own cutting and fitting of plastics and supports.

Covers for single rows are, as we have seen, less practical for use in raised bed gardens than in the conventional row gardens for which they are designed. If they are made by hand instead of from kits they can be designed to accommodate a group of narrow rows. When a raised bed gardener sees how much work is entailed in covering just part of a narrow bed, and how much space is reduced for planting if room must be left for trenches, heavy stones and bunched-up plastic, it doesn't take long before the idea dawns that with just a little more work and a bit more material the whole raised bed could be covered. When this happens, a whole new style of protection has opened up.

Covers for Raised Beds

The gardener who seizes upon the idea of covering a whole bed for late-season protection or the stimulation of early-season growth may be onto more than he or she realizes.

In a 1983 Rodale Research Center study of three plastic row covers and of the vegetables most suitable for growing under them, Rodale researchers were surprised to learn that temperatures in the largest of the three covering structures, which measured 10 feet wide and covered two 5 foot beds, were 2 to 5 degrees higher than under the other two covers, which enclosed one and two rows, respectively. The slight temperature advantage was attributed to the larger volume of energy-holding soil that the structure enclosed. All three row covers tested provided inside air temperatures between 10 and 20 degrees higher than ambient temperatures during an unusually warm Pennsylvania late autumn and early winter, but sank to freezing during late December and January. The three covers gave plantings of oriental brassicas, spinach, and lettuce a five-week advantage over outdoor control plantings in early spring. In construction, the multirow covers were similar to the kit-assembled row covers described earlier, but bent pipe was used to provide a more substantial support than wire hoops would have afforded.

Easy-to-Make Bed Covers

In the autumn of 1984, horticulturists at the Rodale Research Center designed four different sheet plastic and frame structures for use over 4 by 9-foot beds. They were looking for structures that would cover an entire bed and would be relatively inexpensive, easy to build, easy to use, durable, and capable of extending the season.

What follows is a description of each design and the materials it uses.

Plastic Shed This design looks something like an A-frame tent set over a bed. Six-foot-tall posts at either end of the garden bed support a ridge pole. These posts are sunk 2 feet into the soil with 4 feet rising above the ground. A notch in the end posts allows the ridge pole to set securely in place, but it could also be nailed onto the end posts. Plastic sheeting is draped over the ridge pole and held in place on south, east, and west sides by soil or pieces of lumber. A piece of lath nailed over the plastic attaches it to the ridge pole. The plastic is cut longer than the length of the bed so the excess can be used to pull around and cover the exposed ends. Bricks or stones are handy weights to keep these ends closed. For venting, these pieces could be folded back like the flaps on a tent and held in place by the weights. On the north side, the plastic is held down by bales of hay or bags of leaves that can be moved to give access to the plants in the bed. The plastic shed was the second least expensive structure to build when available scrap lumber was used.

Arched Top I This design is for use with raised beds enclosed in wooden sides. Five 10-foot-long aluminum or less expensive PVC pipes are arched to make a tunnel shape that is high enough to provide clearance for reaching into the bed from either short-side end. These pipes are set into holes drilled in the sides of the frame. Screws anchor the pipes in the holes. Six-mil plastic is draped over the arch and anchored to the wooden frame on both long sides with strips of roof lath nailed to the wooden bed sides. Cutting the plastic so it is longer than the bed allows enough excess so that ends can be closed off. Fasten together the plastic on each end with a clothespin when the cover is not being vented. For venting simply roll up the extra plastic until it rests on the first arch on the end of the bed.

Plastic Shed: A plastic sheet draped over a ridge pole covers this garden bed. Bales of hay anchor the loose ends and are easy to move for access to plants.

The arched ribs can be left in place year-round. In the growing season they can support a cheesecloth or Reemay covering that will keep out insects. When the cost of the base is included, this structure is the most expensive of the four to build.

Arched Top II This bed cover follows the same basic design of Arched Top I, minus the wooden bed frame. To anchor the arched 10-foot pipes, ten pieces of 1-inch conduit pipe are sunk into the ground, on opposite sides of the bed. The aboveground pipes slip neatly into these anchoring pipes. The five arches support plastic sheeting that generously extends over the two ends. A slit up the center of these overhanging pieces makes it easy to roll them back for venting or for gaining access to the plants inside. Like Arched Top I, these ribs can be left standing all year, and in summer the plastic can give way to insect-thwarting layers of cheesecloth or Reemay. This structure is the third most expensive of the four to build.

Ground-Hugging Cover This design lies closer to the ground than the others, but it gives easier access to all the plants in the bed at once. A piece of cattle wire fencing is arched over a raised bed. To provide support and add some stability, two notched pieces of wood that stand approximately 2 feet above the ground are set in the bed at each end. The notch allows the fencing to nestle in place securely. On one long side the loose prongs of fencing are pushed into the soil to anchor it.

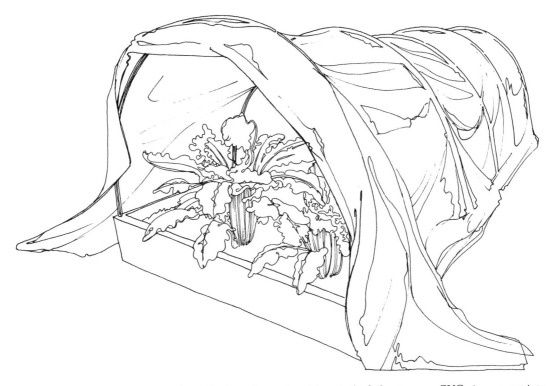

Arched Top I: This cover is designed to fit beds with wooden sides. Arched aluminum or PVC pipes are set into the wooden bed sides. Plastic sheeting is draped over the ribs and nailed into the bed sides with lathe pieces. To vent, roll back the plastic on one end as shown.

On this same side, a sheet of plastic is attached by staples to a 2 by 4, which is laid right next to the base of the fencing. On the other long side the plastic is held down with weights such as stones or bricks. The plastic sheeting should extend over both short ends to allow closing up and venting. Clothespins are handy to join the loose ends of the plastic. To vent, the free end of the plastic can be peeled back. To gain access to the plants you can reach through the opening in the fencing or lift the free side of the arch and prop it up while you're working in the bed. This is the least expensive of the structures.

Materials for all four structures are easily obtained from garden or building supply stores or by salvage from other use. All structures are durable, especially when pressure-treated wood and PVC, bent aluminum, or galvanized steel pipe is chosen. The least durable feature is the plastic sheeting, which must be replaced after a season or two of use. All units were constructed in an hour or less with the aid of a few basic tools. A special tool has to be used for bending aluminum or galvanized steel pipe.

Using the Row Covers

All these structures extended the season and produced healthy crops of lettuce, spinach, and kale that were transplanted into the beds in September and that thrived in a mild fall. In early January, however, a record-breaking freeze destroyed all the crops. Vegetables grown in open air as a con-

Arched Top II: This design is similar to Arched Top I, but it works in beds without wooden bases. Plastic sheeting is cut so that there is plenty of overhang at the ends. A slit in the end makes it easy to roll back one side for venting as shown. A clothespin holds the plastic in place.

trol had begun to show stress as early as mid-December, so it can be said that the raised bed covers kept plants healthy about three weeks longer than they would have remained healthy if unprotected and perhaps as much as two weeks longer than small row tunnels would have kept them. The early freeze of 1984 made comparisons with earlier experiments using row tunnels difficult.

In the plastic shed, which measured 3 to 4 feet high, watering was done by means of a hose and wand. It was accomplished by lifting one short end of the cover and directing the wand to the base of the plants. In the other three structures, which reached a maximum of 4 feet in height, using the wand was more cumbersome, and some watering had to be done by hand after lifting the long sides of the plastic. Plants were watered weekly during a warm November, but later in the season one watering every two weeks was sufficient. Venting was done when air temperatures inside the structures reached 75 to 80°F.

In fall, all of these bed structures are useful for extending the seasons of cabbage, Brussels sprouts, broccoli, kale, lettuce, spinach, and oriental brassicas. In spring, indoor starts of peas, onions, parsley, radishes, broccoli, cabbage, lettuce, spinach, or kohlrabi can be planted two to three weeks earlier than normal by using the structures.

Raised bed covers are also useful for accelerating the early growth of late-spring crops like tomatoes and peppers or for protecting suscepti-

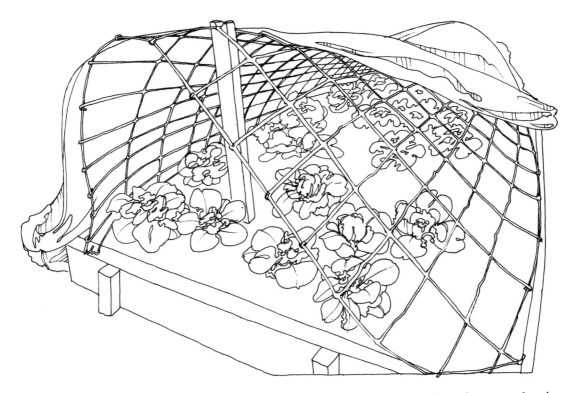

Ground-Hugging Cover: A piece of arched cattle fencing covers the bed. Two pieces of wood, one at each end, support the wire. The plastic is anchored securely on one side, while the other side is held down with bricks or stones. You gain access by moving the bricks and lifting the free side of the cover. Over the course of the season, lifting and lowering may cause the arch to flatten slightly on one side, as shown here.

ble crops like the brassicas and the cucurbits from insect attack. A cheesecloth, fabric, or Reemay cover can be substituted for the plastic to protect against insects in warm weather. However, to assure pollination, plants should always be uncovered before they blossom.

Fabric Covers for Rows and Raised Beds

The introduction of Reemay may have greatly simplified the manufacture and use of row and bed covers. So far, the product is so new that few experiments have been conducted with its use on plants, but it has already proved to be more durable and easier to handle than any variety of polyethylene sheet. It may also have better insulating qualities. Reemay, a DuPont product, is a spun-bonded polyester of very light weight (0.6 ounces to the square yard). Unlike stretched and anchored down polyethylene, which requires a framework structure, it will not weigh down plants if laid directly over them. The thrust of growing plants will lift the material as the plants grow larger. In laying Reemay over rows, however, always leave sufficient slack for the growing vegetables underneath it.

According to researchers at the University of New Hampshire, Reemay has been found to hold enough heat to advance early season growth,

With the Master Gardeners

ONE GARDENER'S SURVEY OF SEASON EXTENDERS

Pernell Gerver is an inquisitive gardener. Not content to rely only on the old standbys, plastic jugs and plastic-swathed tomato cages, he set out to compare the performances of a variety of plant protectors, commercial and homemade. These cloches and row covers ranged from the most expensive types to the least expensive. He set up these informal trials in his award-winning garden on the basis of side-by-side testing with the same conditions.

This 1984 Organic Gardener of the Year gardens in Massachusetts in the Connecticut River Valley. In this climate he found that the tested devices did add considerably to his growing season.

"Our average frost date is Memorial Day, around June 1, so the season has only 120 days," Gerver reports. He can get a two-month head start with early crops in spring and plant warmer-season plants a month earlier than normal by using the best of the season extenders. In the fall, his main emphasis is on trying to get the rest of the harvest in before freeze. On the average, Gerver gets three more weeks of growth after the first frost, which arrives around October 1.

Gerver uses plastic covers over tomato cages to protect the fruit in autumn. If he had a special tomato variety that he wanted to mature very early, however, it is the English glass cloches he's been testing over the last five years that he would choose for the job. Those "probably worked the best of them all," he says. The disadvantage is cost, of course, because of all the glass and the clips.

Recently, Gerver tested both tent and barn cloches placed side by side down the row with a piece of glass capping them off at either end. For ventilation, he removed the tent cloches on sunny days. The more expensive and more spacious barn cloches that he used on tomatoes are held together by a wire, and the roofs have vents. Although he's pleased with the performance of the barn cloche, he regrets to say that this type is "hard to find and expensive."

Gerver's gardening trials also included the circular plastic device made of connected individual tubes of water that provide thermal heat storage. A representative of the company that makes these devices told Gerver that tomato plants could be set out under them two months earlier than normal. "I tried it, and it didn't work," Gerver reports.

Among the larger devices he used were long row covers made of slitted plastic over a wire frame. "I put lettuce under that a little early, and the plastic wouldn't protect it as well as the glass," he says. For comparison, he also tested a setup devised by James Crockett, corrugated fiberglass held together in a quonset shape, like a half-circle, with galvanized wire hoops around the top and a connecting piece underneath. Gerver likes the portable characteristic of this simple tunnel, as well as its comparative low cost and the greater amount of growing space it gives. The commercial tent with the slitted plastic sides, he reports, is, in contrast, hard to move. Fiberglass also outlasts slitted plastic.

"And then," he adds as an afterthought, "there is always the good old standby, the hot cap. I use those, too." Gerver prefers to make his own hot caps out of waxed craft paper. That way, he can make them at least 6 or 8 inches higher for more space and for more ease in covering mature plants. Also, he admits, "I use a lot of milk jugs, too, which are the least expensive."

Home-Style Hot Caps: Start by cutting a circle with at least a 12-inch diameter from waxed craft paper. Make a single cut to the center (this cut will be the height of the cone). Curl the circle into a cone and tack or glue in place. Cut slits along the bottom and fold them out. For ventilation, make slits in the side of the cone. Set the cap over the seedling and anchor by covering flaps with soil.

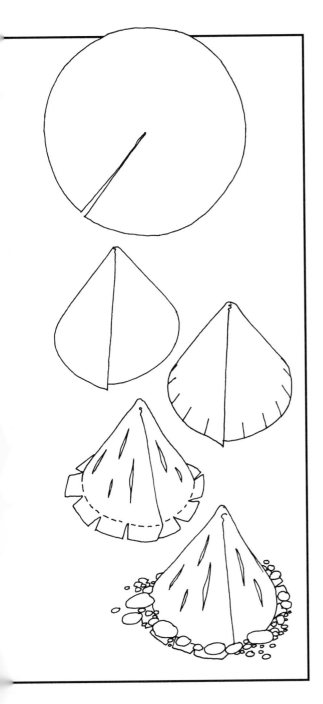

yet it is porous enough to be self-ventilating and to permit the passage of water. It transmits 75 to 80 percent of available light, a percentage higher than that transmitted by wire-reinforced plastic, but lower than that for slitted single polyethylene or double polyethylene. Reemay will shelter seedlings in temperatures down to 28°F, but it is too porous to be depended on for winter frost protection in cold climates. It has been found to confer only 3 degrees of frost protection in spring and 7 degrees in fall. It will, however, offer excellent protection against egg-laying insects.

Reemay can be laid loose over raised beds, but because of its light weight, it should be anchored firmly at all edges to keep it from blowing away. Researchers recommend burying edges under 3 inches of soil. Providing an anchor of stones, bricks, or stakes, or nailing or stapling edges to wooden frames on raised beds would be alternatives to burying. The material biodegrades after three months in bright sunlight, but if used in spring only, it will last two seasons. It adapts to use with bent wire supports, arched pipes, or wooden ridge poles, but must be anchored well over them. Reemay is available at many garden centers in sheets sized for raised bed use. (See the Garden Products section of the Directory of Resources for mail-order suppliers of Reemay.)

The Search Continues

The many sizes, types, and materials of protective devices may seem a bit overwhelming and may raise your hopes. Remember, though, that our quest is not complete. We have looked for, but not yet found, a single device that is guaranteed to take vegetables through a New England winter — or a Michigan, Montana, or Pennsylvania one for that matter — or one that will produce harvests for more than a few weeks out of season. For all the other minor miracles we've asked of protective devices, we have found an abundance of help — some of it better, some of it less good. In the next chapter we will continue with our quest.

8 *Extending the Season with Growing Frames*

Individual glass and plastic cloches, bottomless glass or plastic jugs, growing tunnels, sheet plastic bed covers—we've seen them all, and they all do something to protect plants and to stimulate their early growth. In some parts of the country and for some purposes—such as starting seedlings earlier than normal, or keeping plants frost-free a little longer into fall—these devices may be all you require. What they won't do, however, is maintain a contained microclimate warm enough to protect plants from hard freezes at night or see them very far into winter in northern climates.

What we need, then, is either more heat, or a better way of holding onto the heat we can expect to gather on sunny days. We have already discovered that the larger of the devices we have examined are very efficient at gathering solar heat. Their problem is that they also lose it quickly.

The Manure Hotbed

Let's return again to the experts—the French maket gardeners of earlier centuries. To them, an early vegetable meant more than something to brag about. It could guarantee a doubling of income at the Paris market, where the novelty of vegetables out of season was highly prized by the wealthy epicure.

As a heat source, French gardeners used the high temperatures generated when horse manure ferments in compost. Fresh horse manure reaches 140 to 160°F in the early stages of its decomposition, a temperature much too hot for plants. The French gardeners, however, buried the manure in pits under their vegetable beds, and by carefully mixing fresh manure with dried manure saved from an earlier season and with urine-soaked straw from their stables, they could calculate the amount of heat that would be generated. In winter, according to some ancient sources, a one-to-one mix of dry and fresh manure was used, while in fall or spring the mix approached two dry to one fresh. The task of mixing the manures and straw and forming the mass in the pits below the beds was one of great skill. If it could be called an art, it is now, unfortunately, one of the lost arts.

Of course, the French climate in the market area north of Paris is a milder, more moist one than the climates we enjoy in most parts of North America. That fact may account for some of the difficulty North American gardeners have experienced in trying to replicate the French manure hotbed.

In experiments carried on at the Rodale Research Center in Maxatawny, Pennsylvania, and elsewhere, manure hotbeds accelerated growth to some extent and produced crops earlier than normal in spring when rising air temperatures could be counted on to take over as the heat of fermentation began to dissipate. In fall, manure hotbeds were found to be less successful. Heat from the manure faded before most crops could be brought to maturity. When manure was placed in insulated pits under growing beds to provide

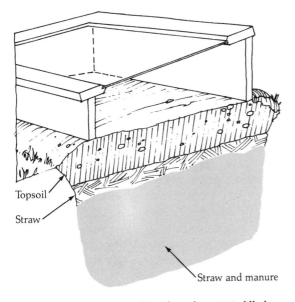

Topsoil

Straw

Straw and manure

Traditional Manure Pit: The 2-foot-deep pit is filled with a blend of straw and fresh manure to within 6 inches of the surface. Next, a layer of straw and one of topsoil are added, and a glass frame is set over the pit.

bottom heat, it could not, obviously, be replenished without disturbing growing plants.

A manure pit is generally 2 feet or more deep and slightly larger than the bed that sits on top of it. Straw is mixed with fresh manure that has heated up to 140°F and then dropped down to 100°F. The mixture is packed into the pit and trampled down 6 inches below the surrounding soil surface. It is watered lightly and then sometimes covered with 2 inches of straw. Six inches of loose topsoil go on top of the manure, or the manure and straw, and make up the growing medium of the bed. Manure hotbeds are always covered with glass frames in winter. After the beds are prepared and the frames are in place, the soil temperature is allowed to rise to 60 to 70°F and seedlings are transplanted into the soil.

An experimental frame used at the Rodale Research Center in 1978 sought to solve the problem of replenishing manure for renewed heat for fall growing. The design incorporated well-insulated movable bins to hold the composting manure above ground. Under 1-foot-deep elevated growing frames, a pair of 2-foot-deep bins of manure were positioned. As temperatures fell, fresh manure was added to the manure bins. Night shutters were used to hold heat inside the frames in cold weather.

Although soon after the manure was added in late November air temperature within the growing frame rose to a peak of 65°F, over a period of time heat diminished radically. By late January, air temperature sank to 40°F in spite of the renewal of the manure. Other structures being tested by the Rodale Research Center at the same time far outperformed the manure-bin frame in terms of vegetable production. One reason for this may have been, however, that the high temperatures generated by the manure released toxic fumes from the newly applied caulk and paint in the frame, which poisoned the plants.

Nick Woodin, a New York State market gardener, feels more optimistic about his own

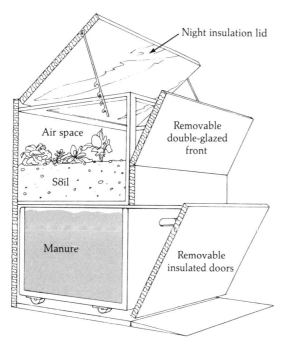

Rodale Manure Frame Design: This frame was designed to make replenishing the heat-providing manure easier. These bins are insulated and movable.

1984 experiment with manure power. Using calf manure, which is less hot than horse manure, he piled a truckload of strawy manure on top of the ground to a depth of 12 to 14 inches and set his 14½ by 9 by 2-foot cold frame over it, adding a thin layer of soil. He banked the outside of the manure pile and later bermed the cold frame with sawdust. After ten days the manure 6 inches into the pile was about 60°F in the early morning and 70°F later in the day. These temperatures remained steady for several weeks, enabling Woodin to harvest peppers from his frame in November in spite of a killing frost in early September.

Woodin attributes his success to constant attention. His hotbed had to be opened for ventilation on sunny days even when the weather was relatively cold. He also shaded it when days were bright and closed it every night. On very cold nights, Woodin gave his frame extra protection by covering the glass with insulating material, a protection comparable to that afforded by the night shutter the Rodale researchers used.

The most practical limitation to the use of manure hotbeds is their "fuel." In many localities, manure is hard to find and, once found, even more difficult to haul unless you own a pickup truck. As more gardeners experiment with manure hotbeds in their attempts to prolong the gardening season, however, perhaps the lost art of the French will be recovered.

Cable-Warmed Beds

The high-tech alternative to the manure hotbed is something a bit sweeter smelling, but, like many modern amenities, it is also costlier. Any simple cold frame or covered raised bed can be made into a hotbed by adding an electric heating cable, assuming a source of electricity is available. Some hardware and garden supply stores carry heating cables. Often, however, it is necessary to look more than one place to find a cable of correct length for a cold frame bed. (See the Garden Products section of the Directory of Resources for the names of companies that carry cables.)

With the addition of a thermostat, the cable can be made to produce the correct amount of heat to maintain ideal growing conditions even in winter weather. Adding insulation to your frame and employing a thermal barrier such as a night shutter will reduce the amount of electricity that is required. Deeply rooted vegetables will not have enough room to grow well in 4 to 8 inches of soil, and it is doubtful that by growing shallow-rooted salad greens alone you could defray the considerable cost of the electricity you would have to use in an average northern winter.

The most economical way to use a cable hotbed is to limit its use to growing the early seedlings that will later be transferred to the first raised beds of spring. A thermostat-controlled cable will give them the correct environment to speed their growth by as much as a month. A good, early supply of cable-accelerated seedlings will lead to heavier yields for some vegetables and to earlier yields for all crops. Earlier yields mean more rapid turnover in the raised beds, which in

turn will make the season more productive.

After the weather has warmed and the cable is no longer necessary, you can continue to grow seedlings in the cable frame by simply disconnecting the heat source.

Cold Frames

From hotbeds we move to cold frames, structures that depend on the heat of the sun for their warmth. These season extenders are workhorses in many gardens, in use every season of the year. There are almost as many variations on cold frame design as there are gardeners, but they all fall into one of two categories—portable or permanent frames.

Portable versus Permanent Frames

Portability is an important quality for frames to be used directly in the raised bed garden. Portable frames can be shifted from bed to bed as the season progresses. Crop rotation can be practiced so that the soil used will always be balanced, full of nutrients and free of disease organisms. A portable frame will pay for itself in higher yields most quickly if it is used in sequence, first over the earliest seedlings of spring, then over later ones, and finally over warm-season crops and those needing protection from early frost into winter. In colder climates no portable frame will promote growth all winter. At best, it will "hold" plants for later harvest or renewed growth in spring.

In order to be easy to lift and maneuver, portable frames should be less heavily insulated than the more soundly built fixed-position cold frames. The angle of the glass must not be so steep that the frame cannot be carried easily.

A permanent position for a frame has the advantage of allowing for heavier, better insulated construction. In winter in northern latitudes, sunlight reaches the earth during most parts of

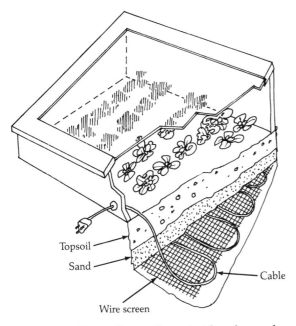

Topsoil

Sand

Cable

Wire screen

Heating Cable Installation: Dig a pit 1 foot deep and remove the soil. Spread the cable in even loops that don't overlap and cover with a piece of wire screen. Add a 2 to 3-inch layer of sand, then fill the pit with 4 to 8 inches of compost-enriched topsoil. Set your cold frame over the prepared pit.

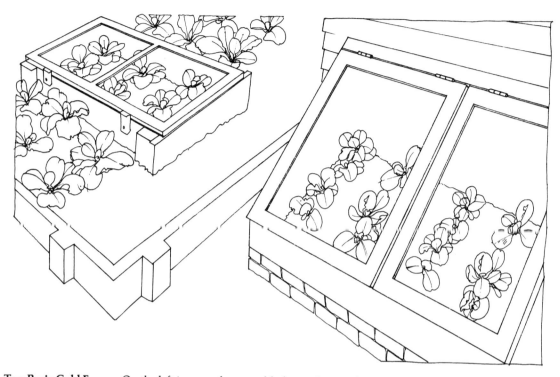

Two Basic Cold Frames: On the left is a wooden portable frame that can be relocated among garden beds as the need arises. The other frame is a permanent one with a masonry base set against the side of a building. If a cold frame is to be used for several years, the masonry base will justify its added expense and labor. Wooden bases are easy to move but offer less insulation, hold heat less readily, and require more maintenance.

the day from low on the southern horizon. If full use is to be made of the sun's rays, the south side of the frame should be low enough to throw very little shadow on the plants inside, and the glazed surface should rise at a slope as high as 45 degrees. Fixed frames accommodate best to steep-angled design. They can be positioned close to a house or other structure for protection from north wind and for additional support on their north side. By facing due south with their steep, glazed side, they catch almost every bit of available sun.

Having a frame very near the house in winter, when most activity has withdrawn from the raised bed garden, assures that daily monitoring and

harvesting can be done without too much discomfort or the expenditure of much time.

In areas with heavy snow, an accumulation of snow or sleet on a portable frame in an exposed place may weigh down the glazing enough to crack, bend, or dislodge it, or to cause it to sag and emit cold air. Thin plastics are ruled out for winter growing in portable plastic frames because of their tendency to sag under snow. Heavy horticultural glass, especially when double glazing is used, will stand up to the weight of snow. In snow-prone areas, fixed frames near a house will be easier to brush free of snow than freestanding portable frames. Steep-angled glazing will also shed snow. House-protected fixed frames will require less year-to-year maintenance than the more exposed portable frames.

Portable Frame Designs

In making a portable frame, your first decision concerns the use you plan for it. The materials you find or can purchase inexpensively will play a large part in your decision, but you should also consider your climate, your latitude, and the seasons of the year when the new frame will be used most over raised beds.

Double Cold Frames In the heyday of the French market gardener, to look down over a field of vegetables was like flying over a huge spread of rooftops composed of hundreds of skylights.

Indeed, the portable glass-paned frames in use in the French fields were called "lights." The modern equivalent, still in use in parts of Europe to this day, is the double cold frame set over beds about 6½ feet wide. Each frame section has a central hinge joining two sashes. On the outside edge of the bed, each sash is set on a "foot," a length of board about 4½ inches high that is affixed roughly perpendicular to the sash. The foot keeps its end of the sash 4½ inches above ground level, while the hinged edge rests on 11-inch-tall blocks placed at intervals down the center of each bed. Beds can be of any length. The ends of the low, tentlike frames are blocked with wooden boards cut to fit the openings and held in place with stakes.

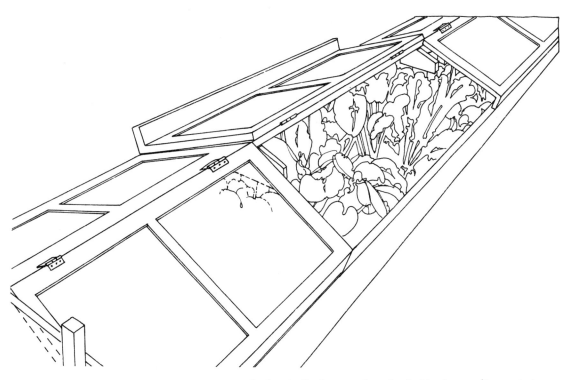

Double Glass Frame: This frame covers an entire bed and affords access from both sides for weeding, watering, and harvesting. T-shaped center supports for the glass frames are anchored in the soil.

EASY PLANS FOR A DOUBLE COLD FRAME

The cheapest and simplest way to construct double frames is to locate a supply of storm windows that are not in use. Ideally, these would measure 24 inches on all sides. Screw lengths of 2 by 4 lumber to one side of the windows and hinge them together in a pair with 3-inch strap hinges. Bevel the base of the sash 16 degrees on top so it will fit tightly. For the sash opener, a separate piece that you position over opposite storm windows to hold them open, use two 27⅝-inch pieces of 1 by 2 lumber and two 5-inch pieces. A dowel inserted into the sash opener fits into a 2½-inch slot routed into the sash base ½ inch deep.

If you cannot find 2-foot-square storm windows, you should be able to size your growing beds to fit the windows you do find. Any reasonably small matched pair of windows will do. Sometimes companies that specialize in installing triple-track aluminum storm windows will tell you how to obtain old wooden-framed storm windows that they have removed when they converted an installation.

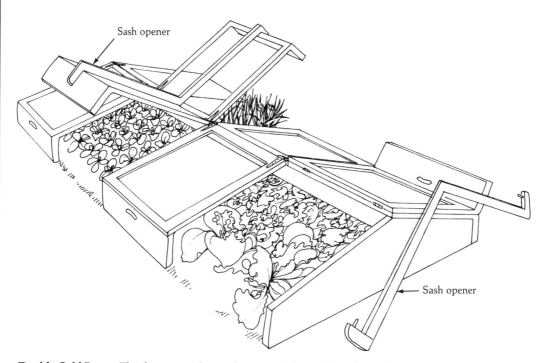

Sash opener

Sash opener

Double Cold Frame: This frame recycles used storm windows. Hinged together at the top, they're vented by a custom-made sash opener that looks like outstretched gull wings. To work in the frame, simply flip over one window to the other side.

It is easy to see how the double glass frame could be made to adapt to narrow raised beds. A 4½-inch foot, or riser, could be attached to each long side of a frame-contained raised bed. The central hinge would allow easy access to the beds. One side is folded back over the other so that one half of the bed is open when weeding, watering, or harvesting are in progress. The center support is a simple "T" made of wood and sunk into the soil. For ventilating on warm days, frames are propped open with blocks of wood or the end panels are removed. In strong winds the frames are better left closed to protect them from breakage. To make French-style double glass frames truly portable—easily lifted by one person—make them in two sections for covering a 9 by 4-foot bed.

Under double glass frames it is generally 40 to 50 degrees warmer than it is outside during the day and 25 to 30 degrees warmer at night, according to David Miskell, an American who worked with the modern counterparts of the original market gardeners while traveling in France in the late 1970s. Miskell is now trying to adapt the frame system to American gardens at his home in Rhode Island.

The French use woven straw mats to cover the glass at night during extreme cold. These mats keep the temperature inside the frame 6 degrees higher than in unprotected frames, which is enough to permit growing straight through the winter in the French climate. Michel LeClaire, the market gardener with whom Miskell worked most closely, claimed that his season was extended three full months by the use of double frames, and Miskell believes that at least a two-month extension is possible in the harsher climate of the United States. More frequent ventilation would also be necessary under the sunnier skies found in most parts of the country.

Double glass frames provide enough head room for all but very tall vegetables like corn. In France they are most often used for carrots, potatoes, cauliflower, green beans, peas, young tomato plants, and zucchini, all intercropped with lettuce. A French-style frame would be suited to spring and early fall use, or for use in the South and mild maritime areas.

Flat-Topped Frames A flat-topped frame will be adequate for your needs for early spring or fall growing. This frame is the easiest style to improvise from found materials. If your raised beds are already framed, you can extend them upward another few inches with additional boards or beams. If your beds are mounded, but not framed, you can enclose them with boards, beams, masonry blocks, cinder blocks, bricks, or even hay bales, or you can construct a simple pen of boards to set around your beds. Storm windows, sheets of flexible but rigid plastic, or corrugated fiberglass are then laid over the top. If you're using corrugated material, be sure that the bed enclosure is topped with wooden filler strips to match the undulations of the corrugated material.

Sloping Top Frames To allow for the drainage of rain and melted snow, you may find it wise to elevate one long edge of your improvised or constructed frame slightly above the other one and to slope the two side ends correspondingly so that the top will fit firmly. Do not extend the sides of framed beds higher than a foot above the mounded soil surface if you wish to continue growing into early winter. High sides will cast chilling shadows on your plants. Set the low side facing south if possible.

The farther north you live and the further into winter you plan to be growing, the more beneficial you will find a sloping glazing surface for your portable cold frame. When one side of it slopes to the south, it allows free passage of warmth-giving sun.

Tent-Style Frames A variation of the low barn-shaped French double frame is a more steeply sloping tent-shaped design. The glazing surface on this model is attached to a supporting wooden

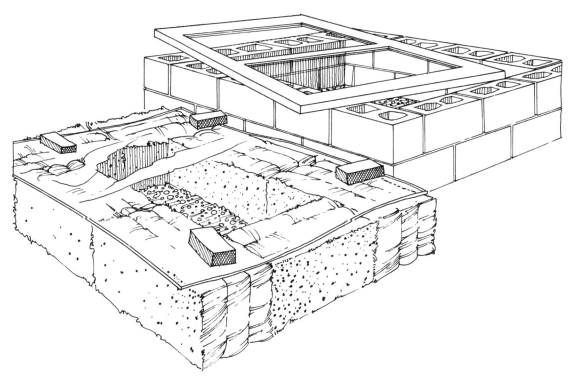

Flat-Topped Frames: These impromptu frames are easy to set up around garden beds. Cinder blocks form the foundation at top, and the storm window frame can be turned for venting. The lower bed is ringed with hay bales and a clear sheet of rigid plastic is held down by bricks.

ridge pole that spans the frame from side to side. (Construct a frame similar to the one used in the plastic shed bed cover discussed on page 239.) The ridge pole supports are sunk into the ground at either short end of the enclosing bed frame. Over this frame, sheets of acrylic, fiberglass, or corrugated fiberglass are nailed or screwed. Additional panels can be set in place to block the two short ends. Leave one end open for ventilation, but close up at night or during a spell of cold weather. The high-rising sides permit an abundance of sun to enter. It may be a little trickier reaching the plants in the center of the bed since the sides aren't hinged like they are on French frames.

Steep-sided tent-style frames are less portable than the other models we have discussed so far, but they will allow the growing of vegetables larger than those that will fit into flat or slightly sloping frames.

Single - Span Frame For in-garden growing in late fall and winter in the North, a portable frame of a single span with a solid north-facing back panel and a south-facing glazed slope of up to 40 degrees is best to use. This design is similar to the most common form of permanent cold frame. It is hinged on the high, solid back near the top corners and propped open for ventilation.

A PORTABLE, EASILY STORABLE COLD FRAME

Jack Ruttle, an editor of *Rodale's Organic Gardening* magazine, came up with an ingenious way to build a portable cold frame from a half sheet of ½-inch exterior plywood, a few screws, and two small, old wooden storm windows given him by a friend. He used ¾-inch scrap lumber for screwing blocks placed in the corners of the frame. More of the scrap was used for reinforcing rails along the top of the front and back pieces. These rails provide a sturdy support for the storm windows. Both the blocks and rails were attached permanently to the front and back pieces with screws and glue. The end pieces were attached to the front and back with a screw in each of the eight corners. The back of the frame is 18 inches high and the front is 6 inches high. Window size determined the width and the angle of the frame.

Ruttle assembles his frame early every spring to house the large quantities of seedlings he starts indoors. To work in the frame he simply removes a window, and to vent he turns a window slightly to create an opening. When the last of the spring seedlings has moved to the garden, he unscrews the frame and stacks the pieces in a neat pile until next season.

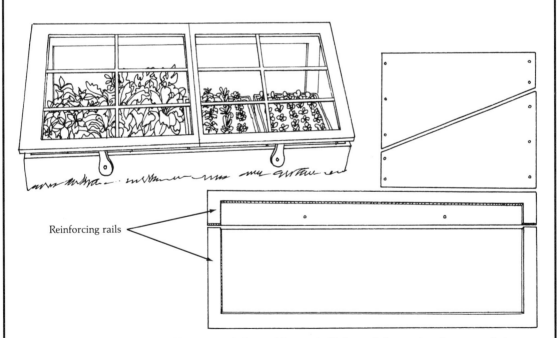

Reinforcing rails

Easy Portable Frame: This cold frame was fashioned from a half sheet of plywood and two recycled wooden storm windows. It's easy to assemble, so you can set it up and take it down as your seasonal gardening needs require.

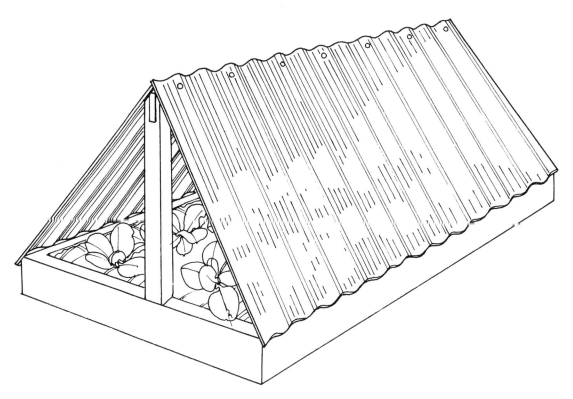

Tent-Style Frame: This bed with wooden sides is covered by a tent made of corrugated fiberglass. The steep sides provide more room for tall vegetables. Use additional panels to close the ends on cold nights.

Single-span frames should always be set over beds that run east to west to attract the maximum amount of light when the sun is low in the southern sky. The most successful of the single-span portable frames are built from rot-resistant or treated wood. If lightness is essential for portability, use sheets of ½-inch exterior grade plywood and, in severe climates, expect to replace the frame every few years. If protection is more important than portability, use heavier wood and, if possible, add a layer of inside insulation. The wood of old discarded house or garage doors is excellent for cold frames.

Lean-To Frame A variation on the single-span frame is the lean-to. The lean-to rises higher over a bed than the conventional single-span frame and

has an even steeper angle, up to 45 degrees. The riser at the front edge of the frame is very low. Because of its high angle, the lean-to frame catches even more winter light than the ordinary single-span frame.

Commercial Frames A visit to a garden supply store or a browse through the pages of a garden catalog will reveal that there are a number of commercial cold frames available, of all levels of sophistication. One model, called the Grow Frame, has recently come on the market from England. The dimensions are 2½ feet wide by 5 feet long, and the shape is like a long, low barn cloche with the peak 11 inches high. The cover is made of PVC clear plastic that will last for five years, and the frame is of galvanized steel. This cold frame

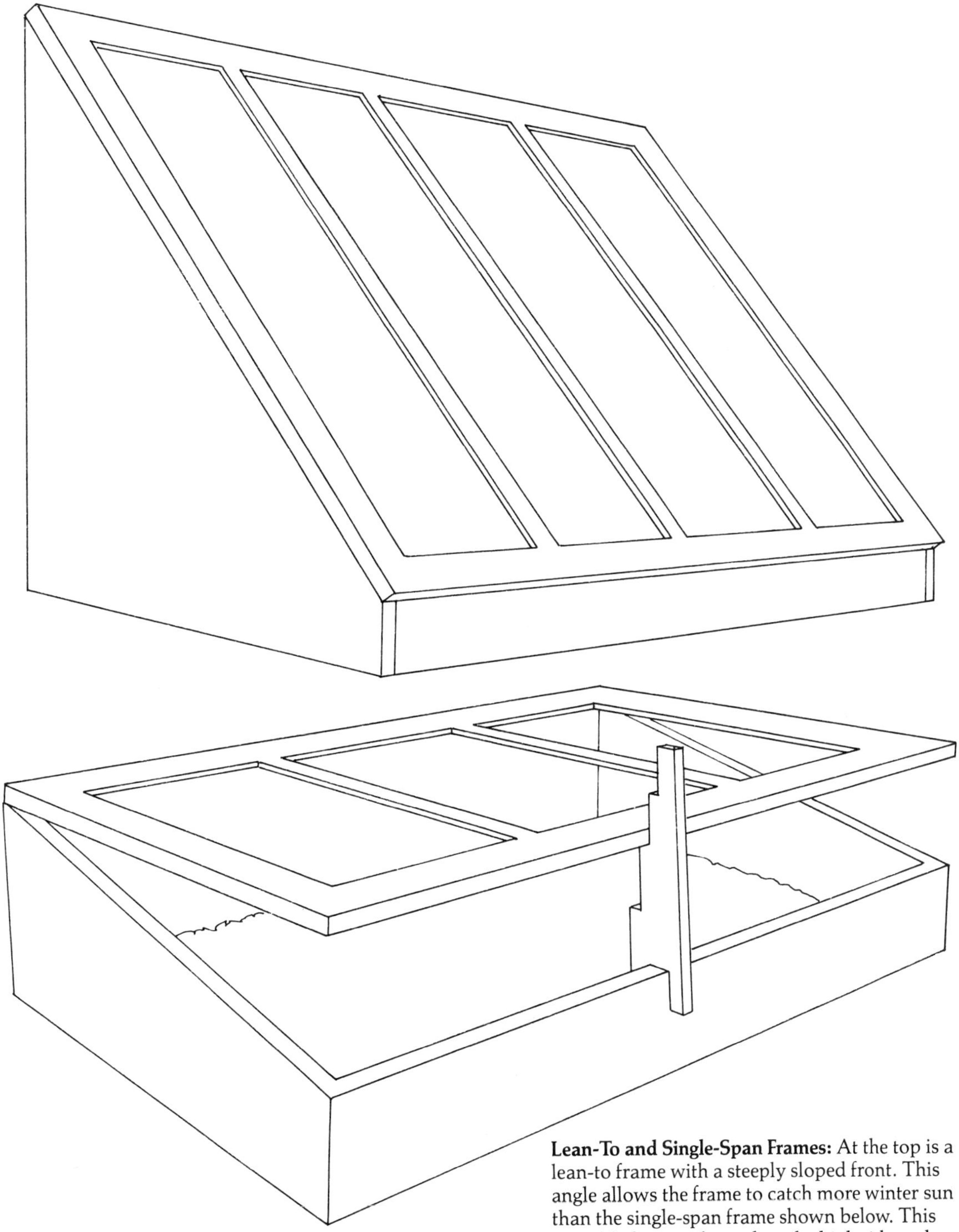

Lean-To and Single-Span Frames: At the top is a lean-to frame with a steeply sloped front. This angle allows the frame to catch more winter sun than the single-span frame shown below. This portable frame is hinged on the high side and propped open for ventilation.

is self-ventilating through special flaps in the roof that also permit the entry of rain water. The assembly is relatively inexpensive.

One popular model, the Ventomatic, has an arched top and comes with a solar-powered automatic ventilator. The sides are also glazed acrylic, but they are only 15 inches high, so the frame will not accommodate the largest plants you may wish to grow. The dimensions of the frame are 36 to 48 inches. Larger commercial frames may cost more than 100 dollars, a price tag sure to sound a bit steep to most gardeners.

Some gardeners may find that commercial frames are more suitable for permanent use than for portable use. When they are to be placed in a separate location there is no need for them to match the dimensions of existing beds.

For a listing of commercially available cold frames and their suppliers, see the Garden Products section of the Directory of Resources.

General Design Pointers Rigid or semirigid plastic may be substituted for glass in window-sash cold frames. Plastic has two advantages over glass. It is less fragile and lighter, allowing greater ease of lifting and permitting the use of larger expanses of unbroken transparent material. The fewer the mullions between panes, the less sunlight is blocked. Its disadvantages are those of any plastic cover—lack of durability, susceptibility to abrasion, some light reduction, and failure to hold in heat during cold nights.

Any cold frame will allow plants to grow longer into winter if the sides and back are insulated, the construction is as airtight as possible, and additional insulation is provided inside or on top of the glazing surface for extra protection during cold nights. The combination of a glass-paned sash for the outer top protection and a layer of sheet plastic on the inside will increase insulation and thereby take plants further into winter. If these measures are not feasible, arrange to cover your whole frame, but especially the glazing surface, with insulating material on very

cold nights. Possible insulators are hay bales, old blankets and quilts, or bags of leaves.

To hold daytime heat into night inside a portable frame, many growers add thermal mass in the form of masonry blocks or jugs of water set against the high north wall. These serve as thermal collectors that release heat slowly during the night. If the solid, north wall of a single-span is painted white or covered with reflecting material, it will bounce light down to the plants growing in the frame.

If you wish your single-span or double-span frame to be removed entirely for efficient storage when not in use, use carriage bolts, pin hinges, and angle-iron side braces in joining the sections and adding the glazing surface.

The Poisson Solar Pod Probably the most efficient of all the newer designs for covering growing beds is Leandre Poisson's Solar Pod, an insulated growing dome that protects vegetables in temperatures down to 10°F when used with a solar collector. The solar collector consists of a 55-gallon drum of water. The pod is designed to cover a 4 by 8-foot permanent bed. Pods are constructed of plywood 2 by 4s and clear, rigid fiberglass that is bent over the wooden frame and set into grooves on the side rails. The cost of a pod is relatively high, but Poisson claims that the investment can be recovered by the savings realized from the vegetables grown over a two-year period. A Solar Pod is expected to last ten years.

The base of the Solar Pod is insulated with a 1 or 2-inch-thick polystyrene board that extends below ground to a depth of 18 to 24 inches. The bottom insulation of the Solar Pod means that this frame is not completely portable. Nor is it designed for a raised bed, since it depends for some of its insulation on a growing surface slightly below ground. The superstructure, however, is designed to be disassembled and removed when not in use, giving a borderline portability to the model. What remains behind is an insulated pit and a 4 by 8-foot fixed frame.

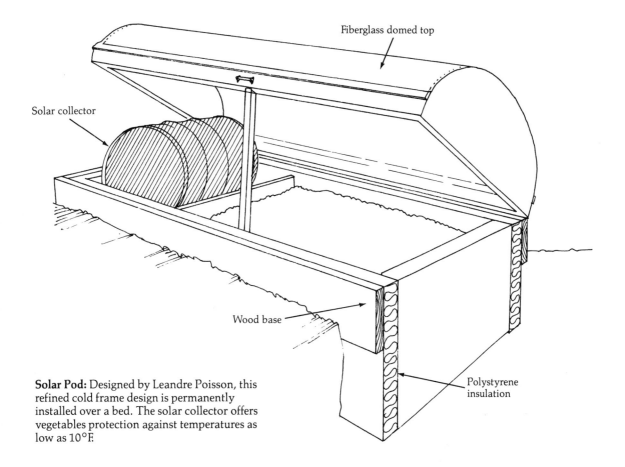

Fiberglass domed top

Solar collector

Wood base

Polystyrene
insulation

Solar Pod: Designed by Leandre Poisson, this
refined cold frame design is permanently
installed over a bed. The solar collector offers
vegetables protection against temperatures as
low as 10°F.

The most efficient use of the Poisson Solar
Pod in a raised bed garden is over one or two
specially prepared beds delegated to winter growing and use in earliest spring. Having two pods
allows for easy rotation. Although dug and prepared with enriched soil in the same manner,
these beds will not be raised like the other beds,
but will consist of dirt filled insulated pits at
least 1 foot deep. When set in place, the top of
the frame will protrude about an inch above
ground level.

One criticism of the pod is that the thermal
storage unit or water drum occupies a large portion of the space meant for growing plants. While
deemed important by its developer, the storage
unit could be eliminated, but only at the loss of
some protection. In New Hampshire, it is claimed,
a properly insulated Solar Pod with a thermal
collector can add as much as six months to the
growing season. If using the pod over a permanent bed, a foundation of concrete blocks might
prove a viable alternative to the deeply sunk
insulated sides.

The domed top and the abundant glazing
area of the pod have the advantage of being able
to catch sunlight from many angles. The design

has been called "elegant," and indeed the curving sides are pleasing to look at and add to the efficiency of the device. The efficient use of sunlight means, however, that the pod heats up rapidly and needs to be vented daily. The design has another drawback. In extremely cold weather it is difficult to further insulate the top surface with mats or to use an interior night curtain because of the curved surface. Kits for the Solar Pod are available through Solar Survival (see the Directory of Resources for the address).

The Permanent Frame

One of the most important aspects of the permanent frame is its site. Whenever possible, the permanent frame should be placed in an unshaded area on the south-facing side of a house or other structure, where it will receive full sun from midmorning to midafternoon during the winter months. The wall of the building just to the north of it will collect heat and will bounce both light and heat rays toward the plants in the frame. The building will also protect the frame from winds and driving rains and snows. The walls of most houses and some garages and sheds also provide a nearby water source to make caring for plants easier.

The ground on which a permanent cold frame rests should be at least as well drained as a raised bed garden. Add soil to the frame with the same care you prepare it for the raised bed. Double digging will probably be unnecessary unless the soil near the house foundation is unusually poor and compacted, but the soil under the frame bed should be loosened to a depth of 18 inches, and compost should be added to enrich the bed. Remove all large rocks. If drainage is poor, add a layer of coarse gravel to the bottom of the hole before soil is returned to it.

A house wall may be fitted with a hook or a hook eye to hold the hinged glazed surface open in an upright position. If this strategy is not feasible, be sure to allow enough space between the back of the frame and the wall to accommo-

date the thickness of the top and to allow for a secure tilt when it is fully raised and leaned backward against the house.

Permanent frames will not have to be moved, so they can be built of heavier materials than portable frames. If possible, use 1-inch lumber. Make sure the wood is decay-resistant or has been pressure treated or treated with nontoxic preservatives. (These are discussed in chapter 1 under Building Sides for Beds.) There is much moisture in a cold frame, and maintenance can become a problem if you don't take preventive measures.

Several factors help you to determine the height of a permanent cold frame at its highest point. It should have an attractive appearance next to the house and not block low windows. It must also be tall enough in the back to accommodate the highest plants you plan to grow. The back of the frame should be no less than 6 inches higher than the front of the frame. The front should be as low as possible to minimize shading The higher the angle of glazing up to around 45 degrees, the more sun will come into your frame during the winter months. If you plan to use the frame for winter growing, build it with the highest back and the steepest angle (up to 45 degrees) that your site will allow. Assuming that the frame will project from the house wall between 3 and 4 feet, the back of the frame can be as high as the frame projects.

If using a masonry, brick, or cinder block foundation, either bolt a 2 by 4 piece of lumber to the masonry, or elevate the masonry 4 to 6 inches above ground and attach a wooden ledge for the glazed surface to rest on. Poured foundations should extend down below the frost line to prevent damage from heaving when the surrounding soil freezes and thaws.

For ventilation a propping stick or a propping block should be used to hold the raised lid in a fixed and stable position. There are several successful systems of propping. One features stepped blocks that rest on the forward edge of the bed.

Permanent Cold Frame: Handles and hinges make this frame easy to open for venting and working in the frame.

Another relies on sturdy notched propping sticks that sit on the ground outside the frame and are attached to the lid and pivot outward. For ease in harvesting, the stick or block should allow the frame to be opened at least 18 inches.

Berming, or piling soil around the frame for solar mass and insulation, will increase a permanent frame's interior heat in winter, but it may still be a poor idea. Unless the frame is quite sturdy and in prime condition, the weight of the berming and the moisture the berming holds will decrease the life of the frame.

Construction Pointers The most sensible size for a frame will be the dimensions of the glazing surface you already have available or can find easily. The larger the interior space, the more stable the interior temperature will be. Standard window sashes will do, up to 3 by 6 feet. Double-glazed glass frames over 6 feet long are too heavy for many gardeners to lift and hold by themselves. If greater length is desired, use two independently hinged sashes. Glass windows that are not divided

into smaller panes are subject to breakage in winds and should be avoided for the sake of safety. A frame made to the size of a 3 by 6-foot sash will accommodate enough winter vegetables for an average family.

The side pieces of the permanent frame should be a little shorter than the width of the top, front to back, because the top will slope toward the front. Generally, the side panels are nearly triangular in shape, resembling half of a steep-roofed barn. With care, they can both be cut from one square of heavy plywood. Window sash handles are useful for opening the frame.

Permanent cold frames with semirigid plastic or fiberglass tops need not be limited in size to standard window frame dimensions, but they will be awkward to use if made much more than 3 feet from back to front. The sides will shade the frame too much if they are much less than 4 feet long.

Many plastics are suitable for glazing cold frames. With lighter plastics, provide double glazing by attaching one sheet to the inside of the

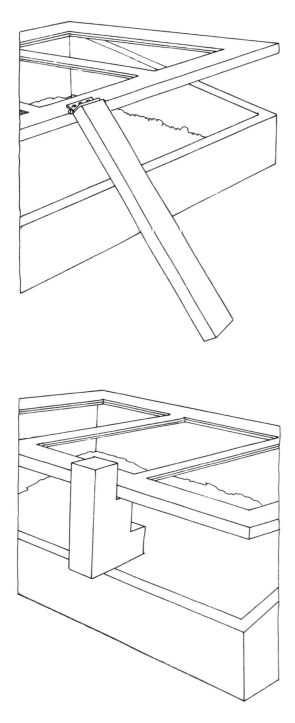

frame cover and a second sheet to the outside. Caulk thoroughly or tape with white vinyl batten tape, available at greenhouse suppliers, to prevent condensation from fogging the plastic between layers. Even when you have used glazing or a window sash, a sheet of 4 or 6-mil plastic film or bubble plastic can be used as a second, inside layer to provide an insulating space.

A lightweight top covering developed at Michigan State University consists of a chicken wire pillow covered with plastic film and tied firmly over the cold frame. Plastic film, it should be noted, provides less insulation than heavier plastic or glass. Rigid or semirigid plastics will generally be the most satisfactory coverings for fixed cold frames. Among these are double-walled polycarbonate, composite Flexigard film, and the flexible acrylics.

All glazing surfaces and all joints—anywhere that air might leak in—should be well caulked with waterproof caulking compound. Anchor weather stripping at the outer edges of all glazing surfaces to make the frame more airtight. The lid should fit firmly and the hinged back edge should show very little light between the hinges. Insulation, in the form of Styrofoam sheets with aluminum backing or a similar material, can be added to all interior walls of a permanent cold frame and laid against masonry foundations to make the frame hold heat better. You might also want to add thermal mass in the form of water-filled jugs or cinder blocks set in the rear of the frame.

Local Cooperative Extension Services often make plans for cold frames available to gardeners. Dalen Products, maker of an automatic ventilator, also offers free plans. (For its address, see the Directory of Resources.)

Propping Devices: The frame on the top has a hinged propping stick that rests on the ground and folds back against the frame when not in use. On the bottom is a stepped block that rests on the forward edge of the bed.

Four Seasons of Cold Frame Growing

However low or high-tech your commercial or homemade frame may be, however inexpensive or costly, you will want it to pay for its keep and them some. If you use it properly and efficiently, the frame should result in healthier, faster growth for plants, and, by allowing for early starts and late finishes, it should greatly increase your total harvest of vegetables.

At each season of the year, a cold frame has its uses. You will have to estimate or learn from experience how much protection your particular frame can be depended upon to afford. Mount a thermometer inside and check the temperature frequently under various weather conditions. If you find your model is not insulated well enough to be used for growing vegetables through winter in your climate, you will find no trouble in making alternative use of it. Store your pulled onions there, for example, or overwinter hardier perennial or biennial crops like dill or leeks in your frame. Semihardy herbs can be dug from your garden and guarded in a cold frame over winter before replanting. Or, instead of moving the plants, you can move a portable cold frame over a section of bed containing the plants.

Perhaps the most popular use of an insulated or uninsulated cold frame is for hardening seedlings started for early spring and destined for growing beds. Move the seedlings from indoors to the frames a week or two before they will go to the beds. This will give you more room in the house for growing more seedlings for later planting, and it will assure satisfactory transplanting with less danger of shock.

With experience, you'll learn how much earlier than normal you can plant fast-maturing, cool-weather vegetables that will give your season an early start and grow to maturity in the cold frame. Begin by using transplanted seedlings of lettuce, beets, carrots, parsley, onions, and spinach and direct-seeded radishes, dwarf peas, and onion sets. Plant dwarf peas only if the back part of your frame is tall enough for them.

In colder regions, an uninsulated portable or permanent frame will add three to five weeks to the spring season, while in warmer areas cold-loving vegetables of moderate to low light requirement can be grown all year. Strawberries can be made to bloom and bear up to a month earlier if grown in a cold frame. Insulated or well-protected cold frames are also good places to germinate seeds in early spring.

In hot summers cold frames, tops open, can be used to start heat-sensitive vegetables like lettuce and to raise them through large seedling stage. A portable frame can be moved to the shadiest, coolest part of the garden for seedling growing. A permanent frame, doomed to a sunny location, can be left fully open and shaded with a grid of laths over the frame. Some gardeners make substitute screening or lath tops with which to replace their hinged glazed tops in summer. In a shaded and well-watered cold frame, lettuce planted in July will sometimes hold into September without bolting.

For early winter use, select vegetables and varieties listed in seed catalogs as tolerant of shade and cold resistant. Plant or start these inside as early as mid-July or August, depending on your climate. Consult the fall seeding dates for eastern Pennsylvania given in the later section on the Solar Growing Frame, and adjust the seedling-starting time to your own locality. Uninsulated cold frames as far north as Pennsylvania will produce salad greens as late as Christmas and may hold oriental brassicas and cold-resistant spinach and mustards into January. Insulated frames often hold oriental greens, leeks, kale, mustard, spinach, winter lettuce, European cabbages, endive, arugula, carrots, and sometimes onions through winter for renewed growth in earliest spring. The more cold-resistant annual herbs, like dill, will overwinter in cold frames, and so will fall-seeded perennial flowers like primulas.

In midspring, heat-loving and long-growing,

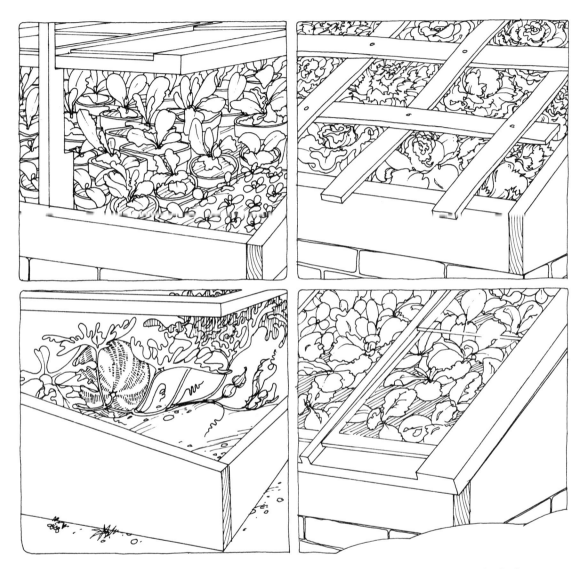

Four Seasons in the Cold Frame: Spring fills the frame with seedlings awaiting a transfer to garden beds. In summer, a lathe top offers shade for light and heat-sensitive crops like lettuce. In fall, a portable frame set over a slow-to-ripen melon can extend the season just long enough for a harvest. Winter finds the frame filled with cold-hardy crops like oriental brassicas, spinach, lettuce, and kale held over for early spring growth.

cool-loving vegetables will have their early growth accelerated if they're started in cold frames. Peppers, tomatoes, eggplants, late cabbages, and fall broccoli all respond well to cold frame starting with healthy growth and earlier yields. The cole crops will benefit more than the tomatoes do,

With the Master Gardeners

FRAME WORK

How do gardeners use their cold frames? Conversations with gardeners across the country revealed that they work their frames the hardest in the spring.

"Before we built our greenhouse," recounts Lynn Coody, a second-place winner along with Jon Davis in the 1984 Organic Gardener of the Year contest, "we grew thousands and thousands of starts in cold frames. Now we use the cold frames right on the beds. They're designed for that. You can just pull them off as the season progresses and move them to the next spot." Coody and Davis are using these portable frames to get a head start on the lettuce season. Their lettuce is ready for market harvest "a month to a month and a half ahead of anybody else's" in Cottage Grove, Oregon. Coody knows the time advantage for a fact, she explains, because her customers always stop buying the cold frame lettuce after four or five weeks, and that is a sure signal that their own garden lettuce is ready to pick. GRAND RAPIDS lettuce, grown in a portable cold frame, is one of the best selling crops they grow.

In Coody and Davis's experience, cold frames are more important for early spring planting than for season extending in fall. "We don't have any frost here until the middle to end of October and by then everything in the winter garden"—a garden of carefully selected hardy varieties—"is already established." However, they do use a cold frame for their fall bok choi and cabbage crops, which are started August 15 and put in the frames in September. To protect this crop from the heat,

Coody covers the frame with laths. She also uses inexpensive nylon netting to keep the cabbage maggot and cabbage butterfly worms out.

Kansan Chris Seitz agrees with Lynn Coody that the real payoff for a cold frame comes in early spring. She figures she advances the season by at least a month. Favorite spring cold frame crops for Seitz are all the coles and also eggplants, peppers, and annual flowers. "It really gets full by the time we take it down."

The best cold frame for use in the fall, Seitz has found, is a portable frame to set over fall beds when it gets to be mid-October. Lettuces (especially Bibb), radishes, and arugula are the best fall frame crops for Kansas, in Seitz's experience. Frames have kept these crops harvestable into the second week of January.

A 1983 finalist in the Organic Gardener of the Year contest, Hugh Matthews says his "absolute favorite" raised bed measures 4 by 8 feet and is framed with beams. It was a simple matter to build a plastic and wood cover for it and turn the whole bed into a cold frame, but the New Hampshire prizewinner has gone a step further. He built a second cover. "I made the other one out of screening," he reports, "so that I could plant my turnips and radishes in the spring and just leave the screening over them." On very cold nights, he uses his plastic and wood frame, but in warmer times he sets the screen in place to keep the flies from laying eggs that become root maggots, a major problem in his garden.

but an early start for tomatoes will at least lead to faster production if not to heavier yields. Cold frames can also be used to start long-season plants like melons that otherwise might fail to mature in the North. In growing warmth-loving crops, close the covers at night until all danger of frost is past, then leave them open, except during cold spells.

Growing in a Cold Frame

Gardeners new to cold frame growing often forget that they are working with a more artificial and controlled environment than they're accustomed to with raised beds and outdoor soil. Cultural practices in a cold frame differ from normal outdoor practices because under glass plants respond differently, and sometimes more strongly,

Spring Cold Frame Crops: Fast maturing, cold-tolerant crops can be spurred on to an early start (and early harvest) in a cold frame. In this frame dwarf peas, lettuce, beets, carrots, parsley, onions, spinach, and radishes are ready for picking.

to changes in light, temperature, moisture, and fertility. Rapid changes in temperature should be offset as much as possible by venting to prevent heat buildup and by adding insulation in the form of blankets, straw, or bagged leaves on top of the frame. Or close a built-in thermal curtain under the frame top when temperatures drop suddenly at night.

In the low light levels of winter, all growth will be slowed. To keep plants healthy, moisture and nutrient levels should be reduced commensurately. Although the soil of cold frames should be prepared with the same care with which you indulge your raised bed, it should not be over-fertile. Use compost to loosen the soil, but don't

add fresh manure. During periods of rapid growth, spring and fall, fertilize with a dilute solution of compost tea, manure tea or seaweed or fish emulsion. Don't feed more frequently than once every two weeks. In winter, reduce the feeding to once a month or less.

Every two or three years, remove and replace the soil in a permanent frame to prevent the buildup of disease organisms and the depletion of nutrients. If many cabbage family members have been grown in a frame over winter and into spring and disease is apparent among them, change the soil annually to prevent buildup of clubroot fungus. Likewise, if damping-off disease has been a problem, change the soil as soon as possible.

VARIETIES FOR WINTER COLD FRAME GROWING

Vegetable	Variety
Bunching onions	IWATSUKI (67).
Chinese cabbage (heading)	NAGAOKA #2 (4) is good for flavor; CHON'S ALL-SEASON (13) is slow to bolt.
Chinese cabbage (nonheading)	KURIHARA (4) and VITAMIN GREEN (72) rate well for flavor.
Chinese celery cabbage (pak choi)	TAI-SAI SEPPAKU (30) tastes good steamed.
Chinese kale	Any available variety will do well; suitable for large frames only.
Chinese mustard cabbage	OSAKA PURPLE (52) is good for color and taste.
Corn salad	Any available variety will do well.
Edible chrysanthemum	Most varieties do well.
Endive	Any variety is suitable.
Kale	PENTLAND BRIG (64), DWARF BLUE CURLED VATES.
Lettuce	WINTER DENSITY (1, 15, 55), GREEN ICE (9), WINTER MARVEL, (1, 15, 55), ARCTIC KING (15), ALPEN (4), ALL YEAR ROUND (1, 15, 55).
Mustard	GREEN WAVE (spectacular in growth), KYO MIZUNA (1, 12, 55), CHINESE BROAD LEAF, FLORIDA BROAD LEAF.
Parsley	Any variety is suitable.
Spinach	WINTER BLOOMSDALE, BENTON #2 (2), KING OF DENMARK (39, 47).
Swiss chard	Any variety will do well.

Water thoroughly and frequently when plants are young, especially in warm weather, but reduce the quantity and frequency of waterings during periods of slow growth in the autumn and winter. Check the moisture of the soil between 1 inch and ½ inch deep. It should remain moist, but not soggy, at all times. Water whenever plants look droopy, but if possible avoid watering on cold, cloudy days. Always water early in the day. Plants and surface soil must not remain wet at night, or fungal diseases may develop. Use water of approximately the same temperature as the soil within the frame, or around 65°F. This is especially important in winter, when cold water from the tap may shock plants grown under glass. Don't neglect watering after the soil outside the frame freezes solid. The inside soil will still be warm and may be dry. In smaller cold frames, precipitation will reach soil in the frame by capillary action, but even after a rain or snowfall, check the soil's moisture level.

Automatic watering with drip irrigation emitters or misters is possible in cold frames. A miniature drip system tailored to the size of a cold frame would be helpful if the frame is to be used principally for starting seedlings in spring and summer or for protecting and accelerating thirsty warmth-loving crops. A winter frame requires so little water and requires so much monitoring that an automatic system would not be justified for it.

The diseases and pests that may be troublesome in a cold frame are the same as those that plague its college-educated cousin, the Solar Growing Frame. (See Caring for Solar Growing Frame Crops later in the chapter.) In addition, in milder climates and during mild seasons, cabbage maggots, imported cabbage worms, and other root worms may find the cold frame a good place in which to prolong *their* lives beyond their normal season. When the frame is open, cover it with cheesecloth, netting, screening, or Reemay to keep egg-laying insects out. If caterpillars become an infestation use *Bacillus thuringiensis*. Don't continue to plant a crop or a variety that has been repeatedly infested with insects. Practice even more thorough garden hygiene in the cold frame than you do in the raised bed, discarding all damaged or sick-looking leaves and plants.

Generous spacing can help avoid disease problems. Spacing in cold frames should be 1½ times as wide as in a raised bed. For example, 9-inch spacing will work for lettuce, but 12 inches or more should be allowed for oriental mustards. This means that if you specialize in large plants for winter growing, you may soon be looking for a second cold frame. The moist conditions in cold frames are prime ones for plant diseases and the warmer the cold frame becomes, up to a point, the more the danger of some diseases. Air circulation is essential to disease control. If your frame is uninsulated and you are using it for full-sized plants only in spring and fall and have had no problem with disease, you can experiment with tightening up your spacing. In no case should you let the leaves of separate vegetables overlap or intermesh with each other. If vegetables are to be grown only to seedling stage, of course, spacings may be tighter. For guidance on spacings of late autumn crops, consult the recommendations made later under Caring for Solar Growing Frame Crops.

Like any growing area, a cold frame should be kept clear of weeds. When possible, encourage them to emerge before you set out your seedling plants and remove them then. For the best use of light, wipe condensation from the inside surface of the glazing daily when you vent the frame and clean the glazing, inside and out, with clear water when it becomes dusty or splashed with mud. When the wooden inside of the frame, especially the back, becomes muddy, wash it with clear water occasionally to restore reflection of light.

When preparing to plant a cold frame in fall or early spring, start seedlings indoors five to seven weeks before transplanting them. Choose the healthiest, stockiest seedlings for frame growing. Keep the cold frame closed to warm it for several days before you set your transplants in place, and especially if the frame is uninsulated, keep it closed, except for rapid venting while the seedlings are getting their start.

Plan the cold frame bed (particularly one with a steeply angled glazing) so that vegetables that will be tallest at maturity occupy the rear space. Use staggered, interplanted rows to make the best use of space. Continue starting and caring for a few seedlings of each variety so that you can replace cold frame plants as soon as they are harvested.

The major chore for any cold frame gardener is temperature control, or, more specifically, preventing heat buildup through venting. On a bright sunny day, whatever the outdoor temperature, inside temperature in an unvented, insulated frame can rise to 100°F or more and wilt or kill plants quickly.

If the morning sun is bright and the sky cloudless, promising continued sun, raise the lid and prop it open 4 to 6 inches. If outdoor temperatures are in the 50s or temperatures inside the frame have risen into the 70s, open the frame all the way to cool it rapidly. If the day is cool and inside temperatures are in the 40s, open the frame only slightly so that cold winds will not chill plants. Follow daily forecasts and your own knowledge of local weather patterns to judge how much air to give your plants.

By two or three in the afternoon in late fall or early spring, or as early as noon in the dead of winter, check the thermometer inside the frame, and if the mercury has fallen into the low 40s, close the lid to conserve daytime heat into the cool night. If the frame is uninsulated and the weather is cold, leave the frame unopened in the morning and late in the afternoon cover it with insulating material. Temperatures should be checked at least twice daily until you are well acquainted with your frame's personality. Wipe away condensation when you open the frame. In insulated frames venting is almost as important for dissipating vapor buildup as for lowering temperature.

To harden-off seedlings in spring, vent the frame a few hours during the warm part of the day, extending the time the frame is open by half-hour increments each day for two weeks and then leaving it open around the clock.

If you're away from home during the day and unable to check the frame, a solar-powered automatic opener will do the opening and closing job for you at preset temperatures. However, it is really no substitute for visual checking of temperature and it will not perform the other daily chore of checking for signs of disease and pests. Small, double-glazed plastic commercial cold frames are available with these solar-powered automatic vents.

Maintain your frame carefully because, as a moist, warm environment, it is subject to rot and rapid deterioration. Whenever paint starts flaking, repaint as soon as the frame is free of plants. Never replant before a newly painted or repainted frame has aired for several weeks. Fumes from the paint may harm the plants. Recaulk as necessary to maintain airtight conditions. When insulating curtains are used, these must be checked for crumbling and breakdown and replaced when necessary. Watch for signs of rusted hardware and nails. Try to use rustproof hardware in construction whenever possible.

Solar Growing Frames

The energy crisis of the 1970s taught us all to look for inexpensive, inexhaustible, and ecologically sound alternatives to electricity and the fossil fuels. Out of our near panic came a new technology of solar engineering that spawned solar homes, solar water heaters, solar greenhouses, and, perhaps most helpful to the average gardener intent on lengthened seasons, the Solar Growing Frame.

Five years of research testing solar greenhouses at the Rodale Research Center, including three years of experimenting with solar frame design, finally produced a solar growing frame just as effective as a solar greenhouse for growing plants with low light requirements. Rodale's Solar Growing Frame, moreover, is a more sensible size for the average family. The cost of the Solar Growing Frame is one-third to one-fourth the cost of a solar greenhouse when the construction of both is done by the owner and when the growing space is comparable.

Rodale researchers found that levels of light within a Solar Growing Frame are higher than in a solar greenhouse and daytime temperatures are warmer. More importantly, the crucial nighttime temperatures in the 4 by 8-foot frame stay just as high as in a solar greenhouse. Small size alone, the Rodale solar research has proven, does not interfere with holding soil-stored heat, as long as there is 1 square foot of south-facing glazing for every square foot of growing bed and as long as the small growing-frame structure is insulated to the same standards as the larger greenhouse. Getting the most heat possible from the sun, and then holding onto the heat through cold winter nights—these are the secrets of the Solar Growing Frame.

Detailed drawings and a materials list for the construction of the Solar Growing Frame are available from the address given in the Garden Products section of the Directory of Resources. The project of building the frame can be completed in three to four weekends, or 20 hours, and requires only basic portable power tools and minimal carpentry skills.

A properly constructed Solar Growing Frame will allow you to grow some vegetables through a winter as cold as those found in New England. It will still not perform the miracle of providing tomatoes in January in northern climates, but only by using an expensive fossil-fuel–heated greenhouse and selecting the right varieties will you ever be able to accomplish that. Lettuce,

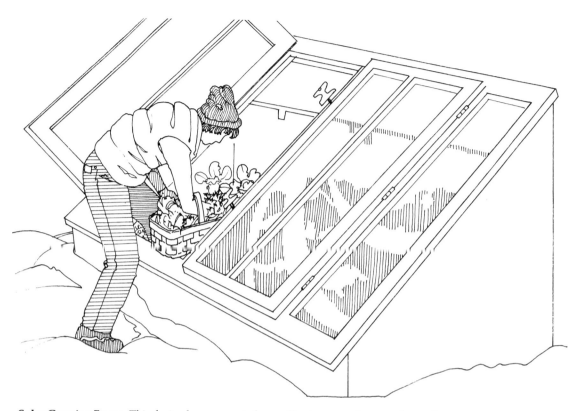

Solar Growing Frame: This design has proven to be as effective as a solar greenhouse for growing plants with low light requirements.

spinach, or Chinese cabbage in January are miracle enough for most northern high-yield gardeners.

To obtain the greatest amount of solar heat, a solar frame should point due south and have a steep slope—a pitch of 40 percent or more—on its south-facing side. The steep pitch allows for full absorption of the low-angled winter sun. Angled glazing captures about twice as much sunlight as horizontal glazing of the same size. A high, vertical back wall, painted white, bounces about 60 percent of the available, captured sunlight back to the leaves of plants. Under ideal conditions, the Solar Growing Frame receives full sunlight from 9 A.M. until 3 P.M. on midwinter days.

For retaining heat, especially during cold nights, the most important feature of the Solar

Growing Frame is its insulation. Its sides are insulated with Styrofoam 2½ inches thick, while beneath the growing bed it is insulated with 1½ inches of Styrofoam. Underground insulation means that the plants have only 18 to 20 inches of root space, considerably less space than roots are given in raised beds, but most of the vegetables suitable for growing at wintertime light levels are shallow-rooted ones.

Further insulation is provided with folding urethane foam shutters, backed with aluminum foil. These insulating shutters, generally used only at night, maintain air temperatures that are 10 degrees warmer than the soil temperatures found 8 inches underground and 6 degrees warmer than in an unshuttered, but identically insulated frame. Under most conditions, plant growth rate is doubled by each 10-degree increase in temperature. Without insulating shutters, much of the heat stored in the Solar Growing Frame would be lost at night.

The Solar Growing Frame is relatively airtight when compared with other frames. It is well caulked, double glazed with glass and fiberglass, and sealed at all joints with weather stripping. Opening the frame for watering and harvesting will not damage plants, because the fresh air introduced in the process heats up rapidly.

Earlier prototypes of the Solar Growing Frame experimented with various heat-storage materials, which were set against the straight, north wall to act as a thermal mass. Researchers found that these materials raised nighttime temperatures inside the frame very little, while reducing the amount of light reflected toward plants and taking up space where more plants could grow. The protected soil inside the frame, insulated on all sides, seems to be its own best solar collector.

Solar greenhouses, of course, offer a more versatile growing environment than a Solar Growing Frame. They provide a better height for working, and, when attached to a house, they add heat and living space to the dwelling. The expense of a greenhouse, however, cannot be justified in terms of food savings alone, while the cost of a Solar Growing Frame can be. The estimated 300 dollar cost of a Solar Growing Frame can be defrayed within five years by the savings the average family can realize by being able to grow winter vegetables.

Raising Vegetables in a Solar Growing Frame

When you have eliminated low temperatures as a problem, the greatest remaining obstacles to winter growing are the short length of winter days and their relative lack of sunlight. Almost as important an obstacle is the fluctuation of temperature that occurs in winter even when a frame is insulated and airtight.

One mistake inexperienced growers often make is to assume that tropical vegetables like tomatoes can be sustained by a solar frame through very cold weather. Another common mistake is to start seedlings for frame growing too late in the season. By the time hard frost arrives in fall, the vegetables you plan to harvest from your frame in winter should be well established. This may mean starting your seedlings as early as July. No false summer will ever last more than an afternoon in a growing frame after truly cold weather arrives. Rather, the artificial climate produced there will be the climate of fall or spring, and it is those cool-season crops you should select to grow there. For production per square foot of space, the oriental brassicas, which include heading and nonheading Chinese cabbage, celery cabbage, and mustard spinach, surpass all other crops for solar-frame growing.

In Rodale Research Center trials, the average vegetable yield from a group of Solar Growing Frames using oriental greens and other crops was 14.7 ounces of greens per square foot of growing surface during the four-month period from January through April. Home gardeners can easily exceed this figure, because the trials included failed warm-weather vegetables and because the experiment used very wide spacing. Even when using the statistics produced by the experiment, however, you can see that with 27 square feet in the Solar Growing Frame, you could produce 25 pounds of fresh greens in an average winter, or enough for 200 fresh winter salads. Production during the winter will be uneven, with far smaller yields in January than in the warmer, longer days of April.

Even during the cold, cloudy first half of January in Pennsylvania, the time of lowest production when air temperatures ranged between freezing in the daytime and 10 to 20°F at night, the researchers picked about 1½ pounds of greens a week. By the end of January, production was up to 2 pounds a week. Total production of Chinese cabbage, to cite one example, rose from a January low of 1 to 5 pounds to a March high of 20 pounds.

To keep production levels up throughout winter, you should have a constant supply of seedlings ready to transfer into the frame when harvesting of mature plants opens up space. Your summertime raised bed garden will have given you all the practice you need at timing your seedlings, but you will find that even under growing lights winter seedling growth is slow.

A long harvest is guaranteed without quite so much transplanting if you harvest only the outer leaves of the salad crops, using the cut-and-come-again method.

The Winter Olympians: Crops for Solar Growing Frames

Fall plantings for Solar Growing Frames should be considered as separate from spring plantings, because certain vegetables with high light requirements, or with a need for steadily increasing temperatures, do better in spring than in fall. Most oriental brassicas, on the other hand, form seedstalks quickly in spring, but make ideal fall into winter plantings because they manage well under low light and tolerate fluctuations in temperature. The boxes Guidelines for Fall and Spring Planting should help you figure your own timetable for planting and harvesting. Keep in mind that careful record keeping and your own experience will be the most useful guides in figuring when to plant.

Joel Rumbolo is a New Jersey gardener who has used a Solar Growing Frame to its full capacity since building it in 1980. He recommends later planting dates than those used at the Rodale Research Center. When he direct-seeded in August, he had trouble getting plants through the winter in New Jersey, either because they bolted in warm fall weather or because mature plants were, in his experience, more susceptible to frost than younger plants. Rumbolo now waits for September to direct-seed Swiss chard, Chinese cabbage, and spinach in rows 6 inches apart and to transplant into the frame established plantings of spinach and parsley. He later thins the direct-sown vegeta-

bles to 3 to 9 inches apart, depending on their mature size.

Rumbolo finds that spinach transplanted from his garden to the frame stays green into January. By that time, the direct-seeded spinach is ready for light harvesting. He begins picking oriental brassicas in November and harvests them straight through May, eating them at least twice a week in salads, steamed or stir-fried.

Yield-Improving Tips

Over their years of observing plants in Solar Growing Frames, Rodale researchers have concluded that the very best way to increase yields is to carefully select varieties that are suited for the conditions found in the frames.

Another important finding is that transplanting has consistently resulted in higher yields than direct-seeding. The Research Center horticulturists also learned that a more continuous supply of table greens was produced when the conventional leafy crops like lettuce and spinach were grown in midfall and were followed in the dead of winter by the heartier oriental brassicas that tolerate both more fluctuation of temperature and less light. Many oriental brassicas survive temperatures of 30°F.

Intensive techniques such as frequent transplanting in succession are suitable to the Solar Growing Frame and will increase production. Intensive spacings, however, must be modified for frame use. Yields of second or third relay crops can be greatly reduced by the consequence of being shaded. A staggered planting pattern will produce more greens than square-centered placement. If you're using the cut-and-come-again method of harvest, spacings can be up to half as large as for whole-plant harvest.

Caring for Solar Growing Frame Crops

Because you're gardening in an artificial environment, and often in seasons that are not naturally conducive to good plant growth, you must modify some of the cultural techniques you practice

GUIDELINES FOR FALL PLANTING

Eileen Weinsteiger of the Rodale Research Center horticultural staff suggests the following crops for fall solar-frame planting. They are listed along with their seed-starting times (in eastern Pennsylvania) and recommended spacings. Choose varieties described in catalogs as low-light tolerant and cold resistant.

Vegetable	When to Seed	When to Transplant	Spacing (in inches)	Harvest†
Broccoli	July 1–14	3–5 weeks later	12–15	Sept. to mid-Nov.
Cabbage	July 1–14	3–5 weeks later	12–15	Sept. to early Nov.
Cauliflower	July 1–14	3–5 weeks later	12–15	Sept. to mid-Nov.
Chinese cabbage	late July	3–5 weeks later	8–10	Oct. to Dec.
Kale	July to Aug.	4–6 weeks later	12	Oct. to Dec.
Kohlrabi	early Aug.	3–4 weeks later	6	late Sept. to early Oct.
Lettuce*	late July to early Aug.	3–5 weeks later	6–8	Oct. to early Dec.
Spinach*	late July to early Aug.	3–5 weeks later	4–6	Oct. to early Dec.
Parsley	June to July	4–6 weeks later	4–6	into mid-Dec.

Swiss chard, Japanese chard, endive, celery cabbage, India mustard, Chinese flowering white cabbage, Chinese mustard, and edible chrysanthemum have also been grown successfully in the fall in Solar Growing Frames. Planting times for these crops will have to be learned through experience. Start the crops listed above in late July or August. If they bolt, try starting them later the next time you plant them. If they fail to mature properly, try planting them earlier. Root crops, including turnips, radishes, beets, and carrots, are generally less successfully grown in solar frames, chiefly because of root maggot damage.

*Use winter varieties
†Final date may be earlier if hard freeze occurs

in the outdoor garden.

Watering For starters, the ground under the insulated foundation of the solar frame should be well drained. Line the excavation with coarse gravel before laying insulation and masonry if drainage is poor.

Immediately after transplanting at any time of year, new seedlings in solar frames will need to be checked every day for water stress, and often they will require daily watering. Oriental brassicas, in particular, have shallow roots and depend on constant soil moisture after transplanting. Don't be misled by the appearance of the soil surface inside the frame or by the evidence of humidity. Condensation inside the glazing may moisten the soil surface without penetrating the soil. Poke

½ inch deep with your finger. Soil at that depth should always be moist to the touch.

After seedlings have recovered from transplant shock, weekly watering will generally suffice to keep the soil moist. Don't be concerned if your transplants lose a few leaves soon after you set them in the frame. They are adjusting to low light levels by shedding excess foliage and are not necessarily water stressed.

If the outside temperature is 10°F or lower, the minimum air temperature inside a frame that is fitted with a thermal shutter will be 30 to 34°F. Occasionally in very cold weather, frame air temperatures sink below this point and plant growth slows to a near halt. With very slow growth, less moisture is required and watering

GUIDELINES FOR SPRING PLANTING

For spring planting in the Solar Growing Frame, the following vegetables are recommended by Eileen Weinsteiger. Planting dates are for eastern Pennsylvania. Choose varieties described as cold resistant in seed catalogs.

Broccoli	Start seedlings indoors in late February or early March and set them into the frame on April 1.
Cabbage	See Broccoli
Carrots	Direct-seed on April 1.
Kohlrabi	See Broccoli
Lettuce	Direct-seed on April 1. To transplant, start indoors in February and set into the frame in March.
Onion sets	Plant in the frame in mid-March.
Parsley	Transplant on April 1.
Peas	Direct-seed into the frame two to three weeks earlier than you would into a garden, or in mid-March.
Radishes	Direct-seed at the beginning of April.
Spinach	Start indoors in February and set into the frame in March.

All spacings for spring crops should be at least half again as wide as spacings recommended for growing beds, because of the danger of fungus disease in the moist, warm conditions of the frame during spring weather.

can be done every two to four weeks, or even less often. It should be noted that with a bottom-insulated growing frame, rain, which may have saturated the surrounding soil, cannot be depended upon to keep beds moist by capillary action. All water will have to be delivered by hand.

Water plants early in the day, using a hose, watering can, or bucket and dipping cup. Watering early will give foliage a chance to dry before nightfall, when temperatures drop. Use water about the same temperature as the soil in your frame. If the frame is working well, the soil temperature will hover around 45°F, whatever the fluctuations of the daytime air temperature. Water colder than 45°F will stress the plants.

Mulching is unnecessary in the moist atmosphere of a solar frame, and it may also block off needed radiation and lower the heat of the soil.

Most beginning solar frame growers underwater their plants. Always remember to increase the amount of water in the spring when temperatures rise and light increases.

Fertilizing Solar frame beds are filled with the same rich, loose soil that is used in raised beds, and they are enriched with compost. Little addi-

tional fertilizer will be required.

In winter, when plants are growing very slowly, heavy feeders like lettuce and other leafy vegetables will benefit from occasional feedings of manure tea or seaweed or fish emulsion. "Occasional" means feed them no more than twice a month. Overfertilizing will cause an unhealthy buildup of salts in the soil.

Venting Until you get used to tending a Solar Growing Frame, the frame will seem to be costing you more time and effort than any raised bed you ever used. You won't be spending most of your time on planting or harvesting, but learning how to regulate the temperature inside the frame. And nothing is more essential to the care of your crops. The highest skill of a solar-frame grower is knowing when and how long to vent the frame.

Excessively high frame temperatures almost always cause more problems to solar-frame growers than do excessively cold ones. The air temperature inside a frame should be checked frequently with a thermometer that hangs there all the time. Never permit the inside air temperature to rise over 85 or 90°F. Tender transplants and mature plants near harvest are the ones most susceptible

Solar Growing Frame Planting Arrangement: Always put your tall growing plants toward the back and the shorter plants near the front. In this frame, broccoli, heading Chinese cabbage, and kale share the back wall. In the front, lettuce, parsley, spinach, and kohlrabi occupy the growing space.

to overheating on a sunny day. Even on a bright cloudy day with cold outside weather, inside temperatures can soar. When the air around them is too hot, plants grow leafy, fail to bear fruit, and are more vulnerable to occasional sudden nighttime dips of temperature.

Most plants grow best if the day-to-night temperature variation is similar to what they would experience in their normal outdoor growing season. For the most suitable solar-frame crops, the best range is between daytime highs in the 50s and nighttime lows in the 30s and 40s.

These crops can tolerate high temperatures in the 80s occasionally, especially when they are in their period of most rapid growth.

To assure regularity of temperature, you must learn when and for how long to ventilate your frame. Beginners often fear that when they open their frames at all, the carefully stored warmth will vanish from the soil. This isn't true.

When the outside temperature is near 40°F, vent the frame by opening the doors 4 to 6 inches. If the outside temperature has reached 50 to 60°F and is still rising, open the doors all the way. On sunny days, vent between 10 A.M. and 2:30 P.M. If clouds develop and the temperature dips, close the frame for the rest of the day to conserve heat for the cold night ahead.

In fall, with generally falling temperatures, frames will be closed for more hours of the day than they are in spring. Generally, frames can be closed at noon on days late in fall. In the depth of winter, whole cloudy days may pass when the frame is never open except for harvesting. Even in winter, however, daily temperature checking is necessary, because threateningly high temperature levels may be reached on some sunny days, even when the outside temperature is near freezing.

In late spring, when you are using your frame to give early starts to heat-loving crops, you can close the frame only at night, or you can let the inside temperatures rise into the high 80s for faster growth. Never let the air inside the frame go much over 90°F.

Weeding Like wide spacing within Solar Growing Frames, weeding is an important preventive measure. Solar-frame environments are moist and warm ones, conducive to diseases and pest infestations. Weeds harbor pests and spread diseases. They also steal nutrients from vegetables.

A good technique is to give weeds a head start by watering the soil of the solar bed before you are ready to plant it. The weed seeds in the soil will sprout and you can pull or cultivate out the newly emerged weeds before you transplant your first seedlings into the frame in early fall.

Diseases and Pests The greatest threats to plants in an airtight solar frame are the mildew and fungi that thrive in moist conditions. The practice of frequent venting not only regulates temperature, but also dispels moisture, preventing mildew and fungi from getting started. Once mildew or a fungal disease is rampant, the best thing to do is to abandon the crop and give the frame a thorough sunning.

Keep your frame clean and maintain it well. Wash it between uses and keep it painted. Remove any leaves that show signs of disease from the frame promptly. Discard all infected plants.

Soil in a solar frame, unlike outdoor soil in a growing bed, is never subjected to freeze. Freeze performs the important function of ridding the soil of many undesirable soil organisms. For this reason, solar-frame soil should be changed once a year. Replacing soil annually also solves the problem of crop rotation. True rotation is, of course, impossible when only one frame is in use.

The soil in solar frames often attracts damping-off fungus. A thin layer of sand, vermiculite, or peat moss spread over the soil of the frame will give some protection from damping-off disease. A weak chamomile tea solution has also been used by some growing-frame gardeners to control damping-off.

Insect problems in a solar frame differ from those you may have encountered in the garden. The most common garden insects — bean beetles, squash bugs, and cabbage worms, for example — will be almost unknown in the frame in the winter, for you will have left their season far behind. Instead, in a closed environment you may experience some of the various plagues of greenhouse operators — insects that reproduce quickly in moist, warm places. Whenever you find insects inside your frame, take action immediately.

In various experiments with frames at the Rodale Research Center, the greatest insect problem was with aphids. Aphids are most easily controlled by washing the foliage of infected plants with lukewarm water and insecticidal soap and rinsing with clear water. Pay special attention to the undersides of the leaves. If an infestation persists, dust with rotenone. (Wait one week after using rotenone before harvesting.) Some varieties of vegetables are more susceptible to aphids than others. Try never to replant repeatedly infested varieties. Good air circulation also helps to control aphids. Introducing ladybugs as aphid predators may help in the fall, but ladybugs seldom linger in the frames in winter. Another trick, frequently used in greenhouses, is to lay strips of aluminum foil between the rows inside the frame. The light reflected onto the undersides of the leaves discourages aphid activity.

Scale insects may attack stems and the undersides of leaves. Pick them off and crush them, or wipe them away with a small sponge soaked in alcohol or soapy water.

The whitefly is a small winged insect common to greenhouses. An easy way to trap them is by setting a yellow plastic or metal tray inside the frame and coating it with a sticky substance like oil, honey, or molasses. In warm weather, replenish the sticky coating often.

Mealybugs are related to scale insects and can be removed in the same way, or they can be killed with a spray of soapy water.

Slugs and snails are great poachers on solar frames. Apparently they find the warmth irresistible and appreciate a winter salad as much as gardeners do. Sand, cinders, wood ashes, or diatomaceous earth can be spread around plants to deter them.

Harvesting Novice frame users often worry that harmful gusts of cold air will rush into their frames if they open them up for harvesting. The worry is generally misplaced. Frames recover heat quickly after being opened for brief periods in winter. Nonetheless, harvesting should be done as rapidly as possible. If you harvest in the morning, the sun will have ample time to restore the frame to cozy warmth by nightfall.

Air circulation helps to control disease, and light is at a premium for winter crops and should not be blocked by crowded spacing. For these reasons, it is wise to harvest all winter-grown plants promptly.

If using the cut-and-come-again method of harvest, leave behind at least six healthy, well-formed leaves when you cut greens. In winter, growth is slower than in the normal season, and plants will recover from cutting more quickly if enough foliage is left behind to sustain them through the shock of partial harvest. If you notice that a plant stem has lengthened and that the leaf flavor has grown markedly stronger, harvest and replace the plant as soon as possible.

Solar Growing Frames rise sharply upward to allow for the best angle for the glazing to catch the sun in winter. This means that in mapping your frame plantings you will need to place your taller crops, like broccoli, heading Chinese cabbage, celery cabbage, and kale, in the back of the frame, and the shorter vegetables, like leaf lettuce or spinach, near the front. Such placement will also make harvesting easier.

Other Uses for the Solar Growing Frame

In regions of high altitude and short seasons, the Solar Growing Frame keeps functioning long after the first early crops go into outdoor beds. Growers at the Windstar Foundation in Snowmass, Colorado, for example, keep their Solar Growing Frame working through summer, planting successions of tomatoes, cucumbers, and bush zucchini in the frame from mid-May on. In this way, they can produce continuous yields instead of the one small harvest of warm-season vegetables that their 60-day growing season usually allows.

The Solar Growing Frame is suitable for seedling starting in spring and for holding seedlings, nurturing them, and hardening them off as they await transfer to outdoor beds. The protection from rain, wind, and insects that the frame affords will benefit seedlings and delicate plants in warm weather as well as in cold. Keep the lid fully open when using the frame in warm weather once all danger of frost has passed.

9 *Special Regional Problems and Their Solutions*

Climate can throw the largest obstacle in the way of a garden's success and productivity. Each part of the country presents some sort of difficulty: problem soil, low rainfall, unpredictable weather, pests, diseases, wind, short season, high water table—and the list could go on and on.

Northerners who envy the long season enjoyed in the Sun Belt probably haven't tried to hoe at midday in a Georgia July or seen crops wither for lack of rain in Arizona or be devoured by an endless succession of pests in Florida. Each geographical area, each locality—or for that matter, each individual garden—has its own problems. Many of these problems can be mitigated by the use of intensive techniques.

In the next few pages we will look at six regions where the gardening isn't easy. We'll also see what gardeners in these areas have done to cope—and make higher yields more likely.

High-Altitude Gardening

The shortest growing season in North America is not in the point furthest north; it's in the highest mountains. Especially in the West, relatively small increases in altitude can change the climate more than longer intervals of latitude. Areas located at high elevation in southern areas have about the same average low temperatures as places of the same altitude much further north, but their growing seasons will be longer. Minimum winter temperatures as low as 0°F are found in high deserts as far south as Southern California and New Mexico. Whatever mountain or high plateau you are perched on, you can automatically add two weeks to the recommended time to begin planting in your zone.

When mountaintops finally do warm up, other troubles begin. The thin, high air provides a poor filter for radiation, and often even hardy cold-weather crops must be protected from sunscald. Wind sweeping the mountaintops can produce drought or can damage plants. But poor air circulation due to thick evergreens on wooded mountains can be just as harmful to plants, for circulating air helps warm the soil. Mountaintop gardeners should look for good air drainage when choosing a gardening spot. In general, a south-facing slope will be warmer and more hospitable to growing plants than a north-facing one.

In areas of strong westerly winds, rain on mountaintops is apt to be erratic, with too much on the windward side and too little on the leeward. Then there are soil problems. The rocky substratum on ridges or peaks often weathers to an acid, compacted soil that requires much organic matter to loosen it. Evergreen needles only increase the acidity, but wood ashes can help bring the pH closer to neutral.

The most limiting factor of all remains the short season. It restricts the number of crops that you can grow successfully, and dictates that you use only quick-to-mature varieties. Intensive techniques are almost obligatory: raised beds to warm the soil and hold the rain; compost and other amendments to loosen and enhance the soil; protective devices to warm and shelter plants (sometimes even through summer); the practice of starting plants indoors and making quick succession plantings; the use of cold frames for hardening-off as well as to extend the season; and relay plantings to make the most of a growing time that seems to pass in the blink of an eye.

Every mountaintop gardener we've been in contact with agrees that all the work is worth it. Vegetables grown in mile-high beds above the clouds win no prizes for size, but their flavor is another matter. Peas ripened in strong sun and cool breezes are sweeter, carrots firmer, and radishes crisper. One gardener recommends that in planting quick-to-mature vegetables like radishes, medium to large-size varieties should be chosen in the hopes of harvesting small, but not minuscule, roots from a mountaintop garden. Beets grown at 8,000 feet seldom exceed 2 inches in diameter, while a 6-inch carrot is considered a monster.

Flavor is not the only advantage of mountain gardening. Lettuce, spinach, and oriental brassicas go through the entire short summer without bolting. Romaine lettuce, endive, and all hardy herbs seem to thrive, and broccoli is made

for the mountains. What's more, when you grow cole crops, you may never see a green caterpillar. Cabbage butterflies appear to prefer lower altitudes, leaving cabbages alone to form small, but tight, solid heads.

Among warmth-loving vegetables, summer squash and cucumbers seem to be the most successful, but you should give cucumbers protection and start both crops indoors. Many high-altitude gardeners find that hybrid zucchini and crookneck squash are the most dependable. Bush squash adapt best to cold late in summer.

Unless your particular mountain is a dry one, use water sparingly. Evaporation in the strong mountain sun cools the soil, and that is the last thing you want to do. One time you want to be generous with water is when you use it to save plants from suspected frost. Shade is both a blessing and a curse in the mountains. Place beds carefully so that the warmth-loving plants are given the sunniest places.

The mountaineering gardener will rarely produce pumpkins or corn for Thanksgiving dinner; the season is simply not long or hot enough to ripen them, even when they're started inside. But with raised beds and the intensive method, the intensely short season will also be intensely satisfying.

Foggy Areas of Coastal Mildness

Fog, like altitude, is a mixed blessing. In coastal British Columbia, for example, it modifies the effects of latitude to give a growing season as long as the Carolinas enjoy. But then it seems to take all that extra time back again. Heavy rains in winter and early spring and a constant high humidity level leave the soil too cool and damp for early tilling and planting. Nights remain chilly until midsummer in this region that closely parallels the climate of England.

In coastal areas nearly every crop has to be planted indoors to give it an early start. Then great care must be taken in hardening-off seedlings.

VEGETABLES FOR MOUNTAIN GARDENS

Here are some useful crops and varieties for seasons of 60 to 100 days. The varieties have been recommended by gardeners in high places. Growers in cool, high desert regions should know about the varieties adapted for spring plantings offered by Native Seeds (44). These include Bantam-type HOPI SWEET CORN, the prolific RED HOPI lima bean, the SANTA DOMINGO WHITE MEATED and ORANGE MEATED melons, and the HOPI YELLOW MEATED watermelon, which can be dry farmed in sand dunes.

Beans
ROYALTY (1, 8, 18) will prosper despite the less-than-ideal conditions. TOP CROP is one of the earliest maturers and a heavy producer.

Broccoli
Start plants indoors in April for setting out in June, or if the ground is clear of snow, start outdoors as soon as the soil can be worked. Use quick-to-develop varieties like GREEN COMET or BRAVO.

Cabbage
EARLIANA has produced from direct seeding in gardens at 8,000 feet. GOLDEN ACRE and RED ACRE are two cabbages very quick to mature.

Carrots
NANTES HALF-LONG, CHANTENAY, and OXHEART will produce small roots. BABY FINGER NANTES matures in a mere 50 days.

Eggplants
EARLY BLACK EGG (51) is one of the earliest to mature, needing 65 days.

Herbs
Good herbs for mountain gardens are basil, chives, dill, mint, parsley, and thyme. These all need an indoor start.

Kale
Start seeds indoors and delay the harvest until fall. HARVESTER (51) has been a reliable producer for high-altitude gardeners, along with DWARF SIBERIAN (9).

Kohlrabi
EARLY WHITE VIENNA and GRAND DUKE usually have enough time to mature in short-season gardens.

Lettuce
Start looseheads indoors. Any romaine does well. BLACK-SEEDED SIMPSON is a reliable leaf type, and loosehead BUTTERCRUNCH is dependable. KAGRAN SUMMER (34), another loosehead, also does well under the intense light levels of mountain areas.

Melons
SWEET GRANITE (51) is a cantaloupe that's been successful for mountain gardeners.

Onions
Onions are well adapted to the Sierras of California, although only sets will have enough time to mature.

Peas
BLUE BANTAM (9), ALASKA, OREGON SUGAR POD (51), and WANDO (17) do especially well. Plant growth often exceeds that at lower altitudes, rising to 5 feet high.

Potatoes
IDAHO and RED RUSSET have survived late summer snows.

Radishes
Middle-sized but quick radishes are best. These include RED GLOBE, WHITE PRINCE (25), and RED and WHITE ICICLE. Plant as early as April in gardens at 7,300 feet.

Spinach
BLOOMSDALE LONGSTANDING and MELODY produce well most of the season. New Zealand spinach needs an indoor start.

Squash
EARLY PROLIFIC STRAIGHTNECK, a summer squash, and PONCA (51), an extra-early butternut, are two good prospects for the short summer season.

Tomatoes
Small or short-season varieties such as SUB-ARCTIC PLENTY (34, 51) and EARLIROUGE (34, 51) do well under protection.

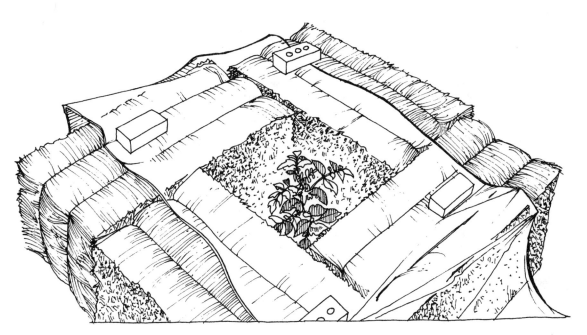

Tomato Nest: Coddle cold-sensitive tomatoes by snuggling them inside an insulating ring of hay bales. At night when the temperature drops, cover with a sheet of plastic.

Some gardeners use permanent mulches and plant through them to avoid waterlogging. Mulch blocks the rain and keeps it from saturating the soil. Raised, deeply dug, well-drained beds are essential.

Protective devices like cloches and tunnels definitely come into their own with a long season and cool soil. Year-round gardening is possible in many coastal areas, with oriental brassicas, lettuce, and spinach the favorite crops. Even on the colder Maine coast, some well-protected overwintered greens give very early spring crops.

Paradoxically, the Pacific Northwest is frequently lacking in rain during June and July, a fact that distinguishes it significantly from the florist's-case climate of England. In August, the rains return, often forcing you to harvest under-ripe tomatoes that would otherwise spoil in the beds. Small melons and summer squash can remain in the garden to ripen in spite of rain, but winter squash and pumpkins are often picked a bit on the early side for indoor ripening. By carefully

timing early crops, you can have them out of the beds by August. Harvest carrots, turnips, and beets promptly or they will split in the ground. Salad crops, on the other hand, can go into winter, benefiting from the long, cool, but well above freezing autumns. In areas where August rains are lighter, carrots, turnips, rutabagas, parsnips, and garlic go through winter mulched, while kale can stand unmulched.

Slugs are a constant problem and one that discourages the use of wooden-sided beds, which give these pests a convenient daytime hideaway. The most common diseases are those that thrive in high humidity: powdery mildew on onions; leaf spot on tomatoes and cucumbers; rust on asparagus; smut on corn and onions; and clubroot on cole crops and turnips. Black rot also wipes out cole crops. The pests you're most likely to encounter include cutworms, root maggots, flea beetles, and aphids. Good sanitation, carefully

(continued on page 294)

VEGETABLES FOR MILD COASTAL GARDENS

Here are a few suggested varieties of vegetables that do particularly well in the Pacific Northwest. Varieties suited to the Maine coastal islands and the fog area around San Francisco will be mentioned only when intensive gardeners in those areas have reported success with them.

Artichokes GREEN GLOBE is a reliable variety. The plants last four years and are set out from January to May in the Bay Area. They need water in dry weather and should be cut back after the bearing season ends.

Beans ROYALTY PURPLE POD (51) does well in cool soil. Short-season bush beans can be planted early in May on the Washington coast. Broad beans like the favas are usually the earliest and hardiest crop in British Columbia, where they are planted in October to go through the winter. Or they can be sown in February. BROAD WINDSOR LONG POD (16, 50) is a good fava bean variety. One Oregon grower recommends SOLDIER (34, 55, 68) and SPECKLED BAYS (63, 68) as fine shelling beans for maritime climates.

Beets Beets need warmer soil for germination than the climate of the Pacific Northwest provides before mid-April. For an early start, sow them indoors. DETROIT DARK RED, RUBY QUEEN, and LUTZ GREENLEAF keep well in damp soil.

Broccoli A hardy broccoli like ITALIAN GREEN SPROUTING or NORTHWEST 29 (31) gives the longest harvest, but it must be protected from heavy moisture in early spring. In milder coastal climates it will come through the winter when planted as late as August. GREEN VALIANT F1 (69) is recommended by an Oregon gardener for its enormous tight heads and 3-inch-long side shoots.

Cabbage This crop will also survive winters in many coastal areas. DANISH BALLHEAD and PENN STATE BALLHEAD (20, 41, 59) are commonly grown in British Columbia. BABY BADGER-HEAD (25) and PRINCESS (63) are other varieties that do well in coastal gardens. JANUARY KING (63) is an exceptionally cold-hardy cabbage that can stay in the garden as late as March. DANRO and CARAMBRA (both available from 62) both remain in good condition in the garden once they've matured; CARAMBRA in particular overwinters well.

Cauliflower Cauliflower does better in the Bay Area than in gardens where summers are dry. In British Columbia, it is sown under glass in January for March transplanting. SNOW CROWN (26, 50) is a rapid grower that produces large heads in maritime regions.

Corn GOLDEN JUBILEE (63) tolerates smog along with cool, moist, and overcast conditions. SENECA HORIZON (53, 63, 69) is an early hybrid that does well in maritime gardens. SUGAR DOTS (63) is called the ideal super-sweet garden corn for the maritime Northwest.

Cucumbers If started indoors, cucumber plants can be set out in mid-May in Washington, but they do better grown under cloches until they begin to climb. STRAIGHT 8, NATIONAL PICKLING, HOKKAIDO EARLY F1 (63), and ROADSIDE FANCY F1 (63) are reported to do well in coastal gardens.

Eggplants DUSKY (9) has been a reliable producer for coastal gardeners. SHORT TOM F1 (64) produces thin-skinned, small oriental eggplants in 75 days in maritime climates.

Garlic Garlic is an excellent plant for the Bay Area, where it is sown 2 inches deep November through January for late summer harvest. It requires dry soil toward the end of its growing period, so it is less suited to the Northwest.

Leeks Leeks will grow well through the winter, or they can be planted in February and hilled for later use. LONDON and AMERICAN FLAG are garden favorites in British Columbia and seem unhurt by winter wetness. DURABEL (63) is bred to handle bad weather and can remain in the garden in good shape until April.

Lettuce GREAT LAKES, GRAND RAPIDS, and the extra-hardy ARCTIC KING (15) are Northwest favorites. Head lettuces should be started inside if garden soil is under 50°F. The harvest ends in July, except in the Bay Area, where it may continue through the rest of the summer if staggered plantings are made. In Maine, ICEBERG, BUTTERCRUNCH, and KAGRAN SUMMER (34) are planted early in spring under cloches and again in August and are unhurt by the cold ocean winds.

Melons HARPER HYBRID (26) cantaloupe has proven itself through many seasons during trials in Oregon's Willamette Valley. It takes about 74 days to mature and can set ten melons on a plant.

Parsnips Parsnips need warmth to germinate and a long growing season so they are usually not planted until late spring for use the following winter. SHORT THICK (40) is one notable exception that matures in 50 days.

Peas Almost any pea grows well in the Northwest if it can be planted early enough without rotting in damp soil. Dwarfs like CORVALLIS (45) bear most abundantly. GREATER PROGRESS (69), with its 65-day season, is a good pea for early bearing. It can be planted by March 1 in British Columbia.

Peppers EARLY PIMENTO, a 55-day variety, sometimes has enough time to mature if protected in its early period. GOLDEN BELL F1 (63) drops fewer blossoms and sets fruit earlier than most varieties under cool night conditions. Try this sweet pepper if you haven't had luck with other varieties. For hot peppers, grow SUREFIRE F1 (63), which remains vigorous even under marginal conditions.

Potatoes In British Columbia, potatoes are sprouted in February for early March planting. WARBA and NORLAND (both from 40) are early-maturing varieties. For late varieties, plant deeper in mid-June. NETTED GEM (2) and NORGOLD RUSSET (20) are varieties that have won gardeners' favor.

Radishes CHAMPION is suited to spring and fall plantings, while SCARLET GLOBE, FRENCH BREAK-FAST, and RED PRINCE (63) withstand summer conditions the best. Radishes are usually sown in late February and make a good intercrop with later germinating parsley.

Spinach KING OF DENMARK (47) and GIANT WINTER (1) are planted in early March in British Columbia. In damp soil the savoy types seem to do best.

Squash GREEN or GOLDEN HUBBARD (3) are both winter types that keep well into fall when set out in mid-May from an indoor start. GREEN BUSH summer squash can be seeded directly when soil is warm. GEM (63) matures in 70 days, making it a very early winter squash.

Swiss chard LUCULLUS will overwinter if sown in late June.

Tomatoes Grown next to a building and covered with a plastic awning on cold nights, HEINZ 1350, ULTRA GIRL (59), and MORETON HYBRID matured early on an island off the Maine coast. FIREBALL and the fast-developing EARLY GIRL are suited to the cool, moist climate of the Pacific Northwest. BEEFSTEAK grows enormous in fogbound Berkeley, California. In one Northwest trial, the top-yielding varieties included BEEFEATER VFN, ULTRA BOY, EARLY CASCADE, VALIANT (8, 14), and IMPROVED WAY AHEAD (35). One Oregon grower recommends KOOTENAI (63) for its fine flavor, better than the Sub-Arctic series tomatoes. Its compact size makes growing under cloches or other protection easy.

tended soil in raised beds, and the individual attention encouraged by intensive methods help combat all of these diseases and pests.

Parts of California's San Francisco Bay Area have 100 days of fog a year. Heavy fog—the kind that closes airports—starts in late September and peaks in January. Light fog lasts from late June until August. Yet the fog makes for the mild temperatures that mean ideal growing conditions for many plants. The minimum temperature is 48°F; the average maximum is 65°F; and the average high in July is 71°F. Intensive techniques, especially the rapid relay planting of short-season crops, produces outstanding harvests throughout the year. Among vegetables that do better in mild fog areas than elsewhere are globe artichokes (treated as perennials south of San Francisco), cauliflower, garlic, fava beans, potatoes, peas, lettuce, endive, Chinese cabbage, kale, mustard, spinach, onions, and leeks.

Fog extends the Bay Area growing season long into fall and winter, sometimes adding August to the list of prime planting months, which begins with April. If you're a Bay Area gardener you'll harvest corn in fall, tomatoes in midwinter, head lettuce (normally a spring and fall crop) in midsummer, and pumpkins as late as December. With protective devices, year-round gardening is easily possible. Particularly tender warm-season vegetables like eggplants, however, are successful only when you grow them under glass.

Anti-Slug Mulches: Protect tender seedlings from the voracious appetites of slugs by ringing the plants with crushed eggshells or sand. You'll need to replenish these barriers throughout the season. Dusting plants with wood ashes is another deterrent.

The Far North

To give you an idea of what gardeners in the farthest reaches of the Far North must contend with, a short 10 to 20 inches below the top garden soil of Alaska the ground temperature holds steady at 32°F all year round. Since most vegetables require soil temperatures over 75°F during some part of their growth, the only way to enjoy anything resembling a growing season in parts of Alaska is to warm the soil artificially. Raised beds and crumbly soil help. So does the use of clear plastic bed coverings, either in place

year-round or set down after the snow melts. Corn can be seeded before the plastic is laid, if the weather is warm enough. When the corn produces small shoots, these are pulled through slits in the bed cover as it's laid in place. Wider-leafed crops are transplanted into holes under slits in the plastic.

Few gardeners have to contend with frozen tundra underfoot or under root, but many successful gardens are planted and harvested in the Far North, from Portland, Maine, to Portland,

Oregon. In a manner similar to mountain climates, the northern temperature range is severely limiting. An experienced gardener as far south as Amherst, Massachusetts, considers any crop that takes more than 90 days to mature a gamble. For him, the gambling involves a race with time to mature as many crops as possible in his 15-bed summer garden. To accomplish this he uses carefully enriched, loose soil; crop rotation among beds to maintain fertility; intercropping; and almost constant transplanting from indoor starts to cold frames and out to the beds. A New York State gardener, faced with a similar short summer, presprouts seeds and uses plastic growing tents directly over the beds, with heating lamps tucked under them on extra-cold nights.

There's no doubt about it—northern climates are harsh. Fewer beneficial soil microorganisms are present to maintain tilth and add nourishment to the soil. In some areas, phosphorus is lacking and acid conditions make growing most vegetable crops difficult. Soils, cold much of the year, become compact and require the addition of much organic matter to loosen and revitalize them. Fortunately, northern areas are often also places where wood ashes are easy to come by before spring tilling. Ashes will supply potassium and counteract soil acidity. Freezes and spring thaws can do as much to stir the soil as an army of earthworms, and cover crops are widely used for soil improvement.

Once the weather breaks into warmth, a swarm of insects descends in the northland, intent on making the most of their own short season with voracious attacks on both plants and gardeners. Your only compensation is the knowledge that these pests will leave just as quickly when autumn approaches.

One of the most important parts of successful northern growing comes in choosing the site for the garden. In many localities it's possible to create gardening microclimates as warm as climates hundreds of miles further south. Avoid north-facing hillsides, shading trees, mucky soils, windswept areas, and low-lying frost pockets. Seek out nearby bodies of water, south-facing slopes, adequate shelter from wind, and light-textured soils.

There are many good things to be said about northern gardening. For one, the days are longer in summer the further north you go. A wise northern gardener will have as much of the garden as possible under way by June, when the growth-accelerating long days reach their climax. In Vermont, this has traditionally meant starting tomatoes inside on the first Tuesday in March, Town Meeting Day. Much earlier starts are preferable for cole crops, lettuce, and spinach that go into gardens soon after the soil can be worked. Well-prepared and covered beds or beds that have been warmed by plastic mulches will speed the transfer outside.

Wider-than-minimum spacing between plants is recommended for early plantings in cool soil, so that the sun's warmth can penetrate to the root zone. Use mulch sparingly and never on long-season or heat-loving vegetables until the ground is thoroughly warm. Cool-season vegetables fare better in spring than in fall and benefit from mulch once they are a few inches high.

In northern Minnesota, an early frost during the first two weeks of September is usual, but so is the Indian summer weather that follows and lasts on into November. Midsummer-planted vegetables like Swiss chard, late broccoli (planted to replace peas), and fall crops of spinach will mature well only if you give them protection from the September frost.

In the Far North and Canada, spring crops will continue to thrive in summer and can be planted repeatedly. Bolt-resistant oriental brassicas, cole crops, lettuce, potatoes, spinach, and radishes are most successful carried over from spring. Cauliflower grows full heads, and lettuce seldom bolts in northern gardens. Corn, tomatoes, melons, and eggplants, on the other hand, require indoor starts, careful protection, and some coddling. The right choice of crops is one important key to northern gardening. Another key is careful planning of successions and relays. Fortunately, although you're required to move like a whirling dervish in summer, the climate has given you plenty of planning time in winter.

Heat and Humidity of the South and Southeast

If the northern gardener seems to be working against time to get a harvest in, then the southern one must feel that gardening never ends. High temperatures spring and fall, mild winters, and plentiful rainfall in summer speed growth, up to the point when midsummer heat waves prove too much for all but the most tropical vegetables. This means one very long growing season for gardens in the places as far south as southern Florida and Louisiana. In subtropical Florida gardeners are taking their summer vacations just when Vermonters move into high gear.

Northerners are often envious, but what they don't always realize is that *everything* in nature keeps growing longer in the South. That includes the organisms that deplete soil fertility and all the diseases and pests that attack plants. The pest-control practice of taking advantage of insect diapause (dormancy) by timing crops to escape insect damage won't work where the pests are present and breeding all year round.

Compost is produced rapidly in hot temperatures and humid conditions, and organic matter, including spoiled fruit and vigorous weeds, is abundant, but the soil, constantly used in production, seems to demand endless replenishment. Fungus diseases unknown in the North dictate special precautions in southern gardens, and the choice of resistant varieties is mandatory. Nematodes are a particular problem in Florida and other citrus growing areas. Some besieged Floridians actually elevate special growing boxes above soil level to avoid nematode infestation.

Heavy rains in summer may cause erosion in beds and may leach and compact the soil. High water tables in places like Louisiana dictate the use of drainage trenches around raised beds.

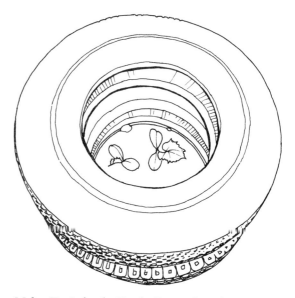

Melon Tactic for the North: Give melons the warmth they crave by insulating them with a stack of heat-absorbing tires. Transplant into a hill of aged manure, add the tires or a black plastic mulch, and your seedlings should get off to a fine start. Remove tires or mulch when threat of frost is over, the air warms up, or the plants have outgrown their tire shelter.

One enterprising Baton Rouge gardener grows a companion crop of frogs in his trenches for insect control. Blistering summer sun and sudden heat in spring, on the other hand, rule out such cool-loving crops as artichokes, asparagus, Brussels sprouts, rhubarb, and rutabagas in Florida, and allow only squash, crowder peas, peanuts, okra, corn, melons, sweet potatoes, and sometimes cucumbers to go through summer.

Many successful northern gardeners dream of retirement gardens in Florida, never realizing that an entirely new kind of planning will be demanded of them there, often with two distinct seasons for which to plan.

The healthier and more nutrient-rich you keep a garden in the Deep South, the longer and better it will produce. Intensive soil preparation is an ideal way to maintain soil quality. You can

VEGETABLES FOR NORTHERN GARDENS

In addition to the crops mentioned here, look at the earlier listing of Vegetables for Mountain Gardens. The varieties recommended there will do well in cool, short-season areas.

Beans   Many kinds of beans, both snap and shell, do well in New England. Boston is not known as the "bean capital" by accident. Northern gardeners have mentioned the snap pole bean KENTUCKY WONDER; the snap bush beans CONTENDER, ROYALTY, EASTERN BUTTER-WAX, and TENDERGREEN; and the shell bush beans FRENCH HORTICULTURAL, DWARF HORTICULTURAL, SOLDIER, JACOB'S CATTLE, RED KIDNEY, and YELLOW EYE, (all available from 68) and favas. Plant all but the cold-hardy favas when frosts are over, continuing into July. Limas are usually impossible in the Far North, although the fast and hardy GENEVA (34) may bring some measure of success.

Beets   LONG SEASON (26), as its name implies, keeps well. EARLY WONDER (34, 59), DETROIT PERFECTED (17), and DETROIT DARK RED are widely used in Wisconsin. FIRST CROP (69) is ready in 45 days, living up to its name.

Broccoli   GREEN COMET keeps producing shoots all summer. Broccoli makes a good fall crop in New England, where it has cool nights for developing flower heads. WALTHAM is a reliable late variety. GREEN MOUNTAIN (5) has a short season and therefore beats the emergence of worms in Vermont.

Cabbage   Late varieties won't mature in Vermont. A good early one with a large head is ALL HEAD EARLY (17). EARLIANA produces smaller heads. DARKRI (48) offers 6 to 8-inch heads a scant 47 days from setting out. STONEHEAD and BADGER MARKET (36) do well in Wisconsin.

Carrots   SPARTAN SWEET (49) is a good long-rooted variety for Wisconsin climates but must be thinned well. CORELESS AMSTERDAM (59) has a shorter root but does well in northern gardens. For heavy soils, use GOLDEN BALL (17, 48, 49).

Cauliflower   If moisture is plentiful, the temperature change gradual, and summers gentle, cauliflower will thrive in cool climates. SNOWDRIFT (16) is planted in spring from indoor starts and SNOWMOUND (59) is direct-seeded for a fall crop where lakes modify cold climates. ALERT (48) is a rapid maturer, ready a mere 48 days from transplanting. Cauliflower seldom needs blanching in the North.

Corn   Use yellow or mixed colored varieties in the North; white ones that generally take longer to mature won't ripen. The best crop is the one planted after the last spring frost. EARLY SUNGLOW, EARLIVEE (34), and NORTHERN X-TRA SWEET (34) are good early varieties. CLASSIC TOUCH (69) is one of the earliest mixed colored corns, ripening in 60 days. For a main crop for Wisconsin climates, try WISCONSIN NATURAL SWEET (35). BUTTER 'N' SUGAR is a good mixed-kernel type.

Cucumbers   In the Far North, cucumbers won't mature unless given extra protection as well as indoor starts. Warm summer days in Wisconsin, on the other hand, are perfect for cucumber growth. GEMINI (59) is a good slicing cucumber, SALVO (34) is fine for pickling, and EARLY FORTUNE (25) will ripen in southern New England if all its late fruits are removed.

Kale   The hardiest of the kales is the high-yielding, phenomenally cold-tolerant hybrid WINTERBOR (34).

(continued)

VEGETABLES FOR NORTHERN GARDENS — *Continued*

Lettuce
Transplanted BUTTERCRUNCH for spring and direct-sown OAK LEAF for fall are favorites. In the Far North, lettuce can be planted all summer, if heading varieties are shaded. NEW YORK NO. 12, WHITE BOSTON, and LOBJOIT'S GREEN COS are New York State favorites (all available from 17). FROSTY (59), a head lettuce, protects itself with disposable wrapper leaves.

Melons
With very short seasons, smaller melons can sometimes be grown to maturity. MINNESOTA MIDGET and NEW HAMPSHIRE MIDGET (9) are small-fruited watermelons. SWEET 'N' EARLY (9) and SWEET GRANITE (51) are small-fruited cantaloupes. Early-maturing melons for chilly places include the heavy-yielding SCOOP hybrid cantaloupe, ready in a phenomenal 61 days, and the 65-day FAR NORTH, 70-day KAZKH, and 75-day EARLY CANADA watermelons (all available from 25).

Onions
Cool soils are good onion-growing soils as long as they dry out in midsummer. Transplants or sets must be used to produce good bulbs in Vermont, especially for SWEET SPANISH and Bermuda types. Let them grow with bulbs showing above ground to help them dry. Pinching off the flowers helps to produce good bulbs in Wisconsin, where varieties like ABUNDANCE (46) can be grown from seed. NORSTAR (69) has been specifically bred for cool northern regions. It matures extra early and is a good keeper.

Peas
LAXTON and LINCOLN are sown in Massachusetts to be out of the ground in time for beets to follow them. Other northern favorites include the tall garden peas FREEZONIAN and FROSTY; dwarf garden peas LITTLE MARVEL, SPARKLE, and KNIGHT; and the dwarf snap pea SUGAR ANN (26, 34). Early plantings in Vermont escape mildew.

Peppers
Peppers will seldom mature fruit in the Far North, but if started indoors in containers, they can sometimes be brought back inside to continue ripening after fall frost. Early peppers include EARLY CALWONDER, KING OF THE NORTH (25), EARLY PIMENTO, NEW ACE HYBRID, and HUNGARIAN WAX (hot).

Potatoes
GREEN MOUNTAIN (27) potatoes are favored in the Northeast for their flavor and texture, but they don't store well. KENNEBEC and KATAHDIN store better, while NORLAND is early. CRYSTAL (25) is a high-yielding, disease-resistant hybrid suited to northern growing conditions. Potatoes do best under mulch. Dig them just after the first fall frost to give them as long a season as possible. Further west, EARLY GEM (47) potatoes are planted in April and SUPERIOR (20, 47) a little later. Late potatoes will seldom grow large.

Spinach
If water is abundant and mulch is used, spinach grows into summer in the North. When harvested early, it can be followed by beans in June. KING OF DENMARK (47) and TENDERGREEN are often used. TYEE (50) is a super-yielding, slow-bolting variety.

Squash
Summer squash are GREYZINI (53), CHIEFINI, and ST. PAT SCALLOP. Winter varieties include BUTTERNUT, TABLE QUEEN (acorn), and TABLE ACE (acorn), which takes only 70 days to mature.

Tomatoes
Early tomatoes include SPRINGSET, EARLIANA, and IMPROVED WAY AHEAD (35). IDA GOLD (34) and SUB-ARCTIC (34, 59) were both developed to stand up to the rigors of growing in the North. Compact, flavorful MOIRA (34) performs well even in adverse weather. NEW YORKER (26) is compact and early and resists verticillium wilt. FIREBALL (26) is one of the most widely grown of extra-early tomatoes in short-season areas. These last three varieties were all bred for abbreviated growing seasons and chilly nights. The prolific Russian tomato SIBERIA (58) is capable of setting fruit at 38°F. PIK-RED (26, 31) produces early beefsteak-type tomatoes on compact, bushy plants; these fruits ripen consistently in cool climates.

eliminate compaction by heavy summer rains by double digging and by conscientiously replenishing organic matter both in spring and fall. Mulching is also valuable to maintain soil structure in heat and rain. Ground-cooling mulches are the ones most used.

In milder areas, beets, leeks, onions, cole crops, radishes, Swiss chard, turnips, and spinach are planted straight through the winter. When the soil is dry, as it often is in winter, lay dampened burlap strips or squares over beds to aid germination. Lightly mulch winter root crops. Deep South gardeners sprout loosehead lettuce inside in February for April through May production. After June, lettuce will seldom survive the heat, and even before then it requires shading canvas or lath structures.

Even further south in the subtropical climate of coastal Florida, two seasons are the rule. When you allow the garden to lie idle in July and August, nematode infestation is reduced, and you can spend the dampest, as well as the hottest, part of the year indoors by the air conditioner.

Plant spring gardens in February using tender to hardy vegetables, but not cool-loving crops like garden peas, which would have too few cool days in spring to remain tender. Plant heat-loving crops like peanuts, okra, sweet potatoes, and black-eyed peas as late as June and they'll go through the summer for October harvest. Tomatoes, squash, and melons are usually started inside so that as each shorter season vegetable, like radishes or lettuce, is harvested, it can be replaced immediately with a heat-loving plant.

In Florida, fall gardens start in late August or early September, when the Deep South rises again from its summer siesta. This time gardeners specialize in cool-season crops like beets, cole crops, garden peas (usually planted as late as November), radishes, carrots, kale, celery, and turnips. Small-fruited tomatoes will mature into winter. Potatoes are planted in January, while February sees the planting of peppers, eggplants, and larger tomatoes for a late spring harvest. March is the planting time for corn, beans, and

(continued on page 302)

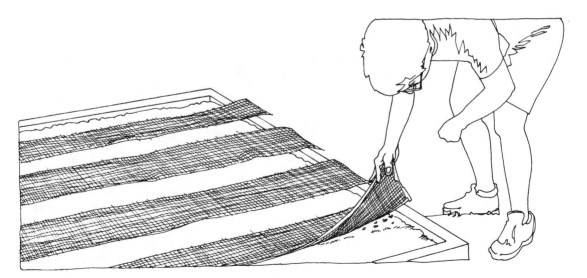

Seed-Starting Trick: Burlap strips laid over newly seeded beds and kept moist can encourage germination. Check daily and lift as soon as green sprouts emerge.

VEGETABLES FOR SOUTHERN GARDENS

Varieties that do best in the muggy heat of the Southeast are often those most resistant to both intense heat and to the various plant diseases that thrive in warm moisture. Because such stress-resistant strains also tend to cope well with cold, damp growing conditions, varieties suited to early spring or late summer in the North often also do well in the South (see these listed earlier in Vegetables for Northern Gardens and in Vegetables for Midwestern Gardens in the section that follows). The varieties mentioned here have been grown by intensive gardeners in the areas indicated.

Beans KENTUCKY WONDER pole beans do well in Virginia. EXTENDER and WADE bush beans thrive in Florida. ROMANO, TENDERGREEN, and EASTERN BUTTERWAX (28) bush beans are favorites in South Carolina, along with JACKSON WONDER (28) lima. Also adapted to hot, moist growing conditions are these bush beans: TENNESSEE GREENPOD (snap), EARLY GALLATIN STRINGLESS (snap), and DIXIE SPECKLED BUTTER (lima), all available from 28.

Beets VERMILION (59) grows well in South Carolina.

Broccoli GREEN COMET is heat resistant in Lousiana.

Cabbage MARION MARKET and KING COLE are popular in southern gardens.

Carrots IMPERATOR does well in Louisiana. South Carolina gardeners find they must dig DANVERS early for best quality.

Celery GOLDEN SELF-BLANCHING is another Louisiana favorite.

Collards GEORGIA and VATES grow well in Florida. MORRIS HEADING is an old southern favorite, often called cabbage collard. The first hybrid collard, HICROP, is compact, disease resistant, and slow to bolt, staying tender and mild flavored even when the temperature soars.

Corn SENECA CHIEF is a popular crop in Florida. WONDERFUL (26), BUTTER 'N' SUGAR, and GOLDEN BEAUTY (10, 14, 17) do well in South Carolina.

Cucumbers POINSETT, ASHLEY, and DIXIE are common in Florida gardens. BURPEE PICKLER is considered a good climber in South Carolina.

Eggplants FLORIDA MARKET thrives in Florida, while KURUME LONG PURPLE (23) grows well in Louisiana.

Herbs Insect-repelling herbs, plants, and flowers are widely used in southern gardens. These include marigolds, chives, chervil, tansy, lovage, mint, hyssop, wormwood, sage, thyme, and garlic.

Lettuce   As a rule, use leaf or loosehead varieties, not tightly heading types. Some favorites are BUTTERCRUNCH, BLACK-SEEDED SIMPSON, and MATCHLESS (15). Other heat and disease-resistant loosehead lettuces worth a try are BALLADE, RED FIRE, and GREEN WAVE (all available from 68). MISSION (48) is a true iceberg type that is unusually heat resistant and is the exception to the rule that loose, leafy lettuces are the only choice for southern gardens.

Melons   Some gardeners find that cantaloupes grown in humid areas taste less sweet than those grown in dry areas. However, CRIMSON SWEET and DIXIE LEE watermelons (both available from 28) are pleasingly sweet and also have disease resistance. Watermelons have time to mature to large sizes.

Mustard   SOUTHERN GIANT CURLED and FLORIDA BROAD LEAF (both available from 36) are popular greens in Florida.

Onions   In Florida, gardeners grow WHITE PORTUGAL for green onions, and TEXAS GRANO, WHITE GRANEX, and TROPICANO RED for bulbs.

Peas   For crowder peas, LADY CREAM and CALHOUN CROWDER are often grown in Louisiana. The snow pea GREY SUGAR and garden peas GREEN ARROW and ALMOTA (68) are good in South Carolina. Many southern gardeners report good luck with WANDO (17), a garden pea. SUGAR BON (9, 48), an early heat and downy-mildew–resistant snap pea, also does well.

Peppers   CALIFORNIA WONDER, YOLO WONDER L, and WORLD BEATER (8) are mild, ANAHEIM CHILI is hot, and all are reported to do well in Florida.

Potatoes   RED LA SODA (47, 54) resists disease in Louisiana.

Radishes   Southern gardeners must be sure to grow these very early or forget about them. SPARKLER and WHITE ICICLE grow well in Florida.

Spinach   VIRGINIA SAVOY (17), DIXIE MARKET, and HYBRID 7 are good choices in Florida. MELODY stands well in South Carolina.

Squash   In Florida, EARLY SUMMER CROOKNECK, COCOZELLE, and PATTY PAN are frequently grown. BUTTERNUT, GOLD NUGGET, and SPOOKIE PUMPKIN are favorites in South Carolina.

Sweet potatoes   CENTENNIAL frequently grows in South Carolina gardens.

Tomatoes   Especially developed for the South are FLORADEL, HOMESTEAD 24, WALTER, MANALUCIE, and TROPIC (all available from 36). BETTER BOY does well in Florida. VEEBRITE and VEEROMA (both available from 59) have a good track record in South Carolina. For fall in Florida, EARLY GIRL and TINY TIM do well. FLORAMERICA HYBRID VF is noteworthy because it resists 17 common tomato complaints. Other southern favorites include STAKEBREAKER VF and RED CHIEF VFN (both available from 28).

cantaloupes, and by April cucumbers are in the ground. To a Northerner, it all seems like a topsy-turvy world, but by avoiding the heat of summer and practicing sensible successions and relays, gardens in the Deep South produce great bounty.

Farther north, between Virginia and Georgia, successions more nearly resemble those of the North, with tomatoes, for example, started inside April through June, for harvest July through November. Peas are sown February through March for May through June harvest.

Southern gardeners must always remember to allow wider spacings in raised beds. When conditions are hot and humid, air circulation is even more important than shading because plants are prone to fungus, and fruit rots quickly. Another good idea is to train as many crops as possible up off the ground. Choose pole beans, for example, over bush beans, and trellis tomatoes, or even squash and melons, to ensure a better quality harvest.

Protective devices are less used in the South than elsewhere, but shading structures are important. In the cooler areas a cold frame may make the difference between an eight-month and a ten-month season or may give you four full months of corn instead of a mere three.

Interior Climate of the Midwest

The Midwest, land of golden grain, would seem logically to offer a golden mean in climate. Instead, removed from the temperature moderating influence of oceans, it is a territory of extremes. Midwestern gardeners share many of the advantages, but also some of the problems, of the Far North and the Deep South. In spring, they must race to catch up with the season, but in summer, their biggest enemy may be extreme heat.

Local areas can be markedly different from each other. Local features like lakes, rivers, hills, and open plains produce separate climates. One common feature of the Midwest, however, is also its greatest limitation: Spring is short. In the northern Midwest, spring follows a severe winter, but even at southern Midwest latitudes, winter seems to jump directly into summer.

Precipitation is generally ideal in total quantity, but it is delivered erratically. Spring floods are common in the enormous drainage area of the Mississippi River. In eastern Indiana, which has almost the same annual rainfall as eastern Pennsylvania, there seems to be no such thing thing as a gentle rain, but only gully-washing storms followed by summer drought. Severe droughts are common in the windswept plains further west, where irrigation is essential in summer.

The soils of the Midwest are known for their fertility and depth, although years of chemical farming and erosion have done much to deplete them. In places that reap the legacy of former prairies, and especially in the fine-textured soil called loess that exists in parts of the upper Mississippi basin, soil nutrients abound. Soil texture, however, is a major problem where glaciers once ground the rocks to impermeable clay and where inland seas and prehistoric lakes left behind clay deposits. Rapidly rising temperatures produce a hard clay crust in summer. Here, the use of raised beds and well-prepared soil is crucial. Good tilth is also important to prevent damage from erosion in the face of likely storms.

Spring is so brief in Iowa that gardeners there report having to plant peas and beans on the same day. Winter also comes all at once, with snowfall and deep freeze arriving soon after Thanksgiving. With such abrupt changes in temperature, early indoor starts, protection from wind, frost and sun, and well-thought-out plant placement are vital weapons in your struggle against the shifting seasons. In the rich soil of raised beds, use close spacing to shade the soil from strong spring and summer sun. This is especially important with cool-loving crops.

Intercroppings demand careful planning and sometimes also the holding back of ready-to-transplant seedlings for relays until the difficult-to-time earlier crops are ready to be replaced. Cold frames are useful for this purpose as well as

Windbreaks: Shown on the top are permanent or semipermanent windbreaks to shelter garden plants. On the left is a hedgerow and row of corn. On the right is a wire fence covered with plastic sheeting and a stone wall. Below you'll see an assortment of portable windbreaks. A section of milk carton (cut diagonally), a burlap screen, and half a plastic bottle are fine for sheltering small groups or individual plants.

for hardening-off. With rapidly changing weather, and planting dates that are seldom regular from year to year because of storms, hardening-off is an important part of midwestern gardening.

In the upper Midwest, a lengthy Indian summer follows the first frost, which comes early in autumn. Movable or fixed bed protection in that climate will save harvests.

Cover crops, which thrive on the former prairie, are often planted to prevent erosion in winter as well as to improve the soil. Soybeans, buckwheat, and alfalfa are favorites. One Iowa gardener advises filling any space with a cover crop if it would otherwise lie open for as much as a month.

Early starts for such crops as peppers, eggplants, and tomatoes and the use of early varieties will prevent damage from hot, dry winds that cause blossom drop. You'll also find that windbreaks are useful. Because winds are usually constant, midwestern gardeners often set up the permanent type, either spaced fencing or rows of trees. Summer mulching is also a wise practice for water conservation and soil shading. Except in low-lying or clay soil areas, soil warms quickly, so you should try to gather spring mulching material in the fall so it will be on hand and ready when you need it. In working against exploding Midwest seasons, relays and careful interplanting schemes will prove the most helpful of the whole battery of intensive skills.

Arid Heat of the Southwest

Gardening in the deserts of the Southwest is an act of oasis-making. Yet arid climates can be among the best for raising vegetables. Sun never lacks, soil can be improved to adequate fertility, tropical plants unknown to other places—dates, papayas, and avocados—add exotic variety, and, at lower altitudes, there are 365 growing days. The limiting factor, however, is water.

To be accurate, we should divide the southwestern United States into subareas. Anyone who has ever been there knows that it is not all desert. A truly arid area is one in which evaporation exceeds precipitation, or rainfall is limited to 5 inches or less per year. At low elevations, conditions are close to tropical in arid places during the rains of late summer and early spring, but only at those times. Arizona gardeners in low deserts time their gardens to begin when the rains come. Summer nights seldom go under 80°F and days can rise to 120°F. Winter lows are over 36°F.

The growing season ranges from year-round near the coast to 302 days in Phoenix. Inland, the planting season begins in fall and lasts only until midspring. Large tomatoes won't fruit in the heat of summer and many vegetables wilt away even when given additional water.

At medium elevations, winters are mild, but there are occasional frosts, and even more damaging, sudden drops in temperature after hot spells. Summer is a little less blazing than in lower land, with nights in the 70s allowing a few more cool-weather crops to grow. Rainfall can reach 15 inches a year. At high elevations, the growing season drops down to 200 days, with winter temperatures as low as 0°F and with rapid swings from hot to cold. The air is so dry that protection alone won't save crops from sudden frost. Cruel day-night temperature variations tax even the hardiest drought-toughened plants. Here, rainfall is greater, but storms are local and often severe and sudden. Dust devil whirlwinds, unblocked by vegetaion, may wipe out whole rows in a garden.

Throughout the Southwest, except in rare cool fog areas, all plants not specifically adapted for desert growing require irrigation and should be planted near a source of water. But water itself can be a problem. In many areas, if not overly alkaline, it is too expensive to use freely. The soil, which is also alkaline, or in some places saline, has a tendency to form a cementlike *caliche*, an impervious hardpan. The soil amost always needs improving before it is fit to garden in.

Faced with these conditions you'll find that using raised, or at least double-dug, beds makes it easier to improve the soil and also to leach out salts and wash them down to a level where they will do less damage to crops. Be sure to keep soil damp in spring during periods of germination and rapid growth. In summer, keep the subsoil moist, but let the tops of beds dry out to act as a dust mulch. In fall, the watering tapers off, except for gardeners who are starting a winter garden.

Drip irrigation, which places water directly into the root zone, is ideal for arid regions. Once

VEGETABLES FOR MIDWESTERN GARDENS

The best rule of thumb is to look for early, stress-resistant plants that can tolerate both heat and cold— and often drought as well.

Beans ROYAL BUSH resists bean beetles. Limas grow well from southern Wisconsin to points further south.

Beets WINTER KEEPER (14) is good for storage.

Carrots IMPERATOR is a heavy producer in Iowa. DANVERS HALF-LONG is better for heavy soil.

Cauliflower SELF-BLANCHE has time enough to grow in all but the northern Midwest. MINI-SNOW beats hot weather.

Corn COUNTRY GENTLEMAN (25, 34), BLACK MEXICAN (52), and ASHWORTH (34), when planted together, give continuous yield for more than two months in Ohio. Midwestern gardeners might also want to try IOCHIEF (9).

Cucumbers POT LUCK and SPACEMAKER produce well on small vines. EARLIEST OF ALL (25) beats the virus season.

Lettuce OAK LEAF stands the heat in Iowa. GREAT LAKES' W.S. (48) is an iceberg type that is highly resistant to tipburn and heat.

Melons Melons for the hot interior climate include the super-yielding IOPRIDE (25) and SHORT 'N' SWEET (48) cantaloupe.

Peas LITTLE MARVEL and LINCOLN produce dependably even in hot spring weather.

Peppers PICK-ME-QUICK (25) was developed for midwestern gardeners at South Dakota State University.

Potatoes KENNEBEC resists disease and pests.

Squash BUTTERCUP (63) keeps well. GREEN STRIPED CUSHAW (22) is extra sweet. Both are winter squash.

Swiss chard RHUBARB is productive and adds a pleasing touch of red to the garden's color scheme.

Tomatoes SUB-ARCTIC (34, 59) and PIXIE (34, 51) produce in late July. EARLY GIRL will give medium-sized fruit a week before the regular size varieties to beat the dry weather in South Dakota. EARLY CASCADE, HYTOP F2 (25), and RUSHMORE (25) have also been successful in South Dakota, where they bear until frost in spite of very hot and dry springs and summers. OXHEART, MARGLOBE, and BEEFSTEAK resist cracking and blight in Illinois. CELEBRITY (9, 26, 50) is a hybrid that has strong disease resistance and bears heavily in blistering heat.

established, it saves you money and precious water resources. Alternatives are soaker hoses under mulch and periodic flooding of garden trenches in which plants are set. In the Southwest, many gardeners reverse the traditional raised bed and turn it into a lowered, or sunken bed. Such beds are also called waffle beds, basin beds, or pans. Pans serve to catch the gully-washing rains when they finally come and thus prevent erosion and runoff. Gardeners often build small adobe walls, or dikes, to contain their sunken pans. If possible, water or flood irrigate at night, when there is less evaporation. In the Southwest, you don't have to worry about creating mildew problems. Whether you water day or night, do it infrequently and deeply to stimulate plants to produce longer roots that can go after moisture on their own. (For more details on flood and basin irrigation, see Watering Devices and Systems in chapter 4.)

Thick mulching is essential to hold in moisture. In dry areas you can use decay-resistant, high-carbon mulches like sawdust and wood chips with less danger to soil nitrogen reserves. The organisms that break down these mulches and use soil nitrogen in the process are less active when water is lacking. If you plan to flood irrigate, add more nitrogen with high-carbon mulches.

Manures contain salts and should be added with caution to soils where the salt content is already high. Open-range livestock, especially, produce manure high enough in some salts as to be harmful in large quantities. Soy meal and alfalfa compost are good alternatives to manures.

Additional southwestern practices are nearly all responses to the need for careful husbanding of the limited water supply. Inside starting not only gets a jump on the summer heat and the autumn chill of higher altitudes, but it's also often the only way to be sure that seeds germinate when the outdoor soil is dry and the evaporation rate high. Crusting soil is a major stumbling block for seeds that are sown directly in the garden. Place shade devices over the soil to keep it from drying and forming a hard layer. One experienced California gardener uses sheets of plywood, burlap, and nylon window screens, in that order, to protect seeds and tiny, newly sprouted plants. He reports that this method works very well for summer-planted carrots. Other southwestern gardeners use soaked burlap or wet newspaper mulch to cover beds while seeds are germinating.

Never locate a vegetable garden near a large tree. A full-sized oak can use up to 3,000 gallons of water a day. If water is scarce, eliminate water and space-demanding crops like sweet corn and standard watermelons. If you can't do without them, plant a miniature variety. Grow leaf instead of heading lettuce unless your water supply is abundant. Heading vegetables and those that set fruit use a lot of water. Whenever possible, use short plants instead of high or vining ones. These will be less exposed to the drying effects of sun and wind. If you're using flood or basin irrigation, you may find interplanting undesirable. With single-crop beds, you can meet the water needs of individual vegetables more economically.

In all but the most coastal and the higher arid areas, gardening is a two-season occupation. Plant cool-season vegetables in late summer to early spring, depending on the severity of the winter. Plant warm-season vegetables, which need heat, but not too much of it if their fruit is to be set, in late winter to early spring, so they can race the heat to maturity. Only gardeners at higher elevations would plant in late spring. Most of your warm-season plants will probably be indoor-started. Some of these warmth-loving crops will behave like true desert plants and go dormant in summer and begin to reproduce again in early fall. A few of the most heat-loving, like melons, squashes, peppers, okra, sweet potatoes, and sometimes small-fruited tomatoes, will continue to set fruit all summer if you give them enough water.

VEGETABLES FOR SOUTHWESTERN GARDENS

Amaranth Amaranth is available in two forms, as a grain crop and a leafy vegetable. It's long been used by Indians in the Southwest and is now gaining popularity among gardeners.

Beans ROYALTY PURPLE POD (51) resists the Mexican bean beetle. DUTCH BROWN (1) is good for drying. Aztec and tepary beans are extremely drought resistant. Local seed companies sell several varieties of them, including some that were found in archeological digs. BLUE SPECKLED and BROWN SPECKLED (51) are developed varieties of tepary bean.

Broccoli CLEOPATRA and GEM are good in the winter garden. SOUTHERN COMET (63) and GREEN COMET are heat resistant and also bear side shoots.

Cabbage COPENHAGEN MARKET, EMERALD CROSS HYBRID (9), and EARLY DUTCH ROUND are good producers in southwestern gardens.

Corn The Papago Indians made wide use of blue corn, which can be eaten fresh or dried and then ground. Among more standard varieties, HOPI WHITE (52), a hominy corn, is native and GOLDEN BANTAM is drought resistant.

Lettuce Quick-maturing varieties need less water. Leaf lettuces have lower water needs than heading ones. SALAD BOWL is a good choice, and BLACK-SEEDED SIMPSON is popular in Southern California. OAK LEAF is heat resistant enough to grow into summer in Oklahoma.

Melons ITSY BITSY SWEETHEART (28), BUSHWHOPPER, FORDHOOK GEM, and HONEY DRIP (63) cantaloupes stand up to heat. Small watermelons (both plant and fruit) use less water than large ones. Among these are SUGAR BUSH (9), BABY FUN (28, 50), and YELLOW DOLL HYBRID (28, 45).

Onions Onions should be salt resistant. GRANEX and NEW MEXICO YELLOW GRANO are good choices.

Peas The University of Arizona's Tucson Center found BLUE BANTAM and LITTLE SWEETIE suitable for the climate. BLUE BANTAM stands up to wind in Oklahoma. PAPAGO (44) is alkali tolerant and can counter Texas root rot.

Peppers In the Southwest, peppers are hot. JALAPENO, LONG RED CAYENNE, NEW MEXICO 64, EL PASO, and SANTA FE GRANDE will take—as well as give—heat. For something a little less blistering, try CUBANELLE (14), PARK'S POT, SWEET BELL BOY, or ACONCAGUA (23).

Spinach Bolt-resistant spinach like MELODY and BLOOMSDALE LONGSTANDING face heat the best. AVON does reasonably well in Southern California.

Squash Among winter squashes, WALTHAM BUTTERNUT, EARLY BUTTERNUT, TETSUKABUTO (23), and ROYAL ACORN are reliable performers. Summer squashes such as GREYZINI, ARISTOCRAT, and STRAIGHTNECK are good, while BLACK MAGIC zucchini is especially salt tolerant.

Tomatoes COLUMBIA and RED CHERRY (9) are among the least susceptible to blossom drop in hot weather. EARLY GIRL seldom fails to set fruit in cool winter nights. PIXIE (34, 51) saves space and therefore water. EARLIROUGE (51) and SUB-ARCTIC PLENTY (34, 51) are early ripening varieties reported to do well in the Southwest.

PART

3 High-Yield Plant Guide

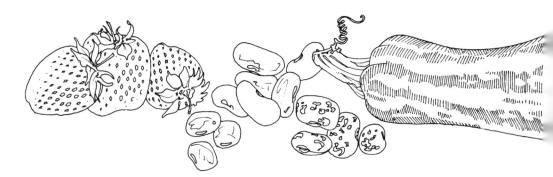

The High-Yield Plant Guide has been written and organized so that you can find thorough, concise growing instructions for 99 vegetables, fruits, and herbs quickly and easily. If you're unsure about a technique that's mentioned, look it up in the index or use the table of contents to direct you to the chapter where it's discussed in more detail.

There are several features of this guide that deserve mention. The Latin forms of plant names are given not to intimidate you, but rather to let you see which plants are related so you can plan rotations in your garden better (related plants tend to succumb to the same pests and diseases).

To help you locate the noteworthy varieties that are mentioned throughout the guide, we've included source numbers. The seed companies (with their addresses) that correspond to the numbers are listed in the Directory of Resources.

Each fruit entry mentions a hardiness zone. Turn to the Hardiness Zone Map on page 386 to find out the boundaries of each zone.

APPLES   *Malus pumila*   Rosaceae

Hardiness Zones:
5 to 7 with some varieties suited to 4 and 8.

Intensive Spacing:
8 to 12 feet for dwarfs, 12 to 18 feet for semidwarfs.

Growing Requirements:
Apples adapt to a wide range of soil types. The basic requirement is that the soil drains well. The pH should be 6.0 to 7.0. Give an annual side-dressing of manure with a sprinkling of wood ashes and bone meal. Critical time for watering is at flowering and near harvest when fruit growth is rapid. Prune to a central leader or open center shape. Some varieties must be cross-pollinated to set fruit and even self-fertile varieties will bear more fruit with cross-pollination.

Pest and Disease Problems:
Insects include aphids, apple fruitworms, apple maggots, codling moths, European apple sawflies, flatheaded borers, leafrollers, plum curculios, and white apple leafhoppers. Diseases are bitter pit, black rot, cedar-apple rust, fireblight, fly speck, powdery mildew, scab, and sooty blotch.

Season-Extending Options:
To promote early bearing, prune back trees severely at planting time so they form low heads. Also, fall-planted trees often begin bearing a year earlier than spring-planted trees. Train trees into an espalier shape against a heat-retaining wall to create a favorable microclimate.

Yield-Improving Techniques:
Alfalfa hay mulch can increase yields. Southern gardeners should look for varieties bred to require few hours of winter chilling.

Harvest and Storage:
Dwarf trees come into bearing in 2 to 4 years. A ripe apple lifts easily from the tree with an upward twisting motion. Store apples in a cool, moist place. A mature dwarf apple yields 1 to 2 bushels of fruit.

Noteworthy Apple Varieties

Variety	Description	Sources
LIBERTY	A semidwarf that is hardy, highly productive and offers resistance to a number of diseases.	83
PRIMA	A dwarf variety with resistance to 4 diseases.	73
STARKSPUR COMPACT MAC	A spur-type genetic dwarf suited for growing in small spaces or containers.	94

APRICOTS   *Prunus* spp.   Rosaceae

Hardiness Zones:
4 to 9.

Intensive Spacing:
8 to 12 feet for dwarfs, 10 to 12 feet for semidwarfs.

Growing Requirements:
Apricots do well in a wide range of soils as long as they are well drained and free of a hardpan layer. The pH is not critical. The important time for watering is during flowering and near harvest when fruit growth is most rapid. Mulch to conserve moisture; trees that suffer from lack of water produce small, mealy fruit. Side-dress yearly with manure and a dusting of wood ashes. Prune plants to an open center shape. Most varieties are self-pollinating, but a few require cross-pollination.

Pest and Disease Problems:
Borers, Japanese beetles, oriental fruit moths, and plum curculios may plague the harvest. Diseases include brown rot fungus, bacterial leaf spot, and canker.

Season-Extending Options:
Fall-planted trees often begin bearing a year earlier than spring-planted trees. Train trees into an espalier shape against a heat-retaining wall.

Yield-Improving Techniques:
Be sure to prune carefully each year to keep the center of the tree open to sun. For healthy, fruiting spurs, sun must reach as many branches as possible.

Harvest and Storage:
Apricots begin bearing in 4 to 9 years. Dead ripe apricots fall from the tree. Extras can be dried or canned.

Noteworthy Apricot Varieties

Variety	Description	Sources
GARDEN ANNIE	A genetic dwarf that grows only 5 to 8 ft. tall.	73
GOLDEN GLO	A genetic dwarf that reaches 4 to 6 ft. tall.	94
MANCHURIAN BUSH APRICOT	A bush type that is very productive in small spaces.	25

ARUGULA (also called rocket) *Eruca sativa* Cruciferae

Propagation:
Sow seeds directly in the garden as soon as soil is workable. Plant seeds ½ inch deep.

Intensive Spacing:
6 to 9 inches. Arugula can be broadcast and grown in wide-rows.

Growing Requirements:
Arugula adapts to a wide range of soils and growing conditions. Treat it the same way you do leaf lettuce.

Pest and Disease Problems:
Slugs and snails can bother plants.

Season-Extending Options:
A good growing frame crop for extra-early spring or late fall greens.

Interplanting Suggestions:
Compact arugula fits in nicely between tall-growing crops.

Succession Planting Suggestions:
Follow this early, quick-maturing green with any warm-season crop like tomatoes, peppers, and eggplants.

Harvest and Storage:
Arugula matures in 40 days. Start to harvest a few outer leaves at a time when they reach usable size. Leaves are best while still young and tender. This cut-and-come-again method will prolong harvesting.

ASPARAGUS *Asparagus officinalis* Liliaceae Perennial

Propagation:
Can be started from seeds or crowns. Plants grown from seed have been shown to produce a larger number of slightly bigger and more tender spears than those started from crowns. Start seeds 12 to 14 weeks before planting out. Soak seeds overnight to improve germination. Set out 12-inch seedlings 4 weeks after the last frost. Plant crowns 2 to 4 weeks before last frost. Set seedlings and crowns in trenches 6 to 10 inches deep. Cover with 2 inches of soil (mound around base of seedlings). As shoots grow, add soil until trench is filled to ground level.

Intensive Spacing:
12 to 18 inches. Give this perennial its own bed or section of bed so it can grow undisturbed.

Growing Requirements:
Adapts well to many types of soil, as long as they're not waterlogged. Grows best in well-drained, sandy loam with a pH of 6.5 to 6.8. Needs full sun. A heavy feeder that benefits from a 6 to 8-inch blanket of compost or manure (composted or uncomposted) spread over the bed. The most drought-resistant of common garden vegetables.

Pest and Disease Problems:
Asparagus beetles are the only common pests. Rust and fusarium wilt can affect plants. Choose resistant varieties to safeguard the health and vigor of your asparagus bed.

Season-Extending Options:
Stretch the harvest by delaying some of the plants in the bed. Let the first spear that emerges from a crown develop completely, to delay the rest for 7 to 10 days. The total yield from the bed will be the same. Also, dig some roots before the soil freezes hard to force indoors.

Harvest and Storage:
Wait to harvest a full 2 seasons after planting. This guarantees good productivity for the life of the bed. Pick for 2 weeks. The next year, pick for 4 weeks, and in following years pick for 6 to 8 weeks. Pick spears less than 1 inch thick with firm, closed tips.

Noteworthy Asparagus Variety

Variety	Description	Sources
BROCK IMPERIAL	Produces 30 percent more than the standard varieties.	25

BASIL *Ocimum basilicum* Labiatae Warm-season annual

Propagation:
Seeds germinate in 5 to 7 days. Basil can be sown directly in the garden after last frost as soon as the soil is thoroughly warm. For transplants start seeds 6 weeks before setting out, which can be done after last frost.

Intensive Spacing:
12 to 18 inches.

Growing Requirements:
Basil will adapt to a range of soils as long as they are well drained. It thrives in a light, medium rich soil that retains moisture well. The pH can range from 5.0 to 8.0. Basil needs full sun.

Season-Extending Options:
Container-grown basil can be set in the garden during the growing season, then brought indoors for a winter harvest.

Yield-Improving Techniques:
Pinch stems periodically to promote bushy growth, which means more harvestable leaves. Pinch off flowers as they appear to keep plants producing good quality leaves.

Interplanting Suggestions:
Grow basil around the base of an ornamental or dwarf fruit tree. Basil is a traditional companion to tomatoes; it is thought to enhance the tomatoes' growth and flavor. It is also reputed to control various bean and cabbage pests.

Succession Planting Suggestions:
Basil can follow an extra-early planting of lettuce, spinach, or peas.

Harvest and Storage:
Basil matures 8 to 10 weeks after planting. Leaves are at their prime before flowers open. Pick a few branches or leaves at a time as needed to ensure continuous production. Some plants may require weekly harvesting from mid-July to maintain good quality leaves. At the end of the season when frost threatens, cut the entire plant. Freeze or dry surplus leaves.

Noteworthy Basil Varieties

Variety	Description	Sources
DARK OPAL	Rich, deep purple leaves make this a handsome plant.	Widely available
SPICY GLOBE	A compact, spacesaving variety well suited to interplanting.	48

FAVA BEANS   *Vicia faba*   Leguminosae   Cool-season crop

Propagation:
Sow seeds directly in the garden up to 7 weeks before the last frost. Plant 1 inch deep.

Intensive Spacing:
8 inches. Favas can be broadcast or grown in wide-rows.

Growing Requirements:
Favas adapt to a wide range of soils, as long as they are well drained and the pH is between 6.0 and 7.5. As warm weather approaches, mulch to keep plants cool.

Trellising or Training Tips:
Provide poles, tepees, or other vertical supports for vining varieties. Dwarf varieties benefit from the support of a piece of twine run around stakes in the corners of the bed or wide-row.

Pest and Disease Problems:
Pests include aphids, bean beetles, and green stink bugs. Diseases are blight and mosaic.

Season-Extending Options:
Favas can withstand light frost. For an extra-early start, raise transplants and have them ready to set out as soon as the soil can be worked. Provide seedlings with protection against heavy frost.

Yield-Improving Techniques:
Treat with bacterial inoculant powder for vetch (*not* for beans and peas) to encourage nitrogen-fixing and vigorous growth.

Succession Planting Suggestions:
Lima beans make good successors to favas.

Harvest and Storage:
Favas take 3 months to mature. Begin harvesting from lowest pods, working up the plant. Pick young for use as snap beans or let beans develop in pods. Cook fresh or dry. Mature beans can also be frozen.

Noteworthy Fava Bean Varieties

Variety	Description	Sources
IPRO	Upright plants produce large, flat beans in 75 days.	29
WINDSOR	3-ft.-tall plants tolerate hot weather.	29

LIMA BEANS   *Phaseolus lunatus*   Leguminosae   Warm-season crop

Propagation:
Seeds take 7 to 10 days to germinate. Sow seeds directly in the garden 2 weeks after the last frost or when the soil has warmed to at least 65°F. Sow seeds 1 inch deep. For transplants, start seeds 3 to 4 weeks before setting out, which can be done 1 to 2 weeks after the last frost. Handle these temperamental transplants with care.

Intensive Spacing:
4 to 9 inches. Bush varieties can be broadcast and grown in wide-rows.

Growing Requirements:
Limas need well-drained soil, rich in organic matter. Soil pH should be 6.0 to 7.5. These nitrogen-fixers have low nitrogen needs and medium phosphorus and potassium needs. The critical time for watering is during pollination, pod development, and pod enlargement.

Trellising or Training Tips:
Be sure to provide vining varieties with tall and sturdy supports.

Pest and Disease Problems:
Insects include aphids, cabbage loopers, corn earworms, cucumber beetles, European corn borers, leafminers, and Mexican bean beetles. Diseases are downy mildew and bacterial spot.

Season-Extending Options:
These beans are extremely cold sensitive. Planting too early before the soil has warmed sufficiently usually means seeds will rot. Try warming soil with plastic or using transplants to get an early start. Or set a portable cold frame over the newly planted bed. Variety selection can extend the season. For early harvests, plant bush varieties. For a later but longer harvesting period, plant pole limas.

Yield-Improving Techniques:
Treat seeds before planting with special bacterial inoculant powder to encourage nitrogen-fixing. Pole beans have been shown to produce abundantly under a mulch of oat straw.

Interplanting Suggestions:
Grow shade-tolerant crops at the base of trellised plants and underneath a bean tepee. Beans also make complementary partners for celery, radishes, and staked tomatoes. Limas can be teamed with corn and squash for a classic combination. Marigolds and potatoes are companion crops that have been shown to keep bean beetles away. Traditional pest-repellent companions also include rosemary and catnip.

Succession Planting Suggestions:
Follow limas with nitrogen-loving crops. Plant in a spot vacated by a quick-growing cool-season crop like leaf lettuce, spinach, or bunching onions.

Harvest and Storage:
Limas mature in 75 to 85 days. Harvest daily to encourage good long-term production. Pick when seeds are bulging in pods, but before pods yellow and deteriorate. Dry or freeze extra beans.

Noteworthy Lima Bean Varieties

Variety	Description	Sources
BRIDGETON	One of the earliest, most productive and disease resistant of the limas.	48
CAROLINA (ALSO CALLED SIEVE)	Early bearing (78 days) variety.	9, 28
GENEVA	Relatively cold-tolerant, early baby bush lima.	34
KING OF THE GARDEN	8-ft. vines produce enormous harvests.	9, 25, 28, 48

SNAP BEANS *Phaseolus vulgaris* Leguminosae Warm-season crop

Propagation:
Seeds take 7 days to germinate. Sow seeds in the garden anytime after last frost. Soil temperature must be at least 60°F; otherwise seeds will rot. Plant seeds 1 inch deep. For transplants, start seeds indoors 3 to 4 weeks before setting out, which can be done 1 to 2 weeks after the last frost. Handle these temperamental transplants carefully.

Intensive Spacing:
4 to 6 inches. Bush varieties can be broadcast; once seedlings are up, thin to 4 to 6 inches apart. Bush beans can also be grown in wide-rows.

Growing Requirements:
Beans need well-drained soil rich in organic matter with a pH of 6.0 to 7.5. These nitrogen-fixers need little nitrogen and moderate amounts of phosphorus and potassium. They do best with full sun but can tolerate some partial shade. The critical time for watering is during pollination, pod development, and pod enlargement.

Trellising or Training Tips:
Pole beans need vertical supports; they'll cling to poles, fences, vertical strings, and even slender tree trunks. Bush beans are self-supporting.

Pest and Disease Problems:
Insects include aphids, cabbage loopers, corn earworms, cucumber beetles, European corn borers, leafminers, and Mexican bean beetles. Possible diseases are anthracnose, bacterial blight, mosaics, and rust.

Season-Extending Options:
Start indoors for a head start on the season. Variety selection can extend the harvesting season. Look for varieties bred to germinate in cool soil that can be planted out a week before last frost. Plant bush varieties for an early harvest and plant pole varieties for a later but longer harvest period.

Yield-Improving Techniques:
Studies have shown that bark mulch increases bean yields and that pole beans do especially well mulched with oat straw. Treat with bacterial inoculant to encourage efficient nitrogen fixing and vigorous growth.

Interplanting Suggestions:
Beans share space well with celery, radishes, and staked tomatoes. They form part of the classic triumvirate—beans, corn, and squash. Pole beans team well with shade-tolerant crops like lettuce, spinach, and bunching onions. Marigold and potato companions have been shown to reduce bean beetle numbers. Traditional insect-repellent companions include rosemary and catnip.

Succession Planting Suggestions:
Follow beans with a nitrogen-loving crop. Plant bush beans to follow an early corn variety. Use bush beans in a series following broccoli and preceding lettuce, or following Chinese cabbage and preceding lettuce and onions. Pole beans can follow lettuce, spinach, or Chinese cabbage.

Harvest and Storage:
Beans are ready to harvest in 40 to 60 days. Keep picking every day to promote continuous production. Beans are best when tender and slim. When seeds bulge in pods, they've passed their prime. Freeze, can, or dry the surplus.

Noteworthy Snap Bean Varieties

Variety	Description	Sources
BOUNTIFUL	Early (46 days) and abundant bush bean.	Widely available
CONTENDER	Good choice for late-season crops.	Widely available
EARLY GALLATIN STRINGLESS	Grows well in hot areas.	28
KENTUCKY WONDER	Vining, vigorous producer of long pods.	9
STRINGLESS BLUE LAKE FM1	Early-bearing, fiberless vining bean.	28, 48

BEETS   *Beta vulgaris*   Chenopodiaceae   Cool-season crop

Propagation:
Seeds can be slow to germinate, taking 7 to 14 days. To speed the process, soak seeds overnight or score seeds with a file. Sow seeds directly in the garden 2 to 4 weeks before last frost. Plant seeds ½ to 1 inch deep. For transplants, start seeds 4 weeks before setting out, which can be done 4 weeks before last frost. Handle these temperamental transplants carefully. For a fall crop, count back 74 days from the first expected frost to determine when to direct-sow.

Intensive Spacing:
2 to 6 inches. Beets can be broadcast and grown in wide-rows.

Growing Requirements:
For the best roots, grow in sandy, well-drained soil rich in organic matter with a pH of 6.5. Beets can tolerate partial shade. This crop needs low amounts of nitrogen, with moderate phosphorus and potassium. Beets need a steady supply of water throughout the growing season.

Pest and Disease Problems:
Generally a problem-free crop. Possible pests include aphids, leafhoppers, leafminers, slugs, and snails. Leaf spot sometimes strikes.

Season-Extending Options:
Beets make great growing frame crops. Direct-seed in frames in late February or early March. Beets can't withstand severe freezing. Put a cold frame over the bed full of storage beets and you can prolong the harvest for an extra month.

Yield-Improving Techniques:
A seaweed mulch has been shown to boost yields.

Interplanting Suggestions:
Beets do well matched with carrots and Swiss chard (give these crops a bed of their own for easy winter harvesting). Beets also pair nicely with corn or kohlrabi. Members of the onion family are considered traditional companions.

Succession Planting Suggestions:
Use this short-season crop to precede or follow a longer maturing midseason crop like bush beans or peppers. Make successive plantings every 3 weeks until midsummer.

Harvest and Storage:
Beets reach maturity in 50 to 60 days. Pull roots while they're still small, from 1½ to 3 inches. Harvest greens throughout the season. Roots can be stored in the garden under a blanket of mulch in areas with mild winters. Dig as needed and be sure to remove all roots when spring arrives. Freeze or can surplus roots.

Noteworthy Beet Varieties

Variety	Description	Sources
BOLTARDY	Extremely cold and bolt-resistant variety.	57, 67
DETROIT DARK RED	Very hardy beet that does well in spring and fall.	Widely available
GREEN TOP BUNCHING	Good choice for late summer and fall greens; roots are not as good as other varieties.	48
LITTLE BALL	Compact root that is ideal for tightly interplanted beds and growing frames.	9
WINTER KEEPER	Long-season beet that stores well under mulch.	14

BLACKBERRIES *Rubus* spp.   Rosaceae

Hardiness Zone:
4 to 10.

Intensive Spacing:
2 feet apart for erect varieties; 6 feet for trailing varieties in northern zones, 8 to 12 feet in more southerly growing areas.

Growing Requirements:
Blackberries adapt well to all soils except those that are acid or poorly drained. Second-year canes are the ones that bear fruit; after the harvest prune these back to ground level. Side-dress annually in spring with manure, and keep plants free of weeds. Blackberries are self-pollinating.

Pest and Disease Problems:
Red spider mites and borers can cause problems. Diseases include a number of different viruses, verticillium wilt, and orange rust. To assure healthy, productive plants, always start with certified virus-free stock.

Season-Extending Options:
Plant early, mid, and late-season varieties to extend the harvest period.

Yield-Improving Techniques:
Mulch can boost yields three to five times. Tip prune first-year canes of erect varieties by 3 to 4 inches; this encourages branching, which means more fruit will be produced.

Interplanting Suggestions:
Plant trellised varieties down the center of a 3-foot-wide bed. The first summer after planting grow beans, peas, and cabbage among the brambles.

Harvest and Storage:
Blackberries begin to bear in abundance 2 to 3 years after planting. They are ripe when they slip easily off the plant. Extras may be frozen, but there is a definite loss of quality. A mature blackberry bush yields 20 pounds of berries.

Noteworthy Blackberry Varieties

Variety	Description	Sources
BLACK SATIN THORNFREE	A heavy yielder with large berries and, better yet, no thorns.	25
DIRKSEN THORNLESS	Similar to Black Satin, but bears 1 week earlier; very hardy, produces large fruit.	5

BLUEBERRIES *Vaccinium* spp.   Ericaceae

Hardiness Zones:
7 to 10 for rabbiteye, 4 to 8 for highbush.

Intensive Spacing:
6 to 8 feet.

Growing Requirements:
Any well-drained, acid soil rich in organic matter will support a healthy stand of blueberry bushes. Highbush plants need a pH of 4.5 to 5.0; rabbiteyes prefer a pH around 4.2. Add a yearly side-dressing of manure and maintain a layer of mulch to keep these shallow-rooted plants moist. Begin pruning after 2 or 3 seasons of growth. Cut out old, less vigorous branches and any that are shading or crowding others. For best yields, plant 2 different varieties for cross-pollination.

Pest and Disease Problems:
Blueberries are relatively problem-free.

Season-Extending Options:
Plant early, mid, and late-season varieties to extend the harvest period.

Yield-Improving Techniques:
Mulches of peat moss or sawdust can boost production.

Interplanting Suggestions:
In a large bed, grow bush squash among the blueberries.

Harvest and Storage:
Wait 6 days to harvest after berries have turned from red to blue. The berries on a single bush will ripen in stages over a period of several weeks, so you won't be faced with a sudden glut. Extra berries freeze well. A mature bush yields 1 to 2 gallons or 8 pounds of berries.

Noteworthy Blueberry Varieties

Variety	Description	Sources
NORTHSKY	A hardy variety that survives cold down to −30°F and stands 18 in. tall.	20
SOUTHLAND	A new hybrid that yields well to the south of Florida.	28, 78
TOPHAT	A self-fertile, hardy variety for the North that grows 24 in. tall.	25

BROCCOLI   *Brassica oleracea*, Botrytis Group   Cruciferae   Cool-season crop

Propagation:
Seeds germinate in 5 to 10 days. Sow seeds outdoors 4 to 6 weeks before the last frost. Plant ½ inch deep. Start transplants 6 to 8 weeks before setting out, which can be done 4 weeks before and 2 to 3 weeks after the last frost. Start transplants for a fall crop 95 days before the first expected frost, and set out when 3 weeks old.

Intensive Spacing:
15 to 18 inches. Give more space to plants allowed to remain in the garden for a crop of side shoots.

Growing Requirements:
Broccoli needs a soil rich in nitrogen. Compost or rotted manure are excellent soil conditioners. Soil pH should be 6.7 to 7.2. Plants can tolerate partial shade. Broccoli needs moderate amounts of nitrogen and phosphorus. The critical time for watering is early in the season to prevent buttoning.

Pest and Disease Problems:
Young plants are bothered by cutworms and flea beetles. Mature plants fall prey to aphids, cabbage loopers, cabbage maggots, harlequin bugs, imported cabbage worms, and leafminers. Diseases include black rot, clubroot, downy mildew, and yellows. Use careful rotations to avoid disease problems.

Season-Extending Options:
Use transplants and plant protectors in early spring. To keep plants grown for summer side shoots from bolting, provide shading devices. Broccoli can be planted in fall and the young plants mulched to overwinter. These will sprout for extra-early harvests in spring. Choose varieties bred specifically for overwintering. Broccoli is also a fine growing-frame crop.

Yield-Improving Techniques:
A seaweed mulch has been shown to increase yields.

Interplanting Suggestions:
Team broccoli with carrots, celery, lettuce, and spinach because of their complementary growth habits. Traditional insect-repelling companions include celery, rosemary, sage, and thyme.

Succession Planting Suggestions:
In long-season gardens, follow broccoli with a planting of corn and cucumbers. In other areas, fit broccoli between early peas and summer squash.

Harvest and Storage:
Broccoli matures 55 to 60 days from transplanting. Cut the main head before yellow florets appear. Return for smaller harvests of side shoots. Can or freeze extra broccoli.

Noteworthy Broccoli Varieties

Variety	Description	Sources
CALABRESE	Hardy variety well suited to overwintering.	Widely available
EMPEROR	Heat-tolerant variety.	34
GREEN COMET	Early, fast-growing broccoli.	Widely available
ITALIAN GREEN SPROUTING	Prolific producer of side shoots.	Widely available
WALTHAM	Heat-resistant variety that does well as a fall crop.	Widely available

BRUSSELS SPROUTS *Brassica oleracea*, Gemmifera Group Cruciferae Cool-season crop

Propagation:
Seeds take 5 to 10 days to germinate. Start transplants 6 to 8 weeks before setting out, which can be done 4 weeks before to 2 to 3 weeks after the last frost. Another way to figure the seed-starting date is to count back 120 days from first expected fall frost. Only gardeners with long growing seasons should sow seeds directly in the garden. Plant seeds ½ inch deep.

Intensive Spacing:
15 to 18 inches.

Growing Requirements:
Brussels sprouts need well-drained soil rich in organic matter. They prefer heavy soil to light and sandy soil. The pH should range from 6.0 to 6.8. Plants need full sun.

Pest and Disease Problems:
Young plants are bothered by cutworms and flea beetles. Aphids, cabbage loopers, cabbage maggots, harlequin bugs, imported cabbage worms, and leafminers are other pests. Diseases include black rot, clubroot, downy mildew, and yellows. Use careful rotations to avoid disease problems.

Season-Extending Options:
This brassica is one of the most cold-resistant garden vegetables. It can stand in the garden, often without mulch, and remain harvestable until late December.

Yield-Improving Techniques:
To encourage most of the sprouts to mature at once, cut off the top rosette of leaves. This will give you a greater quantity to harvest all at once.

Interplanting Suggestions:
Brussels sprouts share space well with parsley, celery, and spinach. Traditional insect-repellent companions include onion family members, rosemary, sage, and thyme.

Succession Planting Suggestions:
This long-season crop doesn't offer much opportunity for successions.

Harvest and Storage:
Brussels sprouts mature in 90 to 95 days. Sprouts taste best when they've been touched by frost. Harvest firm sprouts (working from the bottom to the top of the stalk) over a period of several weeks. Bend plants to the ground (without breaking the stalk) and mulch heavily for a harvest into December. Should any sprouts freeze, cook them before they defrost.

Noteworthy Brussels Sprout Varieties

Variety	Description	Sources
FOCUS F1	Extra-hardy variety that will overwinter unmulched.	64
JADE CROSS HYBRID	Productive, reliable variety.	Widely available
LONG ISLAND IMPROVED	Grows only 20 in. high.	Widely available
ORMAVON	Produces a cabbage head in place of the top rosette.	64

CABBAGE   *Brassica oleracea*, Capitata Group   Cruciferae   Cool-season crop

Propagation:
Seeds germinate in 3 to 10 days. Sow seeds in the garden around the time of the last expected frost. Plant ½ inch deep. Start transplants 6 to 8 weeks before setting out, which can be done 5 weeks before to 2 to 3 weeks after the last frost. For a fall crop, start transplants or sow seeds 99 days before first expected frost.

Intensive Spacing:
15 to 18 inches. Dwarf varieties with smaller wrapper leaves can be spaced more closely. Fall plantings benefit from wider spacing.

Growing Requirements:
Cabbage needs well-drained soil rich in organic matter. The pH can range from 6.0 to 6.8. Provide cabbage with moderate amounts of nitrogen and phosphorus and high amounts of potassium. Cabbage can tolerate partial shade. The critical time for watering is during head development; too much water at the later stages will cause heads to split. The critical time for weeding is during the 3 to 5 weeks following transplanting.

Pest and Disease Problems:
Cutworms and flea beetles bother young plants. Aphids, cabbage loopers, cabbage maggots, harlequin bugs, imported cabbage worms, and leafminers may pose problems. Diseases include black rot, clubroot, downy mildew, and yellows. Use careful rotations to avoid disease problems.

Season-Extending Options:
Give early spring transplants the protection of cloches or growing frames.

Yield-Improving Techniques:
Some early varieties will produce a second harvest. Cut off the head at the base, leaving stalk and roots in place. When small buds appear, remove all except one or two. By late fall these will develop into small, tender heads.

Interplanting Suggestions:
Cabbage fits nicely with peas and lettuce in short rows. It also shares space well with chives, peppers, tomatoes, carrots, lettuce, and spinach. Traditional companions include onion family members, rosemary, sage, and thyme.

Succession Planting Suggestions:
Plant early, mid, and late-season varieties to stagger the harvest. Long-season gardeners can follow plantings of sweet corn, cucumbers, and bush beans with cabbage. Short-season growers can precede and follow midseason varieties with leafy greens.

Harvest and Storage:
Cut heads once they're solid. Left too long in the garden they are likely to split. Varieties noted for being long standing can be mulched heavily and left in the garden for an ongoing winter harvest.

Noteworthy Cabbage Varieties

Variety	Description	Sources
BABY EARLY	Heads mature in 50 days.	50
DARKRI	Compact, fast maturer good for tightly spaced beds in cool, short-season climates.	48
GLORY OF ENKHUIZEN	Good storage variety.	2
MORDEN DWARF	Early-maturing, compact head good for successions and close spacing.	20

CARROTS   *Daucus carota* var. *sativus*   Umbelliferae   Cool-season crop

Propagation:
Seeds take 12 to 14 days to germinate. To speed the process, soak seeds overnight then freeze a week before planting. Sow outdoors 4 to 6 weeks before the last frost date. Plant seeds ¼ to ½ inch deep. Prevent soil crusting by covering with sand, vermiculite, or sawdust. For transplants, start seeds 5 to 6 weeks before setting out, which can be done 4 weeks before the last frost. Handle transplants carefully. For a fall crop, count back 85 to 100 days from the first expected frost to determine when to direct-seed.

Intensive Spacing:
2 to 3 inches. For in-ground storage over the winter, plant a whole block or bed of tightly spaced carrots. These can be harvested by the shovelful. For single-carrot harvesting through the season, wider spacing is suitable.

Growing Requirements:
Carrots need light, sandy loam free of rocks and other obstructions that can make roots fork or split. Soil pH should be around 6.5. They need low amounts of nitrogen, moderate amounts of phosphorus, and high amounts of potassium. Never plant in a bed that's been freshly manured; the roots will become hairy and misshapen. Carrots can tolerate some partial shade. The critical time for watering extends throughout the growing season.

Pest and Disease Problems:
Carrots are seldom bothered. Possible insects include aphids, carrot rust flies, carrot weevils, and cutworms. Diseases include leaf blight and root knot nematodes.

Season-Extending Options:
Use transplants for an early start. Small-rooted varieties do well in growing frames.

Interplanting Suggestions:
Carrots share space well with lettuce and radishes. Another possibility is to plant them with Swiss chard and beets (a trio that overwinters well). Carrots also make a nice neighbor for leeks. Traditional insect-repellent companions include onion family members, rosemary, and sage.

Succession Planting Suggestions:
Make succession plantings every 2 to 3 weeks to stagger the harvest. Make a planting to follow an early corn variety. Southern growers can try a succession of squash, bush beans, and carrots. In short-season gardens, use carrots to follow early peas, lettuce, spinach, or Chinese cabbage.

Harvest and Storage:
Carrots reach full size in 60 to 80 days. The first harvest will probably be slender thinnings from broadcast plantings. Pull carrots whenever they've reached a usable size (judge this by clearing away soil until you see how broad the carrots' "shoulders" are). Carrots store well in-ground as long as winter temperatures don't sink below 20°F. Apply a thick layer of mulch and dig as needed. Or dig and store the surplus in a root cellar. Canning and freezing are also storage options.

Noteworthy Carrot Varieties

Variety	Description	Sources
A PLUS	Extra-rich in vitamin A	35, 38
KURODA CHANTENAY	Well suited to fall plantings.	51
LITTLE FINGER	Fast-maturing variety that's good to use in successions.	9, 50
ORLANDO GOLD	Bolt and crack-resistant and exceptionally rich in vitamin A.	22, 25, 29

CAULIFLOWER *Brassica oleracea*, Botrytis Group   Cruciferae
Cool-season crop

Propagation:
Seeds germinate in about 7 days. Start transplants for the spring crop 6 to 8 weeks before setting out, which can be done 4 weeks before to 2 weeks after the last frost date. Fall crops do well when direct-seeded 12 weeks before the first expected frost. Sow seeds ½ inch deep.

Intensive Spacing:
15 to 18 inches.

Growing Requirements:
Cauliflower needs moist, well-drained soil rich in organic matter. The pH should range from 6.0 to 6.8. Provide low amounts of nitrogen and moderate amounts of phosphorus and potassium. Plants need full sun. The critical time for watering is early in the season to encourage good head formation. As soon as the head begins to develop, pull wrapper leaves together to cover it and hold them in place with a clothespin. Self-blanching varieties make this step unnecessary; they grow best as fall crops.

Pest and Disease Problems:
Young cauliflower plants may be bothered by cutworms and flea beetles. Aphids, cabbage loopers, cabbage maggots, harlequin bugs, imported cabbage worms, and leafminers may also afflict the crop. Diseases include black rot, clubroot, downy mildew, and yellows. Use careful rotations to avoid disease problems.

Interplanting Suggestions:
Cauliflower shares garden space well with carrots, celery, lettuce, and spinach. Traditional insect-repellent companions include onion family members, rosemary, sage, and thyme.

Succession Planting Suggestions:
Follow early-maturing varieties with bush beans or some other heat-loving, relatively quick-growing crop. Precede a fall crop with bolt-resistant lettuce, or spring-growing Chinese cabbage.

Harvest and Storage:
Cauliflower matures in 50 to 115 days depending on variety. Harvest when the head is compact and white. It's past its prime when the head looks yellow or fuzzy (a condition called riceyness). Cauliflower is best when used as close to harvest as possible.

Noteworthy Cauliflower Varieties

Variety	Description	Sources
ALERT	Good choice for cool, short-season climates; matures in 48 days from transplants.	34, 48, 59
EARLY SNOWBALL	Has higher-than-usual amounts of vitamin A.	1, 5
SNOW KING	Early and abundant producer.	9, 22, 35

CELERIAC *Apium graveolens* var. *rapaceum* Umbelliferae Cool-season crop

Propagation:
Seeds take 10 to 21 days to germinate. Presoaking overnight can hasten sprouting. Only long-season gardeners can direct-sow; plant in late summer for a spring crop. Plant seeds ⅛ inch deep. Other gardeners must start celeriac inside 8 weeks before setting out, which can be done anytime after the last frost. (Some gardeners use falling apple blossoms as the sign that it's safe to set out.)

Intensive Spacing:
12 inches.

Growing Requirements:
Celeriac needs a fertile, heavy loam rich in organic matter. The pH can range from 6.0 to 6.5.

Pest and Disease Problems:
Celeriac is generally problem-free. Sometimes aphids, slugs, and snails may be a nuisance. Septoria leaf spot may appear, but not often.

Season-Extending Options:
Use transplants to get a head start on this crop's particularly long growing season.

Succession Planting Suggestions:
This slow-to-mature crop doesn't allow much time for successions.

Harvest and Storage:
Celeriac matures in 110 to 120 days. Harvest roots when they're 2 to 4 inches thick. Celeriac stores well in the ground under a thick mulch for a month after first frost in the North or all winter in milder climates.

Noteworthy Celeriac Varieties

Variety	Description	Sources
ALABASTER	Large, thick roots have creamy white flesh.	Widely available
GIANT SMOOTH PRAGUE	Matures about 10 days earlier than Alabaster.	Widely available

CELERY   *Apium graveolens* var. *dulce*   Umbelliferae   Cool-season crop

Propagation:
Seeds take 10 to 14 days to germinate. Speed the process by soaking overnight then freezing a week before planting. Only gardeners with very long seasons should contemplate direct-sowing. Sow seeds 2 to 4 weeks before the last frost, when the soil registers at least 60°F. Plant seeds ¼ inch deep. Best results are usually had by starting seeds indoors 6 to 8 weeks before setting out, which can be done 3 weeks before to 4 weeks after the last frost. Set out when the temperature dips no lower than 50°F.

Intensive Spacing:
6 to 9 inches.

Growing Requirements:
Celery is a tricky crop to grow, and starting out with good soil can contribute to its success. The soil must be rich and full of organic matter to hold moisture evenly. The pH can range from 5.8 to 6.7. Celery is a heavy feeder that needs large amounts of nitrogen, phosphorus, and potassium. It tolerates partial shade.

Pest and Disease Problems:
Watch for aphids, cabbage loopers, carrot rust flies, carrot weevils, leafhoppers, whiteflies, cutworms, slugs, and snails. Diseases include early and late blights, fusarium yellows, and pink rot.

Interplanting Suggestions:
Celery pairs nicely with spinach or bush beans. It also teams well with parsley, Brussels sprouts, and spinach. As a rule, you can pair it with most brassicas. Cabbage is thought to be a traditional companion.

Succession Planting Suggestions:
This long-season crop doesn't allow much time for successions.

Harvest and Storage:
Celery matures in 90 to 100 days from transplants. Cut a few outer stalks at a time for an extended harvest. Or cut the entire plant off at the base of the crown. Under a thick cover of mulch the celery harvest can continue into the winter.

Noteworthy Celery Varieties

Variety	Description	Sources
FORDHOOK	Standard variety with good growth.	Widely available
GOLDEN SELF-BLANCHING	Stems are white with pale yellow leaves.	Widely available

CELTUCE   *Lactuca sativa* var. *angustata*   Compositae   Cool-season crop

Propagation:
Sow seeds directly in the garden 4 to 6 weeks before last frost, or as soon as soil is workable. Plant them ½ inch deep. Start transplants 4 weeks before planting outside, which can be done 1 month before last frost. For a fall crop, begin sowing 8 weeks before first expected frost.

Intensive Spacing:
18 inches. Celtuce can be broadcast; thin seedlings to 18 inches apart when they're 2 inches tall. This leafy crop can also be grown in wide-rows.

Growing Requirements:
Celtuce prefers a loose, well-drained soil rich in organic matter. Ample amounts of manure or compost promote high-quality harvests. Soil pH should range between 6.0 to 6.8. Keep celtuce well watered, and mulch to stifle weed competition. This green tolerates partial shade.

Pest and Disease Problems:
Occasionally aphids, flea beetles, and slugs may bother the crop. Downy mildew and mold sometimes pose problems.

Season-Extending Options:
Like Swiss chard, celtuce is a heat and frost-tolerant crop. The two-stage harvest (leaves, then edible seedstalk) makes this a productive green in both cool and warm seasons. After the romainelike leaves are harvested, don't discard the plant. Wait for the crunchy seedstalk to emerge. Transplants get an early start on the season, while mulch keeps plants harvestable as fall settles in.

Succession Planting Suggestions:
Sow celtuce at 2-week intervals until midsummer.

Harvest and Storage:
The first harvest begins 45 days after sowing. Pick leaves while they're young by removing them from the outside of the plant. Don't damage the inner leaves. Leaves more than 4 weeks old are too bitter to be palatable. Cut off the central seedstalk when it's 1 inch thick. Peel away the skin to remove any bitterness. Celtuce is best eaten soon after harvest.

CHERRIES *Prunus* spp. Rosaceae

Hardiness Zones:
5 to 8 for sweet cherries, 4 to 8 for sour cherries.

Intensive Spacing:
10 to 15 feet for dwarf and semidwarf sour cherries. 12 feet for dwarf and 18 feet for semidwarf sweet cherries.

Growing Requirements:
Any deep, well-drained loam with a pH of 6.0 to 8.0 is suitable for cherries. Heavy, poorly drained soils will cause undersized fruit to form. Give an annual side-dressing of manure. The critical time for watering is at flowering and near harvest when fruit growth is most rapid. Sweet cherries require cross-pollination, but not all varieties make compatible pollinators. Sour cherries are self-pollinating. Prune dwarf sweet cherries to a central leader shape, standard-size sweets to an open center, and sour cherries to either shape.

Pest and Disease Problems:
Aphids, tent caterpillars, borers, cherry maggots, scale, and birds can cause problems. Brown rot fungus and cherry leaf-spot may afflict trees. Sour cherries are generally less bothered than the sweets.

Season-Extending Options:
Fall-planted trees often begin bearing a year earlier than spring-planted trees. Train trees into an espalier shape against a heat-retaining wall to create a favorable microclimate.

Yield-Improving Techniques:
Careful pruning to expose branches to maximum sunlight ensures an abundant harvest. Southern growers should look for varieties bred to require few hours of winter chilling.

Harvest and Storage:
Dwarf sweet cherries begin to bear within 2 years, and sour cherries in 3 to 5 years. Test for ripeness by tasting full-colored cherries. Sweetness increases the longer cherries remain on the tree (don't let them linger so long that they begin to soften and turn brown). Sour cherries are ripe when they separate easily from their pits. Extra sweet cherries can be canned, and sour ones can be canned or frozen. A mature dwarf sweet cherry tree yields 1 bushel of fruit.

Noteworthy Cherry Varieties

Variety	Description	Sources
COMPACT STELLA	A productive, self-fertile genetic dwarf sweet cherry that grows 10 to 14 ft. tall.	91
NORTH STAR	A genetic dwarf sour cherry that grows 6 to 9 ft. tall.	74, 94
STARKCRIMSON	A self-fertile sweet cherry that is also a genetic dwarf, growing 10 to 14 ft. tall.	94

CHINESE CABBAGE   *Brassica rapa*, Pekinensis Group   Cruciferae
Cool-season crop

Propagation:
Seeds take 10 days to germinate. For spring planting, use transplants only. Start seeds 4 weeks before setting out, which can be done 4 to 6 weeks before the last frost. For fall crops, sow seeds directly in the garden 12 weeks before the first expected frost. Plant seeds ½ inch deep.

Intensive Spacing:
10 to 12 inches.

Growing Requirements:
Chinese cabbage adapts very well to a wide range of soil types. It thrives in moderately rich soil with good amounts of organic matter. Soil pH can range from 6.0 to 6.8. Mulch to conserve soil moisture.

Pest and Disease Problems:
Pests include aphids, cabbage loopers, cabbage maggots, cutworms, harlequin bugs, flea beetles, imported cabbage worms, and leafminers. Diseases rarely pose a problem, but when they do, black rot, clubroot, downy mildew, and yellows are the culprits. Use careful rotations to avoid disease problems.

Season-Extending Options:
Shade spring-planted crops to delay bolting. Fall crops remain in excellent condition in the garden with only a light layer of mulch. Heading cabbages hold better than nonheading ones. Leaves will remain harvestable until November.

Interplanting Suggestions:
Chinese cabbage pairs well with carrots, corn, lettuce, and spinach.

Succession Planting Suggestions:
Use varieties described as bolt-resistant and suited for spring growing for the first planting of the season. All varieties will do well in a fall planting. Follow spring crops with carrots, eggplants, peppers, pole beans, squashes, tomatoes, or turnips. One good four-way relay is to follow Chinese cabbage with bush beans, lettuce, and onions.

Harvest and Storage:
Heading varieties mature in 60 to 85 days, nonheading varieties in 45 to 50 days. Harvest heading Chinese cabbage as soon as it reaches a usable size. Take a few outer leaves at a time from nonheading cabbages for an extended harvest. Keep at least 5 leaves on a plant to ensure continuous production. These cabbages are best when eaten soon after harvest.

Noteworthy Chinese Cabbage Varieties

Variety	Description	Sources
JUNE BRIDE	Heading variety suited to spring planting.	70
KASHIN	Nonheading variety for fall harvesting.	72
MICHIHLI JADE PAGODA	Very heat-resistant nonheading variety.	48
OSAKA LARGE LATEST	Productive, nonheading variety good for spring planting.	52

CHIVES   *Allium schoenoprasum*   Amaryllidaceae   Perennial

Propagation:
Chives can be started from seeds or divisions. Seeds germinate in 10 to 14 days. Start indoors 6 to 8 weeks before setting out, which can be done anytime after last frost. Some gardeners sow seeds directly in the garden in spring, or in late fall for spring germination.

Divisions can be planted in spring as soon as the soil is workable.

Intensive Spacing:
6 inches (for divisions). Give these perennials a permanent site in a bed.

Growing Requirements:
Chives thrive in well-drained soil rich in organic matter. The pH can range between 6.0 and 8.0. Chives tolerate partial shade.

Season-Extending Options:
Container-grown chives can be set in the ground during the growing season. Leave them there to undergo a few frosts before bringing indoors for a winter harvest.

In fall, move a section of the main clump to a growing frame for an ongoing winter harvest.

Yield-Improving Techniques:
Divide established clumps every 4 to 5 years to renew their vigor. In summer, some gardeners cut back the plant to 2 inches to spur a new flush of tender growth.

Interplanting Suggestions:
Chives are traditional insect-repellent companions, particularly with carrots, grapes, tomatoes, and all cucurbits.

Harvest and Storage:
Clip a few spears at a time as needed from the plant for an ongoing harvest. Harvest opened flower heads for vinegar. Chive spears can be frozen or dried.

Noteworthy Chive Variety

Variety	Description	Sources
CHINESE CHIVES (*A. tuberosum*)	A flat-leaved form that is exceptionally hardy and high yielding.	60

COLLARDS   *Brassica oleracea*, Acephala Group   Cruciferae   Cool and warm-season crop

Propagation:
Seeds take 4 to 10 days to germinate. Sow seeds in the garden 3 to 4 weeks before the last frost. Plant them ½ inch deep. Start transplants 6 to 8 weeks before setting out, which can be done 4 weeks before to 2 weeks after the last frost. Start transplants for a fall crop 94 days before the first expected frost.

Intensive Spacing:
12 to 15 inches.

Growing Requirements:
Collards prefer well-drained sandy soil but will adapt to a wide range of conditions. The pH can range from 5.5 to 6.8. Collards need full sun.

Pest and Disease Problems:
Possible insects include aphids, cabbage loopers, cabbage maggots, cutworms, flea beetles, harlequin bugs, imported cabbage worms, and leafminers. Diseases are black rot, clubroot, downy mildew, and yellows.

Season-Extending Options:
To lengthen the growing season in the North, set out transplants in late July or August. Harvesting can begin in 2 months. Give plants protection on cool nights and continue the harvest.

Yield-Improving Techniques:
After you cut the top rosette of leaves, watch for a second smaller rosette to appear in late fall.

Interplanting Suggestions:
Traditional companions include onion family members, rosemary, sage, and thyme.

Harvest and Storage:
Although plants reach full maturity at 70 to 80 days, leaves are ready for harvest as soon as 40 days after planting. Pick them while they're young and tender. Extend the harvest by picking a few leaves at a time from the bottom of the stalk, working upward. Collards are best when used soon after harvest.

Noteworthy Collard Varieties

Variety	Description	Sources
CHAMPION	Heat and cold-tolerant variety with a compact shape well suited to growing frames or closely planted beds.	34
GEORGIA	Dependable crop that won't bolt or toughen.	Widely available
HICROP	Compact, disease-resistant variety that's slow to bolt and stays tender even in hot weather.	48

CORN *Zea mays* Gramineae Warm-season crop

Propagation:
Seeds germinate in 7 to 10 days. To speed the process, soak seeds overnight. Sow early varieties in the garden 2 weeks after the last frost. Plant mid and late-season varieties 2 weeks later. Soil should be at least 50°F for good germination. Seeds planted too early may rot. Sow 1 inch deep. For transplants, start seeds indoors 4 weeks before setting out, which can be done 2 to 3 weeks after the last frost. Handle these temperamental transplants carefully.

Intensive Spacing:
18 inches. Plant corn in blocks of at least 2 or 3 rows to ensure good pollination.

Growing Requirements:
Corn prefers loose, well-drained loam but will adapt to most soil types. The pH should range from 6.0 to 6.8. This crop is a heavy feeder that needs high amounts of nitrogen and phosphorus and moderate amounts of potassium. Because it's shallow-rooted, corn benefits from mulch. The critical time for watering is during tasseling.

Pest and Disease Problems:
Bothersome insects include corn earworms, cucumber beetles, European corn borers, and Japanese beetles. Bacterial wilt and corn smut sometimes pose problems.

Season-Extending Options:
For an early start, use transplants. Warm the soil with plastic mulch.

Yield-Improving Techniques:
Seaweed mulch has been shown to increase yields.

Interplanting Suggestions:
Corn, beans, and squash are a classic combination. Pair Bantam varieties of corn with cucumbers to avoid shading problems. Corn grows nicely with beets, cabbage, and lettuce. Potatoes and soybeans are traditional insect-repellent companions.

Succession Planting Suggestions:
To stagger the harvest, plant early-season varieties every 3 or 4 weeks, up to 3 months before the first expected frost. Or plant a selection of early, mid, and late-season varieties. Follow an early variety with pepper transplants, bush beans, or carrots. Strip the leaves and use the stalk as a pole bean trellis.

Harvest and Storage:
The harvest can begin approximately 60 to 70 days after planting. Corn is ready when the kernels are plump and full of a milky liquid. The silks should be brown and feel damp to the touch. Use corn immediately after picking. Can, freeze, or dry the surplus.

Noteworthy Corn Varieties

Variety	Description	Sources
EARLIVEE	Matures in 63 days, making it a good choice for short-season gardens.	34
GOLDEN JUBILEE	Good variety for cool, damp, overcast regions.	63
GOLDEN MIDGET	Dwarf variety that can be crowded into 8 to 12-in. spacing; yields 4 ears per plant.	Widely available
NORTHERN X-TRA SWEET	Good short-season variety that matures in 75 days.	34

CORN SALAD (also called lamb's lettuce or fetticus)

Valerianella locusta
Valerianaceae
Cool-season crop

Propagation:
Seeds are slow to germinate; be patient. Sow seeds outside as soon as the ground can be worked. Or start seeds indoors 2 to 3 weeks before setting out, which can be done 1 week after last frost. For fall crops, begin sowing in early to late summer. For late fall and early winter crops, sow in early fall. Plant seeds ¼ to ½ inch deep.

Intensive Spacing:
4 inches. Corn salad can be broadcast; thin plants to 4 inches apart when they begin to crowd each other. This green also does well in wide-rows.

Growing Requirements:
Corn salad adapts well to a wide variety of soil types. Provide some shade in the summer to discourage bolting.

Pest and Disease Problems:
Slugs and snails may be occasional pests.

Season-Extending Options:
Corn salad is very cold hardy. Mulch fall crops to keep them growing into winter. For even better protection, transplant them into growing frames or provide them with individual covers or tunnels. For extra-early spring growth, sow seeds in fall right before the ground freezes.

Interplanting Suggestions:
This shade-tolerant green does well at the base of taller crops such as corn, trellised peas and beans, and vertically trained cucurbits.

Succession Planting Suggestions:
To stagger the harvest, make sowings every 2 weeks.

Harvest and Storage:
Leaves are ready for picking 45 days after sowing. For an extended harvest, pick a few outer leaves at a time. Or the whole head can be cut at one time. Corn salad is best when eaten soon after harvest.

CRESSES   *Lepidium sativum* (garden cress)   Cruciferae
Barbarea verna (upland cress)   Cool-season crops (watercress
Nasturtium officinale (watercress)   is perennial)

Propagation:
Seeds sprout in 4 to 5 days. Cresses grow so quickly they're always sown right in the garden. Sow seeds in early spring and again in mid to late summer for fall crops. Plant seeds ¼ inch deep. Watercress can also be started from rooted cuttings.

Intensive Spacing:
6 inches for upland cress and watercress. Garden cress can be broadcast and grows well in dense stands.

Growing Requirements:
Garden and upland cress do well in light, moist soil rich in organic matter. Hot, dry soil promotes exceedingly bitter flavor. Watercress needs the cool, dappled banks of a clean, flowing stream. Plants grow best in partial shade.

Pest and Disease Problems:
Flea beetles and polluted streams (for watercress) pose the most problems.

Season-Extending Options:
Cresses can tolerate mild frosts. Make sowings of garden and upland cress in late summer in growing frames for fall and winter. Or cover late crops with individual protectors or tunnels. They can also be sprouted indoors.

Interplanting Suggestions:
Shade-tolerant garden and upland cresses do well tucked between taller crops, particularly among brassicas. These tidy plants make neat borders along bed edges.

Succession Planting Suggestions:
Make succession sowings every 2 weeks until hot weather arrives.

Harvest and Storage:
Cresses are ready for harvest once they're about 2 weeks old. Cut off leaf tips as needed. The leaves at the tips of watercress branches are the best flavored and most tender. Use cresses soon after harvest.

CROWDER PEAS (also called cowpeas)   *Vigna unguiculata*
Leguminosae
Warm-season crop

Propagation:
Seeds take 7 to 10 days to germinate. Sow seeds in the garden 1 week after last frost. Soil should be at least 60°F. Plant 1 inch deep.

Intensive Spacing:
2 to 6 inches.

Growing Requirements:
Crowder peas adapt well to most soil types as long as they're well drained. The pH should range from 6.5 to 7.0. These soil builders don't need nitrogen, but do need moderate amounts of phosphorus and potassium. The critical times for watering are during flowering and pod formation.

Trellising or Training Tips:
Vining varieties need poles, fences, strings, or other supports. Tie them to these supports, since they have no tendrils. Bush varieties are self-supporting.

Pest and Disease Problems:
Insects include cornworms, Southern green stinkbugs, weevils, and most notably the cowpea curculio. Diseases are root knot, wilt, and various viruses.

Season-Extending Options:
Crowder peas can be thought of as a warm-season substitute for garden peas, particularly the variety QUEEN ANNE. Northern gardeners should look for short-season varieties.

Interplanting Suggestions:
Grow compact, shade-tolerant greens at the base of trellised plants.

Harvest and Storage:
Crowders mature from 50 to 80 days after sowing. Pick pods young and use them as snap beans. When the seeds have enlarged in the pods, shell and cook, or let the pods dry and shell for dried beans.

Noteworthy Crowder Pea Varieties

Variety	Description	Sources
QUEEN ANNE	The crowder that tastes the most like garden peas.	47, 62
TEXAS CREAM #40	Very high-yielding variety.	28
PINK EYE PURPLE HULL	Bush plant that produces 2 crops a season.	28, 47

CUCUMBERS   *Cucumis sativus*   Cucurbitaceae   Warm-season crop

Propagation:
Seeds germinate in 7 to 10 days. Sow seeds in the garden 1 to 2 weeks after last frost, or when the soil is at least 60°F. Start transplants 2 to 3 weeks before setting out, which can be done 2 weeks after the last frost. Handle transplants with care. Plant seeds 1 inch deep in medium-textured soils, 2 inches deep in sandy soils.

Intensive Spacing:
18 to 36 inches. Bush varieties are suited to closer spacing. Situate vining crops toward the side of a bed so they can spill over into the pathway instead of stealing space from neighboring crops.

Growing Requirements:
Cucumbers thrive in well-drained soil rich in organic matter, with a pH of 5.5 to 6.8. These heavy feeders need moderate amounts of nitrogen and potassium and high amounts of phosphorus. They require full sun. These thirsty plants need water particularly during flowering and fruit development. The critical time for weeding is 3 to 4 weeks after direct seeding.

Trellising or Training Tips:
Cucumbers do well as a trellised crop and produce cleaner and healthier harvests. Removing the lateral branches from the bottom 18 inches of stem delays the onset of production but results in greater total productivity over the season.

Pest and Disease Problems:
Troublesome pests are aphids, cucumber beetles, squash bugs, and squash vine borers. Diseases are anthracnose, bacterial wilt, downy mildew, mosaic, powdery mildew, and scab.

Season-Extending Options:
Use gynoecious hybrids (female flowers only) for an early and productive season. Since these plants stop bearing sooner than monoecious varieties (male and female flowers), plant a mixture of both for an early and continuous harvest. Use transplants for a head start, and prewarm the soil with plastic mulch.

Yield-Improving Techniques:
Bark mulch has been shown to increase yields. Cucumbers grown vertically produce twice as much as plants allowed to sprawl. Fifty days before the first expected frost, pinch off all blossoms and immature cucumbers. This allows the plant to channel energy into ripening the remaining ones.

Interplanting Suggestions:
Cucumbers can grow at the base of cornstalks (use a Bantam corn variety to avoid shading problems). Cucumbers also do well next to grapevines. Trellised cucumbers share space well with celery and lettuce. Corn, broccoli, and radish companion crops have reduced striped cucumber beetle populations.

Succession Planting Suggestions:
Long-season gardeners can grow peppers, cucumbers, and cantaloupes in succession. In short-season gardens, cucumbers can follow early peas and spinach.

Harvest and Storage:
Cucumbers should start appearing 50 to 60 days from sowing. Pick every day to encourage continuous production from the vines. Cucumbers left too long turn yellow and signal the vine to stop producing. The only satisfactory way to store the surplus is by pickling.

Noteworthy Cucumber Varieties

Variety	Description	Sources
EXTRA EARLY EXPRESS	An early, abundant variety that produces in 45 days.	17
PIONEER	An early gynoecious cucumber suitable for pickling.	Widely available
SWEET SUCCESS	A self-pollinating gynoecious hybrid with burpless cucumbers.	9, 26
VICTORY	Disease-resistant gynoecious cucumber that yields well in the North.	9, 10, 20

DANDELIONS *Taraxacum officinale* Compositae Perennial grown as annual

Propagation:
Sow seeds in spring as early as the soil can be worked and in midsummer for a fall and early spring harvest. Plant seeds ¼ to ½ inch deep.

Intensive Spacing:
4 inches (if you harvest the entire plant while immature). 10 to 14 inches if you let the plant mature.

Growing Requirements:
These greens adapt to a wide range of soils, as long as they are well drained. Dandelions tolerate partial shade. These are basically a low-maintenance crop. Blanching the heads of plants left to mature in the garden will give you golden, milder tasting greens. Gather the outer leaves and tie them together to cover the inner ones.

Pest and Disease Problems:
Dandelions are seldom bothered.

Season-Extending Options:
Mulch late summer-planted dandelions to overwinter in the North. These plants will send forth tender growth early in spring. Dig mature plants in the fall before the ground freezes to force indoors for fresh winter greens.

Harvest and Storage:
Leaves are ready for harvest 6 weeks after planting. Lift entire plants for these young leaves or take only a few leaves at a time. Plants left in the garden to mature can be blanched. Although these are perennials the harvest is better when you replant each season.

Noteworthy Dandelion Varieties

Variety	Description	Sources
GIANT BROADLEAF	Broader, better quality leaves than the wild dandelion.	3, 15, 17
THICK-LEAVED	Broad leaves are more deeply lobed than those of wild dandelions.	9

DILL   *Anethum graveolens*   Umbelliferae   Warm-season annual

Propagation:
Seeds germinate in 21 days. Sow seeds directly in the garden after last frost. For transplants, start seeds 8 to 10 weeks before setting out, which can be done after last frost. Handle transplants with care. For a fall harvest, sow seeds directly in the garden in July.

Intensive Spacing:
10 to 12 inches.

Growing Requirements:
Dill does best in moderately rich, well-drained, moist soil. The pH can range from 5.0 to 7.0. Dill prefers full sun but will tolerate some shade in the South.

Season-Extending Options:
Dill self-sows readily. These seeds will germinate early and become established quickly in the spring.

Interplanting Suggestions:
Grow dill around fruit trees since it attracts pollinating bees. Dill is a traditional growth-enhancing companion around cole crops, onions, and lettuce. It's also reputed to repel insects from corn.

Succession Planting Suggestions:
Make succession plantings every 3 weeks from May to August for a fresh supply of leaves and seeds.

Harvest and Storage:
Harvest a few leaves as needed from plants throughout the season (they're at their best before flower heads develop). Leaves, known as dill weed, can be dried. Seed heads are ready for harvest 8 weeks after planting. Let them turn completely brown before picking, but catch them before they shatter.

EGGPLANTS   *Solanum melongena* var. *esculentum*   Solanaceae   Warm-season crop

Propagation:
Seeds germinate in 10 days. Direct-seed only in regions with very long warm seasons. Plant seeds ½ inch deep. Transplants are more commonly used. Start seeds indoors 8 to 10 weeks before setting out, which can be done 2 to 3 weeks after the last frost.

Intensive Spacing:
18 to 24 inches. Dwarf varieties are suited to closer spacing.

Growing Requirements:
Eggplants produce well in average loam that's well drained and rich in organic matter. The pH should range between 5.5 and 6.8. These heavy feeders need moderate amounts of nitrogen and potassium and high amounts of phosphorus. Eggplants need full sun. The critical time for watering is from flowering through harvest.

Pest and Disease Problems:
Possible insects include aphids, Colorado potato beetles, cucumber beetles, cutworms, flea beetles, leafhoppers, and tomato hornworms. Diseases that may occur are fruit rot and verticillium wilt. Use careful rotations to avoid disease problems.

Season-Extending Options:
Prewarm soil with plastic mulch.

Interplanting Suggestions:
Eggplants share space well with onions and celery. Traditional pest-deterring companions include green beans, potatoes, and aromatic herbs.

Succession Planting Suggestions:
Eggplants are suitable to follow lettuce, spinach, or bunching onions.

Harvest and Storage:
Eggplants begin to produce in approximately 60 to 70 days. Pick eggplants as soon as they reach a usable size. An eggplant that's past its prime has a dull skin and bitter flavor. Use soon after harvest for there's no satisfactory way to store eggplants.

Noteworthy Eggplant Varieties

Variety	Description	Sources
DUSKY	Compact variety suited to cool, short-season areas.	Widely available
EARLY BLACK EGG	A reliable producer in short-season regions; matures in only 65 days.	51
ICHIBAN	An oriental hybrid that can yield 3 times as many eggplants as standard varieties; fruit is slender and elongated.	9

ENDIVE AND ESCAROLE   *Cichorium endivia*   Compositae   Cool-season crop

Propagation:
Seeds take 10 to 14 days to germinate. Sow seeds directly in the garden as soon as the soil is workable, or 2 to 4 weeks before the last frost. Plant seeds ¼ inch deep. Start transplants 4 to 5 weeks before setting out, which can be done 4 weeks before to 2 weeks after the last fall frost. Time planting for a fall harvest by counting back 142 days from the first expected frost.

Intensive Spacing:
15 to 18 inches. These greens can be broadcast and grown in wide-rows.

Growing Requirements:
Endive and escarole do well in moisture-retentive soils rich in organic matter. The pH can range from 5.0 to 6.8. These greens tolerate partial shade. Mulch these shallow-rooted crops to keep them from bolting. Two to 3 weeks before desired harvest, blanch the heads by gathering the outer leaves together at the top and tying with string. If heads are wet, cover with an inverted clay pot to avoid rotting problems.

Pest and Disease Problems:
Generally pest-free, these greens are sometimes bothered by aphids, cabbage loopers, cutworms, flea beetles, leaf-miners, slugs, and snails. Diseases are rarely a problem.

Season-Extending Options:
Endive, which is hardier than escarole, can be planted in late winter under protective devices for early spring harvesting. Use transplants to get a head start on the season. Endive is an excellent winter growing-frame crop. You can lift roots in the fall before the ground freezes and force them indoors for a harvest of sprouts, known as Belgian endive or chicons.

Interplanting Suggestions:
Endive and escarole are good plants to pair with tall-growing, shade-throwing neighbors in a bed.

Succession Planting Suggestions:
Make succession plantings every 2 to 3 weeks until temperatures start to climb.

Harvest and Storage:
Endive (curly leaved) and escarole (flat leaved) mature in 80 to 100 days. At that time you can cut entire plants off at the base. Before heads are full (about 30 days after transplanting), you can take a few outer leaves at a time for an extended harvest. Use leaves soon after picking.

Noteworthy Endive and Escarole Varieties

Variety	Description	Sources
FULL HEART BATAVIAN	Escarole variety that matures in 90 days.	36
GREEN CURLED	Endive that is easy to blanch.	Widely available
SALAD KING	Slow-bolting endive variety.	Widely available

GARLIC *Allium sativum* Amaryllidaceae Cool-season crop

Propagation:
Plant cloves directly in the garden as soon as the soil can be worked, or 4 to 6 weeks before the last frost. Start indoors 4 to 6 weeks before setting out, which can be done 2 to 4 weeks before to 1 week after the last frost. Set cloves, pointed end up, 1 inch deep.

Intensive Spacing:
2 to 6 inches. Garlic can be grown in wide-rows.

Growing Requirements:
Garlic needs rich, well-drained soil fortified with lots of organic matter. The pH should range from 5.5 to 6.8. This member of the allium family is a light feeder. Garlic needs full sun. Weeding is most critical early in the season when plants are becoming established.

Pest and Disease Problems:
Occasional insect pests are onion maggots and thrips. Plants may be bothered by downy mildew, pink rot, and smut, but this is rare.

Season-Extending Options:
Plant cloves in the fall and mulch for extra-early growth in the spring.

Interplanting Suggestions:
Tuck some cloves under dwarf fruit trees. Garlic's small size makes it easy to pop into open spaces throughout garden beds. Garlic has long been held to have insect-repellent powers and is a favorite companion crop.

Succession Planting Suggestions:
Garlic is a long-season crop that doesn't allow much time for successions.

Harvest and Storage:
Garlic bulbs mature in 90 to 100 days. Throughout the season, snip a few tops for mild garlic-flavored greens. Yellowing and drooping tops signal harvesttime. Stop watering and knock over any tops that have remained upright. Three to 5 days later, dig and let dry in a cool, shady spot.

Noteworthy Garlic Variety

Variety	Description	Sources
ELEPHANT	Massive bulbs can weigh ½ to 1 lb.; has a mild, delicate garlic flavor.	20, 24, 29

GRAPES *Vitis* spp. Vitaceae

Hardiness Zones:
5 to 8.

Intensive Spacing:
7 to 10 feet.

Growing Requirements:
Grapes produce well in rich, well-drained, deeply cultivated soil. The pH can range from 5.5 to 5.7. Grapevines need watering early in the season when shoots are developing and again in midsummer before canes begin hardening-off. Side-dress with manure early in spring. A vine that receives maximum amounts of sun on all its leaf surfaces will be a productive one. There are various patterns of pruning, but all involve training the current season's growth, which is the fruiting wood. All but muscadine grapes are self-pollinating.

Pest and Disease Problems:
Pests include Japanese beetles, grapeberry moths, and birds. Possible diseases are powdery mildew and downy mildew.

Yield-Improving Techniques:
A straw mulch has been shown to increase yields. Light pruning coupled with cluster thinning can produce crops up to 50 percent larger than those that result from traditional heavy pruning.

Harvest and Storage:
Grapes begin bearing in 3 to 4 years. You can spot a ripe grape by a browning and shriveling of the stem and a rich, full color of the fruit. Ripe grapes are also easy to pick from the vine. The best gauge, however, is your taste buds. A mature grapevine can produce 20 to 100 pounds of fruit.

Noteworthy Grape Varieties

Variety	Description	Sources
CONCORD	An American variety that has some disease resistance and is highly productive.	74, 86
FREEDONIA	A highly vigorous hybrid grape for wine.	76
SUFFOLK RED	A heavy-yielding seedless variety.	86

HAMBURG PARSLEY *Petroselinum crispum* var. *tuberosum* Umbelliferae Cool-season crop

Propagation:
To speed the germination process, soak seeds over-night before planting. Sow seeds in the garden around the time of the last frost. Plant seeds ¼ inch deep. Start transplants 6 weeks before setting out, which can be done around the time of the last frost. Handle these temperamental transplants with care.

Intensive Spacing:
4 inches.

Growing Requirements:
Hamburg parsley adapts well to most kinds of soils, as long as they are moisture retentive and free of clods and stones that will interfere with good root development. The pH should range between 6.0 and 7.0. Keep plants well watered and mulched during growth.

Pest and Disease Problems:
Few problems seem to strike Hamburg parsley.

Season-Extending Options:
This hardy plant can survive freezing. Sow seeds directly in the garden in July to overwinter under mulch.

Succession Planting Suggestions:
Don't follow legumes; the excess nitrogen will encourage leafy growth at the expense of root development.

Harvest and Storage:
Hamburg parsley matures in 5 to 6 months, but you can dig roots any time they reach usable size. Clip a few leaves throughout the season to use as a parsley substitute. Roots can be mulched and stored in the ground for an ongoing harvest.

HORSERADISH *Armoracia rusticana* Cruciferae Perennial

Propagation:
As soon as the soil is workable, plant root cuttings in 6-inch-deep furrows. Set cuttings at a 45-degree angle with tops 3 inches below the soil surface.

Intensive Spacing:
10 to 12 inches. Give this perennial its own bed or section of bed and control its invasive growth.

Growing Requirements:
Horseradish prefers deeply prepared, well-drained loam with a pH of 6.0 to 7.0. Potassium is a critical nutrient.

Pest and Disease Problems:
Problems are rare.

Season-Extending Options:
Dig roots in fall before the ground freezes and force indoors for piquant greens for winter salads.

Harvest and Storage:
Delay harvesting until the roots have been touched by frost. Store in a root cellar, or mulch the bed and dig throughout the winter as needed.

Noteworthy Horseradish Varieties

Variety	Description	Sources
MALINER KREN	Large-rooted, vigorous variety.	9
NEW BOHEMIA	Produces large white roots.	Widely available

JERUSALEM ARTICHOKES   *Helianthus tuberosus*   Compositae   Perennial

Propagation:
Plant tubers as soon as the ground can be worked, 4 to 6 weeks before the last frost. Set them 6 inches deep.

Intensive Spacing:
12 inches. Give these invasive perennials their own bed and take measures to keep their growth under control.

Growing Requirements:
Jerusalem artichokes adapt to a wide range of soils as long as they are well drained. The pH should be close to 5.8.

Pest and Disease Problems:
Jerusalem artichokes are rarely bothered.

Harvest and Storage:
Wait to harvest until plants have been touched by frost and tops have died down. Dig and store in the refrigerator. A better quality harvest comes directly from the garden; mulch and dig throughout the winter as tubers are needed. Leave enough stalks to mark location of tubers.

Noteworthy Jerusalem Artichoke Variety

Variety	Description	Sources
SUNCHOKE	Plants are one-third smaller than standard varieties and produce full-size tubers.	64

KALE   *Brassica oleracea*, Acephala Group   Cruciferae   Cool-season crop

Propagation:
Seeds germinate in 5 to 10 days. Sow seeds in the garden 4 to 6 weeks before the last frost, as soon as soil is workable. Plant seeds ½ inch deep. Start transplants 6 to 8 weeks before setting out, which can be done 5 weeks before to 2 weeks after the last frost. For a fall crop, sow seeds 2 months before the first expected frost.

Intensive Spacing:
15 to 18 inches. Dwarf varieties are suited to closer spacing. Kale can be broadcast.

Growing Requirements:
Kale thrives in a loamy soil with a moderate amount of manure or compost. Light sandy and heavy clay soils work against good leaf quality. The pH should range between 6.5 and 6.8. This heavy feeder needs medium to high amounts of potassium. Kale tolerates partial shade.

Pest and Disease Problems:
Insects may include aphids, cabbage loopers, cabbage maggots, cutworms, flea beetles, harlequin bugs, imported cabbage worms, and leafminers. Possible diseases are black rot, downy mildew, and yellows. Kale shows some built-in resistance to clubroot.

Season-Extending Options:
Kale earns the distinction of being the hardiest vegeta-

ble of them all. It remains in good condition for ongoing winter harvests, and only in the most severe climates does it require a mulch or protective covering. In winter gardens, protect frozen kale leaves from sunscale by erecting burlap sunscreens.

Yield-Improving Techniques:
Seaweed mulch has been shown to increase yields.

Interplanting Suggestions:
Kale shares space well with carrots, celery, lettuce, and spinach. Traditional insect-repellent companions include onion family members, rosemary, sage, and thyme.

Succession Planting Suggestions:
For best quality leaves, make two plantings a season, one in spring and one in fall.

Harvest and Storage:
Plants reach maturity 55 to 65 days after sowing, but harvesting can start anytime leaves reach usable size. Pick while leaves are bright green and crisp; old leaves are dark green, bitter, and tough. Kale's flavor is enhanced by frosts. Pick leaf rosettes (always leave the center bud intact) for an ongoing harvest. Or cut the whole plant for a once-and-done harvest. Kale holds up well in the garden over winter. Harvest leaves even if they're frozen; cook before they thaw.

Noteworthy Kale Varieties

Variety	Description	Sources
DWARF BLUE CURLED SCOTCH	Dependable producer that is extra high in vitamins and minerals.	Widely available
KONSERVA	Gives tremendous yields.	34
WINTERBOR	High-yielding, extra cold-hardy variety, well suited to overwintering.	34

KOHLRABI *Brassica oleracea*, Gongylodes Group   Cruciferae   Cool-season crop

Propagation:
Seeds germinate in 5 to 10 days. Sow seeds in the garden 4 to 6 weeks before the last frost. Plant seeds ¼ inch deep. Start transplants 6 to 8 weeks before setting out, which can be done 5 weeks before to 2 weeks after the last frost. For a fall crop, count back 86 days from first expected frost to determine when to sow seeds in the garden.

Intensive Spacing:
6 to 9 inches.

Growing Requirements:
Kohlrabi prefers soil that is rich in organic matter and retains moisture. Soil pH should range from 6.0 to 7.0. This crop is a heavy feeder that needs high amounts of potassium. Kohlrabi tolerates partial shade.

Pest and Disease Problems:
Harlequin bugs and imported cabbage worms are the main pests. Possible diseases are black rot, clubroot, downy mildew, and yellows.

Season-Extending Options:
Kohlrabi can withstand light frost but not hard freezes, so be ready to protect young plants set out early.

Succession Planting Suggestions:
Plant this fast-maturing crop before or after a warm-season crop like bush beans, peppers, or tomatoes. Make succession plantings every 2 weeks until mid-June.

Harvest and Storage:
Kohlrabi matures in 60 to 70 days. The best-tasting bulbs are those that have been touched by a few light frosts. Harvest while still small, no more than 2 to 3 inches in diameter. Slice through the stem 1 inch below the bulb. Fall crops can remain harvestable under a layer of mulch, but don't expect them to last much past late December.

Noteworthy Kohlrabi Varieties

Variety	Description	Sources
EARLY WHITE VIENNA	Cold-resistant variety suited to fall planting; matures in 55 to 60 days.	Widely available
GRAND DUKE	Good spring-planted variety that matures in 45 days.	Widely available
PURPLE VIENNA	Good variety for fall planting; matures in 65 to 70 days.	Widely available

LEEKS *Allium ampeloprasum*, Porrum Group   Amaryllidaceae   Cool-season crop

Propagation:
Seeds germinate in 10 to 14 days. Gardeners in long-season areas have the luxury of sowing seeds directly in beds. Plant in summer for late fall or early winter harvest, or in fall for late winter harvest. Sow seeds ½ inch deep. Gardeners with shorter growing seasons must start with transplants. Start seeds 4 to 6 weeks before setting out, which can be done 5 weeks before to 2 weeks after the last frost.

Intensive Spacing:
2 to 6 inches.

Growing Requirements:
Leeks can adapt to a wide range of soil types but do best in a well-drained, well-limed soil rich in organic matter. Soil pH can range from 6.0 to 7.0. These onion family members are light feeders. As the leeks grow, gradually mound soil around their bases to promote the prized, thick white stems. Leeks tolerate partial shade.

Pest and Disease Problems:
Leeks are generally problem-free but may be bothered by onion maggots or onion thrips.

Season-Extending Options:
Leeks are exceedingly hardy plants. Use transplants to get a head start on the season.

Yield-Improving Techniques:
Some gardeners trim back the fibrous roots before transplanting to encourage vigorous growth and earlier maturity.

Interplanting Suggestions:
Leeks are good growing partners for brassicas. They also share space well with carrots and parsley. Traditional growth-enhancing companions include beets and carrots.

Succession Planting Suggestions:
Leeks can follow an early crop of peas.

Harvest and Storage:
Leeks mature in 75 to 190 days but you can begin harvesting whenever they reach a usable size. Pull or dig the plants from the soil. A layer of mulch keeps leeks in good condition for ongoing winter harvests.

Noteworthy Leek Varieties

Variety	Description	Sources
ELECTRA	Very hardy leek that overwinters well.	26
INVERNO	Good variety for overwintering.	34
KING RICHARD	Early variety that matures in 79 days.	50

LEMON BALM   *Melissa officinalis*   Labiatae   Perennial

Propagation:
Start from seeds, cuttings, or root divisions. Seeds germinate in 14 to 21 days. Sow seeds directly in the garden as soon as the soil can be worked. For transplants, start 8 to 10 weeks before setting out, which can be done after last frost. Set cuttings and divisions out in early spring or in fall before the ground freezes.

Intensive Spacing:
12 inches. Give this perennial a permanent site.

Growing Requirements:
Lemon balm does well on sandy, well-drained soil. The pH can range from 5.0 to 7.0. This herb tolerates partial shade.

Season-Extending Options:
Stop harvesting 1 month before the first expected frost, then harvest lightly after the first frost and continue until leaves die back from the cold.

Interplanting Suggestions:
Plant lemon balm around fruit trees because it attracts pollinating bees.

Harvest and Storage:
Harvest a few stems or leaves at a time as needed. Make light harvests the first year to give the plant time to become established. Leaves for drying should be picked before flowers appear.

LETTUCE   *Lactuca sativa*   Compositae   Cool-season crop

Propagation:
Seeds germinate in 7 to 10 days. For midseason plantings soak seeds overnight and freeze for 1 to 2 weeks. Sow seeds directly in the garden starting 3 weeks before and up to the last frost date. Plant seeds ¼ to ½ inch deep. Start transplants 4 to 6 weeks before setting out, which can be done from 2 weeks before to 3 weeks after the last frost date. For a fall harvest of head lettuce, count back 96 days from the first expected frost to determine when to direct-seed. For leaf lettuce, count back 76 days.

Intensive Spacing:
6 to 9 inches for leaf lettuce; 10 to 12 inches for head lettuce. Leaf lettuce can be broadcast and all kinds of lettuce can be grown in wide-rows.

Growing Requirements:
Lettuce needs rich, well-drained soil. Soil pH can range from 6.0 to 6.8. Lettuce is a heavy feeder that needs moderate amounts of nitrogen and potassium. The critical time for watering head lettuce is during head formation; for leaf lettuce it is throughout the growing season. This leafy crop can tolerate partial shade.

Pest and Disease Problems:
Aphids, cabbage loopers, cutworms, flea beetles, leafminers, slugs, and snails may bother lettuce.

Season-Extending Options:
Have cloches ready to protect transplants set out early. Lettuce thrives under plastic tunnels in colder parts of the season. Overwinter young lettuce plants under mulch or sow seeds before the ground freezes for extra-early growth the next spring. Overwintered crops do well in growing frames.

Interplanting Suggestions:
This compact, shade tolerant crop is a wonderful neighbor to tuck into beds. It teams well with radishes and tomatoes (for a salad bar in a garden bed).

Succession Planting Suggestions:
Fast-growing leaf lettuce is a good crop for the first leg of a relay. Make succession plantings of lettuce every 2 to 3 weeks; use heat and bolt-resistant varieties for summer plantings.

Harvest and Storage:
Leaf lettuce matures in 45 to 55 days, but you can begin harvesting a few outer leaves at a time before plants reach maturity. This method extends the harvest season. Lift entire plants for a once-and-done harvest. Loosehead, head, and romaine lettuces are harvested when the heads are firm and full sized. Loosehead matures in 60 to 75 days, head in 70 to 100 days, and romaine in 75 to 85 days.

Noteworthy Lettuce Varieties

Variety	Description	Sources
BLACK-SEEDED SIMPSON	Reliable leaf variety that has a compact habit and offers an abundant yield per square foot.	Widely available
FROSTY	Head lettuce that protects itself with disposable "wrapper" leaves; good for cold, short-season areas.	59
GREAT LAKES	Head lettuce that is resistant to tipburn and heat.	48
GREEN WAVE	Heat-tolerant loosehead that does well in hot, humid, long-season areas.	68
KAGRAN SUMMER	Loosehead variety that does nicely in short-season areas.	34
LITTLE GEM	6-in.-tall romaine that yields heavily in close quarters.	64
SLO-BOLT	Bolt-resistant leaf lettuce suited to midseason succession plantings.	14, 20

MALABAR SPINACH   *Basella alba*   Basellaceae   Warm-season crop

Propagation:
Seeds can take 21 days to germinate; soaking overnight can speed the process. Sow seeds directly in the garden at least 1 week after the last frost. Make sure the soil is warm. Plant seeds 1 inch deep. For transplants, start seeds 8 to 10 weeks before setting out, which can be done any time after the last frost. Rooted stem cuttings can also be used to start this heat-loving green.

Intensive Spacing:
12 inches.

Growing Requirements:
Malabar spinach needs very rich soil that retains moisture well. The pH can range from 6.0 to 6.7. Keep plants well watered and mulched. Lengthening days can promote flowering, which causes leaf quality to decline. If this should happen, replant so that Malabar spinach can mature during the short days of summer.

Trellising or Training Tips:
Provide vertical supports at least 3 feet tall for these vines.

Pest and Disease Problems:
Malabar spinach is generally problem-free.

Season-Extending Options:
Use transplants for a head start. Warm the soil with plastic before direct-seeding. Cover trellised plants with plastic to protect from early light frosts.

Yield-Improving Techniques:
Keep pinching back growing tips of vines to encourage branching, which increases the number of harvestable leaves.

Interplanting Suggestions:
Plant shade-loving plants at the base of trellised vines.

Succession Planting Suggestions:
Malabar spinach is used by some gardeners as a hot-weather substitute for spinach and lettuce. Follow an early spring crop of spinach or leaf lettuce with a planting of Malabar spinach.

Harvest and Storage:
Plants mature in 70 days, but you can harvest individual leaves once the plant has become established and has started branching. Pick tender, young leaves. A continual harvest stimulates the plant to keep producing leaves.

MELONS　*Cucumis melo*　Cucurbitaceae　Warm-season crop

Propagation:
Seeds germinate in 5 to 10 days. Sow seeds directly in the garden 2 weeks after the last frost date. Plant them ½ inch deep. Start transplants 2 to 4 weeks before setting out, which can be done 4 weeks after the last frost. Handle these temperamental transplants carefully.

Intensive Spacing:
24 to 36 inches. Bush varieties are suited to closer spacing. Situate vining plants near the sides of beds so they can spill over into pathways without crowding neighboring plants.

Growing Requirements:
Melons need light, fertile, sandy or loamy soil rich in organic matter. Avoid heavy, poorly draining clay soils. The pH can range from 6.0 to 8.0. These heavy feeders require moderate amounts of nitrogen and high amounts of phosphorus. Melons need full sun. The critical time for watering is during flowering and fruit development. Wait to mulch until the soil is warm.

Trellising or Training Tips:
Save space with vining varieties by training them to grow up a fence or other support. Tie branches with soft cloth and support melons with slings.

Pest and Disease Problems:
Insects include aphids, squash bugs, and striped and spotted cucumber beetles. Diseases that may afflict melons are fusarium wilt and cucumber mosaic.

Season-Extending Options:
Use transplants to get a head start. Warm the soil with plastic prior to direct-seeding. Short-season gardeners must look for the earliest maturing varieties that are ready in less than 75 days. Use cloches, tents, cold frames, and other protective devices to shelter seedlings from unsettled temperatures.

Yield-Improving Techniques:
Northern growers who seek ripe melons before frost should pinch off blossoms and remove unfruitful branches 50 days before the first frost. This concentrates the plants' energy on ripening the remaining melons. A mulch of salt hay has been shown to increase yields.

Interplanting Suggestions:
Tuck transplants among maturing bunching onions, radishes, carrots, beets, lettuce, and spinach; as these crops are harvested, melon plants will expand to fill the space. Radishes tuck in well among developing melon vines. Traditional insect-deterring companions include nasturtiums and radishes.

Succession Planting Suggestions:
Plant late and early varieties at the same time to provide a succession of melons over a month-long period. Long-season gardeners can grow relays of peppers, cucumbers, and cantaloupes; or corn, tomatoes, and cantaloupes. In short seasons, melons can follow early peas, lettuce, spinach, or Chinese cabbage.

Harvest and Storage:
Cantaloupes begin to ripen 35 to 45 days after pollination. Watermelons ripen in 42 to 56 days. Stems crack as the melons ripen. A stem that has completely cracked and a melon that separates from the vine with a gentle push are reliable signs of ripeness. Use melons soon after harvest since there are no satisfactory storage options.

Noteworthy Melon Varieties

Variety	Description	Sources
ALASKA	Early-bearing cantaloupe that matures in 64 days.	50
BUSH CHARLESTON GRAY	Watermelon with the highest vitamin A content.	25
BUSHWHOPPER	Space-saving bush cantaloupe.	48
CRIMSON SWEET	Very sweet, disease-resistant watermelon bred especially for the South.	26, 28
EARLY CANADA	Early watermelon ready in 75 days.	25

MUSTARD   *Brassica juncea*   Cruciferae   Cool-season crop

Propagation:
Seeds germinate in 5 to 10 days. Sow seeds directly in the garden 2 to 4 weeks before the last frost. Plant them ¼ inch deep. Start transplants 4 to 6 weeks before setting out, which can be done from 5 weeks before to 2 weeks after the last frost. For fall crops, sow seeds in the garden 8 weeks before the first expected frost. Mustard bolts so easily that it is usually grown in fall.

Intensive Spacing:
6 to 9 inches.

Growing Requirements:
Mustard adapts to many soil types but grows best in soil that's moist and rich. Soil pH can range from 5.5 to 6.8. This leafy brassica is a light feeder. Mustard tolerates partial shade. Mulch to keep the soil cool and moist to prevent bolting.

Pest and Disease Problems:
Watch for aphids, cabbage maggots, flea beetles, imported cabbage worms, and whiteflies. Diseases are rarely a problem.

Season-Extending Options:
Use bolt-resistant varieties for early spring plantings.

Interplanting Suggestions:
Plant mustard among taller growing crops.

Succession Planting Suggestions:
Make succession plantings every 10 to 14 days in spring until the temperatures begin to rise.

Harvest and Storage:
Mustard matures in 30 to 50 days. A light frost improves the flavor. You can begin taking a few outer leaves from plants before they mature fully. Small leaves, 4 to 5 inches long, have the best flavor. Cut-and-come-again harvesting spreads out the productive period, but the whole plant can also be cut as needed. Extra leaves can be frozen or canned.

Noteworthy Mustard Varieties

Variety	Description	Sources
FLORIDA BROAD LEAF	Bolt-resistant plant with large leaves and tender ribs.	Widely available
GREEN WAVE	Bolt-resistant variety that's well suited to spring plantings.	Widely available
SOUTHERN GIANT CURLED	Good choice for fall crops.	Widely available

NEW ZEALAND SPINACH   *Tetragonia tetragonioides*   Aizoaceae   Warm-season crop

Propagation:
To speed the germination process, soak overnight in water or rub seeds between sheets of sandpaper. Sow seeds directly in the garden any time after the last frost once the soil has warmed. Plant seeds 1 inch deep. For transplants, start seeds 4 to 6 weeks before setting out, which can be done after the last frost.

Intensive Spacing:
10 to 12 inches.

Growing Requirements:
New Zealand spinach adapts to a wide range of soils, but thrives and produces the best quality leaves in a fertile soil rich in organic matter. Soil pH should be

between 6.5 and 7.0. This green tolerates partial shade. Its sprawling habit makes it self-mulching and somewhat self-shading. Keep soil moist and mulched.

Pest and Disease Problems:
New Zealand spinach is generally problem-free.

Season-Extending Options:
This plant extends its own season by self-sowing and reappearing the next season without any effort from the gardener. If you want to control this self-perpetuating tendency, clip off the hard seed pods before they shatter.

Yield-Improving Techniques:
Pinch growing tips to promote branching, which increases the number of harvestable leaves.

Succession Planting Suggestions:
Use this spinach-substitute to follow an early planting of leaf lettuce or spinach.

Harvest and Storage:
From transplants, harvesting can begin in 1 month. From seed, harvesting begins in 2 months. Once New Zealand spinach is established it will keep producing until frost. Cut 3 to 4 inches from the growing tips for young, tender leaves. Surplus leaves can be frozen.

OKRA *Abelmoschus esculentus* Malvaceae Warm-season crop

Propagation:
Seeds germinate in 7 to 14 days. To hasten the process, soak overnight in water or a dilute chlorine bleach solution. Sow seeds directly in the garden after last frost when the soil has warmed to 60°F. Plant ½ to 1 inch deep. For transplants, start seeds 6 to 8 weeks before setting out, which can be done 3 to 4 weeks after last frost. Handle these temperamental transplants with care.

Intensive Spacing:
12 to 18 inches. Dwarf varieties are suited to closer spacings.

Growing Requirements:
Okra prefers soils that are rich, well drained, and supplied with lots of organic matter. The pH can range anywhere from 6.0 to 8.0. Okra needs full sun. This heavy feeder needs large amounts of nitrogen.

Pest and Disease Problems:
Corn earworms, green stinkbugs, and imported cabbage worms may cause problems. In very hot areas, blight may afflict plants.

Interplanting Suggestions:
Okra shares space well with Swiss chard and cucumbers.

Succession Planting Suggestions:
When okra follows a legume crop it benefits from the accumulated soil nitrogen.

Harvest and Storage:
Okra matures 50 to 60 days after planting. Pick pods when they reach 2 to 3 inches long. Longer pods are more fibrous and less palatable. Keep picking to encourage continuous production. Mature pods left on the plant signal it to stop producing. Use okra soon after harvest since it does not store well.

Noteworthy Okra Variety

Variety	Description	Sources
DWARF LONG GREEN POD	Space-conserving plant that grows only 24 to 36 in. tall.	9, 25

ONIONS   *Allium cepa*   Amaryllidaceae   Cool-season crop

Propagation:
Seeds germinate in 10 to 14 days. Sow seeds directly in the garden 4 to 6 weeks before last frost, as soon as the soil is workable. (This works best for bunching onions, and only in long-season areas for bulbing onions.) Plant seeds ½ inch deep. For transplants of both bunching and bulbing onions start seeds 4 to 6 weeks before setting out. Set out bulbing onions from 6 weeks before to 2 weeks after the last frost; set out bunching onions 4 to 5 weeks before to 2 weeks after the last frost. Plant sets anytime after the last frost date.

Intensive Spacing:
Bunching onions, 2 to 3 inches. Bulbing onions, 4 to 6 inches. Bunching types can be broadcast and all onions can be grown in wide-rows.

Growing Requirements:
Onions require well-drained, well-limed soil rich in organic matter. The pH should range from 6.0 to 6.6. These light feeders require moderate amounts of nitrogen, phosphorus, and potassium. Bunching onions are shade tolerant. The critical time for watering is when bulbs are enlarging. Once the tops fall over, withhold water; otherwise ripening will be delayed. Be sure to remove weeds while plants are becoming established.

Pest and Disease Problems:
Onions are generally problem-free. Occasional pests may include onion maggots and thrips. Downy mildew, pink rot, and smut may afflict plants.

Season-Extending Options:
For fast starts use sets or seedlings; these plants will mature before direct-seeded crops. Sow bunching onions in late fall and protect young plants with a mulch or cold frame; these onions will sprout for extra-early spring growth. Bunching onions make a good winter growing frame crop.

Interplanting Suggestions:
Onion sets do well planted among broccoli, herbs, and marigolds. Bulbing or bunching onions also make a successful team with tomatoes and basil. Onions share space well with carrots, eggplants, peppers, and spinach. Traditional growth-enhancing crops include beets and carrots.

Succession Planting Suggestions:
Onions do well as successors to early peas, lettuce, and spinach.

Harvest and Storage:
Bunching onions, also called scallions, are ready for harvest whenever they reach a usable size. They reach maturity in 60 days. Bulbing onions mature anywhere from 90 to 180 days, depending on variety and whether they were started from sets or seeds. These onions signal maturity by bending over their topgrowth. Once this occurs, leave the bulbs in the ground for 1 to 2 weeks. When the tops have shriveled and browned, dig the bulbs and cure and store.

Noteworthy Onion Varieties

Variety	Description	Sources
BELTSVILLE BUNCHING	Winter-hardy variety suited equally to spring or fall planting.	Widely available
CRYSTAL WHITE WAX	Early-maturing summer onion that doesn't store well.	Widely available
EVERGREEN LONG WHITE BUNCHING	Good variety for overwintering in the garden or in growing frames.	Widely available
SWEET WINTER	Very hardy onion; seedlings can endure temperatures down to −20°F.	48
WALLA WALLA SWEET	In the Northeast can be sown in late summer to overwinter for a harvest the following summer.	34
YELLOW GLOBE DANVERS	Very productive storage onion that needs 16-hour daylengths to mature.	Widely available

OREGANO   *Origanum* spp.   Labiatae   Perennial

Propagation:
Oregano can be started from seeds, stem cuttings, or root divisions. Seeds germinate in 8 to 14 days. Sow seeds directly in the garden after last frost. For transplants, sow seeds 2 to 3 weeks before setting out, which can be done 2 weeks after last frost. Stem cuttings and divisions are the quicker and generally preferred methods of starting plants. Set these out in spring after last frost.

Intensive Spacing:
6 to 8 inches.

Growing Requirements:
Oregano does very well in light textured, well-drained soils rich in organic matter. It requires full sun.

Season-Extending Options:
Stop harvesting 1 month before first expected frost, then harvest lightly after frost until leaves die back from the cold. In most northern areas, oregano must be mulched to carry it through the winter. Container-grown plants can be set out in the garden during the growing season, then brought indoors in fall for a winter harvest.

Yield-Improving Techniques:
Trim back stems after 6 weeks of spring growth to stimulate bushing, which provides more harvestable leaves.

Interplanting Suggestions:
Plant at the base of ornamental or dwarf fruit trees. Oregano is a traditional insect-repellent companion around cole crops.

Harvest and Storage:
Pick stems as needed for fresh use throughout the season. For drying a large quantity of leaves at one time, cut the plant down to its base as blooms begin to appear. There may be enough new growth for a second cutting in late summer.

PARSLEY   *Petroselinum crispum*   Umbelliferae   Biennial

Propagation:
Seeds germinate in 11 to 28 days. To speed the process, soak seeds overnight, then freeze for a week before planting. Or rub between two sheets of sandpaper. Sow seeds directly in the garden about 2 to 4 weeks before the last spring frost. Plant seeds ¼ inch deep. For transplants, start seeds 4 to 6 weeks before setting out, which can be done from 4 to 6 weeks before to 4 to 6 weeks after last frost.

Intensive Spacing:
4 to 6 inches.

Growing Requirements:
Parsley does best in a fertile, moist, sandy loam with good drainage. The pH should range between 6.0 and 8.0. Parsley tolerates partial shade.

Pest and Disease Problems:
Bothersome pests include aphids, cabbage loopers, and carrot rust flies.

Season-Extending Options:
Mulched, parsley can remain in harvestable shape into winter. Potted parsley can be set in the garden during the growing season, then moved indoors for an ongoing winter harvest.

Interplanting Suggestions:
This low-growing, shade-tolerant green tucks in well between tall-growing crops. Team parsley with celery, Brussels sprouts, and spinach for good use of space.

Succession Planting Suggestions:
Parsley goes into the garden early and stays productive all season, so it offers little opportunity for successions.

Harvest and Storage:
Once the plant is established, cut a few sprigs at a time as needed. This cut-and-come-again method can keep the plant producing for a whole season and longer.

Noteworthy Parsley Varieties

Variety	Description	Sources
AFRO	Curly-leaved variety that holds very well in cold weather.	57
FLAT LEAF	Stronger flavored than the curly varieties.	Widely available
TRIPLE CURLED	Curly-leaved variety that is a reliable producer.	Widely available

PARSNIPS *Pastinaca sativa* Umbelliferae Cool-season crop

Propagation:
Seeds germinate in 14 to 21 days. To cut down on this time, presoak seeds and freeze for a week before planting. Sow seeds directly in the garden 2 to 4 weeks before last frost or as soon as the soil can be worked. Gardeners in mild-winter regions can sow in late fall for a spring crop. Plant seeds ½ inch deep. For transplants, start seeds 4 to 6 weeks before setting out, which can be done 4 weeks before to 3 to 4 weeks after the last frost. Handle these temperamental transplants carefully.

Intensive Spacing:
4 to 6 inches.

Growing Requirements:
Parsnips thrive in deep, rich, well-drained soil, preferably a sandy loam. Remove all rocks that may interfere with root development. Soil pH should be 6.0 to 6.8. This root crop requires low amounts of nitrogen, moderate amounts of phosphorus, and high amounts of potassium. Parsnips need full sun. Weed while plants are becoming established to reduce competition.

Pest and Disease Problems:
Parsnips are trouble-free.

Season-Extending Options:
Parsnips are prime season extenders, for these hardy roots remain in excellent shape under a layer of mulch all winter long.

Interplanting Suggestions:
Try planting parsnips at the foot of dwarf fruit trees.

Succession Planting Suggestions:
This long-season crop doesn't offer an opportunity for successions.

Harvest and Storage:
Parsnips mature in 95 to 120 days and always taste better when touched by frost. For an extended winter harvest, mulch deeply and dig as needed. Be sure to remove all ground-stored roots before new growth begins in spring; parsnips' eating qualities begin to decline then.

Noteworthy Parsnip Varieties

Variety	Description	Sources
ALL AMERICAN	Short-rooted variety that matures in 105 days.	Widely available
HARRIS MODEL	Produces long, tapering roots in 120 days.	Widely available

PEACHES AND NECTARINES *Prunus persica*   Rosaceae

Hardiness Zones:
5 to 9.

Intensive Spacing:
8 to 10 feet for dwarfs, 10 to 16 feet for semidwarfs.

Growing Requirements:
Provide a well-drained, loamy soil with a pH of 6.0 to 8.0 for best growth. Side-dress annually with manure when the buds swell. Add a sprinkling of wood ashes. Peaches are sensitive to drought; lack of water causes small and mealy fruit. Critical times for watering are during flowering and near harvest when fruit growth is most rapid. Prune trees to an open center form. Peaches and nectarines are self-pollinating.

Pest and Disease Problems:
Borers, Japanese beetles, oriental fruit moths, and plum curculios may plague trees. Diseases include brown rot fungus and bacterial leaf spot.

Season-Extending Options:
In cold regions where spring warms up slowly, site trees on a southern slope. This allows trees to bloom a little earlier and enjoy a longer growing season before fall frost. Where spring temperatures fluctuate, site on a northern slope. This will slow flowering, reducing the risk of blossoms being caught in a sudden freeze. Or train a tree in an espalier form against a heat-retaining wall to create a favorable microclimate. Fall-planted trees often bear a year before spring-planted trees.

Yield-Improving Techniques:
Don't plant new peach trees on a site where peaches have previously grown. The new trees will languish and in many cases die after several years. Researchers believe this phenomenon is caused by a virus.

Harvest and Storage:
Trees begin bearing in 1 to 3 years. Peaches and nectarines are ripe when the flesh near the stem end yields under pressure. The longer they stay on the tree, the sweeter they become (but left too long they drop). A tree-ripened peach or nectarine only keeps in the refrigerator for several days. Freeze or can a bumper crop. Mature dwarf trees yield 3 bushels of fruit.

Noteworthy Peach and Nectarine Varieties

Variety	Description	Sources
GARDEN GOLD	Dwarf that reaches 5 to 5½ ft. and is suited to container growing.	86
HONEY GLO	Midseason genetic dwarf nectarine.	94
SUN HAVEN	Available as a dwarf, this productive tree gives an early harvest.	86
SWEET MELODY	Genetic-dwarf nectarine that bears in midseason.	94

PEANUTS *Arachis hypogaea*   Leguminosae   Warm-season crop

Propagation:
Seeds germinate in 7 to 14 days. Sow seeds directly in the garden after last frost. Soil should be at least 60°F. Plant seeds 1½ inches deep in heavy soils, and 4 inches deep in light soils.

Intensive Spacing:
12 to 18 inches. Bush or more upright growing varieties are suited to closer spacing.

Growing Requirements:
For best yields provide soil that's warm, loose, and well drained (a sandy loam is ideal). The pH should range between 5.0 and 6.0. Since they're legumes, peanuts are soil builders and need no nitrogen. They do need moderate amounts of phosphorus and potassium. Keep the soil surface loose, and once the runners have implanted there, mulch to cover the runners. Peanuts require full sun.

Pest and Disease Problems:
Peanuts are problem-free.

Season-Extending Options:
In short-season areas, choose varieties carefully, select a south-facing sheltered planting site, warm the soil with plastic, and use transplants. Also use a soil-warming mulch during the growing season.

Succession Planting Suggestions:
Peanuts are a good crop to follow lettuce or spinach. Plant nitrogen-loving crops after peanuts have vacated a bed.

Harvest and Storage:
Peanuts mature in 110 to 120 days. In long-season areas, dig before the first frost once foliage has yellowed and seeds fill the pods. In short-season areas, plants can be touched by a few light frosts before harvest to give pods time to mature. Even after topgrowth has been killed, nuts will continue to mature. Dig or pull plants and use a spade to unearth any peanuts left in the soil. Cure pods in a warm, dry place for about 1 month.

Noteworthy Peanut Varieties

Variety	Description	Sources
EARLY SPANISH	The most dependable variety for short-season areas.	35, 59
TENNESSEE RED-LARGE	Well adapted for long, warm-season areas.	54

PEARS *Pyrus communis* Rosaceae

Hardiness Zones:
5 to 8, with some varieties suited to 4, 9, and 10.

Intensive Spacing:
8 feet for dwarfs and 12 to 14 feet for semidwarfs.

Growing Requirements:
Pears can adapt to any soil, as long as it is not waterlogged, and to a wide range of pH. Side-dress yearly with manure and a sprinkling of bone meal and wood ashes. The critical time for watering is at flowering and near harvest when fruit growth is most rapid. Prune trees with stiff limbs to a central leader shape and those with flexible limbs to an open center shape. Pears need cross-pollination.

Pest and Disease Problems:
Pear psylla and pear slugs may pose problems. Fireblight is the most serious disease.

Season-Extending Options:
Fall-planted trees often begin bearing a year before spring-planted trees. Train a tree in an espalier form against a heat-retaining wall to create a favorable microclimate.

Harvest and Storage:
Dwarf pears begin bearing in 2 to 5 years. Harvest pears before they ripen completely on the tree; by ripening slowly in a cool place they have a less gritty texture. Pick pears while they're still green but separate readily from the tree with an upward motion. Unripe pears can be stored in a cold (just above 32°F) place for up to 3 months before being allowed to ripen. Mature dwarf trees yield 2 to 3 bushels.

Noteworthy Pear Varieties

Variety	Description	Sources
DUCHESS	Available as a dwarf, this is a dependable producer of large pears.	94
MOONGLOW	Semidwarf that is early-ripening and offers resistance to 4 diseases.	74

PEAS   *Pisum sativum*   Leguminosae   Cool-season crop

Propagation:
Seeds germinate in 7 to 14 days. Sow seeds directly in the garden 4 to 6 weeks before the last frost. A soil temperature of 40°F is sufficient for germination. Plant seeds 1 to 2 inches deep. For transplants, start seeds 4 weeks before setting out, which can be done 4 weeks before to 2 to 3 weeks after last frost. Handle these temperamental transplants with care. For a fall crop, count back 70 days from first expected frost to determine when to sow seeds.

Intensive Spacing:
2 to 6 inches. Dwarf peas can be broadcast and grown in wide-rows.

Growing Requirements:
Peas prefer a well-drained and fertile sandy loam, but will adapt to all but heavy, poorly drained soils. The pH can range from 6.0 to 7.5. These legumes are soil builders and require only low amounts of phosphorus and moderate amounts of potassium. Peas tolerate partial shade. The critical time for watering is during flowering and pod development. Mulch helps keep the soil cool and moist, which encourages good growth.

Trellising or Training Tips:
Vining varieties need vertical supports at least 5 feet tall. Even dwarf peas benefit from support. Run string between stakes at corners of the bed or wide-row.

Pest and Disease Problems:
Aphids, cabbage loopers, corn earworms, and cucumber beetles can bother plants. Diseases include ascochyta blight, bacterial blight, damping-off, powdery mildew, and root rot.

Season-Extending Options:
For an early spring start, use well-drained beds in a sunny site in the garden; melt the snow and warm the soil with plastic mulch; and cultivate frequently during early growth. Sow pea seeds in fall before the soil freezes; these will germinate extra early in spring. Fall-planted peas sometimes fail to thrive because temperatures are still too warm. Give them every advantage by mulching the soil, watering frequently, and providing a shading device.

Interplanting Suggestions:
Plant shade-loving, low-growing crops at the base of trellised vines. Group peas with cabbage and lettuce in short rows. Trellised peas share space well with brassicas, turnips, carrots, and radishes. Traditional growth-enhancing companions are carrots and turnips. Cole crop companions have been found to deter pea root rot.

Succession Planting Suggestions:
Plant early, mid, and late-season varieties to stagger the harvest. Follow early peas with leeks, melons, onions, potatoes, squash, or tomatoes.

Harvest and Storage:
Peas are ready for picking in 60 to 75 days. Garden peas are ripe about 3 weeks after blossoms appear. Look for pods that are bulging with seeds and pick before they turn yellow and shrivel. Pick daily to spur continuous production. Snap peas are best when the pods and peas are full sized. Edible-pod or snow peas are in their prime *before* the seeds have matured. Pick the pods when the peas are only tiny bumps. Surplus peas can be frozen.

Noteworthy Pea Varieties

Variety	Description	Sources
DWARF WHITE SUGAR	Bush snow pea.	Widely available
LINCOLN	Late-bearing, heat-resistant garden pea.	Widely available
LITTLE MARVEL	Early-maturing, heavy-bearing garden pea.	Widely available
SUGAR ANN	Dwarf snap pea suited to Northern growing.	26, 34
SUGAR SNAP	Vigorous vines can rise to 6 ft. and produce an abundance of peas.	Widely available
WANDO	Late-bearing, heat-resistant, garden pea variety good for the South.	17, 34, 35

PEPPERS   *Capsicum annuum*, Grossum Group   Solanaceae   Warm-season crop

Propagation:
Seeds germinate in 19 days. Only gardeners in long-season areas can sow seeds directly in the garden 1 week after the last frost. Plant seeds ½ inch deep. For transplants, start seeds 6 to 8 weeks before setting out, which can be done 2 to 3 weeks after the last frost. Don't set out until average night temperatures are 55°F.

Intensive Spacing:
12 to 15 inches.

Growing Requirements:
Peppers grow well in sandy loam that is well-drained and fortified with lots of organic matter. The pH should range from 6.0 to 7.0. These light feeders need only low amounts of nitrogen, phosphorus, and potassium. Peppers need full sun. The critical time for watering is from flowering through harvest.

Pest and Disease Problems:
Insects include aphids, Colorado potato beetles, corn earworms, European corn borers, leafminers, pepper maggots, and tomato hornworms. Diseases that may occur are anthracnose, bacterial spot, blossom-end rot, and mosaic. Use careful rotations to prevent disease problems.

Interplanting Suggestions:
Peppers share space well with cabbage and onions. Carrots are a traditional growth-enhancing companion.

Succession Planting Suggestions:
Use transplants to fill the space vacated by an early corn variety. Long-season growers can follow peppers with cucumbers and cantaloupes. In shorter season areas, peppers can follow lettuce, spinach, bunching onions, or Chinese cabbage.

Harvest and Storage:
Sweet peppers mature from 60 to 70 days. You can harvest immature or leave them on the plant until they reach full size and ripen to a deep red color. Hot peppers are ready any time they reach usable size. Freeze surplus sweet peppers and dry extra hot peppers.

Noteworthy Pepper Varieties

Variety	Description	Sources
EARLY PROLIFIC	Starting at 62 days, this variety offers abundant yields of sweet peppers.	50
KING OF THE NORTH	Early-bearing bell pepper suited to cool, short-season areas.	25
PICK-ME-QUICK	Tolerates extremes of both hot and cold.	25
RED CHILI	Hot pepper that grows 18 to 20 in. tall and fits nicely in closely spaced beds.	Widely available

PLUMS   *Prunus* spp.   Rosaceae

Hardiness Zones:
5 to 7 for European plums, 5 to 9 for Japanese plums.

Intensive Spacing:
8 to 12 feet for dwarf trees, 12 to 14 feet for semidwarf trees.

Growing Requirements:
Plums adapt well to a wide range of soils, even heavier ones. Side-dress yearly with manure and wood ashes. The critical time for watering is during flowering and near harvest when fruit growth is most rapid. Prune to an open center shape. European plums are self-pollinating, Japanese plums require cross-pollination.

Pest and Disease Problems:
Borers, plum curculios, scale, and birds are all plum pests. The most serious disease is black rot.

Season-Extending Options:
Fall-planted trees often begin bearing a year before spring-planted trees. Train a tree in an espalier form against a heat-retaining wall.

Harvest and Storage:
European plums bear in 4 to 5 years, Japanese plums in 3 years. Leave plums on the tree until they're soft to the touch and fragrant. They can be picked earlier when they've just begun to soften.

Noteworthy Plum Varieties

Variety	Description	Sources
BURBANK	Available as a dwarf, this is a hardy and prolific oriental variety.	74
STANLEY	Available as a dwarf, this is a self-fertile European plum that bears early.	74

POTATOES   *Solanum tuberosum*   Solanaceae   Warm-season crop

Propagation:
Plant seed potatoes 2 to 4 weeks before last frost. Set them 4 to 6 inches deep.

Intensive Spacing:
10 to 12 inches.

Growing Requirements:
Potatoes need loose, well-drained soil rich in organic matter. The pH should be between 5.2 and 5.7 for highest yields. These tubers are light feeders and need medium amounts of nitrogen and high amounts of phosphorus and potassium. Potatoes need full sun. Critical time for watering is from flowering to harvest while tubers are developing. As the stems grow, hill up soil around them to give tubers plenty of room to expand.

Pest and Disease Problems:
Insects include aphids, cabbage loopers, Colorado potato beetles, corn earworms, cucumber beetles, European corn borers, leafhoppers, leafminers, potato tuber worms, and tomato hornworms. Possible diseases include black leg, early blight, internal blackspot, late blight, mosaic, rhizoctonia, ring rot, scab, and verticillium wilt. Use careful rotations to avoid disease problems.

Yield-Improving Techniques:
Some gardeners let seed potatoes develop 12-inch-long sprouts before planting and claim that these plants give bigger yields.

Interplanting Suggestions:
As a rule, these sprawling plants don't make good neighbors in a closely interplanted bed. They should have a space all to themselves.

Succession Planting Suggestions:
Potatoes can follow early peas, lettuce, spinach, or bunching onions.

Harvest and Storage:
Potatoes mature in 100 to 115 days, but you can harvest new potatoes any time they reach usable size. For full-size tubers wait to dig until the foliage dies down, around the time of the first frost. Lift the tubers with a garden fork and handle gently for a long storage life. Store in a cool, dark place with high humidity.

Noteworthy Potato Varieties

Variety	Description	Sources
BUTTE	Higher in vitamin C and protein than the standard Russet Burbank.	25
CRYSTAL	High-yielding, disease-resistant plant suited to northern growing.	25

PUMPKINS   *Cucurbita pepo* var. *pepo*   Cucurbitaceae   Warm-season crop

Propagation:
Seeds germinate in 7 to 10 days. Sow seeds directly in the garden 1 week after the last frost. Plant them 1 inch deep. For transplants start seeds 4 weeks before setting out, which can be done 4 weeks after the last frost. Treat these temperamental transplants carefully.

Intensive Spacing:
24 to 36 inches. Bush varieties are better suited to close spacing. Plant vining varieties near the sides of beds, where they can spill over into pathways without overpowering neighboring crops.

Growing Requirements:
Pumpkins need a well-drained sandy loam rich in organic matter. The pH should be 6.0 to 7.0. These heavy feeders require moderate amounts of nitrogen and high amounts of phosphorus. Pumpkins need full sun. Critical time for watering is during flowering.

Trellising or Training Tips:
Save space with vining plants by training them to grow up a support. Tie the vines in place with soft cloth and provide slings for the developing pumpkins.

Pest and Disease Problems:
Insects include cabbage loopers, corn earworms, cucumber beetles, squash bugs, and squash vine borers. Possible diseases are anthracnose, bacterial wilt, downy mildew, mosaic, powdery mildew, and scab.

Season-Extending Options:
Use transplants and warm the soil with plastic before setting them out.

Yield-Improving Techniques:
In short season areas, 50 days before the first expected

frost, pinch off flowers and small fruits to let plants concentrate on ripening the remaining pumpkins.

Interplanting Suggestions:
Pumpkins share space well with sweet potatoes.

Succession Planting Suggestions:
Long-season gardeners can follow sweet corn with pumpkins. In shorter season areas, pumpkins can succeed early peas and Chinese cabbage.

Harvest and Storage:
Pumpkins mature in a lengthy 90 to 115 days. They're ready for harvest when skins lose their sheen. For storage, harvest those that are fully mature with toughened shells. Cure and store in a warm, dry area.

Noteworthy Pumpkin Varieties

Variety	Description	Sources
NAKED SEEDED PUMPKIN	Provides protein-rich edible seeds in addition to usable flesh.	1, 51
SPIRIT HYBRID	Semibush plant that provides abundant yields in 99 days.	9, 50
SPRITE	The only semibush pumpkin to win the All-America Selection award.	38, 50

RADICCHIO   *Cichorium intybus*   Compositae   Cool-season crop

Propagation:
Because plants must mature in the cool days of autumn, sow seeds no sooner than June. If seeds don't germinate well in the warm soil, soak overnight or freeze for 1 week before planting. Sow seeds ¼ inch deep. Start transplants 4 to 5 weeks before setting out in midsummer.

Intensive Spacing:
10 to 12 inches. Radicchio can be grown in wide-rows.

Growing Requirements:
Radicchio adapts well to a wide range of soils. It does best in moisture-retentive soils rich in organic matter with a pH of 5.0 to 6.8. Mulch this shallow-rooted crop to keep it moist.

Pest and Disease Problems:
Wet, humid weather may cause some problems with rotting, but on the whole this chicory is problem-free.

Season-Extending Options:
In the fall, cover plants with cloches or tunnels to protect them for a prolonged harvest. Plants can also be lifted in fall before the ground freezes and set in boxes of sand in a cool basement to be forced.

Harvest and Storage:
Radicchio matures in 85 days. Once leaves have turned red, harvest the entire head by cutting off at ground level, or leave some stump behind from which more leaves may sprout. Use radicchio soon after harvest.

Noteworthy Radicchio Varieties

Variety	Description	Sources
ROSSA DI TREVISO	Slightly less cold hardy than Rossa di Verona.	15, 57
ROSSA DI VERONA	The most well known and commonly grown variety of red chicory.	64
VARIEGATA DI CASTELFRANCO	Variegated form; the heads are streaked with red and white.	15, 57

RADISHES   *Raphanus sativus*   Cruciferae   Cool-season crop

Propagation:
Seeds germinate in 5 to 7 days. Sow seeds for small, early varieties 4 to 6 weeks before last frost, or as soon as the soil can be worked. For fall planting, count back 42 days from first expected frost to determine when to sow seeds. Plant midseason or summer varieties in mid to late spring. Late varieties, or winter radishes, should be sown in the garden 10 weeks before first expected frost. Plant seeds ½ inch deep.

Intensive Spacing:
2 to 3 inches for early varieties; 3 to 5 inches for midseason and late varieties. Small early varieties can be broadcast.

Growing Requirements:
All radishes do best in loose, light, well-drained soil that retains moisture and is rich in organic matter. The pH can range from 5.5 to 6.8. Avoid excess amounts of nitrogen, which will encourage topgrowth at the expense of root development. Radishes tolerate partial shade. The critical time for watering is throughout the entire growing season. Mulch helps cool the soil and conserve moisture, conditions that contribute to good flavor and texture.

Pest and Disease Problems:
Insects include cabbage loopers, flea beetles, harlequin bugs, imported cabbage worms, and onion maggots. Diseases are rarely, if ever, a problem.

Season-Extending Options:
Don't expect early season varieties to last too long into the fall; they can't hold up well under cold temperatures.

Instead, rely upon the winter radishes, also known as daikons, to provide a fall and winter harvest.

Yield-Improving Techniques:
A salt hay mulch has been shown to increase yields.

Interplanting Suggestions:
Small, early varieties are easy to tuck in between vegetables in garden beds. Try some short to medium length varieties at the base of dwarf fruit trees. Early radishes go well with carrots and lettuce and with lettuce and tomatoes. Traditional companions include cucumbers (for insect repellency) and lettuce (for growth enhancement).

Succession Planting Suggestions:
Make successions of early, spring varieties 10 days apart until temperatures rise. Make successions of midseason radishes every 10 days until midsummer.

Harvest and Storage:
Early radishes live up to their name by maturing in 20 to 30 days. Pull them while they're still small, about 1 inch in diameter. Harvest midseason radishes anytime they reach usable size (they mature in 30 to 45 days). Late varieties taste better when they've been touched by frost. They mature in 55 to 60 days, but wait to harvest until after a light frost. Mulch them well for an extended harvest; these roots are not as long lived as carrots and parsnips.

Noteworthy Radish Varieties

Variety	Description	Sources
ALL SEASON	Winter radish that can be harvested from early summer through late fall; well adapted to summer growing.	Widely available
CHERRY BELLE	Quick, round, red root is ready in a mere 22 days.	Widely available
MINOWASE EARLY	This summer radish is ready in 55 days.	34
MIYASHIGE	The best winter radish for storage.	34
MUCHEN BIER	Summer radish that also produces edible seedpods.	64

RASPBERRIES *Rubus idaeus* (red and yellow)   Rosaceae
R. occidentalis (black)

Hardiness Zones:
3 to 10.

Intensive Spacing:
2 to 3 feet apart in rows set 6 feet apart.

Growing Requirements:
Raspberries will tolerate most soils as long as they are well drained. The pH can range from 5.5 to 7.0. The critical time for watering is in mid to late summer. In early fall, excess water will delay hardening off. Mulch to keep roots moist. Prune canes of black raspberries after the harvest. Prune red and yellow summer-bearing raspberries in the same fashion. For red and yellow fall bearers, prune fruiting canes after the summer harvest. Don't cut back canes that fruit in the fall; those will give the following season's first harvest. All raspberries are self-pollinating.

Pest and Disease Problems:
Black sap beetles can injure raspberries. Virus diseases and anthracnose can afflict plants.

Season-Extending Options:
Grow a selection of early, mid, and late-season one and two-crop raspberries to extend the harvest.

Interplanting Suggestions:
In the middle of a 3-foot-wide bed, plant raspberries and provide a trellis. The first summer after planting, let beans, peas, and cabbage share space in the bed.

Yield-Improving Techniques:
Tip prune black and purple raspberries when they reach 2½ to 3 feet tall. This encourages lateral branching, which in turn increases the number of productive canes for the next season.

Harvest and Storage:
Raspberries begin producing in quantity 2 to 3 years after planting. A full, ripe color and a sample berry will confirm when raspberries are ready for harvest. Handle these highly perishable berries gently. Use them soon after harvest. Extras, if there are any, can be frozen. Mature plants produce 2 quarts to 2 gallons of berries.

Noteworthy Raspberry Variety

Variety	Description	Sources
ROYALTY	An unusually disease-resistant hybrid.	9, 48

RHUBARB   *Rheum rhabarbarum*   Polygonaceae   Perennial

Propagation:
Plant crowns in spring as soon as the soil can be worked or in fall before the ground freezes hard. Bury crowns 2 to 3 inches deep.

Intensive Spacing:
24 to 36 inches. Give this long-lived perennial its own bed or section of bed.

Growing Requirements:
Rhubarb does best in a well-drained, sandy loam. Soil pH can range from 5.0 to 6.8. This perennial is a heavy feeder and needs a good supply of phosphorus and potassium. Mulch plants to keep production going; dry soil slows down plants. Rhubarb needs full sun.

Pest and Disease Problems:
A single pest, the rhubarb curculio, may cause difficulties.

Season-Extending Options:
Crowns can be dug and forced indoors over the winter.

Yield-Improving Techniques:
Divide established plants every 5 years to avoid overcrowding and to stimulate the crowns to produce nice, thick stalks.

Harvest and Storage:
Take a few stalks the second season after planting. The third season, the harvest can begin in earnest. Select stalks 12 to 24 inches long. The harvest can continue for 8 to 10 weeks, but be sure to leave at least half the plant intact. To store the surplus, refrigerate for short-term use and cook and freeze for long-term use. Remember that the leaves are poisonous.

Noteworthy Rhubarb Varieties

Variety	Description	Sources
CHIPMAN CANADA RED	Plants produce abundantly and reliably year after year.	Widely available
VICTORIA	Vigorous producer of thick stems.	Widely available

ROSEMARY   *Rosmarinus officinalis*   Labiatae   Perennial

Propagation:
Rosemary can be started from seeds, stem cuttings, or divisions. Seeds germinate in 14 to 21 days. Sow seeds directly in the garden after last frost. For transplants, start seeds 8 to 10 weeks before setting out, which can be done after late frost. Stem cuttings are the preferred method. Set them out in spring after last frost or in fall. Divisions can be planted at the same time.

Intensive Spacing:
Give this perennial a permanent site in a bed.

Growing Requirements:
Rosemary grows best in light, sandy, well-drained soil. The pH is 5.0 to 8.0. It needs full sun.

Season-Extending Options:
Container-grown rosemary can be brought indoors for an ongoing winter harvest. For outdoor plants, stop harvesting 1 month before the first expected frost, then harvest lightly after frost until leaves die back.

Interplanting Suggestions:
Rosemary is a traditional pest-repellent companion. Flowers are reputed to repel moths and flies, and branches strewn in the garden are said to keep away slugs.

Harvest and Storage:
Harvest leaves as needed throughout the season. Dry or freeze leaves for winter use.

Noteworthy Rosemary Variety

Variety	Description	Sources
HUNTINGTON CARPET	Foot-long creeping variety that is highly productive.	106

RUTABAGAS   *Brassica napus*, Napobrassica Group   Cruciferae   Cool-season crop

Propagation:
Seeds germinate in 7 to 15 days. Rutabagas are planted to mature in fall; spring-sown crops grow poorly and taste inferior due to the heat of summer. Sow seeds directly in the garden 15 weeks before the first expected frost. Plant seeds ½ inch deep.

Intensive Spacing:
6 to 9 inches.

Growing Requirements:
Rutabagas thrive in well-limed, medium-heavy soils rich in organic matter. The pH should range from 6.5 to 7.2. This root crop is a light feeder that needs moderate amounts of potassium. Avoid excess nitrogen; that will stimulate topgrowth at the expense of root development. Mulch to keep the soil cool and moist, conditions that promote good growth.

Pest and Disease Problems:
To a minor degree, rutabagas may be bothered by aphids, cabbage loopers, cabbage maggots, cutworms, flea beetles, harlequin bugs, imported cabbage worms, and leafminers.

Season-Extending Options:
This is a frost-tolerant crop, but freezing alters the taste and texture of the root. It provides an ongoing winter harvest when mulched.

Succession Planting Suggestions:
Since this crop goes into the garden toward midsummer, precede it with Chinese cabbage, midseason carrots, early cabbages, and bush beans.

Harvest and Storage:
Rutabagas mature in 85 to 90 days, but taste best when touched by frost. Delay the harvest until after a light frost but do not let roots freeze. These roots can be stored in-ground under a thick layer of mulch for an extended winter harvest. Be sure to dig all roots before topgrowth sprouts anew in the spring.

Noteworthy Rutabaga Varieties

Variety	Description	Sources
AMERICAN PURPLE TOP	Excellent variety for winter storage.	Widely available
LAURENTIAN	Keeps extremely well over the winter.	Widely available

SAGE   *Salvia officinalis*   Labiatae   Perennial

Propagation:
Sage can be started from seeds, cuttings, or divisions. Seeds germinate in 2 to 3 weeks. Sow them directly in the garden as soon as the soil is workable. For transplants, start indoors 6 to 8 weeks before setting out, which can be done after the last frost. Cuttings and divisions allow plants to become established sooner. Plant cuttings and divisions in spring.

Intensive Spacing:
2 feet.

Growing Requirements:
Sage thrives in light, sandy, well-drained soil. The pH should be 6.2 to 6.4. Sage needs full sun.

Season-Extending Options:
Stop harvesting 1 month before the first expected frost, then harvest lightly after frost until leaves die back from the cold.

Yield-Improving Techniques:
Relace plants by stem cuttings or divisions every 3 to 4

years; old plants become too woody and their productivity declines.

Interplanting Suggestions:
Sage is a traditional growth-enhancing companion for cabbage, carrots, strawberries, and tomatoes. It is reputed to repel insects from cole crops.

Harvest and Storage:
Harvest leaves as needed for fresh use throughout the season. Leaves can be dried or frozen.

Noteworthy Sage Varieties

Variety	Description	Sources
DWARF SAGE	This 12-inch-high form is good for small-scale gardens and is less likely to be winter-killed in northern areas.	108
HOLT'S MAMMOTH	This 36-inch-tall plant is fast growing and prolific.	106

SALSIFY   *Tragopogon porrifolius*   Compositae   Cool-season crop

Propagation:
Seeds germinate in 7 to 20 days. Gardeners in the Far North should sow seeds directly in the garden 2 to 4 weeks before the last frost. The soil should be at least 40°F for germination. Gardeners in less severe climates can plant in midspring and gardeners in the South can plant in June for a late fall crop. Sow seeds 1 inch deep.

Intensive Spacing:
2 to 6 inches.

Growing Requirements:
Salsify grows best in a rich, loose, well-drained soil free of rocks and other obstructions. The pH should be as close to 7.0 as possible. A light feeder, salsify benefits from moderate amounts of potassium but is hindered by excess nitrogen. Keep plants cool and moist with mulch to encourage good growth. This root crop tolerates partial shade.

Pest and Disease Problems:
Salsify is generally trouble-free.

Season-Extending Options:
Springtime shoots and leaves that appear on over-wintered salsify can be eaten as an early green.

Yield-Improving Techniques:
A monthly side-dressing of wood ashes or a watering with seaweed emulsion every 3 weeks will encourage thick roots.

Succession Planting Suggestions:
This long-season crop doesn't offer an opportunity for successions.

Harvest and Storage:
Salsify matures in 120 days but can be dug anytime it reaches usable size. Roots touched by frost taste better and have a firmer texture. If mulched they will remain in the garden for an extended winter harvest. Salsify can also be kept in a root cellar but tends to shrivel rather quickly.

Noteworthy Salsify Varieties

Variety	Description	Sources
LONG BLACK	Black-rooted variety that is extremely hardy and thought by many to have a better flavor than white varieties.	Widely available
MAMMOTH SAND-WICH ISLAND	Commonly grown variety with 6-in.-long white roots.	Widely available

SEA KALE   *Crambe maritima*   Cruciferae   Perennial

Propagation:
Plant root cuttings in spring, as soon as the soil can be worked, or in fall before the soil freezes hard. Plant cuttings 1 inch deep.

Intensive Spacing:
12 to 18 inches. Give this long-lived perennial its own bed or section of bed.

Growing Requirements:
Provide light, well-drained soil in a site that receives full sun. Cut off flowers that appear in summer.

Pest and Disease Problems:
Sea kale is generally a problem-free crop.

Season-Extending Options:
Dig crowns in fall and force indoors for a winter harvest of blanched leaf stalks. Forced crowns cannot be put back in the garden and should be added to the compost pile.

Yield-Improving Techniques:
Give plants a boost of seaweed/fish emulsion once each season, after harvesting.

Harvest and Storage:
Wait until plants have been in the garden for 3 seasons before harvesting. In early spring cover crowns with an inverted pot or several inches of leaves. Check in several weeks and harvest blanched leaf stalks when they're 8 inches tall. After the harvest remove the covering and let plants grow.

SHALLOTS   *Allium cepa*, Aggregatum Group   Amaryllidaceae   Cool-season crop

Propagation:
Plant sets 2 to 4 weeks before last frost. In long-season areas they can be planted in the fall. Plant sets so that the pointed tip barely shows above the soil.

Intensive Spacing:
6 inches. Shallots can also be grown in wide-rows.

Growing Requirements:
Shallots need a rich, well-drained soil. The pH can range from 6.0 to 7.0. They need moderate amounts of phosphorus and potassium. Make sure the bulbs have an even supply of water as they're developing. Withhold water once the tops begin to yellow and dry.

Pest and Disease Problems:
Shallots are rarely bothered.

Season-Extending Options:
Plant sets in a container for an indoor harvest of onion-flavored greens throughout the winter.

Interplanting Suggestions:
Tuck in wherever space is available.

Harvest and Storage:
Shallots mature in 100 days, but they can be dug any time they reach a usable size. For storage shallots wait to dig until the tops have withered.

FRENCH SORREL   *Rumex scutatus*   Polygonaceae   Perennial

Propagation:
Sow seeds directly in the garden in spring or fall when soil is at least 60°F. Plant seeds ¼ inch deep. Plantings can also be started by using root divisions.

Intensive Spacing:
18 inches apart. Give this perennial its own bed or section of bed.

Growing Requirements:
French sorrel will adapt to a range of soils, but does best in one that retains moisture well and is rich in nitrogen. The pH can range from 5.0 to 6.8. Mulch in the summer to keep plants cool and moist to prevent bolting.

Pest and Disease Problems:
French sorrel is trouble-free.

Yield-Improving Techniques:
Each spring, side-dress with manure or compost. Divide overcrowded clumps to renew plants' vigor. When seedstalks appear, pinch off so plants devote energy to leaf production.

Interplanting Suggestions:
Plant French sorrel at the base of an ornamental or dwarf fruit tree.

Harvest and Storage:
From seed, French sorrel matures in 70 days. Pick leaves anytime they reach usable size throughout the season. Leaves are at their best when young and tender. Always leave the center rosette of leaves intact for continuous production. Use sorrel immediatelty after harvest.

SOYBEANS   *Glycine max*   Leguminosae   Warm-season crop

Propagation:
Speed the germination process by soaking seeds overnight. Sow seeds directly in the garden 1 week after the last frost, or when the soil has warmed to 65°F. Seeds should be set 1½ inches deep.

Intensive Spacing:
9 inches. Soybeans can be grown in wide-rows.

Growing Requirements:
Soybeans prefer light, well-drained soil not too rich in nutrients. The pH should range from 6.5 to 7.0. These soil builders are hindered by too much nitrogen in the soil; pod production will suffer. Soybeans need full sun. Critical time for watering is from flowering until pods have set.

Pest and Disease Problems:
Insects include cutworms, grasshoppers, Japanese beetles, leafhoppers, Mexican bean beetles, and white grubs. Bacterial blight and downy mildew may also bother plants.

Season-Extending Options:
Warm soil before planting with a plastic mulch. Short-season gardeners should look for early varieties.

Yield-Improving Techniques:
Treat with special soybean inoculant to encourage nitrogen-fixing. If you can't find soybean inoculant, use one recommended for peas and beans.

Succession Planting Suggestions:
Follow soybeans with nitrogen-loving crops.

Harvest and Storage:
Soybeans mature anywhere from 70 to 100 days. For use as a green shelling bean, pick pods when seeds are full size. Pick before the pods yellow and wither. Surplus soybeans can be frozen, canned, or dried. For drying, let pods mature on the plants. Harvest before the pods shatter, shell, and dry the beans until they resist denting by a thumbnail.

Noteworthy Soybean Varieties

Variety	Description	Sources
EDIBLE EARLY HAKUCHO	Plants stand 1 ft. tall and bear an abundance of pods.	48
FISKEBY V	Slightly taller than Early Hakucho; survives well in cool, bright areas with short seasons.	48

SPINACH   *Spinacia oleracea*   Chenopodiaceae   Cool-season crop

Propagation:
Seeds germinate in 7 to 11 days. To speed the process, soak seeds overnight in a dilute vinegar/water solution. For midseason sowing, store seeds in the freezer 1 to 2 weeks before planting. Sow seeds directly in the garden 4 to 6 weeks before the last frost. Soil must be at least 35°F for germination. Plant seeds ½ inch deep. For transplants, start seeds 4 to 6 weeks before setting out, which can be done 3 to 6 weeks before last frost. Handle transplants carefully. For a fall harvest count back 64 days from first expected frost to determine when to sow seeds.

Intensive Spacing:
4 to 6 inches. Spinach can be broadcast and grown in wide-rows.

Growing Requirements:
Spinach adapts to a wide range of soil types but excels in a well-drained, sandy loam rich in organic matter. The pH should be 6.0 to 6.8. This heavy feeder needs moderate amounts of potassium. Plants can tolerate partial shade. Keep beds free of weeds to avoid competition. Mulch to keep soil cool and moist, conditions that encourage good growth and stall bolting.

Pest and Disease Problems:
Aphids, European corn borers, leafminers, and whiteflies can cause trouble. Blight and downy mildew may afflict plants.

Season-Extending Options:
Use heat and bolt-resistant varieties for spring plantings. Mulch young fall plantings to overwinter; in the spring these will put out new growth up to 3 months before last frost. You can also sow seeds in fall before the ground freezes; these will germinate before any spring-sown seeds. Mulch or cover mature plants in fall or dig and transfer them to a growing frame, where they will continue to produce a modest number of leaves. Spinach also does well sown directly in a growing frame.

Interplanting Suggestions:
Compact, shade-tolerant spinach is a good crop to tuck in between taller crops. In particular it does well with Brussels sprouts and celery. It can also be slipped in among strawberry plants very early in the season. Spinach shares space well with onions and brassicas.

Succession Planting Suggestions:
Plant every 2 to 3 weeks until temperatures start to rise. Follow an early crop of spinach with carrots, eggplants, peanuts, peppers, pole beans, potatoes, and tomatoes.

Harvest and Storage:
Spinach matures in 40 to 50 days, but you can begin harvesting once leaves reach usable size. Take a few outer leaves at a time for an ongoing harvest. Or cut the entire plant at ground level. Use leaves soon after harvest. Surplus spinach can be frozen or canned.

Noteworthy Spinach Varieties

Variety	Description	Sources
POPEYE'S CHOICE	Quick-maturing, bolt and heat-resistant variety.	69
WINTER BLOOMSDALE	Cold-resistant, crinkle-leaved variety that can be overwintered successfully.	Widely available

SQUASH *Cucurbita* spp. Cucurbitaceae Warm-season crop

Propagation:
Seeds germinate in 7 to 14 days. Sow seeds directly in the garden 1 week or more after last frost. The soil must be at least 60°F. Plant seeds 1 inch deep. For transplants, start seeds 4 weeks before setting out, which can be done 3 to 4 weeks after the last frost. Handle these temperamental transplants carefully.

Intensive Spacing:
24 to 36 inches for summer and winter squash. Bush varieties are suited to closer spacing. Situate vining plants near the edge of beds so they can spill over into pathways without overtaking neighboring crops.

Growing Requirements:
Squashes thrive in rich, well-drained, sandy loam. Soil pH should be from 6.0 to 7.0. These heavy feeders need moderate amounts of nitrogen and high amounts of phosphorus. They require full sun. The critical time for watering is during bud development and flowering.

Trellising or Training Tips:
To save space, train vining varieties up supports. Tie the vines in place with soft cloth and support the developing squash in slings.

Pest and Disease Problems:
Insects include cabbage loopers, corn earworms, cucumber beetles, squash bugs, and squash vine borers. Possible diseases are anthracnose, bacterial wilt, downy mildew, mosaic, powdery mildew, and scab.

Season-Extending Options:
Warm soil with plastic mulch and get a head start with transplants.

Yield-Improving Techniques:
Starting 50 days before the first expected frost, northern growers should remove all flowers and immature fruits so plants can ripen the remaining squash.

Interplanting Suggestions:
Some gardeners report success with growing squash at the base of dwarf fruit trees. As a rule, these large plants, when allowed to sprawl, make poor partners in a garden bed. When trellised, however, small, shade-tolerant crops can be grown at their base. Squash is part of a classic trio along with corn and beans.

Succession Planting Suggestions:
Squash can follow plantings of early peas, lettuce, spinach, or Chinese cabbage.

Harvest and Storage:
Summer squash appear on plants in 48 to 70 days. Pick them young, tender, and small. Club-size squash may give you more in terms of quantity, but they're lacking in quality. Keep harvesting to assure continuous production. Winter squash mature in 80 to 120 days. Wait to harvest until just before a hard frost (they can withstand a few light frosts, which will improve their flavor). Pick when skin has toughened enough to resist denting. Cure all but acorn squash and store in a warm, dry place. Keep acorn squash cool.

Noteworthy Squash Varieties

Variety	Description	Sources
GOLD RUSH	Space-saving bush summer squash that offers abundant yields.	9
KUTA	Can be harvested as a summer or winter squash; has 2 times the calcium and phosphorus of other varieties.	48
PONCA	Extra-early butternut squash for short-season areas.	51
TABLE ACE	70-day winter squash for short-season areas.	Widely available
VEGETABLE SPAGHETTI	10-ft.-long vines produce up to 18 squash a season.	9, 17, 25

STRAWBERRIES   *Fragaria* spp.   Rosaceae

Hardiness Zones:
Throughout the United States and southerly regions of Canada.

Intensive Spacing:
1 to 1½ feet.

Growing Requirements:
Strawberries adapt well to a wide range of soils, as long as they are well drained and rich in organic matter. Strawberries do best in evenly moist soil and respond well to drip irrigation. The critical watering times are during flowering and runner development. Mulch plants after the soil warms to conserve moisture and keep berries clean. Strawberries are self-pollinating.

Pest and Disease Problems:
Slugs and birds are perennial problems. Verticillium wilt and red stele can afflict plants; buy certified disease-free stock to avoid these problems.

Season-Extending Options:
Site the strawberry bed on a south-facing slope for an early start (only safe in areas where late frosts are not a problem).

Yield-Improving Techniques:
For the delayed gratification of a larger harvest the second season, remove all blossoms the first year. (On everbearers, remove just the first flush of flowers and let the second one mature.) For continued high yields, use rooted runners as replacements for flagging 2 or 3-year-old mother plants. Remove old plants from beds and destroy. Mulches of straw have been shown to increase yields by 10 percent.

Interplanting Suggestions:
Plant strawberries around the base of dwarf fruit trees. Tuck spinach among plants early in spring.

Harvest and Storage:
One month after blooming, strawberries are ripe. Pick with a little bit of stem end still on the berry. Eat soon after harvest or freeze.

Noteworthy Strawberry Varieties

Variety	Description	Sources
BORDURELLA	An everbearing runnerless bush strawberry that is very prolific.	25
OZARK BEAUTY	An incredibly high-yielding everbearer.	25

SUMMER SAVORY   *Satureja hortensis*   Labiatae   Warm-season annual

Propagation:
Seeds germinate in 7 to 14 days. Sow them directly in the garden as soon as soil can be worked. For transplants, start indoors or in a cold frame 8 to 10 weeks before setting out, which can be done after the last frost.

Intensive Spacing:
8 to 12 inches.

Growing Requirements:
Summer savory prefers moderately rich, sandy loam that retains moisture well. The pH can range from 6.5 to 7.5 Savory needs full sun.

Season-Extending Options:
This herb self-sows freely; the seeds germinate and become established long before spring-sown seeds.

Interplanting Suggestions:
Summer savory is a traditional growth-enhancing companion for beans and onions.

Harvest and Storage:
Begin picking a few leaves as needed once the plant reaches 6 inches high. To harvest a large quantity of leaves for drying, cut back the plant one-half to two-thirds its size as flowers appear.

SWEET POTATOES   *Ipomoea batatas*   Convolvulaceae   Warm-season crop

Propagation:
Start from purchased slips or sprout your own. Begin the sprouting 6 to 8 weeks before planting out, which can be done 2 to 3 weeks after the last frost. Night temperatures must stay above 60°F. Set slips 1 to 2 inches deep.

Intensive Spacing:
10 to 12 inches. Bush varieties are suited to closer spacing.

Growing Requirements:
Sweet potatoes adapt well to most soils, but produce the best in light, sandy loams. The pH should be 5.5 to 6.5. Plants need moderate amounts of nitrogen and phosphorus and high amounts of potassium. Sweet potatoes need full sun. Keep weeds at bay during the early stages when plants are becoming established. Plants are very drought tolerant.

Pest and Disease Problems:
Nematodes, sweet potato beetles, sweet potato weevils, and wireworms cause problems mainly in warm regions. Black rot, soft rot, soil rot, and stem rot may bother plants.

Season-Extending Options:
Northern gardeners must pick varieties suited to short-season areas.

Yield-Improving Techniques:
Black plastic mulch has been shown to double yields.

Interplanting Suggestions:
In large beds sweet potatoes can be grown with pumpkins. In general, these sprawling plants aren't well suited to interplanting.

Succession Planting Suggestions:
Sweet potatoes can follow an early planting of peas, lettuce, or spinach.

Harvest and Storage:
Sweet potatoes need 90 to 150 days to mature. You can harvest a few tubers before they reach full size throughout the season. Wait to harvest mature tubers until after the first frost. Dig right away, or if that's not possible, clip off frost-killed vines. Handle tubers carefully and cure them before storing in a warm, dry location.

Noteworthy Sweet Potato Varieties

Variety	Description	Sources
ALLGOLD	Very early, stem-rot–resistant sweet potato that produces in abundance.	Widely available
JEWELL	Early-maturing, heavy yielder that holds its flavor well.	Widely available
VINELESS PORTO RICO	Compact and heavy-yielding variety for small spaces.	68

SWISS CHARD   *Beta vulgaris*, Cicla Group   Chenopodiaceae   Cool and warm-season crop

Propagation:
Seeds germinate in 7 to 14 days. To speed the process, soak seeds overnight before planting. Sow seeds directly in the garden 2 to 4 weeks before last frost. Plant them ½ inch deep. For transplants, start seeds 4 weeks before setting out, which can be done 3 to 4 weeks before last frost. Handle transplants carefully. In long-season areas, sow 10 weeks before first frost for a winter and spring crop.

Intensive Spacing:
6 to 9 inches.

Growing Requirements:
For the finest leaf growth, provide well-drained soil rich in organic matter. The pH can range from 6.0 to 6.8. Swiss chard is a light feeder that needs moderate amounts of nitrogen. This leafy crop tolerates partial shade. This crop is drought resistant.

Pest and Disease Problems:
Problems are rare, but aphids, European corn borers, leafminers, slugs, and snails may bother plants. Possible diseases are blight and downy mildew.

Season-Extending Options:
Swiss chard tolerates frost and hot weather well, so it has a very long productive season. For a head start, use transplants. Cut back stalks in fall and mulch for extra-early fresh spring growth. Or mulch or cover untrimmed plants for an ongoing winter harvest. Swiss chard is a good crop for large growing frames.

Interplanting Suggestions:
Swiss chard teams well with beets and carrots, okra, and cucumbers. Onion family members are traditional growth-enhancing companions.

Succession Planting Suggestions:
Swiss chard can follow early plantings of peas.

Harvest and Storage:
Swiss chard matures in 50 to 60 days. Begin harvesting a few outer leaves 40 days after sowing. Always leave the inner leaves intact to assure continuous production.

Noteworthy Swiss Chard Varieties

Variety	Description	Sources
FORDHOOK GIANT	Vigorous, white-stalked variety.	Widely available
PERPETUAL CHARD	Cut back to 2 inches twice a season, this variety provides an abundant harvest of tender new growth.	9
RHUBARB	Heavy producer with red stalks and leaf veins.	Widely available

TARRAGON   *Artemisia dracunculus* var. *sativa*   Compositae   Perennial

Propagation:
Cuttings and divisions are the preferred way to start this herb. Take cuttings in summer. Divisions can be planted in early spring or early fall.

Intensive Spacing:
Give this perennial space in a bed where it won't be disturbed. Be prepared to control its growth.

Growing Requirements:
Tarragon needs moderately rich, well-drained soil. The pH should range from 6.2 to 6.5. It needs full sun.

Season-Extending Options:
Stop harvesting 1 month before the first expected frost, then harvest lightly after frost until the leaves die back from the cold.

Yield-Improving Techniques:
Divide plants every 3 or 4 years to renew their vigor.

Interplanting Suggestions:
Grow tarragon at the base of ornamental or dwarf fruit trees. This herb can stunt the growth of neighboring herbs, especially thyme. As a traditional companion it is thought to enhance the flavor of vegetables.

Harvest and Storage:
Once plants are established, pick leaves as needed through the season. Dry or freeze for storage.

THYME   *Thymus vulgaris*   Labiatae   Perennial

Propagation:
Thyme can be started from seeds, cuttings, or root divisions. Seeds germinate in 3 to 4 weeks. Sow them directly in the garden as soon as soil is workable. For transplants, sow indoors 8 to 10 weeks before setting out, which can be done after the last frost. Take cuttings in the summer. Plant root divisions in early spring or fall. This method of propagating is the easiest and plants become established the soonest.

Intensive Spacing:
6 to 12 inches. Give this perennial a permanent spot in a bed.

Growing Requirements:
Thyme prefers light, warm, well-drained soil kept on the dry side. The pH can range from 6.0 to 8.0. Thyme needs full sun.

Season-Extending Options:
Stop harvesting 1 month before the first expected frost, then harvest lightly until leaves die back from the cold.

Yield-Improving Techniques:
Divide established plants every 3 or 4 years to renew vigor.

Interplanting Suggestions:
Grow thyme at the base of ornamental or dwarf fruit trees. As a traditional companion, thyme is thought to enhance the flavor of surrounding vegetables and herbs.

Harvest and Storage:
Harvest leaves as needed throughout the season. For a large quantity of leaves to dry, harvest just before flowers bloom for finest flavor. Thyme can also be frozen for storage.

Noteworthy Thyme Varieties

Variety	Description	Sources
CREEPING	This 3-inch-high form is less vulnerable to winter kill in the North.	108
LEMON	A citrus-scented variety that offers a high return for the space.	110
ST. LOUIS	An exceptionally high-yielding variety.	99

TOMATOES   *Lycopersicon lycopersicum*   Solanaceae   Warm-season crop

Propagation:
Seeds germinate in 7 to 14 days. In long-season areas, seeds can be sown directly in the garden after the last frost when the soil is at least 60°F. Sow seeds ½ inch deep. For transplants, start seeds 6 to 10 weeks before setting out, which can be done 4 weeks after last frost.

Intensive Spacing:
18 to 24 inches (for plants trained upright).

Growing Requirements:
Tomatoes thrive in sandy, well-drained loam rich in organic matter. The pH should be between 6.0 and 7.0. These heavy feeders need high amounts of nitrogen and phosphorus and moderate amounts of potassium. Tomatoes must receive full sun. The critical time for watering is from flowering through harvest. An even moisture supply contributes to good production of high-quality fruit. The critical time for weeding is the 5 weeks after transplanting.

Trellising or Training Tips:
Indeterminate plants should be staked to save space and encourage healthier growth. Pinch out suckers to keep growth under control. Determinate plants should not be pruned, but some particularly vigorous ones may benefit from the support of a stake.

Pest and Disease Problems:
Insects include aphids, cabbage loopers, Colorado potato beetles, corn earworms, cucumber beetles, European corn borers, leafhoppers, nematodes, pepper maggots, potato tuberworms, and tomato hornworms. Diseases are anthracnose, bacterial canker, damping-off, early blight, fusarium wilt, late blight, mosaics, and verticillium wilt. Choose varieties with as much disease resistance as possible to ensure high yields.

Season-Extending Options:
Root side shoots from established plants in mid-July for late fall harvesting. (This is a good way to replace plants that have lost their vigor or have been slowed by pests or diseases). Have frost protection ready; plants that can make it through the first light frosts often have a chance to ripen more of their fruit in the Indian summer that follows.

Yield-Improving Techniques:
Foliar sprays of fish emulsion and mulches of peanut hulls have been shown to increase yields. Some garden-

ers find that conscientious removal of suckers promotes earlier and larger tomatoes on the central stem. On seedlings, try cutting back the long taproot and pinching off all but the top rosette and next 2 lower leaves before transplanting. This may encourage earlier fruiting. Studies have shown that transplants grown in 1¾-inch pots give more tomatoes sooner than transplants raised in ⅘-inch pots.

Interplanting Suggestions:
Team staked tomatoes with onions and basil and with lettuce and radishes. Tomatoes also share space well with bush beans and cabbage. Traditional insect-repellent companions include asparagus and basil; parsley is said to enhance tomato growth.

Succession Planting Suggestions:
Plant an assortment of early, mid, and late-season varieties for a harvest that spreads itself over several months. In long-season areas tomatoes can follow corn and precede cantaloupes. In shorter season areas, tomatoes can follow early peas, lettuce, spinach, bunching onions, or Chinese cabbage.

Harvest and Storage:
Tomatoes start ripening 50 to 80 days from transplanting. When frost necessitates picking green tomatoes, set them indoors in a warm spot to ripen. Surplus tomatoes can be frozen, canned, or dried.

Noteworthy Tomato Varieties

Variety	Description	Sources
CLIMBING TRIP-L-CROP	Each 8-ft. vine can produce 2 to 3 bushels.	48
EARLY GIRL	The abundant harvest begins in 54 to 62 days.	Widely available
FLORAMERICA HYBRID VF	Suited to growing in hot, humid, long-season areas; resists 17 common tomato afflictions.	Widely available
LONG KEEPER	Can be picked immature to ripen slowly over a long period indoors to extend the fresh tomato season.	9
MOIRA	Compact, disease-resistant plant produces flavorful crops even under adverse conditions.	34
QUICK PICK VFFNTA	Offers the unbeatable combination of disease resistance and early and very heavy yields.	48
STAKEBREAKER VF	Bred especially for the South but suitable elsewhere.	28
SWEET 100	Tremendous yields of cherry tomatoes appear on the indeterminate vines; rich in vitamin C.	Widely available

TURNIPS *Brassica rapa*, Rapifera Group Cruciferae Cool-season crop

Propagation:
Seeds germinate in 7 to 14 days. Sow seeds directly in the garden 4 to 6 weeks before last frost. Soil temperature must be at least 40°F. For transplants, start seeds 3 to 4 weeks before setting out, which can be done 4 weeks before the last frost. Handle transplants carefully. To time fall planting, count back 9 weeks before first expected frost. Sow seeds ¼ inch deep.

Intensive Spacing:
4 to 6 inches. Turnips grown primarily for greens can be broadcast.

Growing Requirements:
Turnips grow well in rich, loose soil with a pH between 6.5 and 7.0. These light feeders need only low amounts of nitrogen. This root crop tolerates partial shade. Critical time for watering is at the beginning of root development. Mulch to keep soil cool and moist, which will encourage good growth.

Pest and Disease Problems:
Turnips are rarely troubled.

Season-Extending Options:
For a head start, use early maturing varieties and set them into the garden as transplants. Turnips can withstand all but very hard frosts without protection. For late fall greens, use slow-bolting varieties. Mulch and continue to harvest until deep cold stops leaf production.

Yield-Improving Techniques:
A mulch of peanut hulls has been shown to increase yields.

Interplanting Suggestions:
Turnips share space nicely with trellised peas.

Succession Planting Suggestions:
Turnips are a good crop to follow melons at the end of the season.

Harvest and Storage:
Turnip roots mature in 30 to 55 days. Harvest roots while still small, no more than 3 inches in diameter. Once hot weather arrives, the root quality will decline. For greens, harvest a few from each plant throughout the season. Always leave at least 4 leaves intact; otherwise, root development will be hindered. Fall crops can be stored in-ground under mulch but are not as long-lasting and don't remain in as good condition as rutabagas. Surplus roots and greens can be frozen.

Noteworthy Turnip Varieties

Variety	Description	Sources
DES VERTUS MARTEAU	Roots do well for short-term storage since they resist sprouting.	67
SEVEN TOP	Good choice for extra-early or late planting; slow to bolt.	Widely available
TOKYO CROSS HYBRID	Matures in a quick 35 days; does best as a fall crop.	50

VEGETABLE AMARANTH (also called tampala) *Amaranthus tricolor*
Amaranthaceae
Warm-season crop

Propagation:
Sow seeds directly in the garden after last frost. Plant seeds ¼ inch deep. For transplants, start seeds 3 weeks before setting out, which can be done after the last frost.

Intensive Spacing:
6 inches. Amaranth can be broadcast and grown in wide-rows.

Growing Requirements:
Amaranth produces the best leaves when grown in loose, fertile, well-drained soil. It adapts well to a wide range of soil pH. Make sure amaranth receives ample amounts of nitrogen. It also needs full sun. Keep moisture supply steady for a good quality harvest.

Pest and Disease Problems:
Caterpillars and stem borers may bother plants. Leaf curl and stem rot appear on occasion.

Season-Extending Options:
Don't expect much from a fall crop; the shortening daylengths cause plants to bolt.

Yield-Improving Techniques:
When plants are 4 to 6 inches tall, pinch off the top rosette of leaves to encourage bushiness, which means more harvestable leaves.

Interplanting Suggestions:
Amaranth can share space with carrots and onions.

Succession Planting Suggestions:
Follow early plantings of peas, lettuce, and spinach.

Harvest and Storage:
Harvest leaf rosettes from the stem tips as needed. Use young, tender leaves for the best texture and flavor. Extra leaves can be frozen.

Directory of Resources

Seed Sources

Throughout the text, varieties of vegetables, fruits, and herbs have been accompanied by numbers in parentheses. Those numbers correspond to this listing of seed sources. Keep in mind, of course, that many of the outstanding varieties mentioned are available from numerous sources both on and off our necessarily incomplete list. The suppliers keyed are just a starting point for your convenience. Also remember that seed companies change their offerings periodically. There are always new varieties appearing, and sometimes old ones fade quietly from the catalog pages.

We have tried to make this source listing as accurate and up to date as possible. If you should discover that a particular variety is no longer carried by one of the companies listed as a source, check other catalogs. You might also consider writing to the company and inquiring about the fate of that variety. In some seasons, there might be a shortage of seed available for sale to gardeners. Or the company may have decided to drop the variety because of low sales. If enough gardeners write about a specific variety, however, that may prompt the company to carry it again.

Vegetables

1. Abundant Life Seed Foundation
   P.O. Box 772
   Port Townsend, WA 98368

2. Alberta Nurseries and Seeds
   Box 20
   Bowden, Alberta
   Canada T0M 0K0

3. Allen, Sterling and Lothrop
   191 U.S. Route 1
   Falmouth, ME 04105

4. American Takii
   301 Natividad Road
   Salinas, CA 93906

5. Archia's
   106–108 East Main Street
   Sedalia, MO 65301

6. Ball Seed Company
   Box 335
   West Chicago, IL 60185

7. Broom Seed Company
   P.O. Box 237
   Rion, SC 29132

8. Burgess Seed and Plant Company
   905 Four Seasons Road
   Bloomington, IL 61701

9. W. Atlee Burpee Company
    300 Park Avenue
    Warminster, PA 18991

10. D. V. Burrell Seed Growers Company
    Box 150
    Rocky Ford, CO 81067

11. Butterbrooke Farm
    78 Barry Road
    Oxford, CT 06483

12. California Gardeners Seed Company
    904 Silver Spur Road, Suite 414
    Rolling Hills Estates, CA 90274

13. Chon and Son Oriental Products
    P.O. Box 251
    Malaga, NJ 08328

14. Comstock, Ferre and Company
    263 Main Street
    Wethersfield, CT 06109

15. The Cook's Garden
    Box 65
    Londonderry, VT 05148

16. William Dam Seeds
    P.O. Box 8400
    Dundas, Ontario
    Canada L9H 6M1

17. DeGiorgi Company
    P.O. Box 413
    Council Bluffs, IA 51502

18. Dominion Seed House
    Georgetown, Ontario
    Canada L7G 4A2

19. Early's Farm and Garden Centre
    Box 3024
    Saskatoon, Saskatchewan
    Canada S7K 3S9

20. Farmer Seed and Nursery Company
    818 NW Fourth Street
    Faribault, MN 55021

21. Ferry-Morse Seed Company
    111 Ferry-Morse Way
    Mountain View, CA 94042

22. Henry Field Seed and Nursery
    Shenandoah, IA 51602

23. Gleckler's Seedsmen
    Metamora, OH 43540

24. Good Seed Company
    P.O. Box 702
    Tonasket, WA 98855

25. Gurney's Seed and Nursery
    Company
    Yankton, SD 57079

26. Joseph Harris Company
    3670 Buffalo Road
    Rochester, NY 14624

27. Chas. C. Hart Seed Company
    P.O. Box 9169
    Wethersfield, CT 06109

28. H. G. Hastings Company
    P.O. Box 4274
    Atlanta, GA 30302

29. High Altitude Gardens
    P.O. Box 4238
    Ketchum, ID 83340

30. J. L. Hudson, Seedsman
    P.O. Box 1058
    Redwood City, CA 94064

31. Ed Hume Seeds
    P.O. Box 1450
    Kent, WA 98032

32. Island Seed Company
    P.O. Box 4278, Station A
    Victoria, British Columbia
    Canada V8X 3X8

33. Japonica Seeds
    P.O. Box 919
    Jackson Heights, NY 11372

34. Johnny's Selected Seeds
    Albion, ME 04910

35. Jung Seeds and Nursery
    335 South High Street
    Randolph, WI 53957

36. Kilgore Seed Company
    1400 West First Street
    Sanford, FL 32771

37. Kitazawa Seed Company
    356 West Taylor Street
    San Jose, CA 95110

38. Liberty Seed Company
    P.O. Box 806
    New Philadelphia, OH 44663

39. Earl May Seed and Nursery
    Company
    Shenandoah, IA 51603

40. McFayden Seeds
    P.O. Box 1800
    Brandon, Manitoba
    Canada R74 6N4

41. Mellinger's
    2310 West South Range
    North Lima, OH 44452

42. Mountain Seed and Nursery
    P.O. Box 9107
    Moscow, ID 83843

43. Mountain Valley Seeds and
    Nursery Company
    2015 North Main
    North Logan, UT 84321

44. Native Seeds/SEARCH
    3950 West New York Drive
    Tucson, AZ 85745

45. Nichols Garden Nursery
    1190 North Pacific Highway
    Albany, OR 97321

46. Northrup King Company
    P.O. Box 1827
    Gilroy, CA 95020

47. L. L. Olds Seed Company
    P.O. Box 7790
    Madison, WI 53707

48. George W. Park Seed Company
    P.O. Box 31
    Greenwood, SC 29647

49. W. H. Perron Company
    515 Labelle Boulevard,
    Chomedey
    Laval, Quebec
    Canada H7V 2T3

50. Pinetree Garden Seeds
    New Gloucester, ME 04260

51. Plants of the Southwest
    1570 Pacheco Street
    Sante Fe, NM 87501

52. Redwood City Seed Company
    P.O. Box 361
    Redwood City, CA 94064

53. The Rocky Mountain Seed
    Company
    1325 15th Street
    Denver, CO 80217

54. SPB Sales
    P.O. Box 278
    Nash, TX 77569

55. Seeds Blum
    Idaho City Stage
    Boise, ID 83706

56. Seedway
    Hall, NY 14463

57. Shepherd's Garden Seeds
    7389 West Zayante Road
    Felton, CA 95018

58. Siberia Seeds
    Box 3000
    Olds, Alberta
    Canada T0M 1P0

59. Stokes Seeds
    Box 10
    St. Catharines, Ontario
    Canada L2R 6R6

60. Sunrise Enterprises
    P.O. Box 10058
    Elmwood, CT 06110

61. T & T Seeds
    Box 1710
    Winnipeg, Manitoba
    Canada R3C 3P6

62. George Tait and Sons
    900 Tidewater Drive
    Norfolk, VA 23504

63. Territorial Seed Company
    P.O. Box 27
    Lorane, OR 97451

64. Thompson and Morgan
    P.O. Box 100
    Farmingdale, NJ 07727

65. Otis Twilley Seed Company
    P.O. Box 65
    Trevose, PA 19047

66. Unwins
    P.O. Box 9
    Farmingdale, NJ 07727

67. The Urban Farmer
    Box 444
    Convent Station, NJ 07961

68. Vermont Bean Seed Company
    Garden Lane
    Bomoseen, VT 05732

69. Vesey's Seed
    York
    Box 9000
    Charlottetown, Prince
       Edward Island
    Canada C1A 8K6

70. Watanabe
    P.O. Box 4
    Kogota, Milyagi 987
    Japan

71. Willhite Seed Company
    P.O. Box 23
    Poolville, TX 76076

72. Dr. Yoo Farm
    P.O. Box 290
    College Park, MD 20740

Fruits

73. Armstrong Nursery
    1265 South Palmetto Avenue
    Ontario, CA 91761

74. Bountiful Ridge Nurseries
    Box 250
    Princess Anne, MD 21853

75. L. E. Cooke
    Visalia, CA 93277

76. Emlong Nurseries
    Stevensville, MI 49127

77. Ferris Nursery
    811 Fourth Street, NE
    Hampton, IA 50441

78. Florida Vineyard Nursery
    Box 300
    Orange Lake, FL 32681

79. Dean Foster Nurseries
    Route 2, OG-L
    Hartford, MI 49057

80. Inter-State Nurseries
    Hamburg, IA 51640

81. Jackson and Perkins Company
    201 Rose Lane
    Medford, OR 97501

82. Johnson Orchard and Nursery
    Route 5, Box 29J
    Ellijay, GA 30540

83. Kelly Brothers Nurseries
    Dansville, NY 14437

84. Lakeland Nurseries Sales
    340 Poplar Street
    Hanover, PA 17331

85. Henry Leuthardt Nurseries
    Montauk Highway
    P.O. Box 666
    East Moriches, NY 11940

86. J. E. Miller Nursery
    5060 West Lake Road
    Canandaigua, NY 14424

87. National Arbor Day Foundation
    Arbor Lodge 100
    Nebraska City, NE 68410

88. Neosho Nurseries
    900 North College
    Neosho, MO 64850

89. New York State Fruit Testing
    Cooperative Association
    Geneva, NY 14456

90. Pike's Peak Nurseries
    R. D. #1
    Penn Run, PA 15765

91. Raintree Nursery
    265 Butts Road
    Morton, WA 98356

92. Rayner Brothers
    Box 1617G
    Salisbury, MD 21801

93. Spring Hill Nurseries
    Catalog Reservation Center
    P.O. Box 1758
    Peoria, IL 61656

94. Stark Brothers Nurseries
    and Orchards Company
    Box A3441A
    Louisiana, MO 63353

95. Waynesboro Nurseries
    Box 987
    Waynesboro, VA 22980

96. Wayside Gardens
    Hodges, SC 29695

97. Dave Wilson Nursery
    4306 Santa Fe Avenue
    Hughson, CA 95326

98. Wolf River Nurseries
    Route 67, Box 73
    Buskirk, NY 12028

Herbs

99. ABC Herb Nursery
    Route 1, Box 313
    Lecoma, MO 65540

100. Casa Yerba
     Star Route 2, Box 21
     Days Creek, OR 97429

101. Country Herbs
     Box 357
     Stockbridge, MA 01262

102. Fox Hill Farm
     444 West Michigan Avenue,
     Box 7
     Parma, MI 49269

103. Le Jardin du Gourmet
     P.O. Box 30
     West Danville, VT 05873

104. Liberty Herb Farm
     Liberty, ME 04949

105. Otto Richter and Sons
     Goodwood, Ontario
     Canada L0C 1A0

106. Sandy Mush Herb Nursery
     Route 2, Surrett Cove Road
     Leicester, NC 28748

107. Stillridge Herb Farm
     10370 Route 99
     Woodstock, MD 21163

108. Taylor's Herb Gardens
     1535 Lone Oak Road
     Vista, CA 92083

109. Victoria Herb Gardens
     Box 947
     Southampton, PA 19866

110. Well-Sweep Herb Farm
     317 Mount Bethel Road
     Port Murray, NJ 07865

111. Woodland Herb Farm
     Northport, MI 49670

Garden Products

Season Extenders

Cloches

Brookstone
300 Vose Farm Road
Peterborough, NH 03458
Offers a wide variety of gardening aids including Gro-Cones and Gro-Collars.

W. Atlee Burpee Company (see Seed Sources for address)
A source of Hotkaps.

Garden Tech
1150 Great Plain Avenue
Needham, MA 02191
Supplier of the Fabro Expanding Tomato Cover.

Gardener's Supply Company
133 Elm Street
Winooski, VT 05404
Carries a number of season-extending devices including Wall O' Water and Hotkaps.

Mellinger's (see Seed Sources for address)
A source for frosted, plastic plant protectors (in 12 and 15-in.-tall sizes), plant tents, and Hotkaps.

Walter F. Nicke
Box 667G
Hudson, NY 12534
A source for glass tent and barn cloches and for Rumsey clips to make your own glass cloches.

Solar Survival
Box 275
Harrisville, NH 03450
Exclusive suppliers of the Leandre Poisson Solar Cone, which comes fully assembled.

Whiting Enterprises
Route 2, Box 2079
Paul, ID 83347
Maker of the Whiting Mini-Hothouse.

Tunnels

Agrotech
Box 857
Houlton, ME 04730
Offers the Spring Garden Row Cover, which includes a double layer of unventilated polyethylene and preinserted wooden support hoops.

Carefree Garden Products
P.O. Box 338
1400 Harvester Road
West Chicago, IL 60185
Features the Great Vegetable Cover-Up, which includes black plastic mulch along with clear plastic top cover and support wires.

Gardener's Eden
25 Huntington at Copley
Boston, MA 02116
Offers a plastic tunnel kit, called the European Cloche. It consists of three 32-in. sections that snap together and is easily assembled and disassembled for storage.

Gardener's Supply Company (see Cloches for address)
Carries the Tunnel Grow System, which includes black plastic mulch along with clear plastic top cover and support wires.

Green Frame Products
Nasheag Point
Brooklin, ME 04616
Offers the Salad Gardener, an updated version of the European Cloche. It is constructed of rustproof metal tubing and 7-mil cross-laminated plastic. It takes only an hour to assemble, is easily portable, and opens from either side.

Mellinger's (see Seed Sources for address)
Sells tunnel cloche kits.

Sherman Wire
P.O. Box 729
Sherman, TX 75090
Offers Key-Lite, a metal-reinforced plastic, in 3 by 25-ft. rolls.

T & T Seeds (see Seed Sources for address)
Carries the Select Greenhouse Tunnel made from double-layered, unventilated plastic. Plastic-coated metal hoops are included in the kit.

Warp Brothers
110 North Cicero Avenue
Chicago, IL 60651
Features the Warp's Row Cover and Mulch Kit, which includes black plastic mulch along with a single layer of slit polyethylene and metal support hoops.

Materials for Plant Protection

Agplast-LECO
36 Tidemore Avenue
Rexdale, Ontario
Canada M9W 5H4
Offers perforated, slitted, and regular rolled plastic.

Associated Bag Company
160 South Second Street
Milwaukee, WI 53204
Suppliers of Poly-Scrim, a polypropylene-reinforced translucent polyethylene, which makes an excellent floating row cover.

Gardener's Supply Company (see Cloches for address)
Offers Reemay and a special shade cover to protect light and heat-sensitive plants.

Johnny's Selected Seeds (see Seed Sources for address)
Offers a variety of rolled, slitted plastic for plant protection. Also sells Reemay.

KIM International
6448-FG Dawson Boulevard
Norcross, GA 30093
Supplier of the Earth Blanket, a nonwoven mulch/season extender that allows water and air to pass through.

Mellinger's (see Seed Sources for address)
Carries plant protection materials such as Reemay, DuPont's Polyester Row Cover (which is air and water permeable), and slitted plastic.

Territorial Seed Company (see Seed Sources for address)
A source for Reemay.

Soil Heating Cables

Gurney's Seed and Nursery Company (see Seed Sources for address)
Offers the Gro-Quick electric soil heating cables in lengths of 6, 12, and 48 ft.

H. G. Hastings Company (see Seed Sources for address)
Provides electric soil heating cables in lengths of 36, 48, and 60 ft.

Mellinger's (see Seed Sources for address)
Carries the Gro-Quick electric soil heating cables in lengths of 6, 12, 24, 36, and 48 ft.

George W. Park Seed Company (see Seed Sources for address)
Supplies electric soil heating cables in lengths of 12, 24, 36, and 48 ft.

SPB Sales (see Seed Sources for address)
Offers electric Gro-Quick soil heating cables in lengths of 6, 12, 24, 36, and 48 ft.

Cold Frames

Cold frames can be purchased as kits with all the materials included, as kits with certain parts, such as venting hardware, included, or as a set of plans and step-by-step directions for you to follow. We've listed the cold frames below according to those groups.

Complete Kits

Brookstone (see Cloches for address)
Offers the Auto-Vent, which opens and closes according to air temperature, and the Snap-Together Coldframe, which assembles in 10 minutes and provides more than 9 square ft. of growing space.

W. Atlee Burpee Company (see Seed Sources for address)
Features the Ventomatic, which opens and closes according to outside temperatures.

Gardener's Eden (see Cloches for address)
Supplies the Automatic Cold Frame with an automatic open/close feature.

Gardener's Supply Company (see Cloches for address)
Offers the GSC Coldframe, which consists of a galvanized steel frame covered with a "skin" of tough, woven material. Round slits in the roof of the "skin" vent warm air and allow rainwater to enter.

George W. Park Seed Company (see Seed Sources for address)
Carries the Automatic Coldframe with an automatic open/close feature.

Solar Survival (see Cloches for address)
Sells complete kits for the Solar Pod and the Solar Frame, including step-by-step directions and materials lists.

Partial Kits or Plans

W. Atlee Burpee Company (see Seed Sources for address)
Provides the Solarvent Automatic Cold Frame kit which includes the Solarvent automatic ventilator control, directions, blueprints, and materials list.

Dalen Products
201 Sherlake Drive
Knoxville, TN 37922
Offers free plans for solar cold frames. Also sells the Solarvent automatic ventilator control.

Gardener's Eden (see Tunnels for address)
Offers the Automatic Cold Frame, which is portable and easy to assemble.

Walter F. Nicke (see Cloches for address)
Carries the Solar Dome, a 6-foot-high tubular aluminum structure fitted with Fabrene, a special woven material. The frame is lightweight and portable.

George W. Park Seed Company (see Seed Sources for address)
Features a plans kit for building a cold frame. Also sells the Solarvent Cold Frame Opener.

Accessories

Brookstone (see Cloches for address)
Offers the Coldframe Autovent, which automatically opens and closes the cold frame according to preset temperatures. It can lift up to a 26-lb. window.

W. Atlee Burpee Company (see Seed Sources for address)
Carries the Solarvent ventilator for installation in cold frames. This automatic vent will open and close the cold frame according to preset temperatures.

Henry Field Seed and Nursery (see Seed Sources for address)
Supplies the Solarvent automatic window opener.

Mellinger's (see Seed Sources for address)
Offers the Solarvent and the Thermofor, which you set to open and close the cold frame at certain temperatures.

Solar Growing Frame

For detailed drawings and a materials list send a check for $4.95 (payable to Rodale Press, Inc.) to: Solar Growing Frame, Box 155, Emmaus, PA 18049.

Modular Garden Systems

To obtain a complete set of plans for the modular raised bed system, send a check for $3.95 (payable to Rodale Press, Inc.) to Project File, Box 155, Emmaus, PA 18049. Ask for Project File #241.

Plastic Mulches

Agplast-LECO (see Materials for Plant Protection for address)
Offers a heat and light-reflective mulch in two forms. Clear, for maximum light infiltration, and silver, for soil heating and insect control. Also offers a superstrength embossed mulch for high tear resistance. This mulch comes in clear, white, and black.

Blunk's
8923 South Octavia
Bridgeview, IL 60455
Markets Duon Weed Control Mat, which allows both water and air to pass through easily. The mat is made of a nonwoven polypropylene.

Easy Gardener
P.O. Box 21025
Waco, TX 76702
Offers two mulches: Weedblock, which is a long-lasting woven landscape and garden fabric, and Supermulch, a 3-mil polypropylene perforated with thousands of tiny holes. Both allow air and water to pass through, but eliminate weeds. Weedblock is available in 3-ft. widths from 12½ to 250 ft. long. Supermulch is available in 3-ft. widths and lengths of 25, 50, and 100 ft.

Gardener's Supply Company (see Cloches for address)
Supplies the Weed Control Mat, which allows air and water to pass through.

Johnny's Selected Seeds (see Seed Sources for address)
Offers black plastic mulch in 4-ft.-wide rolls.

Tools and Equipment

Gardener's Supply Company (see Cloches for address)
Offers a 10-lb. version of the U-bar called a Soil Digger. The tines are not removable on this model.

Green River Tools
5 Cotton Mill Hill
P.O. Box 1919
Brattleboro, VT 05301
Supplies a U-bar (called the Double-Digger) which has removable tines allowing adjustment for different tasks. Weight is only 9 lbs.

Howard Rotavator Company
Box 7
Muscoda, WI 53573
Sole distributors of the Rotavator, which is a tractor-pulled tiller that shapes, levels, and firms beds.

Luster Leaf Products
P.O. Box 1067
Crystal Lake, IL 60014
Source for the Rapitest soil testing kit, which provides instant results.

Smith and Hawken
25 Corte Madera
Mill Valley, CA 94941
Offers a shorter-handled version of the U-bar with removable tines for adjustment. The weight of this model is 10 lbs.

Watering Devices

Aquatic Irrigation Systems
619e East Gutierrez
Santa Barbara, CA 93103
Offers the Water Chain drip irrigation system. The kit contains 60 ft. of PVC tubing, 32 emitters, and various connectors and other fittings. The system is easily altered and enlarged.

Clapper's
1125 Washington Street
West Newton, MA 02165
Provides a variety of watering devices including sprinklers, nozzles, a Drip Water Systems kit (which includes a soaker hose in addition to the drip hose), and soaker hoses.

Gardener's Supply Company (see Cloches for address)
Carries a number of watering devices such as nozzles, four different size sprinklers, and the Hydro-Grow Watering System. This is a soaker hose system using 70 percent less water than conventional watering systems and can be adapted to various garden designs.

International Irrigation Systems
1555 Third Avenue
Niagara Falls, NY 14304
Supplier for the Irrigro Trickle Irrigation Systems. This system uses only 1 gal. of water per hour, which makes it well suited for dry or drought-prone areas. It can also be converted into a gravity drip system to use rainwater.

George W. Park Seed Company (see Seed Sources for address)
Carries an Irrigro Trickle Irrigation kit consisting of 100 ft. of tubing, connector, and instructions.

Smith and Hawken (see Tools and Equipment for address)
Offers various nozzles, adapters, connectors, and sprinklers, including oscillating, spray, and circle rotary. It also offers the Gardena Drip System Kit, which reduces normal faucet pressure and can use up to 400 emitters and 12 microsprinklers, all from one regulator.

Submatic Irrigation Systems
P.O. Box 246
Lubbock, TX 79408
Carries accessories to equip your garden with a variety of drip irrigation systems. Gives detailed instructions on setting up a system from the planning stage to finished system. Has a number of kits to fit the needs of gardeners with small to large plots. Individual valves, nozzles, and other parts are available to expand the present system.

Plant Supports

W. Atlee Burpee Company (see Seed Sources for address)
Offers the bean and strawberry tower.

Gardener's Eden (see Tunnels for address)
Provides the strawberry tower in 2-ft. and 4-ft. sizes.

Gurney's Seed and Nursery Company (see Seed Sources for address)
Carries the tomato web and the strawberry tower.

H. G. Hastings Company (see Seed Sources for address)
Sells the strawberry tower.

Legume Inoculants

Agricultural Laboratories
1145 Chesapeake Avenue
Columbus, OH 43212
Sells nitrogen-fixing bacteria and prepares special cultures on request.

Recommended Reading

Adams, William D. *Vegetable Growing for Southern Gardens.* Houston, Tex.: Gulf Publishing Co., 1976.

Antill, David. *Gardening under Protection.* Wakefield, West Yorkshire, U.K.: E. P. Publishing, 1978.

Aquatias, A. *Intensive Culture of Vegetables.* Harrisville, N.H.: Solar Survival Press, 1978.

Ball, Jeff. *Jeff Ball's 60-Minute Garden.* Emmaus, Pa.: Rodale Press, 1985.

Bartholomew, Mel. *Square Foot Gardening.* Emmaus, Pa.: Rodale Press, 1981.

Bennett, Jennifer. *Harrowsmith Northern Gardener.* Camden East, Ontario: Camden House Publishing, 1982.

Bresson, Tom. *Drip Irrigation: A User's Manual.* The Urban Farmer, 1982.

Brooklyn Botanic Garden Record, Plants and Gardens. *Handbook on Mulches.* Vol. 13, no. 1. Edited by Paul Frese. May 1978.

Bryan, John E. *Small World Vegetable Gardening.* San Francisco: One Hundred One Productions, 1977.

Bubel, Mike, and Nancy Bubel. *Root Cellaring.* Emmaus, Pa.: Rodale Press, 1979.

Bubel, Nancy. *The Seed-Starter's Handbook.* Emmaus, Pa.: Rodale Press, 1978.

Carr, Anna. *Good Neighbors: Companion Planting for Gardeners.* Emmaus, Pa.: Rodale Press, 1985.

Chan, Peter. *Better Vegetable Gardens the Chinese Way: Peter Chan's Raised Bed System.* Pownal, Vt.: Storey Communications, 1985.

Colebrook, Binda. *Winter Gardening in the Maritime Northwest.* 2d rev. ed. Everson, Wash.: Maritime Publishers, 1984.

Cuthbertson, Tom. *Alan Chadwick's Enchanted Garden.* New York: E. P. Dutton, 1978.

Doscher, Paul; Timothy Fisher, and Kathleen Kolb. *Intensive Gardening Round the Year.* Brattleboro, Vt.: The Stephen Greene Press, 1981.

Editors of *Organic Gardening* Magazine. *The Organic Gardener's Complete Guide to Vegetables and Fruits.* Emmaus, Pa.: Rodale Press, 1982.

Editors of *Reader's Digest. Illustrated Guide to Gardening.* New York: Random House, 1978.

Editors of *Sunset Magazine* and Sunset Books. *Desert Gardening.* Menlo Park, Calif.: Lane Publishing Co., 1967.

————. *New Western Garden Book.* 4th ed. Menlo Park, Calif.: Lane Publishing Co., 1979.

Foley, Daniel J. *Gardening by the Sea, from Coast to Coast.* Philadelphia: Chilton Books, 1965.

Foster, Gertrude B., and Rosemary F. Louden. *Park's Success with Herbs.* Greenwood, S.C.: George W. Park Seed Co., 1980.

The Fundamentals of Gardening for the Northeast. San Francisco: Ortho Books, 1976.

Gardening in Small Spaces. Mount Vernon, Va.: The American Horticultural Society, 1982.

Hastings, Louise. *The Southern Garden Book.* Garden City, N.Y.: Doubleday and Co., 1950.

Head, William. *Gardening under Cover.* Eugene, Oreg.: Amity Foundation, 1984.

Heutte, Frederick. *Fred Heutte's Gardening in the Temperate Zone.* Norfolk, Va.: The Donning Co., 1977.

Hill, Lewis. *Successful Cold-Climate Gardening.* Brattleboro, Vt.: The Stephen Greene Press, 1981.

Jeavons, John. *How to Grow More Vegetables Than You Ever Thought Possible on Less Land Than You Can Imagine.* Rev. ed. Berkeley, Calif.: Ten Speed Press, 1982.

Jennings, Charles. *Drought Gardening.* Portland, Oreg.: Victoria House, 1977.

Kramer, Jack. *Drip System Watering for Bigger and Better Plants.* New York: W. W. Norton and Co., 1980.

Krochmal, Arnold. *Gardening in the Carolinas.* Garden City, N.Y.: Doubleday and Co., 1975.

Langham, Derald G. *Circle Gardening.* Old Greenwich, Conn.: The Devin-Adair Co., 1978.

Larkcom, Joy. *The Salad Garden.* New York: Viking Press, 1984.

Minnich, Jerry. *A Wisconsin Garden Guide*. Madison, Wis.: Wisconsin House Book Publishers, 1975.

———. *Gardening for Maximum Nutrition*. Emmaus, Pa.: Rodale Press, 1983.

Mittleider, Jacob R. *Grow-Bed Gardening*. Santa Barbara, Calif.: Woodbridge Press, 1984.

Nehrling, Arno, and Irene Nehrling. *Easy Gardening with Drought Resistant Plants*. New York: Hearthside Press, 1968.

Newcomb, Duane. *Growing Vegetables the Big Yield-Small Space Way*. Los Angeles: Jeremy P. Tarcher, 1981.

———. *The Postage Stamp Garden Book*. Los Angeles: Jeremy P. Tarcher, 1975.

Pfeiffer, Ehrenfried. *Bio-Dynamic Farming and Gardening*. Translated by Frederick Heckhel. New York: Anthroposophic Press, 1943.

Powell, Thomas, and Betty Powell. *The Avant Gardener: A Handbook and Sourcebook of All That's New and Useful in Gardening*. Boston: Houghton Mifflin, 1975.

Proulx, E. Annie. *The Fine Art of Salad Gardening*. Emmaus, Pa.: Rodale Press, 1985.

Raymond, Dick. *The Joy of Gardening*. Charlotte, Vt.: Garden Way Publishing, 1982.

———. *Wide-Row Planting: The Productive Miracle*. Charlotte, Vt.: Garden Way Publishing, 1977.

Reilly, Ann. *Park's Success with Seeds*. Greenwood, S.C.: George W. Park Seed Co., 1978.

Seymour, John. *The Self-Sufficient Gardener*. London: Faber and Faber, 1978.

Snyder, Leon C. *Gardening in the Upper Midwest*. Minneapolis, Minn.: University of Minnesota Press, 1978.

Staff of *Organic Gardening* magazine. *The Encyclopedia of Organic Gardening*. Emmaus, Pa.: Rodale Press, 1978.

Van Gorder, Steven D., and Douglas J. Strange. *Home Aquaculture*. Emmaus, Pa.: Rodale Press, 1983.

Whealy, Kent, ed. *The Garden Seed Inventory*. Decorah, Iowa: Seed Saver Publications, 1985.

Willis, A. R. *The Pacific Gardener*. Sidney, British Columbia: Grays Publishing, 1964.

Wolf, Ray, ed. *Solar Growing Frame*. Emmaus, Pa.: Rodale Press, 1980.

Hardiness Zone Map

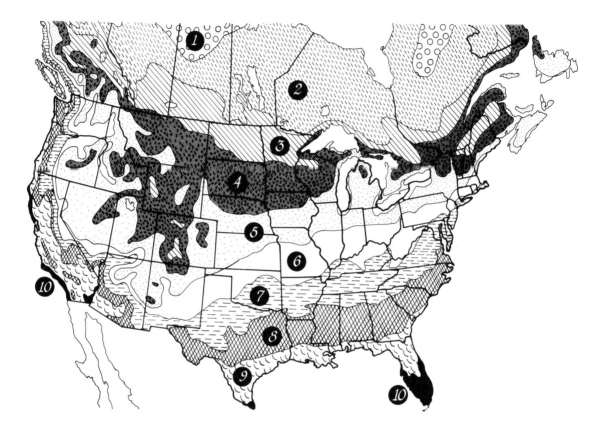

Average Minimum Temperatures for Each Zone

Zone 1	below -50°F	
Zone 2	-50° to -40°	
Zone 3	-40° to -30°	
Zone 4	-30° to -20°	
Zone 5	-20° to -10°	
Zone 6	-10° to 0°	
Zone 7	0° to 10°	
Zone 8	10° to 20°	
Zone 9	20° to 30°	
Zone 10	30° to 40°	

INDEX

Page references in italics indicate illustrations. Bold-faced page references indicate tables.

Rodale Press, Inc., publishes RODALE'S ORGANIC GARDENING®,
the all-time favorite gardening magazine.
For information on how to order your subscription,
write to RODALE'S ORGANIC GARDENING®, Emmaus, PA 18049.